Integrated Information and Computing Systems for Natural, Spatial, and Social Sciences

Claus-Peter Rückemann
*Westfälische Wilhelms-Universität (WWU) & Leibniz Universität Hannover
& North-German Supercomputing Alliance (HLRN), Germany*

Managing Director:	Lindsay Johnston
Editorial Director:	Joel Gamon
Book Production Manager:	Jennifer Romanchak
Publishing Systems Analyst:	Adrienne Freeland
Development Editor:	Myla Merkel
Assistant Acquisitions Editor:	Kayla Wolfe
Typesetter:	Henry Ulrich
Cover Design:	Nick Newcomer

Published in the United States of America by
Information Science Reference (an imprint of IGI Global)
701 E. Chocolate Avenue
Hershey PA 17033
Tel: 717-533-8845
Fax: 717-533-8661
E-mail: cust@igi-global.com
Web site: http://www.igi-global.com

Library of Congress Cataloging-in-Publication Data

Integrated information and computing systems for natural, spatial, and social sciences / Claus-Peter Rückemann, editor.
    pages ; cm
 Includes bibliographical references and index.
 Summary: "This book covers a carefully selected spectrum of issues pertaining to the benefits, dynamism, potential, and challenges of information and computing system application scenarios and components from a wide spectrum of prominent disciplines"--Provided by publisher.
 ISBN 978-1-4666-2190-9 (hardcover) -- ISBN 978-1-4666-2191-6 (ebook) -- ISBN 978-1-4666-2192-3 (print & perpetual access) 1. Computer systems. 2. Information storage and retrieval systems. 3. Systems integration. 4. Science--Data processing. 5. Industries--Data processing. 6. Information technology--Social aspects. I. Rückemann, Claus-Peter, 1967-
 QA76.55.I58 2013
 303.48'33--dc23
                                     2012019278

British Cataloguing in Publication Data
A Cataloguing in Publication record for this book is available from the British Library.

All work contributed to this book is new, previously-unpublished material. The views expressed in this book are those of the authors, but not necessarily of the publisher.

Editorial Advisory Board

Table of Contents

Section 1
Collaboration, Frameworks, and Legal Aspects

Section 2
High End Computing, Storage, and Services

Section 3
Communication, Computation, and Advanced Scientific Computing

Section 4
Big Data Exploration, Visualisation, Education, and Social Media

Detailed Table of Contents

Section 1
Collaboration, Frameworks, and Legal Aspects

This chapter is focused on the present status of Integrated Information and Computing Systems (IICS) for advanced collaboration with complex use cases and system architectures in order to exploit new resources and opening up new cognitive insights for natural sciences' applications. It shows the challenges and strategical significance of creating complex integrated information and computing components and covers state of the art implementation, frameworks, and security issues with these processes and how the overall complexity can be reduced using collaboration frameworks with Distributed and High Performance Computing resources in natural sciences disciplines for building integrated public/ commercial information system components within the e-Society, considering commercial service structures, legal, security, and trust aspects as results from international studies and implementation.

The success of software design, implementation, and operation of information and communication systems are crucially depending on national and international legal regulations. The purpose of this chapter is to identify and analyze the challenges of creating new software in the public cloud due to legal regulations. Specifically, this chapter explores how the Sarbanes Oxley Act (SOX) will indirectly affect the development and implementation process of cloud computing applications in terms of software engineering and actual legality of said software solutions. The goal of this chapter is twofold - to bring attention to the need for specific analysis of legal issues in public clouds as opposed to general analysis, and to illustrate the need for cloud developers to address legal constraint while creating their platforms, in order to increase their viability in the corporate environments.

Creating high end operations' management systems in distributed information and computing environments requires components acting intelligently and in parallel as well as advanced security management. Within this research a management concept for increasingly complex business operations' systems has been created. This chapter presents the results of two use-cases from different domains of operations, an aviation network management and the service-bundling of small enterprises, exemplifying the convergence of new technologies and the organisational and managerial challenges. "Things-that-think" will act autonomously on the Internet, strongly profiting from arising multi-core chip architectures, becoming drivers of massive distribution and parallelisation of stationary and mobile operations' architectures, addressing complexity, criticality, and security by implementing self-awareness as added-value service.

Policies as well as legal and collaborated aspects of information and communication systems are most important when methods and technologies are used for an implementation in e-Government systems as legal, functional, technical requirements, and perception are manifold. This chapter describes an application scenario from the current Singapore e-Government Master Plan. It presents the current status, and provides strengths, weaknesses, opportunities, and threats and allows policy recommendations addressing the challenges when information systems, public, and governmental aspects are integrated for practical use. It addresses practical issues from users' view and research insight for implementing and utilising e-Government and public services based on modern Internet technologies.

The content of this chapter can be applied to many collaboration, workplace, and learning settings that will find benefits from the wide range of applications and the large potential of tablet computers. Tablet computers are already used from the most basic level of medical undergraduate education to specialist care delivery. This chapter focuses on how and where the new technology of tablet computers will find a most effective role in the area of healthcare delivery in the educational setting and a place on the eLearning/ mLearning spectrum, especially it explores the effectiveness in clinical teaching and proposes a suitable pilot study. The chapter compiles a list of recommended medical applications, and a description of challenges and issues when deploying tablet computers to clinical settings.

Section 2
High End Computing, Storage, and Services

Chapter 6

Micha vor dem Berge, christmann informationstechnik & Medien GmbH & Co. KG, Germany
Wolfgang Christmann, christmann informationstechnik & Medien GmbH & Co. KG, Germany

High end computing is characterised by advanced hardware and software environments and large numbers of components. This chapter describes the current state and the ongoing efforts to integrate a monitoring and controlling architecture in modern computing environments. The benefits to be gained from this architecture include increased knowledge about the state of computing resources and the capability to establish a management platform that optimises energy efficiency as well as the availability of the computing environment in a time of a rapidly growing need for compute power. The chapter presents real-life use cases for server virtualisation and High Performance Computing (HPC) where implementations of a management system for energy-efficiency were evaluated, validating the significant increase of energy-efficiency.

Chapter 7

Isabel Schwerdtfeger, IBM Germany

This chapter discusses the challenges high-end storage solutions will have with increased future demands. Large requirements for real-time processing of data access force to address high-end storage solutions. Some most prominent aspects are different high-end storage solutions, suitability to ensure high performance write and retrieval of data in real-time from high-end storage infrastructures, and access from digital archives. This chapter presents a storage review of disk and tape solutions as well as combined disk- and tape storage solutions, focused on available commercial high-end systems, addressing scalability and performance requirements both for online storage and archives. High level requirements aid in identifying high-end storage system features and support extreme scale infrastructures for the amount of data that future high-end storage systems will need to manage.

Chapter 8

Alexander Kipp, High Performance Computing Center Stuttgart (HLRS), Department Intelligent Service Infrastructures, Germany
Ralf Schneider, High Performance Computing Center Stuttgart, Germany
Lutz Schubert, High Performance Computing Center Stuttgart, Germany

Demands for High Performance Computing services are drastically increasing with modern information and computing system infrastructures. Developing and providing complex IT services typically enforces the cooperation of experts from different domains. Beside the domain specific knowledge of the involved experts this typically enforces a profound knowledge of the underlying IT service infrastructures. This chapter shows how a complex HPC service product can be provided in an easy-to-use fashion via a service virtualisation infrastructure. A complex medical simulation use case illustrates the concept. In particular, it is highlighted how a complex IT service can be integrated in a holistic virtual organisation environment and how different experts from different domains can concentrate on their specific domain whilst being enabled to take advantage of the services provided by other experts and domains in a SOA like fashion.

Chapter 9

Architecture for Integration and Migration of Information Systems by Using SOA Services across Heterogeneous System Boundaries

Lars Frank, Copenhagen Business School, Denmark

Rasmus Ulslev Pedersen, Copenhagen Business School, Denmark

This chapter describes how to use SOA services in order to integrate and migrate Enterprise Resource Planning (ERP) systems where local heterogeneous databases are involved. ERP systems are very complex standardized information systems, often vital for the companies using them. Normally it is not possible to integrate different ERP modules from different ERP suppliers, so an overnight switch would be performed. The main focus of this chapter is to illustrate how it is possible to migrate an ERP system module by module and thus minimizing the risk of staying without a functioning system. In this chapter, so called relaxed ACID (Atomicity, Consistency, Isolation and Durability) properties across different database systems or ERP modules are used in order to enable a trust in data, in case of temporary inconsistencies.

Chapter 10

Password Recovery Research and its Future Direction

Vrizlynn L. L. Thing, Institute for Infocomm Research, Singapore

Hwei-Ming Ying, Institute for Infocomm Research, Singapore

There are different directions for securing information systems and access as well as password recovery or access forensics. From a social and technological point of view security, privacy, and recovery are very important issues in Integrated Information and Computing Systems. On one hand, there is human nature and tendency in password selections. On the other hand, users are becoming increasingly aware of the need to adopt strong passwords, bringing challenges to digital forensics investigators due to the password protection of potential evidentiary data. This chapter discusses the existing password recovery methods and identifies promising password recovery approaches. It presents the design, evaluation, and results of a time-memory tradeoff pre-computed table coupled with a new sorting algorithm, two new storage mechanisms, and the proof of feasibility for this technique.

Section 3
Communication, Computation, and Advanced Scientific Computing

Chapter 11

Multiagent Based Product Data Communication System for Computer Supported Collaborative Design

Bernadetta Kwintiana Ane, Institute of Computer-Aided Product Development Systems,
    Universität Stuttgart, Germany

Dieter Roller, Institute of Computer-Aided Product Development Systems,
    Universität Stuttgart, Germany

Ajith Abraham, IT For Innovations - Center of Excellence, VSB-TU Ostrava, Czech Republi

As information and communication technologies advance, Computer Supported Collaborative Design (CSCD) becomes more promising. Designers and engineers on collaborative design environments often work in parallel and independently today, distributed at separate locations, using different tools. Due to unique characteristic of engineering design, interaction during product development is difficult to maintain. This chapter addresses the incompatibility problem by introducing the architecture of a multi-agent based product data communication system, being adaptive and having the capability for autonomous tracking of changes. The chapter describes the architecture and the necessary workflow as well as the complexity and the essential aspects of learning intelligent systems. It enlightens the need for real-time collaborative systems, and the driving force behind Cloud Computing.

Chapter 12

Jelena Mirkovic, Center For Shared Decision Making and Collaborative Care Research, Oslo University Hospital, Oslo, Norway
Haakon Bryhni, Department of Informatics, University of Oslo, Oslo, Norway

For many of today's information services, the mobility aspect is most important as mobile and wireless technologies have great potential to improve efficiency and quality; e.g., in healthcare delivery. This chapter describes the current state of the art in the research field of development and integration of mobile services in the healthcare sector by addressing the two main challenges, usability and security. Main requirements and approaches are investigated for developing highly usable, user-friendly, and well-accepted mobile healthcare services. The chapter identifies and discusses important aspects of security and privacy issues and presents the CONNECT (Care Online: Novel Networks to Enhance Communication and Treatment) project and describes how security and usability issues can be addressed during the development of mobile access to a multi-modal Internet-based patient support system.

Chapter 13

Rasmus Ulslev Pedersen, Copenhagen Business School, Denmark
Mogens Kühn Pedersen, Copenhagen Business School, Denmark

Today's communication and Information System (IS) concepts increasingly have to integrate small systems, which are equipped with sensors, e.g., mobile phones, temperature sensors, GPS tracking, amd emerging nano/ micro-size sensors, which are used by individuals, groups, and organizations. Valuable industry applications range from medicine to manufacturing. This chapter visualises this new class of information systems as fractals growing from established IS and shows how to couple embedded sensor systems with general IS. The merger of these two research areas is an intended new research field and called micro information systems (micro-IS). An initial framework model is established, looking simultaneously at the fundamental IS and ICT aspects. The chapter demonstrates the proposed micro-IS framework with a working open source application of open demand response systems that address the engineering aspects of this work.

Chapter 14

Terje Solvoll, Norwegian Centre for Integrated Care and Telemedicine, Tromsø Telemedicine Laboratory, University Hospital of North Norway & Department of Computer Science, University of Tromsø, Norway

Communication system components are essential for modern medicine but the work setting in hospitals is communication intensive and can lead to significant difficulties related to interruptions from other co-workers. Physicians often need information fast, and any delay for decisions and actions can be critical. The suggested solution for this problem is to implement wireless phone systems, however being known for additional problems related to interruptions, compared to traditional paging systems. But also, the fact that hospital workers prefer interruptive communication methods before non-interruptive methods, amplifies the risk of overloading people when widely deploying phones. This problem causes some hospital staff to resist the adoption of mobile communication, and a key challenge is how to handle the balance between increased availability, and increased interruptions. This chapter presents solutions based on context aware communication systems that aim to reduce interruptions.

Scientific numerical simulation using high performance computing resources is one of the principal tools for exploiting the constraints posed by geological and geochemical surface observations performed by planetary spacecrafts. Thermo-chemical convection is the primary process that controls the large-scale dynamics of the mantle of the Earth and terrestrial planets. This chapter discusses the modeling of active compositional fields in the framework of solid-state mantle convection using the cylindrical/ spherical code, Gaia, and compares an Eulerian method based on double-diffusive convection against a Lagrangian, particle-based method. By using state of the art computing resources and a series of increasingly complex benchmark tests, the chapter shows that the particle method is superior when it comes to model the advection of compositional interfaces with sharp density and viscosity contrasts. This technique is applied to simulate the Rayleigh-Taylor overturn of the Mars' and Mercury's primordial magma oceans.

Scientific modelling is one of the major fields for High Performance Computing. Modelling of geodynamic processes like mantle or core convection has strongly improved over the last two decades thanks to the steady development of numerical codes that tend to incorporate a more and more realistic physics. High-performance parallel computations allow the simulation of complex problems, such as the self-consistent generation of tectonic plates and the formation of planetary magnetic fields. However, the need to perform broad explorations of the parameter space and the large computational demands imposed by the non-linear, multi-scale nature of convection, require several simplifications, in the domain geometry as well as in the physical complexity of the problem. This chapter gives an overview of the state-of-the-art convection simulations in planetary mantles, it present the results, the different models and geometries used, and various methods to simplify the computations.

Section 4
Big Data Exploration, Visualisation, Education, and Social Media

Chapter 17

May Yuan, University of Oklahoma, USA
James Bothwell, University of Oklahoma, USA

The so-called big data challenge poses not only issues with massive volumes of data, but issues with the continuing data streams from multiple sources that monitor environmental processes or record social activities. Statistics tools and data mining methods have been developed to reveal embedded patterns in large data sets. While patterns are critical to data analysis, deep insights will remain buried unless means are developed to associate spatiotemporal patterns to the dynamics of spatial processes that essentially drive the formation of patterns in the data. This chapter discusses the types of dynamics and identifies how to systematically advance space-time analytics to reveal dynamics of spatial processes and presents an example from two General Circulation Models for climate change prediction to highlight potential means of space-time analytics in response to the Big Data Challenge, digging down into massive amounts of spatiotemporal data to derive understanding of spatial dynamics.

Chapter 18

Fabio Gomes de Andrade, Federal Institute of Education, Science, and Technology of Paraíba, Brazil
Cláudio de Souza Baptista, University of Campina Grande, Brazil

Spatial Data Infrastructures (SDI) are currently becoming the solution adopted by many organisations to facilitate discovery, access, and integration of geographic information produced and provided by different agencies. However, the catalog services currently offered by these infrastructures provide keyword-based queries only. This may result in low recall and precision. These catalogs retrieve information based on the metadata records that describe either a service or a dataset. This feature limits the more specific information discovery, such as those based on feature types and instances. This chapter proposes a solution that aims to overcome these limitations by using multiple ontologies to enhance the description of the information offered by SDIs. The proposed ontologies describe the semantics of several features of a service, enabling information discovery at level of services, feature types, and geographic data.

Chapter 19

Belgacem Ben Youssef, King Saud University, Saudi Arabia & Simon Fraser University, Canada

The integration of scientific simulation models and visualisation does provide a number of advanced computing challenges. Visualising time-varying phenomena is paramount to ensuring correct interpretation and analysis, provoking and communicating insights, and acting as a challenge due to the amount of data and the large simulation parameter space. This chapter presents the components of an integrated computing system being developed for the simulation of 3-D tissue growth that would produce computer-aided design tools to facilitate the work of tissue engineers. Visualisation allows the freedom to explore the spatial and temporal domains of such phenomena. The chapter discusses the application of visualisation to the three-dimensional simulation model, using cellular automata, describes components and system architecture, model parallelisation and implementation on parallel machines, and demonstrates the latest results.

In order to reduce risks and increase the speed of new information technology (IT) product or service development as well as to satisfy customers' demand, end users' involvement has become one of the most important issues. This chapter aims at the presentation of the user role in information system development and the activities of prosumers in e-learning. It discusses a concise literature review referring to studies on end users' involvement in the information system (IS) development process and the opportunities of prosumption development on the Internet. The chapter shows up to date e-learning focussed development and IT-supported communication among e-learners as a special domain of IS/IT prosumption. Resulting from the experiences, the chapter covers a proposal of the architecture model as well as it contributes to the discussion on methods of information system design for the prosumption development.

Digital media and the need for information management are omnipresent with information and communication systems today, as the availability of social media has changed the way practitioners handle resources in interactive media contexts and how users interoperate and interact on the Web. Thus, effectively embedding Social Media into information and knowledge management concerns is a central issue. New ways are needed of enriching and annotating content collectively following the wisdom of crowds and helpful intelligent automatic analysis. This chapter discusses the impact of social media concepts and distributed resources in web-based information management, knowledge engineering, and digital media applications, and it shows the relation between traditional web application design, distributed resource utilisation, changes, and challenges in current interactive Digital Media systems.

Preface

Any society is significantly based on information. The importance of its utilisation for the modern society cannot be emphasised strong enough. Every decision relies on the availability and use of information from various sources and fields. Information in natural, spatial, and social sciences and applications is the gold of modern times, driving scientific, industrial, social operations and developments. Future handling of this information and getting an essential surplus value means intelligently using computing resources.

The outlook for the international deployment of informatics and computing in common applications for the next decade is just like undertaking a comprehensive survey on high level topics for some of the most dynamic aspects of modern society, from information sciences, natural sciences, and health sciences, to spatial and social sciences. Where extremes meet, new solutions can be created so the next generation of decision making will get into reach. Future developments for integrated systems have to consider human behaviour and real life usage scenarios. This is important from many different points of view. Today's four stimulations for using advanced information and computing systems are the use of new aspects and approaches, enabling extensions for additional information and computing resources, providing faster and cheaper means, and promoting innovative research. We exigently need optimised integrated computing architectures and decision making processes as complexity arises from the challenging tasks and applications in the leading disciplines we see for the future.

As these processes demand the attention on new chances for future interdisciplinary and multidisciplinary cooperation and developments regarding information we need to gather the top priorities for the key disciplines and understand how information and computing resources are currently used and what outlook the leading experts can give for future system components.

This book on Integrated Information and Computing Systems covers a carefully selected plenitude of issues for a spectrum of prominent topics on these disciplines in order to learn from each other's achievements and to show up answers to the outstanding questions. In this book, the contributing experts for their fields show how information and infrastructures can be modelled, managed, valuated, giving a bright outlook on how information and information technologies can be used for collaboration in networks. As information and computing infrastructures evolve globally, distributed networks expand, and information science is becoming enlivened on all facets of information society, there is an emerging need for creating a base of collaboration, ethics, and a virtual platform for the society lifting business processes, information science and computing to the next level.

With their contribution, the authors in this book show the success of the multidisciplinary collaborative work that has been done in the past. But even more effort has to be undertaken in order to integrate those scientific methods and techniques for integrated systems in the future.

The range of applications spans from integrated information and computing systems for advanced cognition with natural sciences to product data communication systems for collaborative design and social sciences. Therefore this book concentrates on the commonly emerging holistic aspects of data and information processing, information management, ecology, knowledge handling, featuring social media, ontologies, automation, resource discovery up to policies for high-reliability, legal, economical, and financial aspects, e-governance, and software design, smart mobile technologies, intelligent and multi-agent systems and services as well as provision of complex HPC service products, monitoring, accounting, and future energy efficient systems.

This book originates from the contributions and work of a large number of the best experts but what it achieves to unfold it's strength was an editing process of carefully selecting and conjoining all contributions to reveal an interdisciplinary synergism. The authors show how to handle business processes and system management, as well as aspects of service evaluation, networking, and application scenarios from social media, education, and life sciences, from distributed applications to high performance scientific computing and processing.

The initial idea for this book resulted from the international multidisciplinary collaboration and national research projects on communication and computing over a long period of time, starting from the work within the LX Foundation and the Geo Exploration and Information Consortium (GEXI) about years ago. The start was formed at the DigitalWorld umbrella conference 2009 in Cancún, México, especially the International Conference on Advanced Geographic Information Systems & Web Services (GEOWS) and the International Conference on Digital Society (ICDS). Along with the participants, the implementation has been put into life in the following years with well established and newly founded events, workshops, and panel discussions at the DigitalWorld 2010 on St. Maarten, Netherlands Antilles, with the International Conference on Advanced Geographic Information Systems, Applications, and Services (GEOProcessing) and the International Conference on Technical and Legal Aspects of the e-Society (CYBERLAWS). The concluding steps have been prepared during the DigitalWorld 2011 conferences on Guadeloupe, the International Conference on Advanced Communications and Computation (INFOCOMP) 2011 in Barcelona, Spain, the International Conference on Numerical Analysis and Applied Mathematics (ICNAAM) 2011 in Halkidiki, Greece, and the DigitalWorld and GEOProcessing 2012 in Valencia, Spain.

Besides the basic information sciences and software design, geoscientific monitoring and processing, geoscientific and archaeological Information Systems, big data, Spatial Data Exploration, Air Traffic Management systems, simulation, modelling, construction, aerospace design, medical data processing and information visualisation, education and learning environments, knowledge management, documentation, and expert systems as well as data and media exploration, social networks, governance support systems and lots more – all of these are pieces of a large puzzle of components, using and developing information system and computing components that depend on multidisciplinary development and will form the components of the next generation of integrated systems. For example, we need an integration of simulation and information systems plus visualisation and on the other hand an integration of simulation with computing and powerful resources. Moreover, various scenarios demonstrate aspects that information and computing system components are strongly depending on experience and point of view for local context. In some countries the driving force for mobility and distributed applications is the distribution of settlement or the development of the age structure of the society. This book shows that different local and social context will generate different perspectives for distributed and mobile requirements and this is most important to consider for understanding future systems.

There are different directions for collaboration, policy making, and securing information and systems, regarding access, security as well as privacy as these are very important issues in Integrated Information and Computing Systems, for operation and social acceptance. As with security, on one hand user accounts have to ensure security and privacy and at the same time on the other hand, if they are too secure and privacy enhanced, this again may result in new challenges with society and threats. Long-term planning and development of system modules, standardised development and interfaces as well as continuous wide-spread knowledge interchanges and academic and industry collaboration on scientific and technological achievements are the keys for overcoming technological and legal issues and bringing together worlds currently still separated, like information systems, communication technology, mobile services, High End Computing, supercomputing, storage and long-term archiving, networking, and sources in order to make sustainable progress in reaching not only Exascale level infrastructures and services but the next stage of the information society. So presently working on the Integrated Information and Computing System components and features for the future we hope that development of basic structures and components will result in systems that the next generation of collaborative networkers will say "have become state of the art."

STRUCTURE OF THE BOOK

The twenty-one chapters of this book are organised in four sections that address some most essential issues of Integrated Information and Computing Systems for natural, spatial, and social sciences. These issues are ranging from collaboration and technological issues to social and advanced scientific and industrial applications:

Section 1: Collaboration, Frameworks, and Legal Aspects
Section 2: High End Computing, Storage, and Services
Section 3: Communication, Computation, and Advanced Scientific Computing
Section 4: Big Data Exploration, Visualisation, Education, and Social Media

These sections and their chapters cover developments and topics from different disciplines, presenting new scientific insight and showing requirements for resources, services, information systems and knowledge management, and what the scientific and social outcomes and challenges are. They reveal developments and views from industry, for scientific computing and storage, being suitable for "gluing" the pool of multidisciplinary components, and in their multitude of aspects and state-of-the-art case studies presented they enable to have a presentiment on the economical point of the various views and potential and to give an outlook on future horizons.

Section 1 outlines collaborative, technical, and legal frameworks. It describes challenges in creating complex integrated systems, dynamical usage, processing, visualisation, and parallelisation, reducing complexity using collaboration frameworks and concepts with High End Computing systems, Cloud Computing, and security, e-government systems, and knowledge management. It refers to national and international legal aspects for collaboration, development, collaborational teaching, and security, development and implementation issues, transparency, laws and legal regulations. Minimising policies and licensing issues as well as security with centralised and distributed resources and services, cryptography and digital signatures, and privacy and anonymity are some of the focussed topics.

Section 2 presents important topics from High End Computing, High End Storage, and modern services infrastructures. It shows research and application of High Performance Computing, Supercomputing, and Distributed Computing infrastructure, leading to energy efficient systems, modern services, middleware, management, security and password recovery, and Cloud concepts. It shows how to implement and deploy intelligent system components, from academic and industry point of view as well as using, configuring, and managing fast networks and resources.

Section 3 is dedicated to advanced applications making intensive use of communication and computation and implementing high end scientific computing for academic and industry application. It focuses on multiagent systems for collaborative design, deploying supercomputing for advanced scientific computing in geosciences and natural sciences disciplines like computing for planetary physics, communication in hospitals, high end modelling in geodynamics, and an example for an implementation of a future information system landscape.

Section 4 presents advanced applications with focus to spatial sciences, spatial dynamics and Spatial Data Infrastructures, data exploration, tissue growth visualisation, prosumption and education context, networking, and social media. The main focus is on spatial data and big data exploration, ontology based resource discovery in Spatial Data Infrastructures, visualisation regarding tissue growth as well as information system prosumption in e-learning up to the impact of social media in web-based information management and digital media.

TARGET AUDIENCES

The potential audience of this book will be from the information systems, information sciences, informatics and computing non-specific disciplines and fields: geosciences, geoinformatics, planetology, archaeology and archaeo-sciences, health sciences and telemedicine, applied epidemiology and medical geology, resources exploration, higher education, e-learning, social sciences, and digital society. The topics are relevant for high performance computing and distributed computing, future internet management and design, so for participants of European and international programmes, participants in postgraduate study and education programmes of information science and legal informatics as well as industry and small and medium businesses. Nevertheless, the most typical audience is from the fields of advanced scientific computing, information systems, and high end computing. The book will aid to the prospective audience, e.g., to university lecturers and professors, students, researchers, developers of information system components, senior management members in information science and system architects for next generation HEC resources as well as planning agencies, lawyers and governmental and industry decision makers will gain important guidance and overview.

This book is intended to show suitable approaches for components and to answer some key questions: "To what extent does diversity of disciplines challenge the holistic development?", "Is it possible to create complex integrated information and computing systems?", and "How will it be possible to implement international systems respecting the complex legal regulations?" The objective of this book is to show up approaches and to compile answers and results for integration. Therefore this book focuses on the current scope of research and practice for present and future Integrated Information and Computing Systems. The selected chapters for this book escalate the essentials and viewpoints of research, industry, and experts working on natural sciences, technical, and social sciences components for design, development, and implementation of multidisciplinary complex information and computing systems. The multitude of contributions to this book uncovers the why, what, and who for the next generation of system architectures that will impact the information society with their long-term application. Understanding the diversity and how the goal of integrated systems can be reached is one of the main issues of this book. The authors of these chapters reveal the development stage of their contributions to a universal solution for integrated information and computing systems which will serve as a means for building the next generation of Integrated Information and Computing Systems.

Claus-Peter Rückemann
Westfälische Wilhelms-Universität (WWU) & Leibniz Universität Hannover & North German
    Supercomputing Alliance (HLRN), Germany
August 2012

Acknowledgment

This book would not have been possible without the cooperation and support of many people from all continents around the world. First of all I want to thank the authors of the chapters for their excellent contributions to this book project and the outstanding collaboration. I am very grateful to the members of the Editorial Advisory Board and Review Committee for their great support, constructive and fruitful cooperation, for peer reviewing and for giving valuable advice for all of the chapter authors during the double blind review process. This has overall strengthened this book for integrating various disciplines and aligning the complementary topics.

As this book is the result of continuous international collaboration over many years, I am also grateful to the colleagues and participants of the International Conference on Advanced Communications and Computation (INFOCOMP), DataSys, the DigitalWorld umbrella conferences, the International Conference on Advanced Geographic Information Systems, Applications, and Services (GEOProcessing), the International Conference on Technical and Legal Aspects of the e-Society (CYBERLAWS), the International Conference on Digital Society (ICDS), the International Conference on Mobile, Hybrid, and On-line Learning (eL&mL), the International Conference on Information, Process, and Knowledge Management (eKNOW), the International Conference on eHealth, Telemedicine, and Social Medicine (eTELEMED), the DataSys and SoftNet umbrella conferences, the International Conference on Advanced Geographic Information Systems & Web Services (GEOWS), as well as the International Conference on Grid Services Engineering and Management (GSEM), the International Scientific-Practical Conference (HTFR), the International Conference on Numerical Analysis and Applied Mathematics (ICNAAM), and the International Supercomputing Conference (ISC). Starting from the long-term work within the LX Foundation and GEXI Consortium, these conferences have been a central point for scientific collaboration and inspiring discussions on a vast number of interdisciplinary research aspects of integrated communication, information, and computing systems over many years. A large number of issues would not have been enlightened without this active and professional collaboration of international, multicontinental, and multi-disciplinary work groups and joint international expert panels along with many other scientific events beyond regional limitations. It is these international collaborations, with increasing power being the driving force of the innovative development and governance of the future communication, computation, and Internet infrastructure, much more than any edentulous administrative paper tiger workgroup could have done within the last decades.

My thanks go to the scientists in the national and international research groups, scientific and academic associations, and societies for sharing their experiences working with applications scenarios on high end resources as to name the ZIV resources or the North-German Supercomputing Alliance (HLRN) resources, and national funding bodies and alliances that supported parts of the work in the last years, especially there are to name the International Academy, Research, and Industry Association (IARIA), Partnership for Advanced Computing in Europe (PRACE), the Distributed European Infrastructure for Supercomputing Applications (DEISA), the Gauss Alliance, as well as the German e-Science Initiative, and the German Grid Initiative (D-Grid) and for funding of the German High End Computing initiatives thanks go to the German Federal Ministry of Education and Research (BMBF) and the German Research Association (DFG).

I am grateful to the colleagues at the Institute for Legal Informatics (IRI), Faculty of Law, at the Leibniz Universität Hannover, Germany and the postgraduate participants in the European Legal Informatics Study Programme (EULISP), in the postgraduate LL.M. programme in IT-Law and Intellectual Property Law within the last years, especially the participants of the Information Science, Security, and Computing lectures for continuous fruitful discussions and stimulation as well as the colleagues at the Westfälische Wilhelms-Universität Münster (WWU), in the natural sciences, archaeological, and information sciences disciplines for their scientific and technical suggestions and support over the last ten years. A special thanks goes to the private and public supporters who supported this research work by providing communication and computing resources which would not have been available to provide at the local and central institutions.

I also like to thank the team of IGI Global, in particular to Mrs. Myla R. Merkel, Ms. Jan Travers, and Ms. Jennifer Romanchak for their great support and patience. Without their invaluable assistance, this book would have just remained a good idea.

This book shall not be the culmination of collaboration and development for Integrated Information and Computing Systems but the prelude to increased future commitment to these topics. Although in this compilation the space has limited us to a number of representative topics, with these, many concepts have been discussed and put together, ranging from social, technical, and scientific to natural sciences aspects. We will go on with our work in order to bring those integrated systems, components, and infrastructures to life.

Thank you!

Claus-Peter Rückemann
Westfälische Wilhelms-Universität (WWU) & Leibniz Universität Hannover & North German
*   Supercomputing Alliance (HLRN), Germany*
August 2012

Section 1
Collaboration, Frameworks, and Legal Aspects

Chapter 1
Integrated Information and Computing Systems for Advanced Cognition with Natural Sciences

Claus-Peter Rückemann
*Westfälische Wilhelms-Universität (WWU) & Leibniz Universität Hannover
& North-German Supercomputing Alliance (HLRN), Germany*

ABSTRACT

This chapter gives a comprehensive overview of the present status of Integrated Information and Computing Systems for complex use cases and system architectures in order to exploit new resources for opening up new cognitive insights for natural sciences applications. It shows up with the challenges creating complex integrated information and computing components and covers implementation, frameworks, and security issues with these processes and how the overall complexity can be reduced using collaboration frameworks with Distributed and High Performance Computing resources in natural sciences disciplines for building integrated public / commercial information system components within the e-Society. The focus is on using a collaboration framework for integrating computing resources with information system components, interfaces for data and application interchange, based on current developments and embedding development, operational, up to strategical level. Referenced are the case studies within the long-term GEXI project, GISIG framework and Active Source components used in heterogeneous environments. The Collaboration house framework has been created over the last years and is being used for a number of scenarios in research environments, using High End Computing resources. The application of these methods for commercial service structures affords the consideration of various legal, security, and trust aspects. This has already been used by international partners from geosciences, natural sciences, industry, economy, and education though this concept has been found a solution for the component integration and cooperation for information systems, e.g., in natural sciences and archaeology. Nevertheless the different aspects and situations need to be collected in order to provide and disseminate them for wider use. Examples are Envelope Interfaces for geoscientific processing, from advanced scientific computing up to High Performance Computing and Information Systems as well as enabling object security and verification for Integrated Information and Computing Systems.

DOI: 10.4018/978-1-4666-2190-9.ch001

INTRODUCTION

Information systems are based on information but as any real world electronic implementation they need computer systems in order to provide their functions and make them widely usable. Many of these implementations have to provide information based on text, image and manyfold multimedia data, views and structures as introduced with information system cognostics (Edwards, 1996; Montello, 1993; Tversky, 1993). Those implementations have been going ahead and providing interactive or complex information for new insight will need increased computing power (The Exascale Report, 2011; Exascale Project, 2012). This is essential for building cognostic components as for example necessary for geocognostics applications, e.g., for geosciences, environmental sciences, for archaeology and cultural heritage information systems and comparable application scenarios. The prominent "Information System" components still completely ignore these advanced aspects and abilities for integration and computing.

From the high level view the system components are tools for gathering advanced cognition. Cognition is not an ability of a system component but the result of the interaction between user and system components. The more these components integrate multidisciplinary aspects the more potential for new insights can be provided.

After decades of isolated system components many application scenarios do need a change in paradigm on how these systems can be build and operated. The basic question "Which parts are needed for building flexible and sustainable systems based in information and computing systems?" is getting in the focus of many disciplines working towards the goal of complex systems, overcoming the development and operational obstacles and legal-technical issues (Rückemann, 2010) with collaboration and implementation. The experiences with real world development and operation of resources has led to three main columns for this goal.

- Resources (hardware, networking, operational services).
- Services (application services, interactive services, batch services).
- Disciplines (algorithms, dynamical components, information systems, databases).

Once building integrated systems, we will have to support these arrangements and leave space for individual concepts necessary for special cases, using a collaboration framework based on the Collaboration house framework (initially with Grid Computing known as Grid-GIS house framework) for operational to strategical level (Figure 1). The Collaboration house implementation based on geosciences, services, and High End Computing gave insight into the employment of scripting languages and source code based persistent object data for enabling the use of computing resources for geoscientific information systems. It enables sole tenants as well as multiple tenants and groups to configure and operate their applications very flexible and to exploit the available resources to their needs. The basic concept of object graphics based on Active Source has been developed within the GISIG actmap project. Dynamical, event based cartography and visualisation using event-triggered databases and using distributed computing resources have been very successfully adopted for different up-to-date use cases (GEXI, 2012). The results and review of the most prominent issues of development and operation and state of the art dynamical integrated systems regarding information systems and disciplines, resources, and computing have been considered (Rückemann, 2011c).

There are various resources and issues interlinked with these implementations. The next sections categorise them for use with modern collaboration frameworks and will give an impression of which complexity we have to think of when discussing complex systems. This chapter compares implementation case studies from natural sciences in order to show the application

Figure 1. Integrated Information and Computing System Framework (Collaboration house)

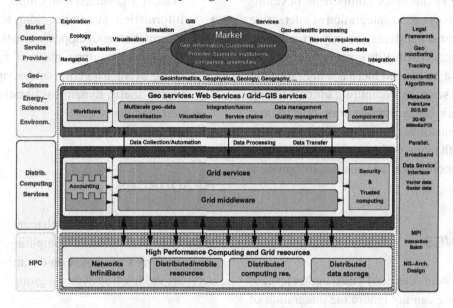

of the collaboration framework. Besides, High End Computing resources like ZIVGrid, HLRN, and resources within the German e-Science framework, have been considered as well as requirements resulting from various specialised information systems. The overall results and conclusions are presented in the following sections of this chapter.

COGNOSTICS AND INTEGRATED SYSTEMS

The integration of geometrical and information systems approaches and cognitive approaches leads to the concept of geocognostics (Edwards, 1996). Geocognostic models in most cases need to have a much more complex structure than solely geometrical models. In many cases this leads to collages of overlays for various views with these higher structures (Tversky, 1993). In addition, from the geocognostics position space and time cannot be separated. This is exactly what integrated systems will have address with their components. In combination with the definition of

data quality to correlate with the classical fitness for use (Goodchild, 1989) for a certain application scenario, these components have to obey common requirements. For example, spatial components need to reduce the constraints of drawing sharp separation and object lines for transition zone and services need to respect the common service structures and policies within collaborations. This classical paradigm has to be extended for complex systems. In any application of the cognitive domain in the future it is necessary to have an option named "it depends". Experience has shown that this has to be considered from development to end-user level.

A theoretical understanding embracing information system aspects and cognitive aspects is needed. Besides the special abilities of integrated spatial components as combination of geometrical and cognitive aspects with topological concepts, cognitive spaces, the combination of spatial models and data structures, handling of statistics, and understanding of space-time relations from real world to cognitive views there are much more essential abilities needed for integrated components in general.

This theory includes component development, system operation, integration of interactive human-computer interfaces, security, error theory, and customisation of quality aspects. As cognitive spaces cannot be imaged there is a high demand for advanced scientific computing and calculating real and virtual humans trajectories, objects, and views, for transformation and projection in order to represent the views of these non-linear spaces in the local geometrical and abstract information system space.

OBJECTIVES

For future systems that need a next higher level of complexity we can not ignore the integration of software and hardware issues anymore. Besides the aspects presented to overcome development and operational obstacles and legal collaboration issues, along with this framework there are various implementation issues with integrated systems covered with this chapter. Long-term case studies with Integrated Information and Computing Systems (IICS) showed that for various application scenarios system components needed a higher level of resources integration and handling of joint issues:

- Integrated external resources usage with interactive components.
- Interactive integration of highly performant resources.
- Trustable operation with information resources.
- Trustable handling of interactive and batch computing requirements.
- Verification of intermediate processes for critical data.
- Ensuring the integrity of large object and file collections.
- Filtering of information content.
- Quantity reduction without loss of information.

- Priority algorithms using links.
- Information structures, long-term usable information encyclopedia creations.
- Dynamical components and applications using event triggering and scripting, providing shells, dynamical libraries, servers, and modules.
- Integrated accounting.

RESOURCES

The resources needed to implement complex Integrated Information and Computing Systems on an overall view are based on disciplines groups, services groups, and systems groups.

Disciplines Resources

These resources are the main information source from which more complex systems are built. Examples for these resources are:

- Information databases.
- Image databases.
- Batch applications.
- Information System components.

Services Resources

Services resources are used to provide mechanisms and interfaces to interweave systems and system components. Web Services is one but not the only and not the most important group. Examples are:

- HyperText Transfer Protocol (HTTP),
- HyperText Transfer Protocol Secure sockets (HTTPS),
- Secure Shell (SSH),
- Secure Copy (SCP),
- Web Pricing and Ordering Service (WPOS),
- Web Processing Service (WPS),
- Web Catalog Service (WCAS),

- Web Coordinate Transformation Service (WCTS),
- Web Resource Service (WRS),
- Web Map Services (WMS),
- Web Feature Services (WFS),
- Web Feature Services – Gazetteer (WFS-G),
- Web Coverage Services (WCS),
- Open Location Services (OpenLS),
- Web 3D Service (W3DS).

Systems Resources

The back end resources that are used from compute systems are the basic resources. Huge High End Computing resources, High Performance Computing and Distributed Computing resources, are built from these resources. An essential idea is to use many of these resources with many resource requests. Examples of these system resources are:

- Central Processing Unit (CPU),
- Memory,
- Disk,
- Inter Process Communication (IPC),
- Network,
- File system buffer cache,
- Devices (drives, graphics devices, mobile devices).

Resources are physically distributed but logically shared. With integrated systems, the logic for using the resources will be handled in the interactive system or in the application using some resources. In case of parallelisation this can be implemented as loosely coupled or massive parallelisation. The management of the CPU and memory resources will have to be done with systems software components. The IPC being most important for interactive communication between components, it is essential that a flexible way for event triggering exists with the framework implementation. With modern implementations, fileevents and channels can be used in very effi-

cient and effective ways, as with Tcl. With modern IPC concepts we do have a number of means of communication, for example:

- Channels: Sockets, Pipes, Files, FIFO and named pipes.
- Shared memory and semaphores.
- Application level message passing.
- Terminals implementations (like pseudo-terminals), databases, message passing (like MPI), Spread, YAMI, signals.

There exist a lot of implementation based on Remote Procedure Call (RPC), service oriented and object oriented IPC, shared state, message passing like POSIX message queues, tmpi, and XPA. Based on the various IPC methods, the communication of local components can be implemented very efficiently. Scheduling and event triggering of loosely coupled components depend on this communication.

ISSUES

The issues for complex systems are reflected by the same groups that deliver and use the resources needed: disciplines, services, and systems respective resources.

Disciplines Issues

- Scientific aspects,
- Data gathering,
- Data preparation,
- Data enrichment,
- Consultancy policies,
- Legal policies.

Services Issues

- Modularisation,
- Provisioning,
- Interfaces.

Systems Issues

- Code optimisation,
- System optimisation,
- System use optimisation,
- Political scheduling,
- Site policies,
- Workload sizing (size, geometry),
- Match site expectations.

Code optimisation is on place one for portable components regarding integrated systems. System and system use optimisation are less important due to fact that commonly there will be no need for resources pinning. Today the impediments of optimised programming for long-term use are far to deep to handle for most disciplines. The jobs and their processes should run efficiently on different resources. With political scheduling and site poli-cies there will most likely be technical measures reflecting constraints. For a typical application scenario common policies should be definable. Mission critical scenarios in such environments will face the fact that different resources provid-ers mostly will not be able to provide identical operations and maintenance conditions.

COMPONENTS AT WORK

The following discussion sums up the results of the various case studies and experiences derived from the developments made within the last years (GEXI, 2012; Rückemann, 2011b) in order to get to a more complete overview of the current state of development, goals and aspects with integrated systems (Figure 2).

A number of case studies have shown demand for fundamental functionalities. Computing case

Figure 2. Overview with application examples from an Integrated System

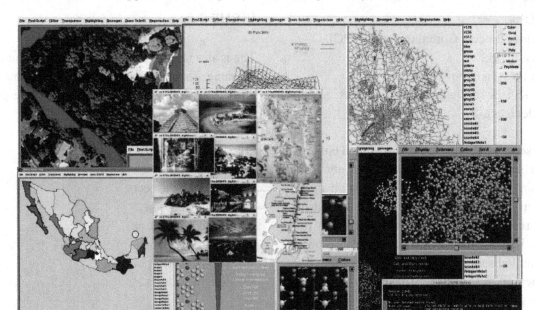

studies have shown demand for flexible integration of interactive and batch jobs into the users data domain (Condor, 2008; D-Grid, 2008; ZIVSMP, 2009; ZIVHPC, 2009; HLRN, 2012). Examples are spanning from precomputation of objects like graphics data operations or compute intensive database requests up to geoprocessing of geophysical data. This means compute jobs and resources cannot be handled like external means, out of range of an information or processing system. The most prominent disciplines on these resources are natural sciences like geosciences, geophysics, physics, archaeology, and many other fields with theoretical and applied usage scenarios (Yin, Shaw, Wang, Carr, Berry, Gross, & Comiskey, 2011). Accounting case studies have shown that distributed systems will need an integrated accounting and billing concept in order to provide application and service focused accounting and billing for resources, services, and content contained in and provided by components (Rückemann, Göhner & Baur, 2007; Göhner & Rückemann, 2006, *"Accounting-Ansätze im Bereich des Grid-Computing"; Göhner & Rückemann, 2006, "Konzeption eines Grid-Accounting-Sys-*

*tems"; Elmroth, Galán, Henriksson, & Perales, 2009). Figure 3 shows examples for accountable data used: application usage (GISIG application) with raster data, vector data, navigation data, surplus commercial data and various secondary data.

Natural sciences and epidemiology case studies have shown that besides computing, the information usage has to fulfill various mission critical demands, for example regarding cryptographic methods and security.

The comparison of the "Trust in Computing" and "Trust in Information" scenarios with Integrated Information and Computing Systems shows the different focus. Although these might be more or less interesting for some disciplines and tasks, modern integrated systems will need to enable user groups and services providers to cover all of these with a unique, holistic concept for resources providing, provisioning, and usage.

This is especially essential for systems that need a large and long-term cooperation and support infrastructures, like environmental, geoscientific, and climatological monitoring and computing systems.

Figure 3. Example GISIG application using various accountable data and interaction

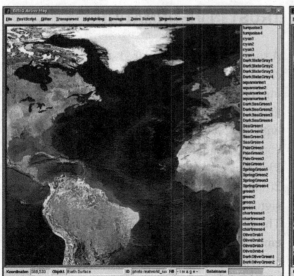 

Today most solutions will need some individual software and hardware configuration. These demands should be reduced with future system architectures. Many of the existing infrastructures are too monolithic and even too much depending on uncoordinated operating system level features. The BOINC infrastructure (BOINC, 2012) for example is used for public resources computing, desktop grid, and trivial parallel computing but like with many other current network computing infrastructures, development for such infrastructures is still much too time consuming and the development of BOINC applications for wider use can only be considered a serious services level task.

In the future integrated systems will certainly still be able to use client and server components, Web Services, approved access methods, and many other well known techniques but the focus of development as well as from users side will be the integration level and how content and context can be handled from application view.

Main aspects of operating these systems in mission critical environments and in combination with social interaction are:

- Reliability in operation.
- Trust in information.
- Trust in computing.
- Privacy of individual data.

Reliability is mostly a matter of implementation in the physical world of operation. For mission critical logistics the information and computing chain has to rely on various prerequisites like sufficient compute, storage, and memory resources, fast and stable broadband networks and a secure network infrastructure in order to avoid shortnesses, bottlenecks, and delays. Information exchange can be handled by means of verification. The implementation of non-closed systems has to consider verification methods like signatures from a Certification Authority (CA) and checksums. It is the purpose of this discussion to focus on logical components and not to show up with the various hardware and implementation issues but for reliable and secure information system and computing usage, any case with mission critical implementations, even more important the more they contain distributed computing and mobile components a fallback solution is essential, based on data replication and emergency procedures.

How have the concepts been realised for basic application components in order to gain cognitive facilities? The following sections will show some important topics and their solutions for special integration problems from existing cases, like with Trust in Information, Trust in Computing, critical data verification in intermediate processes, many-file integrity, content filtering, filealiasing, multilinking.

The overview (Table 1) shows a summary of resources and associated issues regarding the context of High End Computing and some selected examples addressed in the case studies for integrated systems.

As the overall complexity of integrated systems is much higher, from the architecture as well as from operational point of view, even for tasks and interfaces that might seem quite simple, we have choosen a range of different components for the discussion following in the next sections.

TRUST IN INFORMATION

A successful content centred solution for various cases with Integrated Information and Computing Systems, integrating resources, services, and natural sciences disciplines has been developed with the Object Envelopes (OEN). The OEN concept is able to describe any form of object PKI data (Rückemann & Gersbeck-Schierholz, 2011). Various meta data can be used to handle signatures and describe the signed object data. The OEN itself is able to describe any form of embedded or referred meta data. The sample excerpt (Listing 1) shows a simple example for an Object Envelope.

Table 1. Overview of selected resources and components for integrated systems

Resources	Issues	Examples regarding High End Computing	Implementation examples in case studies
Computing Systems	• Trust in computing	• Verification of batch scripts • Verification of system parameters	• Compute Envelopes
Storage	• Trust, reliability, redundancy	• Data reliability and verification	• archivetest • ssedit
Information Systems	• Trust in information • Data verification • Many file integrity • Content filtering • Filealiasing • Multilinking	• Geoscientific databases (LX Project) • Genom databases • Databases with medical data • Databases with climate data • Geoinformation databases • Event databases (GISIG, actmap) • Environmental databases, etc.	• Object Envelopes
Network components	• Reliability • High availability	• Routing, redundancy, monitoring and criticality management	• [commercial solutions]
Appl./ Libraries	• Transparency • Security • Sandboxing • Interfaces	• Software licenses • Program libraries • Dynamical libraries • Library collections for disciplines (mathematics, numerics, parallelisation, geosciences, spatial information, seismics, environmental and medical sciences)	• actlib
Structuring information	• Heterogeneity • Language objects	• Multilingual information	• LX Project databases
Content	• Object handling	• Dynamical components • Multilinking • Image provisioning	• actmap • imageprovisioning • multilink • myWish • asrvProcess
Additional resources	–	• Service components/Service elements • Information systems • QoS parameters (e.g. priorities), etc.	• ISV codes • Special print services • Visualisation • Administration / support, etc.

The OEN solution has been found to be a flexible and extensible solution for creating a secure environment for Integrated Information and Computing Systems. Studies showed that nearly any data structure can be handled with object envelopes in embedded or referred use. The need for modular solutions is reflected by various interdisciplinary cases and scenarios (ICDS-GEO-CYBERLAWS Joint International Panel, 2011; Rückemann, 2011a). Using individual data, privacy issues do not allow to operate these systems in a monopolistic centralised way on one hand. On the other hand individual data may not be spread in distributed environments. The only way

out is to handle this condition privacy-economically restrained, being economic with privacy data and to gather as little information as ever possible. Trust in information concepts can help to realise these complex tasks.

TRUST IN COMPUTING

Envelopes can be used to integrate descriptive and generic processing information. Currently "trust in computing" can cover the "content" aspects (Rückemann, 2010; Rückemann, 2011a). The container concept developed has been called Com-

Listing 1. Object Envelope (OEN)

```
<ObjectEnvelope><!-- ObjectEnvelope (OEN)-->
<Object>
<Filename>GIS_Case_Study_20090804.jpg</Filename>
<Md5sum>...</Md5sum>
<Sha1sum>...</Sha1sum>
<DateCreated>2010-08-01:221114</DateCreated>
<DateModified>2010-08-01:222029</DateModified>
<ID>...</ID><CertificateID>...</CertificateID>
<Signature>...</Signature>
<Content><ContentData>...</ContentData></Content>
</Object>
</ObjectEnvelope>
```

pute Envelope (CEN), inspired by the excellent experiences with the concept of Self Contained applications (SFC). The shown paragraph (Listing 2) lists an excerpt of an CEN embedded into an actmap data set.

With the CEN various items can be controlled, like, for example, information and computing resources instructions, links between the information and computing system, prerequisites of the computing system, processing directives and script elements, input/output data necessary. Besides the algorithmic content and the CEN itself can be signed, the context of the CEN cannot be signed in any way. So, due to the complexity of the environment, the fitness for a specific purpose cannot be guaranteed. In this case geo-location information can be integrated with various geological, archaeological, and context information, e.g., via InfoPoint or additional dynamical features, even when based on compute intensive algorithms.

The concept implements the threefold disciplines, services, resources columns framework. The principal workflow for envelope interfaces making use of these columns can be implemented in a simple and effective way with integrated systems (Figure 4). How CEN and OEN frameworks are used is depicted in Figure 5.

Workflow a) (Figure 4) shows an example for a communication between application components via Inter-Process Communication. Workflow b) illustrates a storage task with request and response using Object Envelopes, and c) illustrates a compute task using Compute Envelopes. Figure 5 explains the compute and storage workflows in detail, respecting the necessary threefold disciplines-services-resources structure.

CRITICAL DATA VERIFICATION IN INTERMEDIATE PROCESSES

Integrated systems do consist of components that will be more or less distributed. With mission critical environments there will be need not only for system security (Chakrabarti, 2007) but also for additional data security. In standard environments one might have backup, archive, checksums and secure access channels. In many cases this is not enough, the more if the level of critical issues increases.

For example with intermediate processes, data will not be controlled by checksums while edited or processed. Once data is corrupted anywhere within the workflow this will lead to problems. Reasons can be communication problems, un-

Listing 2. Compute Envelope (CEN) embedded into a dynamical actmap data set

```
#BCMT----------------------------------------------------
###EN \gisigsnip{Object Data: Country Mexico}
#ECMT----------------------------------------------------
proc create_country_mexico {} {
global w
#   Sonora
$w create polygon 0.938583i 0.354331i 2.055118i ...
#BCMT----------------------------------------------------
###EN \gisigsnip{Compute Data: Compute Envelope (CEN)}
#ECMT----------------------------------------------------
#BCEN <ComputeEnvelope>
##CEN <Instruction>
##CEN <Filename>Processing_Bat_GIS515.torque</Filename>
##CEN <Md5sum>...</Md5sum>
##CEN <Sha1sum>...</Sha1sum>
##CEN <Sha512sum>...</Sha512sum>
##CEN <DateCreated>2010-09-12:230012</DateCreated>
##CEN <DateModified>2010-09-12:235052</DateModified>
##CEN <ID>...</ID><CertificateID>...</CertificateID>
##CEN <Signature>...</Signature>
##CEN <Content>...</Content>
##CEN </Instruction>
#ECEN </ComputeEnvelope>
...
proc create_country_mexico_autoevents {} {
global w
$w bind legend_infopoint <Any-Enter> {set killatleave \
   [exec ./mexico_legend_infopoint_viewall.sh $op_parallel ] }
$w bind legend_infopoint <Any-Leave> \
   {exec ./mexico_legend_infopoint_kaxv.sh }
$w bind tulum <Any-Enter> {set killatleave \
   [exec $appl_image_viewer -geometry +800+400 \
   ./mexico_site_name_tulum_temple.jpg $op_parallel ] }
$w bind tulum <Any-Leave> \
   {exec kill -9 $killatleave }
} ...
```

wanted modifications from third parties or third party components, operating system and hardware failures like memory errors and disk failure. Either on one hand there might be no chance or time to correct the data or on the other hand the backup or archive data might get corrupted.

In standard modular editing processes one relies on the editing process. Data integrity will

Figure 4. Workflow example for envelope interfaces for Integrated Systems

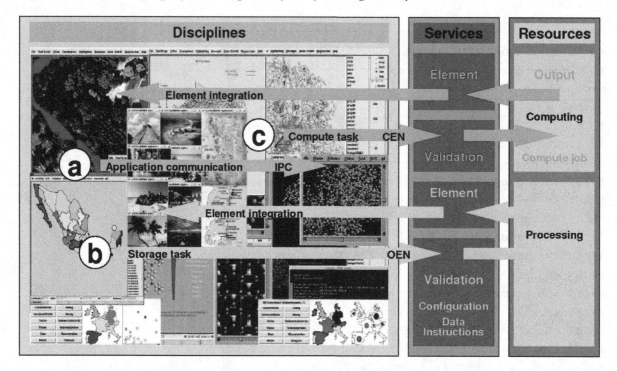

be checked within the database or storage, if at all checked completely. The editing process itself is not wrapped. Neither commercial tools nor free tools have supported the necessary features for dynamical information systems so far.

For integrated systems and applications a secure store edit (ssedit) component has been developed, currently supporting the following features.

- Prepare primary data for provisioning on multiple target platforms (HR devices, smartphones).
- Calculate checksums before accessing data.
- Calculate checksums after accessing data.
- Data verification before and after access.
- Allows logging of data accesses and checksums.
- Can be configured to use any check method.
- Actions can be configured for checksum mismatch.

For graphical as well as for console access a non forking editor access can be achieved for editing data entries. ssedit can be used with any checksum method like md5 or sha512 for example. It can use an accompanying checksum file for the data resource handled. This is important because the part of the data itself, providing trust in information for the overall system components.

The checksum storage and calculation can be done of different resources than the rest of the components used for the integrated information systems itself. The ssedit has been tested within the LX Project (LX Project, 2012) case studies. It showed up to be a valuable support drastically increasing the data reliability. In cases of memory corruption, which is getting an important issue with system memory being increased with all high end systems, it showed automatically while accessing data which parts have been modified by memory errors.

Figure 5. Use of CEN and OEN frameworks with Integrated Systems

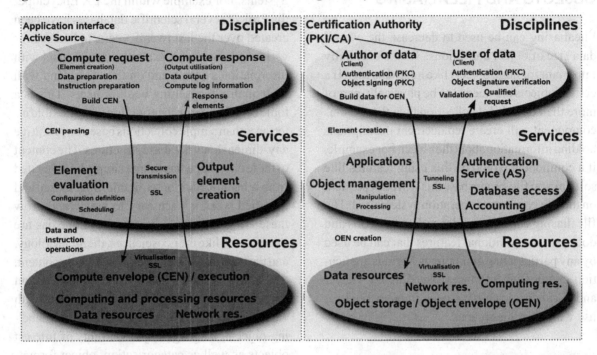

MANY-FILE INTEGRITY

In order to verify the integrity of collections of many files, archive verification methods can be used. This for example includes the hierarchically use of check sums. The archivetest component for example checks the integrity of archive objects as well as of hierarchical object collections. This component can be used in combination with checksums and data verification.

CONTENT FILTERING

Images and video streams used in information systems can be a very valuable good and like other data they should be in the focus of security concerns. The imageprovisioning component, for example, can modify EXIF data, the image size, manipulate the resolution, support the preparation for High Resolution (HR) devices and so on. In general these features are:

- Prepare primary data for provisioning on multiple target platforms (HR devices, smartphones).
- Format conversion.
- Clipping.
- Resolution adaptation.
- Resampling.
- Scaling.
- Codec modification.
- Remove or change secondary data.
- Copyright and licensing data.
- Encrypt data.
- Sign data.

Why would these features be necessary? The information that is contained may be the essential value for some business partner, maybe mission critical or may contain data or information that is in the focus of privacy issues or legal regulations.

OBJECTS AND FILEALIASING

Filealiasing can be used to decrease the overall data size of object collections. This is especially important for huge objects like huge data sets. If a certain objects are needed to be physically part of more than one object collection then the filealias component will create replacement descriptions holding information about the object. For example, if a component would do this using features like soft links on file system base this will be dependent on the file system and operation system used. The filealiasing concept is independent from this and does provide additional features that can be used by any participating component. Various application component interfaces like filealias_viewer and filealias_locate have been implemented for use with existing systems.

OBJECTS AND MULTILINKING

Multilinking is a concept of putting priority and multiplicity on generic data accesses and processes. The multilink component implements multiple instances of objects in a suitable way. For example, if from some object collection a quasi random access is needed by a certain component, may be for displaying a random photo of a group of photos, the component can be used to increase the priority by creating soft links in the file system for prioritised objects.

STRUCTURING INFORMATION

For long-term use complex information creations need to be structured and organised in a flexible and portable way. Not only the size and complexity of such creations themselves will drastically increase over the years but also the internal objects will need structuring and formatting instructions. The encyclopedia creations are an essential source for various Integrated Information and Computing

Systems. For example within the LX Encyclopedia Project several scientific databases have been created over the last twenty years, to be used for various purposes, for example, on one hand with information systems and on the other hand with high quality typesetting book projects. This is a topic centred approach providing more flexible interfaces than simple collections based on primitive any-dimensional database structures. The content of these encyclopedias cannot simply be generated from other information available. Specialised and qualified work is necessary to create and grow these encyclopedias. Various encyclopedias are interwoven, like the geosciences, the archaeology, and the information science encyclopedia content.

Listing 3 shows some excerpt geo content objects from the LX Encyclopedia Project with various properties. This includes content and labeling objects, language objects, Points of Interest objects as well as categorisation, object formatting, and referencing for example via Universal Decimal Classification (UDCC, 2011), indexing, and object internationalisation properties.

DYNAMICAL COMPONENTS

Dynamical components are an essential part of Integrated Information and Computing Systems. The more we focus on interactive information system components that need compute power in time, the more we need dynamical features within these components. These features are needed for triggering event, for providing communication with other components and for interlinking components and applications.

Therefore we need to ask "Is there a unique way how the dynamical requirements of integrated systems can be implemented?" The answer is "Yes, there is a common concept but no common implementation!". The principle is to use meta structures for information and for compute instructions. The way how the interfacing will be

Listing 3. Structuring examples with LX Encyclopedia Project

```
CMP          %-GP%-XX%---: CMP              [Seismik]:

             %-GP%-XX%---:                  Common Mid-Point,

             %-GP%-XX%---:                  ...

             %-GP%-DE%---:                  %%ASC: Ccmp_2D = (1/2)(Anz.d.Kanäle) * x_Geophon / x_shot

             %-GP%-DE%---:                  %%BTe:

             %-GP%-DE%---:                  %%TeX: \begineq{

             %-GP%-DE%---:                  %%TeX: \hbox{$C_{\rm cmp,2D}=\dsty\frac{\hbox{Anz. d. Kan\"ale}}{2}

             %-GP%-DE%---:                  %%TeX:        \cdot\dsty\frac{x_{\rm Geophon}}{x_{\rm shot}}$}

             %-GP%-DE%---:                  %%TeX: }%\end{equation}

             %-GP%-DE%---:                  %%ETe:

             %-GP%-XX%---:                  ...

             %-GP%-DE%---:                  %%ASC: x_2D         als Spurabstand

             %-GP%-DE%---:                  %%ASC: x_2D * y_2D als Basislinie-bin

             %-GP%-DE%---:                  %%ASC: R_Fresnel    als Radius der zentralen Fresnelzone

             %-GP%-DE%---:                  $x_{2D}$ Spurabstand, $x_{2D}\cdot y_{2D}$ Basislinie-bin,

             %-GP%-DE%---:                  $R_{Fresnel}$ Radius der zentralen Fresnelzone

             %-GP%-XX%---:                  ...

             %-GP%-DE%---:                  s. auch CMG, CDP

             %-GP%-EN%---:                  s. also CMG, CDP

Crevasse     %-GP%-XX%---: Crevasse         [Antarktis, Eis]:

             %-GP%-XX%---:                  ...

             %-GP%-XX%---:                  english:  \lxidxlangeins{Crevasse}

             %-GP%-XX%---:                  finish:   \lxidxlangeins{Railo}

             %-GP%-XX%---:                  french:   \lxidxlangeins{Crevasse}

             %-GP%-XX%---:                  german:   \lxidxlangeins{Spalte}, \lxidxlangeins{Gletscherspalte}

             %-GP%-XX%---:                  icelandic: \lxidxlangeins{Jökulsprunga}

             %-GP%-XX%---:                  norwegian: \lxidxlangeins{Bresprekk}

             %-GP%-XX%---:                  russian:   \lxidxlangeins{Lednikovaya treshchina}

             %-GP%-XX%---:                  spanish:   \lxidxlangeins{Grieta}

             %-GP%-XX%---:                  ...

Mondmilch    %-GP%-XX%---: Mondmilch        [Geologie, Speläologie]:

             %-GP%-DE%---:                  Eine weiche, weiße kalkhaltige und plastische Ablagerung, die an

             %-GP%-DE%---:                  ...

             %-GP%-EN%---:                  A soft white calcareous deposit, which occurs on the walls of

             %-GP%-EN%---:                  ...

             %-GP%-XX%---:                  Syn.: \lxidx{Bergmilch}, \lxidx{Felsmilch},

             %-GP%-XX%---:                  Syn.: \lxidx{Elfenmilch}, \lxidx{Bergmehl},

             %-GP%-XX%---:                  Syn.: moonmilk, mountain milk, elf's milk, rock milk, rock meal

             %-GP%-XX%---:                  Syn.: bergmehl, \lxidx{agaric mineral}

             %-GP%-XX%---:                  Syn.: \lxidx{Lublinit}, \lxidx{lublinite}

             %-GP%-XX%---:                       (\engger{partial syn.}{teilweise syn.})

             %-GP%-DE%---:                  s. auch Lublinit
```

continued on following page

Listing 3. Continued

```
        %-GP%-EN%---:              s. also lublinite
        %-GP%-XX%---:              %%SRC: ...
SAB     %-GP%-XX%---: SAB          [Abk, Luftfahrt]:
        %-GP%-XX%---:              Saba (Airport), Netherlands Antilles, The Caribbean.
        %-GP%-XX%---:              %%KML: ...
        %-GP%-XX%---:              %%LOC: ...
        %-GP%-XX%---:              %%SRC: ...
XPL     %-GP%-XX%---: XPL          [Mineralogie, Mikroskopie, Optik]:
        %-GP%-XX%---:              Crossed Polars.\lxidxsmic{Crossed Polars}
        %-GP%-DE%---:              Gekreuzte Polarisatoren.\lxidxs{Polarisator}
        %-GP%-DE%---:              Auch \glqq{}crossed Nichols\grqq{}.\lxidxs{Nichols}
        %-GP%-DE%---:              ...
        %-GP%-EN%---:              Also crossed nichols.\lxidxs{nichols}
        %-GP%-EN%---:              ...
        %-GP%-XX%---:              %%SRC: ...
```

realised, can depend on the application context but it is a matter of the application components!

The excerpt discussed for this is part of a dynamical data set used with the actmap framework. It can be used with dynamical information systems, triggered by events, and handled and extended by scripting means. Various methods have been implemented, from data sets like GAM and GAS data sets to object oriented components based on dynamically used classes like with GOS components (Listing 4).

With the cognostic features this approach enables to seamlessly integrate the relevant views from archaeology and geosciences disciplines for this scenario, information about sites, history, and multimedia data with geological and environmental properties and references.

GISIG Object Source and GISIG Active Map are based on GISIG Active Source. Not only that they can integrate various means of communication, like via IPC, Message Passing Interface (MPI), and Parallel Virtual Machine (PVM), for even more benefits they provide active and portable objects for dynamical applications and can be used as data set components as well as application components. The example shows some of the most important dynamical features with procedures containing spatial data, event handling and bindings.

The GOS components are based on Active Source and inherit all the features. This can include standalone applications, embeddable applications and data sets as well as all of these different qualities at the same time, within the same physical component. On the other hand it is for example possible to use only the data set objects from an executable standalone component.

Shell Environments

One of the most important prerequisites for using local dynamical components are shell environments. Dynamical components are loaded using these shells. Local components can be extended by using flexible software architectures. In the case where general features, basic commands

Listing 4. Dynamical application component (GOS) for use with Integrated Systems

```
#BCMT----------------------------------------------------
###EN \gisigsnip{Object Data: Country Mexico}
###EN Minimal Active Source example with InfoPoint:
###EN Yucatan (Cancun, Chichen Itza, Tulum).
#ECMT----------------------------------------------------
proc create_country_mexico {} {
global w
$w create polygon 9.691339i 4.547244i 9.667717i \
   4.541732i 9.644094i 4.535433i 9.620472i 4.523622i \
   9.596850i 4.511811i 9.573228i 4.506299i 9.531496i \
   4.500000i 9.507874i 4.518110i 9.484252i 4.529921i \
   9.460630i 4.541732i 9.437008i 4.547244i 9.413386i \
   4.553543i 9.384252i 4.559055i 9.354331i 4.565354i \
   9.330709i 4.588976i 9.307087i 4.612598i 9.283465i \
   4.624409i 9.259843i 4.636220i 9.236220i 4.641732i \
   9.212598i 4.641732i 9.188976i 4.648031i 9.165354i \
   4.653543i 9.141732i 4.659843i 9.118110i 4.665354i \
   9.094488i 4.671654i 9.070866i 4.677165i 9.047244i \
   4.688976i 9.023622i 4.695276i 9.000000i 4.707087i \
   8.976378i 4.712598i 8.952756i 4.724409i 8.929134i \
   4.730709i 8.905512i 4.736220i 8.881890i 4.748031i \
   8.858268i 4.766142i 8.834646i 4.783465i 8.811024i \
   4.801575i 8.787402i 4.813386i 8.763780i 4.830709i \
   8.751969i 4.854331i 8.740157i 4.877953i 8.734646i \
   4.901575i 8.728346i 4.925197i 8.746457i 4.937008i \
   8.751969i 4.966929i 8.751969i 4.978740i 8.763780i \
   5.007874i 8.763780i 5.019685i 8.787402i 5.025984i \
   8.805512i 5.031496i 8.817323i 5.049606i 8.846457i \
   5.055118i 8.876378i 5.055118i 9.248031i 5.468504i \
   9.673228i 4.896063i 9.744094i 4.748031i 9.720472i \
   4.553543i \
  -outline #000000 -width 2 -fill green -tags {itemshape province_yucatan}
}

proc create_country_mexico_bind {} {
global w
$w bind province_yucatan <Button-1> {showName "Province Yucatan"}
$w bind province_quintana_roo <Button-1> \
                            {showName "Province Quintana Roo"}
}

proc create_country_mexico_sites {} {
```

continued on following page

Listing 4. Continued

```
global w
global text_site_name_cancun
global text_site_name_chichen_itza
global text_site_name_tulum
set text_site_name_cancun         "Cancún"
set text_site_name_chichen_itza   "Chichén Itzá"
set text_site_name_tulum          "Tulum"
$w create oval 8.80i 4.00i 9.30i 4.50i \
  -fill yellow -width 3 \
  -tags {itemshape site legend_infopoint}
$w bind legend_infopoint <Button-1> \
  {showName "Legend InfoPoint"}
$w bind legend_infopoint <Shift-Button-3> \
  {exec browedit$t_suff}
$w create oval 9.93i 4.60i 9.98i 4.65i \
  -fill white -width 1 \
  -tags {itemshape site cancun}
$w bind cancun <Button-1> \
  {showName "$text_site_name_cancun"}
$w bind cancun <Shift-Button-3> \
  {exec browedit$t_suff}

$w create oval 9.30i 4.85i 9.36i 4.90i \
  -fill white -width 1 \
  -tags {itemshape site chichen_itza}
$w bind chichen_itza <Button-1> \
  {showName "$text_site_name_chichen_itza"}
$w bind chichen_itza <Shift-Button-3> \
  {exec browedit$t_suff}

$w create oval 9.76i 5.20i 9.82i 5.26i \
  -fill white -width 1 \
  -tags {itemshape site tulum}
$w bind tulum <Button-1> \
  {showName "$text_site_name_tulum"}
$w bind tulum <Shift-Button-3> \
  {exec browedit$t_suff}
}

proc create_country_mexico_autoevents {} {
global w
```

continued on following page

Listing 4. Continued

```
$w bind legend_infopoint <Any-Enter> {set killatleave \
  [exec ./mexico_legend_infopoint_viewall.sh $op_parallel ] }
$w bind legend_infopoint <Any-Leave> \
  {exec ./mexico_legend_infopoint_kaxv.sh }
$w bind cancun <Any-Enter> {set killatleave \
                   [exec $appl_image_viewer -geometry +800+400 \
                        ./mexico_site_name_cancun.jpg $op_parallel ] }
$w bind cancun <Any-Leave> {exec kill -9 $killatleave }
$w bind chichen_itza <Any-Enter> {set killatleave \
                   [exec $appl_image_viewer -geometry +800+100 \
                        ./mexico_site_name_chichen_itza.jpg $op_parallel ] }
$w bind chichen_itza <Any-Leave> {exec kill -9 $killatleave }
$w bind tulum <Any-Enter> \
  {set killatleave [exec $appl_image_viewer -geometry +800+400 \
                        ./mexico_site_name_tulum.jpg $op_parallel ] }
$w bind tulum <Any-Leave> {exec kill -9 $killatleave }
}
proc create_country_mexico_application_ballons {} {
global w
global is1
gisig:set_balloon $is1.country "Notation of State and Site"
gisig:set_balloon $is1.color "Symbolic Color of State and Site"
}

create_country_mexico
create_country_mexico_bind
create_country_mexico_sites
create_country_mexico_autoevents
create_country_mexico_application_ballons

scaleAllCanvas 0.8
##EOF
```

or system specific features shall be part of the command execution or interpreter environment, these feature do not need to be implemented in dynamical components or dynamical data sets. The right place can be inside a customised shell, like a "myWish.c". These shell components are most likely to be provided by service providers or more experienced users groups.

Dynamical Libraries, Modules, and Servers

Dynamical libraries can contain component extensions, portable algorithms, and procedures. Like the actlib.tcl these libraries can collect portable procedures and can be embedded into dynamical application components.

Dynamical modules can be used to extend applications and algorithms by components residing on the system level. Modules can be loaded from a system instance on demand. This can be used to optimise performance or to retain control of restricted features.

Besides system specific server implementations, dynamical server implementations can be portable and build on dynamical code base. This works like a portable process communication with a generic interface. The following very simple asrv implementation shows two procedures, asrvProcess (Listing 5) and asrvMy (Listing 6).

This does not need to be started every time the temporary log-watch is started as every instance uses its own process and the component does not need to control processes.

This implements a very simple time limited server-like log-watch. In order to load asrv server procedures from a shell source asrv can be used. A background process can be activated from a shell with asrvProcess. With this it is possible to start a time limited server from the shell with asrvMy.

Now some user or component triggered action can be entered, e.g. in a xterm a remote command can be issued, for example using

```
echo "\$w move germany 50 30" >>asrv.log
```

The command execution will be slightly delayed due to the various actions that are taken. As long as the log-file is not cleaned, it contains a complete history of the commands that have been sent. Remember that if one uses a time limited server, commands will only be evaluated as long as the procedure is running. The time limited server can be reactivated by starting it again for example by calling asrvMy. The asrvProcess is not needed to be run again as long as it is running and as long as there is no need to change anything in it's configuration. Anyway, every program that can be used or modified to append valid commands to the log, like with the actmap framework, might work with this procedure.

EVALUATION

On one hand cognitive multidisciplinary systems can lead to new insights. On the other hand it can be very expendable to create cognitive system components and it can be even very costly to operate these complex systems. This sometimes prevents from the creation of appropriate architectures. Even Cloud Computing, Sky Computing or other recycled systems creation concepts do not help to overcome the mid- and long-term deficits.

Frameworks for integration of components have been found a most valuable means to be considered when using, developing, and operating components for the next generation of integrated systems. The most economic overall results have been found when implementing and operating systems strictly following the underlying framework concept and local policies. The total costs of development and operation did not show additional long-term costs. The holistic total costs of ownership for disciplines, services, and resources have been considered to be drastically reduced with this concept. So this result addresses to funding bodies, too, for which the costs and sustainability of complementary projects in most cases might be an issue with funding.

Any of the main components, e.g., object operations, structuring, dynamical components, libraries and interfaces, can be provided on modular, recyclable, and transparent base. The threefold complementary organisational structure, resources, services, disciplines, lead to a separation of development, operation, and security issues, appropriate for handling in a suitable context. The security issues regard data security and system security.

- Resources and server side (operating system and user space).
- Services and application side (source and binary).
- Disciplines side (data and information).

Listing 5. Simple user space server implementation for dynamical applications

```
proc asrvProcess { } {
  if { [catch {
    exec perl /home/cpr/bin/atchange asrv.log asrvcmd.sh &
  } asrvtmpcatch ] } {
    puts "$asrvtmpcatch"
  }
}
```

For example, components on disciplines level can be extended by defining services interfaces. Resources can be configured and operated in order to adapt to the context requirements. A seamless coverage of cognitive system coverage can be provided that way. Building integrated systems, based on a suitable framework considering the overall life cycle of an integrated system, can provide a valuable fundamental support not only for interdisciplinary but multidisciplinary information and computing systems, integrating natural sciences and social sciences components. Content, interactive dynamical processes and algorithms, e.g., from geosciences, archaeology, and information science disciplines can be easily integrated, as for archaeological geophysics.

With modern applications, requiring interactive and dynamical use of large resources, flexibility for configuration and application is much more important than the number of compute nodes

only. This flexibility has been the case for the ZIVSMP resources as well as some other smaller resources. Many old fashion systems, mostly High Performance Computing resources cannot come up with flexibility of configuration and access necessary for demanding application scenarios. Tender procedures as well as policies, long life cycles, and even sliced monolithic components do not allow an up to date development for the next generation of applications.

The complexity and number of components in High End Computing (HEC) systems is steadily increasing. Computing is beginning to face the next generation of systems with ExaFlop/s range and hundreds of thousands of processors, memory, hard disk, network, and management components. At the same time economical considerations will still be present for the next years, forcing to efficiently handle productive operation and use of these computing, storage, and information system

Listing 6. Time limited server-like log-watch for portable user space servers

```
proc asrvMy { } {
for {set ll 10} {$ll <= 90000} {incr ll 1000} {
  catch {
    after [expr $ll * 1] source asrv.tmp
  }
  catch {
    after [expr $ll * 2] exec echo "" > asrv.tmp
  }
}
}
```

resources, drastically increasing I/O and data sizes at the same time when decreasing overall costs as with broad band, high availability, and redundancy. Providers, users, and developers are facing immense problems with portability, configuration, and effectiveness of their solutions if we will not provide solutions and frameworks in the near future. The major mid-term challenges to be addressed with integrated high end systems for future large scale distributed systems as well as with High Performance Computing systems for computing and processing purposes are:

- Hardware and architecture monitoring interfaces.
- Management solutions for large numbers of hardware and software components.
- HEC memory management on operation system level and communication.

The consequences of these issues are on economic and scientific level, regarding user efficiency, operation efficiency, and funding efficiency.

Performance, quality, and energy optimisation is not possible without overall hardware and software concepts. Monitoring of large system architectures requires hardware interfaces, as well as benchmarking optimisation of large resources requires hardware benchmarking.

The management software components will not only have to address large numbers of hardware and software components, they have to use modular concepts intelligently, for example creating cascading management solutions on systems operation for minimising communication bottlenecks, for example with continuous software distribution and patches in order to be efficient regarding productivity, time, and security. For the next generation of large complex intelligent systems we need fully integrated network and component management solutions addressing autonomous collaborative system components and

fitting into the access, trust, and security policies for provisioning of advanced systems resources. On the hardware side these basic features will have to be supported by intelligent hardware and professional power management, hardware monitoring, and extended configurability. This expresses the need for reliability and integrity solutions as well as for high availability, and buffering concepts, including an intelligent job management with scheduling, batch, accounting, and hardware management and implementing cascading system management with a central point of administration. At the level of complexity of modern systems a software-only or hardware-only solution is absolutely not feasible from the holistic point of view. The integrative aspects of software and hardware architecture regarding these issues are not addressed by the latest computing initiatives, like Grid and Cloud. They have not addressed the software focus and cannot cope with these basic deficits or deliver solutions for scalable and economic handling of growing resources. Even from the content point of view there are unsolved issues as with privacy and security aspects. Securing systems completely towards privacy means introducing new challenges for the society. This is true for content as well as for computing environments, e.g., using approaches of homomorphic encryption and program execution. The situation is comparable to the TSA-Locks we all know from travelling as introduced with the Transportation Security Administration initiatives, having built-in "keys" for authorities. So in case of computing, it is not given if authorities will be suitable at all and if fair overall privacy and security can be possible. These isolated computing concepts are superseded by integrated framework concepts for the next generation of systems, towards and beyond the ExaFlop/s level.

As learned from the case studies, other future applications in advanced scientific computing will, too, significantly profit from a much higher level of abstraction for communication and parallelisation.

For advanced scientific computing applications virtualisation as with the PVM system is, instead of long-winded system-specific rewriting of basic Message Passing use, widely preferred for portable and efficient use of shared and local-memory multiprocessor systems, even with heterogeneous high end resources. So the next generation of systems must be much more efficiently and securely implementing integrated software and hardware strategies in order to increase economic use and flexibility with parallelisation, for loosely as well as for massively parallel computing on user and provider side.

For disciplines the most important lesson learned is that data and information should be organised in modular long-term usable structures, fully equipped with metadata, following best practice guidelines and supporting long-term usable standards. Confirming to this should be strongly forced when national and international funding decisions are made. As on application side with such distributed resources cascading concepts have to be used for reducing bottlenecks with communication and I/O so that the result can be a more efficient operation of widely used large resources. Benefits of these developments will be a convergence of technologies for integrated intelligent system components, as with Multi-Agent Systems (MAS), advanced criticality management, and an ease of use for the overall ecosystem regarding use and development, services, and operation.

CONCLUSION

Implementing Integrated Information and Computing Systems (IICS) has grown attraction over the last years. On the one hand first concepts are available for realising complex systems and on the other hand the resources needed to provide the necessary compute power, networking, and storage are showing up. For the mid-term future common resources should be available in order to build complex integrated systems based on heterogeneous resources and components with distributed strategical level support and based on well structured and maintained data content. Currently, the insight possible has not widely reached the multi-disciplinary level. Therefore the cognitive output is still limited but the integration of information and computing systems has been found to have very high cognitive potential, e.g., for educational purposes and with archaeological geophysics. Developing suitable application components is an ongoing process. It will gain more support by international projects and dedicated funding for various systems. Long-term intended structuring and availability of information is becoming increasingly important. Suitable standards should be a strong constituent with the application scenarios.

Using High End Computing environments, system solutions as presented from the results of cluster experiences, ZIVGrid, HLRN, and various national High End Computing, Grid, and Cloud activities should be built in a more flexible way. The way computing resources are still implemented lead to very inflexible system architectures. In most cases the reasons are not with the hardware developers but on the side of those purchasing resources. Condition like these are a driving factor for intelligent components and criticality management.

The Collaboration house framework supports the flexible implementation of IICS with dynamical and advanced scientific computing components. Usage, development, and operation worked in a very flexible and efficient way for the collaboration partners from various disciplines, services, and resources providers for High End Computing as with future Clouds and Skies.

As many disciplines from natural sciences, medical sciences, and social sciences will need more integrated systems in the future we hope that a basic understanding for the complexity as well as of the potential with an inherently close integration of these systems has been shown.

There will be a lot of paradigm based work to do in order to overcome the present situation with standalone isolated system components but it will be well worth the efforts.

ACKNOWLEDGMENT

I am grateful to all national and international academic and industry partners in the GEXI cooperations for the innovative constructive work, to the members of the boards and the participants of the INFOCOMP, GEOProcessing, ICDS, and CYBERLAWS conferences for their excellent collaboration within the last years. My thanks go to the research colleagues at the Leibniz Universität Hannover, the Institute for Legal Informatics (IRI), the colleagues in the information sciences, geosciences, and archaeological sciences at the WWU, using research capacities on industry and ZIV resources, HLRN, and D-Grid for participating in fruitful case studies and to the participants of the postgraduate European Legal Informatics Study Programme (EULISP) for prolific discussion of scientific, legal, and technical aspects in my lectures and colloquia over the last years.

REFERENCES

BOINC. (2012). *Berkeley Open Infrastructure for Network Computing.* Retrieved March 25, 2012, from http://boinc.berkeley.edu

Chakrabarti, A. (2007). *Grid computing security* (1st ed.). Berlin, Germany: Springer.

Condor. (2008). *High throughput computing.* Retrieved January 2, 2011, from http://www.cs.wisc.edu/condor/

D-Grid. (2008). *The German Grid initiative.* Retrieved October 21, 2008, from http://www.d-grid.de

Edwards, G. (1996). Geocognostics - A new paradigm for spatial information? *Proceedings of the AAAI Spring Symposium 1996.*

Elmroth, E., Galán, F., Henriksson, D., & Perales, D. (2009). Accounting and billing for federated cloud infrastructures. In J. E. Guerrero (Ed.), *Proceedings of the Eighth International Conference on Grid and Cooperative Computing* (GCC 2009), (pp. 268-275). IEEE Computer Society Press.

Exascale Project. (2012). Retrieved March 25, 2012, from http://www.exascale.org.

Exascale Report. (2011). Retrieved November 27, 2011, from http://theexascalereport.com

GEXI. (2012). *Geo exploration and information.* Retrieved January 29, 2012, from http://www.user.uni-hannover.de/cpr/x/rprojs/de/#gexi

Göhner, M., & Rückemann, C.-P. (2006). *Accounting-Ansätze im Bereich des Grid-Computing.* D-Grid Integration project, D-Grid document, 24 pp. Retrieved December 28, 2007, from http://www.d-grid.de/fileadmin/dgi_document/FG2/koordination_mab/mab_accounting_ansaetze.pdf

Göhner, M., & Rückemann, C.-P. (2006). *Konzeption eines Grid-Accounting-Systems.* D-Grid Integration project, D-Grid document, 45 pp. Retrieved December 28, 2007 from http://www.d-grid.de/fileadmin/dgi_document/FG2/koordination_mab/mab_accounting_system.pdf

Goodchild, M. F. (1989). Modelling error in objects and fields . In Goodchild, M. F., & Gopal, S. (Eds.), *The accuracy of spatial databases.* London, UK: Taylor & Francis.

HLRN. (2012). *The North-German Supercomputing Alliance.* Retrieved January 29, 2012, from http://www.hlrn.de

ICDS-GEO-CYBERLAWS Joint International Panel. (2011). *ICDS-GEO-CYBERLAWS Panel on Privacy Invasion and Protection in Digital Society at DigitalWorld 2011,* February 26, 2011, Gosier, Guadeloupe, France, *The International Conference on Digital Society* (ICDS 2011), *The International Conference on Advanced Geographic Information Systems, Applications, and Services* (GEOProcessing 2011), *The International Conference on Technical and Legal Aspects of the e-Society* (CYBERLAWS 2011), February 23-28, 2011, Gosier, Guadeloupe, France / DigitalWorld 2011. Retrieved November 20, 2011, from http://www.iaria.org/conferences2011/filesICDS11/ICDS_2011_PANEL.pdf

LX Project. (2012). Retrieved January 29, 2012, from http://www.user.uni-hannover.de/cpr/x/rprojs/de/index.html

Montello, D. R. (1993). Scale and multiple psychologies of space. In A. Frank & L. Campari (Eds.), *Spatial information theory: A theoretical basis for GIS. Lecture Notes in Computer Science, No. 716*, COSIT'93, (pp. 312-321). Springer.

Rückemann, C.-P. (2010). Legal issues regarding distributed and high performance computing in geosciences and exploration. In *Proceedings of the Fourth International Conference on Digital Society (ICDS 2010),* (pp. 339-344). Retrieved April 30, 2011, from http://www.computer.org/portal/web/csdl/doi/10.1109/ICDS.2010.56

Rückemann, C.-P. (2010). Future geo-exploration information and computing systems created by academia-industry collaboration. In *Proceedings of the 9th International Scientific-Practical Conference 2010 (HTFR 2010),* April 22-23, 2010, (pp. 254-258). Saint Petersburg, Russia: Saint Petersburg University Press.

Rückemann, C.-P. (2011). Envelope interfaces for geoscientific processing with high performance computing and information systems. In C.-P. Rückemann & O. Wolfson (Eds.), *Proceedings International Conference on Advanced Geographic Information Systems, Applications, and Services (GEOProcessing 2011), February 23-28, 2011,* Gosier, Guadeloupe, France, (pp. 23-28). Retrieved April 30, 2011, from http://www.thinkmind.org/download.php?articleid=geoprocessing_2011_2_10_30030

Rückemann, C.-P. (2011a). *Securing privacy for future information and computing systems.* Panel on Privacy Invasion and Protection in Digital Society at DigitalWorld 2011, February 26, 2011, Gosier, Guadeloupe, France, ICDS-GEO-CYBERLAWS Panel, The International Conference on Digital Society (ICDS 2010), February 23-28, 2011, Gosier, Guadeloupe, France / DigitalWorld 2011. Retrieved November 20, 2011, from http://www.iaria.org/conferences2011/ProgramGEOProcessing11.html

Rückemann, C.-P. (2011b). Implementation of integrated systems and resources for information and computing. In C.-P. Rückemann, W. Christmann, S. Saini, & M. Pankowska (Eds.), *Proceedings International Conference on Advanced Communications and Computation (INFOCOMP 2011),* October 23-29, 2011, Barcelona, Spain, (pp. 1-7). ISBN: 978-1-61208-161-8

Rückemann, C.-P. (2011c). Queueing aspects of integrated information and computing systems in geosciences and natural sciences . In Chen, D. (Ed.), *Advances in data, methods, models and their applications in geoscience* (pp. 1–26). doi:10.5772/29337

Rückemann, C.-P., & Gersbeck-Schierholz, B. F. S. (2011). Object security and verification for integrated information and computing systems. In L. Berntzen, A. Villafiorita, & M. Perry (Eds.), *Proceedings of the Fifth International Conference on Digital Society (ICDS 2011), Proceedings of the International Conference on Technical and Legal Aspects of the e-Society (CYBERLAWS 2011),* February 23-28, 2011, Gosier, Guadeloupe, France, (pp. 1-6). Retrieved November 20, 2011, from http://www.thinkmind.org/download.php?articleid=cyberlaws_2011_1_10_70008

Rückemann, C.-P., Göhner, M., & Baur, T. (2007). *Towards integrated grid accounting/billing for D-Grid.* Grid Working Paper.

Tversky, B. (1993). Cognitive maps, cognitive collages, and spatial mental models. *Lecture Notes in Computer Science,* (716): 14–24. doi:10.1007/3-540-57207-4_2

UDCC. (2011). Universal decimal classification. Universal Decimal Classification Consortium (UDCC). Retrieved November 27, 2011, from http://www.udcc.org

Yin, L., Shaw, S.-L., Wang, D., Carr, E. A., Berry, M. W., Gross, L. J., & Comiskey, E. J. (2011). A framework of integrating GIS and parallel computing for spatial control problems - A case study of wildfire control. *International Journal of Geographical Information Science, 26*(4). doi:doi:10.1080/13658816.2011.609487

ZIVHPC. (2009). Retrieved October 23, 2011, from https://www.uni-muenster.de/ZIV/Technik/ZIVHPC/index.html

ZIVSMP. (2009). Retrieved October 23, 2011, from https://www.uni-muenster.de/ZIV/Technik/ZIVHPC/ZIVSMP.html

KEY TERMS AND DEFINITIONS

Collaboration House: Modular collaboration framework for integrated long-term development, operation, and use of high end resources.

Computing System (CS): A resources architecture to provide compute power for certain purposes.

Context: Any information that describes the situation of an entity. Today the context of integrated systems, components and objects, e.g., hardware architecture and complexity of environment, cannot be signed in any way. Methods have to be developed on hardware and software level in order to guarantee the fitness for a specific purpose.

Grid Computing: Grid Computing refers to a hardware and software infrastructure that allows service oriented, flexible, and seamless sharing of heterogeneous network resources for compute and data intensive tasks and provides faster throughput and scalability at lower costs.

High End Computing (HEC): Provision and use of high end resources for computing purposes, High Performance Computing as well as Distributed Computing.

High Performance Computing (HPC): Provision and use of highly performing computer systems at the upper performance limit of current technically possible processing and resources capacity. The formula one of computing.

Information System (IS): A resources architecture to provide information for certain purposes.

North-German Supercomputing Alliance (HLRN): The alliance of the northern states of Germany for providing and use of some standard High Performance Computing resources.

Scientific Computing: Scientific Computing means on top of the pure technical, operational, and provisional level, beyond tools, used for the focus of scientific purposes like for natural sciences application scenarios and algorithms. At the background both capability and capacity computing as well as various computing paradigms can be involved with this.

Security: Security is the characteristic of a safe system to accept only such system states which do not result in unauthorised modification or acquisition of information.

ZIVHPC: Parallel computer system with SMP and non-shared resources, based on AMD Opteron Processors, fast InfiniBand network, and GPFS, Nordrhein-Westfalen, Germany.

ZIVSMP: A flexible multi-processor SMP system for the ZIV-HPC parallel computer, based on AMD processors, fast InfiniBand network, and GPFS, Nordrhein-Westfalen, Germany.

Chapter 2
Software Design for Passing Sarbanes–Oxley in Cloud Computing

Solomon Lasluisa
Rutgers University, USA

Ivan Rodero
Rutgers University, USA

Manish Parashar
Rutgers University, USA

ABSTRACT

The purpose of this chapter is to identify and analyze the challenges of creating new software in the public cloud due to legal regulations. Specifically, this chapter explores how the Sarbanes-Oxley Act (SOX) will indirectly affect the development and implementation process of cloud computing applications in terms of software engineering and actual legality of said software solutions. The goal of this chapter is twofold - to bring attention to the need for specific analysis of legal issues in public clouds (as opposed to general analysis), and to illustrate the need for cloud developers to address legal constraint while creating their platforms, in order to increase their viability in the corporate environment.

INTRODUCTION

Cloud computing has promised to allow not only individuals but also groups of people to access large computing power on demand. Arguably the largest sector needing large computing power on demand in the United States (US) is the corporation. In light of this, it is important to analyze the

feasibility of corporations to actually take advantage of the ever growing area of cloud computing (Armbrust et al., 2009). Research in specific use cases in which companies can use cloud computing have been shown in various approaches (Google App Engine, Windows Azure, Amazon EC2) but what has not been addressed *to the same extent* are the legal issues that cloud computing will face

DOI: 10.4018/978-1-4666-2190-9.ch002

as corporations begin to assess the opportunities that this platform can provide.

The issue of legality as it pertains to cloud computing has been addressed by some (Bowen, 2011), (Jansen & Grance, 2011) but, as will be shown, the need to address legal concerns on a case by case basis uncovers the complexity and challenges that are hidden when only a general outlook is taken. It is our belief that legal concerns will play a major role in the adoption of cloud computing, just as security has been for this new paradigm. This belief comes from two points - that cloud computing can provide major improvements to corporations in terms of return on investment (ROI), reduction to barrier of entry, reduction in task completion times, etc., and as a consequence will need find innovating method remain compliant on all legal regulation. If the legal issues are not addressed corporations will be a large missed market which will not be able, or legally not allowed to use this technology.

The legal issues of cloud computing will impact many individuals within a corporation, but two of the most notable personnel which will have to address them will be the system architect and the software engineer. For the system architect the flow of data will determine the complexity of creating new applications using cloud computing and the integration with other applications. The software engineers will have to program with the constraints of legal issues (SOX in the case of this chapter) in mind in order to deliver a complete solution. In this chapter there will be three use cases that will demonstrate the complexity and limitations that regulations will impose upon the widespread adoption of cloud computing in the corporate environment.

The goal of this chapter is to highlight challenges software engineers will face in the corporate environment when creating software which leverages cloud resources. In order to adequately explain the challenges which arise from SOX related work, SOX analysis, current methods of complying with SOX and use cases are provided.

The related work section includes literature that has explored the effects of legal issues on cloud computing. This section will also serve to show how viewing of legal issues at a distance in software engineering is a stepping stone towards our work. The aim is to show the void of specific legal analysis for cloud computing. In doing so we show why specific legal analysis (in the case of SOX) can be useful for software engineers to account and program with legal concerns in mind. In addition, an overview of SOX is provided to provide a background on the issues which can arise when complying with the act. We will also introduce a technology-agnostic framework to aid in compliance with SOX. A section explaining the inherent problems cloud computing will face due to SOX is provided. This section serves to show that issues which are inevitable in a cloud environment and must be taken into account by software engineers. The use case section is provided to show how to identify SOX issues and design software taking those issues into account.

BACKGROUND AND RELATED WORK

Cloud Computing

The term cloud computing has recently been used in many contexts. For this reason, it is important to qualify what specify components or types of clouds would be affected by SOX. In the context of this chapter cloud computing relates to those resources that are not owned by the corporation itself; the most common used term for such resources is a public cloud. The importance of this clarification is because there is another type of cloud resource that can be owned by the corporation - a private cloud.

The National Institute of Standards and Technology (NIST) defines cloud computing as follows (Mell & Grance, 2011): "Cloud Computing is a model for enabling ubiquitous, convenient, on-demand network access to a shared pool of configurable computing resources (e.g., networks, servers, storage, applications, and services) that can be rapidly provisioned and released with minimal management effort or service provider interaction. This cloud model promotes availability and is composed of five essential characteristics, three service models, and four deployment models. The five essential characteristics are on-demand self-service, broad network access, resource pooling, rapid elasticity, and measured service. The three service models are Cloud Software as a Service (SaaS), Cloud Platform as a Service (PaaS), and Cloud Infrastructure as a Service (IaaS). The four deployment models are Private Cloud, Community Cloud, Public Cloud, and Hybrid Cloud."

As will be shown, a private cloud under SOX would be no different (or have minor differences) from private computing resources today. This will also highlight the differences and similarities between public clouds being "insecure" as has been already studied (Jensen et al., 2009).

The ties between SOX and security will be explored in the SOX section of this chapter. Some of the services that public clouds can provide today and are relevant for legal issues are listed below:

- Information Technology (IT) resources provisioned outside of corporate data center
- Resources accessed over the Internet
- Variable cost of services
- Build and deliver always-on, pay-per-use IT services
- A virtual computing environment (i.e., use of virtualization technology)
- Various service levels exposed i.e., SaaS, PaaS, IaaS.

Due to legal constraints, some or all of these services may be limited for many corporations. This issue will be explored throughout this paper.

Corporation

Since this chapter specifically deals with a legal regulation that corporations must adhere to, it is important to specifically state what a corporation is to better understand the position of this chapter. In this chapter a corporation is defined to be any *publicly traded company*, which must adhere to the Security and Exchange Commission (SEC) regulations. Only publicly traded companies in the US must comply with SOX. This in turn supports the argument that SOX increases overhead for publicly traded companies (Ribstein & Butler, 2006), and puts them at a disadvantage to other, unencumbered competitors. In an extreme case, it could result in the inability for a corporation to use a new technology to better its operations.

Legal Issues in Cloud Computing

The idea to assess the legal obligations that cloud computing must follow is not new. For example, Bowen (2011) showcases many examples of regulations and legal quandaries that face cloud computing. The examples provided range from data privacy and security to jurisdictional issues due to data location. Some examples of the topics that were discussed in the area are analyzed in this chapter.

In the area of US data breaches nonfiction requirements laws Gramm Leach Bliley (Financial Services Modernization Act (Gramm-Leach-Bliley), 1999), and Fair and Accurate Credit Transactions (The Fair and Accurate Credit transactions Act of 2003 (FACT), 2003) acts can be enumerated. These specific laws look to reduce possible financial harm to customers by creating regulations on how corporations may store private data as well as establish procedures as to how costumers must be contacted if their private data is compromised. Specifically, the red flag rules (Gramm-Leach-Bliley Safeguards Rule-Subtitle A, 1999) of the FTC are expanded to sectors outside of the financial sector from which they were created. These laws are one of the many reasons why the cloud computing community has kept data security in mind while developing an infrastructure. On the other hand only taking a broad view of data breach laws will not help engineers to develop applications that are compliant. If these laws are looked into with detail it may be possible to eliminate any risk incurred by using cloud computing simply by identifying a novel software pattern.

Another legal area being address is data locality and issues raised by outsourcing corporate data. This chapter mostly describes the issues involved by cloud computing's heavy use of virtual machines (VM) and the replication of data being seamlessly spread across many regions of the world. One issue discussed is international laws and specifically the European Union's (Gellman, 2009), which could limit the transmission of private data, must have a set level of security involved increasing the overall overhead of cloud computing. This would be due to the fact that the cloud providers would not know which data is considered private and would therefore need to have their entire network compliant with laws such as these.

Our work is complementary to the broad analysis of legal aspects, which is currently being discussed. Our goal is to demonstrate that though broad analysis, engineering concepts can only truly be applied or created once specific regulations are analyzed to know what is deemed as compliant for each law. As such works grow by analyzing individual laws there is the possibility of identifying software patterns or basic building blocks that engineers can learn to use to make their applications compliant across several regulatory bodies.

SARBANES-OXLEY ACT OF 2002

To provide a background for software engineers, the following section provides an analysis of specific sections in SOX. Since SOX is a large piece of legislation, only the relevant sections which can affect the adoption of cloud computing in a corporate environment are provided. Two sections which could be of interest are: section 2, definitions, section 101, provides power to the SEC to create a new oversight board to enforce SOX. Before analyzing SOX it is important to know the history behind the law and why it was enacted. Before analyzing SOX it is important to know the history behind the law and why it was enacted.

The law commonly known as SOX was enacted in July 30, 2002 in order to calm investors in during the Enron and WorldCom scandals. The scandals themselves hurt Enron and WorldCom investors and also shook the confidence in the US's ability to properly protect investors against fraud. As a result the US Congress passed SOX to enforce proper accounting practices by requiring all publicly trade corporations to have suitable internal controls. By enacting SOX Congress hoped to restore the confidence that US corporations were not providing fraudulent accounting reports to the public and hurting investors in the process. Prior to SOX it was common for corporations to hire independent auditors and audit the corporation's financial statements and ensure that generally accepted accounting practices (GAAP) were followed. In this system, no legal requirement to validate a corporation's internal controls existed, thereby creating an opportunity to commit fraud. Upon SOX's enactment all corporations were required to create and maintain internal controls for all financial transactions that posed a material risk to investor if found fraudulent. In addition high level managers were now required to attest to the accuracy of the corporation's financial statements. This requirement would now hold any high level manager accountable for any fraudulent activity that they oversaw. Since most financial transactions in a corporation are digitally approved, executed, and stored, software had to accommodate SOX. SOX has three sections that deal directly with software design, Section 302, Section 404, Section 409.In addition Section 906 has changed the scrutiny that software design is now under.

The following sections from SOX have been determined to have the most impact on the software development process. Although the law does not specifically address software in any form it does address processes that are handled by software. For this reason, in each of the following sections we discuss and analyze how the section ties with software. It must be also stated that the interpretations of these sections are the result of background research, personal interviews, experience and not that of a practicing corporate attorney.

- **Discussion and Analysis:** Although software is never explicitly stated in Section 302 if examined closely it does create new

requirements that the software development process must fulfill. Although a control will be fully explained in the next section, the term will be used throughout this discussion. The two most important pieces of information that should be taken from this section are: reports on internal control must be made and high level executives must attest to their validity. As a consequence of this section the software development process must now include a report on all controls created that maintain the validity of a corporation's financial data. The software development process must now also include reports readable to non-software engineers. The need to communicate with non-technical personnel was not a new problem before SOX, but was

Section 302. Corporate Responsibility for Financial Reports

(a) REGULATIONS REQUIRED.—The Commission shall, by rule, require, for each company filing periodic reports under section 13(a) or 15(d) of the Securities Exchange Act of 1934 (15 U.S.C. 78M, 78o(d)), that the principal executive officer or officers and the principal financial officer or officers, or persons performing similar functions, certify in each annual or quarterly report filed or submitted under either such section of such Act that—
(1) the signing officer has reviewed the report;
(2) based on the officer's knowledge, the report does not contain any untrue statement of a material fact or omit to state a material fact necessary in order to make the statements made, in light of the circumstances under which such statements were made, not misleading;
(3) based on such officer's knowledge, the financial statements, and other financial information included in the report, fairly present in all material respects the financial condition and results of operations of the issuer as of, and for, the periods presented in the report;
(4) the signing officers—
(A) are responsible for establishing and maintaining internal controls;
(B) have designed such internal controls to ensure that material information relating to the issuer and its consolidated subsidiaries is made known to such officers by others within those entities, particularly during the period in which the periodic reports are being prepared;
(C) have evaluated the effectiveness of the issuer's internal controls as of a date within 90 days prior to the report; and
(D) have presented in the report their conclusions about the effectiveness of their internal controls based on their evaluation as of that date;
(5) the signing officers have disclosed to the issuer's auditors and the audit committee of the board of directors (or persons fulfilling the equivalent function)—
(A) all significant deficiencies in the design or operation of internal controls which could adversely affect the issuer's ability to record, process, summarize, and report financial data and have identified for the issuer's auditors any material weaknesses in internal controls; and
(B) any fraud, whether or not material, that involves management or other employees who have a significant role in the issuer's internal controls; and
(6) the signing officers have indicated in the report whether or not there were significant changes in internal controls or in other factors that could significantly affect internal controls subsequent to the date of their evaluation, including any corrective actions with regard to significant deficiencies and material weaknesses.
(b) FOREIGN REINCORPORATIONS HAVE NO EFFECT.—Nothing in this section 302 shall be interpreted or applied in any way to allow any issuer to lessen the legal force of the statement required under this section 302, by an issuer having reincorporated or having engaged in any other transaction that resulted in the transfer of the corporate domicile or offices of the issuer from inside the United States to outside of the United States.
(c) DEADLINE.—The rules required by subsection (a) shall be effective not later than 30 days after the date of enactment of this Act.
(Sarbanes-Oxley Act of 2002, pp. 33-34)

exacerbated by it. In addition, high level executives must also attest to any changes made to internal controls. Taking all these factors into account a new member of the software development cycle must now be included during the development process, the high level executive.

• **Discussion and Analysis:** Out of the selected SOX sections for this chapter, Section 404 directly influences the software design process. Taking this into consideration special attention will be placed on the discussion and analysis. To help understanding the analysis of this section and improve readability specific fragments have been selected for analysis.

To begin our analysis the term "internal control" must first be defined in order to full understand what and how it relates to software. The term internal control is defined in the GAO AIMD-00-21.3.1, "An integral component of an organization's management that provides reasonable assurance that the following objectives are being achieved: effectiveness and efficiency of operations, reliability of financial reporting, and compliance with applicable laws and regulations". Although the definition itself is quite vague in most contexts it is important to keep in mind the frame of reference in which it is being defined. The frame used in our analysis is: what risk is there to the corporation's financial reporting if there were

no control in place for this process? Also, let us further the understanding of an internal control along with the concept of "effectiveness" with an example, a bank vault. The procedure is simple, a person wants to put personal belongings into a bank's vault and retrieve the belongings without much hassle along with the confidence that the belongings are not at risk of being stolen. A control in this example could be a large metal door with a sophisticated locking mechanism. The question is it effectiveness must be dealt on a case by case basis. Let us imagine that this particular bank's walls are made out of breakable glass. In such a case, would the previous control be effective in preventing theft? With this example in mind we can redefine what an internal control to be anything that lowers risk. In the context of SOX an internal control can be defined as anything that can reduce the risk to fraudulent accounting activity.

The other term that we must define is "reporting". For software engineering it can simply be said that reporting is anything that monitors a process and attest to its status. Monitoring is not new in software design and was not implemented due to SOX, but SOX does deem it necessary that all internal controls are special and under no circumstances their status cannot be known.

The next portion of this section that needs to be analyzed is "responsibility of management for establishing and maintaining an adequate internal control structure and procedures for financial reporting" (Sarbanes-Oxley Act of 2002, p. 45).

Section 404. Management Assessment of Internal Controls

(a) RULES REQUIRED.—The Commission shall prescribe rules requiring each annual report required by section 13(a) or 15(d) of the Securities Exchange Act of 1934 (15 U.S.C. 78m or 78o(d)) to contain an internal control report, which shall—

(1) state the responsibility of management for establishing and maintaining an adequate internal control structure and procedures for financial reporting; and

(2) contain an assessment, as of the end of the most recent fiscal year of the issuer, of the effectiveness of the internal control structure and procedures of the issuer for financial reporting.

(b) INTERNAL CONTROL EVALUATION AND REPORTING.—With respect to the internal control assessment required by subsection (a), each registered public accounting firm that prepares or issues the audit report for the issuer shall attest to, and report on, the assessment made by the management of the issuer. An attestation made under this subsection shall be made in accordance with standards for attestation engagements issued or adopted by the Board. Any such attestation shall not be the subject of a separate engagement. (Sarbanes-Oxley Act of 2002, p. 45)

The key word from this portion is "adequate" since it relates directly with our previous analysis of effective internal control. By including the word "adequate" it allows some leeway in terms of not only the amount of internal controls but also their complexity in order to lower risk. The term "adequate" in simple terms deem that software engineers do not have to go "overboard" in their efforts to create a completely risk free system. An example that can illustrate this conclusion is that of an inventory system of a retail store. The procedure is simple: as a retail store sells goods inventory must proportionally decrease. The question posed from this procedure is what would be the "adequate" amount of time before the inventory of the company is updated? In practice there are many determining factors that are involved in determining the time delay in the update of a store's inventory such as number of stores or average transaction per minute. Once again just as the term "effectiveness" was determined on a case by case basis so is "adequate". In both of these cases a SOX auditor will help a corporation determine what is "adequate" and "effective" for each company.

The final portion that should be examined in this section is, "contain an assessment, as of the end of the most recent fiscal year" (Sarbanes-Oxley Act of 2002, p. 45). This portion is quite straightforward but adds to the overhead in designing and updating software for a corporation. An example that illustrates large overhead world be an upgrade or migration of a corporation's enterprise resource planning (ERP) system. This compounded with the increase in the need to test applications more effectively due to their increase in complexity,

Section 409. Real Time Issuer Disclosures

clearly shows that in some circumstances the overhead can be costly.

- **Discussion and Analysis:** In Section 409 it is important to state that the term real time is relative. The term real time in the context of this law is, the length of time the SEC deems adequate to perform a formal audit. Since the term real time is relative as technology advances, the delay in real time will also decrease. This, therefore, also forces software corporation's developers to continue to update older applications if the SEC determines that said applications could pose a financial risk due to the delay providing an opportunity for fraud. Recall the example of a retail store's inventory system from previous discussion. As technology advances the inventory system will have to be updated even if, in theory, the corporation finds it adequate enough for its business. If the SEC determines the inventory system's delay in entering transaction is no longer adequate for a proper audit an update will have to be done. For this reason there is an additional incentive for software engineers to properly identify any bottlenecks in execution time when designing a system.

- **Discussion and Analysis:** The final section (Section 906) that we consider for analysis does not directly affect the software development cycle but emphasizes the message that regulations have severe consequence if not followed. In software engineering there is a common mindset in which an application may not have to work one hundred percent

Section 13 of the Securities Exchange Act of 1934 (15 U.S.C.78m), as amended by this Act, is amended by adding at the end the following:

"(I) REAL TIME ISSUER DISCLOSURES.—Each issuer reporting under section 13(a) or 15(d) shall disclose to the public on a rapid and current basis such additional information concerning material changes in the financial condition or operations of the issuer, in plain English, which may include trend and qualitative information and graphic presentations, as the Commission determines, by rule, is necessary or useful for the protection of investors and in the public interest.". (Sarbanes-Oxley Act of 2002, p. 47)

Section 906. Corporate Responsibility for Financial Reports

(a) IN GENERAL.—Chapter 63 of title 18, United States Code, is amended by inserting after section 1349, as created by this Act, the following:

"§ 1350. Failure of corporate officers to certify financial reports

(a) CERTIFICATION OF PERIODIC FINANCIAL REPORTS.—Each periodic report containing financial statements filed by an issuer with the Securities Exchange Commission pursuant to section 13(a) or 15(d) of the Securities Exchange Act of 1934 (15 U.S.C. 78m(a) or 78o(d)) shall be accompanied by a written statement by the chief executive officer and chief financial officer (or equivalent thereof) of the issuer.

"(b) CONTENT.—The statement required under subsection (a) shall certify that the periodic report containing the financial statements fully complies with the requirements of section 13(a) or 15(d) of the Securities Exchange Act pf 1934 (15 U.S.C. 78m or 78o(d)) and that information contained in the periodic report fairly presents, in all material respects, the financial condition and results of operations of the issuer.

"(c) CRIMINAL PENALTIES.—Whoever—

"(1) certifies any statement as set forth in subsections (a) and (b) of this section knowing that the periodic report accompanying the statement does not comport with all the requirements set forth in this section shall be fined not more than $1,000,000 or imprisoned not more than 10 years, or both; or

"(2) willfully certifies any statement as set forth in subsections (a) and (b) of this section knowing that the periodic report accompanying the statement does not comport with all the requirements set forth in this section shall be fined not more than $5,000,000, or imprisoned not more than 20 years, or both.".

(b) CLERICAL AMENDMENT.—The table of sections at the beginning of chapter 63 of title 18, United States Code, is amended by adding at the end the following:

"1350. Failure of corporate officers to certify financial reports.". (Sarbanes-Oxley Act of 2002, p. 62)

---

of the time but this section serves to show that such a mindset on SOX applications can have severe ramifications.

Public Company Accounting Oversight Board

The Public Company Account Oversight Board (PCAOB) was created under section 101 of SOX once it was enacted. The PCAOB is the organization that the SEC created to have oversight of how SOX would be executed. In this hierarchy of the SEC and PCAOB, the PCAOB is allowed to enforce SOX regulation as they deem appropriate with the SEC having the right to overturn any decision made by the PCAOB. In this section the standard created by the PCAOB, specifically standard 5, will be review in order to have a better understanding as to what are the requirements for an internal control to be deemed SOX compliant. The standard 5 is not provided in this chapter; however, the entire text 5 can be obtained at (Public Company Accounting Oversight Board, n.d.).

The information presented in this section deal with 5 specific elements in standard 5 of the PCAOB: (1) an external auditor, (2) risk of fraud, (3) entity level controls, (4) accounts, and (5) reports. All of these terms and processes are known by reading the SOX act itself and standard 5 clarifies what each means or involves. An additional element that is tackled by standard 5 is the outsourcing of corporate operations to third parties.

The term external auditor is used for any auditor that is hired from an external company. This auditor under standard number 5 is allowed to use the corporation's resources in order to perform his/her audit. In order for a corporation to be deemed compliant all audited internal controls must pass testing and all related paper work related to the testing must be filed future reference. In addition, the process in which these test are conducted must also be provided in order to determine if they are compliant. An example of a case in which the process of testing an internal control would fail would be if a developer was also the quality assurance (QA) personnel that attested to the validity of the results of the control after test scenarios have been run.

Risk of fraud, as stated previously, revolves around the concept of material risk to a corporation's financial records. In standard 5 this is reiterated as to avoid costly overhead by adding internal controls for processes that do not pose a large risk to investors if said processes are found to have fraudulent transactions. This is not to be mistaken to mean that low risk processes are compliant if they have no controls, it simply means that the detail that their controls provide are much less than high risk counterpart. Since risk of fraud is relative to each corporation, auditors and corporate staff must work closely together to explain clearly how the corporation accounts for each financial transaction. For example, if significant portion of all financial transaction go through a particular application, be it for processing or storage, it would be clear that if this application lacks proper internal controls there would be a material risk to the corporation. A more complex example would be: if five percent of all financial transaction passes a particular application, would it still be considered a material risk?

Entity level controls are decided between the auditor and the corporate and subsequently operation level controls are decided if the entity level controls are insufficient. The difference between an operational level control and an entity level control is the granularity. Entities represent entire processes were as an operation is a subtask to a larger process. Operation level controls are normally needed when the entity have complex operations or have "too many" operations creating a need for "checkpoint" controls. An example that illustrates the point is a transaction in which money is moved from one account to another account but has to pass through various operations, e.g., exchange rate, different type of account, etc. In a case such as this each individual operation poses a risk if there is no control which audits the operation. Take for example the exchange rate, if not audited properly the possibility of fraud would be seen as likely.

Standard 5 talks about accounts in terms of the verification process of users and personnel. Here the issue is the need to verify that only authorized users are allowed to access specific data or execute a specific operation. These controls are typical today but cloud computing add a third party with new users that may have access to data that they should not be allowed to access.

Finally, standard 5 addresses process reporting and its role with internal controls. Standard 5 makes necessary that all internal controls report their history of the information that they have been monitoring. This serves three purposes, to test the validity of the control, a type of audit API, and to create a paper trail, which can be presented to the SEC if needed. An example of this would be the complete login history of a database server, or the operations executed by a specific user.

The final issue addressed by standard 5 is that of servers that are not property of the corporation but belong to a third party, in the form of SAS 70. SAS 70 is a SOX audit on a third party company, which interacts with another corporation's financial reports. The most common situations are those where a corporation completely offloads a financial process to another company, such as Salesforce (Manage sales – Salesforce.com, n.d.), and a cloud computing company that handles human resources related jobs for companies. In this example, Salesforce is in charge of handling the accounting of a corporation's employees' benefits and salaries. When a third-party passes a SAS 70 audit it means that all financial processes or services that are performed are compliant with regulation. Unfortunately SAS 70 does not address directly the issue of offloading computing to a third party and, as a consequence, such a process becomes highly scrutinized under audits. An example of this would be doing post processing of financial data on third party server.

COBIT Framework

This section explains how an IT governance framework works and its usefulness in software development with COBIT being our example. Due to space limitation we do not quote all sections that would be useful when creating a new application, instead, we summarize what COBIT is and its usefulness, the entire document can be found at (COBIT – IT Governance Framework – Information Assurance Control | ISACA, n.d.). The goals of COBIT are:

- Making a link to the business requirements
- Organizing IT activities into a generally accepted process model
- Identifying the major IT resources to be leveraged
- Designing the management control objectives to be considered

The goal of COBIT is to create a framework for any project, which may be subject to SOX regulation. For this reason it is necessary to go through the entire document and identify which pieces are the most useful when creating software compliant with SOX in the context of cloud computing.

The most emphasized concepts presented by COBIT are, transparency, prior knowledge of adequacy, understandable to management, process oriented, integrity, availability, compliance, reliability, data preparation and authorization, accuracy, output review, error handling, infrastructure plan, trends (technology), maturity modeling, and quality.

DESIGNING FOR SARBANES-OXLEY COMPLIANCE IN THE CLOUD

The following sections describe some of the inherent issues with cloud computing when SOX is taken into account and provide some use cases to illustrate the areas in which cloud computing can be used effectively as well as the hurdles. A balance must be made between usability and functionality of cloud computing and adhering to legal regulations. The inherent problems of cloud computing cannot be fixed but software engineering can create solutions addressing some of those problems

by taking legal issues into consideration when developing applications using cloud resources.

Software Issues in Cloud Computing

The inherent issues with cloud computing are both obvious and also obscure. This is due to the basic understanding of the law as well as the lack of understanding of the intricacies that are involved in harnessing the computing power in the cloud while complying with SOX. Once it is understood that there need to be controls in order to comply SOX, the next step is to identify where these controls should be place, since incorrect placement will lead to not passing audits. The following are some areas that must be taken into account since cloud computing inherently faces these issues in the context of SOX.

- **Access:** In order to be SOX compliant the following questions must be answered:
  - Who has access to those servers?
  - Who has access to those databases?
  - Who has access to those datacenters?
  - Who has access to the access list?
  - Who has access to my applications?

Etc.

These questions should be at the forefront and answered early on in the design process. We provide a real world example in which an application that was hosted on a third party's server, which also provided maintenance to said server. For example using cloud resources in which the costumer is not allowed to execute commands at the operating system level. After the issue is resolved the application owner could notice extra accounts that did not exist prior to the issue. In such a case any SOX audit would fail due to the possibility of having unauthorized personnel access to the server. Also, it would be in a company's best interest to create controller, which could detect such a scenario either by the application running the server or some secondary application unrelated to the one processing financially sensitive data. Taking this same example and giving its natural extension to other things as the database on the server, the files on the server, the services on the server, etc. and one can begin to see where controls may need to be placed in various locations to be SOX complaint.

- **Control:** There are other different questions related to application authentication of the users such as: How are you assuring me that only the people I want are using the application?

This is straightforward as long as authentication is done at both ends, meaning if there is a local component in the company's data center and there is one in the cloud a user and their transaction must be authenticated at both ends. This will prevent cases where unauthorized users could hop over one or the other to possibly commit fraud.

- **Report:** This part of the compliance can be eased if both sides can find ways to use current tools and technologies that already do reporting for them. Cloud providers can create APIs for their clients to ensure that certain criteria are met, such as which user can access are given to a server. If cloud providers cannot provide such effective tools these issues will have to be taken into account by software engineers.
- **Sprawl:** This should be a major concern as companies begin to explore how much potential space they have and begin to use it. Creating many environments or instances of an application can lead to people forgetting the existence of a VM, for example launching a VM and not terminating when it is no longer needed. This will dramatically increase the

risk of security breaches. Designers should also be aware of such cases and design software that can identify and report itself to avoid problems from forgotten VMs.

- **Testing and Implementation:** Although SOX does not directly address testing it has affected it. In testing it is not only satisfactory that an application passes its functional requirements but it must also follow a process in which appropriate sign offs have been made in terms of handing an application from the developers hands to a testing team. This ensures that all code is tested for any irregularities that can put the company's financial reporting at risk. The testing team must then hand the application off to an implementation team, which can install and attest that all required parties have signed off on the installation. In terms of cloud computing test may have to become more elaborate in terms of identifying where irregularities in the process can occur and test for them.

SOLUTIONS AND RECOMMENDATIONS

The following section provides three use cases to be considered. They have been chosen to illustrate three possibilities of complying with SOX: impossible, doable with design considerations, and straightforward implementation. This covers the two extremes and the middle in an effective way to demonstrate how software engineering practices will have to be modified in order to comply. These use cases also demonstrate that even though cloud computing can provide large benefits in theory, such as raw computing power, it is tempered by regulations, in this case SOX.

Use Case 1: Data Backup of Sensitive Data

One of the most popular services that has emerged as Internet access has become ubiquitous and cloud computing more popular, is data backup (Dropbox, n.d.), (Apple iCloud, n.d.). This service is popular with companies since it provides an important function for them, offsite backups. In general backups are essential for all companies in case a disaster happens in which their data is lost or destroyed either from human error or naturally. For this reason many companies have decided to use cloud computing as a way to backup their data in a safe and reliable manner. Without a doubt data is the most sensitivity asset they have that also affect their balance sheet. One piece of data that can easily be seen as a material risk to a company is its invoices. If pieces of data like invoices are not secure the company will fail any SOX audit. Although their intent of having a backup of this data does have merit, if the method employed is found to be insufficient legal, consequence can occur. As a result, situations like these need a careful balance between a company's desire to have safety measure to service their costumers and adhering to legal regulations.

- **SOX Issues:** Security of data that directly affect a company's balance sheet must answer the following questions when dealing with SOX:
  - Who has access to the data?
  - How is access monitored?
  - Where is the data?

In order to comply with SOX a company must demonstrate that they can control access to the data, as to avoid any unlawful manipulation. The company must also demonstrate that there is a method that can trace all access to sensitive data. Finally, a company must demonstrate that they know where data is at all times when it is in an editable state. This point is important since

if the location of the data is not known it must be demonstrated that the data cannot be falsified and placed back in a matter that can deceive investors and/or auditors. An example would be having a backup of financial data, which in case of an emergency will be used to demonstrate a company's financial transactions. If backups are not secure it is plausible that in an emergency in which data is destroyed, a flooded data center for example, the data would be unreliable and could lead to SEC investigations if accounting does not match what they have on record.

- **Path to Compliance:** In order to successfully answer the previous questions proposed by SOX the following controls need to be created:
  - Controls for the start of the transmission and verifies end of transmission
  - Verify the encryption of the data
  - Identify what data is being transmitted

In this use case it is straightforward how to approach the problem. Since the data is only being backup an not being used, sending only data after is it encrypted should suffices. The type of encryption may have to be changed if it is found to no longer be secure but, in general, once the data is encrypted the data can no longer be retrieved without the key, which must also have controls. With this framework a company has ensured the data cannot be tampered with and if edits are made they can be logged. The last piece that needs to be placed is to ensure only encrypted data is sent offsite.

Use Case 2: Banking in the Cloud

One of the promises that cloud computing wishes to make true is that any company can one day start operating without the need of any own data center. A bank's infrastructure in a cloud would include databases, frontends, and applications that all would be hosted on the cloud, meaning all transactions that the bank processes would also be in the cloud without any need for a bank to invest in any server. This is the ideal scenario in which a bank only needs the money needed to begin lending and host all the transaction on a cloud provider. If a bank also wanted to do any other services such as investment banking this could also be done in the cloud to do complex data analysis. In both of these cases it is obvious to see how companies such as banks could benefit from a cloud infrastructure to provide immense scalability.

- **SOX Issues:** In order to create a bank infrastructure in the cloud the following points would need to be satisfied:
  - All bank transaction need to be verified
  - Any access to a bank account must be controlled
  - All transactions must be logged
  - All related to all transaction must be stored and have access controls

The operations which a bank must perform are fairly straightforward for any bank complications arise when these operations must now be done in a cloud environment. In this scenario it is difficult, if not impossible, to create reliable controls in the cloud. The issue stretch from the shear amount of transaction to the ability to verify who has access to memory of the server in the cloud. One of the major issues that cloud computing has had to face is security. I this use case it would simply not be able to be done while complying with SOX. With security being an issue that cloud computing has not yet been able to solve, all attempts of complying would SOX fail or need an incredible amount of extra controls to prove that banks data is reliable.

- **Path to Compliance:** Simply stated this use case cannot be done in the current cloud due to all the constraints imposed by SOX. The important part of the presented problem is

the shear amount of transactions but how the transactions can be monitored and who has access to the information. Since the operations being performed in this case would be in a cloud there is no way to ensure with one hundred percent certainty that the data can be secure. In this case a company would need to control thousands if not millions of transactions a day to ensure that their balance sheet is correct.

Unfortunately some companies cannot possibly have a complete cloud infrastructure to provide all the benefits that would come from it due to the type of business they provide to their customers.

Use Case 3: Partial Computing in the Cloud

An important service that cloud computing provides is the ability to offload computing to a third party. For a company this is very useful due to the embrace of information technology boom since the 1990s. As a result, many companies have developed complex and time sensitive algorithms that help executives make important decisions about different aspects of the company. We believe that once a standard and SOX compliant framework has been created, companies will begin to use these outside resources to make current processes faster but also allow them to create more complex algorithms, which better describe their business. An example of such a case is advertisement placement on TV and internet and the complexity that each placement contains. There are many constraints to place advertisements on TV as to when specific they can play, what channels they can play on, the contracts that have been signed with the channel (meaning how many viewers are promised to the company paying for the advertisement to play), it can easily become quite complex as to how the ads are placed. It is also important for the reader to know that for some companies their available advertisement spots are considered their inventory and as a result any transaction or operations that decide where each advertisement should be placed will affect their balance sheet, for some companies even as much as more than seventy percent of their revenue.

- **SOX Issues:** In such a case, SOX issues are manageable but some operations are still impossible to be executed in the cloud:
  - ◦ Control which data will be processed on the cloud
  - ◦ Control when outside data can be integrated with internal data

The controls are simple to understand since we have made the assumption that all data once processed has to be integrated with internal data. This is important since, as seen in the previous use cases, when all operations are done in the cloud there is still no grantee that the data will be accurate, to within a reasonable degree of auditing. In this case data can be processed and manipulated outside of a company's data center but will verified before any of this data will be saved and made official on their balance sheet.

- **Path to Compliance:** In this situation there is the opportunity to divide the portions that can be done internally and maintain compliance and outside processing which can then be verified before saving. The proposed solution for such a case is for a company to do complex analysis outside of its data center but allow for a method that can verify that the correct results have taken place. For example, once the results of where the advertisements should be placed a smaller and less complex algorithm can be run to compare the results from the more complex one. In this case any difference can be observed and sign off on

by someone in the company. There can also be another method by which an application is run internally, which can calculate the risk of what the resulting schedule would cost the company.

CONCLUSION

In this chapter we have stated that there is a need for software engineers and the research community to take into account legal aspects as they develop and deploy services in cloud computing. By using SOX as an example of legal regulation which can diminish the large scale adoption of cloud computing in the corporate environment the case for focusing on specific legal issues was highlighted. This was first done by giving a thorough analysis of SOX, extracting key components of the law and elaborating on their significance. Subsequently analyzing the byproduct standards of SOX which have been SEC. This served to partially eliminate ambiguity found originally in SOX legislation. A framework currently being used to handle SOX issues was provided as a tool to identify and solve SOX issues when developing applications. Finally use cases are provided to illustrate the limitations of current cloud computing have due to the legal constraints imposed by SOX. With all these components a strong case for individual analysis of laws was made in order to guide the direction of cloud computing implementation and development.

The area of legal analysis to helping guide research toward areas of consider due to specific laws is important from many aspects. Future work will include other laws cloud computing should consider, software patterns which can be used to handle specific legal considers, and extension to frameworks, such as COBIT, to create applications in cloud computing.

REFERENCES

Apple iCloud. (n.d.). Retrieved March 2, 2012, from http://www.apple.com/icloud/

Armbrust, M., Fox, A., Griffith, R., Joseph, A. D., Katz, R. H., & Konwinski, A. … Zaharia, M. (2009). *Above the clouds: A Berkeley view of cloud computing*. University of California, (UCB/EECS-2009-28), 07-013. EECS Department, University of California, Berkeley. Retrieved March 2, 2012, from http://www.eecs.berkeley.edu/Pubs/TechRpts/2009/EECS-2009-28.html

Bowen, J. A. (2011). *Legal issues in cloud computing* (pp. 593–613). Cloud Computing Principles and Paradigms. doi:10.1002/9780470940105.ch24

COBIT. (n.d.). *IT governance framework – Information assurance control*. ISACA. Retrieved March 2, 2012, from http://www.isaca.org/Knowledge-Center/COBIT/Pages/Overview.aspx

Committee on Financial Services U.S. House of Representatives. (2006). *Sarbanes-Oxley at four: protecting investors and strengthening markets*. Washington, DC: Author.

Dropbox. (n.d.). Retrieved March 2, 2012, from https://www.dropbox.com/

Gellman, R. (2009), Privacy in the Clouds: Risks to Privacy and Confidentiality from cloud Computing, Febuary 23, 2009. Retrieved March 2, 2012, from http://www.worldprivacyforum.org/pdf/WPF_cloud_Priavacy_Report.pdf.

Google App Engine. (n.d.). Retrieved March 2, 2012, from http://appengine.google.com.

Jansen, W., & Grance, T. (2011). *Guidelines on security and privacy in public cloud computing*. Director, 144, 800–144, NIST. Retrieved March 2, 2012, from http://www.securityvibes.com/servlet/JiveServlet/downloadBody/1322-102-1-1327/Draft-SP-800-144_cloud-computing.pdf

Jensen, M., Schwenk, J., Gruschka, N., & Iacono, L. L. (2009). On technical security issues in cloud computing. *2009 IEEE International Conference on Cloud Computing*, (pp. 109-116). IEEE. Retrieved March 2, 2012, from http://ieeexplore.ieee.org/lpdocs/epic03/wrapper.htm?arnumber=5284165

Mell, P., & Grance, T. (2011). *The NIST definition of cloud computing* (Draft), January, 2001. Retrieved March 2, 2012, from http://www.worldprivacyforum.org/pdf/WPF_cloud_Priavacy_Report.pdf

Public Company Accounting Oversight Board. (n.d.). Retrieved March 2, 2012, from http://pcaobus.org

Ribstein, L. E., & Butler, H. N. (2006). The Sarbanes-Oxley debacle: What we've learned; how to fix it. U Illinois Law & Economics Research Paper No. LE06-017. Retrieved March 2, 2012, from http://ssrn.com/abstract=911277

Salesforce.com. (n.d.). *Manage sales*. Retrieved March 2, 2012, from http://www.salesforce.com

Taylor, H. (2006). *The joy of SOX: Why Sarbanes-Oxley and service-oriented architecture may be the best thing that ever happened to you*. Wiley Pub.

United States Congress. (1999). *Gramm-Leach-Bliley safeguards rule-Subtitle A- Disclosure of nonpublic personal information*. Codified 15 U.S.C. 6801-09.

United States Congress. (1999). *Financial Services Modernization Act* (Gramm-Leach-Bliley). Pub. L. No. 106-102,11 Stat. 1338, codified at 15 U.S.C. 6801-09.

United States Congress. (2003). *The Fair and Accurate Credit transactions Act of 2003* (FACT). Pub. L. No. 108-159,117 Stat. 1952.

United States Congress House Committee on Small Business. (2007). *Full committee hearing on Sarbanes-Oxley section 404: Will the SEC's and PCAOB's new standards lower compliance costs for small companies?* Committee on Small Business, United States House of Representatives. Washington, DC: Author.

United States Congress Senate Committee on Banking, Housing, and Urban Affairs. (2009). *The state of the securities markets [electronic resource]: Hearing before the Committee on Banking, Housing, and Urban Affairs, United States Senate, One Hundred Tenth Congress, first session on examining current issues and matters raised in previous securities hearings.* Washington, DC: Author.

Welytok, J. G. (2006). *Sarbanes-Oxley for dummies.* Wiley Pub.

Windows Azure. (n.d.). *Website.* Retrieved March 2, 2012, from http://www.windowsazure.com/

KEY TERMS AND DEFINITIONS

Audit: To examine the financial statements of a business by an independent public account firm following the rules provided by the Security and Exchange Commission (SEC).

Financial Statement: A report on the financial activities of a business which include the buying and selling of assets, as well as current assets and liabilities held.

Financial Transaction: The exchange of good/s and payment between a buyer and seller which are stored for financial statement reporting.

Fraud: To willingly deceive on financial statements in order to deceive the public for financial gain.

Generally Accepted Accounting Principles (GAAP): The guidelines for financial accounting for businesses.

IT Governance: Hierarchy of a corporation as seen by IT the development cycle.

Legislation: A law which has been enacted by a governing body.

Chapter 3

Awareness-Based Security Management for Complex and Internet-Based Operations Management Systems

Udo Inden
*Cologne University of Applied Sciences, Research Centre for Applications of
Intelligent Systems, Cologne, Germany*

Georgios Lioudakis
National Technical University of Athens, Institute of Communication and Computer Systems, Greece

Claus-Peter Rückemann
*Westfälische Wilhelms-Universität (WWU) & Leibniz Universität Hannover
& North-German Supercomputing Alliance (HLRN), Germany,*

ABSTRACT

Grounded on two use-cases from different domains of operations – aviation network management and service-bundling of small enterprises – the authors develop a management concept for increasingly complex business operations' systems. These cases exemplify the convergence of new technologies and with this the arising of new organisational and managerial challenges representing both, risk and chance. Soon so-called "Things-that-Think," profiting from future multi-core chip architectures and autonomously acting in the Internet, will become drivers of massive distribution and parallelisation of stationary and mobile operations' architectures and lead to hybrid networks of humans, things and systems. These developments require elaborating and implementing new principles and mechanisms of operations' management – not at least in order to manage holistic operations' properties raising with the complexity like criticality, resource footprints, or, pars pro toto addressed here, security. The core of the authors' argumentation is that the increase of operations' complexity emerging from this combination of massive heterogeneity, distribution and parallelism, on the other side offers new chances

DOI: 10.4018/978-1-4666-2190-9.ch003

of mastering complexity. For taking this change two concepts are paramount: intelligent peer-to-peer systems and self-aware system behaviour e.g. with regard to performance and for sure: security. Rather than struggling with the finally unavailing undertaking of controlling complexity, this chapter suggests implementing self-awareness as added-value service into complex operations' systems with the goal of managing their "holistic properties" like external effects, criticality, as well as issues of security and trust.

INTRODUCTION

"The machine is the problem: the solution is in the machine" (Poullet, 2006). Since man invented technology it is two-faced: a source of risk and of chance. Fuelled by competition, a race for better technology developed. The sheer complexity of technology grew and now, fuelled by Information and Communication Technology (ICT), it runs at an unprecedented speed. As co-decision-makers in hybrid architectures of widely parallel operations artificial objects (things) to a considerable degree are expected reaching eyes level of its inventors. For basic concepts see Maturana (1984/92) and Kauffman (1995). On examples from commercial and non-commercial service industries we want to illustrate that these features may also become tools of maintaining operations' integrity. Concepts and methodology of implementing principles of technologically enabled self-awareness will be shown in this chapter on the example of security management including considerations regarding the vulnerability of operations' systems which may be organised in the internet.

At this point some basic definitions may be useful: "Operations" comprise the whole network of processes and resources for realising business models which enable subsistence and growth in competitive environments. "Autonomous" means that a system (actor) is able of effectively subsisting on exchanges with its environment, pursuing own objectives and relying on own resources (means to an end).

"Adaptive" systems are able of maintaining their existence under conditions of unexpected, thus unplanned changes in the environment. "Environments" are formed by interactions of systems i.e. are equal to the volume and variety of systems interacting. "Contexts" are relevant backgrounds to acting and interacting, e.g., in terms of different values which derive from the variety of systems. Examples of contradictions may be costs versus quality, or short-term speculative profit versus long-term investor interests. Thus interacting with different systems requires capabilities of standing frictions and balancing conflicts.

Complexity, respectively the uncertainty it produces in terms of lacking information about the operations' scene and of unexpected and thus unplanned events, is the "intimate enemy" of operations' management. Very pragmatically ICT is needed for augmenting awareness and adaptive decision making. But by solving one concern another appears: future technology may even exacerbate the problem:

- Things-that-Think (TtT) are digitally augmented objects like future cars, aircrafts, containers, buildings, refrigerators (Ishi et al., 2010; Günther & Hompel, 2010; Scherer, 2011; C2C-CC Manifesto, 2007; Europe's Information Society, 2011) which – comparable to intelligent software agents (Rzevski, 2011; Koestler, 1967; Chevaleyre et al., 2005; Luck et al., 2005; Sandholm, 1993). I.e. like software agents, things may also have objectives and access to knowledge, may become context- and self-aware and finally able of autonomous decision making.
- Things collect, compute and collaborate in the Internet of Things and Services (IoT/S). IPv6 with $2^{128} = 340.282.366.9$ $20.938.463.463.374.607.431.768.211.4$ 56 (Zivadinovic, 2007) addresses is the backbone for integrating things and ser-

vices at any appropriate resolution, human users and legacy-systems in computing networks (Rückemann, 2010), potentially including auto-parallelised sequential software (Vector Fabrics BV, 2011).

• This comes with distributed multi-core computing capacity (512 logic cores per chip may be available by 2020 (Hochberger et al., 2008) at affordable costs. Grids formed by vast numbers of TtT will provide new options of designing operations' management architectures. Relying on considerable computing power they will consist of massively distributed and parallel applications.

To some degree, this article develops ideas regarding how this could be usefully employed in the future and raises questions about research and developments needed to realise such ideas. Usually for getting control of complexity either "more system" is committed, i.e. more working capital and more staff. Or it is tried to discipline complexity by business and process standards. Obviously both hardly sustain. Nevertheless, many decision-makers consider it less risky to organise firms around proven "standard software." But the installed base of this software unifies behaviour, restricts response to change and finally turns into disadvantages when dynamic capabilities make the difference in competition.

The term "control illusion" indicates that we may focus on the wrong problem: while classical software development explicitly excludes "emergent behaviour" (Müller-Schloer et al., 2008), IBM's vision of autonomous computing hires concepts of self-awareness for overcoming the complexity crisis of software. And SAP, a major provider of business software and standardisation pioneer, currently participates in research on "emergent enterprise software" adapting to changing needs (Knaf, 2011).

"Adaptiveness," the alternative draft to control, employs emergent behaviour rather than fighting

it. Financial markets impressively demonstrate proficiency of prospering with complexity – but also demonstrate urgencies of being (self-)aware and careful about the precipices of personal and organisational greediness or hubris in dealing with it. Conveyed into ICT, self-awareness (Eyal et al., 2004) is a vision of developing autonomous software expected to provide an answer to the problem of the two-faced machine (Kephard et al., 2003), actually by adding complexity to it.

We prefer a pragmatic definition of self-awareness as the "ability of a system to adapt to changes on the base of knowledge about its interactions in a dynamic operations' context with respect to given objectives," whereat "acting on the base of knowledge" means that a system acquires and processes information relevant in terms of its objectives. To be clear this may need some explicit definitions (Figure 1):

As Figure 1 shows, a Multi-Agent System (MAS) is a representation of real world constructed by software agents using the ontology describing their identities (e.g., instance of class "aircraft") with objectives (e.g., "be on time") and relationships to other objects represented by other agents (e.g., instances of airports) and with properties supporting these relationships (e.g., "truck of type #" and "driver with licence type #" – see Figure 2). Agents have states (e.g., agent "aircraft" "is on time" or "is delayed") and states are changed by events (e.g., order of air controller to relinquish a landing slot and go into holding). A continuous flow of real-world data enables continuous mirroring and analysis of real-world states in the virtual world of agents. We call it the "control cycle" which if need be may run close to real-time.

Adaptiveness of MAS works as follows: In case a change of a state affects the satisfaction of at least one agent in terms of his target function, this agent will start negotiations to recover. In consequence other agents will find reason to reconsider their states and finally the deterioration of the global target function may be mitigated,

Figure 1. Architecture of an ontology-based multiagent system (based on: Rzevski, 2011)

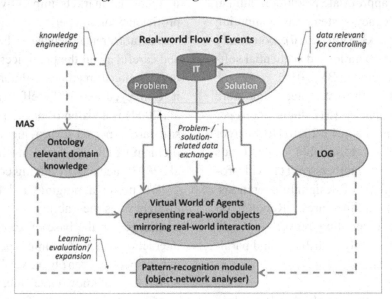

Figure 2. Section of ontology on airport operations with properties matching service requirements

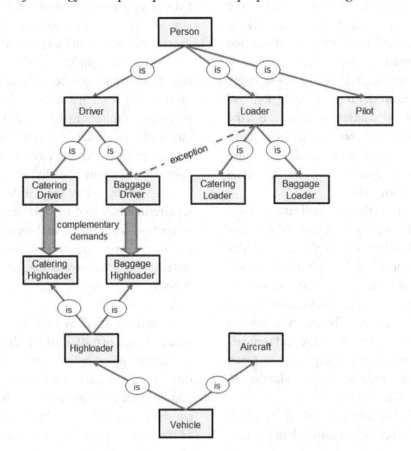

fully recovered or even improved. However while – ceteris paribus – the loss of one agent is also a loss in terms of the global target function the subsequent mitigation, recovery or improvements of the global target function does not mean that there is any "justice": The overall win is the result of a re-distribution of jobs, profits and losses on the level of agents. I.e. some may get "rich" on the "expense" of others. Like in real world the Pareto-principle does not care for the wealth of individuals. But it illustrates that MAS are able of exploiting *any* event as chance to globally improve.

"Behind" the control cycle also "learning cycles" (dotted connectors) can be installed: It is a sort of "back-office" job superimposing agents' operations immediately dealing with the domain and offering three sources of learning. The cycle starts with the engineering of the knowledge stored in the ontology to be used by agents. The second step of the learning cycle is that the system can select and safe protocols of agents' activity: While dashboards are interfaces for human controllers, e.g. dispatchers, providing (almost) real-time information about the progress of real-world operations and MAS control activity, reports go to operations and financial controllers for subsequent analysis and tactical or strategic re-planning. This is the base of collaborative learning. In parallel another module of the MAS can provide basic self-learning capabilities by analysing patterns in the logs of agents' operations feeding results into knowledge engineering processes, actually: the knowledge management system of the respective organisation. This superimposing structure is the base of awareness in terms of a system that "acquires and processes information relevant in terms of its objectives."

Ontology-based MAS, a field of artificial intelligence, are major examples of knowledge processing and autonomous computing. In short, the relation between software-agents and ontologies compares to that between actors of a stage play and their role-script. Ontologies support ob-

ject- and service-oriented modelling of knowledge on relevant level of detail and functionality. I.e. MAS that mimic real-world domains are as real as the ontology has been elaborated. In recent years we gained experimental experience about MAS in a number of industrial as well as research projects, among others learning how ontologies are to be designed according to service-oriented principles in order to systematically ensure feasible and conducive response to unplanned events in a complex operations' environment (Inden & Franken, 2010).

Figure 2 gives an idea how service-oriented ontologies conduct the behaviour of agents: the section refers to airport ground operations including a variety of vehicles and staff, each offering a particular service. Highloaders are specialised for exchanging (un/loading) baggage and cargo or catering trolleys with aircrafts. For service highloaders of the respective type, drivers with the respective licence and loaders with the appropriate training are needed i.e. they offer complementary services.

A simplified scenario may be that agents of highloaders, drivers and loaders coordinate if a flight calls for service. Here it becomes also obvious that object- and service-oriented modelling applies and how: the actual business process emerges from the activity of objects and the services they provide, e.g., as highloaders or drivers or reversely ask – i.e. from their exchange or interaction with their environment. Examples for demand may be that highloaders need fuel and from time to time a slot at the gas station, or that drivers need lunch and a break.

However, rather than technology, our focus of interest is on how advanced ICT enables intelligent organisations. This approach led us thinking about the convergence of developments like Things-that-Think, distributed and parallel processing or the concept of self-awareness. In this chapter we try to bring these aspects together. And, probably even more than performance, the issue of security is to be tackled. For finding reason we suggest a look at the issues of "Security Nightmares" for 2009 and 2012 (Rieger, 2009; Rieger, 2012). We define security as "freedom from risk," i.e. as probabilistic property of a system's relationship to its environment to be provided as inherent property of the architecture.

In research we are interested in learning from further MAS-based experiments in real environments:

- Whether and how exactly "self-aware" ICT will ensure and improve the delivery of expected or promised results, e.g., the provision of feasible (executable in real environment) and conducive (compliant to relevant objectives and rules) answers to unplanned events,
- How self-aware systems are to be designed in order to build trust and support personal and organisational actionability (rather than precariousness),
- How this depends on organisational and managerial frameworks,
- How this may be ensured under conditions of future technology.

Currently we are developing further projects in domains, which structurally may be very different: operations in aviation industry and operations of collaborative networks of rather small companies offering tailored bundles of services. Complexity is the common denominator, asking for and enabling adaptive strategies. Admittedly with the following analysis and ideas we dare an explorative projection of converging technological and organisational developments touching many different disciplines. Therefore, the final result will be a list of open questions rather than an answer.

REFERENCE ARCHITECTURE

We envision an architecture inspired by the model of a multi-agent system in which things, human users (e.g., dispatchers) or – if enabled – legacy software (e.g., a warehouse system if inventory information matters) act as "collaborative objects" (CO) interacting via the Internet (Europe's Information Society, 2011; Rzevski, 2011). The concept compares to a session of computer gamers (we call it a "Collaborative Intelligent Application's Session" - CLIPS) rather than to the "black-box" of MAS running on a single computer – which we do not suggest to implement but to be used as a model. Primarily depending on computing capacity it copes with relevant resolution of object (details modelled as agents) and time (events processed by agents) of real-world, i.e. is able of effective contribution to high-resolution management (Fleisch & Müller-Stewens, 2008).

The MAS model delivers architecture and models of ontologies and agent's protocols which enable purposeful response to unexpected events. Whatever the problem is, it is solved by direct negotiation. Figure 3 drafts a respective architecture of MAS running in the "wilderness" of the internet rather than in the working space of computers – but able of providing the same functionality as described above. Described in MAS terminology, the procedure may be as follows: negotiations will start as soon as an event arrives and produces "meaning" to an agent in the context described in its respective ontology and they propagate along service-oriented relationships. Ontologies instruct, for instance, how to evaluate a specific scenario, which objectives to pursue, what to be settled, with which parties to deal, what resources to make use of, etc. In general, the purpose is to coordinate the process of adaptation to the event, likely to recover a plan of action. This process continues until all agents have returned to the thresholds of their objectives. In a large system this may take a number of iterations (Rzevski, 2011; Hompel, 2008).

Figure 3 shows a session. It is obvious that many of them may run in parallel and that agents may simultaneously participate in several ones. There is also significant computing capacity

Figure 3. Sketch of the reference architecture

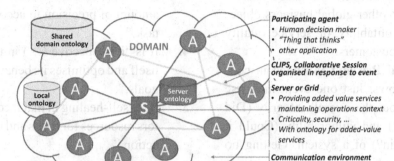

distributed across servers and multi-core chips of future mobile (e.g., aircrafts or smart mobile devices) or stationary Things-that-Think. Acting of individual agents is enabled by local knowledge relevant to their individual operations and shared knowledge which enables collaboration. Shared knowledge is not only stored in ontologies but also e.g., in the form of shared negotiation protocols and formats. As we can see here, the standardisation of business processes will be replaced by the standardisation of communication.

The server infrastructure in the centre of Figure 3 provides added value services to the network referring to tasks which cannot or should not be locally handled. That is, these servers coordinate the context of operations as well as system's properties or states like criticality, security and privacy, or operations' footprints which emerge from local actions but involve the system in its whole: they produce "holistic properties." (In physical systems it compares, e.g., to the average temperature of an object emerging from movements of the particles it consists of.) Methodology of diagnosing and estimating holistic states and properties and policies to respond are subject of ongoing studies.

- **Criticality:** A decisive control parameter of managing complex systems, particularly referring to capabilities of responding to unexpected events. Effective response im-

plies the flexibility of revising the network of contracts, as well as of related "physical" activity. But flexibility is a volatile resource; in this moment it is available, in the next it is "out of stock." And it may depend on butterfly-effects like an infection propagating across the network of peer-to-peer activity. For given constraints, criticality is a holistic parameter: the scale-free point of a phase transition from flexibility to inflexibility or from fluid to frozen (Christensen et al., 2005; Cliver, 2011). "Criticality-awareness" is the aspect of understanding flexibility or "slack" in a system as a valuable resource rather than a subject to cost cutting, as well as being sensitive and responsive to the risk of disability to reasonably respond to unplanned events.

- **Footprints:** In general, total impacts of operations to an environment. For instance, the Global Footprint Network (2011) defines the ecological footprint as the "premier measure of humanity's demand on nature." In a distributed operations' system formed by autonomous objects, this total cannot be managed on local level. As a prominent case take CO_2 emissions or water consumption, since local savings on one end may have to be paid on the other one. "Footprint-awareness," therefore, is the aspect of understanding external effects of operations as a whole and balancing it against other global business objectives like profitability or service quality delivered to customers.

- **Security and Privacy:** Infringed in concrete workflows. Just one event may rise concerns about the overall integrity (Did occur more?) and vulnerability (Could it happens again?) of a system. Getting no or bad answers to one of these questions may turn into serious obstacles of acting. Understanding risk as likelihood of occurrence of undesirable events or states "security-awareness" is a prerequisite of building trust into the integrity of operations in terms of its capability to avoid disliked effects or states. In this respect, security-awareness contributes to criticality management, e.g., by defining and keeping thresholds of capacity provisions.

ON THE CONCEPT OF SELF-AWARENESS

An MIT study (Argarwal, 2010) describes the architecture and behaviour of self-aware computing systems as follows *[shortened]*: "An Organic Operating System (OOS) is the heart of a complete self-aware system. It monitors application execution and hardware parameters, and performs adjustments and optimisations to ensure that the applications are meeting their goals. The four key components of an OOS are the application interface, the hardware interface, the analysis and optimisation engine, and self-aware system services. ... A self-aware ... computer has five major properties":

1. It is "goal-oriented" (meets a user's or application's goals).
2. It "adapts itself to optimise appropriate application metrics" (operationalising the goals).

3. It is "approximate in that it uses the least amount of precision to accomplish a given task."
4. It is "introspective (…) in that it observes itself and optimises its behaviour to meet its goals."
5. It is "self-healing in that it constantly monitors resources for faults and takes corrective action."

Advanced MAS compare to this model of an "Organic Operating System." Petr Skobelev (2010) describes how "bio-inspired" MAS developed in the last decades and shows a number of applications based on the elaboration of that paradigm. These applications are not self-aware in terms of the definition above, i.e. they do not know what they do. For this it would require implementing a second MAS instance providing the capability of introspective analysis and reasoning on the behaviour of the first one. A real- life example may illustrate the meaning of such dual-layered architectures:

In one of our studies we learned about an incident with an 82 years old lady without family and unable to leave her flat on the 5th floor. The nurse, her only social contact, was late and because the old lady became impatient she were coming up to meet the nurse in the staircase, felt down the stairs and died a little later in the ambulance. The nurse was aware of the anxiety of the old lady and had sent a standard "be-a-little-late-message" to the cell-phone the old lady wore on a neckband. But batteries were empty. Changing them was a job on the to-do list of the nurse who since then sends a standard message *and* makes a call to the landline of patients. Some weeks later she got a ticket "because of using phone while driving"; 60 € for distrust in technology. The nurse understood workflow and context. But her *awareness* was focused on the risk of failing technology which – given her dedication to her job – lead her to taking a personal risk: to be caught telephoning. She reflects her behaviour, compares and learns using a picture, or, in the terminology of this paper, an ontology of herself.

This case makes apparent that awareness is an issue of architecture integrating capabilities of acting and capabilities of reflection on acting. In order to match *properties 4 and 5* we suggest continuing the path of bio-inspired computing by implementing two ontologies and agent systems mimicking the brain's capability of parallel acting and reflecting. The first one deals with the operations' domain, the second one with the "dealing," i.e., with the execution of workflows in a context which includes risks and a framework of personal or organisational values to evaluate risk.

A similar, but simpler architecture is also described by the "learning cycle" in Figure 1 above, superimposing immediate agents' operations and linking logs, reports to controllers, dashboard information to, e.g., dispatchers and self-learning capabilities – each considered to be an "added-value service" to tactical and strategic re-planning or knowledge engineering and corporate knowledge management.

In the architecture of Figure 3 the second MAS resides in the central server infrastructure and provides an added value service. Our understanding of self-awareness relies on the fact that the system acquires the knowledge needed for reflecting by co-creating the scene: it is a *participating observer* and is able to analyse current reports and history including its contributions by collecting, filtering and processing data.

Software agents and domain models we have used in previous projects are equal to those described by G. Rzevski (2011) and P. Skobelev (2010) and their underlying architecture, principles of modelling ontologies, as well as of software-agents have been applied to a wide scale of applications, including translation of text, risk management, or logistics and factory planning.

In terms of their microeconomic model, these agents act rationally (Russell & Norwig, 2010) and have measurable objectives and principles of contracting. As backbone of targeted solutions,

they particularise service level agreements (SLA) in terms of time of delivery, costs and price, penalties or running-times. So far, *property 1* is given.

In response to orders and other events or to operations' constraints, agents contract jobs along the supply-chain. The adaptiveness of the system (*property 2*) relies on freedoms of agents to cancel contracts in case they find an opportunity to improve or in the case of obsolescence due to an event or elapsing time. Events appear from outside or from continuous search of agents for better opportunities and their local decisions may cause chains of cancellations and re-contracting (ripple-effects). A global optimum can only be approximated by continuously exploring the space of solutions. Each agent acts with local knowledge, limited capacity of reasoning and under time-restrictions – *property 3* (Simon, 1991).

Properties 4 and 5 require a system to be self-healing due own insights into the way it approximates its goals while adapting to unforeseen events: The system needs to know and evaluate what it does in its whole – and in fact MAS "know" all operations, orders, resources involved, related states and events as well as all relevant parameters. *Pars pro toto* of holistic properties of operations' systems we shall explain in the following how self-healing capabilities emerge from self-aware objects and workflows.

CONSTRUCTING TRUST AND SECURITY-AWARE WORKFLOWS

"Trust is a risky investment into a relationship" (Luhman, 1968). In our vision it is an investment into a relationship to a hybrid management system interacting in a risky environment, the Internet. A technical system, a person, or a currency we don't trust is not expected contributing value. Essentially trust is the fabric of value. It implies the expectation that a system does what it promises to do. Actually it is another holistic property of a system but an attributed one: it emerges from stakeholder's perceptions of operations. And it may take a large effort and a long time building trust but just one event to ruin it.

In hybrid systems, trust refers to the behaviour of technology, of acting humans and to interactions of both – particularly if opaque systems, like the Internet, are involved. From a stakeholder perspective, it is hard to ascribe problems to components. Therefore, implementing a trustworthy design of the system into workflows by well defined service level agreements (SLA) is crucial. Workflows are executed by the activity of resources and SLAs specify contracted services for concrete scenes of operations. They include the following dimensions (Müller-Schloer et al., 2008):

- **Correctness:** Is the SLA correctly formulated and does it actually govern the service?
- **Completeness:** Do SLA and actual operations cover requirements?
- **Performance:** To which qualitative and quantitative level SLA are fulfilled?
- **Dependability:** Under which circumstances or restrictions are service provided – and not?
- **Availability:** What is the likelihood that the service is provided when it is needed?
- **Security:** Is the system able to protect operations' integrity (avoiding infringements of SLA)?
- **Privacy:** Will personal data or information processed as intended and kept confidential?
- **Liability:** Who will be legally accountable for culpable infringements of the SLA?

Essentially, all entities of Figure 3 (humans, software systems, things, etc.) that cooperate, e.g., to fulfil an order, participate in a *workflow* that implements a *business process*. This is not a new concept; other complex operational structures, including virtual enterprises (Mehandjiev & Grefen, 2010) and distributed communications network monitoring (Koukovini et al., 2011), have been seen through a business process management prism. From this point of view, in order to satisfy the holistic property of security, it is the workflow that should be security-aware.

Note that this is different from the concept of "secure workflows" (Bertino et al., 2010; Hafner & Breu, 2009), actually a functional superset. Typically, when referring to workflows, the term security implies the protection of the communication links and the realisation of the objectives of confidentiality, availability, integrity, as well as the assurance that only authorised entities gain access to resources and underlying processes. On the other hand, what we describe in this chapter as "security-awareness," apart from incorporating these "traditional" security goals, goes a step beyond and reflects the property of a complex system to act *for* security, based on the self-awareness and rational behaviour of its components.

Hybrid systems are characterised by large number of collaborative components, with high distribution degree and heterogeneity; this results in a by default loosely-coupled nature of interoperations. The Service-Oriented Architecture (SOA) (Papazoglou & van den Heuvel, 2007) paradigm for software systems has been developed in order to serve exactly the need for loosely-coupled distributed computation, providing a manifold of advantages and potentials. On the other hand, service-orientation and loosely-coupled cooperation patterns come with security concerns; this is not only because of their own vulnerabilities (Bertino et al., 2010; Hafner & Breu, 2009), but also because a potential flaw or failure endangers the overall operation of the system.

In that respect, there is the need for workflows that are *per se* security-aware. Certainly, the bottom-line is the protection of information confidentiality in the context of data exchanges and the capability to verify (i.e., authenticate) the peer at the other side of the link and the integrity of the interoperation procedure. To this direction, there are fairly mature mechanisms that are already international standards (Nordbotten, 2009; Bertino et al., 2010), mostly grounded on the encryption of the underlying communication links and the mutual authentication and authorisation. But this is not enough; trust between agents does not imply a trustworthy system. And this becomes even harder when the involved entities belong to different administrative domains, which is often the case, as reflected by the two use cases documented below. The latter brings to the foreground another dimension of information security, which is about protection of personal privacy and confidentiality of business information. What is the fate of data after their disclosure (even over a protected link and to a trusted party)?

Self-awareness of the entities participating in a workflow can be a significant step fostering security-awareness. The challenge is twofold: on the one hand, to maintain the enforcement of security properties across a complex chain of peers, that may even be unknown at the beginning of the procedure; on the other hand, to enable the overall operation to be self-adaptive, so that failures have minor impact and that the operation is adjusted to the initial goals. In order to meet these challenges, the means leveraged are contextual security policies, rich in semantics, complemented by the appropriate cryptographic primitives.

Contextual Security Policies

Similar to the *subject—verb—object* linguistic pattern, anything that takes place during the function of a system, can be seen as an *operation* of an *actor* over a *resource*. This applies at any granularity level: at the highest level of a business process, a set of actors performs an aggregated super-operation, consisting of elementary operations, over a set of resources; at a low level, an RFID reader executes a "read" operation over an RFID tag. Thus, security policies are intuitively centred around conceptual triples of {*actor*, *operation*, *resource*}, that can be defined either at a concrete or an abstract level, that is, over named,

specific entities or abstractions that encapsulate categories of elements and provide generalisation.

Any security violation and breach certainly includes illicit access to some resources, being systems, data, items, or operations. In that respect, the evolution of security policies has brought access control at the core of the security, but also privacy protection. Beyond the traditional access control models, such as the Discretionary Access Control (DAC), the Mandatory Access Control (MAC) (Samarati & de Capitani di Vimercati, 2001) and the well-adopted Role-Based Access Control (RBAC) (Ferraiolo et al., 2001), the incorporation of features that are specific to privacy protection has resulted in the emergence of the field referred to as Privacy-Aware Access Control (cf. e.g., Antonakopoulou et al., 2012). On the other hand, a recent trend is represented by models that are leveraged for direct management of network security policies (e.g., Preda et al., 2011), in line with and sharing the goals of approaches placed in the area of Policy-Based Network Management (PBMN) (e.g., Basile et al., 2007).

But, in order to effectively regulate the operation of a complex hybrid system and be essentially part of entities knowledge, security policies must incorporate additional features. First, there is the requirement of full abstraction, meaning that all concepts are described at a full abstract level; this enables cohesively treating entities falling under the same conceptualisation. In that respect, RBAC first introduced the *role* abstraction for users, which is the typical pattern followed by most state-of-the-art approaches. On the other hand, only very few approaches support representation using abstractions for all elements (Cuppens & Cuppens-Boulahia, 2008; Lioudakis et al., 2009), while hybrid approaches have just started being investigated.

Second and most important, knowledge, therefore policies, must contain norms regarding what should have happened before and what should provisionally happen next, as well as be bound to events and context. In fact, contextual security policies have been until recently underestimated; while much research has now been done, most policy models reported in the literature only partially support some straightforward contexts, especially temporal (e.g., Joshi et al., 2005; Bhatti et al., 2005), spatial (e.g., Bertino et al., 2005; Cuppens & Cuppens-Boulahia, 2008) and related to history (e.g., Noorollahi Ravari et al., 2010; Cuppens & Cuppens-Boulahia, 2008). Nevertheless, complex hybrid systems should be able not only to behave taking into account contextual parameters, but also to base their operation on events. In other words, events taking place "somewhere" and "somewhen" are interpreted as context whereas the contextual changes should be promptly available to any affected entity and trigger contextual changes that will result in functional adaptation.

In that respect, knowledge must incorporate context, that is, security policies need to be contextual. In addition, the functional logic of the entities comprising a complex hybrid system needs to be *conditional*, i.e., characterised by "contextual branches" enabling the entity to behave in accordance with the underlying context.

Following the *subject—verb—object* metaphor, each {*actor, operation, resource*} triple is characterised as an *action*. Intuitively, actions may represent whatever takes place in the course of time and they can be used for modelling past, present and future context, as well as events. Therefore, rules pertaining to a security policy need to be defined over constructions such as {*action, goal, pre-action, post-action, context*}, surrounded by the appropriate predicates that describe permissions, prohibitions and obligations of the policy enforcing entities. Having a deeper look to this pattern:

- *Action* describes the core of the rule, i.e., what action the rule by definition permits, prohibits or obliges to take place.
- *Goal* reflects the overall objective of the business process. It is essentially a contextual primitive itself; in fact, an operational

decision cannot be taken regardless this parameter which can significantly differentiate an entity's behaviour (e.g., an ambulance acting for "urgency transfer" would negotiate different contracts with traffic lights on the way).

- *Pre-action* reflects actions that should have previously taken place in order for the rule to be activated (a boarding passenger must explicitly follow the "check-in" → "security control" → "go to gate" → "board" procedure).
- *Post-action* similarly implies anything that needs to take place after the enforcement of a rule (an airline pilot's decision to "postpone take-off" following some contextual event, triggers the automatic "notification of the control tower").
- *Context* describes conditions defined over "environmental" properties and states, as well as events ("flight LH1284 sent change request," "ownerless piece of luggage in gate/#," "the time is 15:00 CET," "highloader HL/# is located at gate A15," "the weather is rainy" or "HL/# is dirty").

All these elements should be enabled to be combined using a grammar of logical and domain-specific descriptive operators, in order for complex compositions to be specified ("boarding" is permitted if and only if "check-in" AND "security control" have preceded). Apart from the intuitive advantages this provides, it can be leveraged for the definition of complex structures of tasks, sometimes referred to in the business process management terminology as "worklets" (Adams et al., 2006). Worklets allow for the specification of complex patterns able to model situations such as the one presented later in Figure 5. Enhanced with the appropriate semantics (e.g., temporal), even with some native fuzziness, the expected behaviour of the figure's six jobs can be packaged as a worklet to be part of the knowledge base and be consequently checked and verified against the reported behaviour.

It comes out that a key challenge here is the effective monitoring, collection and dissemination of events and contextual information; thus, the employment of a "context bus" is deemed necessary. This conceptual entity shall be considered as the "broker" for the circulation of context in the complex and heterogeneous environment, assigned with the task of effectively routing such information from the producers (sensors of any type, either humans or software and hardware agents) to its consumers (entities relying on contextual values and events for adapting and/or negotiating their functional behaviour). As an additional service, the context bus should provide for events correlation and the consequent generation of contextual meta-events; this way, the bus fosters facilitation of operation, especially with respect to entities that are characterised by limited resources, as well as reduction of network traffic, redundancy of information and information complexity.

An important feature towards effectiveness and efficiency shall be the ontological "indexing" of information and its consequent ontological routing; that is, information shall travel from producer to consumer based on its semantic characteristics, rather than the network identifiers. This is similar to the primitives of the recent research trend of Content-Centric Networking (e.g., Koponen et al., 2007; Jacobson et al., 2009), which proposes a shift from the network of hosts to a network of content.

The context bus can be provided as an added value service by the server infrastructure of the Figure 3, or as an independent, self-organised overlay peer-to-peer system provided by the participating entities themselves. While a hybrid approach, i.e., a semi-supervised overlay, is rather the optimal approach, in any case there are challenges to be addressed. Two prominent ones concern, respectively, capturing and exploitation of all necessary information semantics and the

employment of the necessary mechanisms for the fulfilment of the legacy security objectives. Some insights regarding these issues are provided in the next sections.

Cryptographic Mechanisms

Cryptography has naturally been the bottom-line for information protection through "hiding," already since the ancient era. The development of public-key cryptography in mid-70s has created new potentials that, together with modern symmetric key algorithms, are nowadays exploited to a great extent for the protection of databases and network links, as well as for strong authentication, authorisation, non-repudiation, information integrity validation, etc.; cryptography lies at the core of information and systems security.

Nevertheless, applied cryptography has started revealing its limitations when dealing with highly distributed and ad hoc computation environments and, therefore, legacy mechanisms, such as SSL and IPSec, are rather insufficient. The problem is not at the encryption algorithms themselves, but mainly concerns the management of cryptographic tokens. In a highly distributed and hybrid environment consisting of a large number of entities of heterogeneous origin, it is, for instance, hard to ground trust on PKI (a rather intuitively obvious solution), due to serious scalability problems, as recently studied within other domains with similar needs, such as the Smart Grid (Khurana et al., 2010).

Therefore, reconsideration is deemed necessary regarding the cryptographic primitives to be leveraged in such complex environments. A possibly promising family of technologies is represented by the mechanisms stemming from the area of Identity-Based Encryption (IBE) (Boneh & Franklin, 2003) and Attributes-Based Encryption (ABE) (Sahai & Waters, 2005); recently, the said cryptographic patterns have been used for incorporating access control policies *into* the data, thus reducing the needs for trustworthiness management and complex schemes for maintaining access policies across the distributed entities. Prominent examples are the Ciphertext-Policy Attribute-Based Encryption (CP-ABE) (Bethencourt, Sahai & Waters, 2007) and Key-Policy Attribute-Based Encryption (KP-ABE) (Goyal et al., 2006).

In that respect, such cryptographic constructions can be leveraged in the context of a complex hybrid system, in fact in conjunction with and for the enforcement of the afore-described contextual security policies. Although probably not immediately obvious, this is again an instantiation of self-awareness; as a matter of fact, following these schemes, the participating entities are empowered with decryption capabilities not by means of holding cryptographic keys, but leveraging their own attributes. That is, an intelligent aircraft is enabled to decrypt a message broadcasted over the air because of being itself the "flight LH1284" AND (as the logical operator, thus capitalised) its captain is "Mr. Orville Wright." In other words, the information "flight LH1284" and "Mr. Orville Wright" *is* the decryption key as LH1284 is the "call-sign" and the description key of a particular flight operated by a particular airline and connected to a set of further information (origin, destination, schedule, crew, flight manifest, etc.).

This can emerge as a critical enabler fostering security in complex hybrid environments. Not only because of ruling scalability issues of key management and reducing the need for trustworthy storage systems, complex infrastructures for policy management (local knowledge shall be enough in most cases) and reference monitors, but also because of enabling controlling access to information despite the dynamic nature of the infrastructure and the lack of knowledge regarding the potential recipients of the data. The specification of the policies at an abstract level and the encryption of information leveraging attributed values provides pretty good assurance that only authorised parties – holders of the appropriate attributes will gain access to data, either personal

(thus protecting privacy), or business (thus protecting business information), or even context (cf. the "dirty vehicle attack" described later).

Yet, there remains the flaw of certifying the cryptographic attributes of the participating entities, since there's still the danger of compromising the associated tokens. A solution to this comes from the technology of Trusted Computing (Felten, 2003); the entities can incorporate a Trusted Platform Module (TPM) (ISO/IEC, 2009) in order to ensure secure storage, remote attestation, certified configurations (e.g., in terms of self-attributes) and tamper-proofness. Nevertheless, not all entities within a complex hybrid system have the capacity for incorporating a TPM; this is a native limitation of constrained devices. However, this can be partially mitigated by means of a microkernel implemented by means of a limited resources smartcard, especially a Java Card (Oracle, 2009); leveraging the cryptographic capabilities offered by the Java Card, the underlying attributes can reside in a cryptographic "sandbox," while certain tasks, like digital signing and data encryption/decryption based on attributes, can be directly executed by the card. This way, constrained devices are enabled to participate in the security functions of the system.

Semantics and Ontologies

An integral part of self-awareness is knowledge about the reality, as well as knowledge regarding how to deal with reality; in this context, ontologies provide a convenient conceptualisation of this reality and a strong potential for inference and decision making. As has been made clear above, this does not leave security unaffected; in fact, the specification of meaningful security policies strongly relies on the semantics of actions, goals and context, including events. And actions contain actors, operations and resources, that have their own and sometimes complex semantics.

In that respect, there are already a number of approaches that make use of the Web Ontology

Language (OWL) (World Wide Web Consortium, 2004) and leverage its rich expressiveness and advanced reasoning capabilities for enforcing security and privacy. As a starting point, OWL has been used to develop policy languages for the Web, such as Rei and KAos (Tonti et al., 2009), and nowadays, there are numerous examples of exploiting OWL ontologies in access control, for purposes such as the ontological implementation of RBAC, privacy preferences modelling and the semantic interoperation of heterogeneous databases. Among the most prominent are the models proposed by Finin et al. (2008), Noorollahi Ravari et al. (2008), Lioudakis et al. (2008), Ferrini & Bertino (2009), Noorollahi Ravari et al. (2010). Moreover, ontologies have been leveraged in order to introduce privacy-awareness in domains such as network monitoring (Lioudakis et al., 2010; Tropea et al., 2011), as well as to describe security alerts, using inference rules to perform the mapping between concrete alerts and contextual provisions (Cuppens-Bulahia et al., 2009).

In our case and as reflected by the general structure of contextual security policies, a variety of ontologies and/or ontological classes is needed capturing associated rules to be described. The particular semantic type characterising a resource constitutes a parameter of significant importance for the determination of the procedures subject of which the resource is and, consequently, of the underlying computational flows. The semantics of the processing operations, the underlying goals, as well as the entities involved as actors, are of equal importance; moreover, security-related decision making takes into account contextual parameters, such as temporal, spatial and history-based ones, as well as events and alerts. Apart from their importance for security (and privacy – business information confidentiality), the semantics are of paramount importance also for the operational consistency and interoperation, at the conceptual level, of the entities participating in the system. Therefore, the system should be grounded on a vast knowledge base implemented by means of

common ontologies shared across multiple domains, enabling not only semantic interoperability among the different actors, but also advanced meta-knowledge extraction and ontology-based intelligent decision making for security.

In more detail, in order to serve the needs for security policies specification, ontologies for a complex hybrid system should capture the following concepts:

- **Operations:** They correspond to the *verb* of the metaphor, describing *what* takes place. They should be organised in hierarchical structures, reflecting inheritance of characteristics, AND-trees and OR-trees. Moreover, the corresponding ontology should provide the means for the definition of complex structures, such as worklets.
- **Resources:** They represent the object of a policy rule and they may reflect a variety of concepts: data, items, orders, documents, even humans (e.g., when delegating an authorisation). A challenge here is to model structures created by combinations of resources; thus, the appropriate semantic relations should be available.
- **Actors:** Many different concepts may play the role of an actor, i.e., of the entity that executes an operation over a resource. Sometimes, an actor is a difficult notion to model, since many actors can be "multiplexed." For instance, within the operation of an airport terminal, the "root" actor may be some authority that creates a chain of authorisations down to the level of a crane that performs a "load" operation over luggage. Therefore, hierarchical relations with rich semantics themselves should be available for capturing the complex chains created and the inheritance of rules and attributes.
- **Context:** An ontological structure for context description should encapsulate and bridge many different contextual types;

these include, for instance, typical contextual parameters, such as temporal and spatial, as well as events and alerts. Each domain has clearly different semantics and presents different challenges. For some contextual types, interesting issues concern how to model certain properties, such as continuous temporal values; for others, e.g., events, of great interest is their mapping to contextual value, as well as their correlation. In all cases, the logical combination of contexts, even heterogeneous, to a single conditional structure and its evaluation generates requirements for flexible contextual modelling.

Use Case 1: Aircraft-Rotation Oriented Air Traffic Management

During 2005 – 2010, two of us, backed by a larger professional background in different fields of aviation industry, were working in a number of projects on the management of airport, flight- and network-related service systems. Almost inevitably we got in touch with current large-scale research programs on improving flight operations' infrastructures in Europe (the SESAR program, Single European Sky ATM Research, Hotham, 2011) and the United States (the NextGen ATM program). After an extensive phase of research SESAR now is about to be implemented and accordingly to planning new technologies and procedures shall be finally deployed by 2020 / 2025. I.e. looking at the pace of change in technology but also at the increasing challenges in global air transport, it is time to start thinking about next steps.

Latest ATM developments include GPS-controlled 4-D flight trajectories, advanced system-wide information management, a higher degree of IT-support for using air-space more efficiently and making flights more economic and safe in spite of significant increases of traffic (Holtham, 2011). As a node of support, the next generations of aircrafts will become "intelligent" (Scherer,

2011) and negotiate routes with controllers and peer-aircrafts in their operations' sectors, support pilots and airline back-offices, or make autonomous decisions.

From the perspective of aircraft and fleet operations effectively maintaining sequences of flights of aircrafts (e.g., on a day) is crucial. These so-called rotations (Belobaba, Odini, & Barrnhart, 2009) are planned among others with respect to demand, aircraft utilisation, direct costs or environmental impacts. Failures propagate across rotations and interfere with crew rotations, maintenance events or inventories of equipment distributed in airline networks. A more extensive description of this case, particularly including considerations on the relevance to High-Performance Computing, is delivered in Inden, Tieck & Rückemann (2011).

Figure 4 shows a rotation with an unplanned event in leg 2; probably an emergency required placing the aircraft in a waiting loop. Now there is a threat that the delay propagates and interferes with the schedule at airport 4. If passengers miss their continuing flights or if baggage is left behind, it will become expensive for the airline in terms of money and of reputation. In this case the intelligent aircraft "invites" related artificial and human agents to a conference, likely organised in the Internet or a proprietary intranet, in order to negotiate opportunities recovering the original plan. Invitees will be the stakeholders along the business process subsequent to the interference, e.g.:

- ATM and airport authorities (systems and officers) along the routes.
- Local ground service providers for aircraft clearance (systems, dispatchers, and things or services).

In a previous project (Inden & Franken, 2010) we have modelled elementary functionalities of interconnected service production, airport ground operations, and rotation and balance of service

Figure 4. High-level scenario of rotation-oriented ATM

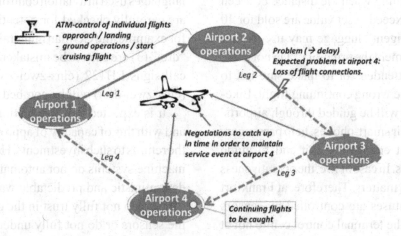

equipment in airline networks on the example of inflight catering services with respect to service generation with SLA per type of flight and aircraft layout. And we included elementary aspects of contingency policies implemented in case of positive evaluation in the economic context of an operations' scene. Flights (respectively aircrafts executing flights) take the role of the order and values of properties of flights like "delay" or "change of aircraft" have immediate impact on service schedules. Thus a change of aircraft may imply a different layout of the galleys (number, measures and organisation of storage positions) and, therefore, require re-organising the whole production process (load assembly) for the respective flight.

The planning and scheduling system for this functionality employs software agents organised in a "conventional" MAS black box. Completing functionality, elaborating details and improving run-time behaviour are, due to the scalability of the underlying SOA-model, a question of effort and access to respective domain knowledge rather than a fundamental problem. And there is no known obstacle to compile these concepts for an open, diverse environment of users interacting via the Internet.

In order to solve rotation-related problems, the "intelligent aircraft" needs to re-negotiate opera-

tions' workflows across the whole environment, formed by aircrafts, ATM- and airport-authorities or ground services. For instance, to catch up with the delay it will send change requests for faster dispatch along its planned trajectory: the last part of leg 2, turnaround at airport 3 and leg 3. With ATM and peer aircrafts it may negotiate a shorter route, for priority in approaches to airports 3 and 4, or an earlier take-off slot. On ground it may ask for a parking position closer to the run-way in order to save some minutes of taxiing, for more staff for cargo loading, for faster transfer of baggage to continuing flights, for parallelising service processes, or skipping others. Thus in the course of negotiations new service contracts with *higher* service levels will be concluded.

Contingency procedures require particularity and diligence. Accordingly, contingency operations are executed by specially trained personnel. Just a little failure, a missing mandatory document, may ruin the service recovery schedule of the airplane and put it at the end of the queue with even more delay. But also a single ownerless piece of luggage may block a terminal for half an hour. Therefore not only security personnel but *all* staff, whether working at check-in counters, in shopping malls and the restaurants or in the toilets, is trained watching for abandoned objects.

Gadgets alarming when the distance between owner and bag exceeds a set value are sold for 40 €. Future "intelligent" luggage may use similar gadgets to implement the principle: "Do not leave your owner unattended" or to make sure not to be loaded into the wrong continuing flight. Likewise passengers will be guided through airports' labyrinths by their smart-phones, help passengers finding the right emergency exit and to guide through safe areas. In case of fire, the operativeness of smoke outlets matters. Therefore, at Frankfurt Airport their statuses are controlled by sensors and reported to the terminal control centre not at least to save time in decision making.

Such concepts need to be carefully integrated into the framework of operations' workflows and controls. Workflows are precisely determined and, in potentially critical areas (e.g., apron field activity) or contexts (e.g., emergency) of operations, certified and subject of, e.g., case-based reviews and checks. As an example for likely most airports in the world, the day of the traffic management department of Cologne-Bonn Airport starts with the questions: What did happen yesterday? What do we have to learn from that? If an issue is identified, appropriate action will be taken and, if need be, forwarded, e.g., to aviation authorities or committees dealing with special operations' domains on national and international levels, like the smoke outlets got into focus of airport security after people asphyxiated in the smoke of a fire at Düsseldorf Airport with 17 casualties (National Fire Protection Association, 1996).

A very formal semantic model used, e.g., in communications between ATM or airport operations' management and the cockpit is another module of strictly rule-based internal proceedings. The purpose, among others, is to avoid misunderstanding or misreading in communication in an international, multi-cultural and multi-lingual environment. It can be explained on the example of "call-sign confusions" (EUROCONTROL Call Sign Similarity Project Update, 2010). A call-sign is the name of a flight, e.g. LH123. In all languages used in aviation control these call-signs are carefully checked for potential misreadings: for example, the German numerals "zwei" (2) and "drei" (3) are easy to be mistaken, thus one of the call-signs LH122 (eins-zwei-zwei) and LH123 (eins-zwei-drei) will be combed out.

It is expected that a reduction of uncertainty and with this of capacity of appropriate acting are the returns to such investments. However, human-machine systems do not automatically work in a deterministic and predictable way: consider that officers do not fully trust in the operativeness of the sensors or do not fully understand how controls work. (Or remember the case of the nurse.) Therefore, much effort is put on the design of human-machine interfaces, on the maintenance of systems and on training.

Finally, the intelligent aircraft will take advantage of such precautions. But hybrid systems formed by self-aware humans and self-aware technology may emerge new challenges and drive requirements for proficient human-machine decision making to an even higher level.

On the other side, there are also issues which cannot be solved by the "intelligent aircraft" or in its peer-to-peer arrangements. So a discussion of the variety of unexpected events and the issue of "butterfly effects" with representatives of Cologne-Bonn Airport is summarised by the statement: "Hardly things happen twice." An example may be the case of a worker towing a passenger stair from a remote place of the airport to the stand of an aircraft already approaching the position. Under pressure of time he took a curve too short around the stand of another aircraft, hit its wing (causing a damage of roughly 500.000 €) and delayed the rotation of the arriving aircraft for about one hour. The problem is not that such events may happen from time to time but that they happen almost any day at some airport, affecting others 3.000 km away. Therefore, criticality but also security cannot be treated only on local level.

In the time of Stuxnet (Chen, 2010), self-aware ICT should also protect against competent, sometimes even professional, hackers or against faults and frauds of insiders. Consider a hack of ATM-systems with the objective of creating chaos by placing series of false change requests. Since aviation networks are highly competitive this is not really absurd. But in a SESAR environment, deviation from planned trajectories will become obvious and faked reports will be sussed. Supervisors will contact the cockpit. Other aircrafts will report the exchange of trajectory data a few minutes ago. Finally, air-fighters will be sent to look after the aircraft.

A more effective attack may target at ground services. Their resources are less precisely tracked, cross-checking is weaker and a faked change request might drive ground operations into chaos. Assumed somebody has found a way to fake change requests to ground services. Particularly in peak-time there is hardly time to verify, thus they will respond, e.g., catering will re-allocate and re-load high-loaders, cleaning will remove a flight from the plan, etc. More critical may be if push-back tractors are shooed around or de-icing trucks in winter. But the integrity-check service of the central server system will work: it is connected to ATM and finds a reason for change requests – or not. Likewise security services will identify change-orders to service providers not fitting into the context of the scene. And for sure contradictions become obvious by digging into history or comparing states.

Use Case 2: Generation Centre Ruhr (GCR), the Problem-Solvers

In terms of inherent complexity and security levels the GCR-case structurally compares to the aviation case. However it does *not* focus on problems of MAS-based problem solving. There are many examples of successful modelling of structurally equivalent problems, e.g., in logistics or risk management. In contrary particularities of hybrid organisational environments are discussed which

rely on personality and circumstances of practical life rather than on formal structures.

The "Generation Centre Ruhr" is a network formed by handicraft firms and service providers offering customised solutions for individuals, families or communities needing to adjust their home and/or their life to the "challenges of aging or illness." It takes advantage from a rich portfolio of offers comprising builders, electricians, fitters, painters, gardeners, homemaking and nursing services or day-clinics, physical therapists, groceries, a municipal savings bank, an insurance, institutes for further training, adult education centre, etc.

In consequence of a number of exploratory studies and extensive analysis of the particularities of their approach to service option bundling, we are currently drilling deeper into the requirements of designing and implementing an organisational setup, including the need for technological support. From the point of view of the ministries funding the GCR-project, it should become a reproducibly strategy and improve the competitiveness of small and medium enterprises.

A case discussed was about a carpenter. He had been contacted by a family to modify the doors in their house for the use of a wheelchair. The carpenter outlined the project, invited a builder for widening the openings, an electrician to reposition light switches and a painter to complete. With access to knowledge-base of the network they found out that the disease, bounding the 30 years old son to the chair, matters with regard to materials used for alterations. After checking with the hospital, further experts were found which consulted on details and processing. During construction it turned out that the availability of special materials was quite poor and the project was to be rescheduled – in coordination with other projects the craftsmen were doing in parallel. After all it took a week more than planned. For the time of construction the family was quartered into a hotel at the Baltic Sea. Costs of the additional week were partly covered by insurance. For the time after the family had returned home, services for homemaking and nursery were prepared.

Another case concerned people being attended by their family except for some hours a day or weeks in the year when they are taken to a day-hospital. Then much is to be coordinated. Children may have to be taken to or picked up from school. A parent is on a business trip or has to do overtime. A traffic jam delays the matutinal taxi. A new driver needs briefing for special equipment. The clinic makes appointments with doctors … Multiply this by 40 patients in a day-hospital and consider "butterfly-effects."

The irritation of the nurse about the functioning of technology occurred at the border between the risk-awareness of the nurse (she called it "worries") and the lacking awareness of the support system acting on the parameter "expected battery lifetime." Instead, by measuring the actual capacity of batteries this system was restarted by a message after batteries had been changed. Thus it failed because batteries were used up earlier than expected. I.e. the control-loop of the system was not complete and after all, the organisation decided instead of trusting technology to check batteries manually every day. Albeit workload was very high, trust in human actors was higher than trust in any machine. In a discussion of ideas to improve technology, the striking argument of the nurse was: "It is irrelevant whether I fail or the system. At the end only I will be responsible." Or in the words of the director of the traffic management department of Cologne-Bonn Airport: "Machines may become risk-aware, but never responsible."

The IT group of craftsman firms discussed issues differently. Their concerns concentrated around protection of calculation and customer databases on one side, as well as project and resource efficiency on the other. The automation of business processes are welcomed as long as these basic demands are fulfilled. A problem in this is that only as a group GCR-partners exceed reaches the scale justifying the investment into automation. I.e. here we encountered a new facet

of awareness: risk to trust in partners. Three of them, the carpenters, are direct competitors. Since just these firms are too small to cover demand and a bigger candidate is not available also quitting is not the best solution. Fortunately, two of them understand the concept of "co-opetition" to collaborate in opening new markets quite well before – still in a fair way – competing for the pray (Brandenburger & Nalebuff, 1996).

The analysis now focuses on automation for the craftsman's group and on added value to nursery services. We envision a network of smart mobile devices providing controlled access to shared knowledge bases and proprietary data and able of dynamically coordinating their activities. Among others, they shall include menus with standard messages (as used by the nurse), re-negotiate schedules on a peer-to-peer base (as required in the case of altering the house or for day-clinics' operations), consult ontologies for finding relevant context of a project (for construction material) – and maintain security and privacy. The current customer database of the GCR holds about 1000 addresses, including outlines of buildings, data on the financial volume of projects and bank-accounts, information about diseases, holiday planning (house is unguarded) … I.e. there is a source of motivation to hack or copy the database.

Besides standard protection (segmenting the database, encryption, strong passwords, etc.) we consider using context-awareness to avoid unauthorised access to databases. In a similar way it also could be applied to scheduling functionality. The context establishes from the contracts, e.g., on a stay in the day hospital, a care service or a construction project, each implying different needs of getting access to client-specific data. For instance, the nurse caring for the old lady does not need outlines of the building, the taxi-driver any information on illnesses. It also matters in which role somebody wants to access the data or from where and at what time. For instance, the nurse will be allowed to access insurance data when she is doing back-office jobs, but only when she is sitting in the office, while the system will alarm if somebody uses her identity for accessing the data when she is doing her domiciliaries. Also mobile devices may only hold data relevant to the current activity. If context changes new data will be downloaded.

WORKING PRINCIPLES OF SECURITY-AWARENESS

In the section on the concept of self-awareness, the need for a two layers' concept for implementing added value services has been introduced. The first one includes workflows, SLA and related knowledge enabling effective and efficient acting in the domain, i.e. to become aware of events, to choose appropriate methods or applying values governing decisions, etc. The second level provides managerial services enabling awareness or evaluation in the light of global operations' standards and if need be corrective action *while* acting in the domain: in the first use-case the aircraft will be updated if a security problem is detected which did not become obvious on the local level. The integration of context information may be arranged by routing all communications through the central system, which will likely produce a bottleneck.

Alternatively the peers will, due to ontologies, filter relevant information to be forwarded to the "security service" for further proceeding. The relevance of information can be understood from the examples and in terms of processing are organised in two categories:

- Information that can be processed by *simple* set-actual comparisons: This refers to the state of smoke outlets (open, closed), to batteries (used, charged) and other readings like the expected and actual position of an aircraft along its planned trajectory, the position of a taxi on its way to the day hospital, the state of a ground service resource or of a capacity-slot of the carpenter

(busy, free) and properties of passengers or baggage (local, transfer). For identifying risks in terms of security, simple rule-based comparisons will be sufficient for guiding decisions. E.g., if there is a fire, smoke outlets are expected to be open and passengers should be not guided through areas where outlets are closed.

- Information that needs to be processed in an *intelligence mode*: This is information the meaning of which is not obvious, i.e. it has to be checked for patterns or indications of risks. This mode will be discussed in the following.

In the first instance the "intelligence mode" is based on the same principles and models as the "simple" one: states of objects, as produced by events or operations, are subject to set-actual comparisons. An example may be the conclusion of a service contract changing the state of the respective resource from idle to busy (process = concluding, event = concluded). Assumed the behaviour of objects is governed (also) by a micro-economic model, the state "satisfied" of an agent will change into "dissatisfied" in case a new opportunity arrives (event) offering a higher profit. The consequence will be that the current contract is cancelled, presumed that there are no constraints as defined in the respective SLA like minimum physical response-time to events, legal aspects, or economic considerations. In the baggage sorter (a logistics context) an RFID-labelled piece of baggage passes a reader (process = passing, event = read) conveying the information that the object "now is 'here'." All these states together represent the context, and the frequency of events and changes of states represents dynamics of an operations' scene with interferences propagating along relationships between objects. E.g., if passengers are "in" a taxi, they together are affected by traffic jam as the staff of the day hospital which is "waiting for" the arrival of passengers.

Figure 5. Gantt-diagram of an operations' scene

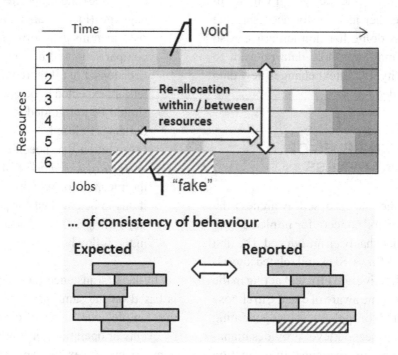

But in the intelligence mode this information becomes subject to more complicated and inter-related comparisons. A Gantt Diagram is a standard of displaying states of resources of processes in time. In Figure 5 one is displayed showing an operations' scene which includes six resources collaborating in a number of jobs (marked by the colours). Note that "resources" may refer to members of the staff, equipment or machinery, the aircraft, a capacity slot, baggage or whatever may be needed for executing an operation. Particularly: we are in a service environment which means that the customer, or at least some of his or her property, needs to take part as a resource in the process.

Voids in Figure 5 mark times when resources are idle (not contracted) and the total of all voids may be a first approximation of the flexibility of the system to respond to events. In case of un-planned events allocations will be revised and flexibility may be consumed. The purpose of criticality management is to avoid "freezing of operations." Thus residual flexibility is continu-

ously estimated. Unfortunately that is not that easy as Figure 5 may suggest: all resources and orders are interconnected in complex patterns and to be characterised by *holistic* parameters like the average response-time of the system, voids per class of resources and in total, density of events in time, measures of interdependencies of activity, etc.

Likewise the attack of hackers is an issue that needs intelligence to be detected. Assumed somebody wants to manipulate the load of an air-catering high-loader (HL, ID = #) destined for a particular flight. Since this business will take some minutes, the perpetrator will have to arrange a slot and since he hardly will ask for clearance of "load bomb" he has to fake another job like the need for cleaning of the truck. But the system is aware of the context, i.e. of the network of all events and states: among others, an event must have been reported that produced the state "HL/# is dirty" and other objects may have been involved in creating it (e.g., a near-accident with another vehicle or a broken trolley). It is also likely that the event has changed the status of other objects. A future IT-enabled catering trolley will know and report that it is fallen over. Bottles of wine (RFID-tagged) should be found "broken." The HL must have made a contract with the cleaning station and it is to be unloaded before cleaning. The time it needs to get to the loading gate and to the station is known, the HL may be GPS-tracked and relevant context parameters (e.g., weather conditions which may impact on decisions) be continuously updated.

When a contradiction has been detected it may have to be verified, at the best by direct communication between security services and concerned objects. In the case of the day hospital we discussed smart-phone applets for automating a policy of mutual verification of punctuality of taxis pick-up of invalids at their homes. The rule was that the taxi driver sends a standardised SMS to the coordination desk if the expected delay is more than 30 minutes. In case the taxi is more delayed, the family sends a message and the control desk calls the driver and, if need be, organises an alternative.

Other policies may be to continue observing the behaviour of the doubtful object, scan for patterns and compare with known ones from history, or to analyse the history of events. The same may be true for validating false negative diagnoses: even if at a first glance the current scene is consistent, history may be not. In sensitive areas operations should be randomly scanned for inconsistency or, depending on available computing capacity, do it online to real-time operations.

These examples may give an idea that the added value service on security-awareness actually is an intelligence application, a kind of "criminal investigation service." This suggests the question: How do famous detectives like *Inspector Colombo* (Inspector Colombo, 1964-2011) work? Actually they have an idea of crime, of scenes and how to find evidence. They carefully search for proofs, hear witnesses, if need be they turn everything upside down, and put pieces together to a pattern.

Suspicion is a part of their nature. They see a picture, find a piece and understand that it marks a crime scene. They understand context, identify and verify contradictions to context, compile the burden of proof and finally take the 'perp' to the court. May be that at an airport more has to be turned upside down than Colombo ever could imagine. But for this reason we have computers. Thus how will "*Colombo-agents*" work?

- Their subject matter is the wrong conduct of operations' principles as defined in ontologies. They continuously scan the flow of states, events and decisions for non-feasible, non-conducive or faked contracts, defective behaviour of objects and respective deviant states of operations.
- They take advantage from the complexity of the system: it is massively distributed, i.e. there are many witnesses to be questioned and to analyse consistency across the local knowledge (logs of decisions-making) of agents. Since agents are self-contained and diverse (human actors, complex software systems, intelligent things, …), as well as organised in massively parallel threads, local knowledge is authentic rather than a copy from other, potentially corrupted sources.
- The complexity of the system also provides build-in firewall functionality which becomes even more effective the more complex and dynamic the scene will become. The effect actually relies on the reversion of a detective's strategy to convict perpetrators by their particular knowledge: corrupting a complex system without leaving explicit marks will need more knowledge about the scene as any perpetrator may ever achieve – particularly if it is to be updated in pace with the dynamics of the scene.
- Since the network of states and events, among others, is organised in the dimen-

sion of time, information passing the context bus is to be synchronised. In highly dynamic environments with a high frequency of events this almost automatically involves implementing principles of real-time management across the whole operations' system.

- Sure turning upside down operations' protocols of potentially hundreds of thousands of self-contained objects in (almost) real-time will need significant computing as well as communication capacity. However, although detective services are organised as a central service, respective server infrastructure and the capacity of potentially hundreds of thousands Things that Think might form a grid allowing for dynamic re-allocation of tasks in order to cut peaks.

CONCLUSION AND FUTURE WORK

Can complexity be exploited in order to manage complexity? We think: Yes, because it is problem *and* resource, but also because a major obstacle of modelling complex operations' systems phrased by the "law of requisite variety" (Ashby, 1957), can be solved. Ashby's variety compares to the resolution of object and time (Müller-Stewens & Fleisch, 2008) which again is matched by the generic scalability of MAS with regard to variety of objects and the frequency and variety of events they cause or which affect them. Ontologies, the compliance to SOA principles and peer-to-peer architecture enable exploring alternatives which may respond to unplanned events by taking advantage of local knowledge.

We presume that this model can be compiled for hybrid as well as massively distributed and parallel acting networks formed by intelligent things, human users and legacy software systems. However this architecture hardly supports concepts like self*-capabilities. Therefore we suggest a dual-layered design of at least two interacting MAS, one for managing the domain and the other providing added value services dealing with holistic context of the operations system such as self-learning or security-awareness.

As mentioned in the intro: our concepts dare an explorative projection of converging technological and organisational developments touching many disciplines of research and technology. Therefore, the result is a list of open questions rather than an answer. And it is an approach towards building contacts and teams interested in further structuring and analysis of the topics addressed:

- Development of a deeper understanding of practical, application-oriented aspects of augmented self-awareness in their organisational and managerial context. With this regard we currently reduce the complexity of analysis by taking the team as the smallest unit of operations into its core. Rather than analysing large-scale application environments, our current approach focuses on domains represented by the GCR case. This finally may shape "professional services" for implementing the technology considered into future intelligent organisations.
- Likely things will become autonomous and self-aware but how could they become legally responsible and liable? Will concluding on a change of a service contract, e.g., between an aircraft and airport ground services, become a juridical act? In the aviation example, pilots, air traffic controllers or service dispatchers will have supervisory positions and make the final decision. And the nursery service decided to trust in manual controls rather than in technology. Thus legal consequences also will depend on the transparency of operations and ergonomic aspects of management interfaces. Or will writing ontologies which instruct agents' behaviour become a legal risk to developers or knowledge engineers. Such

issues are not addressed in this chapter but are to be solved before any serious application can be implemented.

- Also concerns about acceptance are to be addressed, e.g., with regard to the question how investigatory activity of Inspector Colombo will affect privacy, influence assessments of staff or will be judged at the court. Or not at least Things that Think will change job descriptions and workflows, thus affecting labour satisfaction. We should also understand that knowledge processing systems will increase productivity of knowledge workers and likely will cost jobs. What will be the impact to education and labour markets?

- Releasing multi-agent technology from the software box into the wilderness of the Internet and support event- and context-driven ad-hoc conferencing in hybrid collaborative networks of real-world objects which behave like software-agents. This includes revising the design of ontologies and the way they are edited, as well as of the operativeness of service-oriented ontology and object architectures or of the concept service level agreements in such environments. With regard to these topics, we just started in a wider community discussing the usefulness and the opportunities of an open source initiative on the transfer of technological concepts.

- Research on the relationship between coordination of operations on the base of peer-to-peer negotiations on one and of central added value services for managing emergent, holistic operations' integrity, e.g., in terms of security, criticality or external effects of operations. This comprises a careful review of the idea of implementing artificial self-awareness as added value service provided by the means of dual-layered, interacting multi-agent systems.

- Since the volume of agents' communications may increase exponentially with their number and since added value services will consume further resources, likely capacity is the major problem of computing complex of MAS. There are solutions to be considered like the Hadoop filesystem, MapReduce for concurrent and analysis and Chukwa as monitoring system running on top (see Boulon, 2008). On the side of MAS, holonic architectures may contribute to get controllable data volumes (Koester, 1990; Brussels et al., 1998).

- With regard to the design-to-performance, both in terms of effectiveness (delivering valid results) and efficiency (resource consumption) and of the operations' management of large-scale and massively parallel and distributed environments, we expect insights from exchange of ideas and experience with experts in High-End and Grid Computing. Reversely, intelligent added-value services for future complex heterogeneous operations' systems may become a future domain of High-End Computing.

"The machine is the problem: the solution is in the machine" (Poullet, 2006). New technology aims at extending the reach and control of current or imagined operations and frequently also establishes the base of further opportunities, of potential social or economic difference and of stimuli of competition which by then may have not been imagined. These cycles are the more effective the more systems are networked (the most powerful boost has been initiated by the Internet) and it is the way social-economic-technical systems are driving complexity. From this point of view "control illusions" might be explained as result of overemphasising the second part of Poullet's sentence while forgetting the first one suggesting that new technology in its consequence will be the driver of the next generation of problems.

Things are involved in many different ways into almost all kinds of social and economic operations. Our core idea is that intelligent, learning and self-aware things, if need be ad-hoc autonomously collaborating with human users and other systems, will make a difference in the way we can and, because of competition, should and finally will deal with complexity. Hitherto it is prevailingly perceived as source of trouble. In future it also should be perceived as source of chance. As example take the capability of MAS to translate interference into chance to improve or, as another one, the potential opportunity of "Colombo Agents" to exploit complexity as firewall or as source to validate the integrity of operations.

ACKNOWLEDGMENT

The research of G. V. Lioudakis has been supported in part by the European Commission, under the 7th Framework Programme, specifically the project DEMONS (Decentralised, Cooperative and Privacy-Preserving Monitoring for Trustworthiness).

Concepts underlying the architectures of ontologies, multi-agent systems and added-value services enabling self* capabilities have been primed by the Research Centre for Applications of Intelligent Systems of Cologne University of Applied Sciences in the context of the iC-RFID project (intelligent air-Catering, supported by RFID), co-funded by the Research Program on "Convergent Technologies," German Federal Ministry of Economics and Technology, Agency: PT-DLR, German Aerospace Centre, 2007-2010.

REFERENCES

C2C-CC Manifesto. (2007). *Report of the CAR 2 CAR Communication Consortium.* Retrieved June 12, 2011, from http://www.car-to-car.org

Adams, M., ter Hofstede, H. M. A., Edmond, D., & van der Aalst, W. M. P. (2006). *Implementing dynamic flexibility in workflows using worklets.* Technical Report BPM-06-06. BPM Center.

Agarwal, A., Miller, J., Eastep, J., Wentziaff, D., & Kasture, H. (2010). *Self-aware computing.* Retrieved July 11, 2011, from http://www.defensetechbriefs.com/component/content/article/8259

Amir, E., Anderson, M. L., & Chaudhri, C. K. (2004). *Report on DARPA Workshop on Self-Aware Computer Systems.* Retrieved August 18, 2011, from http://citeseerx.ist.psu.edu (document 10.1.1.120.6684.pdf)

Antonakopoulou, A., Lioudakis, G. V., Gogoulos, F., Kaklamani, D. I., & Venieris, I. S. (2012). Leveraging access control for privacy protection: A survey. In Yee, G. (Ed.), *Privacy protection measures and technologies in business organizations: Aspects and standards* (pp. 65–94). Hershey, PA: IGI Global.

Ashby, W. R. (1956). *An introduction to cybernetics.* London, UK: Chapman & Hall Ltd.

Basile, C., Lioy, A., Perez, G. M., Clemente, F. J. G., & Skarmeta, A. F. G. (2007). POSITIF: A policy-based security management system. In *POLICY 2007: Proceedings of the 8th IEEE International Workshop on Policies for Distributed Systems and Networks.* Washington, DC: IEEE Computer Society.

Belobaba, P., Odoni, A., & Barnhart, C. (2009). *The global airline industry.* Chichester, UK: John Wiley & Sons, Ltd. doi:10.1002/9780470744734

Bertino, E., Catania, B., Damiani, M. L., & Perlasca, P. (2005). GEO-RBAC: A spatially aware RBAC. In *Proceedings of the 11th ACM Symposium on Access Control Models and Technologies (SACMAT '06)* (pp. 29-37). New York, NY: ACM.

Bertino, E., Martino, L., Paci, F., & Squicciarini, A. (2010). *Security for Web services and service-oriented architectures*. Berlin, Germany: Springer-Verlag. doi:10.1007/978-3-540-87742-4

Bethencourt, J., Sahai, A., & Waters, B. (2007). Ciphertext-policy attribute-based encryption. In *S&P 2007: Proceedings of the 2007 IEEE Symposium on Security and Privacy* (pp. 321–334). Washington, DC: IEEE Computer Society.

Bhatti, R., Ghafoor, A., Bertino, E., & Joshi, J. B. D. (2005). X-GTRBAC: An XML-based policy specification framework and architecture for enterprise-wide access control. *Journal of ACM Transactions of Information and System Security*, 8(2), 187–227. doi:10.1145/1065545.1065547

Boneh, D., & Franklin, M. K. (2003). Identity-based encryption from the Weil pairing. *SIAM Journal on Computing*, 32(3), 586–615. doi:10.1137/S0097539701398521

Boulon, J. Konwinski, Qi, R., A., Rabkin, A., Yang, E., & Yang, M. (2008). Chukwa – A large-scale monitoring system. In *Proceedings of the First Workshop on Cloud Computing and its Applications (CCA 2008)*. Retrieved February 29, 2012, from http://www.cca08.org/papers/Paper-13-Ariel-Rabkin.pdf

Brandenburger, A., & Nalebuff, B. (1996). *Co-opetition*. New York, NY: Doubleday.

Chen, T. M. (2010). Stuxnet, the real start of cyber warfare? *IEEE Network*, 24(6), 2–3. doi:10.1109/MNET.2010.5634434

Chevaleyre, Y., Endriss, U., Estivie, S., & Maudet, N. (2005). Welfare engineering in practice: On the variety of multi-agent resource allocation problems. In M.-P. Gleizes, A. Omicini, & F. Zambonelli (Eds.), *Engineering Societies in the Agents World V*, (LNAI 3451, pp. 335–347). Berlin, Germany: Springer-Verlag.

Christensen, K., & Moloney, N. (2005). *Complexity and criticality*. London, UK: Imperial College Press.

Cliver, R. (2011). Tremors in the Web of trade: Complexity, connectivity and criticality in the mid-eighth century Eurasian world. *The Middle Ground Journal*, 2, 1–39.

Cuppens, F., & Cuppens-Boulahia, N. (2008). Modelling contextual security policies. *International Journal of Information Security*, 7(4), 285–305. doi:10.1007/s10207-007-0051-9

Cuppens-Boulahia, N., Cuppens, F., Autrel, F., & Debar, H. (2009). An ontology-based approach to react to network attacks. *International Journal of Information and Computer Security*, 3(3/4), 280–305. doi:10.1504/IJICS.2009.031041

EUROCONTROL. (2010). *Call sign similarity project update*. Retrieved May 5, 2011, from www.eurocontrol.int

Europe's Information Society. (2011). *Radio Frequency IDentification and the Internet of Things*. Retrieved July 20, 2011, from http://ec.europa.eu/information_society/policy/rfid/index_en.htm

Felten, E. W. (2003). Understanding trusted computing. *IEEE Security & Privacy*, 1(3), 60–66. doi:10.1109/MSECP.2003.1203224

Ferraiolo, D. F., Sandhu, R., Gavrila, S., Kuhn, R. D., & Chandramouli, R. (2001). Proposed NIST standard for role-based access control. *ACM Transactions on Information and System Security*, 4(3), 224–274. doi:10.1145/501978.501980

Ferrini, R., & Bertino, E. (2009). Supporting RBAC with XACML+OWL. In *SACMAT 2009: Proceedings of the 14th ACM Symposium on Access Control Models and Technologies* (pp. 145-154). New York, NY: ACM.

Finin, T., Joshi, A., Kagal, L., Niu, J., Sandhu, R., Winsborough, W., & Thuraisingham, B. (2008). ROWLBAC: Representing role based access control in OWL. In *Proceedings of the 13th ACM Symposium on Access Control Models and Technologies* (pp. 73-82). New York, NY: ACM.

Global Footprint Network. (2011). *Footprint basics – Overview*. Retrieved October 12, 2011, from http://www.footprintnetwork.org/en/index.php/GFn/page/footprint_basics_overview/

Goyal, V., Pandey, O., Sahai, A., & Waters, B. (2006). Attribute-based encryption for fine-grained access control of encrypted data. In *CCS 2006: Proceedings of the 13th ACM Conference on Computer and Communications Security* (pp. 89–98). New York: ACM.

Günther, W., & ten Hompel, M. (2010). *Internet der Dinge in der Intralogistik*. Berlin, Germany: Springer-Verlag. doi:10.1007/978-3-642-04896-8

Hafner, M., & Breu, R. (2009). *Security engineering for service-oriented architectures*. Berlin, Germany: Springer-Verlag.

Hochberger, C., Waldschmidt, K., & Ungerer, T. (2008). *Grand challenge 6: HW -, SW-Architekturen und Werkzeuge für Multi-Core- und Many-Core-Prozessoren* (p. 41). Grand Challenges der Technischen Informatik.

Hotham, P. (2011). *SESAR & NextGen working together for aviation interoperability*. Presentation to the Royal Aeronautical Society Annual Conference, London, April 14th 2011; Retrieved October 5, 2011, http://www.sesarju.eu/news-press/news/sesar-ju-royal-aeronautical-society-annual-conference-815

Inden, U., & Franken, F. (2011). *Final report: CESSAR – Configuration and evaluation of service systems with RFID*. Gefördert durch das Bundesministerium für Wirtschaft und Technologie (BMWi) Project Number: MT06005) – Cologne Business Working Paper – Publication Series of the Faculty of Economics and Business Administration, Cologne University of Applied Sciences, (in publication) ISSN-Print 2192-7944, ISSN-Internet 2192-7944

Inden, U., Tieck, S., & Rückemann, C.-P. (2011). Rotation-oriented collaborative air traffic management. In C.-P. Rückemann, W. Christmann, S. Saini, & M. Pankowska, (Eds.), *Proceedings of The First International Conference on Advanced Communications and Computation (INFOCOMP 2011)*, October 23-29, 2011, Barcelona, Spain, (pp. 25-30). ISBN: 978-1-61208-161-8

Inspector Colombo. (1962-2011). Retrieved October 12, 2011 from http://www.famous-detectives.com/inspector-columbo.htm

International Organization for Standardization / International Electrotechnical Commission – ISO/IEC (2009). *Information technology – Trusted platform module – Part 1: Overview*. International Standard, Reference number ISO/IEC 11889-1:2009(E).

Ishi, H., Paradiso, J., & Picard, R. (2010). *TTT vision statement*. MIT Media Lab. Retrieved February 29, 2012, from http://ttt.media.mit.edu/vision/vision.html

Jacobson, V., Smetters, D. K., Thornton, J. D., Plass, M. F., Briggs, N. H., & Braynard, R. L. (2009). Networking named content. In *CoNEXT 2009: Proceedings of the 5th International Conference on Emerging Networking Experiments and Technologies* (pp. 1-12). New York, NY: ACM.

Joshi, J. B. D., Shafiq, B., Ghafoor, A., & Bertino, E. (2003). Dependencies and separation of duty constraints in GTRBAC. In *Proceedings of the Eighth ACM Symposium on Access Control Models and Technologies (SACMAT '03)* (pp. 51-64). New York, NY: ACM.

Kauffman, S. (1995). *At home in the universe: The search for the laws of self-organization and complexity.* Oxford, UK: Oxford University Press.

Kephard, J. O., & Chess, D. M. (2003). The vision of autonomic computing. *IEEE Computer, 36*(1), 41–50. doi:10.1109/MC.2003.1160055

Khurana, H., Hadley, M., Lu, N., & Frincke, D. A. (2010). Smart-Grid security issues. *IEEE Security & Privacy, 8*(1), 81–85. doi:10.1109/MSP.2010.49

Knaf, H. (2011). *EMERGENT.* Retrieved September 22, 2011, from http://www.itwm.fraunhofer.de/en/departments/system-analysis-prognosis-and-control/decision-support-in-the-medical-sciences-and-in-technology/emergent.html

Koestler, A. (1967). *The ghost in the machine.* New York, NY: Macmillan.

Koponen, T., Chawla, M., Chun, B., Ermolinskiy, A., Kim, K. H., Shenker, S., & Stoica, I. (2007). A data-oriented (and beyond) network architecture. *ACM SIGCOMM Computer Communication Review, 37*(4), 181–192. doi:10.1145/1282427.1282402

Koukovini, M. N., Papagiannakopoulou, E. I., Lioudakis, G. V., Kaklamani, D. I., & Venieris, I. S. (2011). A workflow checking approach for inherent privacy awareness in network monitoring. In *DPM 2006: Proceedings of the 6th Workshop on Data Privacy Management* (LNCS 7122, under publication). Berlin, Germany: Springer-Verlag.

Lioudakis, G. V., Gogoulos, F., Antonakopoulou, A., Kaklamani, D. I., & Venieris, I. S. (2009). Privacy protection in passive network monitoring: an access control approach. In *Proceedings of the IEEE 23rd International Conference on Advanced Information Networking and Applications (AINA-09)* (pp. 109-116). Washington, DC: IEEE Computer Society Press.

Lioudakis, G. V., Koutsoloukas, E. A., Dellas, N., Kapitsaki, G. M., Kaklamani, D. I., & Venieris, I. S. (2008). A semantic framework for privacy-aware access control. In M. Ganzha, M. Paprzycki, & T. Pełech-Pilichowski (Eds.), *Proceedings of the 3rd International Workshop on Secure Information Systems (SIS'08) – International Multiconference on Computer Science and Information Technology* (pp. 813-820). Los Alamitos, CA: IEEE Computer Society Press.

Lioudakis, G. V., Tropea, G., Kaklamani, D. I., Venieris, I. S., & Blefari-Melazzi, N. (2010). Combining monitoring and privacy-protection perspectives in a semantic model for IP traffic measurements. In E. Gelenbe, R. Lent, G. Sakellari, A. Sacan, H. Toroslu, & A. Yazici (Eds.), *Computer and Information Sciences: Proceedings of the 25th International Symposium on Computer and Information Sciences* (LNEE 62, pp. 187–190). Amsterdam, Netherlands: Springer-Verlag.

Luck, M., McBurney, P., Shehory, O., & Willmott, S. (2005). *Agent technology: Computing as interaction (a roadmap for agent based computing).* Southampton, UK: University of Southampton (on behalf of AgentLink III).

Luhmann, N. (1968). *Vertrauen - ein Mechanismus der Reduktion sozialer Komplexität* (4th ed.). Stuttgart, Germany: Lucius & Lucius.

Maehle, E., & Waldschmidt, K. (2008). *Grand challenge 3: Vertrauenswürdigkeit und Zuverlässigkeit* (p. 30). Grand Challenges der Technischen Informatik.

Maturana, H., & Varela, F. (1992). *The tree of knowledge: Biological roots of human understanding (original: El árbol del conocimiento. Bases biológicas del entendimiento humano)*. Boston, MA: Shambhala Publications, Inc.

Mehandjiev, N., & Grefen, P. (Eds.). (2010). *Dynamic business process formation for instant virtual enterprises*. London, UK: Springer-Verlag.

Müller-Schloer, C., Schmeck, H., Bringschulte, U., Feldbusch, F., Trumler, W., & Ungerer, T. (2008). *Grand Cahallenge 4: 'Organic computing' Techniken*. Grand Challenges der Technischen Informatik.

Müller-Stewens, G., & Fleisch, E. (2008). High-resolution-management: Konsequenzen des "Internet der Dinge" auf die Unternehmensführung. *Führung und Organisation, 77*(5), 272–281.

National Fire Protection Organisation. (1996). *Abschließender Bericht über den Brandhergang - Brand im Terminal des Flughafens*, Düsseldorf, Deutschland 11. Retrieved October 17, 2011, from www.nfta.org

Noorollahi Ravari, A., Amini, M., & Jalili, R. (2008). A semantic aware access control model with real time constraints on history of accesses. In M. Ganzha, M. Paprzycki, & T. Pełech-Pilichowski (Eds.), *Proceedings of the International Multiconference on Computer Science and Information Technology* (pp. 827-836). Los Alamitos, CA: IEEE Computer Society Press.

Noorollahi Ravari, A., Jafarian, J., Amini, M., & Jalili, R. (2010). GTHBAC: A generalized temporal history based access control model. *Journal of Telecommunication Systems, 45*(2), 111–125. doi:10.1007/s11235-009-9239-9

Nordbotten, N. A. (2009). XML and Web services security standards. *IEEE Communications Surveys & Tutorials, 11*(3), 4–21. doi:10.1109/SURV.2009.090302

Oracle. (2009). *Java card 3.0.1 platform specification*. Retrieved October 20, 2011, from http://www.oracle.com/technetwork/java/javacard/specs-jsp-136430.html

Papazoglou, M. P., & van den Heuvel, W.-J. (2007). Service oriented architectures: Approaches, technologies and research issues. *The VLDB Journal, 16*(3), 389–425. doi:10.1007/s00778-007-0044-3

Poullet, Y. (2006). The directive 95/46/EC: Ten years after. *Computer Law & Security Report, 22*(3), 206–217. doi:10.1016/j.clsr.2006.03.004

Preda, S., Cuppens, F., Cuppens-Boulahia, N., Garcia-Alfaro, J., & Toutain, L. (2011). Dynamic deployment of context-aware access control policies for constrained security devices. *Journal of Systems and Software, 84*(7), 1144–1159. doi:10.1016/j.jss.2011.02.005

Rieger, F. (2009). *Security nightmares 2009*. Retrieved Februay 29, 2012, from http://www.golem.de/print.php?a=64350.

Rieger, F. (2012). *Security nightmares 2012*. Retrieved Februay 29, 2012, from http://www.golem.de/print.php?a=88727.

Rückemann, C.-P. (2010). Integrating high end computing and information systems using a collaboration framework respecting implementation, legal issues, and security. *International Journal on Advances in Security, 3*(3&4), 91-103. Retrieved November 06, 2011, from http://www.iariajournals.org/security/sec_v3_n34_2010_paged.pdf

Russell, S., & Norvig, P. (2010). *Artificial intelligence: A modern approach* (3rd ed.). Upper Saddle River, NJ: Prentice Hall/Pearson Education.

Rzevski, G. (2011). A practical methodology for managing complexity. *Emergence: Complexity & Organization, 13*(1-2), 38–56.

Sahai, A., & Waters, B. (2005). Fuzzy identity-based encryption. In R. Cramer (Ed.), *Advances in Cryptology: Proceedings of EUROCRYPT 2005, 24th Annual International Conference on the Theory and Applications of Cryptographic Techniques* (LNCS 3494, pp. 457–473). Berlin, Germany: Springer-Verlag.

Samarati, P., & de Capitani di Vimercati, S. (2001). Access control: Policies, models and mechanisms. In G. Goos, J. Hartmanis, & J. van Leeuwen (Eds.), *Foundations of Security Analysis and Design* (LNCS 2171, pp. 137–196). Berlin, Germany: Springer-Verlag.

Sandholm, T. (1993). An implementation of the contract net protocol based on marginal cost calculation. In R. Fikes, & W. G. Lehnert (Eds.), *Proceedings of the 11th National Conference on Artificial Intelligence* (pp. 256-262) Menlo Park, CA: AAAI Press.

Scherer, C. (2011, January 14). Aircraft must be smart swimmers to make next-gen ATM work. *Flight International*.

Simon, H. (1991). Bounded rationality and organizational learning. *Organization Science, 2*(1), 125–134. doi:10.1287/orsc.2.1.125

Skobelev, P. (2011). Bio-inspired multi-agent technology for industrial applications. In F. Alkhateeb, E. Al Maghayreh, & I. Abu Doush (Eds.), *Multi-Agent Systems - Modeling, Control, Programming, Simulations and Applications*. Rijeka, Croatia: InTech. Retrieved February 29, 2012, from http://www.intechopen.com/articles/show/title/bio-inspired-multi-agent-technology-for-industrial-applications

ten Hompel, M. (2008). *Logistics by design – Ein Ansatz für zukunftsfähige Intralogistik: Serviceorientierte Architektur als Grundlage* (*Vol. 5*, pp. 236–240). Hebezeuge-Fördermittel / HF Forschung.

Tonti, G., Bradshaw, J. M., Jeffers, R., Montanari, R., Suri, N., & Uszok, A. (2003). Semantic Web languages for policy representation and reasoning: A comparison of KAoS, Rei, and Ponder. In D. Fensel, K. Sycara, & J. Mylopoulos (Eds.), *The Semantic Web: Proceedings of the Second International Semantic Web Conference (ISWC 2003)* (LNCS 2870, pp. 419-437). Berlin, Germany: Springer-Verlag.

Tropea, G., Lioudakis, G. V., Blefari-Melazzi, N., Kaklamani, D. I., & Venieris, I. S. (2011). Introducing privacy-awareness in network monitoring ontologies. In Salgarelli, L., Bianchi, G., & Blefari-Melazzi, N. (Eds.), *Trustworthy Internet* (pp. 317–331). Milan, Italy: Springer-Verlag. doi:10.1007/978-88-470-1818-1_24

van Brussel, H., Wyns, J., Valckenaers, P., Bongaerts, L., & Peeters, P. (1998). Reference architecture for holonic manufacturing systems: PROSA. *Computers in Industry, 37*(3), 255–274. doi:10.1016/S0166-3615(98)00102-X

Vector Fabrics, B. V. (2011). *Using vfAnalyst to parallelize your program*. Whitepaper. Retrieved October 3, 2011, from http://www.vectorfabrics.com/

World Wide Web Consortium. (2004). *Web Ontology Language (OWL)*. Retrieved October 20, 2011, from http://www.w3.org/2004/OWL/

Zivadinovic, D. (2007). *IPv6: Das Mega-Netz*. Retrieved August 15, 2011, from http://www.heise.de/netze/artikel/IPv6-Das-Mega-Netz-221708.html

Chapter 4
A New SWOT Analysis of an E–Government System:
Singapore Case

Huong Ha
University of Newcastle, Singapore

ABSTRACT

E-Government is defined as the utilization of the Internet and other technological means to deliver public services to citizens. Following the success of the iGov2010 plan, Singapore has recently launched an e-Government Master Plan 2011-2015 (eGov2015), which opens a new epoch of relationship between government and the public. This chapter aims to (i) discuss the current state of the e-Government system in Singapore, (ii) provide a SWOT (strengths, weaknesses, opportunities and threats) analysis of this e-Government system, and (iii) make policy recommendations on how to address challenges, facing e-Government in order to enhance public trust via the effective and efficient delivery of public services. This chapter is significant as it (i) addresses the issues from a practical perspective and from the view of users, and (ii) provides a better insight for further research in e-Government systems. Finally, neighbouring countries may benefit from the lessons drawn from the Singapore experience in terms of how to achieve a balance between technology adoption, citizen engagement, and delivery of electronic public services.

INTRODUCTION

E-governance embraces e-Government, being defined as the utilization of the Internet and other technological means to deliver public services to citizens and encourage citizen participation. E-Government is one of the most enabling platforms for government to build trust with citizens and allow active citizen engagement in the delivery of public services, as well as in the decision making process. E-Government also promotes openness, transparency and accountability, and, thus, it can

DOI: 10.4018/978-1-4666-2190-9.ch004

change the nature of the relationship between the public sector and the private sector, civil society and citizens.

This chapter aims to (i) discuss the current state of the e-Government system in Singapore, (ii) provide a SWOT analysis of this e-Government system, and (iii) make policy recommendations on how to address challenges, facing e-Government in order to enhance public trust via the effective and efficient delivery of public services.

This chapter will focus on the current strategic framework of Singapore's e-Government system, the strengths and weaknesses of this system, using a SWOT analysis. It also explores the opportunities for e-Government, including the emergence of m-government, a new approach to deliver public services, and the active participation of the citizens in Singapore. A series of cyber-attacks disrupting the government websites in many countries, such as the U.S.A., Malaysia, Estonia, Brazil, etc., has also prompted the author to investigate the growing threats of privacy, security and e-terrorism to the development of an e-Government system.

This chapter is significant as it will (i) address the research questions from a practical perspective and from the view of users (citizens), and (ii) provide a better insight for further research in e-Government and e-Governance, given the growing demand of good public governance and better public services. Finally, neighbouring countries may benefit from the lessons drawn from the Singapore experience in terms of how to achieve a balance between technology adoption, citizen engagement and effective public services.

LITERATURE REVIEW

This section revisits the concept of e-Government, e-Government system and factors affecting this system.

E-Government and E-Government System

There are many definitions of e-Government. According to the United Nations Division for Public Economics and Public Administration (2002), e-Government refers to the delivery of public services and dissemination of government information to the public via the Internet. E-Government is considered as a platform for the government and its citizens to communicate with each other in a timely and cost-effective manner (Angelopoulos, Kitsios, & Papadopoulos, 2010; Evans, & Ye, 2006; Latre et al., 2010). Heeks (2001, 2005) and Rotchanakitumnuai (2008) commented that information technology (IT) is critical to enhance the performance of the public sector in terms of provision of public services. Davies (2007) also affirmed that the value of a government network would be created by using "sophisticated web of technology to support communication and coordination between a diverse network of stakeholders" (p. 11). To make it simple, e-Government is defined as the delivery of the information and services by the public sector via electronic means (Tolbert, & Mossberger, 2006).

Accordingly, e-Government system is the use of IT applications as parts of an integrated architecture framework to deliver public services and to allow various groups of stakeholders to be connected with government and with one another. However, e-Government system is not only about the deployment of technology or techno-based means, but it is about the interconnection and interdependence between the use of technology, strategy, policy, organisational structure, and stakeholders (Angelopoulos, Kitsios, & Papadopoulos, 2010; Yildiz, 2007). These parts of the system must work in a synchronized manner in order to make the system function well, i.e. to transform government as a whole by making it more transparent, responsive, accessible, effective and efficient.

Factors Affecting an E-Government System

An e-Government system can only be successful if it allows quality public services to be delivered and information to be diffused in a speedy, transparent, interactive and cost-effective manner (Angelopoulos et al., 2010). Literature suggests that the effectiveness and efficiency of an e-Government system is affected by the following key variables, namely (i) political, (ii) legal, (iii) resource-based, and (iv) access-related factors. Economic, technological and social factors are embraced in the resource-based and/or access-related variables (Chen, & Knepper, 2005; Ndou, 2004; Rashid, & Rahman, 2010). Table 1 summarises research projects by different authors regarding the determinants affecting an e-Government system.

Political Factors

Political factors embrace leadership commitment and competency, administrative arrangement, and institutions (Rashid, & Rahman, 2010). Bonham et al. (2001), Coursey and Norris (2008), Kettle (2002) and OECD (2003) commented that political commitment is the most important factor for the initiative of an e-Government system. Political leaders must acknowledge and encompass e-Government as a tool and a mechanism to improve the performance of the public service and a platform to connect with the citizens (Council for Excellence in Governance, 2001). Political leaders and government officials must be competent enough to steer the development process of e-Government as it requires a certain level of ICT understanding to appreciate the benefits of IT applications, such as Web 2.0 or cloud computing.

According to Koh et al. (2005) and Singh (2003), administrative capability refers to the ability to set policy and make strategic plans in order to develop e-Government. The size of administration and organisational structure also affect the adoption of technology, which, in turn, will influence the operation and outcome of an e-Government system (Angelopoulos et al., 2010; Moon, 2002; Moon, & Noriss, 2005).

An e-Government system is considered an information network, which is inter-sectorial and interconnected. These information networks are shared by intra- and inter-government departments, and other groups of stakeholders such as the public, business community, and government agencies from other countries. Thus, institutions must be in place to co-ordinate the work of various government agencies and different groups of stakeholders (Rashid, & Rahman, 2010).

Legal Factors

Sound legal and policy frameworks of accessibility to information (i.e. who can access the information, how information can be accessed), and how information is kept confidential is essential for the operations of an e-Government network (Rashid, & Rahman, 2010). An absence of government regulations regarding security and privacy would be a great barrier for knowledge collection and sharing in an e-Government system. In many countries, such as Bangladesh, inadequate regulatory framework has hampered a conducive environment for the development of e-Government (Rashid, & Rahman, 2010). Online security and privacy incidents would reduce public trust in an e-Government system (Tassabehji, & Elliman, 2006). Without trust, the public may decide not to receive public services via e-Government. Also, different practices by different government bodies allow limited and/or non-transparent accessibility to complaint-handling systems and dispute resolution mechanisms (Patterson, 2001). Many countries, such as the U.S.A, the U. K., Australia and Canada, do enact legislation and acts to address issues associated with online security and privacy. Nevertheless, some other countries do not have a legal framework in place to address online security and privacy incidents (Ha, 2011).

Table 1. Determinants and sub-determinants affecting e-government

Determinants	Sub-determinants	Source/s
Political	Leadership commitment and competency	Bonham et al.(2001) Singh (2003) Koh, Ryan and Prybutok (2005) Wescott (2007) Coursey and Norris (2008) Rashid and Rahman (2010) Council for Excellence in Governance (2011)
	Administrative arrangement and organisational structure	Bonham et al. (2001) Singh (2003) Vintar et al. (2003) Koh et al. (2005) Ebrahim and Irani (2005) Wescott (2007) Coursey and Norris (2008) Rashid and Rahman (2010)
	Institutions	Rashid and Rahman (2010)
Legal factors	Security and privacy	Ebrahim and Irani (2005) Wescott (2007) Rashid and Rahman (2010) Ha (2011)
	Regulations and self-regulation	Wescott (2007) Rashid and Rahman (2010) Ha (2011)
	Jurisdiction	Jawahitha (2004) Ong (2005) Ha and Coghill (2006) Wescott (2007)
Resource-based	Financial resources	Wescott (2007) Rashid and Rahman (2010)
	Infrastructure	Heeks (2001) Sharma and Gupta (2002) Vintar et al. (2003) Ebrahim and Irani (2005)
	Human resources	Ha and Coghill (2006) Ojo et al. (2007) Prananto and McKemmish (2007) Wescott (2007) Rashid and Rahman (2010)
	Innovation	Roger (1995) Vintar et al. (2003) Traunmuller (2010)
Access-related	Educational level, technology and technological knowledge, information networks	Sharma and Gupta (2002) Vintar et al. (2003) Ebrahim and Irani (2005) Sipior and Ward (2005) Wescott (2007) Rashid and Rahman (2010)
	Internet connection and affordability of computers	Wescott (2007) Hermana and Sulfianti (2011)

In addition, jurisdiction is also an issue given the transient and cross-border nature of information and the net environment. Jurisdiction concerns are intensified when e-users have to settle a matter with a government agency in overseas (Ha, & Coghiil, 2006; Jawahitha, 2004; Ong, 2005; Wescott, 2007). In many cases, e-users may not be able to communicate with the relevant persons or relevant agencies for settling their problems.

Resource-Based Factors

Resources are critical for the implementation of an e-Government system. Resources refer to both tangible and intangible ones. Tangible resources include financial resources and physical infrastructure for an e-Government system to functions appropriately.

The financial factor is the most important resource-related variable affecting the effectiveness of e-Government (Edmiston, 2003; Norris et al., 2001). A huge amount of capital needed to invest in building IT infrastructure and develop capabilities, in terms of manpower and technological availability, for an e-Government system to be developed and sustained. From the economic perspective, resource-based factors refer to the net benefits received after consideration of all operational and opportunity costs. It is noted that opportunity costs are not easy to be identified and calculated.

Infrastructure is extremely important for an IT-based system to operate successfully. An integrated architecture framework is required for an e-Government system to function satisfactorily as the framework must provide integrated applications and interactive tools in order to facilitate the collection, storage, retrieve and communication of information between government agencies and the citizens, and among government agencies (Ebrahim, & Irani, 2005; Heeks, 2001; Sharma, & Gupta, 2002). Nevertheless, infrastructure can only be developed when there are adequate funds, technology and manpower.

Intangible resources refer to human capital and innovative capabilities. A system can only function well if the operators and users have knowledge about how the system works. Human resources are identified as one of the core competencies of any e-Government network (Chen, & Gant, 2001; Heeks, 2005; Moon, 2002; Taifur, 2006). No matter how well an e-Government system is planned, it is impossible for the system to function without knowledgeable staff who can competently operate and maintain the system. The shortage of IT skilled labour is considered one of the major barriers to develop e-Government. A good example is that many e-Government projects in developing countries, such as Bangladesh, Vietnam, Cambodia, etc. have been delayed due to shortages of IT skilled manpower (Rashid, & Rahman, 2010; Sang, Lee, & Lee, 2009).

Innovation is also one of the priorities to achieve a successful e-Government system. In the early stage of e-Government era, Rogers (1995) discussed the role of innovation and types of innovation in a technology system. Traunmuller (2010) affirmed that the use of innovative web-based applications has produced innovating e-Government networks. The influence of Internet-based means enables the public sector in many countries to improve their performance in terms of administration of feedback, provision of information, citizen participation in policy-making processes, intra- and inter-organisation collaboration, managing knowledge and organisational learning (Traunmuller, 2010).

Access-Related Factors

Determinants associated with access-relatedness include technology, the level of educational and technical knowledge of users, awareness of users, Internet connection and IT-related purchasing power.

Referring to technology, Bonham et al. (2001), Bourn (2002), Dawes and Pardo (2002), Rashid and Rahman (2010) and Taifur (2006) explained that technology is required for the development and maintenance of an e-Government system. Technological capabilities include hardware, software, IT skills and expertise, and the ability to deploy such resources in an effective and efficient manner.

Educational and technical knowledge allows users to easily get information and access e-services on the websites of various government agencies. Low educational performance is considered as one of the factor contributing to widening the digital divide (Sipior, & Ward, 2005). Education and training for government officials, and users are critical success factors of an e-Government system as training enables trainees to understand how and why ICT can revolutionise their work and improve their productivity (Pascual, 2003; Prananto, & McKemmish, 2007).

Also, if the level of awareness of users of an e-Government system is low, it is more difficult for e-Government to be promoted. In some countries, ICT applications are synonymous with luxurious services, which can only be enjoyed by "the elites in the society", and most of the public is "ignorant about the usefulness of ICT" and the benefits to receive public services via an e-Government system (Rashid, & Rahman, 2010, p. 12).

Internet connection allows users to access information and to receive public services online. However, lack of Internet access or high cost of Internet access is a major impediment to active e-Government in many countries, such as Laos People's Democratic Republic, Bangladesh, Iran, etc. (Wescott, 2007).

Finally, IT-related purchasing power refers to the affordability of computers to the citizens. In many countries, namely Korea, Japan, Hong Kong, Taiwan, etc., most of the people have either a computer or a laptop and has access to Internet either via private or public sources (Wescott, 2007). Singapore has a high percentage of the population who has access to a computer (84%) and the Internet (82%) in 2010 (Infocomm Development Authority of Singapore, 2011a). Nevertheless, in some countries where many people live under the poverty line, a computer or a laptop is considered to be luxurious. The digital divide due to techno-disadvantageous and geographical factors has caused e-Government exclusion (Hermana, & Sulfianti, 2011; Sipio, & Ward, 2005).

Singapore's E-Government System

The current state of e-Government in Singapore, the vision and the strategic frameworks of the iGov2010 and the newly launched e-Government Master Plan 2011-2015 in Singapore are explored in this section.

Vision

The concept of e-Government is enriched by the overall vision of the Singapore government, which is to achieve the leading position in e-Government and to better serve the citizens (Ha, & Coghill, 2006).

Following the success of the iGov2010, Singapore has recently launched an e-Government Master Plan 2011-2015 (eGov2015), which opens a new epoch of relationship between government and the people, i.e. from a government-to-you model to a government-with-you model in the delivery of electronic public services (Infocomm Development Authority of Singapore, 2010).

The vision of Singapore's eGov2015 is to "be a Collaborative Government that Co-creates and Connects with Our People" (Infocomm Development Authority of Singapore, 2011b, p. 2). This vision is supported by the three strategic thrusts discussed in the following section. The 10-year master plan of Intelligent Nation 2015 (iN2015) also contributes to enabling the vision of e-Government in Singapore to be materialised (Chung, 2007).

Strategic Thrusts

In Singapore, e-Government has been developed together with the re-inventing of the Public Services in the 21st century since more than 20 years ago. From the technical aspects, Singapore has launched six national strategic ICT plans since 1980 (Chung, 2007). The six national infocomm master plans have contributed to flourish the development of Singapore's e-Government system. These infocomm plans have been introduced concurrently with the four Government Infocomm plans as shown on Table 2. This has demonstrated the capabilities and competencies of Singapore in terms of infocomm planning and development. These have contributed to developing the full potential of e-Government in Singapore.

It is necessary to discuss the strategic framework of the iGov2010 as it is the foundation for the development of Singapore's eGov2015. The Singapore government has introduced four strategic thrusts for the implementation of the iGov2010, which aim to achieve the three key drivers, i.e. (i) managing and governing infocomm, (ii) development of the competency of public sector infocomm, and (iii) development of infocomm infrastructure and safeguarding infocomm security (Infocomm Development Authority of Singapore, 2010).

The first thrust is to enhance the coverage and the depth of e-services in order to enable e-services to reach customers timely and widely, and to provide more sophisticated electronic public services (Chung, 2007). The second focus is to enhance "citizens' mindshare in e-Engagement" (Infocomm Development Authority of Singapore, 2006, p. 2). Information and services must be delivered online in a clear, systematic and value-added manner in order to encourage users to visit and revisit government agencies' websites. Users can be motivated via different tools and mechanisms. For example, Singapore Ministry of Foreign Affairs encourages citizens who travel overseas to provide the information of their travelling and themselves online by offering vouchers to users. Apparently, the government does take into consideration the culture of Singaporeans who love to have monetary rewards for their deeds. Citizens who are encouraged to engage in e-Government would be more confident and willing to provide feedbacks and ideas to relevant government agencies. However, improvement of e-Services and e-Engagement cannot be materialized if relevant government agencies do not have the capacity and capabilities for providing public services via the online platform. Therefore, the purpose of the third thrust is to increase the "capacity and synergy in government" (Infocomm Development Authority of Singapore, 2006, p. 2). The final thrust relates

Table 2. Singapore's infocomm plans and e-Government development

Years	e-Government plans	National infocomm plans
2011-2015	eGov2015	iN2015
2006-2010	iGov2010	iN2005
2003-2006	e-Government Action Plan II	Connected Singapore
2000-2003	e-Government Action Plan I	Infocomm 21
1992-1999	Civil Service	IT2000
1986-1991	Computerisation	National IT Plan
1980-1985	Programme	National Computerisation Plan

Source: Adopted from Chung, M. K. (2007). Singapore e-Government Experience. Paper presented at Asia e- Government Forum 2007, 20 September 2007, Seoul, Korea, p. 6.

to the creation and enhancement of the competitive advantage of the country. From the system perspective, IT infrastructure and security are the key critical success factors of the above strategic thrusts. An e-Government system would not be successful without financial adequacy, which allows Singapore to achieve economic competencies and competitiveness via sectorial transformation. Building capabilities in order to utilize the current resources in a more effective and efficient manner can help a country to achieve national competitive advantage. However, given the transient nature and the issues specially occurring in the online environment, government itself cannot address all problems by itself. Therefore, collaboration between various government departments and between governments and other sectors, such as the private sector, the Infocomm sector, civil society and the public, would facilitate the development e-Government in Singapore. Show cases and promotion of IT solutions for the iGovernment master plan would also contribute to achieve this objective (Chung, 2007).

Developed from the iGov2010, the eGov 2015 master plan focuses on the three-fold strategic framework. The first thrust promotes the co-creation for greater value, i.e. citizens and businesses are engaged and empowered to collaborate with the government to create new e-services (Wong, & Cha, 2009). The government is not only a service provider, but now is transferred to be a platform provider to encourage greater public participation to co-create new content, and innovative and impactful e-services. The second thrust refers to the connection with the public for active citizen participation and deepening the "**e-Engagement** efforts and experiment with new ways to tap on the wisdom and resources of citizens" (Infocomm Development Authority of Singapore, 2011b, p. 10). Consulting with and inviting ideas from the public, and adopting social media as a channel of communication with the public can help government agencies to leverage their capabilities of developing new initiatives and programs to enhance public performance.

Finally, eGov2015 is treated as a catalyst for the "whole-of-government transformation" via the development and conversion of the public sector infrastructure, services, workplace and capabilities (Infocomm Development Authority of Singapore, 2011b, p. 14). The government has also planned to invest in cloud computing or G-Cloud (a private cloud for the public sector) to multiply its capacity in delivering e-services. From the technological perspective, all the thrusts demonstrate that Singapore's e-Government system must work as a whole entity and embrace ICT related technology in the development and transformation process of the public sector.

Other IT-Related Initiatives

In terms of security, the Singapore government has worked with e-Cap, a leading security service provider, to provide round the clock security surveillance technology and service to government agencies. A business intelligent solution, iFAST (Intelligent Food Approval and Safety Tracking System), has been specially developed by Elixir Technology for the food safety authority. OPUS IT, another Infocomm supplier of government agencies, provides "network forensics security solutions" to users (Infocomm Development Authority of Singapore, 2006, p. 3). Added in to this, each government ministry or department does have its own reliable IT vendors and suppliers who support their primary and support activities in the value chain. For instance, Netrust has contributed to the launch of e-passports by Singapore Ministry of Home Affairs, I-magnetron supports the operations of the Singapore Civil Defence Force, and many other examples.

Technologically, Singapore has invested in infocomm infrastructure to support the national e-Government system. A number of programs and projects, such as the Next Generation Nationwide Broadband Network and Wireless@SG have been implemented (Infocomm Development Authority of Singapore, 2010). Singapore was one of the first few countries to "draw together commercial

Grid Service Providers (GPSs) to offer industry and government consumers on-demand and pay-as-you-use access to high performance computing capabilities, software, and immense data strong capacity" (Infocomm Development Authority of Singapore, 2010, p. 7). The Singapore government has also adopted the Web 2.0 as one of the key driving forces for innovation and performance improvement (Lim, & Koh, 2008). New IT applications have enabled collaborative content to be created in different ways. For instance, personal or public blogs are open notes, which are available online for comments from readers, and this enables co-sharing of information online. Such applications can be adopted by the public sector for better performance (Traunmuller, 2010).

Apparently, initiatives by Singapore to develop e-Government are different from e-Government initiatives in other countries. For example, Korea has launched many major e-Government initiatives. These include the establishment of a Government for Citizen (G4C) system, a Social Insurance Information Sharing System (SIIS), a Home Tax Service System, and Government e-Procurement System. E-Approval and e-Document between government agencies have been adopted, and e-Signature and e-Seal have also been introduced (Special Committee for e-Government, Republic of Korea, 2003). Japan has reformed its public administration through the use of IT via e-Government since 1999. E-Government initiatives in Japan have been developed in three stages, namely (i) the initial stage including the introduction of a master plan for using IT in the public sector and the enactment of IT related law, (ii) the development stage embracing programs for building e-Government, and (iii) the promotion stage focusing on programs for promoting e-Government and for future administrative reform (Ministry of Internal Affairs and Communications, n.d.). Japan has also focused on digitization of procedures, which can be offered to the public online. So far, 469.61 million procedures have been digitized, and 159.98 million cases have been used online (Yamada, 2010).

SWOT ANALYSIS OF THE E-GOVERNMENT SYSTEM IN SINGAPORE

A SWOT analysis is employed in this sector to examine the strengths, weaknesses, opportunities and threats of the e-Government system in Singapore. Each of the four components of SWOT analysis is further examined in terms of PEST factors, referring to Political, Economic, Social and Technological determinants.

Strengths and Weaknesses

The analysis of internal environment of the current e-Government system of Singapore identifies the following strengths and weaknesses.

Strengths

Politically, leadership commitment and effective governance are the strengths of Singapore. Commitment and consistent support from political leadership is an important element for successful implementation of an e-Government system (OECD, 2003). Political leaders have shown keen interests in and provided strong supports to IT initiatives since the early stage of the development of e-Government. It is impossible not to mention the technical leadership, which is one of the key drivers of the e-Government development and implementation. Leadership competency is also a significant factor contributing to the success of Singapore's e-Government system. In Singapore, government officials in charge of the development of e-Government and implementation are well-trained. They have the ability to make strategic plans, and incorporate all factors in the planning and development stages. The managerial structure is clear and headed by competent senior government officers (Chung, 2007).

From the administrative and system perspectives, the strengths of Singapore's e-Government lie with the long term systematic planning, especially the introduction of computerization in 1981.

An e-Government system can only function well if all parts of the system work in a synchronized manner. Singapore has invested in infocomm research and development in order to achieve the vision and objectives of its e-Government system. The Infocomm Development Authority of Singapore (IDA) (2010) is the owner of National Authentication Framework, which will help to address online security issues. Singapore also launched the Infocomm Security Master Plan in 2008 to deal with online threats and vulnerabilities (Infocomm Development Authority of Singapore, 2010). For example, the government of Singapore has developed the Public Service Infrastructure (PSI) for the deployment of e-services. Relevant government ministries have also worked with the IDA, National Computer Systems and Ecquaria (IT enterprises) to host more than 2,000 e-services on the PSI (Infocomm Development Authority of Singapore, 2006).

Also, public-private partnership has made the public and private relationships more balanced in terms of diffusion and receipt of information, networking opportunities among several groups of stakeholders, co-sharing public governance, etc. (Traunmuller, 2010). Public-private partnership has been promoted to increase resilience of e-Government system through the launch of programmes such as "Cyber Watch Centre, Code of Practice for Internet Service Providers, Enhancing Government Infocomm Security Situational Awareness and Cyber Security Awareness Alliance" (Infocomm Development Authority of Singapore, 2010, p. 8).

Apart from the public-private partnership, public-public partnerships between various government departments and between governments of different countries have also promoted. Some good examples are the collaboration between the Ministry of Finance (MOF, owner of the e-Government system) and the IDA, partnerships with ICT industry such as working with CrimsonLogic, SQLView, Singapore Technologies Electronics, collaboration with private enterprises

(LawNet, CORENet, TradeNet) and working with other countries, namely Brunei, Thailand, Hong Kong, Qatar, UAE, etc. (Wong, and Cha, 2009). Finally, partnerships with the "people sector" such as schools and communities is also worthy to discuss (Chung, 2007, p. 31). Some examples are the National IT Literacy Programme, e-Citizen Helpers, CitizenConnect Centres (Wong, & Cha, 2009). These partnerships have helped Singapore to achieve Public-Private-People integrated (3Pi) e-services.

From the analysis, Singapore's e-Government system is very robust with the linkages among national and international government agencies, in terms of government-to-government (G2G) collaboration and exchange of information and experience (Infocomm Development Authority of Singapore, 2010). In other words, the strengths of the e-Government system in Singapore lie with the collaboration and cooperation among different agencies, sectors and stakeholders.

Regarding legal aspects, an e-Government system cannot attract users if content exchanged is not safeguarded. Thus, Singapore has introduced various initiatives to help users, enterprises and government agencies create intellectual property. Some of the initiatives are the Infocomm Local Industry Upgrading Programme and Technology Innovation Programme (Infocomm Development Authority of Singapore, 2010).

From the economic perspective, sufficient funds are essential for the development of an e-Government system. Singapore government has invested $1.3 billion in the SOEasy project, and the IDA also works on the Technology Enterprise Commercialization Scheme worth $75 million (Infocomm Development Authority of Singapore, n.d.).

Socially, social media networks are also powerful tools for propaganda of many government-related activities (Traunmuller, 2010). Actually, political leaders in Singapore have engaged in social media for campaigning during the general election in May 2011 and the presidential election in July 2011. The public, especially youngsters have been active in supporting their preferred parties at elections, or disclose the wrongdoings of candidates of other parties via social media networks (Chua, 2011). Nonetheless, security and privacy are some of the side effects of these new communication channels, which will be discussed in the section regarding threats.

Technologically, many channels and mechanisms have been adopted to deliver public services (more than 300 mobile services delivered in 2009), the mobile phone being one of them (Infocomm Development Authority of Singapore, n.d.). Technology has been adopted intensively to build government's capacity and capabilities. The broadband penetration rate in Singapore is very high, at 96% in 2009 (Rab, 2009). This has offered new opportunities for Singapore's e-Government system to further engage the citizens. The Singapore Government Enterprise Architecture (SGEA), the Government Web Services Exchange (GWS-X), the Unique Entity Number (UEN) system are some solutions and programs essential to transform both the front and the back-end of government departments for better synergy among intra- and inter- government agencies (Infocomm Development Authority of Singapore, n.d.). The Standard ICT Operating Environment (SOEasy) project enables Infocomm services provided by various government departments to be consolidated into one single system to make them work seamlessly as the whole unit (Infocomm Development Authority of Singapore, n.d.). Angelopoulos et al. (2010) and Choudrie and Lee (2004) found that the quality of public services can be improved by the adoption of broadband within and between government agencies. Broadband, a high-speed network, allows applications, image and information to be transmitted speedily. It is considered one of the key driving forces of economic growth and national competitive advantage (Kim, Kelly, & Raja, 2010).

New generations X and Y in Singapore are more IT savvy and net-friendly and have made the diffusion of information and knowledge via e-Government networks easier and faster (Traunmuller, 2010). Citizen involvement in government-related activities has been increased via political, social and economic debates online. In addition, Singapore has a pool of IT manpower, i.e. 148,800 people were employed in the infocomm sector in 2009, though more effort is needed to train more IT personnel (Infocomm Development Authority of Singapore, 2010).

Training and development is another forte of Singapore. Two main focuses of training programs are ICT literacy and competency, and e-Government leadership (Chung, 2007). Singapore has established a number of training centers and launched many ICT programs to equip civil servants with the skills and knowledge required for the implementation of an e-Government system (Infocomm development Authority of Singapore, 2002). Employees in the public sector are encouraged to maintain a self-development plan for professional development, and training and development of the labour force has been delegated to the Singapore Workforce Development Authority (WDA) (Ojo et al., 2007). Training on IT security awareness could also increase the users' confidence when they access e-services online (NASCIO, 2007).

Finally, it is impossible to ignore the contribution of the private sector and civil society. The private sector and civil society have also taken many initiatives in this aspect. For example, HP, Intel and Yahoo set up Singapore Centre for Excellence for Open Cirrus Cloud Computing Testbed (2008), AkSaaS, mPlaform Computing Inc and IBM's Cloud Lab launched a SAAS Incubation Centre few years ago (Infocomm Development Authority of Singapore, 2010). A non-profit organisation, Singapore Internet Exchange, has been set up to provide Internet service and content in a non-discriminatory base to telecommunication carriers (Infocomm Development Authority of Singapore, 2010).

Weaknesses

Both Singapore and Japan have introduced master plans for the development of e-Government. Nonetheless, Singapore's e-Government initiatives have focused on technological aspects, whereas Japan has emphasised both IT and legal aspects to build its e-Government. This proposes that one of the weaknesses of the e-Government system in Singapore is the insufficient preparation of a legal framework. This proposition has been evidenced by the fact that Singapore has not enacted any acts or produced any regulation addressing online privacy risks. However, the government is in the process to introduce privacy law to address the issues related to privacy infringement, especially in cloud computing. The Singapore Ministry of Communications and the Arts has called for feedback from the public regarding a legal framework to protect data online (Purnell, 2011).

Also, Japan's e-Government initiatives have been launched and developed in a more systematic manner than the ones adopted by Singapore in terms of preparation, development and promotion of e-Government. Singapore should revise its e-Government master plan in a way that this shortcoming can be addressed.

Added in to the above issues, it is difficult to calculate the opportunity cost, which an e-Government system has incurred. This applies not only to Singapore but also to other countries adopting e-Government. Some other weaknesses are limited human capital resources, such as IT experts, and limited internal capacity to meet high demands for ICT solutions and the tight deadlines for project implementation (Chung, 2007). Insufficient experience and capabilities to implement the e-Government projects, especially at the local and grassroots levels, are also impediments to e-Government (Tolbert, & Mossberger, 206). However, lack of IT skills, lack of interest/no need to use and being too old to learn computer skills are the main reasons for not having access to the Internet of a computer at home. Apparently, many of the people are not aware of the benefits of the Internet. Affordability is also a barrier to IT accessibility as 10% of the respondents in a survey in Singapore cited "too costly to purchase a computer" is a main reason for not having a computer at home (Infocomm Development Authority of Singapore, 2011a, p. 9).

Finally, citizen engagement must be better promoted not by offering monetary rewards, but by providing opportunities for the public to obtain IT education and training and providing low cost computers and IT devices for Internet connection. The master plans focus on the macro level, which provides directions for respective government agencies. However, they do not take into consideration issues at the micro level, for instance, the IT purchasing power of the people, the level of IT savvy of the older generation, etc.

Opportunities and Threats

This section discusses the opportunities for Singapore to develop e-Government by adopting new "government with you" approach to deliver public services, and encouraging active participation of the citizens. It also explores current and future threats to e-Government, such as cyber-attacks, privacy, security and e-terrorism. In other words, external environmental factors are analysed, which shed lights on the opportunities for and threats of the e-Government system in Singapore.

Opportunities

Politically, there are many opportunities for e-Government to grow in Singapore. The political commitment of national leaders and leaders in the region to link national IT networks via building a cyber-highway creates an opportunity for national governments to invest in the development of e-Government. With the support from different governments, human and physical capital resources would be combined to develop strategies for planning, adoption, monitoring, evaluation and modification of e-Government systems within and between countries (Ha, & Coghill, 2006).

The recent political and economic crises increase the distrust of the people to government due to their perception that government is ineffective, inefficient and wasting tax payers' money. This may undermine the rule of law, i.e. regulations and legal framework (Liou, 2011). Thus, e-Government would play a better role in rebuilding public trust to government as an enabling e-Government system can produce accurate and timely information, which allows users to make informed decision. E-Government has, in some ways, increased public trust in government as it provides a channel for citizen assessment of government and enhanced the two-way communication between government and the public (Tolbert, & Mossberger, 2006). In other worlds, e-Government would help to mend the relationship between government and the public as citizen attitudes and mindset have been influenced by the way an e-Government system delivers public services (Chadwick, & May, 2005; Tolbert, & Mossberger, 2006; West, 2004). Better and easy interaction with government via online transactions, e-mails, feedback portals, etc. would allow active participation of citizens (Tolbert, & Mossberger, 2006).

From the economic point of view, limited time is another motivation for the public to adopt e-services. Most people who use e-services can save time, financial resources (e.g. they do not need to send information via mail) and effort. Many Free Trade Agreements, bilateral and multi-lateral trade agreements between Singapore and other have provided opportunities for local enterprises to expand their shares in the global market. Business competition has been more intensive. Thus, information and timing are important factors to leverage firms' competitive advantage and bringing about success in doing business. Businesses also need to collect information and receive public services of both the home and host countries. It is the IT and e-Government networks, which can

help them to access such services from anywhere and at any time (Ha, & Coghill, 2006).

Technologically, new forms of technology, such as Web 2.0 and cloud computing, allow the effective exchange of knowledge, and the management of information flow, such as information storage, checking, retrieval and diffusion. This means the public sector can perform their tasks efficiently, such as making law, drafting legal documents, coordinating with other government departments and other governments (Traunmuller, 2010).

Citizen engagement would be enhanced by the adoption of social media platforms. Social media provides opportunities for the public to be involved in the decision-making process. As e-Government systems are considered information networks, which bridge the information gaps among different government agencies in one country, between government bodies and citizens and businesses in one country, as well as among governments in different countries. New IT applications, such as Web 2.0 and social media provide platforms for citizens to provide feedback and ratings of public services. In many instances, citizens can assist the public sector with monitoring legal enforcement cases. For example, reporting undesirable behaviour such as insult or discrimination against races and the minorities, online scams, spam, online bullying, etc. (Traunmuller, 2010). In Singapore, these instruments contribute to produce new generations of social responsible citizens.

Another opportunity for Singapore is the move from e-Government to m-Government (mobile Government) and from e-Government to i-Government (Integrated Government). Initially, e-Government system aims to integrating public services to reach the citizens timely, effectively and efficiently. Singapore has been in the process to integrate not only services but also processes, information in their e-Government system. By engaging in advanced technology and infocomm solutions, the e-Government system would produce tremendous benefits to citizens and businesses.

Some current benefits of using e-Government are the renewal of road tax, submitting income statement to the tax authority, submitting application for a resale public apartment or balloting for an new public flat (Chung, 2007). Businesses can register a new business online, applying for an entertainment license, submitting building plan and requesting for trade clearance. The lists of activities, which users can perform via the e-Government system would be longer in the future.

Overall, Singapore has adopted more and new IT applications to introduce many public services online and via mobile phone, targeting various groups of users. For instance, national service men can send notification to the Ministry of Defence via online, sms or phone before they make an overseas trip (Ha, & Coghill, 2006; Transport & Travel @ eCitizen, 2010).

Threats

The analysis of the external factors does detect a number of issues, which an e-Government system has to face in the dynamic and changing world. The first key challenge of Singapore's e-Government system includes the increasing expectations of users on e-services. The public expect faster, reliable and comprehensive e-services. In addition, the younger generation of users is more IT savvy. Thus, they would prefer to receive more public services via the online channels, and they also require more sophisticated Infocomm platforms. Hence, the challenge here is how to meet the needs of diverse groups of users.

Another challenge is how to sustain the infocomm competitive advantage of the country and to improve the delivery of public services given the dynamic global infocomm landscape as efficiency and productivity are the key critical success factors of an e-Government system (Infocomm Development Authority of Singapore, n.d.).

Online security and privacy and data protection have always been pressing issues, which need urgent attention of governments in many countries.

Previously, information systems security has focused on the safeguard of information stored electronically in a government agency (Smith, & Jamieson, 2006). However, from the citizens' view, government is seen as one system, and thus a security incident occurring to one government department will be considered as a failure of the whole system (Smith, & Jamieson, 2006). Therefore, concentration on keeping e-documents confidentiality within a government department is inadequate. Mechanisms to ensure a secure environment for the collection, storage and exchange of information between government agencies via online portals must reflect the uniformity feature of an e-Government system, i.e. standardization of methods to ensure the confidentiality of the whole entity. Information security also embraces integrity and availability. Integrity refers to the modification of information by only authorized persons, and information and information processing systems must be ready to collect, store, check, modify and retrieve information when it is needed (Smith, & Jamieson, 2006).

Another critical challenge of the e-Government system is the threat of cyber-crime, which is defined as illegal activities of people "relating to the automatic processing and the transmission of data, use of Computer systems and Networks" (Lunker, 2005, p. 2). An e-Government system is not immune from such cyber misdeeds. To make things worse, cyber-crime is cross border and no national boundaries can prevent the penetration of such cyber wrongdoers. The computer network is a very sophisticated platform for communication exchange between users, but at the same time data can be manipulated for different reasons. After the industrialization wave, due to the revolution of IT, cyberization will be the future trend of socio-economic development. The sophisticated Internet network and advanced IT solutions such as malicious software have offered new avenues for the facilitation of the transition of traditional crimes like fraud, theft, defamation to new forms, which are more difficult to deal with (Chowbe,

2011). In other words, the e-environment also offers opportunities for new forms of mischiefs, namely, hacking, illegal deletion of information, and virus transplantation (Chowbe, 2011). Different from traditional crimes, it is extremely difficult to identify the identity of e-offenders as they can easily hide their identity online (Gercke, 2007). Cyber offenses are easily committed as computer technology can be picked up by fast learners without any formal training. However, it is hard to detect, investigate and take legal actions against such offenses.

How is e-Government affected by these cyber offenses? Firstly, cyber space is cross-border and cyber offenders do not draw a line between committing crimes in a particular jurisdiction. The manipulation of information on government websites would certainly harm the process of trust building with the citizens. Important information such as personal and financial information of users (citizens) may be stolen for unknown reasons or for committing a crime. Confidential information relating national security may also be illegally accessed, i.e. business and military intelligence data may be stolen. This has recently happened when the websites of many governments around the world, for example, USA, Ethiopia, Malaysia, etc., were hacked. According to Chowbe (2001), information in the cyber era is "synonym with either power or source of power.... information is essential" (p. 77). Thus, losing information means losing power. Cyber-criminality has emerged under many new forms such as e-piracy, cyber-bombing, e-mail bombing, e-theft, etc. (Bass et al., 1998). Also, privacy infringements, propagation of undesirable content online, online attacks on critical infrastructure are other forms of threats, which would certainly be harmful too any e-Government system. Secondly, government bodies have been increasingly relied on the use of IT, whereas the prevalence of cyber hackers is more complex and legislation relating to protection of government e-records is inadequate. This has posed another challenge to e-Government when there is no legal framework, which can apply across jurisdiction. Even there is a legal framework, which can apply across nations, enforcement of such law may be infeasible. Finally, the slow response of government in terms of enacting IT related law would undermine the public confidence in government, and impede the development of an e-Government system (As-Saber, Srivastava, & Hossain, 2006).

Other challenges to e-Government include (i) the safeguard of gate-keeping mechanisms given the dynamics and evolving of an e-Government system, (ii) the adoption of IT and advanced technology to reduce the size of the public sector in terms of manpower, (iii) the preparation for employees and citizens to be ready for e-Government and i-Government, (iv) the investment in R&D and human resources to ensure no disruption to the delivery of e-services, and (v) the ability to build capacity and competencies within government agencies to ensure that IT applications and solutions are effectively and efficiently adopted (Andersen, 2006).

Singapore has established a national cyber security centre to identify current and new trends of cyber-attacks and prevent such attacks (Kor, 2011). The government has paid more attention to monitor the cyberspace and to address e-security issues at the national level. Singapore has also provided funds for education programs and cyber-wellness initiatives, which can increase the awareness of the public, especially young people, in terms of online privacy and security, information literacy, etc. (Ministry of Education, Singapore, 2010).

ACHIEVEMENTS OF SINGAPORE'S E-GOVERNMENT SYSTEM

Singapore's infocomm and e-Government plans have produced significant achievements. From an initial limited number of Internet users, Singapore now has 82% of her population connected to broadband and a mobile penetration rate of

144% (Infocomm Development Authority of Singapore, 2010).

Overall, Singapore has obtained international recognition for its successful e-Government system. Some examples are (i) topping the WEF's Networked Readiness Index for five years from 2002 to 2006, (ii) topping the Accenture 2007 Ranking interns of government customer service, (iii) ranked number 7 and number 2 in terms of e-Government Readiness and e-Government Participation in the UN's 2005 e-Government Readiness Report, respectively (Chung, 2007). Singapore has also received many other awards, such as the UN Public Service Awards in 2005, 2006, 2007, 2008 and 2010, the United Nations e-Government Survey 2010 Special Awards (United Nations Public Administration Network, n. d.). Singapore was ranked no. 7 in 2009 in terms of e-readiness by Economic Intelligence Unit (2009). Singapore has also topped the Waseda University World e-Government ranking list in 2009 and 2010. Singapore was ranked second by the World Economic Forum in terms of Networked Readiness Index in 2010-2011 (Dutta, & Mia, 2011). Importantly, the level of acceptance and satisfaction of users of Singapore's e-Government is very high. More than 80% of enterprises and individuals in the e-Government Perception Survey 2006 were happy with the quality of public e-services (Infocomm Development Authority of Singapore, n. d.).

POLICY RECOMMENDATIONS ON HOW TO ADDRESS CHALLENGES FACING E-GOVERNMENT

From the above findings, a number of recommendations are discussed below.

Firstly, it is in the interest of the public sector to actively engage citizens in order to enhance public trust and confidence in government agencies. Adoption of IT applications to allow two-way communication with customers to receive their feedback and ideas for improvement would certainly promote the use of e-Government.

Secondly, process-based trust includes responsiveness and accessibility, and institutional-based trust refers to transparency and responsibility. Both types of trust embrace efficiency, effectiveness and participation (Tolbert, & Mossberger, 2006). Thus, the government should transform themselves to enhance the public sector performance to meet citizen demands. However, governments from different countries may adopt different style of leadership to manage and promote e-Government. Models of public leadership from one country may not apply to another country, which has different political, economic, social and cultural settings and characteristics (Shue, 2011). This principle also applies to Singapore where the limited land, natural resources and political and administrative structures and management make it unique for the analysis of the success and failure of leadership.

Thirdly, strong collaboration among various groups of stakeholders is imperative for the successful development of an e-Government system, which can integrate the operations of various government agencies and enable the government to function as a whole. Nevertheless, it is impossible for e-Government to flourish without leadership commitment and competence, a clear vision and directions, and adequate resources to invest in the development of infrastructure for an e-Government system.

Fourthly, technology is one of the tools for government to fulfil its responsibility to its citizens. Government needs to select and adopt pertinent technological approaches to develop and sustain its e-Government plan. Also, outcomes must be tangible and countable via a well-designed and effective measurement system, which can help to set common objectives, track the progress and evaluation the success of a project (Infocomm Development Authority of Singapore, n.d.).

Fifthly, although a number of threats available online, it is impossible to avoid adopting technology or avoid going online. Hence, one of recommendations is to provide educational programs to users in order to enhance their cyber-literacy and awareness of online incidents (Chowbe, 2011). Citizens have to play an active role in self-protection when going online. Citizen education can empower citizens with knowledge and understanding to exercise precautious in getting information and access public services online. The public and private sectors and civil society can work with one another to provide tailored educational programs to the public in order to increase the level of awareness of their social responsibility and the benefits of accessing public services online.

Finally, advanced technological applications have been employed by government agencies and users to enjoy the benefits of electronic public services. However, cyber wrongdoers also try to make use of high-tech applications to commit offences. The research findings reinforce the fact that utilization of appropriate technological applications can ensure the security of a system. Thus, the use of technology can contribute to enhancing user protection. Also, an e-Government system must be designed in a way that it is both user-friendly and able to prevent and detect online incidents.

CONCLUSION

This chapter has discussed the concept of e-Government and an e-Government system. Determinants affecting the effectiveness of an e-Government system include political, legal, economic, technological and environmental factors. Leadership commitment and competency, administrative leadership, institutions, human and physical resources are sub-sets of the above determinants.

This chapter has analysed strengths, weaknesses, opportunities and threats of an e-Government system, using Singapore as a case study. Apparently, leadership commitment, adequate financial and human resources, adoption of technology and cooperation among sectors are the key strengths of Singapore's e-Government system, whereas the weaknesses include inadequate law and regulation to protect privacy and data, lack of consideration from users' point of view and insufficient citizen engagement.

This chapter has also proposed recommendations on how to improve the performance of an e-Government system. It is important that various groups of stakeholders have to work with each other to provide education to the public to enhance public awareness of the benefits of receiving public services online.

In short, it is not easy to build and maintain a strong foundation for e-Government without sufficient resources and commitment from government agencies. Long-term and holistic strategic plan, leadership commitment and strong co-operation among stakeholders enable the Singapore government to be successful in building infrastructure and planning human capital for its IT and e-Government projects. Yet, the future of Singapore's e-Government depends on many external and internal factors at national, regional and international levels.

REFERENCES

Andersen, K. V. (2006). E-government: Five key challenges for management. *The Electronic. Journal of E-Government, 4*(1), 1–8.

Angelopoulos, S., Kitsios, F., & Papadopoulos, T. (2010). New service development in e-government: Identifying critical success factors. *Transforming Government: People. Process and Policy, 1*(1), 95–118.

As-Saber, S., Srivastava, A., & Hossain, K. (2006). Information technology law and e-government: A developing country perspective. *Journal of Administration & Governance, 1*(1), 84–101.

Bass, T., Freyre, A., Gruber, D., & Watt, G. (1998). E-mail bombs and countermeasures: Cyber attacks on availability and brand integrity. *IEEE Network*, (March/April): 10–17. doi:10.1109/65.681925

Bonham, G., Seifert, J., & Thorson, S. (2001). *The transformational potential of e-government: At the role of political leadership*. Paper read at the 4th Pan European International Relations Conference, University of Kent.

Bourn, J. (2002). *Better public services through e-government*. London, UK: The National Audit Office.

Chadwick, A., & May, C. (2003). Interaction between states & citizens of the age of the internet: E-government in the United States, Britain. *Governance: An International Journal of Policy, Administration and Institutions*, *16*(2), 271–300. doi:10.1111/1468-0491.00216

Chen, Y. C., & Knepper, R. (2005). Digital government development strategies. Lessons for policy makers from a comparative perspective. In Huang, W., Siau, K., & Kwok, K. W. (Eds.), *Electronic government strategies and implementation* (pp. 394–420). Hershey, PA: Idea Group Publishing.

Choudrie, J., & Lee, H. (2004). Broadband development in South Korea: Institutional and cultural factor. *European Journal of Information Systems*, *13*(2), 103–114. doi:10.1057/palgrave.ejis.3000494

Chowbe, V. S. (2011). The concept of cyber-crime: Nature and scope. *Global Journal of Enterprise Information System*, *3*(1), 72–84.

Chua, H. H. (2011, 15 May). Social media: The new voice of GE. *The Straits Times*.

Chung, M. K. (2007). *Singapore e-government experience*. Paper presented at Asia e-Government Forum 2007, 20 September 2007, Seoul, Korea.

Council for Excellence in Governance. (2001). *E-government, the next American revolution*. Washington, DC: Council for Excellence in Governance.

Coursey, D., & Norris, D. (2008). Models of e-government: Are they correct? An empirical assessment. *PAR*, *68*, 523–536.

Davies, P. B. (2007). Models for e-government. *Transforming Government: People. Process and Policy*, *1*(1), 7–28.

Dawes, S. S., & Pardo, T. (2002). Building collaborative digital government systems. In Mclver, W. J., & Elmagarmid, A. K. (Eds.), *Advances in digital government technology, human factors and policy*. Norwell, MA: Kluwer Academic Publishers. doi:10.1007/0-306-47374-7_16

Dutta, S., & Mia, I. (2011). *Global information technology*. Geneva, Switzerland: World Economic Forum.

Ebrahim, Z., & Irani, Z. (2005). E-government adoption: Architecture and barriers. *Business Management Process*, *11*(5), 589–611. doi:10.1108/14637150510619902

Economic Intelligence Unit. (2009). *E-readiness ranking 2009. The usage imperative*. London, UK: Economic Intelligence Unit.

Edmiston, K. D. (2003). State and local e-government: Prospects and challenges. *American Review of Public Administration*, *33*, 20–45. doi:10.1177/0275074002250255

Evans, D., & Yen, D. C. (2006). E-government: Evolving relationship of citizens and government, domestic, and international development. *Government Information Quarterly*, *23*(2), 207–235. doi:10.1016/j.giq.2005.11.004

Gercke, M. (2007). *Internet-related identity theft*. Strasbourg, France: Economic Crime Division, Directorate of Human Rights and Legal Affairs, Council of Europe.

Ha, H. (2011). Security and privacy in e-consumer protection in Victoria, Australia. In Wakeman, I. (Eds.), *IFIPTM 2011, IFIP AICT 358* (pp. 240–252). Berlin, Germany: Springer-Verlag. doi:10.1007/978-3-642-22200-9_19

Ha, H., & Coghill, K. (2006). E-government in Singapore: A SWOT and PEST analysis. [APSSR]. *Asia-Pacific Social Science Review, 6*(2), 103–130.

Heeks, R. (2001). *Understanding e-governance for development*, Working Papers Series, No. 12/2001. Manchester, UK: Institute for Development, Policy and Management Information Systems, Technology and Government, University of Manchester.

Heeks, R. (2005). E-government as a career of context. *Journal of Public Policy, 25*, 51–74. doi:10.1017/S0143814X05000206

Hermana, B., & Sulfianti, W. (2011). Evaluating e-government implementation by local government: Digital divide in Internet-based public services in Indonesia. *International Journal of Business and Social Sciences, 2*(30), 156–163.

Infocomm Development Authority of Singapore. (2002). Equipping public officers for an e-government through ICT education. *eGovernment, 6*(2002), 1-2.

Infocomm Development Authority of Singapore. (2006). *Singapore: A world class e-government.* Singapore: Infocomm Development Authority of Singapore.

Infocomm Development Authority of Singapore. (2010). *Realising the iN2015 Vision. Singapore: An intelligent nation, a global city, powered by Infocomm.* Singapore: Infocomm Development Authority of Singapore.

Infocomm Development Authority of Singapore. (2011a). *Annual survey on infocomm usage in householders for 2010.* Singapore: Infocomm Development Authority of Singapore.

Infocomm Development Authority of Singapore. (2011b). *Singapore egov: Connecting people – Enriching lives.* Singapore: Infocomm Development Authority of Singapore.

Infocomm Development Authority of Singapore. (n.d.). *Singapore's e-Government journey.* Singapore. *Infocomm Development Authority of Singapore.*

Jawahitha, S. (2004). Consumer protection in e-commerce: Analyzing the statutes in Malaysia. *Journal of American Academy of Business, 4*(1/2), 55.

Kettle, D. F. (2002). *The transformation of governance: Public administration for twenty-first century America.* John Hopkins University Press.

Kim, Y., Kelly, T., & Raja, S. (2010). *Building broadband: Strategies and policy for the developing world.* Washington, DC: Global Information and Communication Technologies (GICT) Department, World Bank.

Koh, C. E., Ryan, S., & Prybutok, V. R. (2005). Creating value through managing knowledge in an e-government to constituency (G2C) environment. *Journal of Computer Information Systems, 45*, 32–41.

Kor, K. B. (2011, 22 September). Singapore to set up national cyber security centre. *The Straits Times.*

Latre, M. A., Lopez-Pellicer, F. J., Nogueras-Iso, J., B'ejar, R., & Muro-Medrano, P. R. (2010). Facilitating e-government services through SDIs: An application for water abstractions authorizations. In Andersen, K. N., Francesconi, E., Grönlund, A., & van Engers, T. M. (Eds.), *Electronic government and the information systems perspective* (pp. 108–119). Berlin, Germany: Springer Verlag. doi:10.1007/978-3-642-15172-9_11

Lim, L., & Koh, A. (2008). *The acceleration of SOA adoption in Singapore: Challenges and issues.* Paper read at the 19th Australian Conference on Information Systems, 3-5 Dec 2008, Christchurch, New Zealand.

Liou, K. T. (2011). *The role of governance and evolution of the concept of governance over the last 100 years*. Paper presented at the 3rd International Conference in Public Policy and Management, 23 Oct 2011, School of Public Policy and Management, Tsinghua University, Beijing, China.

Lunker, M. (2005). *Cyber laws: A global perspective*. New York, NY: United Nations Public Administration Network.

Ministry of Education. Singapore. (2010). *Greater support for cyber wellness projects*. Singapore: Ministry of Education, Singapore.

Ministry of Internal Affairs and Communications. (n.d.). *Japan's e-government initiatives*. Japan: Ministry of Internal Affairs and Communications.

Moon, M. J. (2002). The evolution of e-government among municipalities: Rhetoric or reality. *Public Administration Review, 62*(4), 424–433. doi:10.1111/0033-3352.00196

Moon, M. J., & Norris, D. F. (2005). Does managerial orientation matter? The adoption of reinventing government and e-government at the municipal level. *Information Systems Journal, 15*, 43–60. doi:10.1111/j.1365-2575.2005.00185.x

NASCIO. (2007). *Attention state CIOS: It security awareness and training may avert your next crisis!* Lexington, KY: NASCIO.

Ndou, V. (2004). E-government for developing countries: Opportunities and challenges. *Electronic Journal of Information Systems in Developing Countries, 18*, 1–24.

Norris, F., Fletcher, P. D., & Holden, S. H. (2001). *Is your local government plugged in? Highlights of the 2000 electronic government survey*. Baltimore, MD: University of Maryland.

OECD. (2003). *The e-government imperative*. Paris, France: OECD.

Ojo, A., Janowski, T., Estevez, E., & Khan, I. K. (2007). *Human capacity development for e-government*. UNU-IIST Report No. 362. Tokyo, Japan: United Nations University, International Institute for Software Technology.

Ong, C. E. (2005). Jurisdiction in B2C e-commerce redress in the European community. *Journal of Electronic Commerce in Organizations, 3*(4), 75–87. doi:10.4018/jeco.2005100105

Pascual, P. (2003). *E-government*. Philippines and Malaysia: e-ASEAN Task Force and UNDP-APDIP.

Patterson, M. (2001). *E-commerce law*. Paper read at the Free Trade Agreement - Opportunities and Challenges Conference, 21st June, 2001, at Hyatt Hotel, Canberra.

Prananto, A., & McKemmish, S. (2007). *Critical success factors for the establishment of e-government*. RISO Working Paper. Melbourne, Victoria: Faculty of Information and Communication Technologies, Swinburne University of Technology.

Purnell, N. (2011). *Singapore moving on data protection law; Early '12 passage, effective date delay seen*. Bethesda, MD: Bureau of National Affairs, Inc.

Rab, A. (Ed.). (2009). *Information society policies. Annual world report 2009*. Paris, France: UNESCO.

Rashid, N., & Rahman, S. (2010). An investigation into critical determinants of e-government implementation in the context of a developing nation. In Andersen, K. N., Francesconi, E., Grönlund, A., & van Engers, T. M. (Eds.), *Electronic government and the information systems perspective* (pp. 9–21). Berlin, Germany: Springer Verlag. doi:10.1007/978-3-642-15172-9_2

Rogers, E. (1995). *Diffusion of innovations* (4th ed.). New York, NY: The Free Press.

Rotchanakitumnuai, S. (2008). Measuring e-government service value with the E-GOVSQUAL-RISK model. *Business Process Management Journal*, *14*(5), 724–737. doi:10.1108/14637150810903075

Sang, S., Lee, J.-D., & Lee, J. (2009). E-government adoption in ASEAN: The case of Cambodia. *Internet Research*, *19*(5), 517–534. doi:10.1108/10662240910998869

Sharma, S., & Gupta, J. (2002). Transforming to e-government: A framework. *2ⁿᵈ European Conference on E-Government, Public Sector Times* (pp. 383-390), 1-2 October 2002, St. Catherine's College Oxford, United Kingdom.

Shue, V. (2011). *Philosophies and styles of public leadership in China*. Paper presented at the 3ʳᵈ International Conference in Public Policy and Management, 23 Oct 2011, School of Public Policy and Management, Tsinghua University, Beijing, China.

Singh, S. H. (2003). *Government in the digital era and human factors in e-governance*. Paper read the Regional Workshop on e-Government, 1-3 December 2003, Sana'a.

Sipior, J., & Ward, B. (2005). Bridging the digital divide for e-government inclusion: A United States case study. *The Electronic. Journal of E-Government*, *3*(3), 137–146.

Smith, S., & Jamieson, R. (2006). Determining key factors in e-government information system security. *Information Systems Management*, (Spring): 23–32. doi:10.1201/1078.10580530/4 5925.23.2.20060301/92671.4

Special Committee for e-Government, Republic of Korea (2003). *Korea's e-government completion of e-government framework*. Korea: Special Committee for e-Government, Republic of Korea.

Taifur, S. (2006). *SICT's steps towards good governance through ICTs: E-governance strategies. Bangladesh*. Bangladesh: Ministry of Planning.

Tassabehji, R., & Elliman, T. (2006). *Generating citizen trust in e-government using a trust verification agent: A research note*. Paper read at the European and Mediterranean Conference on Information Systems (EMCIS) 2006, July 6-7 2006, Costa Blanca, Alicante, Spain.

Tolbert, C. J., & Mossberger, K. (2006). The effects of e-government on trust and confidence in government. *Public Administration Review*, *66*(3), 354–369. doi:10.1111/j.1540-6210.2006.00594.x

Transport & Travel @ eCitizen. (2010). *NSMen*. Singapore: Singapore Government.

Traunmuller, R. (2010). Web 2.0 creates a new government. In In K. N. Andersen, E. Francesconi, A. Grönlund, & T. M. van Engers (Eds.), *Electronic government and the information systems perspective*, (pp. 77-83). Berlin, Germany: Springer Verlag.

United Nations Division for Public Economics and Public Administration, American Society for Public Administration. (2002). *Benchmarking e-government: A global perspective. Assessing the progress of the UN member states*. New York, NY: United Nations – DPEPA and ASPA.

United Nations Public Administration Network. (n.d.). *United Nations e-government survey 2010 special awards*. New York, NY. *United Nations Public Administration Network*.

Vintar, M., Kunstelj, M., Decman, M., & Bercic, M. (2003). Development of e-government in Slovenia. *Information Polity*, *8*, 133–149.

Wescott, D. (2004). E-government and the transformation of service delivery and citizen attitudes. *Public Administration Review*, *64*(1), 15–27. doi:10.1111/j.1540-6210.2004.00343.x

Wong, P., & Cha, V. (2009). *The evolution of government infocomm plans: Singapore's e-government journey (1980 – 2007)*. Singapore: Institute of Systems Science, National University of Singapore.

Yamada, H. (2010, July). Current status of e-government in Japan and its future direction - Electronic application services. *The Quarterly Review, 36*, 19–33.

Yildiz, M. (2007). E-government research: Reviewing the literature, limitations, and ways forward. *Government Information Quarterly, 24*, 646–665. doi:10.1016/j.giq.2007.01.002

KEY TERMS AND DEFINITIONS

Citizen Engagement: The participation of citizens in public affairs and in the policy making process.

Cyber-Crime: The use of automatic processing, the transmission of data and use of computer systems and networks for illegal activities.

E-Government: The delivery of public services and dissemination of government information to the public via the Internet.

E-Government System: A system using IT applications in an integrated framework to deliver public services and to allow various groups of stakeholders to be connected with government and with one another.

Public Trust: The level of trust and confidence, which citizens have in government as a result of effective delivery of public services.

96

Chapter 5
Accessing Knowledge from the Bedside:
Introducing the Tablet Computer to Clinical Teaching

Douglas Archibald
University of Ottawa, Canada

Colla J. MacDonald
University of Ottawa, Canada

Rebecca J. Hogue
University of Ottawa, Canada

Jay Mercer
University of Ottawa, Canada

ABSTRACT

Tablet computers are very powerful devices that have numerous potential uses in the medical field. Already, the development community has created a wide range of applications that can be used for everything from the most basic level of medical undergraduate education to specialist care delivery. The challenge with tablet computers as a new technology is to find where they fit most effectively into healthcare. In this chapter, the authors focus on how tablets might find a role in the area of care delivery in the educational setting. Included is a discussion on the tablet computer's place on the eLearning / mLearning spectrum, an annotated list of recommended medical applications, a description of challenges and issues when deploying the tablet computers to clinical settings, and finally a proposed pilot study that will explore the effectiveness of using a tablet computer in a clinical teaching setting. The content of this chapter can be applied to many workplace and learning settings that may find tablet computers beneficial such as businesses that require mobile communications, K-12 schools, and higher learning institutions.

INTRODUCTION

In a recent article by Rachel Ellaway, entitled "eLearning: Is the revolution over?" the comment is made that eLearning has "disrupted the status quo in many areas of medical education" (Ellaway, 2011, p. 300). She continues to write that eLearning has been able to provide learners access to resources and convenient learning. Moreover, eLearning has improved the ability for

DOI: 10.4018/978-1-4666-2190-9.ch005

Copyright © 2013, IGI Global. Copying or distributing in print or electronic forms without written permission of IGI Global is prohibited.

clinical teachers to track participant learning and also made an impact at the organizational level, by challenging traditional methods and values. Tablet computers are part of the eLearning revolution and are quickly becoming a popular mechanism for accessing information in a clinical setting. Consequently, as in most professions, technology is changing the way that professionals do business. In this instance, the tablet computer is affecting the way physicians practice medicine.

The Apple iPad® is an example of a tablet computer that offers the convenience of a smartphone and much of the functionality of a laptop or desktop computer. In a recent article in the Journal Annals of Emergency Medicine, entitled "The iPad: Gadget or Medical Godsend?" Eric Berger (2010) notes that many physicians carry smartphones including the iPhone® allowing them to have access to thousands of medical applications (apps). He suggests the iPad is a mechanism with which to connect the world of eLearning with the convenience of mobile learning. "With a large brilliantly lit screen, the iPad has the potential of being a more comprehensive device, pushing physicians away from their desktop computers, where they may eventually be able to perform numerous tasks from viewing radiographs to ECGs" (Berger, 2010, p. 21).

Already, the development community has created a wide range of applications that can be used for everything from the most basic level of medical undergraduate education to specialist care delivery. This chapter begins with a discussion about online learning (eLearning) and mobile learning (mLearning) and where the tablet computer finds a home in the arena of technology assisted medical education. The conversation then proceeds to a commentary on several recent mobile learning studies conducted using tablet computers or smartphones in medicine and other disciplines. This brief literature review is followed with some considerations for implementing tablet computers in clinical settings. The challenge with the tablet computer as a new technology is to find where it

fits most effectively into healthcare. In this case, we will focus on how it might find a role in the area of care delivery in the educational setting. Issues such as managing connectivity, power, and input will be explored. Finally, the chapter concludes with a needs analysis and an introduction to a pilot project, which will explore the use of tablet computers to support rural community specialist preceptors (teachers who teach family medicine residents) with the implementation of the University of Ottawa's revised Family Medicine (FM) Triple C Competency-based curriculum, resources (including medical and general applications), and evaluation tools in an effort to support and enhance effective teaching and learning.

WHERE DOES THE TABLET COMPUTER BELONG?

Before the discussion of how the tablet computer can be used for medical education, it is important to define a few terms. The term eLearning is widely used but can mean different things to different people (Bullen & Janes, 2007). A common understanding of eLearning is as a form of distance education where courses are delivered over the Internet (Bullen & Janes, 2007). However, eLearning is increasingly being described as any electronically mediated learning in a digital format. Bullen and Janes presented an eLearning continuum for formal online learning that provides a useful reference when considering eLearning (see Figure 1). Although this model is an over simplification of eLearning it does lend itself well to show how mLearning can be integrated into the continuum.

The *Mobile Learning Group* at Athabasca University define distance learning as incorporating, "all forms of instruction in which instructor and student are physically removed from one another by time or space from traditional correspondence courses to web-based instruction" (What is Mobile Learning, para. 1), and eLearn-

Figure 1. The eLearning continuum (Bullen & Janes, 2007)

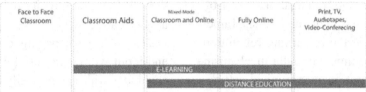

ing includes all forms of online instruction using personal computers. Mobile learning or mLearning, however, involves using small, portable computers that no longer require learners to be constrained to the walls of a classroom, office, or wherever a desktop computer is found, "rather learners are engaged, often synchronously with others and learning resources, while outside the borders of a formal classroom" (Koszlaka & Ntoedibe-Kuswani, 2010, p. 142). The elimination of a formal setting for learning is expressed in *Figure 2* as "Beyond the Classroom." There is a spectrum of mobile devices, ranging from portable computers such as the laptop to mobile phones. Each researcher determines their definition of what constitutes a mobile device. Inclusive definitions include any device, such as laptops, that can be used outside of a standard desk environment.

Generally it is considered that mobile learning involves two-way Internet connections either through wireless or 3G/4G. Therefore, one might consider that mLearning, according to this definition, could span across the entire eLearning spectrum. As the tablet computer has the mobility and convenience of mLearning (especially if it has the capacity of 3G/4G in addition to wireless and

long battery life), and the capability to perform many of the data inputting and retrieval functions of desktop and laptops, then maybe it should be considered a connector between eLearning and mLearning on the continuum (see Figure 2).

The introduction of the tablet computer caused a problem with the definition of mobile learning, as it does not fit within a pocket or purse, but is often considered a mobile learning device. To get around this quandary, Quinn suggests that mobile learning devices are "optimized to run applications for mobile use" (2011, p.31) which deems eReaders and tablets to be mobile devices but laptops and netbooks are not. The advent of new technology will constantly challenge us to define what constitutes a "mobile device."

POTENTIAL FOR CLINICAL TEACHING AND LEARNING

We live in exciting times! Iltifat Husain, editor and founder of iMedicalApps.com indicated in an interview for the *Annals of Emergency Medicine* that he believed the tablet computer will find wide use in clinical teaching and learning. First, he sees physicians and medical students using the

Figure 2. Mobile learning included in the eLearning continuum (after Bullen & Janes, 2007)

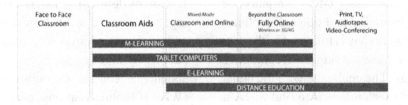

tablet computer as a reference, much as they do already with smartphones. There are a plethora of medical applications that allow clinicians to access the latest evidence-based medicine and clinical procedures. Although smartphones are more portable for retrieving information, tablet computers with their larger screens make reading text much easier. Second, he sees physicians using the tablet computer for patient education. Again there are many medical applications available, at ever increasing rates that have exemplary graphics and video so physicians can explain diseases and treatments to patients. Finally, Husain notes that the most transformative way tablet computers may be used is for viewing and updating patient records. The tablet computer screen is large enough to allow patient charts to be viewed and the resolution is good enough to see detailed medical images. In addition, there are apps available that permit tablet computer users to connect to their desktop. This feature may allow physicians to access electronic orders and prescriptions. No longer will physicians need to go back and forth from the patient to the computer.

Walter Mashman (2011), deputy editor of the Journal of the American College of Cardiology feels the tablet computer is an:

Attractive balance of the right compromises for the market's desires. The iPad [tablet computer] is not a desktop computer, it is not a phone, and it is not a laptop. It is a little of each, but at the same time it really seems to be a new thing. (Mashman, editor's page)

Mashman also indicates that the tablet computer is better suited for retrieving information than producing information. Most may agree with this statement, however, there is potential to input data into the tablet computer and this feature should not be underestimated.

A number of Medical training programs are now issuing tablet computers to their faculty and students. The Ottawa Hospital, for example, has issued iPads to their medical staff. As part of its new iMedEd Initiative, the medical school at UC Irvine in California has recently developed a comprehensive, tablet computer based curriculum. Entering students receive an iPad so they can engage in, "… a completely digital, interactive learning environment" (Vasich, 2012).

According to Elwood et al. (2011) recent surveys indicate that more than 50% of physicians in the United States will own an iPad by the end of 2011. As physicians are adopting tablet computers so is the general public. Many patients, even those who may have limited Internet services, have smartphones or tablet computers. In a recent survey, 85% of physicians stated they would be willing to have patients monitor their health remotely (Elwood et al.). Moreover, it is estimated that over 14% of American adults already use mobile devices to monitor their health (IDC, 2011). As hospitals and medical training centres enter the foray of mobile technology using iPads and other computer tablets, research on the use of the devices is necessary. Moreover, we can anticipate studies exploring mobile health and mobile healthcare education.

RESEARCH ON MOBILE LEARNING DEVICES

As studies emerge involving both the integration of tablet computers into healthcare education curricula and the effectiveness of these devices in clinical settings we can look to the literature on mLearning for direction. There has been a plethora of studies over the last ten years with a dramatic increase since 2008 with the majority being in higher education (Huang & Tsai, 2011). Some interesting studies identified by Huang and Tsai include projects that explore the use of mobile devices to enhance learning in museums and temples (Reynolds, Walker, & Speight, 2010; Chiou, Tseng, Hwang, & Heller, 2010; Hwang & Chang, 2011).

Koszlaka and Ntoedibe-Kuswani (2010) have summarized the literature on mLearning. They noted that Keegan (2002) identified that work in mLearning up to about 2002 had been in its infancy and there had been a scarcity of studies in education that indicated there was a movement toward mLearning. However, Naismith, Lonsdale, Vavoula, and Sharples (2006) noted after examining the work of more than 30 mLearning studies that mLearning could support a variety of activities, but there were numerous implementation and management issues that educators would need to overcome. Barlow-Zambodla's 2009, review of mLearning studies in Africa and Asia highlight data retrieval, access and sharing, and overall phone usage among mobile learners.

Finally, Koszlaka and Ntoedibe-Kuswani (2010) in their own review of literature, indicate there is anecdotal evidence to support that mobile technology is being used to promote both informal and formal learning. They divided their studies into two categories: safe– meaning learners have open access to resources just like going to a computer to find information; and disruptive – meaning learners can participate in collaborative learning, "As active constructors of knowledge, learners search for personal, meaningful, and goal-directed understanding of new situations" (Koszlaka & Ntoedibe-Kuswani, p. 142). This later approach to learning is conducive to social and collaborative constructivism (Garrison, Anderson, & Archer, 2000; Vygotsky, 1978). Furthermore, there are a growing number of studies of mobile learning in medical education contexts. A number of medical education studies have recommendations for future research and cautionary notes for physicians incorporating mobile learning in their teaching and clinical practices. For example, in a very recent study Shamji and Law (2011) caution their readers that the introduction of technology into medical education "is a double-edged sword that can facilitate learning in some cases or create a fog of information that obscures knowledge in others" (p.150). With new technologies, physicians can access much more information quickly; however, there is a risk of too much information. In addition to filtering the information, for example, providing a recommended application (app) list, so that physicians do not need to sort through the over 2000 available medical applications in the app store. Shamji and Law also indicate that physicians need to be shown how to use the devices effectively.

Wu, Li, and Fu (2011) use the technology acceptance model (TAM) to predict the adoption of mobile technology in healthcare. Consistent with other mobile learning experiments based upon the TAM model (King & He, 2006) the two most important predictors of technology acceptance are perceived usefulness an ease-of-use. Mobile devices are "improving the exchange of information, thus reducing medical errors resulting from inadequate access to clinical data" (Lu, Xiao, Sears, & Jacko, 2011, p.410). Recent mobile learning research has shown that actual ease-of-use is a less significant predictor (Liu, Li, & Carlsson, 2010). This change is being attributed to significant improvements in technology and better design of applications. However, physicians often perceive the devices to be difficult to use, creating a barrier to adoption (Wu et al.).

Shamji and Law (2011) recommend training programs to familiarize physicians with technology. A training program in the form of a hands-on workshop, may increase the physician's comfort with using the device, and increase their beliefs in the value of the technology. In addition, selection of specific applications that are easy-to-use and provide immediate benefit to physicians should increase adoption of the technology.

As part of this chapter we suggest recommendations for introducing mobile learning to physicians. Some challenges and considerations in the next section of the chapter come from Dr. Jay Mercer, Medical Director of the Bruyère Family Medicine Centre and Assistant Professor in the Department of Family Medicine at the University of Ottawa. These challenges and considerations are based on experience in incorporating technology in clinical learning environments and include using mobile devices in clinical settings.

CHALLENGES AND CONSIDERATIONS FOR DEPLOYING THE TABLET COMPUTER TO THE CLINICAL SETTING

Choosing the Right Device

Tablet computers come in a variety of ecosystems and device options. Ecosystems refer to the combination of hardware, operating system, and application purchasing method. Presently, the two most common ecosystems are the Apple ecosystem supported on the iPad device and the Android ecosystem supported on a variety of devices such as Samsung Galaxy tablet, HTC Flyer, and Motorola Xoom. Both ecosystems provide a variety of professionally relevant applications. Apple has slightly more expensive devices; however the iPad is homogenous making it easier to support. In other words, the ecosystem is contained with a limited number of platforms and a commitment to continued vendor support. Alternatively, the Android ecosystem supports a variety of devices, with a variety of form factors (for example, 7 inch and 10 inch screen options), which some users might prefer. This variety and the slightly lower cost of the Android devices, makes it attractive. However, using a variety of different devices increases complexity to the deployment process and increases support costs. Finally, if an organization is considering building their own applications, the process for including them into the ecosystem must be taken into account. Although it is typically faster to deploy applications to the Android market, the variety of supported platforms means additional effort must go into programming and testing. The choice of ecosystem and devices impacts not only the initial cost of implementation, but also the ongoing costs of the deployment, and should be fully considered.

Establishing a Constellation of Professionally Relevant Applications

The first challenge with any new device is getting the user to use it. To accomplish this, the device needs to provide a certain level of perceived utility to the user. Intrinsically, the tablet computer is quite limited. Its email, Web browsing and other basic functions are performed quite well by existing laptop and desktop computers. The tablet computer could try to compete with this basic functionality, but would find itself very dependent on either complex or expensive connectivity to the Web. To avoid this dilemma the tablet computer must contain a collection or constellation of applications that are immediately relevant to either the care delivery or teaching mission of the user. Examples might include a drug database, textbooks and clinical calculators.

Establishment of this constellation on the device has numerous critical implications. First, it will dramatically increase the probability that the device will be carried with and used by the provider. Users are also more likely to make sure the device is charged to operate and that they are adept at operation of the components of their application. The results will create the necessity to have the tablet on hand when patient care is provided or education is carried out.

Another group of applications are those that depend on connectivity to function. Web-based applications or those that reside on proprietary intranets are examples. In the medical field, the electronic patient record is a good example. While complex to deploy and use, this may be the most critical application to entice new users.

Establishing a Constellation of Personally Relevant Applications

The second constellation that needs to be on the tablet computer is composed of applications that are personally relevant. As a general rule, if a user can think of an area that interests him or her they are likely to find an application for it. By demonstrating how the tablet computer can be valuable to the user personally as well as professionally, the likelihood of the physician using the device will increase. Providing the opportunity for the physician to 'play with' the tablet computer outside the workplace will increase their comfort and skill using it and facilitate their understanding of its capabilities. This will have a direct impact on the degree to which the tablet computer can be used in the clinical setting and the speed with which the adoption will occur.

Managing Connectivity

The tablet computer's connectivity is one of the features that fundamentally differentiate it from its predecessors. With a SIM card, the device has access to the same networks used by the ubiquitous smartphone. This approach while highly effective at improving usability is expensive and limited by some lingering issues with the interaction between cell phone transceivers and sophisticated equipment in critical care areas. There are also areas in most hospitals where cell phone service is simply not available. In some cases, it is a direct result of the type of shielding required to permit safe operation of x-ray machines and other imaging devices. Consequently, applications must be able to operate while disconnected from the Internet or the tablet computer must offer alternative approaches to network connectivity.

The simplest solution is to provide a WiFi network within the healthcare facility as an alternative to the cell phone network. Whether this is done in a small portion of the facility or throughout, it is a complex undertaking that requires detailed planning, testing and support. In some cases the WiFi network is provided as an adjunct to the cell phone network. If the tablet computer is set up properly, it will preferentially use the WiFi network when it is available, which both saves battery life and reduces the reliance on the cell phone network.

An interesting alternative approach involves tethering the tablet computer from a cellular telephone. For example, the iPad's sister product the iPhone makes this task exceptionally easy as the implementation on both devices is very straightforward even for the novice user. It results in the iPad being able to exploit the cell phone network access available to the iPhone. If the user already has a phone of this type then a second data plan is not required. While this is a very effective approach to providing connectivity to the iPad, it creates significant power demands on the iPhone. Since its WiFi and cell network transceivers must be operational all the time, some users may experience a dramatic decrease in battery life. While there are certainly ways to manage this, it adds a layer of complexity to the iPad deployment.

Managing Power

Often it is very mundane issues that can cause major problems with technology implementations. In the case of the tablet computer, one of the key issues that must be considered is available power. Due to excellent design, most tablet computers have a very long battery life so this will not be an issue for many users. However, if there is extensive use of either the cellular or WiFi network then battery life will be shortened. To avoid this becoming a usability problem, it will be necessary to recharge the device in the locations where it is primarily used. For most clinicians this will mean having a charger at home and in their office. While this is a simple solution, it is one that will increase the total cost of ownership for the device and should be considered as part deployment plan. If the primary user of the device is highly mobile, then a portable charging solution may also be necessary.

The method for providing Internet connectivity can have an impact on power consumption as well. When the tablet computer is tethered to a cell phone, the cell phone will have dramatically increased power requirements. This will require sharing the charger for the tablet computer if a compatible device is used, carrying an additional charger, or carrying an external battery for the phone that will allow it to operate for a longer period of time. If an external battery is selected as a solution, it will also have charging requirements. These requirements and the cost of the battery itself will need to be considered as part of a total cost of ownership for the tablet computer deployment.

Managing Input

Getting data into small devices can be a challenge. With the tablet computer this is mitigated somewhat by the fact that the on-screen keyboard is quite large. Unfortunately, there is a lack of tactile sensation that results in a speed decrease for most users. For small amounts of data entry this is not a significant problem. However, it can become an issue if lengthy narrative must be entered. Alternatives include an external keyboard or voice recognition software. Many of the external keyboards available are either wireless (via a Bluetooth connection) stand-alone devices or combinations that are typically both keyboards and cases. These devices make data entry easy, but increase the weight and generate additional power requirements. The devices also have some cost and training implications for the organization that is deploying them.

Managing Output

The most typical output modalities for a tablet computer are data presentation on the screen, audio, video (via an external screen) or a combination of these. Printing, from the device is certainly possible, but requires careful pre-planning due to the fact that the tablet will need specialized wireless capable printers and appropriately configured applications.

Physical Protection

Portable devices such as the tablet computer are exposed to numerous physical hazards that can never be fully mitigated. Organizations that deploy them need to have a plan in place for when the device is dropped, scratched, or exposed to water. Some protection is provided by hard covers or combined keyboard/covers, but these add costs to the deployment and do not protect from all perils. Regardless of what protection is provided, it must be assumed that some of the tablet computers will be lost, damaged or stolen. If the organization wants the tablet computer to remain fully integrated into the provider's practice, they will need to have fully configured replacements prepared and available.

When a tablet computer is used in the healthcare setting, specific plans must also be made to ensure that it does not become contaminated with bacteria or viruses. Consideration should be given as to how the device can be used in the context of an outbreak. In that instance, it may not be possible to take the tablet computer into patient rooms and this may require a change in the physician's workflow. Innovative companies such as *Seal Shield* (http://www.sealshield.com/) are now providing antimicrobial protection for mobile devices such as the tablet computer.

Data Protection

Once the tablet computer has been fully configured by the user and in use for any length of time, the value of the data on the device becomes more valuable than the device itself. To ensure continued usability and to avoid frustration, a strategy must be in place to protect all of the applications, configurations and data on the tablet computer. This can be accomplished with backup to a proprietary local network, backup to a personal computer (PC) or backup to a commercial service. In each case the issues of confidentiality, integrity and availability of data must be considered by the organization that is conducting the deployment. Leaving the creation of a strategy for this up to an inexperienced user is a risky proposition. Typically, the data on the device is either exposed to privacy compromise, or not adequately protected. The tablet computer offers several ways to protect each of the data types on the device, and these must be fully implemented.

CONDUCTING A NEEDS ANALYSIS TO DETERMINE THE FEASIBILITY OF TABLET COMPUTER DEPLOYMENT IN A RURAL TEACHING HOSPITAL

Before the pilot, *Using Tablet Computers to Support Community Specialist and Family Medicine Preceptors*, was to be undertaken, a needs analysis was conducted in June 2011 to determine the extent to which physicians used mobile online technology and their preferences for medical apps. The needs analysis survey was distributed to 13 specialist and family medicine preceptors (clinical teachers) in a rural teaching hospital. The findings from the survey were used to inform the choice for mobile medical and general applications to be pre-loaded onto the iPads for the pilot. The survey contained questions for the physicians about the technology they used at home and work, Internet connectivity, medical software programs they most commonly used, and how they used their mobile devices.

Essentially, all of the physicians (preceptors) were keen to try using a tablet computer for clinical teaching. They felt that the iPad would be a convenient interactive tool for retrieving and inputting information relating to the revised family medicine curriculum, including resident evaluations. Moreover, the physicians were unanimous about using medical apps with residents in their clinical teaching. However, only about half of the preceptors indicated they would consider using a tablet for taking clinical notes.

Table 1 is a list of medical apps either confirmed beneficial for clinical use by the authors or suggested by preceptors. The reviews are taken directly from the personal experiences of the authors.

USING TABLET COMPUTERS TO SUPPORT COMMUNITY PRECEPTORS: A PROPOSED PILOT

The authors of this chapter decided it would be of value to share how we plan to investigate the feasibility and usability of tablet computer in clinical settings. It is our feeling and of other researchers mentioned earlier in the chapter, that tablet computers have tremendous potential in many teaching and learning environments. The results of the pilot will be disseminated in the near future so feasibility and usability successes, barriers, issues and lessons learned can be shared.

The purpose of our pilot is to explore the use of tablet computers to support rural community specialist preceptors with the implementation of the University of Ottawa's new Family Medicine (FM) Triple C Competency-Based curriculum, and access resources (including medical and general applications), and evaluation tools in an effort to support and enhance effective teaching and learning. The tablet computer chosen for this study is the iPad as there are more medical apps available for it than any other model.

iPads will be pre-loaded with the revised Family Medicine curriculum framework and tagged learning objectives, new and revised resident evaluations (including an innovative field note), and preferred medical applications. The iPads will be introduced to physicians at a half-day workshop and then used for clinical teaching.

Although some community family physicians have been involved in the FM curriculum revisions, few specialists have had the opportunity to become aware of the revised curriculum, the new learning objectives, and the companion teaching

Table 1. Suggested medical apps for mobile devices

App	URL	Review
Lexicomp Clinical Suite	http://webstore.lexi.com	Subscriptions run about $175 US per year. Includes 5 of Lexicomp's most popular data bases: Lexi-Drugs, Lexi-Interact, Lexi-Lab & Diagnostic Procedures, Harrison's Practice, and Lexi-CALC. Well worth the subscription fee.
UpToDate Mobile	http://www.uptodate.com/home/about/mobile-access.html	Free with subscription to UpToDate (about $500 per year). UpToDate is an ongoing peer reviewed database that includes over 9,000 topics across 19 specialties addressing questions that arise in clinical practice. Each topic has evidence-based recommendations that clinicians can use at the point of care.
iMedical apps	http://www.iMedicalapps.com	iMedicalApps is a website that contains reviews of medical apps as they become available. Many reviews are of free or inexpensive apps that may be worth trying.
Colour Atlas of Family Medicine	http://itunes.apple.com/ca/app/the-color-atlas-family-medicine/id385223695?mt=8	This is a native app (you don't need to connect to the internet to view the contents). It contains thousands of photographs of common and uncommon diseases. Very worthwhile for teaching and learning.
Oxford Handbook of Clinical Medicine	http://oxfordmedicine.com/about.dtl	This is one of a suite of valuable, point of care references that have been created for the web and mobile platforms.
Visible Body	http://www.visiblebody.com	Sophisticated anatomy teaching and reference tool that can either be deployed onto certain mobile devices or used on a device with web access.
SCAT2	http://www.scat2.org/	Sport Concussion Assessment Tool

and evaluation tools, and resources. Despite efforts to involve all stakeholders and end users in the design and delivery process of the new curriculum, reception to and implementation of organizational change is often perceived as difficult. In order to facilitate the implementation of the revised curriculum, this pilot was supported by and extended the efforts of the department of FM by focusing on the adoption of the innovation with specific attention to community specialist preceptors.

To this end, the objectives of this pilot are to:

- Ensure community preceptors in all specialties receive faculty development critical to their knowledge and understanding of their roles as teachers of FM residents;
- Facilitate an awareness, understanding of, and adoption by community specialist preceptors of the new FM Triple C Competency-Based curriculum;

- Save the community specialist preceptors time and make their job as teachers more effective by providing them with and supporting them to use an iPad containing all the new curriculum learning objectives, strategies and evaluation tools;
- Generate increased communication and a community of practice to facilitate knowledge mobilisation, exchange, and use between the community specialist preceptor and the resident; and the community specialist preceptor and the DFM;
- Provide an environmentally friendly, paper free, convenient, flexible learning environment;
- Enhance relationships between community specialist preceptors and the DFM, by providing an opportunity for team-building and mentorship;

- Situate FM at the forefront of innovation in health education;

All community preceptors who specialize in family medicine, obstetrics and gynaecology, internal medicine, paediatrics, orthopaedic surgery, general surgery, psychiatry, and emergency medicine, at the identified rural teaching hospital with whom they share the teaching responsibilities of the family medicine residents, will be invited to a local half-day workshop geared to providing faculty development critical to their roles as teachers (residents will also be able to participate in the workshop). The purpose of the workshop will be two-fold: first, to introduce participants to the iPad and provide them with an opportunity to explore how it works and second; to introduce the revised curriculum and resources.

During the workshop, the following information will be presented: an overview of the revised FM curriculum, the FM conceptual framework, organization of curriculum into eight domains (specific to each specialty), learning objectives, teaching strategies, evaluation strategies, and using the iPad to facilitate the teaching and learning of FM residents. Each community specialist, family medicine preceptor and resident will be given an iPad. In order to receive an iPad preceptors and residents will agree to partake in the evaluation of the pilot study by completing two surveys, taking field notes, and participating in a follow-up interview.

The following research questions are to be addressed:

1. How does the use of the iPad affect the implementation and adoption of a new curriculum among community specialist preceptors and their FM residents?
2. How does the use of the iPad affect the content, delivery, service, structure and outcomes of the FM curriculum with community specialist preceptors and their FM residents?

The research design will be an intrinsic case study (Stake, 2005). The case study approach is used if there is interest in understanding a particular case, such as this example of a rural clinical teaching site. Case studies are often used in education and exploratory research to gain an in-depth understanding of a single case.

Various means of quantitative and qualitative data collection will be used in this pilot to allow the participants' experiences to be captured in addition to obtaining objective evidence regarding the participants' perceptions of the use of the iPad in facilitating the adoption of the revised FM curriculum. These will include observations, note taking (using the notepad and voice recorder functions on the iPad), survey, and semi-structured interviews. The researchers involved in this pilot are also conscientious of the busy schedules and time commitments that often constrain preceptors and residents and will incorporate the evaluation procedures into the learning process as much as possible to avoid being time consuming or inconvenient. The multiple data sources will enable triangulation.

Data analysis will be an ongoing process throughout the project. The qualitative data will be analyzed inductively and deductively. The research questions will be used as a framework from which to search for themes and meanings emerging from the data. The categories, themes and patterns that emerge in this process will be evaluated for their credibility. At the same time, the evaluators will search through the data for disconfirming instances and alternative explanations. Direct quotations will be used throughout the reports in order to preserve the voice of the participants. Quantitative data analysis will involve calculating frequency and descriptive statistics for the learners' responses on the closed-answer survey items.

FUTURE RESEARCH DIRECTIONS

As organizations begin to deploy tablet computers in the workplace we will begin to see studies involving their integration and application. Some questions to explore will be how effective the tablet computer is in making clinical teaching more effective. We may also be reading in the near future of studies that explore the use of the tablet computer for improving patient education. Finally, an area of future research may be to explore the use of the tablet computer for inputting electronic orders and prescriptions. However, if the tablet computer is to be used for the handling of confidential patient information, security needs to be a focus. As technology progresses so will security features.

CONCLUSION

Mobile Health is an area that is growing at an increasing rate. Indeed it will be interesting to see the affect iPads and other tablet computers have on clinical teaching and learning. With the rapid adoption of mobile technology by physicians and patients there will be many attempts to use of the tablet computer to foster clinical teaching and communication. Already, smartphones are making their way into the clinical setting. Medical students, residents and practising physicians are quick to use their mobile devices to access the latest medical procedures, drug database and calculators. Is there a place for the tablet computer in the clinical setting? Studies such as the proposed intervention mentioned in this chapter will provide us with more insight into the feasibility of using tablet computers in the clinical setting – time will tell.

REFERENCES

Barlow-Zambodla, A. (2009). Mobile technology for learner support in open schooling. *SAIDE Newsletter, 15*(1). Retrieved October 20, 2011, from http://www.saide.org.za/resources/newsletters/Vol_15_no.1_2009/Content/Mobile%20Technology%20for%20Learner%20Support.htm

Berger, E. (2010). The iPad: Gadget or medical godsend? *Annals of Emergency Medicine, 56*(1), 21A–22A. doi:10.1016/j.annemergmed.2010.05.010

Bullen, M., & Janes, D. P. (2007). Preface. In Bullen, M., & Jane, D. P. (Eds.), *Making the transition to e-learning: Strategies and issues* (pp. vii–xvi). Hershey, PA: Information Science Publishing.

Chiou, C.-K., Tseng, J. C. R., Hwang, G.-J., & Heller, S. (2010). An adaptive navigation support system for conducting context-aware ubiquitous learning in museums. *Computers & Education, 55*(2), 834–845. doi:10.1016/j.compedu.2010.03.015

Ellaway, R. (2011). eMedical teacher. *Medical Teacher, 33*, 258–260. doi:10.3109/0142159X.2011.561696

Elwood, D., Diamond, M. C., Heckman, J., Bonder, J. H., Beltran, J. E., Moroz, A., & Yip, J. (2011). Mobile health: Exploring attitudes among physical medicine and rehabilitation physicians toward this emerging element of health delivery. *The American Academy of Physical Medicine and Rehabilitation, 3*, 678–680.

Garrison, D. R., Anderson, T., & Archer, W. (2000). Critical inquiry in a text-based environment: Computer conferencing in higher education. *The Internet and Higher Education, 2*(2-3), 87–105. doi:10.1016/S1096-7516(00)00016-6

Hwang, G. J., & Chang, H. F. (2011). A formative assessment-based mobile learning approach to improving the learning attitudes and achievements of students. *Computers & Education, 56*(1), 1023–1031. doi:10.1016/j.compedu.2010.12.002

Hwang, G. J., & Tsai, C. C. (2011). Research trends in mobile and ubiquitous learning: A review of publications in selected journals from 2001 to 2010. *British Journal of Educational Technology, 42*(4), 65–70. doi:10.1111/j.1467-8535.2011.01183.x

IDC. (2011). *IDC predictions 2011: Welcome to the new mainstream.* Retrieved October 20, 2011 from http://www.idc.com/research/viewdocsynopsis.jsp?containerId=225878

Keegan, D. (2002). *The future of learning: From eLearning to mLearning.* Retrieved October 20, 2011 from http://learning.ericsson.net/mlearning2/project_one/book.html

King, W. R., & He, J. (2006). A meta-analysis of the technology acceptance model. *Information & Management, 43*(6), 740–755. doi:10.1016/j.im.2006.05.003

Koszlaka, T. A., & Ntloedibe-Kuswani, G. S. (2010). Literature on the safe and disruptive potential of mobile technologies. *Distance Education, 31*(2), 139–157. doi:10.1080/01587919.2010.498082

Liu, Y., Li, H., & Carlsson, C. (2010). Factors driving the adoption of m-learning: An empirical study. *Computers & Education, 55*, 1211–1219. doi:10.1016/j.compedu.2010.05.018

Lu, Y.-C., Xiao, Y., Sears, A., & Jacko, J. (2004). A review and framework of handheld computer adoption in healthcare. *International Journal of Medical Informatics, 74*, 409–422. doi:10.1016/j.ijmedinf.2005.03.001

Mashman, W. (2011). Editor's page. The iPad in Cardiology: Tool or toy? *JACC: Cardiovascular Interventions, 4*(2), 258–259. doi:10.1016/j.jcin.2011.01.001

Mobile Learning Group. Athabasca University. (n.d.). *Mobile learning and pervasive computing.* Retrieved October 1, 2011, from http://adlib.athabascau.ca/

Naismith, L., Lonsdale, P., Vavoula, G., & Sharples, M. (2006). *Literature review in mobile technologies and learning (Futurelab Series Report 11).* Bristol, UK: Futurelab.

Quinn, C. N. (2011). *Designing mLearning: Tapping into the mobile revolution for organizational performance.* San Francisco, CA: Pfeiffer.

Reynolds, R., Walker, K., & Speight, C. (2010). Web-based museum trails on PDAs for university-level design and evaluation. *Computers & Education, 55*(3), 994–1003. doi:10.1016/j.compedu.2010.04.010

Shamji, A., & Law, M. (2011). The role of technology in medical education: Lessons from the University of Toronto. *UMTJ, 88*(3), 150–153.

Stake, R. E. (2005). Qualitative case studies. In Denzin, N. K., & Lincoln, Y. S. (Eds.), *The Sage handbook of qualitative research* (3rd ed., pp. 443–466). Thousand Oaks, CA: Sage.

Vasich, T. (2012). *The age of electronic medicine.* Retrieved January 27, 2012 from http://www.uci.edu/features/2010/08/feature_ipad_100813.php

Vygotsky, L. S. (1978). *Mind in society.* Cambridge, MA: Harvard University Press.

Wu, I.-L., Li, J.-Y., & Fu, C.-Y. (2011). The adoption of mobile healthcare by hospital's professional: An integrative perspective. *Decision Support Systems*, *51*, 587–596. doi:10.1016/j.dss.2011.03.003

KEY TERMS AND DEFINITIONS

CanMEDS-FM Roles: Family Medicine Expert, Communicator, Collaborator, Manager, Health Advocate, Scholar and Professional which identify the knowledge, skills and attitudes necessary to become a well-rounded, competent family physicians who can provide effective primary healthcare to patients (http://www.cfpc.ca/up-loadedFiles/Education/CanMeds%20FM%20Eng.pdf).

Curriculum Domains: The University of Ottawa FM program content is organized around four human life cycle topics (Maternity/Newborn Care; Care of Children/Adolescents; Care of Adults and Care of the Elderly) and an additional four healthcare related topics (Procedural Skills; Behavioural Medicine and Mental Health; End-of-Life Care and Care of Special Populations).

Curriculum Framework: An organized plan or roadmap that identifies processes, content, supports and expected outcomes in a curriculum.

Family Medicine Competency-Based Curriculum: A curriculum designed to emphasize the development of competencies in the four principles of family medicine and the CanMEDS-FM Roles as defined by the College of Family Physicians of Canada.

Preceptor: A clinician teacher who has a faculty appointment in the DFM and who is responsible for supervising the learning of one or more assigned postgraduate or undergraduate learners for the duration of their training.

Principles of Family Medicine: The Family Physician is (1) a skilled clinician and (2) a resource to a defined practice population; (3) FM is a community-based discipline and (4) the patient/physician relationship is central to the role of the Family Physician (http://www.cfpc.ca/Principles/).

Resident: An individual who has received a medical degree and is registered in a recognised postgraduate training program. In family medicine, this training program is usually two years in length.

Tethering: A technology that will allow the use of a cell phone as a modem for another device such as a laptop or tablet computer.

Triple C Curriculum: Comprehensive, focused on continuity, and centred in family medicine. The College of Family Physicians of Canada (CFPC) recommends that all family medicine postgraduate training programs in Canada adopt this competency-based curriculum. (http://www.cfpc.ca/triple_C/)

Section 2
High End Computing, Storage, and Services

Chapter 6
Energy–Efficient Monitoring and Controlling of Computer Systems

Micha vor dem Berge
christmann informationstechnik & medien GmbH & Co. KG, Germany

Wolfgang Christmann
christmann informationstechnik & medien GmbH & Co. KG, Germany

ABSTRACT

This chapter aims to describe the current state and the ongoing efforts to integrate a monitoring and controlling architecture in modern computing environments. Benefits to be gained from this architecture include: More knowledge about the available computing resources and the capability to establish a management platform that optimizes energy efficiency as well as the availability of the computer environment in a time of a rapidly growing need for computer systems. In two use cases, namely server virtualisation and High Performance Computing (HPC), implementations of a management system for energy-efficiency were evaluated, showing that it is possible to increase the energy-efficiency by more than 10%, depending on the use case and the workload.

INTRODUCTION

Many of today's computer systems are set up with a strong focus on availability and reliability on the one hand and low acquisition costs on the other hand. When customers have to choose which computer systems to buy, the Total Costs of Own-

ership (TCO) are often thrust aside as if they were of lower importance than the purchasing price, although they are the proper measure for overall costs. The TCO usually consist of the acquisition or depreciation costs, maintenance and service costs as well as disposal costs or resale value. In case of a computer system that has to provide

DOI: 10.4018/978-1-4666-2190-9.ch006

high availability, costs resulting from downtime can be considered as well. Most server systems are running 24 hours a day, 7 days a week and 365 days a year. Because of this, the energy costs for operation and cooling are among the biggest expenses during the lifetime of a server. These costs can be reduced by managing all servers in a sensible and energy-efficient way.

Another aspect of the reduction of energy consumption is the accompanying reduction of CO_2 emissions. The worldwide CO_2 emissions of data centres are already approximately equal to the total CO_2 emissions of airlines and account for almost 2% of global production and has a rapidly growing trend. The worldwide data centre electricity consumption grew up from 70.8 Billion kWh in the year 2000 to 152.2 Billion kWh in 2005 (Koomey, 2008).

Thus, the efficiency of IT systems and data centres becomes a priority for research and industry. High Performance Computing is considered one of the major issues to be addressed in this context. Companies like Google or Facebook know the problems of running thousands of servers (which regularly show up in the form of an immense electricity bill). They have begun to build their own energy-efficient servers.

In this chapter we are going to explain how complex HPC environments can be monitored and managed in an energy-efficient way while keeping the additional payload for the entire system as small as possible. This can be done via standardized software and hardware access layers or by new monitoring and controlling architectures that enable the user to reach a maximum of energy efficiency. One new type of monitoring and controlling architecture for cluster servers will be introduced, which was developed by the German company Christmann, see Christmann (2012).

BACKGROUND

As described in the introduction, the increasing worldwide demand on energy for data centres is becoming a serious problem. If the energy required running modern data centres would increase at a constant rate over the next years, we would theoretically need all power plants of the world just to run the data centres in a few years. For this reason, the European Council has confirmed the objective to save 20% of the EU's energy consumption compared to projections for 2020 (CEC, 2009), while the Climate Group (2008) has estimated that ICT-enabled improvements could save about 15% of total carbon emissions by 2020, even in other sectors than the ICT sector. Every IT company must deal with this emerging problem that more and more companies are already aware of. By now there are several rather conventional factors that can increase the energy efficiency of data centres, which will be briefly presented in the following passage.

The first possibility to increase energy efficiency is to scrutinise existing data and applications. Often it is possible to shut down some servers just because the running application or existing data is no longer used, but in many scenarios the necessity of applications is not monitored, which makes it impossible to evaluate the necessity of servers. Also, the amount of resources used by different programs might vary a lot and should be compared critically.

The second factor is to use server virtualisation. By doing so it is possible to migrate old servers to virtual machines (VM) and to consolidate several VMs on one physical server (host). In most cases, a prerequisite is a newer hardware with CPU support for Virtualisation Technology (called Intel VT or AMD-V, see details at AMD

(2005)). Customers reported an energy drop of up to 80% in BMU (2009) while increasing the utilization of the hosts from 5-10% to 60-80%.

A third factor with a strong effect on energy efficiency is the IT hardware itself. A typical customer might have a strong link to his standard hardware supplier and might buy new hardware because of a special feature or to integrate it smoothly into the existing manufacturer-specific infrastructure. But a very important fact is that the energy efficiency of a piece of hardware has a strong impact on its TCO, which makes it very important to be considered in the decision process as well. Since 2007, an international benchmark for measuring the energy efficiency of servers exists, called SPECpower, see SPEC (2008) and SPEC (2008-2010), which helps customers choosing an energy-efficient server model, at least in this specific benchmark. Although this benchmark cannot be generalised, it is a good starting point while looking for energy-efficient servers. As stated in Koomey's Law by Koomey et al. (2010), the energy efficiency of micro processors grows with the same rate predicted by Moore's Law, see Moore (1965), meaning it doubles every 18 months, there are still big differences between different server models.

A further factor is a highly efficient, correctly dimensioned Uninterruptable Power Supply (UPS). Modern large-scale UPS have an efficiency of up to 99%, whereas smaller systems reach about 90%. An important point is the right dimensioning – UPS should always be operated in the upper third of their workload because this is where their efficiency reaches its maximum level. Furthermore, Rasmussen (2011) highlighted that some UPS have special energy-efficiency modes.

Air-conditioning is the fifth factor that can help reduce the required energy. As stated by Patterson (2009), air-conditioning consumes about one third of the overall energy in a typical data centre. Another third is used by the servers themselves, the last third is distributed to the Power Distribution Units (PDU), UPS and other infrastructure

components. Commonly proposed improvements are the increase of the cooling air temperature, the use of geothermics and the separation of cold and warm areas and a continuous housing of these areas. There are several further recommendations like direct water cooling of all main-components in a server, which is described by Kranzlmüller (2011), or cooled rear-doors which cool the outlet air of servers down so that the rack gets climatic neutral, see Patterson & Fenwick (2008). Increasing the temperature of the server room leads to less energy consumption of the cooling units while often the server lifetime is not impacted, see Patterson, M. K. (2008).

The sixth factor in which the overall energy efficiency can be optimized is the active use of wasted heat to heat buildings and a sensible construction of buildings with regard to energy aspects. An example is the position of the heat exchanger, which should be on the cold side of the building. In the northern hemisphere it would be the northern side of the building.

A seventh factor is the power source that produces the electrical energy used for the entire infrastructure and the servers. If the power generator is for example a coal power station, the CO_2 emissions will be immense, whereas the CO_2 emissions of a hydroelectric power plant are very low. This way, CO_2 emission is less, whereas the used energy remains constant.

All of these factors are implemented hundreds of times and cause a significant increase in energy efficiency, which often yields a fast return on investment. The Code of Conduct on Data Centres Energy Efficiency, see European Commission (2010), contains good standard indications to reach scrutinise the energy-efficiency in data centres. The main topic of this chapter is the active management of existing hardware through a sensible use of a monitoring and controlling infrastructure. Through this management, the servers can operate in an energy-efficient way, and an increase in efficiency of 10-20% can be achieved, depending on the typical workload as shown in GAMES D7.4

(2010) and own tests. Besides these approaches to saving energy, some software packages for the management of virtualized environments have already implemented energy-efficient scheduling mechanisms for VMs. Examples are the virtualisation solutions by Citrix and VMware, market leaders in the proprietary sector. Also open source solutions like openQRM, see openQRM (2012), show attempts at energy-efficient management for high available systems by building up an N+1 failover cluster. Some older virtualisation management solutions are only able to build N+N failover cluster, which wastes a lot more energy.

ENERGY-EFFICIENT MANAGEMENT OF SERVERS

Managing servers in an energy-efficient way can be regarded as working in a loop:

1. We have to monitor the servers and applications that run on the servers.
2. The monitoring data that is now available has to be processed in a sensible way.
3. The processed data leads to management decisions.
4. Now the servers can be controlled as decided in the previous step.
5. Afterwards the servers are behaving differently than before, which can be monitored once more.

These steps will be discussed in the following sections after a look at existing management solutions and virtualisation as one main technique facilitating dynamic management.

Energy-Efficiency through Virtualisation

Virtualisation is probably the technique that has changed the data centre's daily business the most over the last years. As almost all modern data centre environments are based on virtualisation, it

is obvious to use this technique to increase energy efficiency. Through migration of old servers to VMs and the consolidation of many VMs on a few hosts, energy efficiency was greatly increased in recent years.

When talking about management solutions we usually have a virtualised environment in mind, which is easily manageable due to the advantages of the virtualisation layer. Alternatively it must have been ensured that all applications are aware of changes to the cluster. The virtualisation layer lets us transparently move workloads off a server that can then be put in a low-energy state without notifying the applications.

With virtualisation, we now have the possibility to dynamically manage the VMs on the hosts. An essential basis for the management is a fully virtualised server infrastructure with a central storage. This allows for live migration of the VMs without having to transfer the VM's hard drive image between two hosts, which would slow down the migration process drastically. If the hard drive images reside on a central storage, only the VM's actual state (which is its RAM, CPU state and established TCP connections) have to be transferred between the source and target host. This happens very fast over a quick interconnect such as 10 Gigabit Ethernet. Basically, live migration can be implemented in various ways, but the main steps are the following:

- Copy the VM's file system from one host to another if it resides on local storage. For a shared storage this point can be left out. While copying data, files can be modified on the source host which has to be logged for a later synchronisation.
- Pause the VM. The VM stops immediately, maybe while executing some commands.
- Synchronize the file system if files have changed since the first copy job.
- Transfer the RAM, network statuses and the CPUs registers to the destination host.
- Copy the VM-specific configuration, like RAM size, hard drive size etc.

- Start the VM on the destination host. A network broadcast is also needed, which publishes the way to access the VMs via the new host's MAC address.
- If the start of the VM on the destination host was successful, delete the VM on the source host.

The technique of live migration as described above is also the basis for efficient backups, which can be made while the VM is running. These backups happen nearly in the same way as live migration. The essential difference is that the destination host is not another host but a backup target. This helps to reduce the downtime of the VM. Otherwise, VMs must be stopped to avoid problems with inconsistent files that were accessed while the backup was running.

Management Approaches to Improve the Energy-Efficiency

In this section we will describe different management approaches to improving energy-efficiency. The main idea of management for energy-efficiency is to detect when system resources are not used and then put these resources in a low-energy state. This can be done by shutting off parts of the hardware (like hard drives) or entire hosts. Shutting down hosts can only be accomplished when there are no services running on them.

As an example for a virtualised management solution we will describe the basic idea of the Distributed Power Manager (DPM) from VMware as stated in VMware (2010). The DPM is an add-on module for a multi-host virtualisation cluster environment and enables the cluster to carry out an automatic resource management. Before being able to use DPM, it has to be ensured that every single host that is part of the cluster can be switched on by Wake-On-LAN, IPMI or HPs proprietary management solution. If switched on, DPM can be configured to behave in a conservative or aggressive manner, which will influence

thresholds that are part of the decision process. Enabling the user to modify these thresholds individually, DPM is configurable to meet the desired performance / energy-efficiency trade-off. By default, the utilisation range (an artificial metric that contains information about CPU and memory load) of the hosts should be between 45% and 81%. If the average utilisation of the last five minutes was above 81%, a new host is powered up to quickly react to the growing resource needs, whereas powering down hosts is less reactive. If the utilisation is below 45% for a longer period of time, the VMs are being migrated and the host is put in a low-power state.

With the Moab Adaptive Computing Suite by Adaptive Computing, a very different solution shall be briefly introduced here, see Adaptive Computing (2011). Adaptive Computing offers a virtualisation environment, but a suite designed to manage a data centre by automating provisioning, chargeback, reporting and managing. This is done by analysing available information about resources, workloads, service-levels and users in real-time. Information can be extracted by the suite itself or by external monitoring solutions like Nagios. Although the implementation details of most management parts are not publicly available (from the users' perspective), the management of high energy efficiency seems to be similar to VMware's described above. It can also analyse the workload of hosts and shut them down when they are not needed, and is also able to turn them on again.

The Problem of Managing Thousands of Servers

One problem that might arise while trying to monitor and manage servers is that the overhead of monitoring and controlling might be greater than the benefit of the energy-efficiency management. The problem gets bigger the more servers are to be managed. Especially the network overhead of the monitoring data that has to be pulled from every single host and sometimes even from every single VM might lead to a serious performance drop. In some cases it is even impossible to monitor all available servers, each running 10-20 services. This problem is well known, also to the popular monitoring software Nagios which fires an 'overlapping request' error in this case. In data centres whose main goal is High Performance Computing, almost no monitoring is done because of the problem that the increasing network load which will also lead to an increasing latency for messages, which is not acceptable (especially for HPC). Administrators as well as users are afraid of uncontrollable performance drops or even worse problems that may result in financial losses.

Of course it is not possible to control what is not even measurable. A fine-grained measurement of the main values of every host and VM is inevitable. As described above, gathering the monitoring data, processing the data, finding decisions and controlling the servers and VMs is a loop. The frequency at which this loop is processed is a highly important parameter, because it defines the management overhead. As long as monitoring all servers is still possible from the monitoring software's point of view, doubling the frequency increases the management overhead in a linear way. But the benefit will usually not be doubled; we will experience a steep increase in efficiency when enabling the management in very long periods. When the frequency rises up

from a few hours to 30 minutes, we will again experience a performance boost, but probably a time span between 30 minutes and 30 seconds will not make that much of a difference – depending on the workload. If the workload is changing very slowly, it is necessary to also monitor the servers in a long interval. If the workload changes quickly, you should be able to monitor this quick change. Based on a locally bound "office worker" workload, servers are utilized from roughly 7am to 10pm and under-utilized during the remainder of the time. In Figure 1 you can see a sine-like utilization curve over the time, which is typical for mainly locally used servers, such as web servers for a national audience. This sine-like curve suggests an interval of 5-30 minutes.

Running into overlapping requests when reducing the cycle time is one problem, a delayed reaction to varying workloads is a completely different problem.

Pre-Aggregation of Monitoring Information

The problem of monitoring thousands of servers can be addressed by two different measures. The first one is to set up a completely separate monitoring network and the second one is the aggregation of monitoring data before sending it over the network. Both approaches combined can guarantee an effective monitoring and thus

Figure 1. Typical load curve of a nationally used server

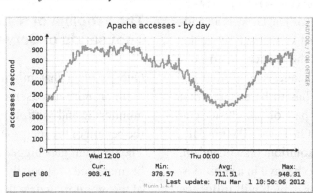

form the basis for an efficient management. Keeping in mind that the overhead for building up a dedicated monitoring network is quite big, the best cost-to-benefit ratio seems to be a sensible pre-aggregation of all monitoring data before sending it to the management server.

By pre-aggregating monitoring data, the number of information requests from a single server can be reduced from the full number of requested values to only one value. Let's assume we would need 10 values, for example. The payload size of a single monitoring packet sent over the network would be ten times bigger than a standard monitoring packet, if all raw-data is aggregated and then sent in one packet. But because a TCP/IP packet has a payload size of 1460 Bytes, and one dataset is just a few Bytes long in most cases, only one packet would be required. This way the interfering network traffic for monitoring can be kept as small as possible. Another benefit would be that the monitoring server had the potential to monitor ten times more servers without the problem of overlapping requests. Of course these aggregated values have to be processed individually, which causes some overhead for splitting them into single information packages again. But the splitting happens inside of a database, which is much faster than transferring them individually over the network, so there will most likely still be an improvement induced by the pre-aggregation.

The type of pre-aggregation described above is a consolidation of many requests into only one request and therefore not an aggregation in the literal sense. A real pre-aggregation would not only pack the monitored data to one TCP/IP packet, but would also aggregate the sensor values themselves. Useful aggregated values are the average value over the time x that corresponds to the cycle time of the managing system. Another interesting value is the trend of the values, which can go downwards or upwards or remain constant. This additional information is useful for a sensible energy-efficiency management, and the pre-aggregation on the host relieves the manage-ment server because it doesn't have to extract this information by itself.

To make sure the pre-aggregation does not cause an additional payload on the hosts themselves, which is unacceptable, there has to be a little extra hardware on every host doing the pre-aggregation. This is why Christmann has designed an 18-node cluster server with an integrated monitoring and controlling infrastructure. Of course this integrated monitoring- and controlling-infrastructure must also be funded, but because it is only micro controller-based, the costs are very low for all 18 nodes. It is possible to run a little monitoring- and controlling-system on this extra hardware, which is interacting with its equals. This makes it possible to set up a cascaded management solution consisting of a local loop that monitors and controls the hardware directly, and an overall management system called 'global loop' that monitors and controls all available resources from a higher layer, for example at the level of operation systems. This allows for a short-cycle local control loop that reacts very fast at the hardware layer and the operation system layer. Furthermore it allows for a long-cycle global loop that adapts to long-term changes on the hardware-, operation system-, virtualisation- and application layers. The principle of a cascaded control system is that the local loop acts in a self-determined manner and that the global loop perceives the local loop not as a control system, but merely as a part of the controlled system. In other words, the local loop is a black-box for the global loop, acting on its own. Thus both loops must have well-defined responsibilities, which usually may not overlap. An approved distribution of responsibilities would be the following: The local loop controls the hardware power states of the CPU, hard drives and possibly the RAM, in addition it pre-aggregates and consolidates all monitoring values for the global loop. The global loop controls the state of the whole host, meaning it can be shut down or put the VMs and the applications into hibernation.

Scheduling Approaches to Improve the Energy-Efficiency

Assuming that live migration works, and monitoring is also running efficiently, the next important step for setting up energy-efficiency management is sensible data mining combined with a scheduler that determines the right actions for the VMs and hosts. The data mining shall not be examined very intensively here, because a simple but effective scheduler works with only very little data mining intelligence, as our test proved. In this test we implemented (as described later on in more detail) a very simple scheduler that was based on only few variables, and reached a 10% improvement in energy-efficiency. Simple data mining can even be integrated into the monitoring solution with pre-aggregation (as described above). For the envisaged scheduler, the actual monitoring values plus the average values provided enough information to make good decisions.

The few existing implementations of energy-efficient management systems for VMs differ in many aspects, which will be highlighted here. A very simple - and in many cases also effective - scheduling works as follows: All existing VMs are transferred to one host until the resources of this host are exhausted - until it is 'full'. This happens until every host is 'full' and no more VM can be migrated. Now 'empty' hosts can be put into a low-energy state. When a high load situation arises, the hosts will be started immediately, which can be done via different techniques like Wake on LAN, IPMI, AMT/vPro or a manufacturer-specific command. If the new host has booted up, one of the VMs will be live-migrated to this host until the work load reaches an acceptable range again.

The simplicity of this scheduler is advantageous on the one hand, because it has very low demands on the monitoring and data mining. On the other hand it has some clear disadvantages. Once all VMs are consolidated to a few hosts and all other hosts have been shut down, significant energy efficiency can be achieved. If a high workload suddenly emerges, one VM has to be migrated from a host that is already under high workload and which will be strained even more by the migration process. This does not flatten the load peak, it even worsens it. Such behaviour is only tenable in two cases: If the load peaks are absolutely unpredictable, which makes a more intelligent behaviour impossible, or if the load peaks are very long and the additional load at the beginning (through the migration of the VM) can be tolerated. This might be the case in temporally widely distributed HPC scenarios, where a calculation is made every few days that takes hours or maybe even days to complete.

A general problem of this simple scheduler is its reactive character: It can only react when an excessive workload already occurred or when the load was very low for a longer period of time. An alternative approach is a proactive scheduler, which has its basis in sophisticated data mining that tries to predict future workloads. Generally, a prediction can be more accurate the more uniform the workload curves are. Assuming that the managed servers are mainly used by employees of a company that have an eight-hour work day, the prediction will be very accurate due to the similarity of every day and week. It is important that a prediction is made for a complete week, so that the weekend time is also under observation. A different but very effective way of prediction in stable and uniform environments is the manual prediction, which takes into account much more variables (like holidays) than automatic data mining could ever do. Of course it requires a person who regularly evaluates the varying workloads and the demands from the user-side and brings these two perspectives together as effectively as possible. A trade-off between automatic and manual prediction is a hybrid scheduling that acts dynamically within a user-defined scope. As mentioned before, a prediction can only be accomplished when the workload is somehow predictable and not chaotic (at least from the limited point of view of a data mining solution), which might be the case in an internationally oriented workload.

Cost-Benefit Analysis

In addition to the scheduler's and data mining problem of when to move VMs and when to shut down hosts, there is another problem to deal with. Let's call it 'cost-benefit analysis'. The challenge is to maximize the time that hosts will remain in low-energy states, keeping in mind that every action has its own costs. Albers (2010) describes how different algorithms can influence energy-efficiency by dealing with the problem of when to put resources in a lower energy state. If β defines the costs to wake up a system from a lower-energy state, r defines the energy usage of a resource in its actual energy state, and T defines the possible idle period, then a transfer to a lower energy state is only rational if $\beta < rT$. An algorithm that knows T in advance is able to act in an optimized way and needs minimal energy.

Albers proposes different algorithms, the behaviour of which is nearly optimal and which need no more than the c-fold energy, as an optimal algorithm would need. The first algorithm puts the resource to a low- energy state after an idle time of β/r and needs $2c$ of energy. A slight variation of this algorithm needs only $e/(e-1)c \approx 1.58c$ of the ideal energy consumption as described (Karlin et al., 1994). Interestingly, it is based on a function that puts the resource into a low-energy state after a random time between $t = 0$ and $t = \beta/r$. A self-learning algorithm that learns to predict the time β/r will need at most the $e/(e-1)c$-fold of the ideal possible energy.

Up to now, the implicit assumption was that the resource has only two energy states, namely an active state and an energy-saving state. This is not the case on modern computer systems that have more than a dozen energy states. For example, most modern CPUs have 12 or more so-called p-states that regulate the CPU's frequency and voltage settings. Starting from an ideal system there are usually the following possibilities to run the system in:

- Normal mode
- Scale down the CPU in several steps
- Stop the hard drive
- Suspend the computer system
  - to RAM
  - to hard drive
- Shut down the complete system

In general, it can be assumed that a deeper energy state uses less energy than a higher energy state. Furthermore, the costs to get back up to a higher state are greater the deeper the actual state is – for example, it takes more energy to completely boot up a server than to wake it up from a sleep state.

In 2003, Irani et al. proved that this algorithm has $2c$ of the theoretical optimal energy efficiency. In this context, a generalisation of the previously introduced self-learning algorithm does not need more than the 1.58-fold energy compared to an ideal algorithm.

Quality of Service

One aspect that has not been addressed directly so far is the quality of service that should remain at a maximum level without (and also with) dynamic management. The necessary trade-off between maximum energy efficiency and constant high performance might not lead to compromises that impair the overall performance, user experience or even defined Service Level Agreements. For this reason, the typical workload and workload spikes of every single VM should be monitored and analysed carefully. If a VM tends to produce extremely fluctuating workloads, this should be recognized. A suitable reaction would be to preserve necessary resources on the host for this VM to depress the occurring variances.

A very promising approach was published by Rodríguez-Haro et al. (2009), describing a multi-process scheduler that is able to guarantee quality of service policies for VMs. The basic idea is to define the minimum requirements of every VM regarding its computing power. Based on this information, it is possible to implement a multi-process scheduler that can both maximize the workload on the host and guarantee quality of service policies. This is of great importance, especially in heterogeneous environments, where one VM might be used as a Virtual Desktop that needs high responsiveness and another VM might be used for HPC simultaneously, utilising all available system resources. Usually both use cases preclude each other, but thanks to the scheduler, they can be combined.

One more point that found nearly no response in publications up to now is the difference between workload demands. One VM might be CPU-bound, another one might be I/O or RAM-bound, compare Asanovic et al. (2006). All these different demands can be combined on one host if the scheduler and the hardware architecture are suitable. In this context, 'suitable' means that both the hardware and the scheduler are in the position to handle these various demands synchronously, which can be done in the best way by modern multi-processor systems. A combination of several VMs with various demands on one host leads to a maximisation of the system's resource usage, because all available hardware components are utilised. In contrast, a pure CPU-bound application often does not require many resources from the RAM or hard drives, which is a waste of the available resources and - because it also still has to be electrically supplied - of energy.

Testbed with 18-Node Cluster Server

As described above, a sensible pre-aggregation of monitoring data is one of the key features necessary for managing a great number of servers in an energy-efficient way. As shown in Figure 2, our testbed consists of a cluster computer system with 18 nodes, an internal network server, an imager server, a network-attached storage (NAS) and a frontend server. All these parts are connected via a Gigabit interconnect network. The two main components of the testbed are the cluster system called RECS (Resource Efficient Computing System) and the frontend server introduced by Christmann (2009). The frontend server is supposed to collect the required information for the management framework by monitoring the energy consumption, application status and other obligatory parameters, whilst executing submitted jobs and deployed services as described in GAMES D7.4 (2011). The GAMES Application Server is supposed to run the monitoring environment Nagios. More important, the runtime controller of the management framework should then be able to adjust the configuration of the test bed and leverage workloads among computing nodes according to the adaptation methodologies.

In order to evaluate the described testbed in operation, a fine-grained monitoring solution has been developed, allowing a detailed inspection of the entire testbed. In order to avoid influencing the evaluation results by affecting the testbed environment with the related monitoring actions, a new monitoring infrastructure was developed as part of a research project funded by the German federal ministry for economy and technology, for which the University of Paderborn and Christmann designed the RECS, see Christmann (2009). The concept of this monitoring approach is to reduce the network load, avoid the dependency of polling every single compute node at the operation system layer, and to build up a basis on which new monitoring- and controlling-concepts can be developed. To meet these requirements, there is a specially designed central backplane for the RECS with an integrated master-slave system of microcontrollers.

The status of each compute node within the testbed is connected to an additional independent microcontroller in order to manage the measured data. The main advantage of the RECS system is to avoid the potential overheads caused by measuring and transferring data, which would consume lots of computing capabilities, particularly in a large-scale environment. This approach

Figure 2. HPC testbed infrastructure for energy efficiency analysis

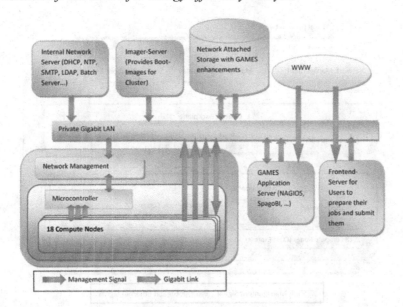

can play a significant role. On the other hand, the microcontrollers also consume additional energy. Compared with the potentially saved energy, it is expected that the additional energy consumption could be neglected. This microcontroller-based monitoring architecture is accessible to the user via a dedicated network port and has to be read out only once to get all the information about the installed computing nodes. When a user monitors 10 metrics on all 18 nodes, he would have to perform 180 pulls, which can now be reduced to only one, because the master microcontroller does a pre-aggregation (in the sense of consolidation) of the monitoring data and is extensible to do more pre-aggregation. This example shows the immense capabilities of a dedicated monitoring architecture, which can also (partly) be found in other multi-socket hardware solutions like blade centres.

In order to allow for monitoring the energy consumption of the infrastructure servers (which don't have integrated power meters), an external power meter can be installed in the environment as well. A similar type of microcontroller-based architecture is used for the power meter. We use power meters that can monitor five single power lines, two thermal sensors, as well as some additional digital and analogue signals. All this information can be read out with the help of a Nagios plugin, with only one pull, just like the RECS (Figure 3).

The novel monitoring technique of the Cluster System is realized by a dedicated master-slave microcontroller architecture that collects data from connected sensors and reads out the information that every mainboard provides via SMBus and I²C (as seen in Figure 3). The Cluster Server consists of 18 CPU-Modules in the COM Express design, each mounted on a baseboard. Each baseboard is equipped with a thermal and current sensor. At the current state, the system-specific metrics that can be captured are: The operation status of the mainboard, network-status, -speed and -activity, fan rotational speed and potentials on the mainboard itself. All sensor data are read out by one microcontroller per baseboard, acting as a slave and thus waiting to be pulled by the master microcontroller. The master microcontroller and the whole monitoring- and controlling capabilities are accessible to the user by a dedi-

Figure 3. RECS monitoring and controlling architecture

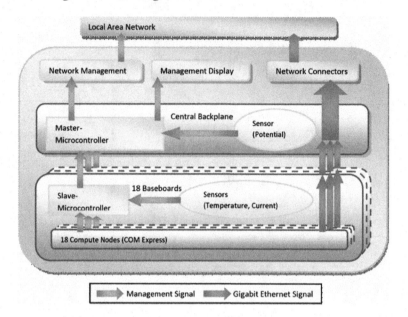

cated network port and additionally by a LCD display at the front of the server enclosure.

In addition to the monitoring approach, the described infrastructure can be used to control every single compute node. It is possible to switch each mainboard on and off, which is like virtually pressing the power- and reset-button of each mainboard. This enables the management framework to control more energy saving states of the hardware than possible with common systems, because the framework can wake up sleeping compute nodes and turn on completely switched-off nodes even if Wake-on-LAN is not supported by the mainboard. It is even possible to have a mixed setup of energy consumption, where some nodes are under full load, others are completely switched off, and some nodes are waiting in a low-energy state for computing tasks.

Proof of Concept in a Virtualised Environment

In the past we had the chance to test different types of energy-efficient management approaches on various hardware setups. In the following section we will present two different management approaches that gear towards very different use cases. The first one was developed on the basis of a complete virtualised infrastructure and the possibility of moving VMs from one host to another via live migration, shutting down and starting hosts as needed. The second one was developed within the research project GAMES (see www.green-datacenters.eu) that is funded by the European Commission, and examines the impact of IT energy consumption in medium and large organizations from a holistic perspective. The goal of the GAMES project is to develop methodologies, models and tools to reduce the environmental impact of such systems. The basis (and at the same time a typical use case) for the development of the second test are High Performance Computing (HPC) environments, which usually refuse to use virtualisation because of a slight performance loss. For the first implementation within the virtualized environment, we chose only a few metrics for data mining and the scheduler, which led to a simple proof-of-concept implementation:

- Actual and average CPU usage of every host and VM
- Actual and average memory usage of every host and VM

- Actual and average overall system load (consisting of CPU & IO usage) of every host and VM

The implementation was based on a scheduler on the basis of principles described in a section of "Management approaches to improve the energy-efficiency": First the VMs were packed together onto a few hosts and then free hosts were shut down. In case of an increasing workload, a new host was booted up and one or more VMs were migrated to that host. As already mentioned, this was only a proof-of-concept implementation that had various issues remaining that would render it insufficient for real-world scenarios. The monitoring, data mining and scheduler had a frequency of five minutes, which appeared to be a good trade-off between responsiveness for the user, execution time for actions and additional load induced by the management. A faster interval would have led to more responsiveness, but might also have induced a lot more management overhead due to overly short monitoring intervals and too fast actions. The migration of a VM took usually 1-4 minutes and thus was just inside the management interval. A slower interval might have been too slow for a user-driven environment.

In the testbed, this management ran on 10 Linux servers with Proxmox installed. Proxmox is a web-based open source virtualisation and cluster management suite that has no automation for any kind of VM management. Nagios was used as a monitoring solution, running in its default five-minute cycle. To gather all necessary data, some Nagios plugins were developed. Additionally to the 10 servers, there was a central Network Attached Storage (NAS), where the virtual hard drives of the VMs were located. All components were connected through a Gigabit Ethernet LAN. The measured time was about 6.6 hours (=79 management cycles) and after the 40th Cycle, the management was activated. The results can be seen in Figure 4. Right at the beginning, the average power usage was about 415 Watts for all 10

servers. After the initial start of the management, a slight increase can be observed, which is caused by the additional load through the migration of the VMs. After some cycles, enough migrations were executed to shut down one host. This led to a drop of the required energy to roughly 400 Watts – another host was shut down at cycle Nr. 64, which led again to an energy usage drop to about 375 Watts for all 10 servers. Through the use of this very simple management implementation, the energy-efficiency of the first testbed could be improved by about 10% even in an actively used server setting. If the servers were used to a lesser extent, the improvement would have been even higher, a general possible improvement from 10%-20% even in highly used environments can be assumed if the management is completely implemented and well equilibrated.

Proof of Concept in a HPC Environment

The second implementation of an energy-efficient management was tested within a HPC environment (which was described in 2010 in GAMES D7.4), where all compute jobs run directly on the hardware, without virtualisation.

The possibility of managing a HPC environment in an energy-efficient way is quite different than managing a virtualized environment. Cluster computer systems used for HPC run compute tasks directly, but are usually not utilized all of the time. During the time the systems are not utilized, there is the chance to lower the energy consumption by putting as many system resources into a low-energy state as possible. Depending on the specific hardware, these are usually different p-states of the CPUs and sometimes the local hard drives.

Besides the fact that the HPC test case lacks a virtualisation layer, there is another major difference. The first test case used the global knowledge of all VMs and hosts to make a decision, the impacts of which are globally ideal. The second test case monitors only one local host and reacts

Figure 4. Measured energy consumption with and without management

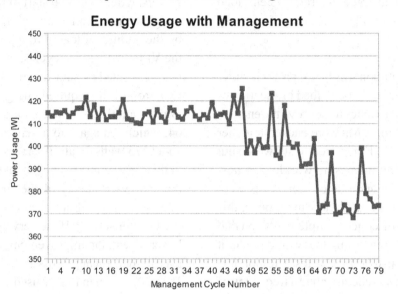

the Green Performance Indicators in GAMES D2.1 (2010) that allow for an extensive analysis and optimisation of the respective hardware and software settings.

The example testbed, consisting of the 18 node cluster server RECS, is also monitored by a Nagios instance that stores the data to a data base. In the GAMES project, this was carried out with the help of an energy sensing and monitoring interface (ESMI), which is described in GAMES D5.1 (2010). Its goal is to enhance the limited capabilities of monitoring solutions like Nagios. The initial monitoring data set on energy consumption can be composed of the following metrics:

to its workload very quickly, but lacks the global view. The reason for this is simple: In a HPC environment there is no possibility to manage the workload globally without access to the compute queue scheduler. Two assumptions can be made. First, usually these schedulers simply deploy the pending compute tasks to the computers that are available. Second, only one compute task runs on one computer at the same time. So the scope of action for the energy-efficient management is restricted to one computer and the possibility to be triggered by the queue scheduler when insufficient resources are available. Therefore this management is called a local control loop, whereas the management of the first test case is a global control loop.

In this second test case, much more monitoring information is available for the local control loop than for the global control loop in the first test case, because of the special hardware. The fine grain monitoring solution of the 18 node cluster server RECS that was presented above is the backbone for this kind of analysis and optimisation of the environment in order to achieve specific goals like high energy efficiency. This monitored information can be used to compute

- Mainboard Temperature of each single mainboard
- Central input voltage, which is the same for all installed compute nodes
- Power consumption (in Watts) of each compute node
- Status of the Mainboard: on or off
- CPU occupation of a compute node including %user, %nice, %system, %iowait and %idle values
- Memory usage of a compute node

- Resource usage of the simulation process, including its CPU Usage, Memory Usage and CPU time

The first four values in particular are measured directly from the master microcontroller of the RECS through one single pull by using a developed Nagios plugin. The output of the collected information of the related plugin is structured as follows in Box 1:

The last three values are measured in a traditional way by using three different Nagios plugins running on the Linux OS which forms the basis for the compute nodes. It has to be noted that the data that is monitored here is only a sub-set of what is possible with today's monitoring techniques. Other metrics like Storage Usage or I/Os per second (which can be relevant, in particular for HPC environments), are also available, but not necessary for this evaluation.

In the previously introduced research project GAMES, two types of local control loops (LCLs) for the HPC use case were evaluated, namely a fuzzy logic and a bio-inspired local control loop, which are described in detail in GAMES D4.1 (2010). The general idea of both implementations is that the energy consumption optimization process can be achieved by identifying the server's over-provisioned hardware resources and executing Dynamic Frequency Scaling (DFS) actions to the CPUs to put them into low-power states. In order to build a baseline to compare the impact of the GAMES framework with respect to the entire energy consumption, the evaluation results of the HPC use case execution have to be reflected first, without enabling the GAMES framework. The explicit description of the HPC usage case, including the theoretical background and its computing characteristics, is presented in GAMES D7.2 (2010).

For the evaluation of the GAMES local control loops, we applied three different scenarios, namely the execution of the simulation without any controller, as well as with the local control loops implementing different internal reasoning, learning and decision taking mechanisms. In order to assess the differences between executions using different local control loops, the following aspects of the IT environment have been monitored and evaluated:

- Power consumption (using the system energy usage metric)
- CPU usage (using the CPU usage metric)
- CPU frequency (monitoring the frequency mode of the CPU)

These three aspects allow for a performance assessment of the energy-aware controllers. Furthermore, in order to eliminate the influences of unknown factors and disturbances, the trial has been executed five times for each use case, with same computational conditions. The results are the mean values of these five executions. Through the nature of the used cancellous bone simulation process, described in GAMES D7.2 in 2010, it was not predictable when a specific computing node got occupied by a certain compute job, although the

Box 1. Plugin output

```
{OK, all 18 boards available|
nr_boards=18|
boards_status=1;1;1;1;1;1;1;1;1;1;1;1;1;1;1;1;1;1|
boards_temp=31;27;28;28;26;27;27;26;28;33;32;33;31;31;30;30;30;30|
central_voltage=11.78|
boards_power=23;24;24;21;21;19;21;19;18;11;20;14;16;13;16;17;16;26}
```

same computation has been executed in all cases. By taking into account the mean values for the entire cluster, this effect is also considered within our measurement, making sure that the following evaluation results allow a good comparison of the corresponding execution modes. Figure 5 depicts the CPU behaviour and the related power consumption of the entire cluster without any power management.

For the evaluation, we considered the mean values of all test runs with one specific setting by measuring the entire cluster. Since the data (particularly in regard to power consumption as seen in Figure 6) has been measured in a real time environment by physical sensors and plugins, the measurement deviation has to be taken into account. For this reason, we employed the Standard Error (SE) to estimate the possible measurement error and give a scope of the error for processing data. The influences of both controllers can be evaluated more precisely with consideration of the SE. A detailed overview about the measured values is given in GAMES D7.4 (2010).

In Figure 6 the average power consumption of the GAMES cluster without any LCL is com-

pared to both management implementations. The comparisons regarding CPU Usage/Frequency are left out because they are very implementation-specific and don't have a vivid meaning. In addition, the power consumption is the main criterion for assessing the performance of controllers in order to compare the effectiveness of the different settings. We determined that there are different phases in the simulation process, where the local control loops show a better behaviour in order to achieve improved energy efficiency compared to the normal optimisation done by the Linux operating system's own power scheduler. There are also phases where the LCLs show less energy-efficiency. This fact can be explained when dividing Figure 6 in two parts: In the first 45 minutes, a high-load scenario can be observed, whereas the second part obviously shows a low-load scenario. The LCLs are designed with typical HPC scenarios in mind, where medium-load scenarios are very rare. In high-load scenarios, the servers are expected to offer a maximum compute capability, whereas in the low-load scenarios very low energy consumption is expected. The LCLs meet these demands, which leads to higher energy

Figure 5. CPU behaviour and power consumption without LCLs

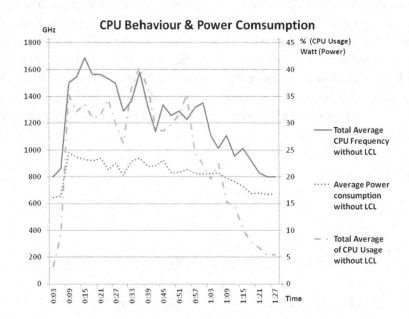

Figure 6. Average power consumption of the HPC testcase with and without LCLs

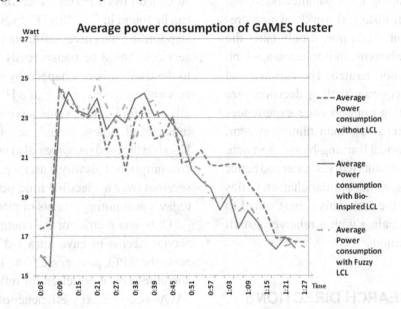

consumption in high-load scenarios and lower energy consumption in low-load scenarios compared to the default Linux power scheduler.

The average power consumption of the entire evaluation (with the local control loops) is as follows:

- Without local control loops: 20.61 Watts per node. The standard error is 4.17%
- With Fuzzy Logic Controller, 20.45 Watts per node. The standard error is 4.20%
- With Bio-inspired Controller, 20.56 Watts per node. The standard error is 4.04%

Although this evaluation shows just a small improvement of the overall energy efficiency, some aspects were determined that can be enacted as Green Actions, which will be described in the following paragraphs. They allow us to improve the entire energy efficiency for the second release of the local control loops within the GAMES project.

Both LCLs try to reduce the servers' high energy consumption by adjusting the CPUs' p-states according to the actual workload variation. As comparisons with other hardware have shown,

the Local Control Loops' energy-saving potential is directly influenced by the number of p-states that the servers' CPUs offer. As a consequence, a higher number of power states will enable the LCLs to be more accurate at controlling the CPUs power consumption, which will consequently result in more energy savings. The processors that were used in the HPC testbed were Intel P8400, which have only three p-states. As was already mentioned, modern CPUs have up to 12 p-states, which will be evaluated in the second trials.

Another potential optimization can be achieved by making the local management aware of the workload dependencies and predictability of specific HPC use cases. In this approach, when one LCL decides to change a processor's p-state, it will also take into account the state of the neighbouring dependent processors. For example, if a server's processor is treated intensively, it might be highly probable that other processors will also be used immediately. Thus all neighbour processors will be pushed to the highest p-state, preparing for the emerging calculation jobs.

Both LCLs have individual capabilities for improvement. The Fuzzy Logic LCL will be enhanced by changing some parameters, so that it takes more of the historical workload measurements into account. Right now it only takes the current and last measurements into account, which seems to be too short-termed. The Bio-inspired LCL dynamic frequency-scaling decisions are gathered by learning from previous experiences in a similar manner to the human immune system. Through this historical learning-based approach, the energy savings results will get better and better the more workloads with similar characteristics have appeared in the past. This is best suited to a HPC use case dealing with a relatively small number of applications.

FUTURE RESEARCH DIRECTIONS

In general, the future of computing will be influenced by energy-efficiency for the next decades. As the development of new applications focuses more and more on a wide variety of mobile devices, which do not have the resources to host applications themselves, many applications will run remote in a data centre. This is one reason why the need for more computing power in data centres will grow significantly. The efforts to reduce the overall energy consumption (and thus the costs of servers) will surely be one of the main goals of the server hardware suppliers, data centre management software developers and data centre owners. To effectively reduce energy consumption, all possibilities have to be exhausted.

We are sure that effective monitoring and controlling is one of the key technologies (besides virtualisation) to reach a high load of all servers, which is necessary for high energy-efficiency.

Future research and development can concentrate on a lot of different aspects in this area.

Already development and published metrics for energy-efficiency are a first starting point to sensitise data centre's personnel to energy-efficiency. One of the outcomes of the GAMES project is the development of such metrics. A description of the

so called Green Performance Indicators (GPIs) can be found in GAMES D2.1 (2010). To go one step further, the energy-efficiency of servers and services should be transparently communicated to the user. This can happen by redesigning the accounting. Today, a user of a HPC service usually pays for booking some servers for a specified time period. A new, flexible accounting could be based on the used resources, also including energy consumption. This way, a user would pay for used services over a specified time period, similar to today's accounting models of cloud services.

Only one metric for the energy-efficiency of servers seems to have attracted attention right now, the SPECpower_ssj2008. This metric has sometimes been criticised for reflecting only the JAVA-specific energy-efficiency of a server, which can not always be adapted to the performance of a file-, database-, print- or web-server. An extension of this benchmark to measure various load scenarios could solve this issue.

Focusing on management for high energy efficiency, a perfect solution should act transparently without user interaction and reach an optimum of energy efficiency while taking Quality of Service and Service Level Agreements into account. These requirements seem to be mostly fulfilled by Adaptive Computing's suite and also by VMware's DPM. In how far these solutions act optimal, or whether there is still room for improvements, can't be said without extensive tests. But usually there is still some room for improvements left in terms of achieved energy-efficiency and response. Both can most likely be enhanced by adding a workload prediction.

To be prepared for every possible kind of workload and to optimise the behaviour of the scheduling, management solutions must be self-learning. With the bio-inspired LCL, a first proof-of-concept implementation was introduced in this chapter. This approach has the advantage of being self-optimising and thus able to adapt to various scenarios quickly and without user interaction.

The integration of monitoring and controlling capabilities into the hardware itself is a further research field. Christmann's RECS can be seen as a proof-of-concept that allows for a fine-grain monitoring while reducing the network load significantly. An important step is the integration of the metrics available on the operation system level into the monitoring. These metrics, like the CPU usage, are of great importance, but still have to be measured in a traditional way. If they could also be measured through the microcontroller monitoring architecture, this would be a great benefit.

If the concept of the integrated Master-Slave microcontrollers is improved further, a complete management solution can be implemented on a hardware layer. Concrete examples to implement are variations of the Local Control Loops as described above. With this implementation on a hardware level, a self-optimising hardware would have been created.

The lifetime reduction that can be induced by power-cycling a server multiple times a day might also be an interesting research field, because as far as we know there is no scientific study about this relation. At least classical hard drives are known to have a limited resistance against power cycles, especially when they are several years old.

CONCLUSION

As mentioned in the introduction and the background paragraph, the increasing energy requirements of data centres become a serious problem. This was realized by data centre owners and distributors of commercial and open source software. Many approaches have been addressed in this chapter on how to create energy-efficient computer systems based on very different techniques and addressing various use cases. One key technology for improved energy efficiency is virtualisation, as it allows not only consolidating servers, but also to dynamically react on varying workloads, shutting down as many hosts as possible. Especially for the HPC environment, a dedicated and very

effective monitoring solution is necessary to avoid disturbing the computations. With the help of the microcontroller-based monitoring and controlling approach of the RECS, a basis was created to allow for a granular monitoring without interfering with the HPC goals. In different use cases and proof-of-concept implementations it was possible to show an increase in energy efficiency of up to 10%. Based on this increase, it is highly likely that an increase of up to 20% in energy efficiency is realistic for well-tested systems.

REFERENCES

Adaptive Computing. (2011). *Moab adaptive computing suite data sheet. Retrieved* March 1, 2012, from http://www.adaptivecomputing.com/docs/1450

Albers, S. (2010). Energy-efficient algorithms. *Communications of the ACM, 53.*

AMD. (2005). *AMD secure virtual machine architecture reference manual,* Rev. 3.01.

Arnone, D., Lazzaro, M., & Rossi, A. (2010). *GAMES deliverable 5.1 [GAMES D5.1], Specification of the ESMI interface.* Retrieved March 1, 2012, from http://www.green-datacenters.eu

Asanovic, K., Bodik, R., Catanzaro, B. C., Gebis, J. J., Husbands, P., et al. (2006). *The landscape of parallel computing research: A view from Berkeley.* Retrieved March 1, 2012, from http://www.eecs.berkeley.edu/Pubs/TechRpts/2006/EECS-2006-183.pdf

Bundesministerium für Umwelt, Naturschutz und Reaktorsicherheit (BMU). (2009). *Energieeffiziente Rechenzentren, Best-Practice-Beispiele aus Europa, USA und Asien.*

Christmann. (2009). *Description for resource efficient computing system* (RECS). Retrieved March 1, 2012, from http://shared.christmann.info/download/project-recs.pdf

Christmann. (2012). *Christmann website.* Retrieved March 1, 2012, from at http://christmann.info/

Commission of the European Communities (CEC). (2009). *Commission recommendation of 9.10.2009 on mobilising information and communications technologies to facilitate the transition to an energy-efficient, low-carbon economy.*

Deliverable, G. A. M. E. S. 7.4. (2011). *First GAMES trial results.* To appear on http://www.green-datacenters.eu

European Commission. (2010). *EU code of conduct for data centres.* Retrieved March 1, 2012, from http://re.jrc.ec.europa.eu/energyefficiency/html/standby_initiative_data_centers.htm

Irani, S., Sandeep, S., & Gupta, R. (2003). Strategies for dynamic power management in systems with multiple power-saving states. *ACM Transactions on Embedded Computing Systems, 2*(3), 325–346. doi:10.1145/860176.860180

Jiang, T., Kipp, A., et al. (2010). *Layered green performance indicators definition.* GAMES Deliverable 2.1 [DAMES D2.1]. Retrieved March 1, 2012, from http://www.green-datacenters.eu

Karlin, A. R., Manasse, M. S., McGeoch, L. A., & Owicki, S. S. (1994). Competitive randomized algorithms for nonuniform problems. *Algorithmica, 11*, 542–571. doi:10.1007/BF01189993

Kipp, A., Schubert, L., Liu, J., et al. (2011). Energy consumption optimisation in HPC service centres. *Proceedings of the Second International Conference on Parallel, Distributed, Grid and Cloud Computing for Engineering*, Ajaccio, Corsica, France, (pp. 1-16). Retrieved March 1, 2012, from http://www.ctresources.info/ccp/paper.html?id=6281

Koomey, J. (2008). Worldwide electricity used in data centers. *Environmental Research Letters, 3*(034008).

Koomey, J., Berard, S., Sanchez, M., & Wong, H. (2010). Stanford University implications of historical trends in the electrical efficiency of computing. *Annals of the History of Computing, 33*(3), 46–54. doi:10.1109/MAHC.2010.28

Kranzlmüller, D. (2011). *SuperMUC – PetaScale HPC at the Leibniz Supercomputing Centre* (LRZ). Retrieved March 1, 2012, from http://www.nm.ifi.lmu.de/~kranzlm/vortraege/2011-10-17%20Linz%20-%20SuperMUC%20-%20PetaScale%20HPC%20at%20the%20Leibniz%20Supercomputing%20Centre.pdf

Liu, J., Kipp, A., Arnone, D., vor dem Berge, M., et al. (2010). *Validation scenarios.* GAMES Deliverable 7.2 [GAMES D7.2]. Retrieved March 1, 2012, from http://www.green-datacenters.eu

Moore, G. E. (1965). Cramming more components onto integrated circuits. *Electronics Magazine, 4.* openQRM. (2012). *OpenQRM website.* Retrieved March 1, 2012, from http://www.openqrm.com/

Patterson, M. K. (2008). The effect of data center temperature on energy efficiency. *Thermal and Thermomechanical Phenomena in Electronic Systems, ITHERM, 2008.* doi:10.1109/ITHERM.2008.4544393

Patterson, M. K. (2009). *Data center energy: Going forward.* The Green Grid Technical Forum.

Patterson, M. K., & Fenwick, D. (2008). *The state of data center cooling.* Retrieved March 1, 2012, from ftp://download.intel.com/technology/EEP/data-center-efficiency/state-of-date-center-cooling.pdf

Rasmussen, N. (2011). *Eco-mode: Benefits and risks of energy-saving modes of UPS operation.* Retrieved March 1, 2012, from http://www.apc.com/whitepaper?wp=157

Rodríguez-Haro, F., Freitag, F., & Navarro, L. (2009). Enhancing virtual environments with QoS aware resource management. *Annales des Télécommunications, 64,* 289–303. doi:10.1007/s12243-009-0106-1

Salomie, I., Cioara, T., Anghel, I., et al. (2010). *Run-time energy-aware adaptivity model.* GAMES Deliverable 4.1 [GAMES D4.1]. To appear on http://www.green-datacenters.eu

SPEC. (2008). *SPECpower_ssj2008 description.* Retrieved March 1, 2012, from http://www.spec.org/power_ssj2008/index.html

SPEC. (2008-2010). *All published SPECpower_ssj2008 results.* Retrieved March 1, 2012, from http://www.spec.org/power-ssj2008/results/power-ssj2008.html

The Climate Group on behalf of the Global eSustainability Initiative GeSI [Climate Group]. (2008). *SMART 2020: Enabling the low carbon economy in the information age.*

VMware. (2010). *VMware distributed power management: Concepts and usage.* Retrieved March 1, 2012, from http://www.vmware.com/files/pdf/Distributed-Power-Management-vSphere.pdf

Chapter 7
High-End Storage

Isabel Schwerdtfeger
IBM, Germany

ABSTRACT

This chapter discusses the challenges high-end storage solutions will have with future demands. Due to heavy end-user demands for real-time processing of data access, this need must be addressed by high-end storage solutions. But what type of high-end storage solutions address this need and are suitable to ensure high performance write and retrieval of data in real-time from high-end storage infrastructures, including read and write access from digital archives? For this reason, this chapter reviews a few disk and tape solutions as well as combined disk- and tape storage solutions. The review on the different storage solutions does not focus on compliance of data storage management, but on available commercial high-end systems, addressing scalability and performance requirements both for online storage and archives. High level requirements aid in identifying high-end storage system features and support Extreme Scale infrastructures for the amount of data that high-end storage systems will need to manage in future.

INTRODUCTION

Today, due to huge data growth, more digitization needs, mobile devices producing more data, faster supercomputer power and applications, end users expect to store and archive their data in real time and have continuous real-time access to that data. According to recent studies by IDC, the worldwide data volume in the year 2020 will be 35 Zettabytes (Erickson, 2010). Data growth is expected to increase by factor 45 compared to the existing volume. One Zettabyte is a one followed by 21 zeros. Keeping up with this fast-growing demand of user behavior of "self-service" real-time data access, common and established IT-infrastructures are put under stress. Storing everything on disks becomes too large to create a backup, which leads to long backup windows and

DOI: 10.4018/978-1-4666-2190-9.ch007

increasing energy costs for the power consumption of disks systems. This becomes even more critical to evaluate, if some data has to be stored for at least 10 years or longer.

This chapter describes some high-end storage systems for real-time processing and will describe storage solution scenarios. First, there will be an overview of high-end disk-based storage systems and the general characteristics of storage infrastructures. This part includes a short overview over the developments of hard disk drives (HDD) and introduces the alternative of Solid-state disks (SSD). As it is important what type of hardware technology is supporting high-end storage solution, it is also important to ensure data integrity in storage solutions; file system programs play a vital part of a storage solution for data integrity. A file system is necessary to enable access to data by file name or directory and needs to be able to directly access data regions on a storage device (Wikipedia.org, 2012). For the purpose of this analysis two worldwide well-known file systems programs, as characterized as distributed parallel fault-tolerant file systems, IBM General Parallel File Systems (GPFS) and Lustre, an open source file system, will be shortly described.

The second part covers high-end tape-based storage systems, while the third part discusses combined disk- and tape-based solutions, including high-end storage software for archiving and hierarchical storage management (HSM) solutions. As for Future analysis, it will be discussed how the project approach on "Pergamum", an approach for a only Disk-Based Archival Storage, is a viable alternative to Tape-only based for archival storage.

OVERVIEW OF HIGH-END STORAGE AND SOLUTIONS

High-End Disks and Disk Subsystems Overview

High-end disk systems exist in organizations and companies that need high performance and huge storage capacity. These types of complex storage infrastructures need solid management and often include features such as replication, virtualization and support for multiple storage tiers (Perkins, 2007). International Business Machines Corp. (IBM) has a broad range of storage systems available, addressing various needs for storage infrastructures, i.e., for open systems and optimized for z/OS and System i, for block-based or file-based storage infrastructures. The strategy of the IBM System Storage products is aligned to the need of delivering the right system "fit for purpose" for any workload.

High-end storage components are subject to the same characteristics as any storage solution. Therefore, the main characteristics of storage infrastructures are:

- Availability of overall storage infrastructure
- Backup and Recovery policies as well as existing data centre infrastructures to be included into the overall IT environment,
- Systems Management and Service Management tools in use,
- Performance criteria to be met by desired trough-put and end user expectations,
- Capacity planning and sizing to meet expected needs in data growth,

- Scalability in terms of horizontal or vertical scaling possibilities,
- Reliability in terms of data integrity,
- Security in terms of data protection and security measures,
- Service Level Agreements for sustained quality of service,
- Flexibility for the rate of changes and dynamic adaptation,
- Cost efficiency to the required storage infrastructure, and
- other.

High-end storage products are usually defined by research institutes, such as Gartner's Magic Quadrants, e.g., "Gartner Magic Quadrant Midrange and High-End Modular Disk Arrays" and naturally, from detailed information of the vendors about their product specifications in terms of capacity, performance and other characteristics. "Since the market's ability to absorb new technology, services and messages is limited, Magic Quadrants include both forward- and backward-looking evaluation criteria" (Luethy, 2011). Typical high-end systems from IBM are the IBM System Storage DS8000, IBM XIV Storage System series and IBM Scale Out Network Attach Storage (SONAS). The following Figure 1 shows the available vendors for high-end disk storage products, as of 2010:

To derive official, vendor-independent lists on high-end storage systems is difficult. Some can be found in official rankings for high-end storage disk products, either from research institutes or from official rankings such as "Product of the Year". According to the latest Storage magazine/SearchStorage.com *Quality Awards* for enterprise arrays ("NetApp tops-enterprise-arrays-field-

Figure 1. Gartner's magic quadrant for midrange and high-end modular disk arrays, November 2010

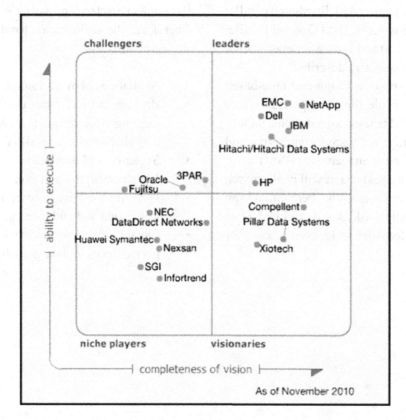

again", 2011), these are recently surveyed high-end disk and disks subsystems of different vendors available in 2010, providing a good overview on what disk systems are available for high-end disk storage:

- 3PAR InServ Storage Server T400/T800 or S400/S800
- EMC Symmetrix, DMX/DMX-3/DMX-4, V-Max
- Fujitsu Eternus DX8400/DX8700*
- Hewlett-Packard XP Series or StorageWorks P9000 Series
- Hitachi Data Systems USP/USP V/VSP Series
- IBM DS8000 Series or XIV Storage System
- NetApp FAS6000 Series or V6000

A typical characteristic of a high-end storage disk system is its capacity by single system. SONAS, e.g., is designed as a single global repository to manage multiple petabytes of storage and up to a billion files under a single file system securely and efficiently. It provides a policy-driven file lifecycle management, driven by a robust policy engine and automated storage tiering (disk and tape) for operational efficiency, ease of management and cost savings. The SONAS appliance, based on IBM General Parallel File System (GPFS) technology, is a clustered NAS solution that can scale from small size to a nearly unlimited number of nodes. A single SONAS appliance scales up to a billion files in a single file system, and up to 256 file systems. Assuming 2 TB disk drives, such a system has 14.4 petabytes (PB) of raw storage and billions of files in a single large file system (Lovelace, Boucher, Nayak, Neal, Razmuk, Sing, & Tarella, 2010). IBM announced on February 11, 2010 that SONAS is able to provide access to billions of files, no matter where they reside (Darcy, 2010).

However, the IBM System Storage DS8000 is also a high-end disk system, due to its innovative

and market-proven IBM POWER® microprocessors in dual two-way or dual four-way shared Symmetric Multi-Processor (SMP) complexes ("IBM System Storage DS8000 series", 2011), but it supports 5 TB to over 2,300 TB of physical capacity, upgradeable without system disruption. Compared to the SONAS appliance (in terms of capacity), the DS8000 appears to be small. However, the usage type for SONAS in storage infrastructures is different from using a DS8000.

We must differentiate between what storage network is in place and what type of data is being stored. If the main focus of the storage infrastructure is (for example) to support data from research experiments, it is to be expected to have lots of file sets, called unstructured files, so that it runs better via a file-based CIFS or NFS on a i.e., a SONAS appliance. In contrast, block-based sets of data exist, generated by multiple database servers of e.g., an SAP database infrastructure, that fits better on a e.g., DS8000 and is more concerned about the performance of the storage system. A disk subsystem is available throughout the network for all servers, and hence for its end users, when the disk subsystem is connected and uses an additional method that decides on either a file-based storage (via SMB/CIFS), NFS or a block-based storage via iSCSI/LUN/SAN, or one of the newer introduced methods with Fiber-Channel Over Ethernet (FCoE). For a high-end storage product such as the DS8000, this storage system can primarily store block-based structured data sets. Currently the DS8000 is one of the most capable disk systems in terms of Input/Output Operations per Second (IOPS).

Aspects of Hard-Disks Drive (HDD) and Solid-State Drive (SSD)

In 1956, IBM invented the first magnetic hard disk drive called "RAMAC" (Random Access Method of Accounting and Control). This was part of the computing system RAMAC 305 with its disks subsystem RAMAC 350. Over decades, all futures developments on hard disks, with their continuous objective to increase capacities, shorten access times, increase data transfer rates, but lower costs per stored megabytes (MB), were based on this invention. The velocity of the technological development of hard disks drives from 1956 until 2010 can be derived from the decline in price for one MB per Euro, as described in Table 1, following (Gerecke, 2010):

As of today, multiple types of hard disk technologies are available in either 2,5" or 3,5" form, as follows: Advanced Technology Attachment (ATA), Serial ATA (SATA)[1], Serial Attached SCSI (SAS), Fibre-Channel (FC)-disks. Without the discovery of the Giant Magneto resistance effect, discovered in 1988, and with the acknowledgement of the Nobel Prize award in physics in 2007 for Peter Gruenberg from KFA Juelich and Albert Fern from University of Paris, currently available hard disk capacities would never exist (Gerecke, 2010).

As real-time processing and fast access (as well as high performance) is the key for certain high-end storage solutions, this increases the demand for the recently developed Solid-State Drives (SSD) that are able to fulfill the demand for even faster read-and-write of data on storage systems. SSD use microchips which retain data in non-volatile memory chips and contain no moving parts. They are typically less susceptible to physical shock, silent, have lower access time and latency, but are more expensive per gigabyte (GB) (Solid-state drive, n.d.). SSD retail prices have decreased since 2007 in US-Dollar/GB compared to HDD by a sustained yearly price reduction of 50%, but SSD remain expensive compared to a 2,5" HDD by the factor 12 (Luethy, 2010).

To compare SSD vs. HDD, a couple of criteria must be taken into account. The read performance of SSD is different than that of a HDD. The read performance of SSD does not change based on where data is stored, while on HDD, if data is written in a fragmented way, reading back the data will have varying response times (Solid-state drive, n.d.). During demonstrations in advancements of high-end storage solutions, SSDs were able to demonstrate, using IBM General Parallel File System (GPFS) technology and parallel processing, to successfully scan 10 billion files in 43 minutes (Freitas, Slember, Sawdon, & Chiu, (2011). In context of high-end storage, SSDs have to be considered, despite the fact that they are expensive. According to the SNIA Organization, accurate and meaningful calculations of storage costs at the enterprise level must necessarily include more variables – one of the most important being performance (Ekker, Coughlin, & Handy, 2009, p.7)

Distributed Parallel Fault-Tolerant File Systems

Distributed and Fault-Tolerant Computing has been always a key topic for research and development. The file systems programs developed for storage systems are grouped in different categories: file system for disk-based file systems, distributed file systems, and special purpose file systems (Wikipedia.org, 2012). Starting with a local file system, over time, additional file systems appeared focusing on specialized requirements such as data

Table 1. Price development of hard disks drives, Gerecke 2010, p. 9

Year	1956	1964	1975	1987	1991	1997	2000	2006	2009
Euro/MB	12,000.00	8,000.00	70.00	12.00	9.00	1.00	0.25	0.015	0.0054 (FC Disk) 0.0025 (SATA)

sharing, remote file access, distributed file access, parallel file access, HPC, archiving, security, etc. Due to the dramatic growth of unstructured data, files as the basic unit for data containers are morphing into file objects (Harmer &Bandulet, 2011). Figure 2 shows in an applicable diagram, how file systems can be categorized.

This chapter focuses on high-end storage systems that only use network based file systems as for high performance and extreme scalability storage solutions. A network file system is any file system that supports sharing of files over a computer network protocol between one or more file system clients and a file system server (Harmer & Bandulet, 2011). Two major known network distributed file systems are Lustre, an open source based file system and GPFS from IBM. Lustre is one of the most widespread parallel file systems in modern HPC environments, but user must start to look for different support options, if it runs on Non-Oracle hardware (Snell, 2011). GPFS from IBM however, has a worldwide support organization to support users in their support needs, either remote or on-site. In specific HPC environments, GPFS and Lustre provide very similar performance for large cluster, though GPFS can be used for a wide variety of workload

for HPC as well as mission critical commercial applications. GPFS has a wide variety of features, extensive API support and support for 3rd part applications. If you need a large file system for high performance sequential data access you can use GPFS or Lustre (Hiegl, 2009).

The file system is a crucial part of any IT infrastructure. When the appropriate file system is selected, then the entire cluster is defined or the database, that runs the file system. In consequence, the support of the file system becomes more important than for the redundant installed hardware components (Hiegl, 2010). Future directions will focus on very fast and reliable parallel file systems with focus on the discussion from "Silent Data Corruption" vs. "End-to-End Data Integrity".

Tape-Based Systems for High-End Storage Infrastructures

Ideal for long-term storage of large amounts of data are tape technologies. Due to the availability of open standards with Linear Tape-Open (LTO) as magnetic tape data storage technology (originally developed in the late 1990s), it is accepted to archive long-term data. LTO-cartridges have a shelf live of 30 years. However, tape-based archi-

Figure 2. File system taxonomy, Harmer & Bandulet, 2011

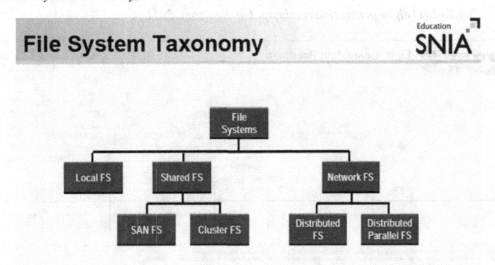

137

val systems suffer from poor random access performance, which prevents the use of inter-media redundancy techniques and auditing, and requires the preservation of legacy hardware (Techrepublic.com, 2011). In contrast, many disk-based systems are ill-suited for long-term storage, because their high energy demands and management requirements make them cost-ineffective for archival purposes (Techrepublic.com, 2011). Therefore, tape technologies must be considered, especially to address the huge requirements in data growth.

Today, tape systems are primarily used for backup and disaster recovery, as well as for long-term archiving. Tape storage is intended for data protection and long term retention. IBM invented the concept of magnetic tape computer storage back in 1952 and continues to lead the industry in tape innovation. Due to the standard specification of LTO, starting as LTO-Tape technology 2000, Ultrium 1, with 100GB native capacity on single-tape cartridges, was increased to 200GB in 2003 as LTO-2 (Gerecke, 2010), up to the fifth generation of LTO-5 in 2010. Tape has remained solid and reliable for more than a decade. The third generation of LTO-3 in 2005 included not only the read/write-backward compatibility to former LTO generations, but also introduced WORM-cartridges: Write Once Read Many, a compliance-

relevant functionality to avoid overwriting or changing existing data on a tape cartridges. By 2011, LTO-5 is widely in use, as it provides very high storage capacity per tape cartridge. One tape cartridge provides native 1,5TB capacity, and when compressed then 3,2TB. Compressed capacities for the LTO-5 generation assume a compression ratio from 2:1. Figure 3 provides the storage capacity per LTO generation as well as the corresponding compression rate, known as the development of the Ultrium LTO Eight -Generation Roadmap. Ultrium is a consortium founded by Hewlett-Packard (HP), IBM and Quantum. The LTO Program was founded in 1997.

In current research studies, for example from the Data Mobility Group, tape is becoming *the new hot storage technology for 2011* (Martins, 2011). Due to tape being low in energy consumption and able to store massive capacities, tape becomes more relevant than ever (Martins, 2011).

Martins (2011) stated the following as a factor underlying this belief:

- Trends in data storage and information management.
- The traditional advantages of tape.
- Advances in tape technology increase performance, capacity, and reliability.

Figure 3. Ultrium LTO eight-generation roadmap, Ultrium.com, 2011

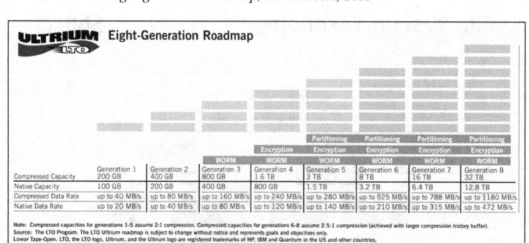

- A vibrant ecosystem of software solutions expanding the utility of tape.
- Tape is ideally suited for archive storage.

Tape plays a vital role in IT infrastructures for high-capacity storage backup. The unique tape attributes support storage requirements and is low in energy consumption.

According to IBM (2011) Tape is:

- **Removable:** store it away to help protect it from viruses, sabotage and other corruption
- **Scalable:** add more cartridges, not drives
- **Portable:** move it to another site to avoid destruction in the event the first site suffers threat or damage
- **Fast:** lightning fast — up to 280 megabytes per second (with 2:1 compression) for IBM's LTO® (Linear Tape-Open®) Generation 5 systems
- **Reliable:** trust IBM servo technology, read after write verification and advanced error correction systems, to help maintain reliable and dependable storage

Tape supports compliance requirements with its WORM applications, and it has a low total cost of ownership, costing up to 10 times less than disk (IBM Tape, 2011).

Combinations of Disk- and Tape-based Storage Infrastructures

Businesses value more and more archival data, so that storage tiering solutions receive greater attention, while IT budgets are squeezed or cut. If all data must be stored in the same high accessible type of hardware and on expensive high available storage technologies, or should it rather be classified according to usage access behavior and types of data? In order to derive how data is being used in an organization, a data classification model, supported by storage software, is being used to address these questions. This includes all types of storage technologies in place up to high-end hierarchical storage management (HSM) solutions. Data Management requirements are usually dependent on organizational specifics and applications used in these organizations. A large organization (in terms of high data volume and variety of applications generating lots of data) gets involved in high-end storage solutions, as various needs of data management solutions arise. These organizations need to address the growing needs for different characteristics of usage behavior, data integrity and archiving needs, to store long term data (if that data is of value for the organization), or must even put appropriate policies in place that allow the deletion of data and information after a certain period of time, to keep control of the overall storage infrastructure. One measure to achieve better control and overview is to conduct a data classification analysis, usually conducted as a consulting engagement.

According to Gartner (Couture, 2009), a typical investment of $50,000 to $100,000 in professional storage services, supported by tools and methods to analyze the current storage infrastructure, is able to free up wasted storage capacity, improves storage efficiency and avoids millions of dollars of new hardware acquisition costs, driving higher utilization of existing storage systems. Kemptner (2007, p.3) already put the basic principles for a storage infrastructure in place: It is always the first question what is to be stored, and the second question how and where. The type of data being stored decides the type of storage technology required for the storage infrastructure. One way to derive a solution for complex organizations with lots of data storage needs is to conduct a professional services engagement, e.g., an "Application-to-Infrastructure Alignment", available from IBM for example. It is the business and technical analysis of an environment to determine the 'right-tier' for each application from a storage and data protection perspective. The key is that the business department decides upon the value of the data and usage pattern, while technical requirements are linked to available storage technologies for the needed data usage pattern. IBM studies conducted by the "Application-to-Infrastructure" alignment study for "right-tiering" showed potential savings in engagements of ca. 11% by using different Storage-tiering.

"Right-tiering" within storage infrastructures cannot be accomplished without appropriate storage software technology. There are multiple software technologies available on the market. Only a few software products are highlighted (e.g. from IBM) that are available to either set up a tiered storage environment, control a tiered-storage environment, or enable the user directly with automated functions within the storage solution:

- IBM Tivoli Storage Productivity Center (TPC) for setting up a tiered storage infrastructure, used for data classification and monitoring.
- IBM Tivoli Storage Manager (TSM) for management and control of a tiered storage infrastructure including backup and archiving in addition to its HSM components.
- IBM SAN Volume Controller (SVC), a virtualization storage software to control and move freely among installed storage capacities including non-IBM storage hardware components.
- IBM General Parallel File System (GPFS), a clustered file system for high-performance and parallel computing for massive scale.
- High Performance Storage System (HPSS) is hierarchical file system software designed to manage and access many petabytes of data at high data rates.

In today's storage infrastructures, a smart combination of characteristics and usage of software tools as stated above is one of the key success criteria for obtaining storage efficiency and optimizing storage utilization, enabling organizations to quickly and dynamically adapt to changing environments. Performance, the cost of chosen storage solution and benefit to the organization and the IT- budget are among the main criteria for receiving a respectable storage infrastructure. This was frequently addressed by the introduction of a storage strategy based on "information lifecycle management" (ILM) for data management. Basically, storage technologies were used to accomplish that. However, rarely effective governance models and execution are lacking the sound implementation of an ILM strategy in many organizations. Storage optimization assessments and consulting engagements based on a proven methodology and with adequate software tools, analyze the organizational, technological and operational changes necessary to implement an ILM strategy. An ILM strategy is always accompanied by policies, processes, rules, regulations, and responsibilities. However, stringently implementing this in a large organization with different needs and behaviors is not a simple task.. In the past years, lots of ILM strategies have failed or only had minimal effects, so that organizations realized the need for analysis with emphasis on new rules for storage infrastructures. Technologies are widely available for all kinds of data management needs. However, what to combine for which use case is becoming the key question in a dynamically changing world.

High performance computing (HPC) usually demonstrates the potential advancements for new developments in general purpose IT at early stages. This also applies to IBM's GPFS history, which was originally developed in 1996 by Frank Schmuck and Roger Haskin, both working at IBM Research Almaden, San Jose, California. First was the "Tiger Shark" file system, which was then named GPFS in 1998. GPFS is a Shared-Disk File System for Large Computing Clusters (Kraemer, 2011, p. 6). By 2011, more than 20 clustered file systems have been developed (Kraemer, 2011, p.8), all addressing the basic need to move data more efficiently among storage systems and infrastructures. Today, GPFS is part of many commercially available products, e.g., SONAS, which now addresses not only HPC customers, but also commercial organizations.

ILM tools in GPFS (Figure 4) allow you to define file level policies that determine where the data is physically stored regardless of its placement in the logical directory structure (Kraemer, 2011, p.23). Key benefits of GPFS are:

- One global file system namespace across a pool of independent storage
- Files in the same directory can be in different pools
- Files placed in storage pools at creation time using policies
- Files can be moved between pools for policy reasons

- Can be used for hierarchically arranged storage based on files
- Allows classification of data according to Service Level Agreements (SLAs)

According to IBM, GPFS already powers many of the world's largest scientific supercomputers and commercial applications, requiring high-speed access to large volumes of data such as:

- Digital media
- Engineering design
- Business intelligence
- Financial Analytics
- Seismic data processing
- Geographic information systems
- Scalable file serving

Figure 4. Information lifecycle management with GPFS, IBM, 2010

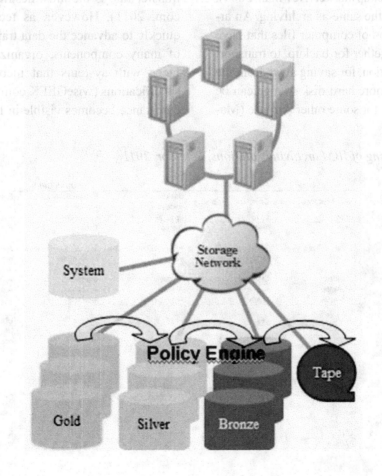

Actually, GPFS includes a policy engine to conduct ILM, however it does not include a HSM function without help of additional software like TSM. Its policy engine allows moving data from high-end storage to low-end storage within disk systems. However, to combine it with tape infrastructures, TSM is needed to deploy a combined disk- and tape based infrastructure. In contrast, HPSS includes the functionality to read and write directly through the storage network between end users' computer networks, directly to the data on tape and on disks in parallel.

However, combinations of disk and tape storage infrastructures do not fulfill the requirement of fast writing and retrieval access to data at an adequate speed, as today's end users require "real-time" processing and availability. De-duplication means reducing the amount of data even further, because de-duplication technology is now commonplace in the backup market (Newman, 2009). But backup is not the same as archiving. An archive is a collection of computer files that have been packaged together for backup, to transport to some other location, for saving away from the computer so that more hard disk storage can be made available, or for some other purpose (Mahendra, 1998). An archive can include a simple list of files or files organized under a directory or catalog structure (depending on how a particular program supports archiving) (Mahendra, 1998).

For archiving needs, Figure 5 shows eleven requirements and possible archive solutions from IBM. The products and solutions are: IBM NSeries, IBM Information Archive (IA), IBM TSM and Tivoli Storage Manager for Space Management (TSM/HSM), SONAS with GPFS, and HPSS. According to the type of archiving requirement and scenario, Figure 5 describes what storage solution is applicable and possible to select. As for high-end storage, the solutions SONAS and HPSS are to be considered.

How fast data from applications is running is defined by its data transfer rate to the storage infrastructure. In a world where programs and files are becoming ever larger, the highest data transfer rate is the most desirable (wiseGEEK. com, 2011). However, as technology moves quickly to advance the data transfer rate (DTR) of many components, organizations are often faced with systems that incorporate varying specifications (wiseGEEK.com, 2011). This circumstance becomes visible in Figure 4. DTR is

Figure 5. Positioning of IBM archiving solutions, Schnoor, 2011

Requirement	nSeries	IA	TSM	SONAS/GPFS	HPSS
1. Customer need	NAS Appliance	Compliance Appliance	Backup & File Repository	Extrem Scale NAS Appliance	Extreme Scale HSM (inkl GPFS Support)
2. Maximum Capacity	up to 2PB	up to 304TB	up to 3PB	up to 14PB	Extreme (over 100 PB)
3. Maximum Bandwith	limited	limited	limited	Extreme	Extreme
	~ max. I/O of a single server	~ max. I/O of Server (up to 3 within appliance)	~ max. I/O of a single server	900 MB/s per node: up to 30 nodes	1000(s) MB/s per mover, over 100 movers
4. Availability					
- No Single Point of Failure	Standard	Standard	Available	Standard	Available
- High Availability	Available	Available	Available	Available	Available
- Data Mirroring	Available	Available	Available	Available	Available
5. Security					
- Authentification	yes	yes	yes	yes	UNIX, Kerberos
- Autorisation	yes	yes	yes	yes	UNIX, DES
- Compliance	SnapLock	SSAM/WORM	SSAM/WORM	no	no
6. Interfaces	CIFS, NFS	TSM-API, NFS	TSM-API	CIFS, NFS, SFTP	FTP, PFTP, HPSS-API, RHEL-VFS (CIFS, NFS, SFTP, HTTP), GPFS, div. 3rd Party
7. Storage Media	Disk	Disk, Tape, Optical	Disk, Tape, Optical	Disk, Tape and Optical via TSM only	Disk, Tape
8. Storage Hierachies	no	yes	yes	yes	yes
9. Hardware Independent	no	no	yes	no	yes
10. Storage Solutions OS	ONTAP	RHEL	multiple	RHEL	RHEL, AIX
11. Client OS	multiple	multiple	multiple	multiple	multiple

the speed at which data can be transmitted between devices. This is sometimes referred to as through-put (wiseGEEK.com, 2011). The data transfer rate of a device is often expressed in kilobits or megabits per second, abbreviated as kbps and mbps respectively. It might also be expressed in kilobytes and megabytes, or KB/sec and MB/sec (wiseGEEK.com, 2011).

Disk-Based Archival Storage Research

Tape-based infrastructures are in some organizations and businesses sometimes not desired to use for archiving purposes or no experience is internally available so that the common use and usual behavior to store everything on disk systems is widely spread. Hence, developers and researches, seek in times where data volumes are growing also solutions that enable a pure Disk-based approach of archival storage. The project Pergamum represents one of this kind approach as it aims at replacing tape with an energy efficient, reliable disk-based archival storage solution (Storer, Greenan, Miller, & Vorugati, 2008). Based on the assumption that hard disk drives have dropped in prices relative to tape, Pergamum achieves via a network of intelligent, disk-based, storage appliances reliable data storage and energy- efficiency.

But in order to measure the entire benefits, it is necessary to take into account all costs associated with the storage infrastructure procurement and operations. The Total Cost of Ownership (TCO)/Performance not the unit Price/Performance is the key to value if to use a pure disk-based archival storage solution or a combined disk/tape-based archival storage solution. For a full TCO analysis the following aspects need to be considered, at least:

- Purchase price (balanced reliability, capacity and I/O)
- Recurring maintenance
- Power
- Cooling

- Administration / Management
- I/O Infrastructure to balance capacity and I/O requirements
- Footprint
- Site/specific and political...(Watson, 2009)

However, the approach by the Pergamum project aims more at due to better development of commoditized hardware components, to realize a significant cost savings by keeping the vast majority, as many as 95%, if the disks spun down while still providing reasonable performance and excellent reliability (Storer, Greenan, Miller, & Vorugati, 2008). The used technology in this project enables to greatly reduce the energy usage, but still requires certain overall different technology architecture for the storage system. Still being a research project at the Storage Systems Research Center at the University of California, Santa Cruz, Pergamum represents a revolutionary design for a cost effective, disk-based archival storage solution, but is not yet commercially available (Mottram, 2008).

CHALLENGES OF HIGH-END STORAGE FOR REAL-TIME PROCESSING

Real-Time Processing in High-End Storage

Real-time processing as defined by Wikipedia:

Each transaction in real-time processing is unique. It is not part of a group of transactions, even though those transactions are processed in the same manner. Transactions in real-time processing are stand-alone both in the entry to the system and also in the handling of output ("Transaction_processing_system", n.d.).

Figure 6 explores a simple idea: How to position each storage solution by its data volume to be stored into a single system ("high" as in greater than 15 PB, "low" as below 1 PB data volume), and by which favorable processing type ("batch" vs. "real-time"). This positioning does not account for the type of network used and assumes a standard file- size of ~ 160 MB (Hulen & Jaquette, 2011). This is an average file size for a typical HPSS installation.

All of these components can be positioned in entry, midrange or enterprise storage systems, and be enriched with so-called "Storage Optimizers", i.e., SAN Volume Controller (SVC), Easy Tier, or IBM Random Access Compression Engine (RACE). Storage and archiving strategies are defined by their usage requirements, either for compliance need, regular batch processing backup and archive (i.e., for databases, applications systems like SAP, Oracle, etc.), or for long-term archiving, including clustered HSM file repositories. One of the available HSM-clustered file repositories is HPSS for extreme-scale environments.

Quadrant A positions the storage systems and solutions that most apply for real-time processing and which are able to store more than 1 PB

per single system. Quadrant B positions storage systems and solutions that are rather batch-oriented as processing type of data. However, newer features in metadata management of the utilized relational databases will make these solutions more applicable for real-time processing. Quadrant C positions storage systems and solutions that have a lower possibility to store less than 1P and are more likely to be seen as "Storage Optimizers" and thus not applicable for long-term archiving, which needs storage solutions for high data volumes. Furthermore, Quadrant D positions NAS filer storage systems that have a high real-time processing capability, but lack the vertical scalability in storage capacity. In addition, RACE is an appliance in front of the Storage Area Network (SAN) and not used as a single storage system, rather reflecting a "Storage Optimizer" as described earlier.

High Performance Storage System (HPSS)

HPSS is Software that manages PB of data on disk and robotic tape libraries. HPSS provides

Figure 6. Positioning archive systems by data volume vs. processing type (batch vs. real-time), Schnoor, 2011

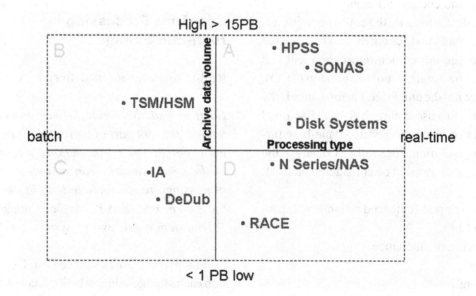

highly flexible and scalable hierarchical storage management that keeps more recently used data on the disk and older data on tape. HPSS uses cluster, LAN and/or SAN technology to aggregate the capacity and performance of many computers, disks, and tape drives into a single virtual file system of exceptional size and versatility (HPSS Collaboration.org, 2011). This approach enables HPSS to easily meet otherwise unachievable demands towards total storage capacity, file sizes, data rates, and number of stored objects (HPSS Collaboration.org, 2011). HPSS is known to be the leading archival storage software system for fulfilling extreme scale requirements (National Energy Research Scientific Computing (NERSC), 2009). Speeds are limited only by the underlying computers, networks, and storage devices. HPSS can manage parallel data transfers from multiple network-connected disk arrays at hundreds of megabytes per second. These capabilities enable new data-intensive applications such as high-definition digitized video, at rates sufficient to support real-time viewing (Hulen, n.d.). At the German Climate Computing Center (DKRZ, 2011), the implemented HPSS (as data archive) has an available bidirectional bandwidth of 3 GigaByte/s (sustained), and 5 GigaByte/s (peak). A central technological goal of HPSS is to move large files between storage devices and parallel or clustered computers at speeds many times faster than today's commercial storage system software products (Gerry, Hulen, Schaefer & Coyne, 2009).

HPSS supports striping to disk and tape (Figure 7). At 100 MB/s, it takes almost 3 hours to write a 1 TB file to a single tape. Using an 8-way tape stripe, that time is cut to less than 25 minutes (Gerry et al., 2009)! Commercially available 2,5" disks based on MLC chips, solid state storage featuring a SATA (3 Gb/sec.) interface, have data transfer rates of 150 MB/sec. (read) and 90 MB/sec. (write) (Logic Supply Inc., 2011). It must be differentiated between reading data and writing data to demonstrate real-time (or near real-time) data storage access. Writing data to storage is sometimes called "data ingestion" (H. Hulen, personal communication, June 17, 2011). A typical day of writing data to the archive at the European Centre for Medium-Range Weather Forecast (ECMWF) is ~ 42 TB (Richards & Dequenne, 2010). Reading from the archive is ~ 19TB per day (Richards & Dequenne, 2010).

The focus of HPSS is the network, not a single server processor as in conventional storage systems. HPSS provides servers and movers that can be distributed across a high performance network to provide scalability and parallelism. The basis for this architecture is the IEEE Mass Storage System Reference Model, Version 5 (Hulen, n.d.), see Figure 6. Once a transfer session is established, the actual data transfer takes place directly between the client and the storage device controller (Hulen, n.d.).

HPSS achieves high data transfer rates by eliminating overhead normally associated with data transfer operations. In general, HPSS servers establish transfer sessions, but are not involved in the actual transfer of data. For network-attached storage devices supporting IPI-3 third party transfer protocols, HPSS Movers deliver data at device speeds. For example, with a single HiPPI attached disk array supporting IPI-3 third party protocols, HPSS transfers a single data stream at over 50MB/sec (Hulen, n.d.).

The HPSS Application Program Interface (API) supports parallel or sequential access to storage devices by clients executing parallel or sequential applications. HPSS also provides a Parallel File Transfer Protocol. HPSS can even manage data transfers in situations where the number of data sources and destinations are different. Parallel data transfer is vital in situations that demand fast access to very large files (Hulen, n.d.).

Due to the fact that HPSS does not have volume-based licensing, the investment for such a high performance archiving solution is costly for the first year, but after it is in operation, the pay-off is clear, as only the costs for the tape library and media have to be calculated in future

Figure 7. Architecture of high performance storage system, HPSS-Collaboration.org, 2011

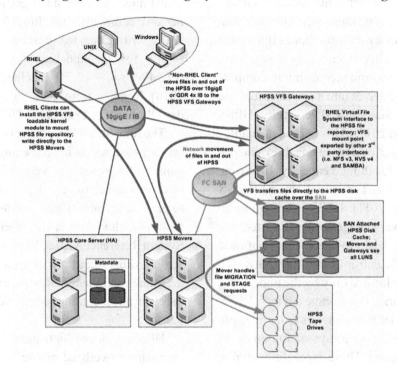

years. At the UK Met Office, the payoff of HPSS for research data was clear: In 2010, the archive size was approx. 3PB, but with a forecast to the year 2013 by 20PB (Francis, 2010), the UK Met Office needed a solution that supported Extreme Scale Computing, storing and keeping data as a central asset for research; but at the same time to be Energy efficient and affordable in the long term. The use of HPSS is thus technically and commercially attractive for this type of storage and archiving demands.

Solutions and Recommendations

Researchers get the brightest ideas, and with better equipment to analyze, research, discover, and exploit, the possibilities for new ways of developing fundamental experiments or create new simulations are promising. Due to this type of research, high amounts of data are generated and need to be stored and archived in large file systems. Real-time applications are common in

weather forecast, measuring seismic activity, applications for simulating new developments in airplanes, air traffic control systems, or railway switching systems, etc. In the future, due to new compression mechanisms, i.e., IBM RACE can perhaps reduce the Terabytes (TB) or even Petabytes (PB) managed in archives.

Hence it is made easier even for NAS environments to become applicable for long-term archiving. But for certain industries, i.e., for basic research organizations or governmental institutions, there is a clear need to grow in data by far more than 60 PB by 2016 (H. Weber, personal communication, February 22, 2011). Real-time compression may come in use for unstructured files and hence in use for NAS environments. Relating this to archives, real-time compression in primary storage may help reduce the amount of data to be archived, i.e., for databases, IBM Lotus Notes®, Text, CAD, or VMware VMDK files (IBM Systems and Technology Group, 2010), with a compression rate of up to 80 percent.

It is interesting that new and innovative results for commercial IT environments can often be derived from high performance computing and extreme scale environments. As a recent study by the German Federal Ministry of Education and Research shows, 43 percent of german businesses were participating in the first governmental subsidized research on developments in HPC-Software for scalable parallel computing (Bundesministerium für Bildung und Forschung (BMBF), 2009). The formed Gauss-Alliance fosters this necessary exchange of new results among businesses and research institutes, as of current, research organizations are developing the first petaflop HPC computing systems and exascale storage systems.

The recommended use of HPSS is for storing data sets that require high availability and need long-term storage. It is not intended for real-time access or short-term storage of temporary data [18]. Therefore, the team "near real-time" for HPSS is introduced by Harry Hulen, IBM Global Services – Federal, Houston, Texas (H. Hulen, personal communication, June 17, 2011). He describes the possibility of using HPSS for a near real-time application as follows:

"A good example of near-real-time data ingestion is when a scientific experiment is running and producing data that must be captured, such as a high energy physics experiment or a satellite that is sending down data that must be ingested and put on tape. There are two cases: "bursty" data that requires high rate ingestion for a period of time, and then stops for a while. In this case a disk cache usually takes care of the real time part of the problem, and then data migrates to tape when the burst of ingestion is complete. A tougher case is when there is a steady stream of data for a long period of time. In this case the tape system must operate at close to real time for a long period. An example of this kind of data would be the satellite that continually downlinks data.

Usually the read side of the problem is defined by response time and not data rate. If data is on disk and the storage system is not suffering from queuing, then the response is quick. The best example to think of is Yahoo or Google. If data has migrated to tape and then purged from disk, then the user may have to wait for minutes instead of seconds or sub-second responses. This reading of data is real-time, or near real-time, in the sense that the answer closely follows the interrogation; however, the terms "real time" and "near real time" are used less often for this type of transaction. A distributed system like HPSS are valuable for high data rate near real time data ingestion because a cluster can keep data flowing to more disks and tapes than a monolithic, single-computer storage system can manage.

When designing a tape system for near-real-time storage, it is necessary to accommodate the non-real-time characteristics of tape, particularly what happens when a tape is full. At that point the tape cartridge must be unmounted and another tape mounted. This process can take two to three minutes in a modern robotic tape library. There must be sufficient tape drives so that other tapes are waiting and ready to go, or there must be sufficient disk to catch and hold the ingested data. In any case, it is necessary to over-provision a near real time system when compared with a system that can gracefully allow longer queues to develop.

HPSS supports near-real-time data ingestion for both bursty data and steady state data with its distributed data mover architecture and its ability to write stripes of data across multiple tape drives."

FUTURE RESEARCH DIRECTIONS

The future is Exascale environments in combination with Extreme Scale archival storage, as petascale environments are currently in place. But how does this relate to the Extreme Scale archival storage? The challenge will be clearly achievable high data throughput and reliable metadata management. If IDCs projection that in the year 2020 the global data volume will be 35 Zettabytes is correct, then actual numbers and scientific research results should give a good future outlook on the coming developments. According to the Advanced Scientific Computing Advisory Committee (ASCAC) Subcommittee, Exascale computing is expected to start in 2018 (U.S. Department of Energy, 2010). However, scientific research already conducted by the U.S. Department of Energy (DOE) stated the need for Exascale archival storage (based on actual figures derived from their installed base) for the year 2015 (U.S. Department of Energy, 2009). Extreme Scale archival storage is needed to support Extreme Scale Computing, storing and keeping data as a central asset for research, but at the same time it must be energy-efficient and affordable in the long term. HPSS is poised to be one of those Extreme scale archival solutions to support this direction.

Within HPSS, file metadata is maintained in DB2, IBM's real-time database system (University Corporation for Atmospheric Research (UCAR), 2011). Furthermore, other major application domains such as real-time data collection also require such extreme-scale storage. The HPSS architecture and basic implementation built around a scalable relational database management system (IBM's DB2) is well positioned to take on this challenge (Boomer, Broussard, & Meseke, 2011).

First prototypes from the HPSS development team have shown that the new architecture provides 10x performance of the HPSS V7 single metadata server architecture (Boomer et al., 2011). Therefore, HPSS will accommodate both: End user expectations to have access to data in real-time

(or at least "near real-time") and store them long-term, and for IT-Managers, HPSS demonstrates a viable alternate disk and tape solution scenario, saving costs for future extreme-scale storage data growth requirements.

CONCLUSION

This chapter provided an overview of current high-end storage disk and tape systems as well as storage software solutions. As of today, these storage solutions are "high-end". But as society and the IT industry are confronted with further advancements and challenges, higher technological barriers must be overcome. Exascale is compelling for science and economic opportunities, and Extreme Scale storage solutions will become vital to support as early as possible, even before Exascale computing is deployed.

As digital data growth will remain "a stable fact" due to the end users' changed behavior, rising digitization requirements, increasing usage of mobile devices and applications spur off continuously. Researchers face a growing number of problems where experiments are impossible, dangerous, or inordinately costly (U.S. Department of Energy, 2010), providing enough reason to support the further development of high-end systems and high-end storage for future needs.

From the perspective of current high-end storage availability, the "highest-end" of storage solutions must be put front and center, to enhance in design, advance significantly in development for new storage products and spur creativity at unprecedented speed and fidelity (U.S. Department of Energy, 2010). Combinations of existing high-end storage systems and technologies support these future developments.

REFERENCES

Boomer, D., Broussard, K., & Meseke, M. (2011). *HPSS 8 metadata services evolution to meet the demands of extreme scale computing* [PDF document]. Retrieved June 26, 2011, from http://www.pdsi-scidac.org/events/PDSW10/resources/posters/HPSS8.pdf

Bundesministerium für Bildung und Forschung (BMBF). (2009). *Ergebnisse der ersten HPC-Fördermaßnahme, HPCSoftware für skalierbare Parallelrechner* [PDF document]. Retrieved June 23, 2011, from http://www.pt-it.pt-dlr.de/_media/HPC_Infoblatt.pdf

Couture, A. W. (2009). *Invest in storage professional services, not more hardware.* Gartner RAS Core Research Note G00165133. Retrieved October 18, 2011, from http://www.gartner.com/DisplayDocument?doc_cd=165133&ref=g_rss

Cox, R. W., Rinnen, P., Zaffos, S., & Chang, J. (2010, November 15). *Magic quadrant for midrange and high-end modular disk arrays.* Gartner RAS Core Research Note G00207396. Retrieved October 18, 2010, from http://www.gartner.com/technology/media-products/reprints/hitachi/vol3/article2/article2.html?WT.ac=us_hp_sp1r21&_p=v

Darcy, M. (2010, February 11). *IBM announces new scale-out storage system to access billions of files.* IBM Press Release. Retrieved October 16, 2010, from http://www-03.ibm.com/press/us/en/pressrelease/29786.wss#release

Deutsches Klimarechenzentrum (DKRZ). (2011). Data archive. Retrieved June 18, 2011, from http://www.dkrz.de/Klimarechner-en/datenarchiv

Ekker, N., Coughlin, T., & Handy, J. (2009). *Solid stat storage 101: An introduction to solid state storage,* (p. 7). Storage Networking Industry Association (SNIA). Retrieved October 18, 2011, from https://members.snia.org/apps/group_public/download.php/35796/SSSI%20Wht%20Paper%20Final.pdf

Erickson, T. (2010). *IDC prognostiziert 35 Zettabyte für das Jahr 2020.* SearchStorage.com. Retrieved October 18, 2011, from http://www.searchstorage.de/themenbereiche/management/daten/articles/262827/

File System. (n.d.). In *Wikipedia.* Retrieved January 22, 2012, from http://en.wikipedia.org/wiki/File_system

Francis, M. (2010). *High performance storage user forum* (HUF). UK Met Office, September 28, 2010, Hamburg, Germany.

Freitas, R., Slember, J., Sawdon, W., & Chiu, L. (2011). *GPFS scans 10 billion files in 43 minutes.* IBM Advanced Storage Laboratory, IBM Almaden Research Center, San Jose, CA [PDF document]. Retrieved October 18, 2011, from http://www.almaden.ibm.com/storagesystems/resources/GPFS-Violin-white-paper.pdf

Gerecke, K. (2010). *IBM systems storage-Kompendium.* Mainz, Germany: IBM Deutschland GmbH.

Gerry, J. A., Hulen, H., Schaefer, P., & Coyne, B. (2009). *High performance storage system overview* [PDF document]. Retrieved from http://www.hpss-collaboration.org/documents/HPSSIntroduction2009.pdf

Harmer, C., & Bandulet, C. (2011). *The file system evolution*, (p. 3). [PDF document]. Retrieved January 22, 2012, from http://www.snia.org/sites/default/education/tutorials/2011/fall/FileSystemsManagement/CraigHarmer_File_Systems_Evolution_v1-3.pdf

Hiegl, M. (May 5, 2009). *IBM general parallel file system*. Blog. Retrieved January 22, 2012, from https://www-304.ibm.com/connections/blogs/Martin_Hiegl/tags/gpfs?lang=en_us

Hiegl, M. (April 23, 2010). *Sun/Oracle bereitet das Ende von Lustre vor* [Blog]. Retrieved January 22, 2012, from https://www-304.ibm.com/connections/blogs/Martin_Hiegl/tags/gpfs?lang=en_us

HPSS Collaboration. org, (2010). *What is high performance storage system?* Retrieved June 18, 2011, from http://www.hpsscollaboration.org/index.shtml

http://science.energy.gov/~/media/ascr/ascac/pdf/reports/Exascale_subcommittee_report.pdf.

Hulen, H. (n.d.). *Basics of the high performance storage system* [PDF document]. Retrieved June 18, 2011, from http://www.isi.edu/~annc/classes/grid/papers/HPSS-Basics.pdf

Hulen, H., & Jaquette, G. (2011). *Operational concepts and methods for using RAIT in high availability tape archives* [PDF document]. Retrieved June 8, 2011, from http://www.storageconference.org/2011/Papers/MSST.Hulen.pdf

IBM System Storage DS8000 series. (2011). Retrieved October 16, 2011, from http://www-03.ibm.com/systems/storage/disk/ds8000/overview.html

IBM Systems and Technology. (2010). *Optimize storage capacity with IBM Real-time compression* [PDF document]. Retrieved June 18, 2011, from ftp://public.dhe.ibm.com/common/ssi/ecm/en/tsb03020usen/TSB03020USEN.PDF

Kemptner, H.-P. (2007). *Storage Architekturen – Datenmanagement im Mittelpunkt*, V3, (Unpublished). IBM Deutschland GmbH, Mainz.

Kraemer, F. (2011). *Advanced clustered and parallel storage system technologies in action* [PDF document]. Retrieved October 16, 2011, from http://www.linuxtag.org/2011/fileadmin/www.linuxtag.org/slides/Frank%20Kraemer%20-%20Advanced%20Clustered%20and%20Parallel%20Storage%20System%20Technologies%20in%20Action.pdf.

List of File System. (n.d.). In *Wikipedia*. Retrieved January 22, 2012, from http://en.wikipedia.org/wiki/List_of_file_systems#Distributed_parallel_fault-tolerant_file_systems

Logic Supply Inc. (2011). *Transcend commercial 2.5" SATA SSD, 64 GB*. Retrieved July 3, 2011, from http://www.logicsupply.com/products/64gssd25s_m

Lovelace, M., Boucher, V., Nayak, S., Neal, C., Razmuk, L., Sing, J., & Tarella, J. (2010, November 17). *IBM scale out network attached storage: Architecture, planning, and implementation basics*, (p. 9). IBM Redbook SG24-7875-00 [PDF document]. Retrieved October 16, 2011, from http://www.redbooks.ibm.com/redpieces/pdfs/sg247875.pdf

Luethy, R. (2010, December 17). *Price trends of HDDs Vs. SSDs*. Retrieved October 16, 2011, from http://rogerluethy.wordpress.com/2010/12/07/price-trends-of-hdds-vs-ssds/

Luethy, R. (2011, January 18). *Gartner magic quadrant midrange and high-end modular disk arrays*. Retrieved October 16, 2011, from http://rogerluethy.wordpress.com/2011/01/18/gartner-magic-quadrant-midrange-and-high-end-modular-disk-arrays/

Mahendra, J. (1998). *What is archive? Definition from "Whatis.com"*. Retrieved June 17, 2011, from http://searchstorage.techtarget.com/definition/archive

Martins, J. (2011, March 1). *The hot new storage technology for 2011 is... tape?* Data Mobility Group [PDF document]. Retrieved October 17, 2011, from http://public.dhe.ibm.com/common/ssi/ecm/en/tsl03052usen/TSL03052USEN.PDF

Mottram, B. (2008). *Pergamum – "New age" storage clustering takes aim at disk based archival storage, a brief.* [PDF Document]. Retrieved January 22, 2012, from http://www.veridictusassociates.com/images/Pergamum_Brief.pdf

National Energy Research Scientific Computing (NERSC) Facility. Extreme Scale Workshop. (2009). *HPSS in the extreme scale era* [PDF document]. Retrieved June 18, 2011, from http://www.nersc.gov/assets/HPC-Requirements-for-science/HPSSExtremeScaleFINALpublic.pdf

Newman, H. (2009). *LBL HPSS Workshop for DOE/SC, CTO/Instrumental Inc.,* July 2009.

Perkins, M. (2007). *High-end storage array specifications*. SearchStorage.com, Retrieved October 16, 2011, from http://searchstorage.techtarget.com/tutorial/High-end-storage-array-specifications

Richards, M., & Dequenne, F. (2010). *HPSS at ECMWF: High performance storage system user forum* (HUF), September 28, 2010, Hamburg, Germany.

Schnoor, I. (October 23, 2011). Real-time processing and archiving strategies. In *Proceedings International Conference on Advanced Communications and Computation* (INFOCOMP 2011), October 23-29, 2011, Barcelona, Spain, (pp. 155-160). ISBN: 978-1-61208-161-8

Snell, A. (April 8, 2011). *LSI und Whamcloud bieten gemeinsam Lustre Support Service für HPC Storagesysteme*. Press Release LSI Corp. Retrieved January 23, 2012, from http://www.lsi.com/emea/newsroom/Pages/ge_20110408pr.aspx

Solid-state drive. (n.d.). *Wikipedia, the free encyclopedia*. Retrieved October 16, 2011 from http://en.wikipedia.org/wiki/Solid-state_drive.

Storage magazine/SearchStorage.com (2011, March). *NetApp tops enterprise arrays field again*. Retrieved October 16, 2010, from http://searchstorage.techtarget.com/magazineContent/NetApp-tops-enterprise-arrays-field-again.

Storer, M. W., Greenan, K. M., Miller, E. L., & Voruganti, K. (2008, February). *Pergamum: Replacing tape with energy efficient, reliable, disk-based archival storage*. [PDF Document]. Retrieved January 22, 2012, from http://www.ssrc.ucsc.edu/Papers/storer-fast08.pdf

Tape, I. B. M. (2011). *Why IBM?* Retrieved October 16, 2011, from http://www-03.ibm.com/systems/storage/tape/why/index.html

Techrepublic.com. (2011). *Pergamum: Replacing tape with energy efficient, reliable, disk-based archival storage*. Retrieved June 17, 2011, from http://www.techrepublic.com/whitepapers/pergamum-replacing-tape-with-energy-efficient-reliable-disk-based-archival-storage/1294097.

Transaction_processing_system. (n.d.). *Wikipedia, the free encyclopaedia*. Retrieved June 17, 2011 from http://en.wikipedia.org/wiki/Transaction_processing_system

University Corporation for Atmospheric Research (UCAR). (2011). *CISL HPSS*. Retrieved June 18, 2011, from http://www2.cisl.ucar.edu/book/export/html/964

U.S. Department of Energy (DOE). (2009). *HPSS in the extreme scale era* [PDF document]. Retrieved October 19, 2011, from http://www.nersc.gov/assets/HPC-Requirements-for-Science/HPSSExtremeScaleFINALpublic.pdf

U.S. Department of Energy (DOE). (2010). *The opportunities and challenges of exascale computing* [PDF document]. Retrieved October 19, 2011, from

Watson, D. (2006). *Yes, Virginia, there is an HPSS in your future*. [PDF Document]. Retrieved January 24, 2012, from http://www.hpss-collaboration.org/documents/WatsonSalishan2007.pdf.

wiseGEEK.com. (2011). *What is data transfer rate?* Retrieved June 23, 2011, from http://www.wisegeek.com/what-is-datatransfer-rate.htm

KEY TERMS AND DEFINITIONS

Archive: A collection of computer files that have been packaged together for backup, to transport to some other location, for saving away from the computer so that more hard disk storage can be made available, or for some other purpose.

Backup: Making copies of data which may be used to restore the original after a data loss event.

Byte: Unit of digital information.

Exabyte: 1 EB = 1 000 000 000 000 000 000 B = 10^{18} bytes = 1 billion gigabytes = 1 million terabytes.

HPSS: High Performance Storage System.

HSM: Hierarchical Storage Management.

Petabyte: 1 PB = 1000 000 000 000 000 B = 10^{15} bytes = 1000 Terabytes.

Terabyte: 1000 Gigabytes.

Tier: In computer programming, the parts of a program can be distributed among several tiers, each located in a different computer in a network. Such a program is said to be tiered, multi-tier, or multi-tiered.

Zettabyte: 1,000,000,000,000,000,000,000 bytes = 10^{21} bytes.

ENDNOTES

[1] Enables higher data transfer rates than previous standard based on ATA.

Chapter 8
Encapsulation of Complex HPC Services

Alexander Kipp
High Performance Computing Center Stuttgart (HLRS),
Department Intelligent Service Infrastructures, Germany

Ralf Schneider
High Performance Computing Center Stuttgart, Germany

Lutz Schubert
High Performance Computing Center Stuttgart, Germany

ABSTRACT

Developing and providing complex IT services typically enforces the cooperation of several experts from different domains. Beside the domain specific knowledge of every involved expert this typically enforces a profound knowledge of the underlying IT service infrastructures. In this chapter, the authors show how a complex (HPC) IT service product can be provided in an easy-to-use fashion via a service virtualisation infrastructure by referring to a complex medical simulation use case. In particular, they highlight how such a complex IT service can be integrated in a holistic virtual organisation environment and show how different experts from different domains can concentrate on their specific domain whilst being enabled to take advantage of the services provided by other experts/domains in a SOA like fashion.

INTRODUCTION

Meanwhile the Internet has become an integral part of our everyday life. Beside the opportunity to use the Internet as a source for information it has become common to use the "Web" also as interaction platform for the provisioning of services. Furthermore, with the trend towards cloud computing the Internet has become additional attraction towards a communication platform allowing for the provisioning of almost any kind of resource by using the relevant communication standards. Taking into account this kind of infrastructure allowing integrating a wide range of services and resources, which might also be distributed all over the world, the concept of Virtual Organisations (VO) has been coming up at the beginning of the 21th century. These VO

DOI: 10.4018/978-1-4666-2190-9.ch008

models, like exemplary defined in (Dimitrakos et al., 2007), foresee to handle virtual resources, being typically made available via the Internet, to provide an aggregated, complex product consisting of different, orchestrated services. This approach has been considered in a large variety of research project, e.g. Akogrimo (Jähnert et al., 2010), BEinGRID, TrustCoM and BREIN (Taylor et al., 2009). In particular the enabling of such VOs towards a dynamic environment, allowing reacting by itself on unforeseen events, like e.g. the underperformance or the failure of a subcontracting service provider, has been considered within these research projects. However, the management of such dynamic environments, in particular taking into account the technical aspects that have to be considered e.g. when a service provider is replaced by another one, has been seen as one of the most challenging tasks. This is furthermore true for the internal management of resources within an organization. Enterprise Resource Planning (ERP) and Enterprise Application Integration (EAI) are getting more and more important for the efficient usage of the internally available resources, whilst facing similar challenges when operating a VO consisting of external services.

The conceptual solution for these issues has been faced with the upcoming of the Service Oriented Architecture (SOA) paradigm, which mapped the established and proven idea to provide standardised interfaces abstracting from the underlying realisation of the relevant functionality from electronic engineering to the software engineering world. To allow for this approach, web service technologies have been seen as the enabler for a real SOA in a distributed environment whilst being based on web technologies. However, this approach has only been successful in a limited way, since, due to a rank growth of a lot of relevant web service standards, the original goal, to decouple the interface definition from the related service implementation whilst enabling a service consumer by just invoking the relevant interface methods, has not been achieved. So far,

only technically versed people are able to realise processes based on web services or consume the relevant services. In particular taking into account the differing IT experience of users shows that the current available environment are not satisfying the concrete needs of the relevant users.

Within this chapter we are going to present an infrastructure allowing for the best suitable support for such kind of virtual organisations allowing for the provision of complex IT service products. Therefore, we are going to describe the concrete requirements for such an infrastructure by taking into account that cooperation between organisations is usually driven by the intention to optimise the mutual benefits. Typically cooperation between business entities takes place because each involved entity can benefit from the collaboration. Additionally, typically with the provision of a service according to expert knowledge is sold as well, because the underlying processes realising the relevant service are usually the essential part distinguishing service providers, e.g. one service provider can provide a specific service cheaper, or with better Quality of Service (QoS) properties than another one. So this knowledge about the structure of a service or a process can be seen as the competitive advantage between them.

In order to keep this advantage in comparison with his competitors a service provider usually wants to hide this details about how a service is provided from his customers, and in particular from his competitors. The provision of such specialised services usually requires also a specialised environment and specialised knowledge. In particular in High Performance Computing (HPC) environments a detailed knowledge of the relevant systems is of essential importance, because otherwise there will be a significant decrease of performance, and thus increase of the corresponding costs. However, most users of such infrastructures are not aware of the technologies they are using, and thus potentially wasting time and money.

Within this chapter we are going to show such a complex IT product by describing the process of a cancellous bone simulation whilst showing how such a complex service can be provided in an easy-to-use fashion via a service virtualisation infrastructure. This kind of simulation is a very complex process, requiring a lot of detailed knowledge about the computing infrastructure as well as the necessary setup. With this example we are going to show how such a complex process can be sold as an "IT product" by allowing for the virtualisation of the underlying infrastructure and environments, allowing finally for the invocation of the simulation process within a common workflow language, like e.g. the Business Process Execution Language (BPEL). This will allow in particular also users with little IT knowledge to consume such complex services, without the burden to acquire in a first instance a detailed knowledge about the corresponding environments. However, in some cases a user might require to know some details about the infrastructure in order to allow for a smooth execution of a service. This might be the case e.g. within HPC environments, where a user might want to know in detail how the system is working or be enabled to configure the system respectively to optimise the entire performance, whilst a "manager" typically just wants to run the service. In such a scenario differing pricing schemes would be provided, where the "premium" service allowing for a simple invocation by "hiding" the necessary knowledge within the user interface would be more expensive than a "native" service where the customer has to do most of the configurations and setups by themselves.

Finally, we are going to highlight how such a virtualisation environment allows for the provision of a real SOA environment, which has to be seen as the key-enabler for such kind of collaborations.

Therefore, we are analysing the specific requirement for scientific workflow environments, in particular with respect to common workflow languages and runtime environments, like be-

ing available for e.g. BPEL in the first instance. Afterwards, we are presenting a typical HPC usage case highlighting the complexity of such a service. In the following section we are reflecting how complex services can be orchestrated by applying a messaging infrastructure, namely the so-called Enterprise Service Bus. In the following section we are presenting briefly our virtualisation infrastructure and show, how this infrastructure can be applied to concrete environments in order to allow for a smooth integration of scientific workflow systems. Finally, we are showing how the previously presented simulation process can be encapsulated within a BPEL process by using a common visual design tool and are concluding this chapter with a summary.

RELATED WORK

In this section we are going to analyse the requirements for scientific workflows, and highlight, in how far the de-facto standard for workflows in the eBusiness domain, BPEL, can be used for such processes.

Requirements for Scientific Workflow Environments

Scientists are typically specialised for a specific domain and are not aware of the underlying IT and service infrastructure they are using for their experiments and simulations. However, since current environments enforces, in particular within the HPC and simulation domain, to have at least a basic knowledge of the relevant IT infrastructure and the software environments, scientists are often forced to gain this basic knowledge as well in addition to their specialised domain knowledge. However, this basic knowledge is typically not sufficient to execute the simulation processes in an optimal way, or to face specific problems within the IT infrastructure, e.g. if the environment does not behave as expected. This enforces the support of experts, which typically causes delays and inconveniences for both, the scientists as well as the system administrators. Therefore, it is sensible to allow for a decoupling of the infrastructure and the application logic, which is reflected in the scientist's applications and services. In particular, this decoupling allows for a professional management of the IT infrastructure environment, whilst scientists can concentrate on their research.

Furthermore, scientists are also interested in controlling the workflow execution, since, during the simulation, in particular in case of unforeseen phenomena, it is of interest to suspend, eventually change some parameters and resume the simulation. In addition, in case of such unforeseeable phenomena it is also of interest to extract the intermediary results.

Beside this, during execution of a simulation process, a refinement of the workflow structure might be required, due to the intermediary simulation results gained during the execution of the simulation. This evolution due to intermediary simulation results is due to the unforeseeable behaviour of specific materials or environments which are not predictable, and thus building the base for the need of such kind of simulations.

Another issue that have to be considered in the context of scientific simulation environments is that these processes are often characterised as long-running processes. Furthermore, the infrastructure of such HPC compute jobs is replaced periodically due to the fast development and improvement in the IT hardware sector. Due to this development allowing for better compute power by consuming less energy, typically after approximately 5 years the systems have to be replaced by new architectures, because the old systems do not allow for a sensible compute power in relation to the consumed energy, in particular with respect to continuously rising electric power prices and an increasing interest of the public in the energy consumption of such systems, especially with respect to the environmental impact. So, the ad-

aptation of IT infrastructure is a common issue, enforcing in current environments also an evolution of the related simulation environments due to changed hardware environments (e.g. new IT infrastructures allowing for some performance for a specific job whilst allowing for a better energy efficiency). Furthermore, in HPC environments often heterogeneous environments are provided in order to face the differing requirements of varying compute jobs, causing an additional overhead for the scientists in order to determine the optimal configuration for a specific job.

This idea of scientific workflows is not new. Actually, there are a lot of workflow management systems (WfMS) available. However, these approaches are typically specialised and thus limited to the specific domain, causing problems in case of collaborations within inter-disciplinary domains, like e.g. Taverna (Oinn et al, 2006), Pegasus (Deelman et al., 2004) or Triana (Shield & Taylor, 2006). A detailed overview about the specific features and specialities of these environments is given in (Görlach et al., 2011). In this domain, GriCol has been established as a reference language for scientific workflows (Currle-Linde et al, 2006). However, GriCol faces some gaps as the other mentioned frameworks.

Furthermore, in these environments scalability is also not well addressed. In addition, choreographies are not considered at all within scientific workflow environments. Choreographies allow for the assembling of different instances of workflows, in particular with respect to cross-domain collaborations (Görlach et al., 2011).

Another peculiarity of scientific workflows it that the required results are often achieved by several executions of the simulation process with varying parameters (parameter study) in a trial-and-error manner (Sonntag & Karastoyanova, 2010). This proceeding is due to the fact that for most real-world problems it is difficult to find a mathematical model in order to describe the entire problem statement. Therefore, simulations, in particular parameter studies, are executed in order to find the optimal solution by trying various different settings.

Once a result is achieved, it is also of significant importance to allow for the reproducibility of the achieved results, allowing for the traceability of the results at a later point in time.

Applying Common Workflow Description Languages to the Scientific Computing Domain

Simulation processes follow a well defined flow, which can be described within common workflow languages (Görlach et al., 2011). In particular, the de-facto standard for web service based workflows, namely BPEL, is in general usable for scientific workflows. The major target of common workflow environments is the automation of well defined processes, which maps theoretically to the principle of parameter studies. These studies are reflected by the execution of the same process with varying input parameters, until a specific goal is achieved.

Typically, within scientific processes large amounts of data have to get processed (Ludäscher et al., 2009), so the corresponding handling is a fundamental issue (Deelman & Chervenak, 2008). However, since BPEL mainly concentrates on the control flow but not on the data flow, BPEL shows some gaps with this respect. Namely, BPEL is missing the required support for the handling of large data sets at workflow level, pipelining, the sharing of data between different and potentially distributed instances, as well as different abstraction views on the corresponding data sets (Sonntag et al., 2010). In addition, these data sets are often of heterogeneous nature, so, in order to allow for the usage of a workflow engine in this context, the explicit passing of links between these data sets, as well as the potential mapping of the different data types, has to be integrated in a transparent way.

Within such environments, scientists typically act as modeller, user, administrator and analyst of the workflow (Görlach et al., 2011). Often, the development of scientific workflows is typically done in a "trial-and-error" manner, whilst these classical workflows describe the control flow of an application / process not considering the related data flow. The major gap here is that common workflow languages do not provide sensible mechanism to handle large datasets, which have to get processed during execution of the scientific workflow (Sonntag et al., 2010) (Deelman & Chervenak, 2008).

The mentioned workflow technologies are already established in the eBusiness domain, where the major focus relies on the description of well known processes. Due to the well-structured proceeding within simulation environments, allowing for an adaptation of these common established workflows technologies, the scientific community is getting more and more interested in workflow technologies (Deelman et al., 2009) (Taylor et al., 2007). These workflows, in particular in combination with a SOA based environment, allow for the execution of experiments within highly heterogeneous environments. In particular in HPC environments this is a very challenging issue, since within these environments typically a lot of different machines for different job types are involved.

This is due to the fact that specific simulations tend to run on specific platforms (hardware and software environment) differently, in particular with respect to the execution performance. So, it might be sensible to execute the different phases of a simulation process (which are described in detail for a specific simulation job in the following section) on different compute machines, eventually with different settings. This shows once again that for an optimal usage of the corresponding environments a fundamental knowledge of the underlying infrastructure is of essential importance, however, most scientists do not have this knowledge and are also not interested in gaining this knowledge. They typically prefer to focus on the development of their simulation processes, so an environment allowing scientists to concentrate on the design and the flow of the simulation process instead of the technical details of the environment is essential to face this issue.

Flexibility is crucial issue in scientific workflows as well. Due to changes in environments and the unpredictable and dynamic behaviour of the application, an environment for such simulation processes must be able to allow for the transparent usage of the corresponding resources. This required flexibility is twofold: on the one hand, an adjustment of the workflow itself might be necessary, due to received intermediary results, e.g. showing that specific branches of a simulation should be taken into account in more details. On the other hand, it might be necessary to adjust the service infrastructure, since it has been detected during execution that some processing steps could be performed in a more efficient way if being deployed on specific systems or by adapting the runtime environment respectively.

From a technical perspective, this issue can be faced by providing the HPC resources in a SOA like fashion. Therefore, an interoperable access to resources via web service technologies, namely the Web Service Description Language (WSDL) and SOAP, would allow in the first instance to enable an interoperable and more abstract access to the required resources by hiding, at least to some degree, the technical peculiarities of the underlying infrastructure. In the following, these resources can be orchestrated with state-of-the art workflow languages, like e.g. BPEL.

The transparent usage of workflow and service infrastructures requires an automated data transformation and service discovery, since common web service based environments do not allow for this due to the needed technical background. As discussed before, conventional scientific workflow languages are mainly data driven and are typically provided within a hybrid language.

In summary, scientific environments can benefit from the robustness of proven, common workflow technologies, in particular by taking advantage of the proven and grown integrated mechanisms for recovery, exception handling and flow control. However, most common scientific environments just allow for changing the input parameters, but not the server infrastructure.

BPEL is widely accepted in industry and research, enables also for the integration of legacy applications via web service interfaces. Furthermore, there is a broad tooling support, allowing for the visual design of workflows and thus make it quite easy to build up complex workflows. In particular the visual support allows also users with little IT background to model corresponding processes.

As it has been shown in (Akram, Meredith & Allan, 2006) BPEL can be applied for scientific workflows. The control flow capabilities of BPEL have already been discussed in this section. In order to close the remaining gaps with respect to the handling of large data sets in scientific workflow environments, an extension to BPEL has been announced, namely BPEL-D (Khalaf, 2007). The BPEL-D extension allows for the description of data dependencies (Khalaf, 2007) within BPEL processes. However, these dependencies are translated into standard BPEL before execution, so these dependencies are not available during runtime. This makes this approach not usable within dynamic environments at all. Another approach to handle big amounts of data in BPEL processes in described in (Wieland et al., 2009). This approach allows for the integration of references to datasets across web services. This approach enables to refer only the relevant data sets for a specific simulation, and thus allowing transferring only the required data sets to the corresponding compute nodes, if required. However, it is not described how these data sets should be transferred, in particular with respect to the transport protocol to be used for the data transfer, as well as how the data source should be accessed. Typically, this data is protected and thus, in order to access the data sets remotely, this information has to be provided as well.

An architecture for scientific workflow is described in (Görlach et al., 2011). The reference implementation currently relies on the apache AXIS2 framework and does not allow for an abstraction of the integrated resources and thus, does not allow for the dynamic, transparent evolution of scientific workflows. Therefore, the realisation of an extended service bus allowing for the invocation of virtual web services has to be integrated as described in the following.

HPC USE CASE

The Computer-Aided simulation of complex scenarios of real-world problems provides a significant improvement in the development of new methods and new technologies, whilst minimizing the related costs and efforts. This is in particular the case with respect to the simulation of processes

- That are unsolvable by traditional and experimental approaches, like e.g. the prediction of future climate changes or the fate of underground contaminants
- Which are too hazardous to study in laboratories, like e.g. the characterisation of the chemistry of radionuclides, other toxic chemicals or the distribution and effect of medicine within a human body
- That are time consuming or expensive to solve by traditional means, e.g. car crashes, development of new materials or aerodynamic optimisations (requiring a physical model for each potential change)

In summary, such simulations provide a significant impact in the engineering, environmental and medical sector allowing for a detailed analysis of the relevant method or prototype whilst not affecting the environment at all.

Typically application in HPC environments are parameter studies in order to archive the best suitable solution for a given problem statement.

Therefore, specific characteristics of e.g. a surface have to be simulated by varying input parameters following the trial and error principle, since for a lot of real-world problems no formal procedure exists in order to achieve specific goals. So, in order to find the optimal solution for a given problem, different variants have to be tested.

Although the general procedure within parameter studies for different domains is similar, these complex procedure enforce a lot of detailed knowledge of both, the simulation itself as well as the appropriate IT infrastructures and the corresponding software environments. Current environments enforce engineers and scientists to have this knowledge, beside the knowledge of their relevant domain, as well, which is a big problem. Following the idea of SOA it is advantageous to have experts for each of the mentioned domains allowing for an optimised knowledge, and thus operation, of these environments.

As an example for such a complex simulation process the micro-mechanical simulation of cancellous bone tissue, to determine its macroscopic elastic material properties on the continuum scale, is presented.

Nowadays implant and prosthesis development is mostly done on experimental basis. So the choice of type, size and positioning of the implant is based mainly on the experience of the surgeon, which is a source of potential errors. This is also reflected by the fact, that most postoperative mechanical complications are not explainable respectively cannot be quantified, like e.g.

- The Z-Effect of intramedullary implants with 2 proximal fixation devices
- Cut-out of gliding screw
- Loosening (about 12% revisions of placed implant are required per year in Germany)

In order to minimise, or ideally even eliminate, these drawbacks, an extended support is needed in order to

- Chose the correct type of implant
- Support the correct positioning of the implant
- Predict the healing process
- Predict and quantify possible mechanical complications

That continuum mechanical simulations of bone-implant-systems have the potential to provide this support is shown by the work of numerous research groups during the past years. For static Finite Element simulations of bone-implant-systems in general three prerequisites are essential. (1) The bone geometry, (2) the forces acting on the bone structures which includes body- as well as muscle forces and (3) a detailed modelling of the inhomogeneous, anisotropic material distribution of the bony structures.

The process of micromechanical simulations of cancellous bone tissue aims at the third of the above mentioned prerequisites and becomes necessary due to the lack of resolution of nowadays clinical imaging techniques. To separate the micro structures of cancellous bone, which have a diameter of ≈ 0.1mm, from volumetric imaging data, an isotropic resolution of ≈ 0.02mm would be necessary. Since this resolution is approximately 20 times higher than the one achievable with modern, clinical, dual source computer tomography (CT) an additional modelling step has to be introduced to enable continuum mechanical simulations with anisotropic material data on the resolution scale of clinical CT-data.

The general process of this additional modelling step for one element is show in Figure 1.

In detail, the following steps are processed:

1. In the first step, a representative volume element (RVE) is selected and loaded from the initial data set.

Figure 1. Direct mechanical simulation proceeding of a cancellous bone

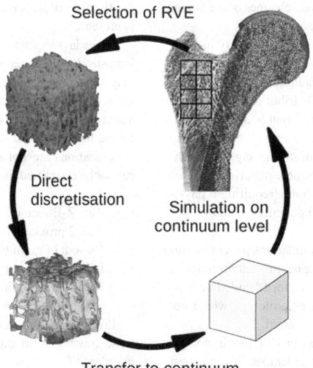

Selection of RVE

Direct discretisation

Simulation on continuum level

Transfer to continuum

2. Now this RVE is discretised and boundary conditions are applied in order to proceed with static simulations. In this step a domain decomposition has to be processed by conducting a 2D-3D algorithm splitting. Therefore, the domain is decomposed with cutting planes in a normalised way to the global coordinate axis. Then, the resulting sub-domain faces are analyzed for iso-lines with 2D marching cubes, in order to allow for the meshing of the iso-lines with 2D advancing fronts. These iso-lines are attached to each sub-domain connected to the corresponding face. For each of these sub-domains closed seed fronts are constructed. Finally, this described 3D advancing fronts algorithm is executed in each sub-domain on the closed front. Afterwards, the geometry setup is processed as depicted in Figure 2.

3. After the direct discretisation the RVE is simulated in 6 different load cases to gain the local microscopic strain and stress distributions on the microscopic level. The procedure is depicted in Figure 3.

4. The simulation results are transferred back to the continuum level by calculating the effective stiffness tensor for the RVE. In detail 4 connections between local microscopic and averaged macroscopic elastic properties have to be considered to determine the effective stiffness tensor of the RVE.

The average strain over a RVE $\bar{\varepsilon}_{ij}$ is computed as the integral average of the local strain field ε_{ij} by

$$\bar{\varepsilon}_{ij} = \frac{1}{\left|V_{RVE}\right|} \int_{V_{RVE}} \varepsilon_{ij} dV_{RVE} \tag{1}$$

The connection between the local microscopic strains and the average strain is further given by the linear transformation

$$\varepsilon_{ij} = M_{ijkl} \bar{\varepsilon}^{kl} \tag{2}$$

with M_{ijkl} being the so called local structure tensor (Hollister & Kikuchi 1992)

Now, starting from the generalized Hooke's low on microscopic level

$$\sigma_{ij} = C_{ijkl} \varepsilon^{kl} \tag{3}$$

with σ_{ij} the local strain field and C_{ijkl} the local stiffness tensor, it can be derived (c.f. Hollister & Kikuchi 1992) that the so called effective stiffness tensor of the RVE $\bar{C}_{ijkl}$ is given by

$$\bar{C}_{ijkl} = \frac{1}{\left|V_{RVE}\right|} \int_{V_{RVE}} C_{ijmn} M_{mnkl} dV_{RVE} \tag{4}$$

Executing the procedure over an entire bone, (4) becomes

$$\bar{C}_{ijkl} = \bar{C}_{ijkl}(x,y,z) \tag{5}$$

allowing for a correlation to measures derived from clinical-CT data

$$\bar{C}_{ijkl}(x,y,z) \sim CT(x,y,z) \tag{6}$$

The effective stiffness is represented as a tensor of rank four $\bar{C} = \bar{C}_{ijkl} e^i \otimes e^j \otimes e^k \otimes e^l$, depending on four bases (coordinate systems) e^i, e^j, e^k and e^l. All these four bases are equal to the global coordinate system. Due to symmetries the 81 coordinates of the effective stiffness tensor can be reorganized in a symmetric 6x6 matrix. So, for each of the 6 simulated load-cases one column of the matrix can be calculated, resulting in a dense matrix in general. This proceeding is depicted in Figure 4.

Figure 2. Geometry setup

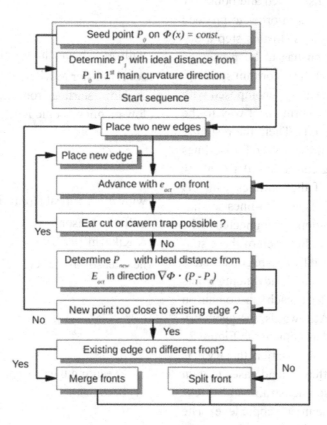

Finally, the computed results have to be correlated to the relevant clinical-CT data in order to enable a detailed analysis of the cancellous bone behaviour for the processed forces and implant positions on the continuum level. This correlation takes place with multivariate statistics and is done via a cluster analysis and linear discriminant analysis.

This rough description of the simulation process shows the complexity of the entire processing of such kind of simulations, often overburden experts with a detailed medical knowledge background. Therefore, in order to face this issue, we are going to show in the following sections how our virtualisation approach in combination with common workflow languages can close this

Figure 3. Static simulation processing

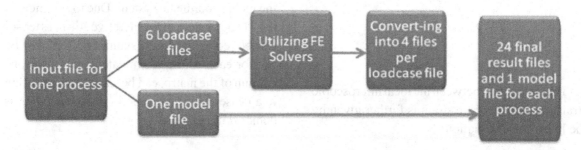

Figure 4. Calculation of the effective stiffness matrices

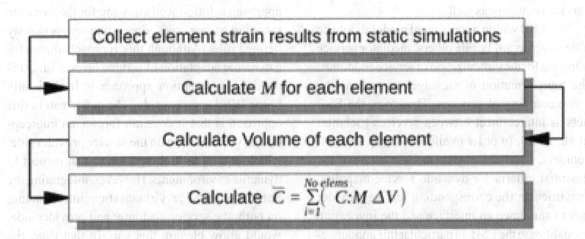

gap. In particular by allowing for the realisation of such complex processes without requiring all the knowledge as depicted in this section. In the following section we are showing how this complex procedure can be encapsulated in a SOA like manner, allowing all involved domain experts to concentrate on their expertise, in order to provide this internal process knowledge as an easy-to-use IT product to external customers.

PROVISION AND INTEGRATION OF COMPLEX IT SERVICES: THE ENTERPRISE SERVICE BUS (ESB)

Increasing business dynamics, changing customer preferences, and disruptive technological shifts pose the need for two kinds of flexibility that inter-enterprise information systems must address--the ability of inter-enterprise linkages to support changes in offering characteristics (offering flexibility) and the ability to alter linkages to partner with different supply chain players (partnering flexibility) (Gosain, Malhotra & Sawy, 2004). From a technical perspective this enforces a new kind of infrastructures allowing for the transparent communication interception as well as the corresponding transformation considering the business partners needs correspondingly.

In order to allow for such a dynamic SOA based environment, the essential backbone of such an environment is the communication infrastructure, namely the so-called Enterprise Service Bus (ESB). This communication infrastructure should allow for both, the interconnection of local services within a domain, as well as the orchestration and integration of services from external service providers. In particular the latter one should be possible without the burden to consider the service providers runtime environment and used technologies. Typically, a service consumer just wants to use the service and get back the corresponding results. However, current environments based on web service technologies only provide a limited support for such kind of environments. Therefore, the ESB has to provide some essential functionality, however, current ESB systems have some significant gaps making their usage a limiting factor in such dynamic environments.

First of all, common ESB Systems have problems in recovering from unforeseen errors. This is mainly due to the missing support for evolution during runtime (Astrova, Koschel & Kruessmann, 2010). Furthermore, most ESB are designed to allow for an orchestration and integration of services within a specific domain. Typically, the ESB „ends" at the boundaries of an organisation (Graf & Hommel, 2010), which makes it quite complex task to integrate services from external service providers as well.

The ESB within a conceptual model should be able to act as an, beside others, mediator service allowing for the virtualization of service endpoints, the transformation of messages as well as the loose coupling of services. Therefore, the ESB acts as interconnect between services (Schmidt et al., 2005). In order to allow for such an environment, Service metadata is seen as one of the essential criteria for dynamic service mapping. In particular, the corresponding service provider has to announce an interface and the invocation modalities to the ESB. In particular this announcement of interfaces allowing for the invocation of services enforces the service consumer to have a concrete knowledge about the services he intends to invoke, namely the service location as well as the syntactical interface.

In order to tackle this issue of this closed binding between services, in (Li, Muthusamy & Jacobsen, 2010) a new architecture is proposed for distributed workflow execution. Therefore, a mapping of BPEL elements to pub/sub semantics is introduced, allowing realising a defined BPEL process within a distributed agent environment. Therefore, every agent takes over a specific task within the workflow. The message routing is realized with a hierarchical message broker infrastructure. However, this approach does not allow for the provision of complex, aggregated IT services. Furthermore, the hiding of the underlying infrastructure by the published service endpoint of a service provider is not considered as well. However, combining this approach with the introduced gateway infrastructure would allow for a decoupled approach allowing for a dynamic environment.

Other approaches facing this challenging issue of dynamically mapping service invocations to potentially changing service providers is introduced in (Moser, Rosenberg & Dustdar, 2008). The authors propose a new approach for monitoring and dynamic service selection for BPEL processes. Therefore, an Aspect-Oriented Mapping approach is introduced allowing for the dynamic mapping of messages, depending on previously defined rules. Although this approach allows for a dynamic adaptation of service invocations, this message interception approach is limited only to the BPEL process side. The major gap in this approach is that it does not foresee an interception or virtualisation on the service provider side, which is a quite limiting aspect with respect to dynamic environments. However, integrating the introduced service virtualisation infrastructure on both, the service customer and provider side, would allow closing this gap. In that case, the AOP message transformation component could get coupled with the gateway infrastructure.

To summarise, an ESB is mainly driven by concrete IT and Business needs, namely the need to support loosely coupled and distributed business units and business partners automating supply chains (Chappel, 2004). Experts have been disappointed by common approaches like CORBA and EAI whilst focusing on a loosely coupled, distributed SOA environment. However, most EAI (Degenring, 2005) and ESB solutions are of proprietary nature.

The key-parts of the ESB is the Message Oriented Middleware (MOM), allowing for a robust and reliable transport of messages, an efficient movement of data across abstract data channels as well as a reliable end-to-end connection. A specific support should be given to web service based environments, which is a "technical" realisation of the SOA approach. In particular, the integration and usage of abstract business services and entities should be supported in order to allow for the required dynamicity support. To this respect, an intelligent routing have to be supported, in particular with respect to message routing based on the content, context and / or on business rules. Furthermore, in order to allow for the dynamic replacement of services within a VO, a transformation support should be given respectively. This allows for the transparent replacement of services in a running environment without affecting the invoking applications / services at all.

In summary, in order to allow for a dynamic VO environment whilst taking into account the integration of domain internal services as well as of services from external service providers, the integration of applications / services has to be done via abstract service endpoints in order to hide the technical details of an applications / services. This procedure allows for a logical abstractions of applications and services, for the internal usage e.g. in order to form new applications based on existing services, as well as for the external service provisioning. In particular the latter one allows for the provision of complex IT products by

- Orchestrating existing internal and external services.
- Allowing for the provision of this aggregated, complex IT service to external customers in a transparent way.
- Allowing for the integration of explicit domain knowledge (process knowledge).

Furthermore, an ESB has to provide an extensive support for.

- Security issues, in order to ensure that only authorised users are allowed to access and consume services, as well as to ensure data privacy and protection.
- Adapters, in order to allow for the integration of legacy applications with no web service interconnection, as well as for the transformation of messages and data.
- Management and monitoring opportunities, in order to allow adjusting the environment during runtime, whilst also ensuring to provide a detailed overview of the current runtime state. The latter one can also be taken into account in order to adjust the ESB setting correspondingly, e.g. in order to invoke services with a better energy-efficiency behaviour for specific

tasks. This could be determined by taking into account the corresponding monitoring information.

- Process orchestration, in order to allow for the combination of existing internal and external services.
- Complex event processing, in order to allow for an intelligent steering of events and the corresponding actions, in particular in order to support the processing, the correlation as well as pattern matchings for the raised events.
- Integration tooling. Ideally, this tooling should enable user to define their processes and flows within a graphical user interface. Furthermore, an extensive support should be given for deploying and testing the corresponding services.

In the following section, we are depicting the architecture of such a virtualization environment enabling the simplified assembling of complex IT services.

SERVICE VIRTUALISATION INFRASTRUCTURE

In this section the architecture of the virtualisation gateway is briefly introduced. A detailed description of the virtualisation infrastructure is given in (Kipp et al., 2012), (Kipp & Schubert, 2011) and (Kipp et al., 2009). As mentioned before there is a concrete need in service virtualization and thus consequently in an abstraction layer. This abstraction layer operates as an intermediary service between consumer and the actual service logic by intercepting and analysing invocations and mapping them to the corresponding service(s). This mapping can also involve the necessary transformation steps as the virtualization infrastructure does not focus on a specific interface description.

General Architecture

Since the gateway acts as a single entry point to not only local service logics, but potentially also to the whole virtual collaboration environment, it also provides the functionality to encapsulate services.

Through using "double-blind virtualisation" mechanisms, i.e. by deploying the gateway on both consumer and service provider side, it is possible to alter resources and providers without affecting the calling applications.

Figure 5 presents a sample deployment of the Gateway infrastructure. The dashed line denotes an indirect link (as the gateway extends the message channel).

Figure 6 shows the structure of such a gateway. This structure enables service provider to *encapsulate* and *hide* their infrastructure in a way that also allows for *virtualization of products*. With the gateway being extensible, it provides the basis to non-invasively enact *security, privacy* and *business policies* related to message transactions. With the strong SOA approach pursued by the virtualization gateway, the structure furthermore meets the requirements of *minimal impact* and *maximum deployment flexibility*; through its filters, it furthermore supports the *standardized messaging support*. The gateway is furthermore

constructed in a way that allows for participation in *multiple collaborations* at the same time without requiring reconfiguration of the underlying infrastructure.

In effect, this virtualisation technology thus acts as an enhanced messaging infrastructure which can serve the following purposes:

- **Policy Enforcement:** The gateway can enforce policies upon message transactions since it allows the definition of criteria that must be fulfilled before a potential consumer is authorized to access a specific service. To this end, policy decision points can be inserted into the message chain (see below). For example, it is possible to differentiate service consumers based on their reputation, so as to estimate the relative trustworthiness, the effort worth investing etc.

- **Message Security, Identity and Access Management:** In an ideal world, all deployed client applications and web services support the corresponding specifications like WS-Security, WS-Trust and WS-Federation. Ideally, each client application should be able to fetch security tokens that are necessary for service access, and each deployed service should

Figure 5. Sample deployment of the Gateway infrastructure

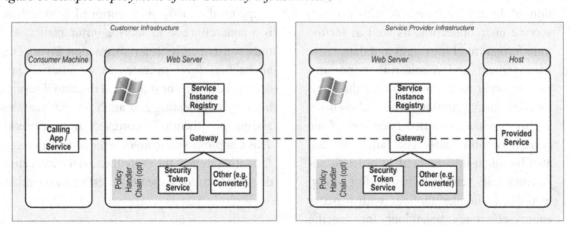

Figure 6. Gateway structure

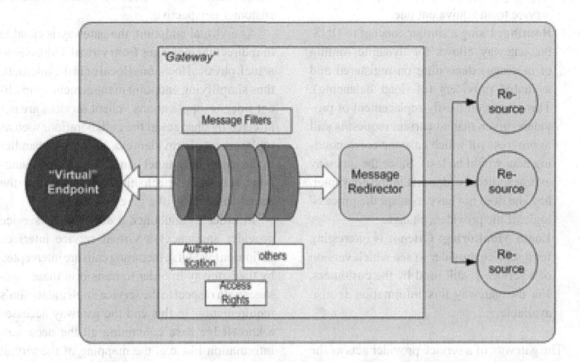

be able to authorize an incoming request using a claims-based security model with fine-grained authorization. Unfortunately, many applications in production today do not yet adhere to these principles, and the gateway can serve as a migration path towards broader adoption of the claims-based access model. The customer-side gateway can authenticate internal requestors, request security tokens on their behalf and protect (i.e. encrypt) outgoing messages. A service-side gateway can act as a policy-enforcement point to authenticate and authorize incoming calls. For example the gateway can establish a secure connection to the service consumer while the concrete client application does not support any secure data transmission.

- **Protocol Translation:** Not only are web service protocol specification subject to constant changes, but also a broad scope of protocols serve similar needs, thus lead-

ing to recurring interoperability issues between customers and providers. With static interfaces, the consumer has to ensure that his/her service invocation is compatible with the specifications of the provider…

- **Transformation:** Since the gateway provides a universal interface for the underlying services a transformation has to be done before the message is forwarded to the corresponding service. Transformation actions can be done as a following step of the protocol translation, in particular regarding the transformation of service specific parameters.

- **Filtering and Information Leakage Protection:** The gateway can detect and remove private information from a request, offering a hook to install information leakage detection and prevention mechanisms.

- **Load Balancing and Fail Over:** The gateway can act as a load balancer. If e.g. one service is currently heavy in use the gateway may decide to forward requests to this service to an equivalent one.

- **Routing:** Using a similar concept to DNS, the gateway allows for dynamic routing of messages depending on registered and available providers (cf. load balancing). This allows on-the-fly replacement of providers, given that no current request is still in progress (in which case the corresponding data would be lost). Since the gateway exposes virtual endpoints to the consumer, he / she does not have to adapt the process' logic, if the providers change.

- **Login Monitoring:** Often it is interesting for a service provider to see which version of a service is still used by the customers. Via the gateway this information is also available.

The gateway of a service provider acts as the virtualization endpoint of the services exposed by the respective organization. Its main task consists in intercepting incoming and outgoing messages to enforce a series of policies related to access right restrictions, secure authentication, transformation etc. thus ensuring that both provider and collaboration specific policies are maintained in

transactions. Figure 7 shows the gateway from a customer perspective.

As a virtual endpoint, the gateway is capable of redirecting messages from virtual addresses to actual, physical locations (local or in the Internet), thus simplifying endpoint management from client side, i.e. applications / client services are not affected by changes in the collaboration, such as replacement of providers etc. An intrinsic handler in the gateway channel hence consists in an endpoint resolution mechanism that identifies the actual destination of a given message.

In order to announce a service, the service provider announces a virtual service interface definition (WSDL). Incoming calls are intercepted by the gateway in order to transform these messages with respect to the service implementation's requirements. To this end the gateway accesses a knowledge base containing all the necessary information like e.g. the mapping of the virtual name to a concrete service endpoint and the transformation of method names and parameters. As the gateway can route to any number of physical endpoints, this approach allows the provider to expose multiple WSDLs for one and the same service, as well as the other way round, namely to expose multiple services via a single (virtual) web

Figure 7. The Gateway principle

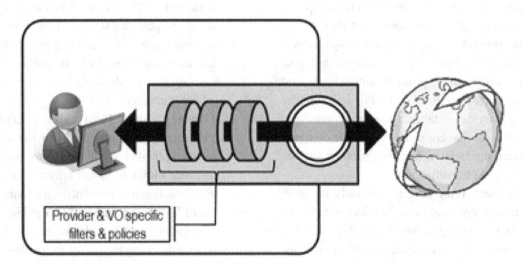

service interface. This allows not only to distinguish between various (potentially user specific) instances of a single web service, as is currently being exploited by cloud service farms, but it also enables the service provider to dynamically move service instances between resources, as well as to compose new services through combination of existing applications, without having to rewrite the corresponding logic. It is hence also possible to provide services dynamically – e.g. by announcing new virtual interfaces, or by altering the service logic without having to change the interface.

These aspects simplify service management significantly, as it removes the issue of having to cater for individual instances and their representation. For example if used in a cloud like fashion, updates initiated at the breeding site would automatically spread across the network over time.

A detailed evaluation of this approach is given in (Kipp & Schubert, 2011).

Applying the Gateway Infrastructure to Different logical Domains

As described before the virtualisation gateway infrastructure allows for a transparent and flexible usage of services and applications being provided via a web service interface. In this section we are describing how the gateway can be applied in order

to face the challenging issue about the provisioning of complex IT service products. In particular, we are depicting how the Gateway infrastructure can be applied to concrete environments following a hierarchical approach. This proceeding allows for a concentration of expertise within the involved domains, whilst enabling experts from these domains to use the corresponding services of the other domains in an easy and transparent way. Therefore, we reflected such an environment in Figure 8. As depicted, the gateway infrastructure has been applied to the following domains:

- The service customer.
- The service provider.
- The service infrastructure (acting as a local gateway not being foreseen for external usage).

In this environment, the service customer has designed a local workflow in order to orchestrate different locally as well as remotely provided services. As depicted, all invocations are done via virtual service endpoints, which are intercepted by the corresponding customer gateway. The virtualisation gateway logic decides in the next steps to which destination and in which format the intercepted message should get routed. Since these invocations are done via virtual service end-

Figure 8. Applying the virtualisation infrastructures to different domains

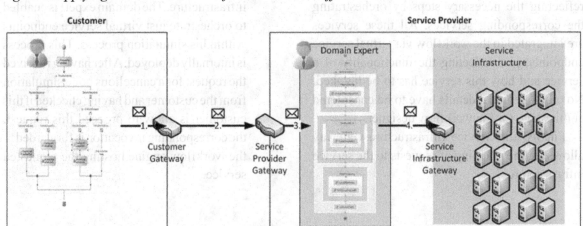

points, the change of a concrete service endpoint does not affect the customer's workflow at all, since, besides the transparent routing of messages, the gateway allows for a transparent message transformation as well. So, in case of changing a service endpoint for a virtual service endpoint, the gateway enables for the integration of rules in order to map the common invocations to the new service interface. In particular, for the designer of the customer workflow it does not matter if the service is executed locally or remotely. The process designer can concentrate on the design of the process flow without the need to take into account the concrete service infrastructure.

The service provider domain is divided into two sub-domains, since the service provider provides both, complex IT services as well as the corresponding infrastructure. Of course, the presented approach allows also for the integration of an external infrastructure provider. In that case the Service Infrastructure Gateway would be located at a third party infrastructure service provider. However, this would not affect the workflow orchestration of the domain expert of the service provider, since the invocation of the service infrastructure is also encapsulated within the gateway infrastructure by using the announced virtual service endpoints.

The complex IT service product is provided by allowing a domain expert, in our case an expert for medical simulations, to design a workflow reflecting the necessary steps by orchestrating the corresponding services. All these services are integrated in the workflow via virtual service endpoints, just reflecting the functionality of a service and how this service has to be invoked. No other technical details have to be considered at this stage for the workflow designer.

Finally, the Service Infrastructure Gateway allows for the mapping of requests to the service infrastructure.

In the following, we are presenting the processing of this hierarchical gateway infrastructure by following a concrete service invocation from the service customer.

1. As part of the customers' workflow reflecting the simulation of a specific region of a human body a cancellous bone simulation process should be triggered. The customers' workflow engine invokes a virtual service endpoint.

2. The corresponding message is intercepted by the customer's gateway and forwards this request to the corresponding service provider, which haves a contract with the customers' company for this kind of simulations. The workflow designers as well as the execution environment are not aware about which service provider is going to process the corresponding step in his workflow. Typically, service customers don't want to get bothered with these details. They just want to have the results of the computation.

3. The domain expert of the service provider designed a process for the simulation of cancellous bones by applying the corresponding functions, applications and data flows in the correct order. By taking advantage of the internal Service Infrastructure Gateway the domain expert does not have to take into account the technical details of the service infrastructure. The domain expert is enabled to orchestrate just virtual service endpoints within his simulation process. This process is internally deployed. After having received the request for a cancellous bone simulation from the customer and having checked if this customer is allow to proceed this request, the corresponding invocation is forwarded to the workflow engine hosting the requested service.

4. Finally, the activities of the local workflow of the service provider are transmitted via the Service Infrastructure to the corresponding compute nodes.

Figure 9 depicts in detail how the mapping of requests to the service infrastructure is handled. The virtualisation gateway has been realised with .NET 3.5, implementing the entire routing and managing logic. However, most IT infrastructure environments do not allow for the deployment of .NET services, so in order to steer the invocation of application and services on the IT Service Infrastructure, an additional Cluster Controller has been realised. The cluster controller is realised as a light-weighted gSOAP (gSOAP, 2012) application, allowing for the execution of local system operation which can be triggered via a web service interface. Furthermore, the Cluster Controller allows for passing references to data sets to the corresponding compute nodes and clusters respectively. These references include

*   The data transfer protocol and the location of the required data set.
*   Optional a query allowing for the selection of specific elements of the dataset. This proceeding allows for the reduction of the amount of data that have to get transferred to the compute nodes
*   The accounting information being required to access the data set

These references allow for an intelligent management of large data sets respectively, whilst following a SOA based approach.

PROVIDING A CANCELLOUS BONE SIMULATION SERVICE VIA BPEL

As depicted in before common workflow languages face the specific requirements of scientific workflows as well, however, the realisation of this kind of workflows with BPEL is still facing some

Figure 9. Applying Gateway to handle local service infrastructure

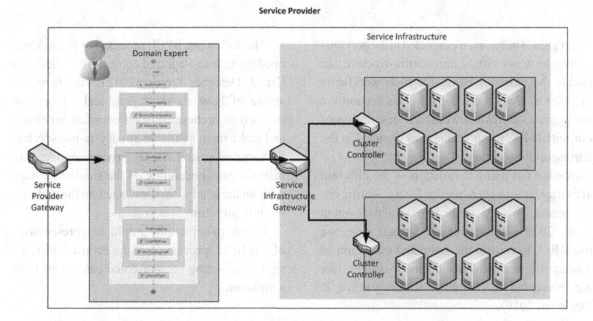

Figure 10. BPEL process for a cancellous bone simulation

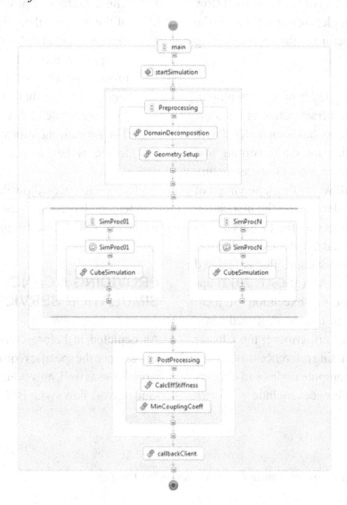

major gaps. Therefore, we depicted in the previous section how our virtualisation infrastructure can enable the usage of BPEL for such workflows in order to close these gaps. In this section we are going to provide a workflow description of our initial HPC usage scenario as depicted in the corresponding section.

We are not going to reflect how the different activities have to get modelled for a scientific environment. This is described in detail in (Sonntag et al., 2010). Within our HPC usage case, we use BPEL to control the setup and execution of a scientific workflow management system, like e.g. presented in (Sonntag, Karastoyanova & Deelman, 2010).

The following BPEL process has been developed using the integrated eclipse BPEL designer (BPEL Designer Project, 2012). This is an example of how standard graphical editors can be used to orchestrate such complex processes and make them available as easy-to-use services for external customers. By proceeding like this, scientist can concentrate on the simulation itself without the need to take into account the underlying infrastructure.

Figure 10 depicts the graphical representation of this BPEL process from the eclipse BPEL designer, reflecting our presented cancellous bone simulation.

The process is started by receiving the invocation message via the corresponding web service interface by triggering the startSimulation method. In the following the defined activities of the simulation process are executed, namely

- The preprocessing
- The simulation itself
- The postprocessing of the simulation results

Therefore, the required functionality of the corresponding steps is provided by separate applications, which can be invoked via a virtual service interface. These invocations are mapped in the next step to concrete service endpoints, or might be forwarded to an external party. However, the scientist designing this process does not have to be aware of the location of these services. He can concentrate on the orchestration of the required functions in the BPEL process and the virtualisation infrastructure takes care that the corresponding invocations are send to the correct services. In particular, the involved experts does no longer have to gain knowledge about the underlying service infrastructure, since the services are all provided and invoked via virtual service endpoints. So, even in case of replaced service providers or new runtime environments this does not affect the workflow itself, since the service virtualisation environment enables to adapt the corresponding requests to fit the potential new, service specific requirements.

CONCLUDING REMARKS

In this chapter we highlighted the gaps of common scientific and eBusiness workflow environments towards the provision of complex IT service products. Therefore, in order to overcome the identified gaps, we have shown how our virtualisation infrastructure can be applied to allow for the design, development and execution of scientific workflows in a SOA like manner. Finally, we applied the presented virtualisation infrastructure in different domains and presented the design of a reference workflow for a specific medical usage case, which can be provided as an easy-to-use service product to external customers.

As an outlook for future developments we think it would be interesting to apply the presented approach to different types of IT infrastructures in order to reflect the specific requirements, in particular with respect to the corresponding knowledge domains. This chapter mainly concentrated on applying the gateway infrastructure within a HPC environment.

Recently, we enhanced the gateway in order to automatically determine errors in service invocations, e.g. in case of a machine crash, an automatic re-routing of the corresponding invocation to another corresponding resource is applied. This approach is currently operating on syntactical level, so, for future developments, also semantic annotations have to be considered in order to find resources providing the corresponding functionality. Another interesting research issue is the semantic mapping between interfaces for increased interoperability. Actually this mapping is done on a syntactical basis. In particular, the mapping is done by providing concrete rules describing which method has to be mapped to which target operation. This is also the case for the corresponding data sets respectively. A semantic enhanced mapping would minimize the effort to provide such rules, since a high-level as well as human understandable description of the corresponding service interfaces would allow for an autonomic determination of fitting partner services to reach a common goal as well as a reduced manual overhead in order to reconfigure the infrastructure respectively.

REFERENCES

Akram, A., Meredith, D., & Allan, R. (2006). Evaluation of BPEL to scientific workflows. *Sixth IEEE International Symposium on Cluster Computing and the Grid (CCGRID'06)*, (pp. 269-274). IEEE. doi:10.1109/CCGRID.2006.44

Astrova, I., Koschel, A., & Kruessmann, T. (2010). Comparison of enterprise service buses based on their support of high availability. *Proceedings of the 2010 ACM Symposium on Applied Computing - SAC '10*, (p. 2495). New York, NY: ACM Press. doi:10.1145/1774088.1774605

BPEL Designer Project. (2012). Retrieved February 10, 2012, from http://www.eclipse.org/bpel/

Chappel, D. A. (2004). In Hendrickson, M. (Ed.), *Enterprise service bus: Theory in practice* (1st ed., p. 352). O'Reilly Media.

Currle-Linde, N., Adamidis, P., Resch, M., Bos, F., & Pleiss, J. (2006). GriCoL: A language for scientific grids. *2006 Second IEEE International Conference on e-Science and Grid Computing (e-Science '06)* (pp. 62-62). Amsterdam, Netherlands: IEEE. doi:10.1109/E-SCIENCE.2006.261146

Deelman, E., Blythe, J., Gil, Y., Kesselman, C., Mehta, G., & Patil, S. (2004). Lecture Notes in Computer Science: *Vol. 3165. Pegasus: Mapping scientific workflows onto the grid* (pp. 131–140). doi:10.1007/978-3-540-28642-4_2

Deelman, E., & Chervenak, A. (2008). Data management challenges of data-intensive scientific workflows. *2008 Eighth IEEE International Symposium on Cluster Computing and the Grid (CCGRID)*, (pp. 687-692). IEEE. doi:10.1109/CCGRID.2008.24

Deelman, E., Gannon, D., Shields, M., & Taylor, I. (2009). Workflows and e-science: An overview of workflow system features and capabilities. *Future Generation Computer Systems, 25*(5), 528-540. Elsevier B.V. doi:10.1016/j.future.2008.06.012

Degenring, A. (2005). Enterprise service bus. *JavaSPEKTRUM, 4*, 16-18. Retrieved February 10, 2012, from http://www.sigs-datacom.de/fachzeitschriften/javaspektrum/archiv/artikelansicht.html?tx_mwjournals_pi1[pointer]=0&tx_mwjournals_pi1[mode]=1&tx_mwjournals_pi1[showUid]=1612

Dimitrakos, T., Golby, D., & Kearney, P. (2004). *Towards a trust and contract management framework for dynamic virtual organisations*. eAdoption and the Knowledge Econ- omy: eChallenges 2004. Retrieved February 10, 2012, from http://epubs.cclrc.ac.uk/bitstream/701/E2004-305-TRUSTCOM-OVERVIEW-FINAL[1].pdf

Görlach, K., Sonntag, M., Karastoyanova, D., Leymann, F., & Reiter, M. (2011). Conventional simulation workflow technology for scientific conventional workflow technology for scientific simulation. In X. Yang, L. Wang, & J. Lizhe (Ed.), *Guide to e-science* (pp. 0-31).

Gosain, S., Malhotra, A., & El Sawy, O. A. (2004). Coordinating for flexibility in e-business supply chains. [Armonk, NY: M. E. Sharpe, Inc.]. *Journal of Management Information Systems, 21*(3), 7–45.

Graf, S., & Hommel, W. (2010). Organisationsübergreifendes Management von Föderations-Sicherheitsmetadaten auf Basis einer Service-Bus-Architektur. *Informationsmanagement in Hochschulen* (4th ed., pp. 233-246). Retrieved February 10, 2012, from http://dx.doi.org/10.1007/978-3-642-04720-6_20

gSOAP. (2012). Retrieved February 10, 2012, from http://www.cs.fsu.edu/~engelen/soap.html

Jähnert, J., Mandic, P., Cuevas, A., Wesner, S., Moreno, J. I., & Villagra, V. (2010). A prototype and demonstrator of Akogrimo's architecture: An approach of merging grids, SOA, and the mobile Internet. *Computer Communications*, *33*(11), 1304–1317. doi:10.1016/j.comcom.2010.03.003

Khalaf, R. (2007). *Note on syntactic details of split BPEL-D Business Processes Institut für Architektur von Anwendungssystemen, Elektrotechnik Und Informationstechnik* (p. 13). Stuttgart. Retrieved February 10, 2012, from http://elib.uni-stuttgart.de/opus/volltexte/2007/3230/index.html

Kipp, A., Jiang, T., Liu, J., Fugini, M., Anghel, I., & Cioara, T. (2012in press). Energy-aware provisioning of HPC services with virtualised web services. In Khan, S. U., & Kolodziej, J. (Eds.), *Evolutionary based solutions for green computing*. Berlin, Germany: Springer Verlag.

Kipp, A., & Schubert, L. (2011). eBusiness interoperability and collaboration. In E. Kajan (Ed.), *Electronic business interoperability: Concepts, opportunities, and challenges* (pp. 153-184). Hershey, PA: IGI Global. doi:10.4018/978-1-60960-485-1

Kipp, A., Schubert, L., & Geuer-Pollmann, C. (2009). Dynamic service encapsulation. *Proceedings of the First International Conference on Cloud Computing* (pp. 217-230). Munich. doi:10.1007/978-3-642-12636-9_15

Li, G., Muthusamy, V., & Jacobsen, H.-A. (2010). A distributed service-oriented architecture for business process execution. *ACM Transactions on the Web*, *4*(1), 1–33. doi:10.1145/1658373.1658375

Ludäscher, B., Altintas, I., Berkley, C., Higgins, D., Jaeger, E., Jones, M., & Lee, E. a, et al. (2006). Scientific workflow management and the Kepler system. *Concurrency and Computation*, *18*(10), 1039–1065. doi:10.1002/cpe.994

Ludäscher, B., Weske, M., McPhillips, T., & Bowers, S. (2009). Lecture Notes in Computer Science: *Vol. 5701. Scientific workflows: Business as usual?* (pp. 31–47).

Modafferi, S., Mussi, E., Maurino, A., & Pernici, B. (2004). A framework for provisioning of complex e-services. *Proceedings IEEE International Conference on Services Computing, SCC 2004* (pp. 81-90). IEEE. doi:10.1109/SCC.2004.1357993

Moser, O., Rosenberg, F., & Dustdar, S. (2008). Non-intrusive monitoring and service adaptation for WS-BPEL. *Proceeding of the 17th International Conference on World Wide Web - WWW '08*, (p. 815). New York, NY: ACM Press. doi:10.1145/1367497.1367607

Oinn, T., Greenwood, M., Addis, M., Alpdemir, M. N., Ferris, J., & Glover, K. (2006). Taverna: Lessons in creating a workflow environment for the life sciences. *Concurrency and Computation*, *18*(10), 1067–1100. doi:10.1002/cpe.993

Schmidt, M.-T., Hutchison, B., Lambros, P., & Phippen, R. (2005). The enterprise service bus: Making service-oriented architecture real. *IBM Systems Journal*, *44*(4), 781–797. doi:10.1147/sj.444.0781

Shields, M., & Taylor, I. (2006). Programming scientific and distributed workflow with Triana Services. *Concurrency and Computation: Practice & Experience - Workflow in Grid Systems, 18*(10), 1-10. doi:10.1002/cpe.v18:10

Sonntag, M., Currle-Linde, N., Görlach, K., & Karastoyanova, D. (2010). Towards simulation workflows with BPEL: Deriving missing features from GRICOL. *21st IASTED International Conference on Modelling and Simulation MS 2010*. ACTA Press.

Sonntag, M., & Karastoyanova, D. (2010). *Next generation interactive scientific experimenting based on the workflow technology.* 21st IASTED International Conference Modelling and Simulation (MS 2010). ACTA Press.

Sonntag, M., Karastoyanova, D., & Deelman, E. (2010). Lecture Notes in Computer Science: *Vol. 6470. BPEL4Pegasus : Workflows combining business and BPEL4Pegasus : Combining business* (pp. 728–729). doi:10.1007/978-3-642-17358-5_75

Taylor, I. J., Deelman, E., Gannon, D. B., Gannon, D., Shields, M., & Taylor, I. (2007). *Workflows for e-science - Scientific workflows for grids.* Springer Business. Retrieved February 10, 2012, from http://books.google.de/books?hl=de&lr=&id=-ZEtM2YKwEYC&oi=fnd&pg=PR7&dq=Workflows++for++e-+Science&ots=HMdPzLt37Q&sig=l65IfOlX9Km2GOOn3kKpFMAiruw#v=onepage&q&f=false

Wesner, S. (2005). Towards an architecture for the mobile grid (Architektur für ein Mobiles Grid). *it - Information Technology, 47*(6), 336-342. doi:10.1524/itit.2005.47.6.336

Wieland, M., Gorlach, K., Schumm, D., & Leymann, F. (2009). Towards reference passing in web service and workflow-based applications. *2009 IEEE International Enterprise Distributed Object Computing Conference,* (pp. 109-118). IEEE. doi:10.1109/EDOC.2009.17

KEY TERMS AND DEFINITIONS

Business Communication: Communication within a supply chain, e.g. between a service consumer and the corresponding service provider.

Communication System Operations and Management: Infrastructure needed for the provision of communication channels within a supply chain.

Dynamic eBusiness Workflows: Workflows allowing for a dynamic adaptation without the need of manual actions.

Dynamic Service Integration: Infrastructure allowing for the dynamic adaptation of resource infrastructures without affecting the corresponding resource consumers.

Virtual Organization: (eBusiness) entity which operates primarily via electronic means.

Chapter 9
Architecture for Integration and Migration of Information Systems by Using SOA Services across Heterogeneous System Boundaries

Lars Frank
Copenhagen Business School, Denmark

Rasmus Ulslev Pedersen
Copenhagen Business School, Denmark

ABSTRACT

The objective of this chapter is to describe how it is possible to integrate and/or migrate information system where local heterogeneous databases are involved. ERP (Enterprise Resource Planning) systems are very complex standardized information systems, and they are often vital for the companies that use them. Therefore, the authors use integration and migration of ERP systems as an example. Normally, ERP systems are migrated/converted overnight as it normally is not possible to integrate different ERP modules from different ERP suppliers. This is very risky as many types of industries cannot function without a running ERP system. The main focus of this chapter is to illustrate how it is possible to migrate/convert an ERP system module by module and thus minimizing the risk of staying without a functioning ERP system. In central databases, the consistency of data is normally implemented by using the ACID (Atomicity, Consistency, Isolation and Durability) properties of a DBMS (Data Base Management System). This is not possible if heterogeneous databases are involved and the availability of data also has to be optimized. Therefore, in this chapter, the authors use so called relaxed ACID properties across different database systems or ERP modules. The objective of designing relaxed ACID properties across different database systems is that the users can trust the data they use even if the involved database temporarily are inconsistent.

DOI: 10.4018/978-1-4666-2190-9.ch009

INTRODUCTION

Database transactions are any logical operation on the data of the database. The ACID properties of a database are delivered by a DBMS to make database recovery easier and make it possible in a multi user environment to give concurrent transactions a consistent view of the data in the database. The ACID properties are consequently important for users that need a consistent view of the data. Information systems that use different DBMS systems can be integrated by using more or less common data and/or by exchanging information between the systems involved. In both situations, the union of the databases of the different systems may be implemented as a database with so called relaxed ACID properties where temporary inconsistencies may occur in a controlled manner. Therefore, the objective of implementing relaxed ACID properties it is that from a user's point of view it must still seem as if traditional ACID properties were implemented in order to keep the local databases trustworthy for decision making.

In the following part of the introduction, we will first give an overview of how relaxed ACID properties may be implemented. Next, we will give an overview of how an ERP system with relaxed ACID properties across its modules may be used to migrate ERP modules one by one. Finally we will describe the objective of the chapter in more details.

Relaxed ACID Properties

The Atomicity property of a DBMS guarantees that either all the updates of a transaction are committed/executed or no updates are committed/executed. This property makes it easier to make database recovery. In distributed databases, this property is especially important if data are replicated as inconsistency will occur if only a subset of data are replicated. The Atomicity property of a DBMS is implemented by using a DBMS log file with all the database changes made by the transactions. The global Atomicity property of databases with relaxed ACID properties is implemented by using compensatable, pivot and retriable subtransactions in that order. This is explained in in more details in section 2.1. As explained in section 2.2 the global Consistency property is not defined in databases with relaxed ACID properties because normally such databases are inconsistent. However, this inconsistency may be managed by using countermeasures in the same way as isolation anomalies may be managed by using countermeasures.

The Isolation property of a DBMS guarantees that the updates of a transaction cannot be seen by other concurrent transactions until the transaction is committed/executed. That is, the inconsistencies caused by a transaction cannot be seen by other transactions. The local Isolation property of a DBMS may be implemented by locking all records used by a transaction. The global Isolation property of databases with relaxed ACID properties may be implemented by using countermeasures against the inconsistencies/anomalies as explained in section 2.3.

The Durability property of a DBMS guarantees that the updates of a transaction cannot be lost if the transaction is committed. The local Durability property of a DBMS is implemented by using a DBMS log file with all the database changes made by the transactions. The global Durability property of databases with relaxed ACID properties is implemented by using the local Durability property of the local databases involved.

Data replication is normally used to decrease local response time and increase local performance by substituting remote data accesses with local data accesses (Frank, 2010). At the same time, the availability of data will normally also be increased as data may be stored in all the locations where they are vital for disconnected operation. These properties are especially important in mobile applications where the mobile user often may be disconnected from data that are vital for the normal operation of the application Kurbel et. al, 2005. See Coratella at al., 2002 for a framework that addressee such challenges. The major disadvantages of data replication are the additional costs of updating replicated data and the problems related to managing the consistency of the replicated data.

In general, replication methods involve n copies of some data where n must be greater than 1. The basic replication designs storing n different copies of some data are defined to be n-safe, 2-safe, 1-safe or 0-safe, respectively, when n, 2, 1 or 0 of the n copies are consistent and up-to-date at normal operation. An overview of replication in distributed systems can be found in (Stockinger, 1999). In mobile computing, we recommend using only the 1-safe and 0-safe replication designs, as these use asynchronous updates which allow local system to operate in disconnected mode.

Therefore, in this chapter we will only use asynchronic replication designs with relaxed ACID properties to increase the autonomy of heterogeneous application modules.

A *heterogeneous modular* ERP *architecture* is an integrated set of ERP systems in different locations where each ERP module can use the resources of the other ERP modules in its own or in other ERP locations. In a heterogeneous modular ERP architecture, the ACID properties must be relaxed both across locations and across modules in the same location. That is, within a module the traditional ACID properties of a DBMS may be used. Relaxed ACID properties are implemented by the modules themselves for all accesses/updates across modules. Each ERP module has full autonomy over its own resources/tables. That is, the tables of a module may be recovered independently of the tables owned by other ERP modules.

In this chapter, we use the following two different integration techniques for databases.

1. The first technique uses asynchronous data replication as the communication tool between heterogeneous systems/modules/databases. By using this technique it is possible for the involved information systems to stay autonomous. However, as the data replication is asynchronous it is important to use countermeasures against the anomalies that may occur when only relaxed ACID properties are used across the heterogeneous system boundaries. This integration method is only recommended for database tables with relatively few updates.

   As an example, the employee table and the department table are updated relatively rare from a single module (e.g. the HRM module) but may be used by many different modules. Therefore, such tables may be updated manually (or replicated automatically by using retriable updates) in both the old and new ERP systems in the period of migration as illustrated later in this chapter.

2. The second technique uses SOA services as a communication tool between heterogeneous systems/modules/databases. This integration method is recommended for database tables with many updates where asynchronous real-time replication therefore is costly. This integration method may also be useful if many different systems/modules have to update the same table because if only a single copy exists it is easier to manage the consistency. Tables like stocks of money (account tables) or products (stock tables) are updated by many different modules and therefore, we will later use these tables as an example where retriable and/or compensatable SOA services are used for updating a remote database table.

Both these Integration techniques for tables are illustrated later in this chapter.

Objective

The objective of this chapter is to describe how it is possible to use the architecture of a heterogeneous modular ERP system to integrate and/or migrate any information system over a longer or shorter time period.

When the migration is over it is possible to convert to back to a traditional central Information system for all modules that use the same DBMS system. However, the best of breed ERP module for a special line of business may for example be heterogeneous with the accounting module of the company and in this situation the module for the special line of business should not be converted. Another situation, where the heterogeneous systems may be optimal is if the information system has bottlenecks. In this situation, it may be convenient for some of the modules to keep the distributed heterogeneous modular ERP architecture as the bottlenecks may disappear if the modules are operated in different computers.

Mergers & Acquisitions (M&As) are situations where different companies more or less voluntary agree on integration into one company. Such a combined organization cannot function effectively until the information system of the acquired business unit is integrated with the acquirer's existing information system (Giacomazzi et al., 1997; Robbins and Stylianou, 1999; Wijnhoven et al., 2006; Mehta and Hirschheim, 2007). This assumption is supported by Accenture (2006) and McKinsey (Sarrazin & West, 2011) that report that 45-60% of the expected benefits from acquisitions are directly dependent on post-acquisition information system integration.

The chapter is organized as follows: First, we will describe the transaction model used in this chapter. In section 3, we will describe the properties of a heterogeneous modular ERP architecture that are necessary for migrating ERP modules independently of each other. In section 4, we will use the sales and accounting modules as examples to illustrate how it is possible exchange

an ERP module or to migrate to another central or distributed ERP system by using a heterogeneous modular ERP architecture. Section 5 gives an overview of the most important replication design that may be used to manage redundancy between tables from different ERP systems. Finally, we have conclusions and future work.

Related Research: The transaction model used in this chapter is *the* countermeasure *transaction model* (Frank, 2010). This model uses the relaxed Atomicity property as developed by Garcia-Molina and Salem, 1987, Mehrotra et al., 1992; Weikum and Schek, 1992, and Zhang, 1994. How to use countermeasures against consistency anomalies are described by Frank (2011c). The model uses countermeasures against the isolation anomalies. These anomalies are described by Berenson et al., 1995 and Breibart et al., 1992. How to use countermeasures against isolation anomalies was first systematized by Frank and Zahle (1998). In the countermeasure transaction model the problem of implementing the Durability property is solved as describe by Breibart et al., 1992.

Like Zhang et al. 1994, we might just as well have called our transactions '*flexible transactions*' as the only new facility is the use of countermeasures to manage the missing consistency and isolation properties. Many researchers (e.g. Hohpe and Woolf, 2004; Linthicum, 2004; Gold-Bernstein and Ruh, 2005; Zhu, H., 2005; Henningsson et at., 2007; Tanriverdi and Uysal, 2011) have dealt with Integration patterns/architectures. However, to our knowledge they either assume the integration can take place overnight or they only take the atomicity property into account and do not deal with the ACID properties in general when they are more or less missing in the period of migration. An early version of our migration architecture has been described by Frank, 2008. How to integrate heterogeneous distributed databases in general by using our transaction model and SOA services are described by Frank, 2011b. How to integrate ERP modules of special lines of business with a heterogeneous ERP system has been described by Frank and Munck, 2008, and Frank, 2011, for different lines of business.

Strategic values and challenges in M&A are described by Harrell and Higgins, 2002; Sudarsanam, 2003; Wijnhoven et al., 2006; Mehta and Hirschheim, 2007; Sarrazin and West, 2011 and Tanriverdi and Uysal, 2011. Research overviews on M&A integration have been made by Barkema and Schijven, 2008; Haleblian et al., 2009; and Lee, 2010.

BACKGROUND: THE TRANSACTION MODEL

Many transaction models have been designed to integrate local databases without using a distributed DBMS. In such distributed databases *Global transactions* (Gray and Reuter, 1993) access data located in more than one local database. The countermeasure transaction model (Frank and Zahle, 1998) has, among other things, selected and integrated properties from these transaction models to reduce the problems caused by the missing ACID properties in a distributed database. In the countermeasure transaction model, a global transaction involves a *root transaction* and several single site *subtransactions* that are executed in database locations. The subtransactions may be nested, i.e. a subtransaction may be a *parent transaction* for other subtransactions. All communication with the user is managed from the root transaction, and all data is accessed through subtransactions. In the following subsections, we will give a broad outline of how relaxed ACID properties are implemented.

The Atomicity Property

Updating transactions have the *atomicity property* and are called *atomic* if either all or none of their updates are executed. In the countermeasure transaction model, the global transaction is partitioned into the following types of subtransactions executed in different locations:

The *pivot* subtransaction that manages the atomicity of the global transaction. The global transaction is committed when the pivot subtransaction is committed locally. If the pivot subtransaction aborts, all the updates of the other subtransactions must either not be executed or the updates must be compensated.

The *compensatable* subtransactions that all have the property that they may be compensated. Compensatable subtransactions must always be executed before the pivot subtransaction is executed to make it possible to compensate them if the pivot subtransaction cannot be committed. A compensatable subtransaction may be compensated by executing a *compensating* subtransaction.

The *retriable* subtransactions that all have the property that they are designed in such a way that the execution is guaranteed to commit locally (sooner or later) if the pivot subtransaction has been committed.

As described earlier, the global atomicity property is implemented by executing the compensatable, pivot and retriable subtransactions of a global transaction in that order. For example, if the global transaction fails before the pivot has been committed, it is possible to remove the updates of the global transaction by compensation. If the global transaction fails after the pivot has been committed, the remaining retriable subtransactions will be (re)executed automatically until all the updates of the global transaction have been committed.

The Consistency Property

A database is *consistent* if its data complies with the consistency rules of the database. If the database is consistent both when a transaction starts and when it has been completed and committed, the execution has the *consistency property*. Transaction *consistency rules* may be executed by a DBMS as control programs that reject the commitment of transactions, which do not comply with the consistency rules.

The above definition of the consistency property is not useful in distributed databases with relaxed ACID properties because such a database is almost always inconsistent. However, a distributed database with relaxed ACID properties should have *asymptotic consistency*, i.e. the database should converge towards a consistent state when all active transactions have been committed/compensated. Therefore, the following property is essential in distributed databases with relaxed ACID properties:

If the database is asymptotically consistent when a transaction starts and also when it has been committed, the execution has the *relaxed consistency property*.

How to implement relaxed consistency by using countermeasures are described by Frank (2011c).

The Isolation Property

The isolation property is normally implemented by using locking or optimistic concurrency control. Optimistic concurrency control cannot per definition be used in integrating autonomous local databases. In the countermeasure transaction model, long duration locks cannot instigate isolated global execution as retriable subtransactions may be executed after the global transaction has been committed in the pivot location. Therefore, only *short duration locks* (or local optimistic concurrency control) are used, i.e. locks that are released immediately after a subtransaction has been committed/aborted locally. To ensure high availability in locked data, short duration locks should also be used in compensatable subtransactions, just as locks should be released before interaction with a user. This is not a problem in the countermeasure transaction model as the traditional isolation property in retriable subtransactions is lost anyway. If only short duration locks are used, it is impossible to block data. (Data is *blocked* if it is locked by a subtransaction that loses the connection to the "coordinator" (the pivot subtransaction) managing the global commit/abort decision). When transactions are executed without isolation, the following so-called *isolation anomalies* may occur (Berenson et al., 1995 and Breibart, 1992).

- *The lost update anomaly* is by definition a situation where a first transaction reads a record for update without using locks. Subsequently, the record is updated by another transaction. Later, the update is overwritten by the first transaction. In extended transaction models, the lost update anomaly may be prevented, if the first transaction reads and updates the record in the same subtransaction using local ACID properties. Unfortunately, the read and the update are sometimes executed in different subtransactions belonging to the same parent transaction. In such a situation, a second transaction may update the record between the read and the update of the first transaction.

- *The dirty read anomaly* is by definition a situation where a first transaction updates a record without committing the update. Subsequently, a second transaction reads the record. Later, the first update is aborted (or committed), i.e. the second transaction may have read a non-existing version of the record. In extended transaction models, this may happen when the first transaction updates a record by using a compensatable subtransaction and later aborts the update by using a compensating subtransaction. If a second transaction reads the record before it has been compensated, the data read will be "dirty".

- *The non-repeatable read anomaly* or *fuzzy read* is by definition a situation where a first transaction reads a record without using locks. Later, the record is updated and committed by a second transaction before the first transaction has been committed. In other words, it is not possible to rely on the data that have been read. In extended transaction models, this may happen when the first transaction reads a record that later is updated by a second transaction, which commits the update locally before the first transaction commits globally.

- *The phantom anomaly* is by definition a situation where a first transaction reads some records by using a search condition. Subsequently, a second transaction updates the database in such a way that the result of the search condition is changed. In other words, the first transaction cannot repeat the search without changing the result. Using a data warehouse may often solve the problems of this anomaly (Frank, 2003).

The countermeasure transaction model (Frank and Zahle, 1998) describes countermeasures that reduce the problems of the anomalies. Later in this capture, the *Pessimistic View Countermeasure* may be used to eliminate the risk of using dirty and/or the non-repeatable data, and therefore, the idea of this countermeasure is explained in the following:

- The pivot or compensatable subtransactions for updates that "limit" the users' options. That is, concurrent transactions cannot use resources that are reserved for the compensatable/pivot subtransaction.
- The pivot or retriable subtransactions for updates that "increase" the users' options. That is, concurrent transactions can only use increased resources after the increase has been committed.

Example

When updating stocks, accounts, vacant passenger capacity, etc. it is possible to reduce the risk of reading non-available stock values. These pessimistic stock values will automatically be obtained if the transactions updating the stocks are designed in such a way that compensatable subtransactions (or the pivot transaction) are used to reduce the stocks and retriable subtransactions (or the pivot transaction) are used to increase the stocks. That is, for attributes with stock like values the compensatable subtransactions that reduce the stock may be used to "limit" the users' options and the retriable subtransactions that increase the stock may be used to "increase" the users' options.

The Durability Property

Updates of transactions are said to be *durable* if they are stored in a stable manner and secured by a log recovery system. In case a global transaction has relaxed atomicity, the relaxed durability property will automatically be implemented, as it is ensured by the log-system of the local DBMS systems (Breibart et al., 1992).

DESCRIPTION OF THE PROPERTIES OF HETEROGENEOUS MODULAR ERP ARCHITECTURE

A traditional ERP system consists of modules like Sale, Production, Procurement, Accounting, CRM, HRM, etc. with the applications that are common for most types of industry. These modules may be extended with specific line of business modules like e.g. the hospital sector, the transport sector, and university administration in order to make it possible for the ERP system to function as an integrated system that support all the administrative functions of a specialized organization. In a traditional ERP system the whole database is common for all the modules of the ERP system even though special modules may have suppliers of their own. That is the applications of the ERP system may have full ACID properties. In a heterogeneous modular ERP architecture, each module may own its own database tables and applications. The applications of a module may access the tables of its module directly. In contrast, when an application in one module needs data from another module it must use e.g. SOA services and not access the data directly. Applications that only use data owned by their module may have full ACID properties. The applications of a module that use services from another module can only have relaxed ACID properties. Each ERP module has full autonomy over its own tables and its tables may be recovered independently from the tables owned by other ERP modules. The modules of a distributed modular ERP system may be mobile as it should be possible for them to operate in both connected or disconnected mode with respect to the other ERP modules depending on whether the ERP module has access to the tables of the other ERP modules or not.

It should be possible to have different versions of the same module. The different module versions may be developed by different software suppliers that have specialized in software for different lines of business. That is the modules may be heterogeneous. It should be possible to build ERP applications in the same way as package-deal houses by using different standard components/ modules that may be delivered by different suppliers that in turn may use different databases.

In order to implement integration flexibility (fault tolerance in case a backup unit is used) between the ERP modules of different companies, it is not acceptable that the different modules communicate directly with each other. All communication between different modules must be executed by applications offered as e.g. SOA services. In order also to implement relaxed ACID properties between the modules each module should offer the following types of services (Frank 2001lb):

- Read only services that are used when a local internet system wants to read data managed by another local internet system.
- Compensatable update services that are used when a local internet system wants to make compensatable updates in tables managed by another local internet system.

- Retriable update services that are used when a local internet system wants to make retriable updates in tables managed by another local internet system.

By using these three types of services from other local internet systems it should be possible for any local internet system to make distributed updates with relaxed ACID properties.

Description of How to Migrate by Using a Heterogeneous Modular ERP Architecture

In a heterogeneous modular ERP architecture we define the Accounting module as the module that owns the Account, Account item, the Product stock tables and possible other tables where the balances have to be updated by compensatable and retriable subtransactions managed from many different modules. In order to prevent having different versions of tables that have many updates it is important that the tables and applications of the accounting module are the last to be migrated from the old accounting system. Therefore, the first step in the migration process is to expand the accounting module with read, compensatable, and retriable services that makes it possible to implement relaxed ACID properties in the modules that read or update the tables of the accounting module (Frank, 2008). This is illustrated in the right part of Figure 1.

The second step in the migration process is to replicate all tables with relatively few updates where the tables are used from both the accounting module and other modules. Such tables may e.g. be tables with Employee and Organization and/or department information if these tables are necessary in both the new ERP system and in the old ERP accounting module. This is illustrated by the redundant department tables in Figure 2. We will recommend updating the replicated tables by using retriable subtransactions.

Figure 1. Illustration of the integration of the accounting tables with a sales module

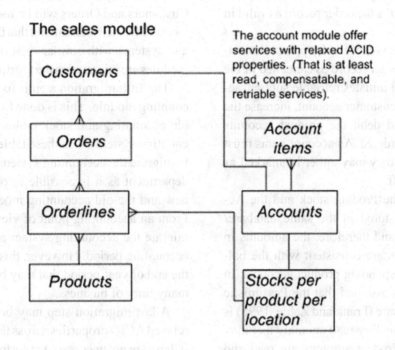

The Product stock table is at least updated by the Sales module, the Procurement module, and the Production module as these modules change the amount of products in the stocks. These modules may now be migrated as the third step in the migration process as the relationships and update procedures to the accounting module now are in place.

A sales transaction may be implemented by first reading the customer record of the customer. Next, the customer/salesman may search the product table and for each selected product, compensatable subtransactions are used for creating an order-line, debit the customer account, reduce the product stock, and credit the product account for the products ordered. After having controlled

Figure 2. Illustration of module integration with redundancy management of departments

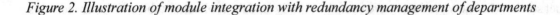

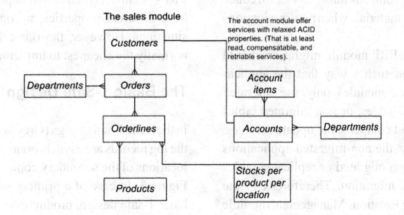

possible additional payment conditions, the pivot subtransaction marks the order record as valid in the sales location.

If the order later is cancelled, a pivot subtransaction marks the order record as cancelled in the sales location, and initiates retriable subtransactions to credit the customer account, increase the product stock, and debit the product accounts for the products ordered. As account items must never be deleted, they may either be marked as cancelled or set off.

In this case, the Product stock and the Account tables are stored in the same database/module location, and therefore, the amounts in the Product stocks are consistent with the balances of the corresponding product accounts. In this example, it is assumed that the Pessimistic view countermeasure (Frank and Zahle, 1998) is used to manage the dirty read anomaly that may occur when the Product amounts are read and updated. That is the Sales system, the Procurement system and the Production system cannot update the Product stocks directly as the applications of these systems do not belong to the accounting module with the Product stock table. However, the sales application can e.g. use a compensatable SOA service to reduce the Product stocks, and the Procurement system can a use retriable SOA service to increase the Product stocks when new products arrive. In the same way, the Production system can use the retriable service to increase the Product stocks when new products have been produced and the compensatable service to reduce the stocks of raw materials when new productions are planned.

The order of ERP module migration should be determined in such a way that the applications of migrated modules only use migrated tables, replicated tables, or non-migrated tables with retriable and compensable update services. In the same way, the non-migrated applications must only use non migrated or replicated tables in the period of migration. Therefore, e.g. the CRM (Customer Relations Management) module should be migrated after the Sales system as the Customers and Orders will be used by the CRM module. We will recommend that the CRM system and systems with similar relationships to other modules are migrated as the fourth migration step.

The fifth migration step is to migrate the accounting module. This is done by converting the old accounting and stock tables as the new accounting system owns these tables. It is possible to migrate the accounting system department by department as it is possible to operate both the new and the old accounting module in parallel. From an accounting point of view it is easier to migrate the accounting system at the end of an accounting period. However, this period is often the end of year period that may be very busy for many lines of business.

A last migration step may be to remove the relaxed ACID properties across the ERP modules if these are not necessary for performance or flexibility reasons.

OVERVIEW OF REPLICATION METHODS FOR HETEROGENEOUS DATABASES

As described earlier, we will in our integration architecture only use the asynchronous replication methods. Therefore, the replication methods described in this section can all be used to automatically update replicated tables in heterogeneous ERP systems. As the different replication methods have different properties, no one is best in all situations. However, the Basic 1-safe design is normally the cheapest to implement and operate.

The Basic 1-Safe Design

In the basic 1-safe design (Grey and Reuter, 1993), the log records are asynchronously spooled to the locations of the secondary copies as illustrated in Figure 3. In case of a primary site failure in the basic 1-safe design, production may continue by

Figure 3. The basic 1-safe database design

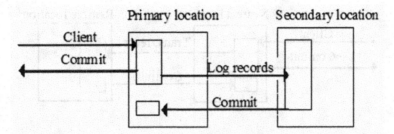

selecting one of the secondary copies but this is not recommended in distributed ERP systems as it may result in *lost transactions*, because some of the updates may not have reached the secondary that would have been used as the new primary copy.

The 0-Safe Design with Local Commit

The *0-safe design with local commit* is defined as n table copies in different locations where each transaction will first go to the nearest database location, where it is executed and committed locally (Figure 4).

If the transaction is an update transaction, retriable subtransactions propagates asynchronously to the other database locations, where the transaction is re-executed without user dialog and committed locally at each location. This means that all the table copies normally are inconsistent and not up to date under normal operation. The inconsistency must be managed by using countermeasures against the isolation anomalies. For example, to prevent lost updates in the 0-safe design, all update transactions must be designed to be commutative (Frank and Zahle, 1998).

The 1-Safe Design with Commutative Updates

The 1-safe design can transfer updates to the secondary copies in the same way as the 0-safe design. In such a design, lost transactions cannot occur because the transaction transfer of the 0-safe

design makes the updates commutative. The properties of this mixed design will come from either the basic 1-safe or the 0-safe design. The 1-safe design with commutative updates does not have the high update performance and capacity of the 0-safe design. On the other hand, in this design the isolation property may be implemented automatically, as long as the primary copy does not fail. Normally, this makes it much more economical to implement countermeasures against the isolation anomalies because it is only necessary to secure that "the lost transactions" are not lost in case of a primary copy failure.

The 0-Safe Design with Primary Copy Commit

The "*0-safe designs with primary copy commit*" is a replication methods where a global transaction must first update the local copy closest to the user by using a compensatable subtransaction. Later, the local update may be committed globally by using a primary copy location. If this is not possible, the first update must be compensated. The primary copy may have a version number that can be replicated. This may be used to control that an updating user is able to operate on the latest version of the primary copy before an update is committed globally in the location of the primary copy. If an update cannot be committed globally in the primary copy location, the latest version of the primary copy should be returned to the updating user in order to repeat the update by using the latest version of the primary copy.

Figure 4. The 0-safe database design

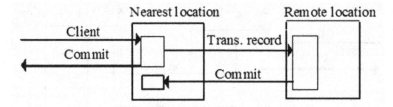

DISTRIBUTED SYSTEM SUPPORT

The design outlined in the previous sections can be supported by the 2nd generation web services models. These models are the specifications that start with the letters "WS-". They include web services for trust, policies, and transactions. We do not focus on security (in the terms of cryptography) in this paper, but the WS-TX (web services transaction) protocols do include partial support for distributed transactions. The WS-Coordination serves as a coordinator mechanism for WS-AtomicTransaction and WS-BusinessActivity. Both standards by OASIS Web Services Transaction (WS-TX) Technical Committee have support for transactions involving two or more distributed parties. The WS-AtomicTransaction includes roll-back mechanisms, which mimics the traditional ACID properties. More interestingly, the WS-BusinessActivity protocol have support for longer (as in duration) transactions. Therefore there is not explicit roll-back support in this protocol, but the lack of this feature is the *compensable* activity that is executed if the main activities cannot complete. This protocol is therefore one possible way to implement the relaxed ACID properties for heterogeneous information systems.

CONCLUSION AND FUTURE RESEARCH

ERP systems are very complex software products and it is very difficult to integrate different ERP systems. Converting from one ERP system to another may be even worse as it is very risky if the conversion has to take place overnight. However, it may be necessary if different companies fuse to a single company or if best of breed software for a special lines of business is selected. Therefore, we have in this chapter used relaxed ACID properties to illustrate how it is possible to integrate and / or migrate heterogeneous ERP systems/modules.

In this chapter, we have also described the architecture of a heterogeneous modular ERP system. This architecture may be viewed both as a tool for migrating heterogeneous ERP systems and as an architecture for permanent integration of heterogeneous ERP modules. In the future, it is our intension to analyze more examples of the usefulness of our heterogeneous modular ERP architecture.

We believe that in the future all users should have the possibility to be mobile and even have the possibility to operate in disconnected mode. We believe that the heterogeneous modular ERP architecture described in this chapter is well suited for such integration as retriable updates from remote mobile users may be asynchronous and have relaxed ACID properties. A recent focus on small heterogeneous systems can be exemplified with wireless sensor networks, and the continuous data streams associated (Pedersen, 2007) with such architectures. However, such architecture needs to be analyzed in much more details possibly with implementation support by SOA oriented protocols such as specified by WS-BusinessActivity.

ACKNOWLEDGMENT

This research is partly funded by the 'Danish Foundation of Advanced Technology Research' as part of the 'Third Generation Enterprise Resource Planning Systems' (3gERP) project, a collaborative project between Department of Informatics at Copenhagen Business School, Department of Computer Science at Copenhagen University, and Microsoft Business Systems.

REFERENCES

Accenture. (2006). *Executives report that mergers and acquisitions fail to create adequate value.* Accenture.

Barkema, H., & Schijven, M. (2008). How do firms learn to make acquisitions? A review of past research and an agenda for the future. *Journal of Management, 34*(3), 594. doi:10.1177/0149206308316968

Berenson, H., Bernstein, P., Gray, J., Melton, J., O'Neil, E., & O'Neil, P. (1995). A critique of ANSI SQL isolation levels. *Proceedings of the ACM SIGMOD Conference,* (pp. 1-10).

Breibart, Y., Garcia-Molina, H., & Silberschatz, A. (1992). Overview of multidatabase transaction management. *The VLDB Journal, 2,* 181–239. doi:10.1007/BF01231700

Coratella, A., Hirsch, R., & Rodriguez, E. (2002). A framework for analyzing mobile transaction models. In K. Siau (Ed.), *Advanced topics in database research,* Vol. 2, ed. Hershey, PA: IGI Global.

Frank, L. (2003). Data cleaning for datawarehouses built on top of distributed databases with approximated ACID properties. *Proceedings of the International Conference on Computer Science and its Applications,* National University US Education Service, (pp. 160-164).

Frank, L. (2004). Architecture for integration of distributed ERP systems and e-commerce systems. [IMDS]. *Industrial Management & Data Systems, 104*(5), 418–429. doi:10.1108/02635570410537507

Frank, L. (2008). Smooth and flexible ERP migration between both homogeneous and heterogeneous ERP systems/ERP modules. *Proceedings of the 2nd Workshop on 3rd Generation Enterprise Resource Planning Systems,* Copenhagen business School.

Frank, L. (2010). *Design of distributed integrated heterogeneous or mobile databases* (pp. 1–157). Germany: LAP LAMBERT Academic Publishing AG & Co. KG.

Frank, L. (2011). Architecture for ERP system integration with heterogeneous e-government modules. In Chhabra, S., & Kumar, M. (Eds.), *Strategic enterprise resource planning models for e-government: Applications & methodologies.* Hershey, PA: IGI Global. doi:10.4018/978-1-60960-863-7.ch007

Frank, L. (2011b). Architecture for integrating heterogeneous distributed databases using supplier integrated e-commerce systems as an example. *Proceedings of the International Conference on Computer and Management* (CAMAN 2011), May, Wuhan, China.

Frank, L. (2011c). *Countermeasures against consistency anomalies in distributed integrated databases with relaxed ACID properties. Proceeding of Innovations in Information Technology (Innovations 2011).* Abu Dhabi: UAE.

Frank, L., & Munck, S. (2008). An overview of architectures for integrating distributed electronic health records. *Proceeding of the 7th International Conference on Applications and Principles of Information Science* (APIS2008), (pp. 297-300).

Frank, L., & Zahle, T. (1998). Semantic ACID properties in multidatabases using remote procedure calls and update propagations. *Software, Practice & Experience, 28*, 77–98. doi:10.1002/(SICI)1097-024X(199801)28:1<77::AID-SPE148>3.0.CO;2-R

Garcia-Molina, H., & Polyzois, C. (1990). *Issues in disaster recovery. IEEE Compcon* (pp. 573–577). New York, NY: IEEE.

Garcia-Molina, H., & Salem, K. (1987). Sagas. *ACM SIGMOD Conference*, (pp. 249-259).

Giacomazzi, F., Panella, C., Pernici, B., & Sansoni, M. (1997). Information systems integration in mergers and acquisitions: A normative model. *Information & Management, 32*, 289–302. doi:10.1016/S0378-7206(97)00031-1

Gold-Bernstein, B., & Ruh, W. A. (2005). *Enterprise integration: The essential guide to integration solutions*. Addison-Wesley.

Gray, J., & Reuter, A. (1993). *Transaction processing*. Morgan Kaufman, 1993.

Haleblian, J., Devers, C., Mcnamara, G., Carpenter, M., & Davison, R. (2009). Taking stock of what we know about mergers and acquisitions: A review and research agenda. *Journal of Management, 35*(3), 469. doi:10.1177/0149206308330554

Harrell, H., & Higgins, L. (2002). IS integration: Your most critical m&a challenge? *Journal of Corporate Accounting & Finance, 13*(2), 23–31. doi:10.1002/jcaf.1220

Henningsson, S., Svensson, C., & Wallén, L. (2007). *Mastering the integration chaos following frequent m&as: Is integration with SOA technology*. In 40th Hawaii International Conference on System Science Waikoloa, Hawaii, US.

Hohpe, G., & Woolf, B. (2004). *Enterprise integration patterns*. Addison-Wesley.

Kurbel, K., Jankowska, A. M., & Dabkowski, A. (2005). Architecture for multi-channel enterprise resource planning system. In J. Krogstie, K. Kautz, & D. Allen (Eds.), *Mobile information systems II*, 191, (pp. 245-259). New York, NY: Springer-Verlag. Retrieved from http://www.springerlink.com/content/6717916mw6081610/

Lee, A. (2010). Retrospect and prospect: Information systems research in the last and next 25 years. *Journal of Information Technology, 25*, 336–348. doi:10.1057/jit.2010.24

Linthicum, D. (2004). *Next generation application integration*. Addison-Wesley.

Mehrotra, S., Rastogi, R., Korth, H., & Silberschatz, A. (1992). A transaction model for multidatabase systems. *Proceedings of the International Conference on Distributed Computing Systems*, (pp. 56-63).

Mehta, M., & Hirschheim, R. (2007). Strategic alignment in mergers & acquisitions: Theorizing is integration decision making. *Journal of the Association for Information Systems, 8*(3), 143–174.

Pedersen, R. U. (2007). TinyOS education with LEGO MINDSTORMS NXT. In Gama, J., & Garber, M. M. (Eds.), *Learning from data streams* (pp. 231–241). Springer. doi:10.1007/3-540-73679-4_14

Polyzois, C., & Garcia-Molina, H. (1994). Evaluation of remote backup algorithms for transaction-processing systems. *ACM TODS, 19*(3), 423–449. doi:10.1145/185827.185836

Robbins, S., & Stylianou, A. (1999). Post-merger systems integration: The impact on is capabilities. *Information & Management, 36*, 205–212. doi:10.1016/S0378-7206(99)00018-X

Sarrazin, H., & West, A. (2011). Understanding the strategic value of it in m&a. *McKinsey Quarterly*.

Stockinger, H. (1999). Data replication in distributed database systems. *CMS Note*. Retrieved from http://cdsweb.cern.ch/record/687136

Sudarsanam, P. (2003). *Creating value from mergers and acquisitions: The challenges: An integrated and international perspective*. Prentice Hall.

Tanriverdi, H., & Uysal, V. (2011). Cross-business information technology integration and acquirer value creation in corporate mergers and acquisitions. *Information Systems Research, 22*(4). doi:10.1287/isre.1090.0250

Weikum, G., & Schek, H. (1992). Concepts and applications of multilevel transactions and open nested transactions. In Elmagarmid, A. (Ed.), *Database transaction models for advanced applications* (pp. 515–553). Morgan Kaufmann.

Wijnhoven, F., Spil, T., Stegwee, R., & Fa, A. (2006). Post-merger it integration strategies: An IT alignment perspective. *The Journal of Strategic Information Systems, 15*(1), 5–28. doi:10.1016/j.jsis.2005.07.002

Zhang, A., Nodine, M., Bhargava, B., & Bukhres, O. (1994). Ensuring relaxed atomicity for flexible transactions in multidatabase systems. *Proceedings of ACM SIGMOD Conference*, (pp. 67-78).

Zhu, H. (2005). *Building reusable components with service-oriented architectures*. In 2005 IEEE International Conference on Information Reuse and Integration (IEEE IRI-2005), Las Vegas, Nevada, USA.

KEY TERMS AND DEFINITIONS

Data Streams: Continuous flow of data from sensor systems.

Enterprise Resource Planning Systems: Integrated and holistic system to handle the majority of company functionality.

Heterogeneous Databases: Databases that differ with respect to elements related to system integration such as data models or location.

Modular Systems: Subdivision of a system into its smaller parts.

Relaxed Acid Properties: A set of properties that allows integration of heterogeneous databases.

SOA: Service oriented architecture which is both a paradigm and also a set of supporting web service standards.

Chapter 10
Password Recovery Research and its Future Direction

Vrizlynn L. L. Thing
Institute for Infocomm Research, Singapore

Hwei-Ming Ying
Institute for Infocomm Research, Singapore

ABSTRACT

As users become increasingly aware of the need to adopt strong password, it brings challenges to digital forensics investigators due to the password protection of potential evidentiary data. On the other hand, due to human nature and their tendency to select memorable passwords, which compromises security for convenience, users may select strong passwords by considering a permutation of dictionary words. In this chapter, the authors discuss the existing password recovery methods and identify promising password recovery approaches. They also present their previous work on the design of a time-memory tradeoff pre-computed table coupled with a new sorting algorithm, and its two new storage mechanisms. The results on the evaluation of its password recovery performance are also presented. In this chapter, the authors propose the design of a new password recovery table by integrating the construction of common passwords within the enhanced rainbow table to incorporate the two promising password recovery approaches. They then present the theoretical proof of the feasibility of this technique.

INTRODUCTION

Being the most common authentication method, passwords are widely used to protect valuable data and to ensure a secure access to systems/machines. However, the use of password protec- tion presents a challenge for investigators while conducting digital forensics examinations.

In some cases, compelling a suspect to sur- render his password would force him to produce evidence that could be used to incriminate him, thereby violating his right against self-incrim-

DOI: 10.4018/978-1-4666-2190-9.ch010

ination. Therefore, this presents a problem for the authorities. It is then necessary to have the capability to access a suspect's data without expecting his assistance.

While there exist methods to decode hashes to reveal passwords used to protect potential evidence, lengthier passwords with larger characters sets have been encouraged to thwart password recovery. Awareness of the need to use stronger passwords and active adoption have also rendered many existing password recovery tools inefficient or even ineffective.

The more common methods of password recovery techniques are based on brute force, precomputed tables, dictionary attack, breaking hashing algorithms and more recently, using rainbow tables.

In the brute force attack, every possible combination of the password characters in the password space is attempted to perform a match comparison. It is an extremely time consuming process and recovering a strong password could take weeks or even months. However, due to its exhaustive generation and search, the password will be recovered eventually if sufficient time is given. Cain and Abel (Cain and Abel, 2012), John the Ripper (John The Ripper, 2012) and LCP (LCPSoft, 2012) are some popular tools which support brute force attacks.

The precomputed tables, on the other hand, hold all the possible passwords in the password space and their corresponding hash values, which were generated beforehand. The tables were then sorted and stored. Given a password hash, the corresponding password can be easily retrieved from the tables. The disadvantage is the need for an extremely large storage space. For example, to generate precomputed tables for 10-character passwords whereby the characters can be any printable ASCII characters, and the hash output for each password is 16 bytes (e.g. MD5 hash), the precomputed tables will be 1.317ZB (Zetta Bytes).

Therefore, this method is not feasible for strong password (e.g. within a large password space).

The dictionary attack method composes of loading a file of dictionary words into a password cracking tool to search for a match of their hash values with the stored one. It is a subset of the precomputed tables as only commonly used passwords were stored in the file. If the password is not a dictionary word, the recovery would fail.

Research attempting to discover and identify the weaknesses of hashing algorithms have also been useful in the application of passwords or encryption keys recovery. This method is based mainly on the collision of hashes in specific hashing algorithms (Contini, 2006; Fouque, 2007; Sasaki, 2007; Sasaki, 2008). However, they are too complex and extremely time-consuming to be used for performing password recovery during forensics investigations. The methods are also applicable to specific hashing algorithms with inherent weakness only.

In the time-memory tradeoff method (Hellman, 1980), a hybrid of brute force attack and precomputed tables is used. Large number of different passwords are repeatedly hashed and reduced to forms password chains. Only the head and tail of these chains are stored in tables. During a recovery, the password hash goes through a series of reduction and hashing until a match with one of the stored tails is found. The chain which generates this password hash can be identified and the password can be recovered. The storage space and recovery speed can be adjusted flexibly by setting the rounds of hashing and reduction, and the available storage space, accordingly. This method can be applied to retrieve Windows login passwords encrypted into LM or NTLM hashes (Todorov, 2007). Passwords encrypted with hashing algorithms such as MD5 (Rivest, 1992), SHA-2 (NIST, 2002) and RIPEMD-160 (Dobbertin, 1996) are also susceptible to this recovery method.

The rainbow table method (Oechslin, 2003; Thing, 2009; Ying, 2011) falls under the class of time-memory tradeoff method. The difference is that different reduction functions are used at each step of the chain generation, so as to minimise the collision of merging chains. Therefore, the success rate of password recovery can be higher. Existing rainbow table based password recovery tools (Ophcrack, 2012; RainbowCrack, 2012; Shmoo, 2012) are based on the method by Oechslin (Oechslin, 2003). As a hybrid of brute force attack and precomputed tables, rainbow tables have shown significant improvement in the success rate (ranging from 75% to 99%), storage requirement (typically few Megabytes to Gigabytes) and recovery time (in terms of seconds to minutes).

In this article, we present our time-memory tradeoff rainbow table method, which show promising performance and results (that is, in terms of success rate and recovery speed) during password recovery. We propose the future directions in the area of password recovery research, through the integration of permutated dictionary words and our rainbow table techniques, by taking into consideration the human nature and their tendency in password selections. We present the theoretical proof of the feasibility of the core mechanism. We also discuss challenges and how the technological advances may aid in password recovery research.

BACKGROUND

Before proceeding further, we state some definitions which will be used in this section, in Table 1.

The idea of a general time-memory tradeoff was first proposed by Hellman in 1980 (Hellman, 1980). In the context of password recovery, we describe the Hellman algorithm as follows.

We let X be the plaintext password and Y be the corresponding stored hash value of X. Given Y, we need to find X which satisfies $h(X) = Y$, where h is a known hash function. However, finding $X = h^{-1}(Y)$ is feasibly impossible since hashes are computed using one-way functions, where the reversal function, h^{-1}, is unknown. Hellman suggested taking the plaintext values and applying alternate hashing and reducing, to generate a precomputed table and storing only the first and last columns (the initial and final plaintext values in each row). During a recovery, a reducing operation is performed on the hash and a search of the computed plaintext value attempting to match one in the stored last column is conducted. Alternate hashing and reducing operations are performed till a matching plaintext value is found and the corresponding row is reconstructed to trace back to the correct plaintext value which produced the given hash.

Table 1. Definition of symbols

Symbol	Definition
X	Plaintext password
Y	Hashed value of X
x_i	Initial value of a chain
$y_{i,j}$	Hashed value of a password in a chain (i is chain number, j is column number of hashed values)
$z_{i,j}$	Reduced value of a hash
c_i	Final value of a chain
h	hash function
r_i	Reduction function
n	Number of reduction functions
m	Number of chains

For example, the corresponding 128-bit hash value for a 7-character password (composed from a character set of English alphabets), is obtained by performing the password hashing function on the password. With a reduction function such as $H \bmod 26^7$, where H is the hash value converted to its decimal form, the resulting values are distributed in a best effort uniform manner. For example, if we start with the initial plaintext value of "abcdefg" and upon hashing, we get a binary output of 0000000....000010000000....01, which is 64 '0's and a '1' followed by 62 '0's and a '1'. $H = 2^{63} + 1 = 9223372036854775809$. The reduction function will then convert this value to "3665127553" which corresponds to a plaintext representation "lwmkgij", computed from $(11(26^6) + 22(26^5) + 12(26^4) + 10(25^3) + 6(26^2) + 8(26^1) + 9(26^0)$.

After a pre-defined number of rounds of hashing and reducing (making up a chain) as shown in Figure 1, only the initial and final plaintext values are stored (as shown in Figure 2). Therefore, only the "head" and "tail" of a chain are stored in the table. Using different initial plaintexts, the hashing and reducing operations are repeated, to generate a larger table (of increasing rows or chains). A larger table will theoretically contain more pre-computed values (i.e. disregarding hash collisions), thereby increasing the success rate of password recovery, while taking up more storage space. The pre-defined number of rounds of hashing and reducing

will also increase the success rate by increasing the length of the "virtual" chain, while bringing about a higher computational overhead.

To recover a plaintext from a given hash, a reduction operation is performed on the hash and a search for a match of the computed plaintext with the final value in the table is conducted. If a match is not found, the hashing and reducing operations are performed on the computed plaintext to arrive at a new plaintext so that another round of search can be made.

For example, we would like to find the password corresponding to a password hash, v. We apply one round of reducing operation to the password hash, v, and obtain a plaintext, w. We perform a search and find a match of w to the final value of the 212th chain in the rainbow table shown in Figure 3 (that is, $w = c_{212}$). The chain is then computed from its initial value, x_{212}, till the password hash, v, which is equal to $y_{212,3000}$, is reached. The password, which is the plaintext, $z_{212,3000}$, just before the password hash, $y_{212,3000}$, can then be obtained from the chain.

In the event that no matching value can be found on the rainbow table, it is deduced that the particular password does not exist within the table and cannot be recovered. To increase the success rate of recovery, the number of reduction functions (that is, n) and chain count (that is, m) have to be increased. However, this will at the same

Figure 1. Hellman's table

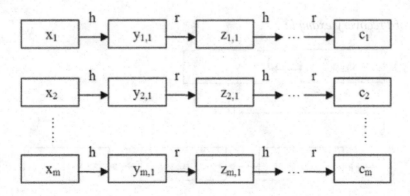

Figure 2. Stored values in a time-memory tradeoff password recovery table

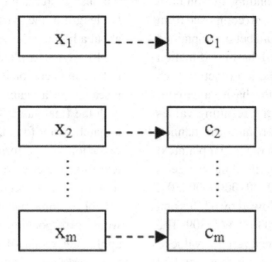

time, increase the computational complexity and storage requirement significantly.

The maximum number of rounds of hashing, reducing and searching operations is determined by the chain length. If the hash value is found in a particular chain, the values in the chain are then worked out by performing the hashing and reducing functions to arrive at the plaintext giving the specific hash value.

Unfortunately, there is a likelihood that chains with different initial values may merge due to collisions. These merges will reduce the number of distinct hash values in the chains and therefore, diminish the rate of successful recovery.

The success rate can be increased by using multiple tables with each table using a different reduction function. If we let $P(t)$ be the success

rate of using t tables, then $P(t) = 1 - (1 - P(1))^t$, which is an increasing function of t since $P(1)$ is between 0 and 1. Hence, introducing more tables increases the success rate but also cause an increase in both the computational complexity and storage space.

In (Denning, 1982), Rivest suggested a method of using distinguished points as end points for chains. Distinguished points are keys which satisfy a given criteria, e.g. the first or last q bits are all '0's. In this method, the chains are not generated with a fixed length but they terminate upon reaching pre-defined distinguished points. This method decreases the number of memory lookups compared to Hellman's method and is capable of loop detection. If a distinguished point is not obtained after a large finite number

Figure 3. Password recovery example

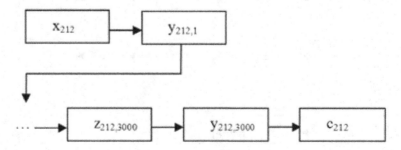

of operations, the chain is suspected to contain a loop and is discarded. Therefore, the generated chains are free of loops. One limitation is that the chains will merge if there is a collision within the same table. The variable lengths of the chains will also result in an increase in the number of false alarms. Additional computations are also required to determine if a false alarm has occurred.

In 2003, Oechslin proposed a new table structure (Oechslin, 2003) as shown in Figure 4, to reduce the probability of merging occurrences. These tables with the new table structure were named the rainbow tables. The chains in the rainbow table were generated using multiple reduction functions instead of the same function so that there will only be merges if the collisions occur at the same positions in both chains. An experiment was carried out and presented in Oechslin's paper. It showed that given a set of parameters which is constant in both scenarios, the measured coverage in a single rainbow table is 78.8% compared to the 75.8% from the classical tables of Hellman with distinguished points. In addition, the number of calculations needed to perform the search is reduced as well. Rainbow tables have been well-known to provide an efficient way of recovering a password.

However, as cyber crimes are continuously rising, people become increasingly aware of the need to adopt stronger security to protect their data. At the same time, this brings challenges to the digital forensics investigators as it becomes increasingly difficult to access password-protected evidentiary data. Therefore, researchers are looking into methods to increase the success rate of password recovery despite the challenges.

IMPROVING PASSWORD RECOVERY

The key objectives in enhancing password recovery to meet the challenges of strong password-protected evidentiary data are to improve (or maintain satisfactory) success rate and speed of password recovery. Utilizing the hybrid approach of the brute force technique and precomputed table has proven to be the most cost-efficient way (that is, achieving the maximal success rate using a minimal amount of time) to perform password recovery. Therefore, to improve password recovery performance, further research to increase the success rate and reducing the recovery time of rainbow tables should be conducted while taking into consideration stronger passwords adopted by common users.

On the other hand, it has been shown that humans are tempted to choose passwords which are easy for them to remember (Google News, 2009; Narayanan, 2005). Such passwords could be based on a combination of common key se-

Figure 4. Rainbow table

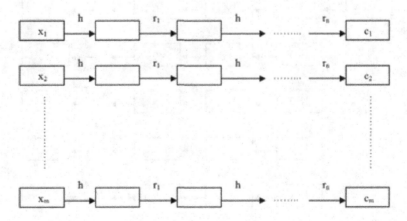

quences on the keyboard layout, dictionary words, and a combination of dictionary words. Another common approach to strengthen the passwords while maintaining their memorability is to include numbers and special characters in the passwords. Therefore, by taking into consideration the human nature and their tendency in password selections, and incorporating such knowledge into the design of a new method to perform password recovery would improve password recovery performance significantly.

In the following sub-sections, we briefly describe our recent work on the enhancement of rainbow tables (Thing, 2009; Ying, 2011). Next, we propose a new approach of the integration of memorable passwords with the enhancement rainbow tables and present the proof of the feasibility of the approach.

Enhancement of Rainbow Tables

In (Thing, 2009; Ying, 2011), we proposed an enhanced rainbow table design with a novel sorting algorithm. In the design, the same reduction functions as in the rainbow table method are used. The first novelty lies in the chains generation technique. Instead of taking a large set of plaintexts as the initial values, we systematically choose a much smaller unique set. We choose a plaintext and compute its corresponding hash value by applying the password hash algorithm. We let the resulting hash value written in decimal digits be H. Following that, $(H+1) \bmod 2^j$, $(H+2) \bmod 2^j$,......, $(H+k) \bmod 2^j$ for a variable k, where j is the number of bits of the hash output value, were computed. For example, in MD5 hash, $j = 128$. These hash values are then noted as the branches of the above chosen initial plaintext. We then proceed by applying alternate hashing and reducing operations to all these branches. We call this resulting extended chain, a block (as shown in Figure 5). The final values of the plaintexts are then stored with this 1 initial plaintext value. We perform the same operations for the other plaintexts. These sets of initial and final values make up the new pre-computed table.

To recover a password given a hash, we apply reducing and hashing operations alternatively until we obtain a plaintext that corresponds to one of the stored final values, as in the rainbow table method. After which, we generate the corresponding branch, till the value of the password hash is reached.

Figure 5. Enhanced rainbow table

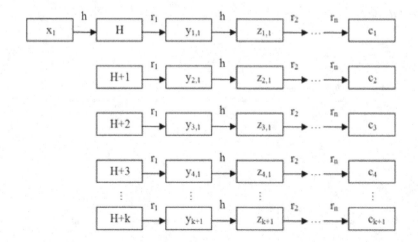

Comparisons Between the Designs of Enhanced Rainbow Table and Rainbow Table

We identify and list the differences and similarities between the design of our new method and the rainbow table method as follow:

- Both use *n* reduction functions.
- Instead of storing the initial and final values as a pair as in the rainbow table, the initial value is stored with multiple output plaintexts after a series of hashing and reducing operations. This results in a large amount of storage conservation in the new method.
- The hashes H, $(H+1)$ mod 2^j, $(H+2)$ mod 2^j,......, $(H+k)$ mod 2^j are calculated in order to generate subsequent hashes, resulting in the uniqueness of the values in the 1*st* column of hashes in the new method. The uniqueness of the hash values is guaranteed unless the total number of hashes is greater than 2^j. This situation is not likely to happen as it assumes an extremely large table which fully stores all the possible pre-computed values.
- In this new design, the recovery of some passwords in the first column is not possible as they are not stored in the first place. However, we have shown in our analysis and evaluation (Thing, 2009) that the effect is negligible.

The main drawback of the proposed enhanced rainbow table is that each password search will incur a significant amount of time complexity. The reason is that the passwords cannot be sorted in the usual alphabetical order now, since in doing so, the information of its corresponding initial hash value will be lost. The lookup will then have to rely on checking every single stored password in the table. However, this inefficient search will result in a significant degradation in the password recovery speed. To solve this problem, we propose a novel sorting algorithm so that the password lookup in the stored tables can be optimized. For the rest of the article, we follow the definition of the symbols as shown in Table 2.

We require a sorting of the "tail" passwords to achieve a fast lookup. Therefore, we introduce the use of special characters that cannot be found on the keyboard, which are the non-printable ASCII characters, for rainbow table sorting. There are a total of 161 such characters and we assume that these non-printable ASCII characters do not form any of the character set of the passwords since they could not be keyed in by users to form passwords. We insert a number of these special characters into the passwords that we store.

The way in which these special characters are inserted will provide the information on the original position of the passwords in the rainbow table after the table has been rearranged in alphabetical order. The consequence is that this these inserted special characters will incur storage space. However, we illustrate in (Ying, 2011)

Table 2. Definition of symbols for enhanced rainbow table sorting

Symbol	Definition
Y	Total number of special characters available
w	Number of special characters in password
m	Length of password
x	Special character in password (labelled x_1, x_2,.....), $1 \leq x_i \leq Y$
p	location of a special character within password (labelled p_0, p_1,.....), $0 \leq p_i \leq m$, where x_i is placed at location p_{i-1} within a password

that the increase in storage space is minimal and is also significantly lesser than the original rainbow table's storage requirement. The advantage of this sorting algorithm is that the passwords in the table can now be sorted and thus a password lookup can be optimized.

As an example, we let 0000000 denote a 7-character password. The 161 non-printable ASCII characters are used as special characters $x_1, x_2,........, x_{161}$, and are represented by numeric values from 1 to 161, respectively. The 8 possible locations of the special characters in a password are represented by underlines in _0_0_0_0_0_0_0_. Each location can hold more than one special character.

For example, 0000000 does not carry any special character and is at position 0. In $0000000x_1$, x_1 is the first (scanning from rightmost) special character in the password, as denoted by its subscript value of 1. The position of this password depends on the numeric value represented by the special character, x_1. Therefore, the position is from 1 to 161 depending on which of the 161 special characters is used (that is, $0000000x1$ is

at position 1 if $x_1 = 1$, and at position 161 if $x_1 = 161$). Continuing in this manner, $000000x_{10}$ is at position 162 if $x_1 = 1$, and at position 322 if $x_1 = 161$. Therefore, $x_1 0000000$ is at position 1128 if $x_1 = 1$, and at position 1288 if $x_1 = 161$.

After covering all the locations for special characters in the password by using only 1 character but without completing the allocation of special characters for all the passwords in the password space, we can increase the number of allocated special characters in the password, one at a time. For the insertion of 2 characters, $0000000x_2 x_1$ is at position 1289 if $x_1 = x_2 = 1$. $0000000x_2 x_1$ is at position 1290 if $x_2 = 1$ and $x_1 = 2$. $0000000x_2 x_1$ is at position 1291 if $x_2 = 1$ and $x_1 = 3$. Continuing in this manner, $0000000x_2 x_1$ is at position 27209 if $x_2 = x_1 = 161$, $000000x_2 0x_1$ is at position 27210 if $x_2 = x_1 = 1$, and so on.

We derive the formulas in Figure 6 for the computation of the original position of a password in the rainbow table.

In addition, we also proposed two new storage methods for the enhanced rainbow table. In method 1, the passwords are still stored side by

Figure 6. Password position computation

w=1: Original position of password
$$Yp_0 + x_1$$

w=2: Original position of password
$$Yx_2 + x_1 + Y^2\binom{p_1+1}{2} + Y^2 p_0 + Ym$$

w=3: Original position of password
$$Y^2 x_3 + Yx_2 + x_1 + Y^3\binom{p_2+2}{3} + Y^3\binom{p_1+1}{2} + Y^3 p_0 + Y^2\binom{m+1}{2} + Y^2 m + Ym$$

w=4: Original position of password
$$Y^3 x_4 + Y^2 x_3 + Yx_2 + x_1 + Y^4\binom{p_3+3}{4} + Y^4\binom{p_2+2}{3} + Y^4\binom{p_1+1}{2} + Y^4 p_0 + Y^3\binom{m+2}{3} + Y^3\binom{m+1}{2} + Y^3 m + Y^2\binom{m+1}{2} + Y^2 m + Ym$$

For a general w, the original position is given by
$$\sum_{i=0}^{w-1}\left(Y^i x_{i+1} + Y^w\binom{p_i+i}{i+1}\right) + \sum_{i=0}^{w-2}\sum_{j=0}^{i} Y^{i+1}\binom{m+j}{j+1}$$

side as in the original rainbow table method. Retrieval of passwords for checking is performed at a specific fixed length. The w used in method 1 must be a fixed length too. The total number of positions that can be identified is reduced as they do not include positions that can be identified for number of special characters smaller than w. In storage method 2, we propose storing the passwords line by line. Therefore, a special character has to be used for delimitation purpose. A good choice would be the line feed character. Y is then reduced to 160. The w used in method 2 can be of a variable length. The total number of positions that can be identified still includes positions that can be identified for number of special characters smaller than w.

In (Ying, 2011), the sufficiency of the available special characters for use in sorting, the storage requirements, and the success rate of password recovery were evaluated. We showed that for a password length of 10 characters, only 5 special characters are needed to sort the entire table. As the length of the password increases, the required number of special characters required for performing sorting increases very slowly. This is due to the simultaneous increase in the number of special characters insertion spaces in a password as the length of the password increases. We also evaluated the 2 storage methods and found that both methods have comparable requirements on w for the same length of passwords. Therefore, it is advisable to use storage method 1 as the password retrieval for lookup has a lower complexity due to the use of fixed length per password storage.

Maintaining the same storage space requirements for both the enhanced rainbow table and the original rainbow table, the enhanced rainbow table is able to achieve an improvement of up to 26.13% and 23.60%, for the recovery of alpha-numeric passwords and passwords containing any of the printable ASCII characters, respectively, over the original rainbow table.

Maintaining the same success rate of recovery for both the tables, the enhanced rainbow table is able to achieve up to 28.57% in storage space conservation compared to the original rainbow table in the case of the alpha-numeric passwords recovery. In the case of the recovery of passwords containing any of the printable ASCII characters, the storage space conservation can reach 25%.

Next, we propose the integration of permutated dictionary attack within the enhanced rainbow table to take into consideration the human tendency to select memorable passwords.

Integration of Permutated Dictionary and Enhanced Rainbow Table

In rainbow tables, passwords were generated based on the hashing and reduction functions. Therefore, the generation is very random and a large percentage of passwords may contain special characters at random places and non-dictionary words. Such passwords have a very low memorability level and users who chose such passwords usually create the passwords using strong password creation tools. Most users also need to note down the passwords and store them separately to prevent them from forgetting their own passwords for subsequent accesses. However, users tend to want to avoid the trouble of choosing a password of such high complexity and worry about forgetting it later. Therefore, they usually try to choose passwords which are memorable. These passwords are usually dictionary words, common keyboard layout key sequences or information related to themselves (for example, their name, spouse's name or birthdays).

A simple approach is to conduct a dictionary attack first and then the rainbow table password recovery if the dictionary attack fails. However, both the computational overhead and storage requirement will be high. Instead, in this article, we propose a novel approach to incorporate common passwords into the rainbow table so that the percentage of common passwords can be higher resulting in a higher success rate even in the scenario whereby the length of the passwords is large and the storage capacity is limited. The aim of the integration of permuted dictionary and the enhanced rainbow table is to construct the table where by it can contain as many permutated dictionary words as possible (in both stored elements and the virtual chains).

The simplest method to create the hybrid table is to generate permutated dictionary words as the initial column of passwords. However, this is only applicable for the case of the original rainbow table as the initial column is also discarded in the enhanced rainbow table.

Instead, the approach we have to adopt is to have the first reduction function generate permutated dictionary words in the first virtual column, which in the enhanced rainbow table, will be recoverable. However, in this case, the possible number of "initially generated" permutated dictionary words is limited by the number of chains in the table. The recovery speed may also suffer for such passwords as they fall under the first virtual column. Therefore, next, we additionally propose constructing a chain where all the entries are possible common passwords.

Suppose we identify x number of the most common passwords that we would like to incorporate in the virtual chain, other than those we have already included in to first virtual column of the other chains. We want to ensure that these x passwords can be generated from our rainbow chain. One way to do this is that starting with any password, hash and choose an appropriate reduction function R_1 which reduces the hash to one of the x number of words in the list. Continuing with the chain generation, hash this result and choose an appropriate reduction function R_2 which again reduces the new hash to another one of the words in the list. Continue doing so until all the remaining words in the list have been generated in the chain. As long as x is not too large relative to the total password space, we will always almost certainly be able to choose such reduction functions, R_i, and thus, generate such a chain which contains all the common passwords.

As an example, suppose we want to recover a 7-character password where the character set consists of all the lower case alphabetical letters and the passwords are hashed using the MD5 algorithm. In addition, we want to ensure that the common passwords are recoverable. For example, given that "letmein", "abcdefg" and "testing" are three common 7-character passwords, the goal is to include these passwords in the rainbow chains so that they can be recovered.

Starting with the password "testing" and upon hashing it, its hashed value will be H_1 = ae2b1f-ca515949e5d54fb22b8ed95575. Converting this value to the decimal representation and apply a reduction function R_1 to H_1 where $R_1(H_1) = H_1 +$ 4938209469 mod 267. Converting $R_1(H_1)$ back to the password representation will correspond to the password "letmein". The next step of the chain is to hash "letmein". This will result in H_2 = 0d107d09f5bbe40cade3de5c71e9e9b7. Then, apply a reduction function R_2 to H_2 where $R_2(H_2)$ $= H_2 + 3129034064$ mod 267. Converting $R_2(H_2)$ back to the password representation will correspond to the password "abcdefg".

Therefore, in this example, we set the design of the reduction function R_i to be ($p_{i+1} - a_i$ mod N), where p_{i+1} is the password to be generated from one round of hashing and reducing p_i using H_i and R_i, respectively, a_i is the generated hash from hashing p_i with H_i, and N is the total password space.

To ensure that collision would not arise from using the same R in the table, we perform a simple proof of the uniqueness of R for the example cases, as follow.

Proposition 1: Any given 3 common passwords can be generated regardless of the size of the password space and the hash applied using unique reduction functions.

Proof: We let the size of the password space be N, and let the hash function be denoted by H. For simplification, we define "=" to represent "≡ mod N" for the subsequent parts of the proof. To prove the proposition, we show that there exists at least one arrangement to insert these 3 passwords such their corresponding reduction functions will be distinct.

We let the 3 passwords be p_1, p_2 and p_3, and the results of $H(p_1)$ mod N, $H(p_2)$ mod N, and $H(p_3)$ mod N, be a_1, a_2 and a_3, respectively. Suppose for all 6 arrangements, each arrangement results in having an identical reduction function. Thus, we obtain, the following system of equations:

1. $p_2 - a_1 = p_3 - a_2$
2. $p_3 - a_1 = p_2 - a_3$
3. $p_1 - a_2 = p_3 - a_1$
4. $p_3 - a_2 = p_1 - a_3$
5. $p_1 - a_3 = p_2 - a_1$
6. $p_2 - a_3 = p_1 - a_2$

Comparing equations 1 and 3, we get $p_1 + p_2 = 2p_3$

Comparing equations 2 and 5, we get $p_1 + p_3 = 2p_2$

Comparing equations 4 and 6, we get $p_3 + p_2 = 2p_1$.

Solving these 3 new equations, we obtain $p_1 = p_2 = p_3$. This is a contradiction since p_1, p_2, p_3 are distinct modulo N; thus proving Proposition 1.

Proposition 2: Any given 4 common passwords can be generated regardless of the size of the password space and the hash applied using unique reduction functions.

Proof: We let the size of the password space be N, and let the hash function be denoted by H. Again, for simplification, we define "=" to represent "≡ mod N" for the subsequent parts of the proof. We let the 4 passwords be p_1, p_2, p_3 and p_4, and the results of $H(p_1)$ mod N, $H(p_2)$ mod N, $H(p_3)$ mod N, and $H(p_4)$ mod N, be a_1, a_2, a_3 and a_4, respectively.

We consider the 3 passwords p_1, p_2 and p_3 to be placed in the first 3 entries of the chain, as shown

in the above case. Applying Proposition 1, there exists an arrangement which will result in distinct reduction functions for each of the password generation. Without loss of generality, we assume that the first 3 passwords in the chain are (p_1, p_2, p_3) in that order such that the corresponding reduction functions are distinct. Therefore, p_4 will be in the 4th entry of the chain. Suppose that $p_4 - a_3 \neq p_2 - a_1$ and $p_4 - a_3 \neq p_3 - a_2$. Then (p_1, p_2, p_3, p_4) is the desired order to place the passwords which ensures that the reduction functions are distinct.

Suppose either $p_4 - a_3 = p_2 - a_1$ or $p_4 - a_3 = p_3 - a_2$.

Case 1: $p_4 - a_3 = p_2 - a_1$

Consider the arrangement (p_4, p_1, p_2, p_3). If $p_1 - a_4 \neq p_2 - a_1$ and $p_1 - a_4 \neq p_3 - a_2$, the proof is completed. Otherwise, either $p_1 - a_4 = p_2 - a_1$ or $p_1 - a_4 = p_3 - a_2$.

Case 1(a): $p_1 - a_4 = p_2 - a_1 = p_4 - a_3$.

Consider the arrangement (p_1, p_3, p_4, p_2). Suppose not all the reduction functions are distinct, then $p_3 - a_1 = p_2 - a_4$. Next, we consider the arrangement (p_4, p_1, p_3, p_2). If not all the reduction functions are distinct, then $p_3 - a_1 = p_2 - a_3$. This implies that $a_4 = a_3$ and thus, $p_1 = p_4$, which is therefore, a contradiction.

Case 1(b): $p_1 - a_4 = p_3 - a_2$ and $p_4 - a_3 = p_2 - a_1$

If $p_1 - a_4 = p_1 - a_3$, then $a_3 = a_4$. Thus, (p_4, p_3, p_1, p_2) will be the desired arrangement. If $a_3 \neq a_4$, we consider the arrangements (p_4, p_2, p_3, p_1), (p_1, p_3, p_4, p_2), (p_4, p_1, p_3, p_2), (p_2, p_4, p_1, p_3) and (p_1, p_4, p_2, p_3) in the order as stated. If none of these arrangements result in having distinct reductions functions, then by considering arrangement (p_2, p_4, p_1, p_3), we obtain $p_3 - a_1 = p_4 - a_2$, and by considering the arrangement (p_1, p_4, p_2, p_3), we obtain $p_4 - a_1 = p_3 - a_2$.

Hence, $p_3 = p_4$, which is a contradiction.

Case 2: $p_4 - a_3 = p_3 - a_2$

Case 2(a): $p_4 - a_3 = p_3 - a_2 = p_1 - a_4$

Consider the arrangement (p_3, p_4, p_2, p_1). If this arrangement results in having distinct reduction functions, then $p_2 - a_4 = p_1 - a_2$. Next, we consider the arrangement (p_4, p_2, p_3, p_1). If this arrangement does not result in having distinct reduction functions again, then we must have $p_2 - a_4 = p_1 - a_3$. Hence, $a_2 = a_3$ which imp

Case 2(b): lies $p_3 = p_4$, which is a contradiction.

$p_1 - a_4 = p_2 - a_1$ and $p_4 - a_3 = p_3 - a_2$

Consider the arrangement (p_4, p_1, p_3, p_2). If $a_1 = a_3$, then we consider the arrangement (p_3, p_2, p_1, p_4).

If this is not the desired arrangement, then $a_2 = a_4$. Finally, we consider the arrangement (p_2, p_1, p_3, p_4).

If $a_1 \neq a_3$, we consider the arrangements (p_2, p_1, p_3, p_4), (p_3, p_2, p_4, p_1) and (p_2, p_3, p_1, p_4) in this order. Using a similar argument as in case 1(b), we obtain $p_1 + p_2 = p_3 + p_4$ and $p_2 - p_1 = p_3 - p_4$. Thus, $p_2 = p_3$, which is a contradiction.

This proves Proposition 2.

FUTURE RESEARCH DIRECTIONS

As technology advances, it aids in the progress of password recovery research. The future of password recovery research should focus on designing methods and mechanisms which utilize and integrate promising existing and new technologies. As demonstrated in this article, we provide a simple design of the integration of the permutated dictionary and rainbow table to maximize the potential of each method, after considering the trend in users' password choices. Other future directions in the research of password recovery could also take into consideration the increasing speed of computing hardware, increasing storage capacity, and the utilization of parallelism processing, cloud storage and cloud computing resources to optimize the password recovery performance despite stronger passwords adoption.

CONCLUSION

In this article, we first explained the need for password recovery in the field of digital forensics, where suspects or criminals can make use of password protection techniques to protect their data and hinder the investigation process. We then discussed the existing password recovery methods, such as the brute force attack, the precomputed tables approach, the dictionary attacks, cryptanalysis of hashing algorithms to break them for the purpose of generating password hash values collisions, and the rainbow tables approaches. We then identified the promising password recovery approaches as the rainbow table approaches and the permutated dictionary attack. The reason is that the rainbow table approach can be considered the most cost-efficient way (that is, achieving the maximal success rate using a minimal amount of time) to perform password recovery, while the dictionary attack takes into consideration the tendency of humans to choose passwords that are memorable. In addition, we discussed the use of permutated dictionary words. Permutated dictionary words are commonly used by humans to combine dictionary words, include/change special characters at specific locations (for example, numbers as a suffix to the words, replacing 'i' with '1') and include common keyboard layout key sequences (for example, 'asdfghjkl;'), to enhance the strength of their weak chosen passwords.

We presented our previous work on the design of a time-memory tradeoff pre-computed table coupled with a new sorting algorithm, and its 2 new storage mechanisms. Maintaining the same storage space requirements for both our enhanced rainbow table and the original rainbow table, we were able to achieve an improvement of up to 26.13% and 23.60%, for the recovery of alphanumeric passwords and passwords containing any of the printable ASCII characters, respectively, over the original rainbow table. While maintaining the same success rate of recovery for both the tables, our enhanced rainbow table was able to achieve up to 28.57% in storage space conservation compared to the original rainbow table in the case of the alpha-numeric passwords recovery. In the case of the recovery of passwords containing any of the printable ASCII characters, the storage space conservation can reach 25%.

We then proposed the design of a new password recovery table by integrating the construction of common passwords within our enhanced rainbow table to incorporate the two promising password recovery approaches. We then presented the theoretical proof of the feasibility of this technique. We also pointed out the future research directions of password recovery research to focus on the design of hybrid systems and mechanisms to integrate other promising algorithms, utilizing the high-speed hardware and parallelism of the processing.

REFERENCES

Cain and Abel. (2012). *Password recovery tool*. Retrieved February 15, 2012, from http://www.oxid.it

Contini, S., & Yin, Y. L. (2006). Forgery and partial key-recovery attacks on HMAC and NMAC using hash collisions. *Proceedings of the Twelfth International Conference on the Theory and Application of Cryptology and Information Security (AsiaCrypt), Lecture Notes in Computer Science, 4284,* December 3-7, 2006, Shanghai, China, (pp. 37-53). ISBN 3-540-49475-8

Denning, D. E. R. (1982). *Cryptography and data security*. Addison-Wesley Publication.

Dobbertin, H., Bosselaers, A., & Preneel, B. (1996). Ripemd-160: A strengthened version of RIPEMD. *Proceedings of the Third International Workshop on Fast Software Encryption, Lecture Notes in Computer Science, 1039,* (pp. 71-82). February 21-23, 1996, Cambridge, United Kingdom. ISBN: 3-540-60865-6

Fouque, P. A., Leurent, G., & Nguyen, P. Q. (2007). Full key recovery attacks on HMAC/NMAC-MD4 and NMAC-MD5. *Proceedings of the Twenty Seventh International Cryptology Conference, Lecture Notes in Computer Science, 4622,* August 19-23, 2007, Santa Barbara, California, United States of America, (pp. 13-30). ISBN: 978-3-540-74142-8

Google News. (2009). *Favorite passwords: '1234' and 'password'*. Retrieved December 20, 2009, from http://www.google.com/hostednews/afp/article/ALeqM5jeUc6Bblnd0M19WVQWvjS-6D2puvw

Hellman, M. E. (1980). A cryptanalytic time-memory trade-off. *IEEE Transactions on Information Theory, IT-26*(4), 401-406. ISSN: 0018-9448

John the Ripper. (2012). *Password cracker*. Retrieved February 15, 2012, from http://www.openwall.com

LCPSoft. (2012). *LCPSoft programs*. Retrieved February 15, 2012, from http://www.lcpsoft.com

Narayanan, A., & Shmatikov, V. (2005). Fast dictionary attacks on passwords using time-space tradeoff. *Proceedings of the Twelfth ACM Conference on Computer and Communications Security,* November 7-11, 2005, Alexandria, Virginia, United States of America, (pp. 364-372). ISBN: 1-59593-226-7

National Institute of Standards and Technology. NIST. (2002). Secure hash standard. *Federal Information Processing Standards Publication, 180*(2), 1-75. Retrieved February 21, 2012, from http://csrc.nist.gov/publications/fips/fips180-2/fips180-2.pdf

Oechslin, P. (2003). Making a faster cryptanalytic time-memory trade-off. *Proceedings of the Twenty Third International Cryptology Conference (CRYPTO), Lecture Notes in Computer Science, 279,* August 17-21, 2003, Santa Barbara, California, United States of America, (pp. 617-630). ISBN: 978-3-540-40674-7

Ophcrack. (2012). *Ophcrack rainbow tables*. Retrieved February 15, 2012, from http://ophcrack.sourceforge.net/tables.php

RainbowCrack. (2012). *RainbowCrack project*. Retrieved February 15, 2012, from http://project-rainbowcrack.com

Rivest, R. (1992). *The MD5 message-digest algorithm*. IETF RFC 1321, Retrieved February 21, 2012, from http:// www.ietf.org/rfc/rfc1321.txt

Sasaki, Y., Wang, L., Ohta, K., & Kunihiro, N. (2008). Security of MD5 challenge and response: Extension of APOP password recovery attack. *Proceedings of RSA Conference, The Cryptographers' Track, Lecture Notes in Computer Science, 4964, Topics in Cryptology,* April 8-11, 2008, San Francisco, United States of America, (pp. 1-18). Retrieved February 21, 2012, from http://www.springerlink.com/content/y368t967v5168586/

Sasaki, Y., Yamamoto, G., & Aoki, K. (2008). Practical password recovery on an MD5 challenge and response. *Cryptology ePrint Archive,* Report 2007/101, (pp. 101-111), Retrieved February 21, 2012, from http://eprint.iacr.org/2007/101.pdf

Shmoo. (2012). *The Shmoo Group rainbow tables*. Retrieved February 15, 2012, from http:// rainbowtables.shmoo.com

Smyth, S. M. (2009). Searches of computers and computer data at the United States border: The need for a new framework following United States V. Arnold. *Journal of Law, Technology and Policy, 2009*(1), 69-105. Retrieved February 21, 2012, from http://papers.ssrn.com/sol3/papers.cfm?abstract_id=1345927

Thing, V. L. L., & Ying, H. M. (2009). A novel time-memory trade-off method for password recovery. *International Journal of Digital Forensics and Incident Response, 6,* S114-S120. Retrieved February 21, 2012, from www.dfrws.org/2009/proceedings/p114-thing.pdf

Todorov, D. (2007). *Mechanics of user identification and authentication: Fundamentals of identity management*. Auerbach Publications. doi:10.1201/9781420052206

Ying, H. M., & Thing, V. L. L. (2011). A novel rainbow table sorting method. *Proceedings of The Second International Conference on Technical and Legal Aspects of the e-Society* (CYBERLAWS), February 23-28, 2011, Gosier, Guadeloupe, France, (pp. 35-40). ISBN: 978-1-61208-122-9

KEY TERMS AND DEFINITIONS

Cryptanalysis: Analytical methods to circumvent cryptographic algorithms.

Digital Forensics: Forensics Science encompassing the acquisition, reconstruction and analysis of digital evidence.

Enhanced Rainbow Table: A enhanced form of precomputed table where only the final columns are stored by incorporating specially designed sorting and storage methods. Used to derive the plaintext from its hash value (that is, reversing the one-way hash functions).

Password Recovery: Process, techniques, or methods to find a password which results in the similar hash so as to gain access to a system, device, data or network.

Permutated Dictionary Attack: Enhanced form of dictionary attack to consider the recovery of passwords which combine dictionary words, include/change special characters at specific locations and include common keyboard layout key sequences to enhance the strength of their weak dictionary passwords.

Rainbow Table: A precomputed table where only the initial and final columns are stored. Used to derive the plaintext from its hash value (that is, reversing the one-way hash functions).

Section 3
Communication, Computation, and Advanced Scientific Computing

Chapter 11
Multiagent Based Product Data Communication System for Computer Supported Collaborative Design

Bernadetta Kwintiana Ane
Institute of Computer-Aided Product Development Systems, Universität Stuttgart, Germany

Dieter Roller
Institute of Computer-Aided Product Development Systems, Universität Stuttgart, Germany

Ajith Abraham
IT For Innovations - Center of Excellence, VSB-TU Ostrava, Czech Republic

ABSTRACT

Today, designers and engineers on collaborative design environments often work in parallel and independently using different tools distributed at separate locations. Due to unique characteristic of engineering design, interaction during product development is difficult to maintain. As the information and communication technologies advance, computer supported collaborative design (CSCD) becomes more promising. Nevertheless, a potential problem remains between the product design and manufacturing, which primarily lies on the geometric shape of products that exists inherent in mass-customization. Meanwhile, each CAD/CAM technology has its own authoring tools, which govern the use of independent language and format for expressing various features and geometry. This condition creates incompatibility and has significant impact to the product costs. This chapter is to address the incompatibility problem by introducing the architecture of a multiagent-based product data communication system. The developed system is adaptive and has a capability for autonomous tracking of design changes. The tracking model is able to support forward and backward tracking of constraint violation during the collaborative design transactions.

DOI: 10.4018/978-1-4666-2190-9.ch011

BACKGROUND

Today's industry requires massive computer-supported technologies to address the increasingly complex product development tasks and the high expectations of customers. As the information and communication technologies advance, the application of collaborative engineering to product design, so-called computer supported collaborative design (CSCD), becomes more promising.

Sprow (1992) defines CSCD, or so-called cooperative design, as the process of designing a product through collaboration among multidisciplinary product developers associated with the entire product life cycle. CSCD is carried out not only among multidisciplinary product development teams within a company, but also across the boundaries of companies and time zones, with increased numbers of customers and suppliers involved in the process.

Accomplishing a design task and delivering the results to manufacturing requires immense and complex information. Currently, most CAD/CAM technologies govern independent authoring tools in different proprietary formats. Meanwhile, a potential problem between design and manufacturing remains in the geometric shape of products, which mainly exists inherent in mass-customization. For instance, creating 'thread' on a screw using the *thread* feature operation in the

Autodesk Inventor as depicted in Figure 1. This feature often cannot be recognized when the design is transferred and read using another CAD/CAM system (e.g., Solidworks). Or, in some cases it will be recognized with certain deviation of dimensions and tolerances. This condition creates incompatibility problem. Failures in the final design requires engineer to perform design rework, which has significant impact to the product costs. Furthermore, if failures are recognized after the design being manufactured, it will result in such condition the whole products to be rejected.

In collaborative design environment, the design – build – test cycle is performed by designers and engineers who work with various application systems in geographically distributed locations. When change is applied on a part, changing of shapes or dimensions will create constraints propagation to the adjacent parts that might affect the overall performance of the product. In this regard, the ability to tracking design changes becomes important. Therefore, the synchronization of product data communication along product development process is necessary to take place.

This chapter aims to address the incompatibility problem in the collaborative design environment. To support design exchange, a multiagent based product data communication system is introduced. The adaptive system is developed on the Cloud technology, where a shared server

Figure 1. Screw: (a) original design created by Autodesk Inventor, (b) original design read in Solidworks, (c) translated design to neutral file in Solidworks

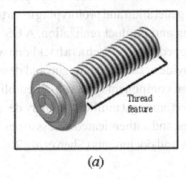 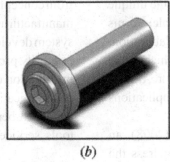 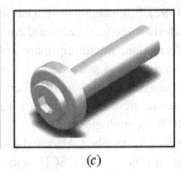

(a)   (b)   (c)

provides resources, software and data to designers and engineers to perform on-demand real-time collaborative work at remote locations. The data communication network is designed based on the seven-layers ISO/OSI model. The ISO/OSI network is an Open System Interconnect (OSI) model developed by the International Standards Organization (ISO) in 1984 (ISO, 1992) as a conceptual framework for communication in the network across different equipment and applications by different vendors. Today, ISO/OSI model is considered as the primary architectural model for intercomputing and internetworking communications.

In the following paragraphs, Section 2 describes the conceptual framework of computer supported collaborative design (CSCD) and the applications of Cloud Computing and agent-based technologies, Section 3 explains the architecture of the multiagent based product data communication system, Section 4 provides an illustration on the system's capability for tracking of design changes. Finally, Section 5 provides the conclusion of current work and a direction for future works.

COMPUTER SUPPORTED COLLABORATIVE DESIGN

Many researchers consider CSCD as an application of computer supported cooperative work (CSCW) in design. The term CSCW was first used by Greif and Cashman in 1984 to describe a way to support people in their work arrangements with computers (Greif, 1988; Schmidt and Bannon, 1992). Engineering design has some unique characteristics (e.g., diverse and complex forms of information, interdisciplinary collaboration, and heterogeneous software tools), which make interactions difficult to support. Therefore, design has become one of the most important applications of CSCW technologies.

According to Shen, Hao and Li (2008), an important objective of CSCD is to address the insufficient or even absent manufacturability checks concurrently by detecting and considering conflicts and constraints at earlier design stages. To support collaborative design, information and communication technologies are used to augment the capabilities of the individual specialists, and enhance the ability of collaborators to interact with each other and with computational resources.

With the rapid advancement of Web-based technology, CSCD has progressed dramatically. The depth and breadth of CSCD applications are far beyond the traditional definition of concurrent engineering. Moreover, the application of agent-based technology has been investigated to be effective to enhance communication, cooperation and coordination amongst design team as well as software tools. Today, the need to dynamically provide resources of various kinds as services which are provisioned electronically in the collaborative design environment has lead to the use of Cloud Computing. In this framework, services should be available in a reliable and scalable way so that designers and engineers can use them, either explicitly upon request or simply as and when required.

Web-Based Technology

The Web was originally developed for information sharing within internationally dispersed teams and the dissemination of information by support groups. Since its emergence in the early of 1990s, the Web has been quickly adopted into the collaborative design environment to publish and share information relevant to the design process, from concept generation and prototyping to virtual manufacturing and product realization. A CSCD system developed with the Web as a backbone will primarily provide access to catalogue and design information on components and sub-assemblies, communication amongst multidisciplinary design team members, and authenticated access to design tools, services and documents (Shen et al., 2008).

The Web can be integrated with other related technologies and used for product data management.

Along with the Web, a number of associated representation technologies have been developed, such as Hyper Text Mark-up Language (HTML), eXtensible Mark-up Language (XML), and Virtual Reality Mark-up Language (VRML) to enable better cross-platform and cross-enterprise exchange of multimedia information and design models (Ane and Roller, 2011). Many early collaborative design systems were developed using the Blackboard architecture (Jagannathan, Dodhiawala, & Baum, 1989) and distributed-object technologies like CORBA (Common Object Request Broker Architecture) (Object Management Group, 2008), COM (Component Object Model) (Box, 1998), and DCOM (Distributed Component Object Model).

A blackboard architecture is a distributed computing architecture, where distributed applications modeled as intelligent agents share a common data structure, called the "blackboard", and a scheduling/control process. The Common Object Request Broker Architecture (CORBA) is an architecture and specification for creating, distributing, and managing distributed program objects in a network. Developed by the Object Management Group (OMG), CORBA allows programs at different locations and developed by different vendors to communicate in a network through an "interface broker." The Component Object Model (COM) is an architecture and infrastructure for building fast, robust, and extensible component-based software. The COM is merely a language-independent binary-level standard defining how software components within a single address space can efficiently rendezvous and interact with each other and, at the same time, retaining a sufficient degree of separation between these components so that they can be developed and evolved independently. While, the Distributed Component Object Model (DCOM) is a seamless evolution of COM, developed by Microsoft. DCOM (Distributed Component Object

Model) provides a set of concepts and program interfaces, in which client program objects can request services from server program objects on other computers in a network in a reliable, secure, and efficient manner.

Most Web-based collaborative design systems are developed using Java and CORBA (Jagannathan, Almasi, & Suvaiala, 1996; Wallis, Haag, & Foley, 1998; Huang and Mak, 1999a). Some others are developed using Common Lisp, i.e., WWDL (Zdrahal and Domingue, 1997), and Prolog, i.e., WebCADET (Caldwell and Rodgers, 1998). In addition to HTML and Java Applets, ActiveX (Huang, Lee, & Mak, 1999; Huang and Mak, 1999b) and VRML (Zdrahal and Domingue, 1997; Wallis et al., 1998) are widely used for developing client-side user interfaces.

In Figure 2, a Web-based collaborative design system on three-tier communication framework is illustrated. In this framework, the wide-area networks and the internet-based WWW infrastructure allow to develop intelligent knowledge servers. Using the knowledge-based expert system running on servers, a large-scale group of users can communicate with the system over the network (Xuan, Xue, & Ma, 2009).

However, the Web technology alone is not a complete solution to collaborative design systems, although it makes remote communication physically viable through a common network. Collaborative design involves not design activity solely, but also the translation of terminology amongst disciplines as well as locating and providing distributed engineering analysis services. Thus, the Web servers should not only be a repository of information, but also provide intelligent services to assist users to solve design problems. In this regard, the application of software agents offers potential to improve the efficiency of collaborative design.

Figure 2. Web-based collaborative design on three-tier communication framework (Source: Xuan, Xue, & Ma, 2009)

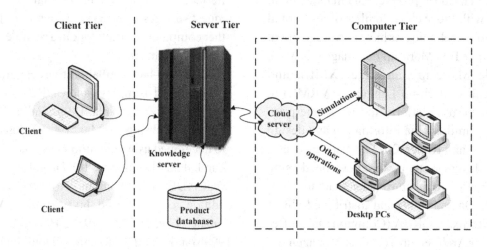

Agent-Based Technology

In agent-based collaborative design, software agents are mostly used for supporting cooperation amongst designers, enhancing interoperability between traditional computational tools, or allowing better distributed simulations. An agent-based collaborative design system is a loosely coupled network of problem solvers that work together to solve complex problems that are beyond their individual capabilities (Shen et al., 2008). Software agents in such systems are communicative, collaborative, autonomous, reactive (or proactive), and intelligent.

Conceptually, an agent is defined as a computer system that is situated in some environment, and that is capable of autonomous action in this environment in order to meet its design objective (Weiss, 1999). *Autonomous* means that agents are able to act without the interventions of humans and other systems. They have control both over their own internal state and over their behavior.

An agent in collaborative design plans and solves the local problems of modular design by the design-related knowledge. Each agent is a knowledge system which solves the modular design problem based on their knowledge base. But

the complexity of the solved problems and the size of knowledge base are less than the requirements of centralized design. Figure 3 illustrates an agent structure model for collaborative design. The main components comprise of human-computer interaction interface, sensor, effectors, executable controllers, functional module, evaluator, communication mechanism and agent private knowledge base (Ming, Jinfei, Qinghua, & Yuan, 2010).

Agents will typically sense their environment, i.e., by physical sensors or software sensors, and will have available a repertoire of actions that can be executed to modify the environment, which may appear to respond non-deterministically to the execution of these actions. An intelligent agent is one that is capable of flexible autonomous action in order to meet its design objectives. In this definition, the term of *flexibility* refers to reactivity, pro-activeness, and social ability. Reactivity represents the ability of the intelligent agents to perceive their environment, and respond in a timely fashion to changes that occur in it in order to satisfy their design objectives. Pro-activeness means that the intelligent agents are able to exhibit goal-directed behavior by taking the initiative in order to satisfy their design objectives. Social ability refers to the capability of the intelligent

Figure 3. Agent structure model for collaborative design (Source: Ming, Jinfei, Qinghua, & Yuan, 2010)

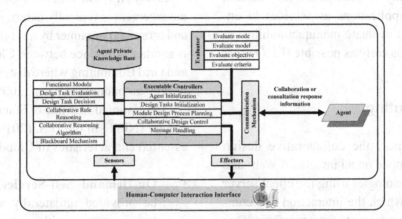

agent to interact with other agents (and possibly humans) in order to satisfy their design objectives.

Agents operate and exist in some environment, which typically is both computational and physical. At times, the increasing interconnection and networking of computers makes such situation rare, in the usual state of affairs the agent will interact with other agents. Then, it is more convenient to deal with them collectively, as a *society of agents*. Multiagent systems are the best way to characterize or design distributed computing systems. Multiagent environments have some characteristics: (1) typically open and have no centralized designer, (2) provide an infrastructure specifying communication and interaction protocols, and (3) contain agents that are autonomous and distributed, and may be self-interested or cooperative. The rationale for interconnecting computational agents and expert systems is to enable them to cooperate in solving problems, to share expertise, to work in parallel on common problems, to be developed and implemented modularly, to be fault tolerant through redundancy, to represent multiple viewpoints and the knowledge of multiple experts, and to be reusable.

Prior research projects have demonstrated the application of software agents to collaborative design (Shen et al., 2008). PACT (Cutkosky et al., 1993) was considered as one of the earliest

successful projects in this area. The interesting aspects of PACT include its federation architecture using facilitators and wrappers for legacy system integration. SHARE (Toye, Cutkosky, Leifer, Tenenbaum, & Glicksman, 1993) was concerned with developing open, heterogeneous, network-oriented environments for concurrent engineering, particularly for design information and data capturing and sharing through asynchronous communication. DIDE (Shen & Barthes, 1995) was developed to study system openness, legacy systems integration, and distributed collaboration. ICM (Fruchter, Reiner, Toye, & Leifer, 1998) developed a shared graphical modelling environment for collaborative design activities. A-Design (Campbell, Cagan, & Kotovsky, 1999) presented a new design generation methodology, which combines aspects of multi-objective optimization, multi-agent systems, and automated design synthesis. It provided designers with a new search strategy for the conceptual stages of product design that incorporates agent collaboration with an adaptive selection of design alternatives.

A successful implementation of CSCD needs a series of new strategies for efficient communication amongst multidisciplinary groups, an integration of heterogeneous software tools to realize obstacle-free engineering information exchange and sharing. In addition, a strategy is also needed for interoperability to manipulate downstream manufacturing applications as services to enable designers to evaluate manufacturability or assembleability as early as possible (Li, Ong, & Nee, 2006).

Cloud Computing

In current practice, the collaborative design systems is developed on an integrated Web- and agent-based technologies using the client/server architecture, in which the interaction and communication between agents are predefined. Due to the nature of collaborative design, the dynamic design tasks are usually involving complex and non-deterministic interactions on heterogeneous and distributed systems. This yields results that might be ambiguous and incomplete. On the other hand, designers and engineers intend to perform real-time collaborative works, where multiple users are able to share files and work on the same document simultaneously. This requirement becomes the driving force behind the use of *Cloud Computing* in collaborative design.

Baun, Kunze, Nimis, & Tai (2011) defines Cloud Computing as a technology that provides scalable, network-centric, abstracted information technology (IT) infrastructures, platforms, and applications as on-demand services, by using virtualized computing and storage resources and modern Web technologies. These services are billed on a usage basis. In this context, Cloud Computing uses virtualization and the modern Web to dynamically provide resources of various kinds as services which are provisioned electronically. These services should be available in a reliable and scalable way so that designers and engineers can use them either explicitly on-demand or simply when required.

However, this definition does not specify whether the services are provided by a distributed system or a single, high-performance server. This is in contrast to *Grid Computing* which always uses a distributed system. In general, Cloud ser-

vices rely on a distributed infrastructure, but their management is typically determined in a central and proprietary manner by a single provider. This is another difference between Cloud Computing and Grid Computing where distributed nodes are usually autonomous (Wang, 2009).

The National Institute of Standards and Technology (NIST) in the U.S. (2010) specifies five essential characteristics of Cloud environment:

- **On-Demand Self-Service:** Services can be provided unilaterally and on-demand to consumers without requiring human interaction.
- **Broad Network Access:** Services are available over the network in real-time through standard mechanisms.
- **Resource Pooling:** The resources are pooled to enable parallel service provision to multiple users (multi-tenant model), while being adjusted to the actual demand of each user.
- **Elasticity:** Resources are rapidly provisioned in various, fine-grained quantities so that the systems can be scaled as required. To the users, the resources appear to be unlimited.
- **Measured Quality Of Service:** The services leverage a quantitative and qualitative metering capability so that usage-based billing and validation of the service quality are possible.

Some of Cloud technologies that suitable to make effective use of the resources through different varieties of Cloud provision in the collaborative design environments are:

- **OpenNebula:** This is a fully open-source toolkit to build an 'Infrastructure as a Service' (IaaS), whether private, public or hybrid. The toolkit orchestrates storage, network, virtualization, monitoring and security technologies to enable the dynamic placement of multi-tier services on distributed infrastructures (OpenNebula, 2010). The benefits include centralized management, higher utilization of existing resources, scalability of services to meet dynamic demands and seamless integration of IT resources (Mahmood and Hill, 2011).

- **CA 3Tera AppLogic:** This is an application-centric Cloud Computing platform and a key component of Cloud solutions provided by the CA Technologies (CA Technologies, 2010). It allows for composing, running and scaling distributed applications and uses virtualization technologies to be completely compatible with existing operating systems, middleware and Web applications. The platform eliminates the binding of software and hardware through virtualization. The applications are assembled using completely self-contained independent software components (Mahmood & Hill, 2011).

The collaborative design systems, unlike distributed systems which are interconnected over local networks, they use the distributed Cloud Computing systems that integrate heterogeneous resources, which could be located at any place on this earth where an Internet connection is available. In such environments, it is recommended to use a loosely coupled, asynchronous, message-based communication via Web services (Mahmood & Hill, 2011).

Web Service

As defined by the Web Services Architecture Working Group of the World Wide Web Consortium (W3C), a Web service is a software application identified by a uniform resource identifier (URI), whose interfaces and binding are capable of being defined, described and discovered by XML artifacts and supports direct interactions with other software applications using XML based messages via internet-based protocols (W3C, 2002). Meanwhile, Wohlstadter and Tai (2009) define Web services as distributed middleware, which enables machine-to-machine communication on the basis of Web protocols.

The Web services are determined by the intended use of technology to provide services for the specified needs. They propagate a compositional approach for application development. Functions can be integrated into an application using external or distributed services.

With regard to interoperability, the Web services describe the standards required to format and process messages as well as the standards for service interfaces. There are two approaches of interoperability. The first approach is SOAP/WSDL-based Web services. SOAP is a messaging protocol and WSDL (Web Services Description Language) is an interface description language. Thus, SOAP/WSDL-based services have programmatic interfaces. The second approach is RESTful (REpresentational State Transfer) services. REST describes a style of software architecture, which is built on top of HTTP. RESTful services can only be invoked from the uniform HTTP interface. Both SOAP/WSDL-based Web services and RESTful use uniform resource identifiers (URIs) to identify the required services (Baun et al., 2011).

MULTIAGENT-BASED PRODUCT DATA COMMUNICATION SYSTEM

In order to solve the existing problem of incompatibility that exists in collaborative design, in this section the architecture of multiagent-based product data communication system is introduced. The system is developed on a private Cloud network using the integrated Web- and agent-based technologies that enables communication and coordination amongst multiple users in the collaborative design environment.

The system architecture uses a centralized database that can be shared during the collaborative design transactions. The product database is designed on an active semantic network (ASN), i.e., a network of nodes and links, where the nodes represent objects of the real world and the links relations amongst these objects. The ASN can handle and manage the increasing amount of knowledge during the design process (Roller, Eck, Bihler, & Stolpmann, 1995; Roller & Eck, 1997; Thiel, Dalakakis, & Roller, 2005). The active component is able to make inferences and activate external actions (e.g., at a graphical user interface). Considering the complexity of engineering parts, feature taxonomy and data dictionary are built as reference in the database.

In this architecture, as it has been mentioned the data communication network is designed on the seven-layers ISO/OSI network model. The OSI model defines the communications process into seven layers, which divides the tasks involved with the moving information between networked computers into smaller and more manageable task groups. A task or group of tasks is then assigned to each of the seven OSI layers. In the following paragraphs, each component of the system is discussed.

The ISO/OSI Communication Network

The seven-layers OSI model divides the communication process into seven layers, i.e., physical, data-link, network, transport, session, presentation, and application layers. Each layer is reasonably self-contained so that the tasks assigned to each layer can be implemented independently. This enables the solutions offered by one layer to be developed and replaced without adversely affecting the other layers. Figure 4 describes the ISO/OSI Product Data Communication Network.

Layers 1 to 3 deal with communications between network devices. The physical layer defines the electrical and mechanical specification of data transmission devices. This layer performs major function and service for the establishment and termination of a connection to a communications medium. It also performs modulation, or conversion, between the representation of digital data in user equipment and the corresponding signals transmitted over a communications channel. The data-link layer provides frames across a single local area network (LAN), which functions to define the resolution of contention for the use of

Figure 4. ISO/OSI product data communication network

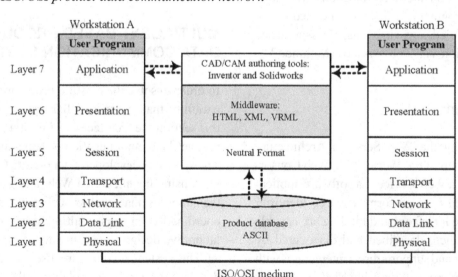

shared transmission medium, delimitation and selection of frames addressed to given nodes, detection of noise through frame-check sequence, and any error correction or retries performed within the LAN. The network layer provides the functional and procedural means of transferring variable length data sequences from a source host on one network to a destination host on a different network, while maintaining the quality of service requested by the transport layer.

Layers 4 to 7 deal with end-to-end communications between data source and destinations. The transport layer provides transparent data transfer between end-users, providing reliable data transfer services to the upper layers by ensuring that data units are delivered error-free, in sequence, with no losses or duplications. The session layer controls the dialogues between computer systems during a communication session. This layer establishes, manages and terminates the connections between the local and remote application. It provides full-duplex operation, and establishes check-point, adjournment, termination, and restart procedures. The presentation layer establishes context between application-layer entities, in which the higher-layer entities may use different syntax and semantics if the presentation service provides a mapping between them. Finally, the application layer defines the user interface for communication process and data transfer in a network. It interacts with software applications (e.g., Autodesk Inventor, Solidworks, etc.) which implement communication components. This layer functions for determining resource availability as well as synchronizing communication process.

When data is sent from workstation A to workstation B, it goes down the layers. At each layer, a control message is appended to the data. Then, the complete data is transmitted through the ISO/OSI medium to workstation B. At each layer of workstation B, the control message is stripped and proper actions are taken to convert the data into a proper format. In our network model, two CAD/CAM/CAE authoring tools are implemented at the application layer, i.e., Autodesk Inventor and Solidworks. At the presentation layer, the engineering design is then communicated through a middleware on HTML, XML, and VRML formats. In this layer, design intent is further encoded/decoded into the neutral format for data storage and retrieval purposes. Finally, the design entities are encrypted/decrypted and store in the database in ASCII (American Standard Code for Information Interchange) code. The product database divides into three object-oriented databases (OOD), i.e., design, manufacturing, and process planning databases. The active OOD allows users to specify actions to be taken automatically by agents given certain rules when certain conditions arise (Roller and Eck, 1998). In the following subsection, the concept of multiagent system is discussed.

Multiagent System

On the aforementioned architecture, the product data communication system runs on an intelligent knowledge server, which embodies two capabilities of intelligent and learning agents. The intelligent agent is responsible to identify the part identity (i.e., part name, ID, date of creation, creator, model, and sub-assemblies), design (i.e., geometry, topology, dimensions, and constraints), and function based on the existing data dictionary built in the system, as well as to define similarity of a part amongst others based on its function or model. When a new design is introduced, the learning agent acts to learn the new function. Then, the agent measures similarity of the new part in comparison with the existing ones, extract related design information, create new identity and, finally, register and store it as a new entity in the data dictionary.

The aspect of learning is essential for agents. Agents are assumed to be situated in a flexible environment which they can modify while pursuing their own goals. In this environment, the agents are proactive in that they may initiate certain goal-oriented behavior. A learning agent can easily adapt with a changing environment by extending and modifying its behavior according to its own experience, i.e, by changing existing rules or adding new rules (Borghoff & Schlichter, 2000). Figure 5 describes learning triggered by a user agent. The user agent learns either by interacting with other agents, or by communicating with the users (e.g., designers, engineers, managers, etc.). The learning process can be based on user feedback, explicit user programming by examples, or by observing user interactions with the applications.

The product data communication system is developed as an adaptive system. Here, the term of adaptive represents the ability of agents to adapt with changes in environment that commonly source from the changing of product database, application programs, data structure and formats, in such a manner in order to improve the system's future performance (Ane & Roller, 2011). Based on the ability of the learning agent to modify or add rules, the design knowledge can be up-dated on regular basis, thus, they are reusable. Since the design knowledge is developed on an active database system, hence, in the following subsection the active semantic network is going to be discussed.

The Active Semantic Network

The Active Semantic Network (ASN) is a shared database system developed for supporting designers during product development and is realized as an active, object-oriented database system. The ASN uses mechanisms of distributed database systems to distribute design objects in a heterogeneous environment and to allow distributed access to shared data. The goal of the ASN is to represent all knowledge relevant to the product development process and to support geographically distributed product design teams (Roller, Eck, Bihler, & Stolpmann, 1995).

Concepts of cooperative transaction models allow a group-oriented access to shared objects by multiple users (Roller, Bihler, & Eck, 1997). The objects in the database consist of three parts: the data itself, a set of associated rules, and locking objects for realizing the cooperative transaction system. Cooperative access to shared objects is realized by extended locking mechanisms which use knowledge about users and user groups in the knowledge base to support collaborative works.

Figure 6 depicts the structure of the ASN. The most important parts in this structure are a meta model to specify the structure of the ASN,

Figure 5. Learning of a user agent (Source: Borghoff & Schlichter, 2000)

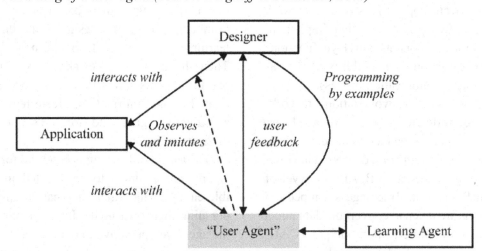

a database-independent programming interface, an active component for rule processing, a cooperative transaction model and a distributed object management. The active component of the ASN is able to propagate changes at one node of the semantic network across the whole network, as well as to signal inconsistencies and conflicts to the responsible users, and start external actions (e.g., at the graphical user interface).

Before a constraint can be propagated, it has to be modelled. As illustration, a basic geometric constraint problem of piston is described in Figure 7. The performance of a piston is affected by the rotation of crankshaft that is supported by the piston rod. The crankshaft is represent as a circle where the center of the circle will be the axis of the crankshaft and the circumference represents the rotation of the center of the journal. The piston rod is represented as a straight line. The piston and the top of the piston rod travel at the same vertical velocity. Representation of piston in the object-oriented product model is described in

Figure 8. In this representation, there is a dependency between a piston and a rod, which is a simple constraint between different objects.

In the following step, rules are used to evaluate parameters inside the 2-dimensional geometric objects (e.g., ellipse, triangle, etc.) and define the geometric constraints. Here, constraints propagation is realized through the Event-Condition-Action (ECA) rules. According to McCarthy and Dayal (1989), the ECA rules have the following attributes:

- An *Event* triggers a rule.
- A *Condition* is a collection of queries that are evaluated when the rule is triggered.
- An *Action* is executed when the rule is triggered and its condition is satisfied.
- Using the ECA rules, the geometric constraints can be modeled in the following way:
- Event is a write operation on one of the variables of a constraint.

Figure 6. Structure of the active semantic network

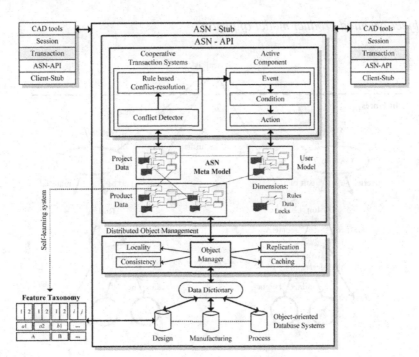

Figure 7. Piston: (a) product model, (b) definition of design problem

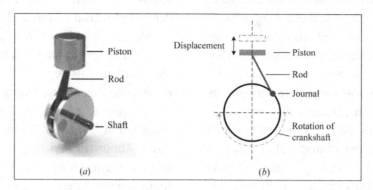

- Condition is a collection of queries that check if the constraint is satisfied.
- Action is executed if the constraint is not satisfied. in order to satisfy it.

Applying the ECA rules, constraints between different objects of piston can be modeled in the ASN. In constraint modeling, a new object is created which represents the geometric constraint itself. Objects in the network which model no real item in the real world but properties like 'relationships' or 'constraints', are called "virtual

objects" in the ASN. Figure 9 shows the virtual object "Constraint =". The constraint concept "Identical" describes the identity of two geometry parts, and the instance of this concept models the fact that the instances "piston" and "rod" have the same geometry.

The complete specification of all dependencies amongst all variables of a constraint is only possible, if the constraint describes in mathematical objects well represents the geometric objects. Here, the piston-crankshaft mechanism can be abstracted as a geometric constraint solving prob-

Figure 8. The object-oriented product model of piston

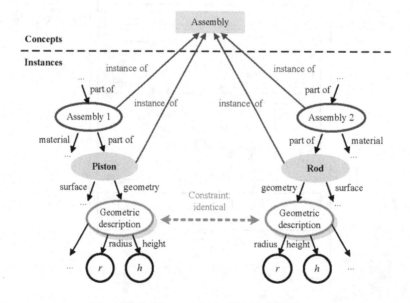

Figure 9. Representation of constraints in active semantic network

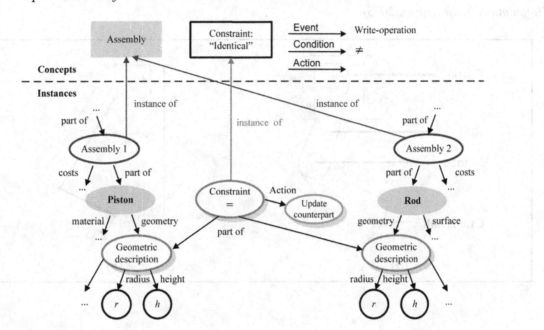

lem comprising five points p_i, $1 \le i \le 5$, and a straight line l_i. Figure 10 depicts geometric constraint for the piston-crankshaft mechanism (Cundy & Rollet, 1961; Hoffmann & Joan-Arinyo, 2005).

In the following process, a set of constraints which includes point-to-point distances, dpp(.), and coincidences, on(.), can be defined:

$$
\begin{aligned}
\mathrm{dpp}(p_1,\ p_2) &= d_1 & \mathrm{on}(p_1,\ l_1) \\
\mathrm{dpp}(p_2,\ p_3) &= d_2 & \mathrm{on}(p_2,\ l_1) \\
\mathrm{dpp}(p_3,\ p_4) &= d_3 & \mathrm{on}(p_3,\ l_1) \\
\mathrm{dpp}(p_4,\ p_5) &= d_4 & \mathrm{on}(p_5,\ l_1) \\
\mathrm{dpp}(p_1,\ p_5) &= d_5 &
\end{aligned}
$$

Based on given constraints, a constraint graph is developed to study the propagation of a constraint across the network as depicted in Figure 11. Furthermore, the constraint graph can also be used to analyze whether a system of equations is under-, well- or over-constrained from the system structure.

In the piston-crankshaft mechanism, the speed of a piston is significantly affected by the connecting rod, $s = ((d_1 - d_5) + d_2)$. For instance, if p_5 is modified from p_1, this condition affects constraint d_5 that propagates to constraints d_1 as well as the optimal distance, s. Using the Law of Cosines (Rollins, 2012), finally, the optimal s can be found:

$$b^2 = s^2 + r^2 - 2rs\cos\left(\theta\right) \tag{1}$$

$$s = r\cos\left(\theta\right) + \sqrt{b^2 - r^2\sin(\theta)^2} \tag{2}$$

$$s = d_3\cos\left(\theta\right) + \sqrt{d_4^2 - d_3^2\sin(\theta)^2} \tag{3}$$

During design communication, designer needs information about product and sub-assemblies in order to establish and make transaction on the ASN. This type of information is provided in the Data Dictionary. In the following subsection, the structure of data dictionary is discussed.

Figure 10. Piston and crankshaft mechanism: (a) actual mechanism, (b) geometric problem (Source: Hoffmann & Joan-Arinyo, 2005)

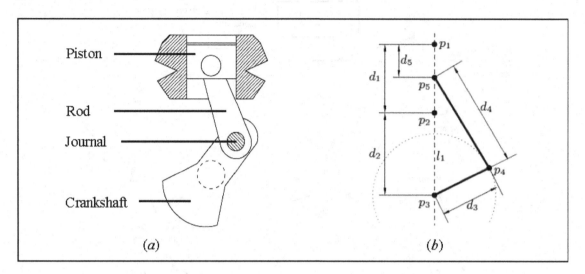

(a) (b)

Data Dictionary

A data dictionary, or also called metadata repository, is a centralized repository of information about data such as meaning, relationships to other data, origin, usage, and format (IBM Dictionary of Computing, 2008). Data dictionary is an integral part of the product database. It holds information about the database and the type of data that it stores, i.e., the metadata. It provides a collection of

Figure 11. Constraint graph of piston-crankshaft mechanism

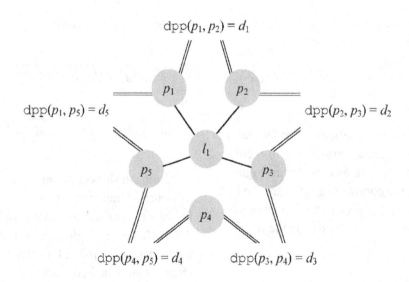

descriptions of the data objects or items in a data model for the benefit of designers and engineers who need to refer to them.

In the proposed architecture, data dictionary is not hidden from users that differ from most database management systems. However, the use and retrieval of data requires authorization in order to prevent them from improper use that might accidentally destroy the contents. The integrated data dictionary is called active since it controls access to the database and automatically updates as changes occur in the database.

For illustration, a data dictionary that adopts the electronic parts catalogue (ETK) of the BMW Group is presented. It provides interfaces for users to interact and access data related to vehicles model and object relationships of parts and sub-assemblies. It consists of record types (i.e., images and tables) created in the database by systems generated command files, tailored for each supported back-end product database management system. The 'back-end' refers to the database that resides in the intelligent knowledge server. Typically, entry of a data dictionary are: name of table, name of fields in each table, data type of each field (e.g., text, date, integer, image, etc.), length of each field, default value of each field, type of field (i.e., 'nullable' or 'not nullable'), and constraints applied to each field.

Using a descriptive name or Product-ID, an object in real world (e.g., gearshift, brake, wheel, etc.), its relationship with other objects, and the type of data (e.g., text, binary value, image, etc.) can be identified. Figure 12 shows data structure of vehicles parts in the data dictionary, in which the design of a crankshaft connecting rod can be accessed. The data dictionary opens a window started from layer 1 (i.e., 'Vehicle Parts') that provide information on engine object amongst a set of collection of vehicle parts. Afterwards, it continues respectively to open windows in layer 2 which provide information on the connecting rod amongst related sub-assemblies of an engine, layer 3 information on the engineering design and,

finally, layer 4 information on the specification of connecting rod.

When a new design is introduced in the system and previously does not exist in the database, this will invoke the learning agent to study about the new entity through feature recognition. The recognition algorithm works by recognizing a new entity from its geometric shape based on specification in the feature taxonomy. In the following subsection, the structure of feature taxonomy is described.

Feature Taxonomy

Generally speaking, feature means the generic shapes or characteristics of a product with which designers and engineers can associate certain attributes and knowledge useful for reasoning about given product. Many of the feature definitions are abstract in the sense they do not designate classes intended to be instantiated. Instead, they are present to give a clear structure to the feature taxonomy and to take benefit of inheritance. Therefore, it is important to outlining the higher-levels of feature taxonomy.

Referring to Shah & Mantyla (1995), feature taxonomy can be defined as a hierarchical classification of features used in design and manufacturing that gives a natural structure for developing the feature library, as well as to simplify and encourage the extension of the library. In this context, the taxonomy is oriented to feature-based manufacturing. The outline of the feature taxonomy is depicted in Figure 13. It is initiated by the root class feature that has direct subclasses basic-feature, transition, billet, container-feature, and surface. These abstract classes form the roots of subtaxonomies of features for the following purposes:

- **Basic-Feature:** This class consists of regular features appearing as detail features in the feature models, i.e., texture, hole, rotational-feature, and prismatic-feature.

Figure 12. Structure of data dictionary (Adapted from ETK - BMW Group, 2010)

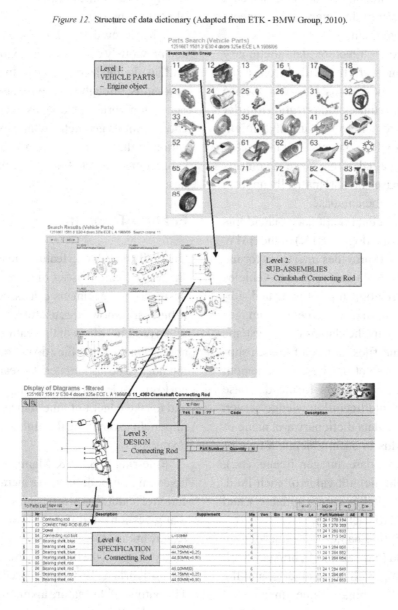

Figure 12. Structure of data dictionary (Adapted from ETK - BMW Group, 2010).

- **Transition:** This class consists of regular features corresponding with various types of roundings and blends between two regular features.
- **Billet:** This class is the root of features representing various kinds of "base objects" that form the basis of feature-based designs and also act as initial workpieces for machining applications. Typical billets include block, L-block, and more complex solids such as special castings.
- **Container-Feature:** This class is the root of all feature types that are made of other simpler features, such as compounds, patterns, and also whole parts and assemblies.

Figure 13. Feature taxonomy (Source: Shah & Mantyla, 1995)

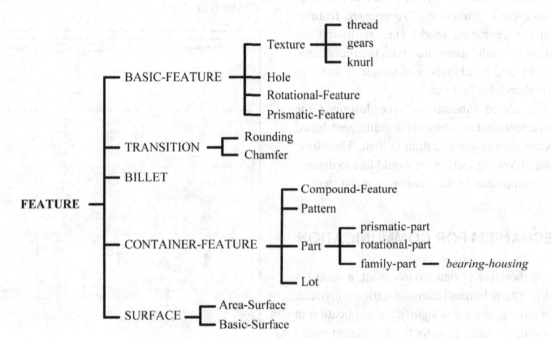

- **Surface:** This includes surface types. Surfaces are used to denote areas of features for recording feature containment relationship. Surfaces are also useful to model certain manufacturing processes applied to a planar or cylindrical area.

The definition of abstract feature classes can be described as follows in Box 1:

The definition of the above subclasses defines the instance-slots position and orientation in the class feature. This means, all features subclasses will also contain instance-slots position and orientation. These definitions give the *x*, *y*, and *z* translations and rotation angles about *x*-, *y*-, and *z*-axes of the feature with respect to the part coordinate system. The class slot sign of the frame basic-feature states that by default, all basic features are considered 'negative' in that they denote removal of material from a basic part. In contrary, all billets are marked 'positive'. The slot parent-surface-def states that by default, basic features are oriented along the 'normal direction' of the

surface they are contained in. Finally, it is defined that all surfaces will contain a 'working allowance'.

The features classes and subclasses in the feature taxonomy are implemented in conjunction with the feature library in the product database management system for feature creation and feature recognition purposes. A feature library contains generic definitions of feature classes. This might include a list of faces, which is needed to create or recognize a feature and the relationship between them. Table 1 depicts a generic feature library. Each feature is defined by its generic shape as described by the parameterized sketch. The parameters are organized into three groups: independent dimension, derived dimensions, and parameters needed in positioning the feature with respect to other features.

In feature recognition, the geometric model is compared to pre-defined generic features in the feature library in order to identify instances that match the pre-defined ones. Specific tasks in feature recognition might include the identification of feature geometry (i.e., edge/face growing, closure, etc.), extraction of recognized features from the geometric model (i.e., removing the portion of model associated with the recognized feature), and combination of simple features to get higher-level features.

The above subsections have described the components and structure of the multiagent-based product data communication system. Therefore, in the following section we would like to discuss the communication mechanism of the system.

MECHANISM FOR COMMUNICATION

In collaborative design environment, a complex Web of interaction and communication is to occur. This circumstance has significant implication in the design of interaction for the multiagent-based communication system.

Synchronous Bidirectional Communication

In the aforementioned product data communication system, the interaction is designed as bidirectional communication that supports information flow from sender to receiver, and vice versa. Typically, this provokes a 'request-answer' scheme as the pattern for the data exchange. The request consists of the name of a requested service operation together with the needed parameters. The answer contains the result the receiver has obtained by executing the requested service operation using the submitted parameters.

In this design, the data exchange is synchronous. The process blocks a sender until the receiver has effectively received the message. In analogy, the receiver is blocked until the message is stored into the receiver's buffer.

Any communication between a sender and a receiver is subject to losses of request messages, losses of answer messages as well as crashes of the sending or receiving sites. In order to detect

Table 1. Generic feature library (Source: Shah & Mantyla, 1995)

Feature and Sketch	Independent Dimensions	Derived Dimensions	Positioning
Block	Length, width, height	None	World coordinates or on the face of another block
Wedge	Length, width, height 1, height 2	None (optional; length and width derived from parent block)	World coordinates or on the face of another block
Thru-Hole	Diameter	Depth (distance between entry and exit faces)	On entry face; specify x, y distance from reference edges on entry face
Blind Hole	Diameter, depth, radius	None	Same as thru-hole
Feature and Sketch	**Independent Dimensions**	**Derived Dimensions**	**Positioning**
Double C-bore Hole	Dia, dia.1, dia.2, len.1, len.2	Length (optional; fixed ratios for dia.1/dia and dia.2/dia)	Same as thru-hole
Base	Height, width, length, T		Positioned in WCS
Blind Slot	Depth, width, length	Radius = width/2	On planar face; along an edge, specify distance from the reference vertex
Taper Pocket (Thru)	Length, width, R, taper_angle	Depoth (determined; by distance between entry and exit faces)	On entry face; specify x, y position of centerpoint / axes wrt edges (optional; specify orientation)
Boss	Dia., height		On entry face; specify x, y position of centerpoint wrt edges
Recess	Depth, width	in_dia (= hole_dia) out_dia (= in_dia + 2*depth)	Distance from entry face of hole
Feature and Sketch	**Independent Dimensions**	**Derived Dimensions**	**Positioning**
Rib	Height, length, width	Radius (= 0.5 width)	On support face and start face as shown specify distance from reference edge

and handle the unexpected events, the product data communication system uses an 'exactly-once' call semantics, i.e., the requested service operation is

Box 1. Abstract feature classes

```
(defframe feature
  (instance-slots (position (0 0 0)) (orientation (0 0 0)))
)
(defframe basic-feature
  (is-a feature)
  (sign NEGATIVE)
  (parent-surface-def (constraints (axis_normal_c)))
)
(defframe transition
  (is-a feature)
  (instance-slots the-surfaces)
)
(defframe billet
  (is-a feature)
  (sign POSTIVE)
)
(defframe container-feature
  (is-a feature)
)
(defframe surface
  (is-a feature)
  (instance-slots working-allowance)
)
```

processed exactly once. If repeatedly sent requests exist by a sender, at the receiving site the receiver keeps a list of current requests. Each request in the list is tagged with a unique identifier. Requests are not deleted from the list until the sender has acknowledged the correct reception of the result submitted by the receiver. Repeatedly sent requests from a sender for the same service operation are answered with the result of the first successful service operation. In any case, the receiving site does not process the same request twice. Figure 14 illustrates a communication process between a sender and a receiver, where the reception of the third request results in answering with the result obtained from processing the second request.

However, a failure of the receiver might occur that leads to an infinite blocking of the sender.

Sender and receiver might end up in a cyclical blocking state and have to deal with the problem of deadlocks. To remedy this drawback, some sort of decoupling of sender and receiver must be performed. This decoupling can be achieved by using lightweight processes, or also called 'threads' (Borghoff & Schlichter, 2000).

Assuming a sender has invoked an operation send (message *M*) to receiver *R*, then the receiver invokes an operation of the form receive (message *M*, sender *S*, buffer *B*). When using remote-invocation send, a sender suspends execution until the receiver has received and processed a submitted request that was delivered as part of the message. In the receiver site, the reception of a message is performed in a conditional case. In the conditional reception, the resumption of

Figure 14. A request-answer scheme under an exactly-once semantics (Source: Borghoff & Schlichter, 2000)

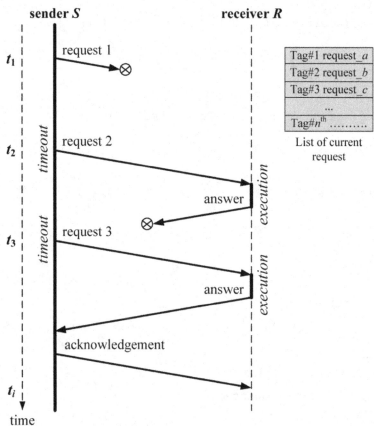

execution by the receiver is dependent upon the existence of an arriving message. A precise description of this situation is described in the following algorithm in Box 2.

If the expected message of a sender has arrived, the function receive returns true, otherwise false.

The sender and receiver must have a similar understanding on the agent communication language being used. In the multiagent systems environment, an agent must represent its knowledge in the vocabulary of a specified ontology. All agents that share the same ontology for knowledge

Box 2. Conditional reception

```
Code fragment (Operation receive)
function receive(message M, sender S, buffer B): errorcode;
        if ($ message M of sender S) then
                copy message M into buffer B;
                return true
        else return false;
```

representation have a common understanding of the "words" in the agent communication language.

In this regard, the agents need a shared ontology to be able to communicate meaningful. Thus, an ontology should be created and be accessible to the agents who are communicating.

Ontology

An ontology is a representation of knowledge of some part of the world. Ontologies provide a natural, declarative way of identifying concepts and terms that can serve as the basis for communications. Generally, an ontology is defined as a specification of the objects, concepts, and relationships in the area of interest.

Product ontology classifies the design objects into *parts*, *features*, *requirements*, and *constraints*. Axiom is used to describe the constraints and relationships amongst the objects. In this context, the design activity is a process of constructing the objects and axioms in the ontology as well as evaluating the satisfaction of requirements and constraints by the product structure and parameter values.

In the product ontology, each object is associated with a unique name that can be thought of as its ID. There are two types of objects, i.e., *class* objects and *instance* objects. A class is used for representing a generalized type or category of object, and instance for a specific member of a class. An instance and a class are related by the predicate instanceOf(.,.). Afterwards, each of these classes can be further divided into subclasses. The subclass relationships are denoted by the predicate subclassOf(.,.).

Given an example of Torus-Primitive. The term Torus represents a concept and the term On represents a relationship. Concepts can be represented in the first-order logic as unary predicates. While, the higher-arity predicates represent relationships. The idea of a torus is a primitive object can be described in the following first-order logic expression:

$$\forall x(\text{Torus } x)\square(\text{PrimitiveObject } x)$$

There are other more general representations. Instead of (Torus T), the expression (instanceOf T Torus) can be used. Both T and Torus are now objects in the universe of discourse, and relationship instanceOf and subclassOf can be introduced (Box 3).

The last statement is a rule that expresses the notion of a type hierarchy. Looking at the product hierarchy, if two agents agree on the upper nodes of a taxonomy, they can jointly traverse the taxonomy until they find the location of a newly introduces concept. Thus, they can build a shared understanding of their content language.

In the product hierarchy, a 'part' is a component of the artifact being designed. The artifact itself is also viewed as a part. The structure of a part is defined in terms of the hierarchy of its component parts. The relationship between a part and its components is captured by the predicate component_of, which can be defined by axioms in Box 4(Lin, Fox, & Bilgic, 1996).

Design is an evolutionary process, in which changes might occur frequently during the process. Before reaching its maturity, each object of parts, features, and constraints might undergo many

Box 3. instanceOf and subclassOf relationship

```
(class Torus)
(class PrimitiveObject)
(subclassOf Torus PrimitiveObject)
∀x,y,z (instanceOf xy) ∨ (subclassOf yz) " (instanceOf xz)
```

Box 4. Axioms

Axiom 1: Between two parts p and p', relationship of p is a component (subpart) of p'can be expressed in:
```
component_of(p, p')
```
Axiom 2: The relation component_of is transitive, i.e., if a part is a component of another part that is a component of a third part, then, the first part is a component of the third part:
```
(∀p1,p2,p3) component_of(p1,p2) ∧ component_of(p2,p3)
            ⊃ component_of(p1,p3).
```
Axiom 3: The relation component_of is non-reflexive and anti-symmetric. This means a part cannot be a component of itself, and it is never the case that a part is a component of another part which in turn is a component of the first part:
```
(∀p) ¬ component_of(p,p),
(∀p1,p2) component_of (p1,p2)⊃¬ component_of(p2,p1).
```
Axiom 4: A part can be a subcomponent of another part. However, each part has a unique ID (i.e., its name), then, it cannot be a subcomponent of two or more distinct parts which are not components of each other:
```
(∀p1,p2,p3) component_of(p1,p2) ∨ component_of(p1,p3)
  ⊃ p2 = p3 ∧ component_of(p2,p3)∧ component_of(p3,p2).
```
Parts can be made from the same model and be identical copies, and can be used as different assemblies.

Axiom 5: Part1 and Part 2 are identical copies of Part that treated as different instances of the same class and associated with different ID:
```
        instanceOf(Part1, Part),
        instanceOf(Part2, Part).
```
Parts are classified into two types, depending upon the component_of relationship it has with the other parts in the hierarchy. The two types are primitive and composite.

Axiom 6: A primitive part is a part that cannot be further subdivided into components. This type of parts exist at the lowest level of the artifact decomposition hierarchy. Therefore, a primitive part cannot have subcomponents:
```
(∀p) primitive(p) ≡¬ ($p') component_of(p',p).
```
Axiom 7: A composite part is a composition of one or more other parts. A composite part cannot be a leaf node in the part hierarchy; thus any part that is composite is not primitive.
```
(∀p) composite(p) ≡¬ primitive(p).
```
Axiom 8: Most composite parts are assemblies that are composed of at least two or more parts:
```
(∀p) assembly(p) ≡(∃p1,p2) component_of(p1,p)
 ∧ component_of(p2,p) ∧ p1 ¹ p2.
```
Sometimes a designer may need to find out the direct components of a part. A part is a direct component of another part if there is no middle part between the two in the product hierarchy.

Axiom 9: p1 is a direct component of p2 if p1 is a component of p2 and there is no p' such that p1 is a component of p' and p' is a component of p2:
```
(∀p1,p2) direct_component_of(p1,p2) ≡ component_of(p1,p2)
 ∧¬ (∃p') component_of(p1,p') ∨ component_of(p',p2).
```
The component_of relation relates objects at lower-level in the component tree to the objects at higher-level. By the relation, it is possible to traverse upward in the component tree. However, there is also a need to traverse downward in the component tree.

Axiom 10: A relation of object that traverse downward in the component tree is defined as component, which is the inverse relation of component_of:

Box 4. Continued

```
(∀p1,p2) has_component(p1,p2) ° component_of(p2,p1).
```
    A part might have different kind of features, e.g., geometrical features, functional features, assembly features, mating features, physical features, etc. Here, features refer to the geometrical features such as hole, slot, channel, groove, boss, pad, etc.. They are also called form features.

    Axiom 11: A part and its features are related by the predicate feature_of:
```
feature_of(f,p).
```
    Axiom 12: There can be a composite feature of f' which are composed of several sub-features, f1, f2, ..., fi:
```
subfeature_of(f1,f).
```
    Axiom 13: A subfeature f1 of a feature f2 of a part p is also a feature of the part:
```
(∀f1,f2,p) subfeature_of(f1,f2) ∨ feature_of(f2,p)
⊃ feature_of(f1,p).
```
    Axiom 14: The feature_of and subfeature_of have inverse relations has_feature and has_subfeature:
```
(∀f1,f2) has_feature(f1,f2) ≡ feature_of(f2,f1),
(∀f1,f2) has_subfeature(f1,f2) ≡ subfeature_of(f2,f1).
```

transformations and revisions. Therefore, versions of design need to be created as objects to record the history of designs.

By understanding the architecture and communication mechanism of the multiagent-based product data communication system, in the following subsection we provide an illustration on the capability of the multiagent-based communication system to perform tracking of design changes.

TRACKING OF DESIGN CHANGES

In collaborative design environment, designers deal with many possibilities and complexities of design changes. During design transactions, they must assess the impacts of a design change on the other design objects and notify other parties promptly. In most design environment, due to the lack of tracking of design changes, designers have to manually perform a consistency check for a proposed design change as well as to identify all the impacts of the change. This condition makes design consistency and accuracy are not

guaranteed and the productivity of design team is compromised (Wang, Shen, Xie, Neelamkavil, & Pardasani, 2000).

In order to solve this drawback, an approach to the tracking of design changes in a unified framework (Xie, 2001) is introduced. This approach enables a team of designers work on a Web-based collaborative design in distributed remote locations to visualize, manipulate and evaluate the impacts of changes to a design.

Product Data Driven Approach

From the perspectives of product variation and product improvement, design changes are imperative in order to meet the requirements of product specification, safety standards, or to reduce manufacturing or maintenance costs. Due to the associated relationships between elements in a product, a design change might have an impact on certain geometric constraints that might propagate to other elements of the product. In this approach, the mechanism for tracking of design changes is based on product data and the

Figure 15. E-R diagram for change tracking model (Source: Xie, 2001)

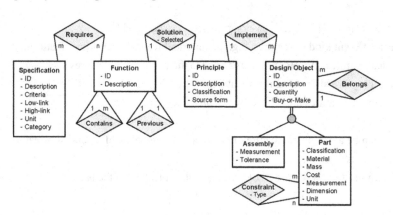

relationships generated during various stages of a product design process.

The product data contains product descriptions for product specification, function decomposition structure, solution principles, layout design, assemblies, and parts. The relationships are established between two or more elements having geometric constraint relationships to one another. Here, the geometric constraint relationship defines three types of constraint between parts, i.e., fit, contact, and consistent constraints. The fit constraint exists if there is a tolerance requirement between parts. The contact constraint represents a physical contact between two parts. The consistent constraint exists if two parts hold a dimensional constraint without a physical contact.

The product data driven approach enables designers to identify the total impacts of a proposed design change on an entire product. It provides a fundamental mechanism to support forward tracking and backward tracking of a design change. Forward tracking identifies the impact of the change on later design stages if a design change occurs at an earlier stage. On the other hand, backward tracking identifies the impacts of changes on previous stages, if a change occurs at a later stage. These operations can be implemented with database support.

To make the necessary design information available, product data information is extracted

from various stages of design process and represented in a data model. A data model is a set of concepts that can be used to describe the structure of a database (Elmasri and Navather, 1989). In this process, an entity-relationship (E-R) model is used to describe product data with such concepts as entities, attributes, and relationships.

The entities and attributes describe an abstract object with its properties. The change tracking model includes five types of entities, i.e., *Specification*, *Function*, *Principle*, *Design_Object*, *Assembly*, and *Part*. These entities are associated to 19 attributes, i.e., *ID, Description, Criteria, Low-limit, High-limit, Unit, Category, Source-form, Selected, Quantity, Buy-or-make, Measurement, Tolerance, Classification, Materials, Mass, Cost, Dimension, and Type.*

The relationships represent a set of associations amongst entities. They limit the possible combinations of entity instances. Cardinality ratio constraints specify three common combinations for binary relationship types, i.e., *one-to-one* (1:1), *one-to-many* (1:M), and *many-to-many* (M:N). The change tracking model includes seven types of relationship, i.e., *Requires, Contains, Previous, Solution, Implement, Belongs*, and *Constraint*. Figure 15 describes the relationships between entities and their associated attributes. In order to provide better understanding on the change tracking model, the following subsection illustrates

Figure 16. Displacement of elements: (a) deflected shapes of individual elements, (b) disparity of displacements along juncture line connected elements, and (c) reduction of displacement gap by refinement of gridwork (Source: Gallagher, 1975)

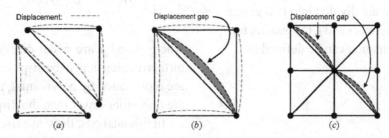

the forward tracking process of design changes on a motor-body.

Case Study

The initial design of the motor-body is cylinder shape made from alloy steel (SS) with mass 1.751 kg and volume 0.000227 m³. The motor-body is designed must be at a fixed position inside the vehicle engine compartment. During operation, the force produced by the electrical motor inside the motor-body is uniformly distributed from center to boundary. Therefore, three fixtures are applied at the bottom, and left- and right sides to clamp the motor-body at the fixed position.

The real structure of motor-body sustains a distributed state of stress. The stress is represented by forces at the element joints or nodes. Correspondingly, the displacement of these points is employed in the characterization of displaced state of the element.

To describe nodes of finite element in a continuum structure, they are assumed in the triangular elements that vary quadratically over the surface of the elements. When the elements are joined, there will be a general lack of continuity of the edge displacement of the elements along the juncture line as described in Figure 16. The joining of the elements at the vertices enforces the continuity of displacements only at those points. The three points of a triangular element define uniquely the shape of displacement. Since only the two end

points of the element interface have influence in defining the shape of displacement along an edge, then, the displacements of the edges of the respective elements will differ for each case. As more elements are used, the disparity of the displacement of the adjacent element edges is reduced and the error in the solution due to this condition is reduced as well.

Most structural analysis problem can be treated as linear static problem under assumptions small deformation (i.e., loading pattern is not changing due to the deformed shape), elastic material (i.e., no plasticity), and static load (i.e., the load is applied to the structure in a slow of steady operation). To estimate the possible occurrence of shape deformation, the force-displacement analysis is applied. The relationship between the joint forces and the joint displacements of finite elements should satisfy the following stiffness function,

$$\{F\} = [k] \{D\} \qquad (4)$$

where {F}: element force, {D}: displacement vectors, and [k]: element stiffness matrix. An individual term of the [k] matrix, k_{ij}, is an element stiffness coefficient. If the displacement D_j is imposed at unit value and all other degree of freedom (d.o.f.) are held fixed against displacement ($D_k = 0$, $k \neq j$), then the force F_i is equal in value to k_{ij}.

During the design optimization, the displacement analysis is performed using the mixed force-displacement equation that defines a relationship between vectors containing both force and displacement. If the forces and corresponding d.o.f. of an element are divided into two groups, designated by subscripts s and f, the general form of a mixed representation can be defined as,

$$\begin{Bmatrix} F_f \\ \Delta_f \end{Bmatrix} = \begin{bmatrix} \Omega \end{bmatrix} \begin{Bmatrix} F_s \\ \Delta_s \end{Bmatrix} \tag{5}$$

The force-displacement analysis produces an average deformation scale at $1.7250e^{+8}$ and a prediction of location where the deformed mesh are most possible to occur. The resultants displacement shows the minimum condition 0 mm is at location (3.969 cm, -0.499 cm, -11.000 cm) and the maximum condition $6.76612e^{-8}$ mm at location (-3.373 cm, -3.291 cm, -0.099 cm). The analysis predicts that two most possible deformed locations likely to occur at the lower-part of cab-screw holes. This condition makes the cylinder shape has more possibility to slip from its position and fixtures.

Applying the stress analysis, a convenient mode of selection of stress fields that satisfy the equilibrium differential equations can be determined by using the stress functions. Stress functions are parameters which, when differentiated in accordance with certain rules, give stress components that automatically satisfy the differential equations of equilibrium.

Stresses can be evaluated at any point, both inside the element and at the nodes. For small strain and small rotations,

$$\varepsilon_x = \frac{\partial u}{\partial x}, \quad \varepsilon_{yx} = \frac{\partial v}{\partial y}, \quad \gamma_{xy} = \frac{\partial u}{\partial y} + \frac{\partial v}{\partial x} \tag{6}$$

or, in matrix form

$$\begin{Bmatrix} \varepsilon_x \\ \varepsilon_y \\ \gamma_{xy} \end{Bmatrix} = \begin{bmatrix} \partial/\partial x & 0 \\ 0 & \partial/\partial y \\ \partial/\partial y & \partial/\partial x \end{bmatrix} \begin{Bmatrix} u \\ v \end{Bmatrix}. \tag{7}$$

where u and v are nodal displacements. Based on this relationship, if the displacements functions are represented by polynomial, thus, the stresses are one-order lower than the displacements.

In this analysis, the von Mises stress function is applied (Liua et al., 2005)

$$\sigma_e = \frac{1}{\sqrt{2}} \sqrt{(\sigma_1 - \sigma_2)^2 + (\sigma_2 - \sigma_3)^2 + (\sigma_3 - \sigma_1)^2} \tag{8}$$

where σ_1, σ_2, and σ_3 are three principle stresses at the considered point in a structure. For a ductile material, the von Mises stress (σ_e) and the yield stress of the material (σ_y) must satisfy the following constraint

$$\sigma_e \leq \sigma_Y. \tag{9}$$

For 2-dimensional problem, the two principle stresses in the plane are determined by

$$\sigma_1^P = \frac{\sigma_x + \sigma_y}{2} + \sqrt{\left(\frac{\sigma_x - \sigma_y}{2}\right)^2 + \tau_{xy}^2}$$

$$\sigma_2^P = \frac{\sigma_x + \sigma_y}{2} - \sqrt{\left(\frac{\sigma_x - \sigma_y}{2}\right)^2 + \tau_{xy}^2} \tag{10}$$

Thus, the von Mises stress can be expressed in terms of the stress components in the xy coordinate system as

$$\sigma_e = \sqrt{(\sigma_x + \sigma_y)^2 - 3(\sigma_x \sigma_y - \tau_{xy}^2)}. \tag{11}$$

Table 2. Forward tracking for change of Design_Object

ENTITIES	ATTRIBUTES	STATUS	DESIGN VALUES	
			INITIAL	OPTIMAL
Function	ID	No change	part#1	part#1
	Description	No change	Motor-body	Motor-body
Principle	Classification	No change	Motor protection	Motor protection
	Source Form	No change	In-house production house	In-house production
Design_Object	Quantity	No change	100 pieces	100 pieces
	Buy-or-Make	No change	make	make
Specification	Criteria	No change	mechanic – static	mechanic – static
	Low-limit	Change	3.04976e-006 N/mm^2	3.43238e-007 N/mm^2
	High-limit	Change	0.000572322 N/mm^2	0.00139487 N/mm^2
	Unit	No change	1	1
	Category	No change	automotive part	automotive part
Part	Material	No change	alloy steel (SS)	alloy steel (SS)
	Mass	No change	min 1.750 – max 1.860 kg	min 1.750 – max 1.860 kg
	Cost	No change	USD 367.82 - USD 375.00	USD 367.82 - USD 375.00
	Measurement	No change	millimeter (mm)	millimeter (mm)
	Dimension	Change	d: 82.5mm, l: 110 mm	w: 82.5 mm, h: 82.5 mm, l: 110 mm

Figure 17. Initial design: (a) cylinder motor-body, (b) 3D cross-section of deformed mesh, (c) estimated deformed mesh, (d) estimated strained mesh

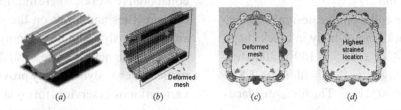

Figure 18. Optimal design: (a) block motor-body, (b) 3D cross-section of deformed mesh, (c) estimated deformed mesh, (d) estimated strained mesh

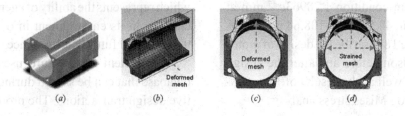

The result of stress analysis estimates minimum stress $3.04976e^{-6}$ N/mm^2 (MPa) at location (4.170 cm, -0.470 cm, -6.750 cm) and maximum stress 0.000572322 N/mm^2 (MPa) at location (3.524 cm, -3.385 cm, -0.350 cm). The stress is distributed from the inner cylindrical mesh boundary to the outer boundary with the highest strained locations are found at the elements adjacent to the four cab-screw holes. This condition makes the initial design has high potential failure (i.e., crack) during the assembly and product use. Therefore, the initial design needs to be improved.

Based on prior design history, designers decide to change the design of motor-body from cylinder to block shape. The change of *Design_Object* from cylinder to block shape has driven direct changing of *assembly*, *part*, and *constraint* respectively. In this case, tracking of design changes is performed based on entities, attributes, and relationships, which have been determined in the E-R diagram. Changing of geometry has an impact to constraints of four cab-screw holes which, in its turn, propagate to the changing of dimensions and positions of those holes on the modified shape. The progress for forward tracking of change of *Design_Object* is described in Table 2.

As a result, the collaborative design produces an optimal design of motor-body in block shape with dimension 82.5 x 82.5 x 100 millimeters using material alloy steel (SS) with mass 1.859 kg and volume 0.000241 m^3. The force-displacement analysis of the new design generates an average deformation scale $8.59488e^{+7}$, i.e., 50.18% better than the initial design. On the block shape, the deformation has been localized at the upper-front to upper-middle of finite mesh. The resultants displacement shows the minimum condition 0 mm is at location (41.25 mm, 23.25 mm, 0 mm) and the maximum condition $1.28963e^{+7}$ mm at location 0.09 mm, 44.50 mm, -108.64 mm). Figure 17 and Figure 18 describe the design of motor body in comparison before and after the design optimization, as well as the results of force-displacement and von Mises stress analysis.

CONCLUSION

Today, product development is inevitable must be performed as an integrated process design to manufacturing. In a collaborative design environment, design activity might take place at distributed geographic locations that involves multidisciplinary design team work with various CAD/CAM application systems. This circumstance has driven a need for better communication and coordination amongst design team during the design process. As the information and communication technologies advance, the application of collaborative engineering to product design, so-called computer supported collaborative design (CSCD), becomes more promising.

In collaborative design environment, Web technology makes remote communication physically viable through a common network. Furthermore, an integrated Web- and agent-based CSCD is able to support cooperation amongst designers and engineers, enhancing interoperability between authoring tools, and allow better communication of modular design tasks. In current practice, designers and engineers intend to perform real-time collaborative works, where multiple users are able to share files and work on the same document simultaneously. With the support of Cloud technology, designers can use virtualization and the modern Web to dynamically provide resources of various kinds as services for collaborative design, which are provisioned electronically.

In this chapter, architecture of multiagent-based product data communication system has been introduced. The multiagent system runs on an intelligent knowledge server, which embodies two capabilities of intelligent agent and learning agents. It is developed as an adaptive system, which represents the ability of agents to adapt with changes in its environment in order to improve the system's future performance.

The system architecture uses a centralized database that can be shared during the collaborative design transactions. The product database is designed on an active semantic network (ASN) that can handle and manage the increasing amount of knowledge during the design process. The product database is coupled with data dictionary and feature taxonomy. Data dictionary provides a collection of descriptions of the data objects or items in a data model for users who need to refer to them during the design transaction. When a new design is introduced and previously does not exist in the database, the learning agent will be invoked to perform feature recognition. Here, the recognition algorithm works by recognizing a new entity from its geometric shape based on specification in the feature taxonomy.

The data communication network is based on the seven-layer ISO/OSI network model. During communication, the interaction is designed as bidirectional communication that supports information flow from sender to receiver, and vice versa. Since an agent must represent its knowledge in the vocabulary of a specified ontology, hence, product ontology is created that must be accessible to the agents who are communicating. Thus, all agents that share the same ontology for knowledge representation have a common understanding in the agent communication language.

In practice, design changes are imperative in order to meet the requirements of product specification, safety standards, or to reduce product costs. The product data communication system provides an ability to the tracking of design changes in a unified framework. The mechanism for tracking of design changes is based on product data and their relationships. The product data driven approach provides a fundamental mechanism to support forward tracking and backward tracking of a design change. This approach enables designers work on a Web-based collaborative design in distributed locations to visualize, manipulate and evaluate the total impacts of a proposed design change on an entire product.

ACKNOWLEDGMENT

This research project is organized under the financial support of Institute of Computer-aided Product Development Systems, Universität Stuttgart and The Alexander von Humboldt Foundation, Germany.

REFERENCES

Ane, B. K. (2010). *Automation of design for reverse engineering in a collaborative design environment: Development of STEP neutral format translator for product data exchange. Research Report*. Stuttgart, Germany: IRIS, Universität Stuttgart.

Ane, B. K., & Roller, D. (2011). An architecture of adaptive product data communication system for collaborative design. *Proceedings of the 4th International Conference on Advances in Computer-Human Interactions (ACHI'11)*, (pp. 182-187).

Baun, C., Kunze, M., Nimis, J., & Tai, S. (2011). *Cloud computing: Web-based dynamic IT services*. Heidelberg, Germany: Springer-Verlag.

Bernd, B., Heiko, G., & Michael, W. (2007). Aktives Semantiches Konstruktions- und Zuverlässigkeitsnetz . In Bertsche, B., & Bullinger, H.-J. (Eds.), *Entwicklung und Erprobung Innovativer Produkte-Rapid Prototyping: Grundlagen, Rahmenbedingungen und Realisierung* (pp. 130–158). Berlin, Germany: Springer-Verlag.

Borghoff, U. M., & Schlichter, J. H. (2000). *Computer-supported cooperative work: Introduction to distributed applications*. Heidelberg, Germany: Springer-Verlag.

Box, D. (1998). *Essential COM*. Upper Saddle River, NJ: Addison-Wesley.

Caldwell, N. H. M., & Rodgers, P. A. (1998). WebCADET: Facilitating distributed design support. *Proceedings of the IEEE Colloquium on Web-Based Knowledge Servers*, (pp. 9/1–9/4).

Campbell, M. I., Cagan, J., & Kotovsky, K. (1999). A-design: An agent-based approach to conceptual design in a dynamic environment. *Research in Engineering Design, 11*, 172–192. doi:10.1007/s001630050013

Cundy, H. M., & Rollet, A. P. (1961). *Mathematical models* (2nd ed.). Oxford, UK: Oxford University Press.

Cutkosky, M. R., Engelmore, R. S., Fikes, R. E., Genesereth, M. R., Gruber, T. R., & Mark, W. S. (1993). PACT: An experiment in integrating concurrent engineering systems. *IEEE Computer, 26*, 28–37. doi:10.1109/2.179153

Elmasri, R., & Navather, S. B. (1989). *Fundamentals of database systems*. New York, NY: Benjamin Cummings Publishing Company Inc.

ETK - BMW Group. (2010). *Electronic parts catalogue. Database version: ETK 2.32*. Munich, Germany: BMW Group.

Fruchter, R., Reiner, K. A., Toye, G., & Leifer, L. J. (1996). Collaborative mechatronic system design. *Concurrent Engineering . Research and Applications, 4*, 401–412.

Gallagher, R. H. (1975). *Element analysis: Fundamentals*. Prentice Hall.

Greif, I. (1988). *Computer-supported cooperative work: A book of readings*. San Mateo, CA: Morgan Kaufmann Publishers.

Hague, M. J., & Taleb-Bendiab, A. (1998). Tool for management of concurrent conceptual engineering design. *Concurrent Engineering . Research and Applications, 6*, 111–129.

Hoffmann, C. M., & Joan-Arinyo, R. (2005). *A brief on constraint solving*. West Lafayette, IN: Purdue University.

Huang, G. Q., Lee, S. W., & Mak, K. L. (1999). Web-based product and process data modelling in concurrent 'Design for X'. *Robotics and Computer-integrated Manufacturing, 15*, 53–63. doi:10.1016/S0736-5845(98)00028-3

Huang, G. Q., & Mak, K. L. (1999). [a]). Web-based morphological charts for concept design in collaborative product development. *Journal of Intelligent Manufacturing, 10*, 267–278. doi:10.1023/A:1008999908120

Huang, G. Q., & Mak, K. L. (1999). [b]). Design For manufacture and assembly on the internet. *Computers in Industry, 38*, 17–30. doi:10.1016/S0166-3615(98)00105-5

Huang, K., Li, X., Cao, S., Yang, B., & Pan, W. (2001). Co-DARFAD: The collaborative mechanical product design system. *Proceedings of the 6th International Conference on Computer Supported Cooperative Work In Design*, (pp. 163-168).

Hummel, K. E., & Brooks, S. L. (1986). Symbolic representation of manufacturing features for an automated process planning system . In Lu, S., & Komanduri, R. (Eds.), *Knowledge-based expert systems for manufacturing* (pp. 233–243). ASME.

IBM Dictionary of Computing. (2008). *IBM terminology*. Retrieved January 20, 2011, from http://www-01.ibm.com/software/globalization/terminology/d.html

International Standard Organization (ISO). (1992). *Industrial automation system and integration – Product data representation and exchange. Technical Report*. Geneva, Switzerland: ISO Central Secretariat.

Jagannathan, V., Almasi, G., & Suvaiala, A. (1996). Collaborative infrastructures using the WWW and CORBA-based environments. *Proceedings of the IEEE Workshops on Enabling Technologies Infrastructure for Collaborative Enterprises (WET ICE '96)*, (pp. 292-297).

Jagannathan, V., Dodhiawala, R., & Baum, L. S. (1989). *Blackboard architectures and applications*. San Diego, CA: Academic Press.

Li, W. D., Ong, S. K., & Nee, A. Y. C. (2006). *Integrated and collaborative product development environment: Technologies and implementation*. Singapore: World Scientific.

Lin, J., Fox, M. S., & Bilgic, T. (1996). *A requirement ontology for engineering design*. Unpublished technical report, University of Toronto, Canada.

Liua, C. L., Lua, Z. Z., Xub, Y. L., & Yuec, Z. F. (2005). Reliability analysis for low cycle fatigue life of the aeronautical engine turbine disc structure under random environment. *Materials Science and Engineering A*, 218–225. doi:10.1016/j.msea.2004.12.014

Mahmood, Z., & Hill, R. (2011). *Cloud computing for enterprise architectures*. London, UK: Springer-Verlag.

McCarthy, D. R., & Dayal, U. (1989). The architecture of an active database management system. *Proceedings of ACM SIGMOD International Conference on Management of Data*, (pp. 215-224).

Ming, C., Jinfei, L., Qinghua, K., & Yuan, Y. (2010). Study on collaborative product design based on modularity and multi-agent. *Proceedings of the 2010 14th International Conference on Computer Supported Cooperative Work in Design*, (pp. 274-279).

National Institute of Standards and Technology. (2012). *The NIST definition of cloud computing*. Retrieved February 3, 2011, from http://csrc.nist.gov/publications/nistpubs/800-145/SP800-145.pdf

Object Management Group. (2008). *Common object request broker architecture (CORBA) Specification: Version 3.1*. Needham, MA: OMG.

OpenNebula. (2010). *About the OpenNebula technology*. Retrieved March 3, 2012, from http://www.opennebula.org/about:technology

Roller, D., Bihler, M., & Eck, O. (1997). SN: Active, distributed knowledge base for rapid prototyping. *Proceedings of 30th ISATA - Volume "Rapid Prototyping in the Automotive Industries"*, (pp. 253-262).

Roller, D., & Eck, O. (1997). Constraint propagation using an active semantic network. *Proceedings of 1st International Workshop on Geometric Constraint Solving & Applications*.

Roller, D., & Eck, O. (1998). Constraint propagation using an active semantic network . In Brüderlin, B., & Roller, D. (Eds.), *Geometric constraints solving and applications*. Berlin, Germany: Springer-Verlag. doi:10.1007/978-3-642-58898-3_3

Roller, D., Eck, O., Bihler, M., & Stolpmann, M. (1995). *An active semantic network for supporting rapid prototyping. ISATA Proceedings on Mechatronics - Efficient Computer Support for Engineering* (pp. 41–48). Manufactoring, Testing & Reliability.

Rollins, J. M. (2012). *Speed of a piston*. Retrieved March 15, 2012 from http://www.camotruck.net/rollins/piston.html

Schmidt, K., & Bannon, L. (1992). Taking CSCW seriously. *Computer Supported Cooperative Work*, *1*, 7–40. doi:10.1007/BF00752449

Shah, J. J., & Mantyla, M. (1995). *Parametric and feature-based CAD/CAM: Concepts, techniques, and applications*. Toronto, Canada: John Wiley & Sons, Inc.

Shen, W., & Barthes, J. P. (1995). DIDE: A multi-agent environment for engineering design. *Proceedings of the 1st International Conference on Multi-Agent Systems (ICMAS'95)*, (pp. 344-351).

Shen, W., Hao, Q., & Li, W. (2008). Computer supported collaborative design: Retrospective and perspective. *Computers in Industry, 59*, 855–862. doi:10.1016/j.compind.2008.07.001

Sprow, E. (1992). Chrysler's concurrent engineering challenge. *Manufacturing Engineering, 108*, 35–42.

Technologies, C. A. (2010). *Turnkey cloud computing*. Retrieved September 14, 2011, from http://www.3tera.com/AppLogic

Thiel, S., Dalakakis, S., & Roller, D. (2005). A learning agent for knowledge extraction from an active semantic network. *World Academy of Science, Engineering and Technology, 7*.

Toye, G., Cutkosky, M., Leifer, L., Tenenbaum, J., & Glicksman, J. (1993). SHARE: A methodology and environment for collaborative product development. *Proceedings of the IEEE 2nd Workshop on Enabling Technologies: Infrastructure for Collaborative Enterprises*, (pp. 33-47).

Verroust, A., Schonek, F., & Roller, D. (1992). A rule oriented method for parametrized computer aided design. *Computer Aided Design, 24*, 531–540. doi:10.1016/0010-4485(92)90040-H

Wallis, A., Haag, Z., & Foley, R. (1998). A multi-agent framework for distributed collaborative design. *Proceedings of the IEEE Workshops on Enabling Technologies Infrastructure for Collaborative Enterprises (WET ICE '98)*, (pp. 282-287).

Wang, L. (2009). *Virtual environments for grid computing*. Karlsruhe, Germany: Universitaetsverlag Karlsruhe.

Wang, L., Shen, W., Xie, H., Neelamkavil, J., & Pardasani, A. (2000). Collaborative conceptual design: A state-of-the-art survey. *Proceedings of the 6th International Conference on Computer Supported Cooperative Work in Design*, (pp. 204-209).

Weiss, G. (1999). *Multiagent systems: A modern approach to distributed artificial intelligence*. Massachusetts, USA: MIT Press.

Wohlstadter, E., & Tai, S. (2009). *Web services, reference entry. Encyclopedia of Database Systems (EDBS)*. Heidelberg, Germany: Springer.

World Wide Web Consortium. (2002). *Web services architecture requirements*. W3C Working Draft 29 April 2002. Retrieved February 10, 2011, from http://www.w3.org/TR/2002/WD-wsa-reqs-20020429

Xie, H. (2001). Tracking of design changes for collaborative product development. *Proceedings of the 6th International Conference on Computer Supported Cooperative Work in Design*, (pp. 175-180).

Xuan, W., Xue, S., & Ma, T. (2009). Architecture of collaborative design based on grid. *Proceedings of the Third International Conference on Genetic and Evolutionary Computing*, (pp. 244-247).

Zdrahal, Z., & Domingue, J. (1997). The world wide design lab: An environment for distributed collaborative design. *Proceedings of the 1997 International Conference on Engineering Design*, (pp. 19-21).

KEY TERMS AND DEFINITIONS

Active Semantic Network (ASN): A shared database system developed for supporting designers during product development and is realized as an active, object-oriented database system. ASN comprises a network of nodes and links, where the nodes represent objects of the real world and the links relations amongst these objects.

Adaptive: The ability of the intelligent agent to adapt with changes in its environment that commonly sources from changes of structure, program, or data (i.e. based on its input or in response to information) in such a manner that the expected future performance will improve.

Agent: An autonomous, reactive, pro-active computer system, typically with a central locus of control, that is at least able to communicate with other agents via some kind of communication language. Another common view of an agent is that of an active object or a bounded process with the ability to perceive, reason, and act. Various attributes are discussed in the context of agent-based systems.

Cloud Computing: By using virtualized computing and storage resources and modern Web technologies, cloud computing provides scalable, network-centric, abstracted information technology (IT) infrastructures, platforms, and applications as on-demand services. These services are billed on a usage basis.

Computer Supported Collaborative Design: The process of designing a product through collaboration among multidisciplinary product developers associated with the entire product life cycle.

Feature Taxonomy: A natural structure of feature-based manufacturing used to develop the feature library and to simplify and encourage the extension of the library.

Data Dictionary: A centralized repository of information about such data like meaning, relationships to other data, origin, usage, and format.

ISO/OSI Model: An Open Systems Interconnection (OSI) model developed by ISO (International Organization for Standardization) in 1984, defines a networking framework for implementing protocols in seven layers. Control is passed from one layer to the next, starting at the application layer in one station, and proceeding to the bottom layer, over the channel to the next station and back up the hierarchy.

Multiagent System: A collection of software agents that communicates and works in conjunction with each other. They may cooperate or compete with others, or some combination of cooperation and competition, to solve a complex problem which is beyond the capability of each individual system.

Web Technology: The platforms and technologies which are used to develop a mechanism that allows two of more computer devices to communicate over a network through alternatives Web sites and Web applications.

Chapter 12
Development, Integration, and Deployment of Mobile Information Services in Healthcare:
Usability and Security Challenges and Opportunities

Jelena Mirkovic
*Center for Shared Decision Making and Collaborative Care Research,
Oslo University Hospital, Oslo, Norway*

Haakon Bryhni
Department of Informatics, University of Oslo, Oslo, Norway

ABSTRACT

The use of mobile and wireless technologies has great potential to improve the efficiency and quality of healthcare delivery. The main goal of this chapter is to describe the current state of the art in the research field of development and integration of mobile services in the healthcare sector by addressing the two main challenges: usability and security. The authors investigate the main requirements and approaches for developing highly usable, user-friendly, and well-accepted mobile healthcare services. In addition, they identify various ways of addressing security and privacy issues in mobile healthcare services and discuss the advantages and shortcomings of each approach. Finally, the chapter presents the CONNECT (Care Online: Novel Networks to Enhance Communication and Treatment) project and describes how security and usability issues can be addressed during the development of mobile access to a multi-modal Internet-based patient support system.

DOI: 10.4018/978-1-4666-2190-9.ch012

INTRODUCTION

Mobile devices, such as mobile phones and tablet PCs, are widely popular today, and they are accepted as an important part of people's everyday lives. They allow people seamless access to numerous services and the possibility to stay connected independent of location and time. The use of mobile services has increased in many application areas such as learning, government, and business, and the healthcare sector is also slowly beginning to recognize and leverage the advantages of ubiquitous and seamless information systems.

The use of mobile and wireless technologies in the healthcare sector can result in higher efficiency and quality of healthcare services and decrease healthcare-related spending (Shieh, Tsai, Arash, Wang, & Lin, 2007; Gollol Raju, et al., 2004). All stakeholders in the healthcare sector (e.g., healthcare providers, patients, and healthcare institutions) can benefit from the introduction of mobile access to healthcare information systems (HISs). For example, healthcare providers could access patients' medical information and databases containing medical knowledge and references independent of the their current time and place. Patients could be offered all times available services for consultations with healthcare personnel and experts in various medical fields. Moreover, patients can be offered the possibility of continuous monitoring of their health conditions, being more active participants in the medical decision-making process, and keeping communications channels with healthcare providers open at all times.

However, before mobile devices are ready for wide deployment in healthcare, many challenges and issues must be addressed and resolved. The limited capabilities of wireless and cellular communications networks and mobile devices (e.g., display, processing power, and input characteristics) and the large diversity of mobile devices and their capabilities are only some of the challenges introduced by emerging mobile and wireless tech-

nologies. Additionally, the development of new and advanced technologies will introduce new issues and new contexts in the already-identified problem space. In addition to the limitations of mobile devices and networks, numerous issues are still unresolved regarding security, privacy, organization and legislation in healthcare systems and services.

In the literature, there is a large body of research in this area that is addressing various challenges and introducing new knowledge regarding the development, integration and deployment of mobile devices and services in HISs, as showed in (Mirkovic, Bryhni, & Ruland, 2009). The main goal of this chapter is to provide overview of the identified challenges and issues in developing and deploying useful and well-integrated mobile healthcare services with a focus on usability and security. Through overview of these two specific topics we will present different approaches how identified challenges can be addressed and resolved. Finally, we will demonstrate how security and usability are addressed during the development of mobile access to a Internet-based patient support system in the CONNECT (Care Online: Novel Networks to Enhance Communication and Treatment) project.

BACKGROUND

Numerous countries define their healthcare strategies and policies by stressing the importance of using new and emerging technologies. For example, in Norway, the government has defined a National eHealth strategy called "Interaction 2.0," which focuses strongly on the development of network-based services for patients and the general public, patient access to summarized medical information, telemedicine, and the electronic exchange of information and knowledge (Helse-og omsorgsdepartementet, 2008). In addition, the number and popularity of mobile healthcare applications available on online application stores (e.g., iTunes Store, and OviStore) is growing. Kailas, Chia-Chin, & Watanabe (2010) and Dolan (2010) state that the number of standalone smartphone healthcare applications today is more than 7000 and this number is steadily increasing. This proves a recognized potential of mobile healthcare services and presence of technologies that can be used for their implementation and delivery. However, mobile devices are usually just standalone systems today and they are not integrated in HIS and accepted as a standard means for healthcare service delivery. Examples can be found in which some hospitals are beginning to accept mobile and wireless technology (e.g.,(Microsoft Case Studies, 2011b; Microsoft Case Studies, 2011a; University of Cambrige, & China Mobile, 2011)), but these are only isolated instances. Integrating mobile devices and services with HIS remains an open issue and a topic that requires further research.

Beyond the limitations of mobile and wireless technologies, additional challenges and unresolved issues influencing the wide deployment and acceptance of mobile healthcare services in everyday healthcare delivery identified by Standing and Standing (2008) include the following:

- **A Centralized System:** HISs today usually store patients' medical information on one closed, centralized system. However, this type of system does not comply with distributed healthcare systems in practice today, resulting in the dispersal of patient health information among various HISs and a failure to provide a medical record that contains all of a patient's health-related data. Many countries today are working on developing standard national electronic healthcare record (EHR) system that can gather all patients' data in one place and provide easy access to information at the point of need not just for healthcare personnel but also for patients (e.g., (Kannoju, Sridhar, & Prasad, 2010; Spil & Katsma, 2007; "ASIP Santé project", 2011; "An

Electronic Health Record for every South African", 2011)).

- **Integration with Complex Healthcare Systems:** A HIS is a large, complex system that is specific and poorly integrated with other services and information systems. Integrating additional services therefore requires many resources, especially if data from various systems are used. Today many research projects work on addressing issues of integration and interoperability between different HISs, communication networks, and device types. For example, epSOS project are addressing cross-border interoperability issues and aim to design, develop, and evaluate a service infrastructure that provides easy sharing and cooperation between EHR in different European countries (Thorp, 2010). One more example is global initiative with name Integrating the Healthcare Enterprise that works on developing the framework for exchanging health information seamlessly between different applications, systems, and settings (Wein, 2003).

- **Critical Information:** Information regarding patient health is highly critical and thus requires a high level of reliability when managing and processing the information. Some countries have special organizations charged with controlling the quality and functionalities of healthcare services available through new and emerging technologies (e.g., the Food and Drug Administration in the USA).

- **Conservatism:** The healthcare sector accepts changes slowly, ensuring that the change is needed and that any risk taken is minimal when innovations are accepted and integrated. Therefore, the healthcare sector is able to avoid potential problems and emerging issues, but at the same time, it misses out on the advantages that can result in better organization and productivity.

- **Fear of Control:** Various mobile and wireless services can enable users to stay connected and use various services independent of location and time. However, with the introduction of such technologies as position systems, the issue arises of people's right to privacy, especially in the healthcare sector.

- **Security and Legal and Regulatory Implications:** Using mobile devices in healthcare raises major concerns about security and the protection of patients' private medical information. The implementation of security mechanisms on mobile devices can differ greatly from such mechanisms on standard personal computers, introducing the question of whether the protection of users' information is sufficient. There is a large body of research that is using different approaches for addressing numerous security challenges and developing advanced security mechanisms for enabling secure access to patients' private data over mobile devices. However, there is no standard security solution for mobile access to HISs defined today, mainly due to different requirements and rules set by different countries to ensure required level of security for people's private and sensitive data.

In addition to the issues concerned with the use and integration of emerging mobile and wireless technologies in complex HISs, another important topic is end-users and their acceptance of the system. In the literature, numerous studies can be found that investigate users' acceptance and willingness to use mobile devices for accessing healthcare information services. Different projects report different results. For example, Challenor and Deegan (2009) reported that patients in a research study have accepted a mobile phone, followed by text and letter format, as the most convenient method for receiving clinic results. Luo, et al. (2009) reported that the majority of people who are SMS and Internet users are comfortable in using these technologies for the delivery of healthcare information. However, a study by Kleiboer, et al. (2010) identified which methods of remote symptom assessment cancer patients would use. The results showed that most patients do not feel comfortable using technology such as websites, email, and mobile phone texting. Furthermore, Pinnock, Slack, Pagliari, Price, and Sheikh (2006) found that both clinicians and patients had concerns about clinical benefits, impact on self-management, and workload and cost when considering the acceptance of electronic self-monitoring systems. Therefore, various studies have been performed to identify the most important factors influencing the acceptance of mobile healthcare services by different user groups. Wu, Wang, and Lin (2007) showed that healthcare providers' acceptance and intention to use mobile services are influenced mostly by compatibility with other components of the information system, perceived usefulness and perceived ease of use. On the other side, Lin and Yang (2009) reported that patients' acceptance of using an e-health mobile services is primarily predisposed by their attitudes, perceived usefulness, subjective norms, perceived ease of use, and innovativeness. In the literary survey by Or and Karsh (2009), variables that are associated with patient acceptance of new technologies in health management were reported. The presented variables were related mostly to patient characteristics, human-computer interaction, organization and environment. From these examples it can be concluded that user-friendliness and usefulness are one of the most important factors influencing end-users intention to use the eHealth and mHealth services and acceptance of these services in people's everyday activities and health management process.

An additional challenge when implementing mobile services in healthcare systems is handling mobility issues. When developing services with support for access over different types of terminals and different communications networks, an important issue is how to adapt one service to different contexts of use. Although today most mobile services are developed as standalone systems, and they are not integrated with other systems and HIS, with further development and improvement of new technologies, the issue of adaptability will present an important challenge for the implementation of seamless and ubiquitous healthcare services.

Here, we have identified numerous unresolved challenges and obstacles that influence the large-scale acceptance and utilization of mobile services in healthcare. As can be seen, this is a broad problem space that includes numerous topics and research areas that must be thoughtfully addressed and resolved before mobile devices can achieve their potential and begin to be used in everyday healthcare delivery. In the next sections, we will direct our focus on two topics that we have identified as highly important for the development of useful, safe, and well-accepted mobile healthcare services: usability and security.

USABILITY AND SECURITY ISSUES FOR MOBILE HEALTHCARE SERVICES

In this section, we will describe two specific challenges faced when developing mobile healthcare services: (1) ensuring usability and user-friendliness of the system and (2) implementing security mechanisms to protect confidentiality, integrity, and privacy of patient's medical information. In the next section, we will briefly describe how usability and security issues are addressed in the CONNECT project.

Usability

One standard approach for developing highly usable and well-accepted information and communication systems is by using user-centered design method. User-centered design focuses on

involving users in the design of computerized systems from the first phase of system development process and identifying their requirements and expectations (Abras, Maloney-Krichmar, & Preece, 2004). Not just end-users should be involved in the design process. Multidisciplinary experts and various stakeholders in the system (e.g., software developers, usability experts, and healthcare professionals) can also give valuable contributions in identifying end-users requirements and developing highly user-friendly system. Numerous usability evaluation methods can be used to include different types of stakeholders in the application design, implementation, and evaluation phases. The most common organization of the usability evaluation methods is as follows:

- **Usability Inspection:** A process by which usability experts (e.g., specialists, software developers, users and other professionals) test and examine usability-related aspects of a user interface .
- **Usability Testing:** A process by which a list of standard tasks are performed by typical users, and usability experts use a different method to identify how to adapt the application to users' needs and expectations.
- **Usability Inquiry:** A process by which users' feedback regarding system usability is gathered by talking to users or watching how they use the system in real life.

Different methods have different characteristics, and they are used in different phases of the process of application development (Nielsen, 1995; Shneiderman, 1986). The major factors that influence the selection of a usability evaluation method are the usability requirements as defined for a specific system, the phase in the development process, and the types of participants who are available to perform the evaluation. The approach that is generally recommended is to use different evaluation methods during one system design and development process with the goal of identifying and addressing the requirements of different stakeholders and of more efficiently creating a system that is highly effective and user-friendly (Mayhew, 1999; Norman, 2002).

In the literature, numerous studies can be found that employ different usability evaluation methods and combinations thereof during the development of the design and the implementation of mobile healthcare services. For example, Lorenz and Oppermann (2009) presented the development process of a mobile system for monitoring vital parameters (blood pressure, in this case). Because of the complexities of supporting a broad user group, the study adopted a user-centered design approach and organized numerous cycles for specification of the problem space and application functionalities, development of mock-ups, gathering of user feedback, and a refinements phase. As a result, the authors identified a list of design guidelines they considered as vital for the development of successful patient monitoring systems. Additionally, they concluded that developing one single solution would not fit the needs of all users and recommended the development of different interface versions for different user groups.

Another example given by Siek, et al. (2011) describes the development process of a web-based personal health application that runs on a tablet PC and provides older adults and their caregivers the ability to manage health-related information during care transition. The authors organized six usability studies during four design cycles: user needs assessment, low-fidelity prototyping, high-fidelity prototyping, and functional prototyping. Through these cycles, the study identified interdisciplinary research and collaboration among all stakeholders—patients, caregivers, health professionals, designers, and health "informaticians"—as an important prerequisite to developing an effective personal health application. In conclusion, the authors reported their findings and suggested guidelines for developing these types of mobile services, including encouraging researchers to first install mobile applications

with basic functionalities on user terminals and gradually adding features as users become more proficient in interacting with the services.

Perhaps the most important group of potential users of (mobile) healthcare services is the elderly (Or & Karsh, 2009; Heart & Kalderon, 2011; Lorenz & Oppermann, 2009). Developing mobile healthcare services for the elderly can be especially demanding because of the group's limited expertise in using new technologies (Verhaeghen & Salthouse, 1997; Poynton, 2005; Marquie, Jourdan-Boddaert, & Huet, 2002) and poorer cognitive and perception abilities (Charness & Bosman, 1990; Rabbitt, 1993). However, research such as (Conci, Pianesi, & Zancanaro, 2009), (Venkatesh, Morris, Davis, & Davis, 2003), and (Plaza, et al., 2011) shows that the elderly are willing to accept and adopt technology when it meet their needs and expectations. In the literary overview presented by Plaza, et al. (2011), the main reasons that the elderly are ready to accept mobile phones in their everyday lives are described. The identified reasons are an increased feeling of safety and security, aids for memory and activities of daily living, communication functionalities, and a freer and healthier independent life. However, there are still issues related to usage of mobile phones by the elderly, such as the passive usage of mobile phones, the fear of consequences of their use (e.g., disease, addiction, and tendency to have accidents), and design-related issues (e.g., device size, text size, and buttons) (Kurniawan, 2008). The conclusion of the review by Plaza, et al. (2011) is that mobile applications present an important and powerful tool that can improve the quality of life for the elderly, although their requirements and adaptations have not been sufficiently investigated. Some of the shortcomings suggest directions for further research, such as more effective integration of end users in the application development process, the development of products that are especially tailored to the elderly, advanced mobile service support and training, and more research regarding evidence of the impact of mobile healthcare applications (Plaza, et al., 2011; Heart & Kalderon, 2011).

In conclusion, we can say that developing interface for mobile healthcare services and choosing functionalities to be supported still presents a major challenge. Numerous challenges remain that must be addressed before mobile devices can find their place in everyday healthcare delivery. Even though there is a large body of research addressing the identified issues, there are still no generic frameworks or proposed solutions that are applicable to numerous types of applications and types of users. The approach that we recommend and that is shown to be most effective in numerous studies is using a user-centered and participatory design method during the process of mobile application development and implementation. Thus, developers can ensure that they are taking into consideration end-user requirements and that they are adjusting mobile services and devices to users' capabilities and expectations and implementing useful and required functionalities.

Security

One of the most critical issues that must be resolved before mobile devices and services can be used in healthcare on a large scale is security. There is a large body of research that is working on identifying security requirements and developing security mechanisms and frameworks that can be used for protecting patients' private data. However, there is still no standard, widely accepted approach for secure storage and delivery of patients' private data using mobile networks and devices. Various approaches for enabling secure mobile access to peoples' private information can be found in the literature, and in this section we will present a brief overview of those approaches.

A basic approach in a majority of studies today is integrating standard security mechanism(s) (such as Public Key Infrastructure, password authentication, or data encryption) into the mobile application architecture. One example of this ap-

proach is shown by Pitsillides, et al., (2006) and Panteli, Pitsillides, Pitsillides, and Samaras (2010), in which a security framework is described for the provision of end-to-end security of e-health mobile applications that support the networked collaboration of healthcare professionals. Authentication of the user is implemented in two stages. First, the user performs authentication on the device using a strong PIN number. Then the user is authenticated for the application through a digital certificate and a strong password. Digital certificates are installed on all mobile devices and, in addition to authentication, they are used for the encryption of sensitive data during transmission and integrity control on information exchanged over the Internet. Brechlerova and Candik (2008) shows how the more advanced security mechanisms and technologies, such as XML Security and Security Assertion Markup Language (SAML), can be used for enabling secure communication and integrity and confidentiality of exchanged information. For example, Yu, Gummadikayala, and Mudumbi, (2008) describe a specification of security and privacy framework that can provide secure access to ubiquitous healthcare services to the patients in rural or remote areas from distant hospitals. The proposed framework uses SAML security assertions for exchanging the secured user identification information between the server and mobile clients and enables single sign-on functionality to end-user. Adding standard security features and mechanisms as part of a project's implementation provides developers with a high level of flexibility and control because they are not dependent on any third-party solution to implement and control security functionalities. In addition, developers can choose which level of security they will implement with the appropriate security mechanisms (and their combination) currently available. However, when using this approach, developers are required to perform a substantial amount of work during the integration of selected mechanisms and their maintenance. Additionally, all standard security mechanisms have shortcomings and limitations that must be taken into consideration and properly addressed if the desired security level is to be accomplished (e.g., static passwords are highly vulnerable to different types of attacks, and digital certificates can greatly impact system scalability and complexity because they must be installed and maintained on each specific client device).

Another approach to handle security is to take advantage of the existing technologies of mobile network operators that implement various standard security mechanisms. One example of this approach is given by Shanmugam, Thiruvengadam, Khurat, and Maglogiannis (2006), where authentication of a mobile device user is performed using the Generic Bootstrapping Architecture (GBA) mechanism implemented by the mobile network operator. GBA is a framework for mutual authentication of users and network applications, and it consists of a single authentication infrastructure that can be used for all of the potential services on a mobile device ("The 3rd Generation Partnership Project", 2011). The user is authenticated based on long-term credentials present in the Subscriber Identity Module (SIM), which are protected from unauthorized access. Additionally, MacDonald (2008) demonstrated how the GBA mechanism can be improved to provide a higher level of security and privacy for healthcare applications. Standard security solutions provided by mobile network providers can offer benefits such as easy integration of well-established and approved security solutions without the need for additional development and maintenance. However, they also introduce drawbacks such as less control and flexibility because the third party is controlling the security features that protect access to private medical data. An additional problem can be the numerous mobile network providers in each country, entailing cooperation agreements and a need for all of the mobile providers to define and agree on the security policies to enable access to healthcare services for all potential users.

Furthermore, mobile device hardware additions can be developed for upgrading the performance of security mechanisms. One example of this approach is given by Matsuoka, Schaumont, Tiri, and Verbauwhede (2004), which describes a design approach that optimizes Java-based cryptographic applications in resource-limited embedded devices by moving performance-critical components of the security applications to hardware acceleration units. Additional protection of critical components is implemented by applying a special dynamic differential logic style, which makes the secure modules resistant to attack by side channels. As a result, an architecture is developed in which all sensitive operations are restricted to the secure co-processor and overall performance is raised 25x compared to a pure Java implementation. Although higher performance of demanding security operations can be achieved using this approach, developing specific hardware additions is usually a demanding and costly process that requires adaptation of the entire mobile device hardware. Therefore, work on improving the security features of legacy mobile devices and SIM cards hardware are usually done by mobile device manufacturers and operators. Some examples of advanced technologies are Near-Field Communication technology, which can be used to facilitate user authentication, and cryptographic SIM cards, which provide secure storage of a user's certificate and support for performing encryption and signing operations. Security features built into mobile device hardware can help developers to implement and improve advanced security mechanisms and provide better protection of users' private data without requiring additional development efforts. However, they introduce additional dependency of security mechanisms to mobile device hardware, which can result in delivery of healthcare services to only a group of users who poses mobile devices with required hardware functionalities.

Limited computational capacity and power supply of mobile devices have resulted in the recent popularity of research related to external services such as cloud computing and agent technologies for performing security algorithms on mobile applications. For example, Nkosi & Mekuria (2010) described a framework that uses a cloud computing protocol management model that aims to provide heavy multimedia and security algorithms as a service to mobile devices. The described framework uses next-generation networks and IP multimedia subsystems with cloud computing to reduce the organizational and implementation burden of existing mobile health monitoring systems. Another example is given by Sulaiman, Xu, & Sharma (2009), who established a new security mechanism for online communications using mobile agents. A mobile agent, as defined by White (1996), is a program that can migrate or move from one home platform to another, carrying its code and data. Sulaiman, Sharma, Wanli, and Tran (2008) described how a previously established Multilayer Communication approach is extended to introduce mobile agents in e-health services. We believe that using external services such as cloud computing and mobile agents has great potential to enable developers to improve the security capabilities of mobile healthcare applications and overcome existing mobile device limitations. However, work in this area is still in the early stages, and much more research is required before these types of mechanisms will be in use for everyday healthcare services.

To ensure that patients' private data are protected from unauthorized use and different types of security attacks, each country defines its own privacy laws and regulations. For example, the Health Insurance Portability and Accountability Act (HIPAA) in the USA established standards for the electronic storage, retrieval, and transmission of patient healthcare information applicable not only to hardwired computer devices and networks, but also to mobile and wireless devices (Appari, Anthony, and Johnson, 2009). HIPAA privacy and security rules ensure the confidentiality, integrity and availability of all "individually identifiable

health information", and protect data against any reasonably anticipated threads and accidental disclosure of the information (U. S. Department of Health and Human Services, 2003; U.S. Department of Health and Human Services, 2003). For a system to comply with defined security rules different protection mechanisms can be applied; however, implementation rules and strength of required security mechanisms are not defined by HIPAA standards. As a result, security level implemented in a HIS may vary from one system to the other. Other example of setting security and privacy regulations can be seen in Norway where the government established guidelines for implementing electronic services and interactions on the Internet (Fornyings-, administrasjons- og kirkedepartementet, 2008). In that document, four security levels of user authentication are defined, and requirements are established for the implementation of different types of Internet services. The highest security level, which entails the obligatory use of a Public Key Infrastructure for performing authentication, encryption, and signing of sensitive data, is required for healthcare services and other services in the public sector. In this manner security measures that must be present in one system are more specifically defined, even though implementation could still vary among various solutions. For this reason, each solution considered to be at the highest security level must be submitted to the Norwegian Post and Telecommunication Authority, which checks to see whether the requirements are met. From this example we can see how security regulations may vary from one country to other. Due to this reason it is important to ensure that electronic data security laws and standards are carefully studied and addressed when developing mobile healthcare services. Formal methods that can be used for verification of security, privacy, and patient safety policies implemented in HISs can be found in literature. For example, Mathe, et al. (2007) introduce a model-based design technique combined with the development of high-level modeling abstractions that can be used for analysis of the HISs and investigation of unforeseen and unintended privacy and security breaches. Other example is given by Podgurski (2010), where it is used evidence-based validation methods to analyze a combination of usage data, clinical data, and execution data and measure and enhance safety and efficiency of HISs.

One important consideration when selecting security mechanisms for protection of HIS must be usability and user-friendliness of the entire system. Security features of one system are usually seen as contradictory to user-friendliness, and keeping in mind that potential users of healthcare systems are patients and/or healthcare providers, both the usability and the security of the system are highly important requirements. Numerous surveys can be find in literature that demonstrate how different user groups accept various security mechanisms (e.g., (Jones, Anton, & Earp, 2007; Clarke, Furnell, Rodwell, & Reynolds, 2002; Clarke & Furnell, 2005)). However, because of the high diversity of users and their various capabilities and expectations (especially related to healthcare applications), our recommendation is to involve potential end users in the application development process and to identify their needs and acceptance of security mechanisms (especially authentication) for each specific system. Thus, it is possible to determine how seriously users perceive security and privacy issues of healthcare systems and what they are willing to do to preserve the security of their private information. If users' perception of security and protection requirements for their private information differs from security mechanisms required and implemented in the system, the result can significantly influence the system's usefulness and acceptance. If users believe that their private data are not protected well enough, the result can be lower acceptance or rejection of the system. However, if users perceive the implemented security measures to be unnecessary, they will attempt to circumvent them and in the process can introduce new security vulnerabilities to the

system. For this reason, it is critical to know the users and to ensure that they understand and accept the security requirements and mechanisms implemented in the system.

CONNECT PROJECT

In this section, we will present a brief overview of the CONNECT project and describe how we addressed previously identified issues of usability and security in mobile healthcare applications.

The goal of the CONNECT project is to identify key factors that are related to successful adaptation, implementation, and maintenance of Internet-based support systems for communication and information sharing between and among patients and care providers. For this reason, it is developed a patient portal that integrate a suite of context-sensitive, multi-modal, Internet-based tools and provide patients with seamless and secure access to their medical information and connection with care providers. The underlying application in the CONNECT project is called WebChoice. WebChoice is a web application through which patient patients can: 1) monitor their symptoms through the Internet over time, 2) access evidence-based self-management options and advice tailored to their reported symptoms, 3) use communication area where they can ask questions to a clinical nurse specialist and 4) exchange experiences with other patients with the same diagnosis (Ruland, Borosund, & Varsi, 2009; Jeneson, Andersen, & Ruland, 2007; Andersen, Ruland, Slaughter, Andersen, & Jacobsen, 2005). The system is currently more adapted for chronic or serious long-term illnesses, but the general idea can be implemented on a wide range of cases. The randomized clinical trials tested different parts of the system, and the results show less symptom distress, depression, and better self-efficacy for the patients with access to the developed patient support system (Ruland, Borosund, & Varsi, 2009; Ruland, et al., 2007).

Here, we will focus on the work done as part of the CONNECT project, in which functionalities from a developed patient support portal are adapted and implemented for use on mobile terminals. In our work we identified and addressed the main challenges for mobile application development, deployment and integration. In the following we will give an overview of how usability and security issues are addressed, as these are the main topics of this chapter.

Usability

We previously described why it is highly important to identify and develop interface design and application functionalities in accordance with users' needs. Through our work on the CON-NECT project, we addressed research questions regarding the development of user-friendly mobile application, users' expectations and requirements for the patient support system, and users' acceptance of mobile applications for everyday health management (Mirkovic, Bryhni, & Ruland, 2011a). To develop the mobile application, we used an interaction design model described by Preece, Rogers, and Sharp (2002) and user-centered design and usability evaluation methods that consisted of interviews, usability testing, and heuristic evaluation. In the evaluation process, different types of participants (patients, design and software development experts, and medical personnel) were recruited.

Phases of the design, development and evaluation process were:

1. Development and evaluation of the application interface design,
2. Low fidelity usability testing and semi-structured interviews with patients,
3. Development of a user interface,
4. Heuristic evaluation,
5. High fidelity usability testing and semi-structured interviews with patients.

Some screenshots of the final mobile application are shown in the Figure 1.

Through the process of mobile application development, we identified the main usability and functionality requirements that must be taken into consideration when enabling mobile access to patient support systems (e.g., the organization of interface elements; the size of text; and the use of icons, colors, and images). Additionally, we concluded that when developing mobile services as one type of access to a patient support system, it is enough to implement support only for a limited set of functionalities. Thus, the mobile application can be simple and provide only the features that require access at all times. The results also showed that patients accepted the mobile application in addition to the web application. They found the mobile application to be useful, and they did not have any major usability issues with the final mobile application. The patients additionally identified numerous new scenarios in which the mobile application might be more suitable than the web application (e.g., they can use the system while lying or resting, while in transit or waiting for appointment, or while walking and relaxing outside). We concluded that currently available services for providing patient support during long-term and chronic illness (such as phone calls or appointments at hospitals) are not sufficient. The implementation of ubiquitous patient support systems that provide seamless access to healthcare services is needed to meet increasing patient requirements and to provide healthcare management information at the point of need.

During the final phase of usability evaluation, the targeted user group was composed of women between 20 and 50 years of age who were under treatment for breast cancer. An additional value of the study is that potential future users were given the opportunity to test the application and they could see a real need for this type of systems. In further research, we plan to adapt mobile services for a larger user group (especially the elderly and

Figure 1. Screenshots of the final mobile application interface

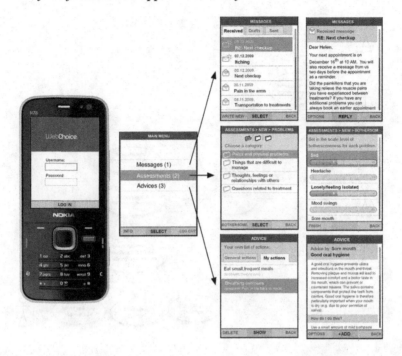

users with special needs caused by their specific requirements) and make the mobile application more useful, user-friendly and adaptable for users with different needs. Additionally, we continue our work on adapting the application to different contexts (e.g., different terminal types and communications networks characteristics).

Security

As part of the research on development, integration, and deployment of mobile services in real life healthcare systems, we worked on identifying and reviewing the security mechanisms necessary to provide secure mobile access to healthcare services. We created and evaluated a security architecture that complies with identified security requirements without affecting usability and accessibility of the system. In (Mirkovic, Bryhni, & Ruland, 2011b), we describe a proposed secure solution (Figure 2). User protection is enabled through strong multi-factor authentication over

two communication channels using Encap's Confirm-by-PIN solution (Hagalisletto & Riiber, 2007; Raddum, Nestås, & Hole, 2010) and utilization of a secure HTTPS connection. The proposed solution provides multiple security features to a legacy system: protection against unauthorized access to the patient's medical information, protection of confidentiality and integrity of the transferred and stored data and the mobile application, protection against session hijacking and brute-force attacks, as well as protection against copying the application data and their unauthorized usage on other devices. The solution is not dependent on the mobile network provider and the type of mobile device the application is running on. Additionally, the user is not required to posses any additional authentication token (entailing technology such as a one-time password generator or a code card).

Authentication process is performed in couple of steps (Figure 2). Four actors participate in the authentication process:

Figure 2. Use case diagram of proposed authentication process

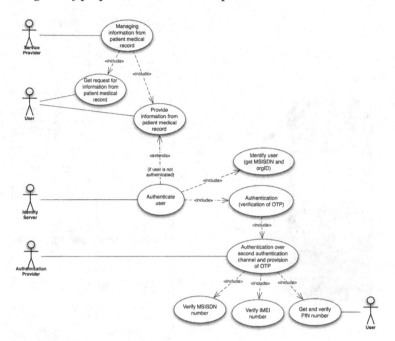

1. **User:** Which is the patient with an installed mobile application on his/hers private mobile phone.
2. **Service Provider:** Which stores and manages patient medical records and provide healthcare information services.
3. **Identity Server:** Which performs authentication of the user for Service Provider.
4. **Authentication Provider:** Which performs additional authentication of the user over a second communication channel and perform delivery of a One Time Password (OTP).

The user sends a request for private data from the medical record to Service Provider over a secure HTTPS channel. If the user is starting a new session, and he is not authenticated before, request is forwarded to Identity Server who is in charge for performing user authentication for Service Provider. The user is identified using MSISDN (the telephone number uniquely identifying a subscription in a GSM or a UMTS mobile network as defined by the E.164 standard (International

Telecommunciation Union, 2010)) and orgID (the code that identifies type of user). Authentication of the user is performed over two communication channels. Using the second authentication channel the user's personal PIN number, the mobile device identifier, and the user's private MSISDN number are verified. If all credentials that are provided are correct, OTP is generated and verified over main HTTPS-based communication channel.

As described previously, Norway has strict security requirements and corresponding legislation for protecting patients' private data. In (Mirkovic, Bryhni, & Ruland, 2011b), we discussed how the proposed architecture meets these requirements, identified additional improvements and adaptations that might be required and proposed how these requirements can be properly addressed. Additionally, we developed a test bed based on a description of the security architecture deployed in University Hospital in Oslo. Thus, we proved the feasibility of the solution and showed how the proposed architecture could be deployed and adapted for a real life hospital information system.

By testing the implemented solution, we identified possible bottlenecks and areas for improvement and also concluded that the load on the mobile phone when authentication is performed is not problematic and scalability of the system is not considerably to be affected.

Finally, we can say that many considerations and requirements must be addressed when developing security architecture for use in healthcare. In our project, we demonstrate how these requirements can be addressed and how security on the highest level can be obtained without affecting usability, mobility, and accessibility of the system. To additionally evaluate acceptance of the proposed security solution as future research, we plan to perform usability evaluations of the proposed security mechanism and to identify potential users' understanding and requirements regarding protection of their private medical information.

CONCLUSION

In this chapter, we discussed the main challenges and obstacles that must be addressed when developing, integrating, and deploying mobile services for HISs. We found that using mobile devices and services in the healthcare sector can provide numerous advanced features to various potential users. However, despite the obvious advantages of these types of services and the fact that the technology for their development is currently available, numerous challenges remain for their integration in complex HISs. The two main challenges we discussed most closely are usability and security. We identified possible approaches and methods to meet these challenges but also concluded that there are still no standard, widely accepted solutions for addressing these issues during the development of mobile healthcare services.

Potential of ubiquitous systems that are accessible over various user terminals and communications networks and that are adaptable to the current context of users' requirements and preferences are today fully recognized by various parties (e.g., academia, industry, and governments). However,

before these types of systems can be implemented on a large scale, security standards and general practices for protecting users' private data must be developed and accepted in everyday practices. Additionally, the standard security solutions must enable access to private information for both patients and healthcare providers in a user-friendly and secure manner. As a part of the CONNECT project, we developed security architecture that resolves currently identified security requirements and does not affect the usability and accessibility of the entire system, and we propose that the security architecture based on proposed solution be accepted as standard solution for enabling secure mobile access to patients' private information. We claim that binding security solution to external provider (such as, mobile network provider, mobile device manufacturer) is not acceptable, since it can result in less control over the system's security and limit the accessibility to the system. Additionally, since a mobile phone is highly personal device today we propose that it can be used as both authentication token and access terminal, and in this manner provide highly usable and user-friendly solution without decreasing security of the whole system.

For developing useful and well-accepted mobile healthcare applications, general rules and guidelines for user interface and application functionalities must be defined. Through our work on the CONNECT project, we demonstrated how usability issues can be addressed through user-centered design methods and by including potential end users in the process of application development, in which users' requirements and needs for these types of systems are identified. However, additional challenges will emerge with development of new technologies and new usage contexts. Therefore, we propose the development of standard general frameworks and design guidelines for the development of mobile healthcare applications for different developer platforms, communication networks, and types of users. These types of standardized frameworks can ease further development of new and advanced user-friendly and useful mobile information services.

REFERENCES

Abras, C., Maloney-Krichmar, D., & Preece, J. (2004). User-centered design. In Bainbridge, W. S. (Ed.), *Berkshire encyclopedia of human-computer interaction*. Great Barrington, MA: Berkshire Publishing Group.

An Electronic Health Record for every South African. (2011). Retrieved December 28, 2011, from http://ehr.co.za/main.php

Andersen, R., Ruland, C., Slaughter, L., Andersen, T., & Jacobsen, W. (2005). Clustering techniques for organizing cancer-related concepts into meaningful groups for patients. *AMIA Annual Symposium Proceedings*, (p. 882).

Appari, A., Anthony, D. L., & Johnson, E. M. (2009). *HIPAA compliance: An examination of institutional and market forces*. Paper presented at the 8th Workshop on Economics of Information Security, London.

ASIP Santé project. (2011). Retrieved January 09, 2012, from http://esante.gouv.fr/en

Brechlerova, D., & Candik, M. (2008). *New trends in security of electronic health documentation*. Paper presented at the ICCST 2008, 42nd Annual IEEE International Carnahan Conference on Security Technology, 2008.

Challenor, R., & Deegan, S. (2009). What service users want: a new clinic results service. Can we satisfy both patients' needs and wants? *International Journal of STD & AIDS, 20*(10), 701–703. doi:10.1258/ijsa.2009.009077

Charness, N., & Bosman, E. A. (1990). Human factors and design for older adults. In Birren, J. E., & Schaie, K. W. (Eds.), *Handbook of the psychology of aging* (3rd ed., pp. 446–463). San Diego, CA: Academic Press.

Clarke, N. L., & Furnell, S. M. (2005). Authentication of users on mobile telephones - A survey of attitudes and practices. *Computers & Security, 24*(7), 519–527. doi:10.1016/j.cose.2005.08.003

Clarke, N. L., Furnell, S. M., Rodwell, P. M., & Reynolds, P. L. (2002). Acceptance of subscriber authentication methods for mobile telephony devices. *Computers & Security, 21*(3), 220–228. doi:10.1016/S0167-4048(02)00304-8

Conci, M., Pianesi, F., & Zancanaro, M. (2009). *Useful, social and enjoyable: Mobile phone adoption by older people*. Paper presented at the 12th IFIP TC 13 International Conference on Human-Computer Interaction: Part I.

Dolan, B. (2010). *Number of smartphone health apps up 78 percent*. Retrieved August 3, 2011, from http://mobihealthnews.com/9396/number-of-smartphone-health-apps-up-78-percent/

Fornyings-, administrasjons- og kirkedepartementet. (2008). *Rammeverk for autentisering og uavviselighet i elektronisk kommunikasjon med og i offentlig sektor*. Retrieved July 25, 2011, from http://www.regjeringen.no/nb/dep/fad/dok/lover-og-regler/retningslinjer/2008/rammeverk-for-autentisering-og-uavviseli.html?id=505958

Gollol Raju, N. S., Anthony, J. P., Jamadagni, R. S., Istepanian, R., Suri, J., & Laxminarayan, S. (2004). *Status of mobile computing in health care: An evidence study*. Paper presented at the 26th Annual International Conference of the IEEE Engineering in Medicine and Biology Society (IEMBS '04).

Hagalisletto, A., & Riiber, A. (2007) *Using the mobile phone in two-factor authentication. UbiComp 2007 Workshop Proceedings*.

Heart, T., & Kalderon, E. (2011). Older adults: Are they ready to adopt health-related ICT? *International Journal of Medical Informatics, 8*, 8.

Helse- og omsorgsdepartementet. (2008). *Samspill 2.0 Nasjonal strategi for elektronisk samhandling i helse- og omsorgssektoren 2008 – 2013.* Retrieved August 3, 2011, from http://www.helsedirektoratet.no/samspill/publikasjoner/samspill_2_0__nasjonal_strategi_for_elektronisk_samhandling_i_helse__og_omsorgssektoren_2008___2013_744694

International Telecommunication Union. (2010). *The international public telecommunication numbering plan.* Retrieved July 19, 2011, from http://www.itu.int/rec/T-REC-E.164/en

Jeneson, A., Andersen, T., & Ruland, C. M. (2007). *Comparing messages in an online communication forum for cancer patients with patients' messages to a clinical nurse specialist.* Paper presented at the Medinfo 2007 Congress, Brisbane.

Jones, L. A., Anton, A. I., & Earp, J. B. (2007). *Towards understanding user perceptions of authentication technologies.* Paper presented at the 2007 ACM Workshop on Privacy in Electronic Society.

Kailas, A., Chia-Chin, C., & Watanabe, F. (2010). From mobile phones to personal wellness dashboards. *Pulse, IEEE, 1*(1), 57–63. doi:10.1109/MPUL.2010.937244

Kannoju, P. K., Sridhar, K. V., & Prasad, K. S. R. (2010). *A new paradigm of electronic health record for efficient implementation of healthcare delivery.* Paper presented at the 2010 IEEE EMBS Conference on Biomedical Engineering and Sciences (IECBES).

Kleiboer, A., Gowing, K., Holm Hansen, C., Hibberd, C., Hodges, L., & Walker, J. (2010). Monitoring symptoms at home: What methods would cancer patients be comfortable using? *Quality of Life Research, 19*(7), 965–968. doi:10.1007/s11136-010-9662-0

Kurniawan, S. (2008). Older people and mobile phones: A multi-method investigation. *International Journal of Human-Computer Studies, 66*(12), 889–901. doi:10.1016/j.ijhcs.2008.03.002

Lin, S. P., & Yang, H. Y. (2009). Exploring key factors in the choice of e-health using an asthma care mobile service model. *Telemedicine Journal of Electronic Health, 15*(9), 884–890. doi:10.1089/tmj.2009.0047

Lorenz, A., & Oppermann, R. (2009). Mobile health monitoring for the elderly: Designing for diversity. *Pervasive and Mobile Computing, 5*(5), 478–495. doi:10.1016/j.pmcj.2008.09.010

Luo, N., Koh, W. P., Ng, W. Y., Yau, J. W., Lim, L. K., & Sim, S. S. (2009). Acceptance of information and communication technologies for healthcare delivery: A SingHealth Polyclinics study. *Annals of the Academy of Medicine, Singapore, 38*(6), 529–528.

MacDonald, J. A. (2008). *Cellular authentication - Key agreement for service providers.* Paper presented at the Second International Conference on Pervasive Computing Technologies for Healthcare, 2008 (PervasiveHealth 2008).

Marquie, J. C., Jourdan-Boddaert, L., & Huet, N. (2002). Do older adults underestimate their actual computer knowledge? *Behaviour & Information Technology, 21*(4), 273–280. doi:10.1080/0144929021000020998

Mathe, J. L., Duncavage, S., Werner, J., Malin, B. A., Ledeczi, A., & Sztipanovits, J. (2007). Towards the security and privacy analysis of patient portals. *SIGBED Review, 4*(2), 5–9. doi:10.1145/1295464.1295467

Matsuoka, Y., Schaumont, P., Tiri, K., & Verbauwhede, I. (2004). *Java cryptography on KVM and its performance and security optimization using HW/SW co-design techniques.* Paper presented at the 2004 International Conference on Compilers, Architecture, and Synthesis for Embedded Systems.

Mayhew, D. J. (1999). *The usability engineering lifecycle.* Paper presented at the CHI '99 Extended Abstracts on Human Factors in Computing Systems.

Microsoft Case Studies. (2011a). *Egyptian Ambulance Organization: Ambulance agency improves emergency service delivery with electronic fleet management.* Retrieved August 03, 2011, from http://www.microsoft.com/casestudies/Case_Study_Detail.aspx?CaseStudyID=4000010726

Microsoft Case Studies. (2011b). *First choice home health and hospice of Utah, home health provider saves $500,000 annually, doubles cash flow, with mobile solution.* Retrieved July 19, 2011, from http://www.microsoft.com/casestudies/Case_Study_Detail.aspx?CaseStudyID=4000010753

Mirkovic, J., Bryhni, H., & Ruland, C. (2009). *Review of projects using mobile devices and mobile applications in healthcare.* Paper presented at the Scandinavian conference on Health Informatics, Arendal, Norway.

Mirkovic, J., Bryhni, H., & Ruland, C. (2011a). *Designing user friendly mobile application to assist cancer patients in illness management.* Paper presented at the eTELEMED 2011, The Third International Conference on eHealth, Telemedicine, and Social Medicine, Gosier, Guadeloupe, France.

Mirkovic, J., Bryhni, H., & Ruland, C. M. (2011b). *Secure solution for mobile access to patient's health care record.* Paper presented at the 2011 IEEE 13th International Conference on e-Health Networking, Applications and Services, Columbia, Missouri, USA.

Nielsen, J. (1995). *Usability engineering.* San Francisco, CA: Morgan Kaufmann Publishers Inc.

Nkosi, M. T., & Mekuria, F. (2010). *Cloud computing for enhanced mobile health applications.* Paper presented at the IEEE Second International Conference on Cloud Computing Technology and Science (CloudCom 2010).

Norman, D. (2002). *The design of everyday things.* Basic Books.

Or, C. K., & Karsh, B. T. (2009). A systematic review of patient acceptance of consumer health information technology. *Journal of the American Medical Informatics Association, 16*(4), 550–560. doi:10.1197/jamia.M2888

Panteli, N., Pitsillides, B., Pitsillides, A., & Samaras, G. (2010). An e-healthcare mobile application: A stakeholders' analysis experience of reading. In Khoumbati, K., Dwivedi, Y. K., Srivastava, A., & Lal, B. (Eds.), *Handbook of research on advances in health informatics and electronic healthcare applications: Global adoption and impact of information communication technologies* (pp. 433–445).

Pinnock, H., Slack, R., Pagliari, C., Price, D., & Sheikh, A. (2006). Professional and patient attitudes to using mobile phone technology to monitor asthma: questionnaire survey. *Primary Care Respiratory Journal, 15*(4), 237–245. doi:10.1016/j.pcrj.2006.03.001

Pitsillides, A., Samaras, G., Pitsillides, B., Georgiades, D., Andreou, P., & Christodoulou, E. (2006). Ditis: Virtual collaborative teams for home healthcare. *Journal of Mobile Multimedia*, 23-26.

Plaza, I., Martin, L., Martin, S., & Medrano, C. (2011). Mobile applications in an aging society: Status and trends. *Journal of Systems and Software, 84*(11), 1977–1988. doi:10.1016/j.jss.2011.05.035

Podgurski, A. (2010). *Evidence-based validation and improvement of electronic health record systems.* Paper presented at the FSE/SDP Workshop on Future of Software Engineering Research.

Poynton, T. A. (2005). Computer literacy across the lifespan: A review with implications for educators. *Computers in Human Behavior, 21*(6), 861–872. doi:10.1016/j.chb.2004.03.004

Preece, J., Rogers, Y., & Sharp, H. (2002). *Interaction design* (1st ed.). New York, NY: John Wiley & Sons, Inc.

Rabbitt, P. (1993). Does it all go together when it goes? The Nineteenth Bartlett Memorial Lecture. *The Quarterly Journal of Experimental Psychology. A, Human Experimental Psychology, 46*(3), 385–434. doi:10.1080/14640749308401055

Raddum, H., Nestås, L. H., & Hole, K. J. (2010). *Security analysis of mobile phones used as OTP generators.* Paper presented at the Workshop in Information Security Theory and Practice.

Ruland, C. M., Borosund, E., & Varsi, C. (2009). User requirements for a practice-integrated nurse-administered online communication service for cancer patients. *Studies in Health Technology and Informatics, 146*, 221–225.

Ruland, C. M., Jeneson, A., Andersen, T., Andersen, R., Slaughter, L., & Bente Schjodt, O. (2007). Designing tailored Internet support to assist cancer patients in illness management. *AMIA... Annual Symposium Proceedings / AMIA Symposium. AMIA Symposium, 11*, 635–639.

Shanmugam, M., Thiruvengadam, S., Khurat, A., & Maglogiannis, I. (2006). *Enabling secure mobile access for electronic health care applications.* Paper presented at the Pervasive Health Conference and Workshops, 2006.

Shieh, Y. Y., & Tsai, F. Y. Arash, Wang, M. D., & Lin, C. M. C. (2007). *Mobile healthcare: Opportunities and challenges.* Paper presented at the International Conference on the Management of Mobile Business, Toronto, Canada.

Shneiderman, B. (1986). *Designing the user interface: Strategies for effective human-computer interaction.* Boston, MA: Addison-Wesley Longman Publishing Co., Inc. doi:10.1145/25065.950626

Siek, K. A., Khan, D. U., Ross, S. E., Haverhals, L. M., Meyers, J., & Cali, S. R. (2011). Designing a personal health application for older adults to manage medications: A comprehensive case study. *Journal of Medical Systems, 12*, 12.

Spil, T. A. M., & Katsma, C. P. (2007). *Balancing supply and demand of an electronic health record in the Netherlands; Not too open systems for not too open users.* Paper presented at the 40th Annual Hawaii International Conference on System Sciences, 2007 (HICSS 2007).

Standing, S., & Standing, C. (2008). Mobile technology and healthcare: The adoption issues and systemic problems. *International Journal of Electronic Healthcare, 4*(3-4), 221–235. doi:10.1504/IJEH.2008.022661

Sulaiman, R., Sharma, D., Wanli, M., & Tran, D. (2008). *A security architecture for e-health services.* Paper presented at the 10th International Conference on Advanced Communication Technology (ICACT 2008).

Sulaiman, R., Xu, H., & Sharma, D. (2009). *E-health services with secure mobile agent.* Paper presented at the Seventh Annual Communication Networks and Services Research Conference (CNSR '09).

The 3rd Generation Partnership Project. (2011). *The mobile broadband standards.* Retrieved September 23, 2011, from http://www.3gpp.org/

Thorp, J. (2010). Europe's E-health initiatives. *Journal of American Health Information Management Association, 81*(9), 56–58.

U. S. Department of Health and Human Services. (2003). *Summary of the HIPAA privacy rule.* Retrieved January 06, 2012, from http://www.hhs.gov/ocr/privacy/hipaa/understanding/summary/index.html

U. S. Department of Health and Human Services. (2003). *Summary of the HIPAA security rule*. Retrieved January 06, 2012, from http://www. hhs.gov/ocr/privacy/hipaa/understanding/srsummary.html

University of Cambridge, & China Mobile. (2011). *Mobile communication for medical care - Final report. Case study A: mHealth in Guangdong Province*. Retrieved August 3, 2011, from http://www.csap.cam.ac.uk/media/uploads/files/1/mobile-communications-for-medical-care.pdf

Venkatesh, V., Morris, M., Davis, G., & Davis, F. (2003). User acceptance of information technology: Toward a unified view. *Management Information Systems Quarterly, 27*(3), 425–478.

Verhaeghen, P., & Salthouse, T. A. (1997). Meta-analyses of age-cognition relations in adulthood: Estimates of linear and nonlinear age effects and structural models. *Psychological Bulletin, 122*(3), 231–249. doi:10.1037/0033-2909.122.3.231

Wein, B. B. (2003). IHE (Integrating the Healthcare Enterprise): A new approach for the improvement of digital communication in healthcare. *Rofo, 175*(2), 183–186. doi:10.1055/s-2003-37238

White, J. (1996). *Mobile agent white papers*. Retrieved March 25, 2011, from http://www.klynch.com/documents/agents/

Wu, J. H., Wang, S. C., & Lin, L. M. (2007). Mobile computing acceptance factors in the healthcare industry: A structural equation model. *International Journal of Medical Informatics, 76*(1), 66–77. doi:10.1016/j.ijmedinf.2006.06.006

Yu, W. D., Gummadikayala, R., & Mudumbi, S. (2008). *A web-based wireless mobile system design of security and privacy framework for u-Healthcare*. Paper presented at the 10th International Conference on e-health Networking, Applications and Services (HealthCom 2008).

KEY TERMS AND DEFINITIONS

eHealth: Represents utilization of communication and information technologies and sources (such as Internet, computers, and mobile phones) in the healthcare sector with the goal to improve access, efficiency, effectiveness, and quality of healthcare systems.

Heuristic Evaluation: A usability inspection method used to identify usability problems in the computer program user-interface design. Heuristic evaluation is usually performed by design experts who review the system design according to previously defined guidelines. Through the process the goal is to identify interface elements that are not compliant with defined rules so they can be fixed and adapted in further application development process.

Information Security: Represents protection of data in one information system from unauthorized access and modification ensuring in this manner system confidentiality, integrity, and availability.

mHealth: Represents utilization of mobile telecommunication and multimedia technologies and devices in medical care.

Mobile Device: A term used to refer to a great number of different devices present today that allow people to access information and services independent of their current place and time. This includes cell phones, smartphones, tablet PCs, and portable devices.

Patient Support System: An information system that help patients to better understand and manage their illness, become more engaged in their own health care and the decisions they face, and improve communication with their care providers.

Seamless Access: Means allowing the users access to the system anywhere, at any time, and over all access networks and devices without interruptions.

Ubiquitous System: An information system that is present everywhere in the people environment and people use it all the time. This type of system is usually thoroughly integrated into everyday objects and activities that people use them without thinking about the access tool. In this manner technology is made effectively invisible to the users, and users are more focused on tasks on hand.

Usability: Matching products and systems design and functionalities to user needs and re-

quirements and making systems easier and more convenient to use in people everyday lives.

XML Security: A standard that defines XML vocabularies and processing rules in order to ensure authenticity, integrity, and confidentiality of parts of XML documents. It utilizes standard security and cryptography technologies together with emerging XML technologies to provide secured access to private information.

Chapter 13
Micro Information Systems:
New Fractals in an Evolving IS Landscape

Rasmus Ulslev Pedersen
Copenhagen Business School, Denmark

Mogens Kühn Pedersen
Copenhagen Business School, Denmark

ABSTRACT

We are increasingly surrounded by and using small systems, which are equipped with sensors. Mobile phones, temperature sensors, GPS tracking, emerging nano/micro-size sensors, and similar technologies are used by individuals, groups, and organizations. There are valuable applications for industries such as medical and manufacturing. These new sensor applications have implications for information systems (IS) and, the authors visualize this new class of information systems as fractals growing from an established class of systems; namely that of information systems (IS). The identified applications and implications are used as an empirical basis for creating a model for these small new information systems. Such sensor systems are called embedded systems in the technical sciences, and the authors want to couple it with general IS. They call the merger of these two important research areas (IS and embedded systems) for micro information systems (micro-IS). It is intended as a new research field within IS research. An initial framework model is established, which seeks to capture both the possibilities and constraints of this new paradigm, while looking simultaneously at the fundamental IS and ICT aspects. The chapter demonstrates the proposed micro-IS framework with a working (open source) application of open demand response systems that address the engineering aspects of this work.

INTRODUCTION

The title of the chapter includes the word fractals; that is because we see the use of sensors systems as new fractals growing off a main IS "body" as illustrated in Figure 1. By observation and with extensive experience from working with sensor systems, it has become apparent to us, that there exist kinds of system that will provide significant value to IS. These sensor systems will change how business as a whole is conducted into a better informed organization, while it may also have

DOI: 10.4018/978-1-4666-2190-9.ch013

Figure 1. Mandelbrot fractals (Wikipedia:Mandelbrot:Set)

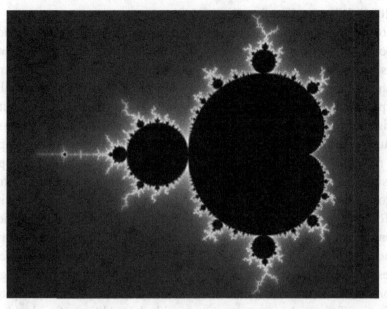

significant impact at the group and the individual levels. If IS recognizes the value of sensor data present in many natural science/social science/computer science etc. scenarios, then we believe that new levels of insight might emerge over time.

We suggest micro-IS as a prolific new research area for IS research. First, we consider embedded systems are different in many aspects from PC and server-based systems. An embedded system is customized toward a specific task, and furthermore it is subject to a different set of demands and interfaces than its PC and server-based counterparts. Embedded systems are almost always equipped with various sensors that process a sensation for a target IS. It also enables new and rejuvenated IS processes; seamless collaboration over great distances in virtual meeting rooms is

one example that would use micro-IS to create a shared (virtual) context.

A second path to introduce micro-IS can be to consider the introductory words of Richard T. Watson in his brief historic overview of information technology (Watson, 2001). Our Table 1 extends Watson's Table 1 (in which he links fundamental communication technologies to the human senses) by adding an *embedded systems* row to it.

It is another way to show that embedded systems add the hearing, sight, touch, smell, and taste senses to IS systems. We note that smell and taste are more complicated inputs than sound and light, and would involve more techniques such as sensor fusion.

The set of micro-IS applications later in the chapter each interfacses one or more of these senses. The integration of embedded systems with

Table 1. Extending Watson's (Watson, 2001) communication technology table with embedded systems

Communication technology	Human Senses				
	Hear	**See**	**Touch**	**Smell**	**Taste**
Embedded systems with sensors	Microphone:✓	Light and color sensors:✓	Touch sensors:✓	Open research	Open research

physical processes is put forward by Edward E. Lee (E. E. Lee, 2006). What he describes from a technical point of view is also fundamental to our micro-IS proposal. Yet, we need add one more aspect to Watson's senses which is "speech" that has received much attention throughout the 20th Century due to explosive developments in radio- and cables transmission expanding human speech by a kind of "virtual proximity." Though speech is not considered a "sense" it is by far the most important synthesis of senses by which human beings are able to represent and communicate with each other. Tools that overcome the natural distance limitations to talk between human beings have been the most important extension of human capabilities the last 100 years as seen in telecommunication networks, and in mobile and wireless communication. To a very large extent we see sense-sensitive embedded systems in mobile and wireless devices that merge telecommunications and IS.

Now that we have indicated the versatility of embedded systems in Table 1 it is possible to present our argumentation for their practical impact upon information system. Our thesis is that micro-IS has an important role to play in IS: in order to support this claim, we conduct an inductive argumentation starting with some example applications where sensors obviously play important roles. Then we follow up with a second premise in the form of probable implications to several fields within or close to the IS core (Sidorova, Evangelopoulos, Valacich, & Ramakrishnan, 2008). A section on sensors and an expansion of the fractal idea is presented, which leads up to an initial model of micro-IS that captures and generalizes both the applications and the implications for IS. In this model we shall relate the tight duality between IS processes and ICT technologies from a micro-IS perspective using our set of applications and implications.

SENSOR CONNECTED IS SYSTEMS

The embedded systems provide to IS systems what ears, eyes, fingers, nose, and tongue provide to humans. With these information channels we are able to do an amazing number of things. The same is true for IS systems; with the sensing capabilities of embedded systems, the capabilities are expanded. Sensors will capture real properties like temperature, motion, pictures, etc. This information can be distilled from raw data, to information, then to content, into a knowledge database. Micro-IS will provide new layers of connectivity to existing IT infrastructures: we again relate this to how fractals evolve in Figure 2.

Today's computers are logically connected mainly by means of internet protocols. However, with the addition of embedded systems to the existing and future IT systems, the scene will be different. Figure 2 shows how an existing system with only a few PC nodes expanded into a larger network with more micro-IS nodes. The additional nodes are connected via new layers: the first layer symbolizes the wired/wireless connection to a micro-IS system, while the second layer represents some physical connection to sensors and actuators. All layers are connected logically by different communication protocols.

In the concept of the networked firm the digital exchanges have been drivers whereas in ubiquitous computing, context was all inclusive. In a micro-IS enabled IS understanding the acquisition of pre-structured data in contrast to human un-structured inputs holds potential for a "creative destruction" of the field of IS. In actor-network theory actors may be "machines" or pre-programmed sensors. In IS we now have the micro-IS performing meaningful tasks within a wider setting as in peer-to-peer interchange of innocuous knowledge in a differentiated network (M. K. Pedersen & Larsen, 2005). We only need to add that agency

Figure 2. The existing networked IT infrastructure will get new layers of fractal-like connectivity with embedded sensor systems

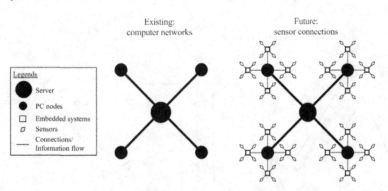

of peers may also be performed by micro-IS like sensors. An example of this is found in the case of distributed knowledge management systems where micro-IS would provide data production on a regular basis on logistics and product-state in a digital construction and maintenance model for the construction industry (M. K. Pedersen, 2007).

Some decades ago it was not common for companies to have mainframe computer power at their disposal: today, it is the case. Similarly, the field of embedded computing and the notion of sensors have not yet emerged in many business systems contexts, even though micro-electronics is already a large industry. But several factors have changed over the last decade (just as in the case of computational resources); first, embedded sensor technology is becoming more approachable and secondly, the widespread use of embedded systems is evident to most people, as in the use of GPS, temperature sensors, etc. Therefore we are moving toward the future connections in Figure 2. Potential application for these sensor data systems can be found in a very active research field called wireless sensor networks (WSN) (Culler & Hong, 2004). A WSN can capture any kind of data, but also has the capability to store, process, and wirelessly deliver information to ERP/CRM and other systems.

TOWARD A PRELIMINARY MICRO-IS MODEL

We propose a model (see Figure 3) to reach a deeper understanding of embedded sensor systems in an IS context. In the implications section (below), it is stated that some of the problems faced by micro-IS systems are to relay correct information to the ERP system in an efficient manner. It is an example of why we need to include several constraints in the model to contain the challenges. These constraints are problems that must be overcome in order to deploy a successful micro-IS system to support a specific IS process, such as the need for a greener computing.

On the other hand, there are also great potential in micro-IS applications, as we see in the energy management example (below), so there are output arrows in Figure 3 indicating the opportunities for positive social and business impact.

There are two aspects to micro-IS, which are important to see: one is the support for IS processes, and the second one is the ICT technology. There is a close interrelationship between these two parts, as is the case (below) with the temperature logger application that supports better medicine development, using cutting-edge ICT technologies.

Figure 3. Micro information systems model overview

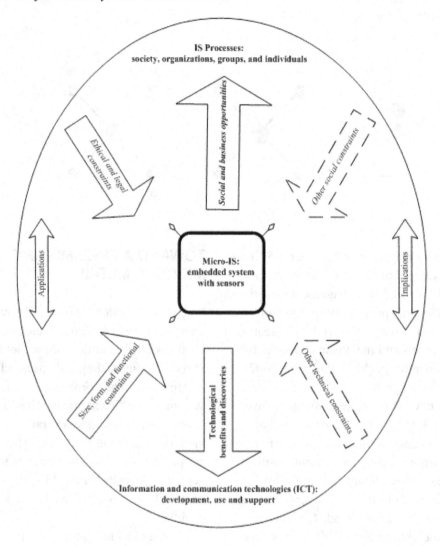

Micro-IS systems are composed of a number of components as illustrated in Figure 2 and Figure 3. The micro-IS component is central to the model because it is the combination with IS that produces our new research artifact. There is frequently an intelligent systems component that enables these systems to work autonomously. A number of constraints dominate the technological design of embedded systems and thus also micro-IS systems. It is mainly the size, form, and functional constraints that are emphasized here. The art of designing micro-IS systems will be the correct tradeoff between these constraints as demonstrated

with cases in Table 2. From a social science perspective the ethical and legal constraints can be identified as important when applied in business models. The task of designing a micro-IS system is inherently dual: We should strive to find innovative ways to support new IS processes, while working within the ICT related technological and ethical boundaries that are challenged when we add micro-IS in information processes. Micro-IS systems represent a significant tool that responds to all the principles of computation addressed by Peter Denning (Denning, 2007).

MICRO-IS APPLICATIONS

To justify our claim that many existing IS systems contain micro-IS systems with sensors, we provide some examples hereof. The list is not intended to be exhaustive in any respect, because we believe that this is only the beginning of a new development. However, we have selected examples that represent a spectrum of the rich opportunities for development of applications. Below, we now present a range of possible micro-IS applications that we summarize in Table 2.

Clinical Test Trial Support

Temperature control in pharmaceutical companies is assisted by embedded systems with sensing capabilities (Figure 4). The addressed problem is when these companies distribute medical products on a clinical trial protocol subject to temperature swings during transport to globally distributed test sites.

One example of a relevant embedded system is an ELPRO product in Figure 4, which is a small device equipped with a temperature sensor and the capability to store these temperature loggings. A LIBERO can be put in each box together with the medicine, and upon arrival to the test trial location it is collected for subsequent data analysis with respect to the temperature curves while in transport. This system is also used for monitoring food storage temperatures.

Human Genome Profiling

IBM's "DNA Transistor" (IBM_Press_Room, 2009) is a research project involving nano-technology and micro-electronics that seek to develop a device which can be used for personal DNA genome analysis. The idea, as depicted in the Figure 5 multimedia clip, is that human DNA can pass through very small sensor holes.

The goal of the project is to make it more affordable for individuals to perform a DNA analysis. From a micro-IS perspective it serves as a glimpse of the opportunities provided by nano-technology and bio-technology that are on the rise.

RFID for Library Systems and Logistics

One of the important technologies of the last decade is possibly RFID (Figure 6), and a company such as Philips has used this technology to optimize the supply chain with their certified products.

Other RFID applications include library support for managing book check-out and check-in processes. The RFID system chips are placed in the books, which then are managed by a self-service system.

Intelligent Energy Management

Sentilla and Arch Rock are located in the Silicon Valley area, and these companies produce corporate energy management systems. Such systems allow companies to match energy usage and consumption. The Sentilla Energy Manager for Data Centers™ and the Arch Rock Energy Optimizer™ monitor individual machines in the data centers and thus provides a real-time view of energy consumption (Figure 7). The Arch Rock Energy Optimizer product has been discontinued by Cisco after its acquisition of Arch Rock (Figure 8). Energy monitoring can also be done for governmental buildings and commercial buildings.

This is an example of an embedded system that uses sensors to provide value to both the company directly using it while at the same time addressing a global quest for green computing and governmental claims on management to document compliance to environmental regulations. We demonstrate a design science framework within this green computing context later in the chapter.

Table 2. Micro-IS model mapping of selected IS and ICT aspects in relation to applications and implications grouped by unit of analysis and subject (Dwivedi & Kuljis, 2008)

Unit of Analysis & Applications / Topics & Implications	Society	Organization		Individual		
	Intelligent energy management	A mobile temperature sensor system	RFID for library support	Mobile phone w/sensors	Intelligent (educational) toys	A human DNA transistor
IS management:						
New business models	Addressing profitability while at the same time contributing to a global need.	Conversion of a manual IS process to a micro-IS supported ICT platform.	Saving on manual processes by allowing self-service.	New programs use built-in sensors for geo-aware services.	Interaction with 3rd party sensors for expanded and shared business models.	Affordable personal DNA profile instead of costly centralized analysis.
Outsourcing	Wireless sensor network applications are not mature enough for outsourcing.	Possible challenges in outsourcing embedded systems development.	RFID is a standard component as is the library support: ready for outsourcing.	Sensors are probably developed in Asia, but software is likely to be programmed by Apple.	The software part is likely to be internalized, but electronic components are off-the-shelf.	Internal research, which is not ready for outsourcing.
Ethics and CSR	A case of CSR where people, planet, and profit are all addressed.	The temperature logger ensures better clinical trials and thus safer products.	Possible hacking of systems with implications of privacy.	Careful selection is necessary to avoid intrusive use of sensor-enabled phone.	Can be used to prototype examples of systems which have ethical dilemmas.	Case of something with both a side and possibly unintended uses.
IS Design, development, and use:						
Security	Precautions must be taken if the system manages energy rather than just monitoring it.	Access to logged data must be secured.	Ensure that RFID signals are not captured by malicious systems.	Ensuring that phone sensors do not unintentionally log GPS or movements.	Some sensors can jam or capture information.	Device with the (future) DNA transistor must protect information.
ISD	Example of data from a sensor-driven problem area in a traditional user domain.	Very difficult to fix bugs in shipped micro-IS systems, so extra QA measures are needed.	Can be addressed with standard ISD methods and techniques.	Traditional ISD development methods supports a number of IS process scenarios.	Innovative tools have been developed to let a wider group gain ISD understanding.	Engineering research efforts and also many future IS applications.
Design science and SSM	Energy management can be designed into other corporate processes for regulatory compliance.	Possible to investigate how other sensors can assist the clinical trials.	Determine other ways to incorporate RFID support.	Determine new applications combinations of on-phone sensors.	How to design new playware that accomplishes stated features of the toy.	Investigate what artifacts would this transistor work with.

continued on next page

Table 2. Continued

Unit of Analysis & Applications — Topics & Implications	Society	Organization		Individual		
	Intelligent energy management	A mobile temperature sensor system	RFID for library support	Mobile phone w/sensors	Intelligent (educational) toys	A human DNA transistor
HCI	Future energy systems can predict (from behavioral patterns) when to switch energy on/off.	Good example of small system with small display and PC analysis software.	Valuable system with combined use of an embedded system and a PC.	Perfect use of sensors to make an existing artifact (phone) more useful and interactive (speech recognition).	Designing toward specific age groups, such as young, adult IS students.	An interesting illustration of *human* computer interaction.
IS planning:						
Information management	New type of streaming information over time.	Necessary with redundant measures to ensure loggings.	Straightforward integration into existing library systems.	Apple had to make choices as to how sensors are available to programmers.	Fine way of seeing the difficulty in storing information for later retrieval.	Difficult to capture, store, and prepare information for IS use.
ERP and resource management	A set of applications ready for integration in SAP environmental compliance ERP modules.	Evolvement of temperature critical processes toward ERP integration.	Established and already in use for good tracking, etc.	This device can also function as a PDA for entering and tracking many types of equipment.	ERP systems can interface to LEGO factories, and valuable hands-on experience be acquired.	Applicable also in animal meat production facilities with detailed tracking of herd profiles.
IS research and education:						
IS education	Motivational application that demonstrate the good things of micro-IS.	Students and professionals can see how micro-IS can help in industry sectors.	Example of how a costly process has been automated.	Relevant discussion emphasizing sensor possibilities.	Hands-on experience with intelligent toys can sharpen innovation skills.	Good case to discuss and prepare for new kinds of micro systems.

Figure 4. ELPRO temperature datalogger (ELPRO)

Figure 5. IBM DNA transistor information video (IBMSocialMedia)

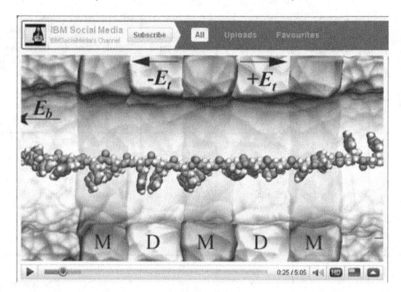

Mobile Phone with Sensors

Mobile phones, such as the iPhone, have started to be equipped with sensing technology. This popular mobile phone is equipped with sensors that enhance the user experience (Figure 9). One sensor turns off the screen when the IPhone is close to the head such that the touch (sensor) screen is not accidentally activated by touching of the ear.

The phone automatically knows when it should be in landscape or portrait mode; it is handled by a three-axis gyro sensor as illustrated in Figure 9. A light sensor automatically controls the bright-ness of the screen, to make is lighter when it is dark. The built-in compass sensor assists with navigation. So even the mobile phones are turning into sensor equipped systems.

Intelligent Toys

LEGO™ is a large Danish toys manufacturer. They have produced a robotics invention kit called LEGO™ MINDSTORMS™. The first version peaked from 1999 to 2006 with over 1,000,000 kits sold and the sales of the new version — called NXT — is likely to sell even more in a shorter time frame (Figure 10).

Figure 6. Package logistics control with RFID chips (Philips)

It is a perfect example of a micro-IS experimental platform as it can easily be constructed and integrated into almost any perceivable service, business process, or technological artifact.

Most embedded systems platforms consist of similar parts to those shown in Figure 10: (1) small computer, (2) touch sensor, (3) microphone sensor, (4) light sensor, (5) distance sensor, and (6) motors. There exist many more sensors (R. Pedersen, 2008) for this experimental platform, and many of the before mentioned industrial applications could easily be prototyped with this system.

Several of these applications spark implications in areas such as ethics, security, HCI, object oriented analysis and design, and even corporate social responsibility. Now we shall turn to some application-triggered implications.

MICRO-IS IMPLICATIONS TO IS

Micro-IS presents many new implications for business models, outsourcing, information management, HCI, ethics, and corporate social responsibility (CSR) amongst others. It is possible to include some of these important areas in this section, but micro-IS will influence many other areas of IS than what we can address here. Table 2 summarizes the following sections.

New Business Models

Companies become increasingly information connected to their environments. This means that the organization will possibly be more agile and able to react quickly to changes in its business surroundings consisting of flows of people, products and services and their logistic interrelationships. There are still digital gaps to be bridged and micro-IS can help closing it. This is also true for a related paradigm of ubiquitous systems (Fleisch & Tellkamp, 2006). One example could be that it is not quite the same having a phone conversation with a person from a different department as talking face-to-face with that same person. However some future micro-IS systems could provide enough (virtual) physical context (presence) in order for the two rooms to appear as one setting. It is examples like this and many other new cases that will lead to new revenue streams providing higher efficiency and new income sources for businesses along with identification of further value-creation opportunities in actions and impacts in their business environments.

ERP and Resource Management

Electronic commerce and electronic data interchange (EDI) are interesting in terms of micro-IS. Previously, data was created on demand from

Figure 7. Sentilla monitors in perk kit

Figure 8. Arch Rock energy manager monitor screen (Arch-Rock)

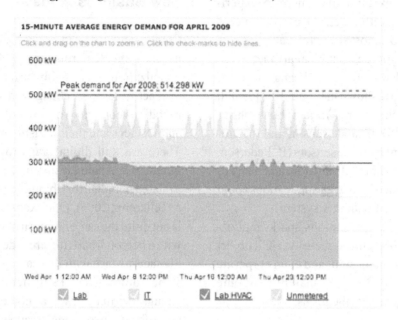

people and systems. In the new era we see data being created from unobtrusive sensors of the environment in a much broader meaning than the one defined by previous data sets. We can label our era as "from unobtrusive bits and bytes to bottom line." The sensor systems capture unobtrusive bits and bytes that are turned into valuable information that directly affects the bottom line in a positive

way. As micro-IS becomes available in various forms, it also opens doors for new ways of using EDI, XML, and for populating semantic webs with sensors as systems extensions and so on. We can imagine a shipping container equipped with a micro-IS that is programmed to capture and log position, and movements. Such a container could automatically deliver a summary of its information

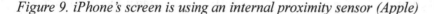

Figure 9. iPhone's screen is using an internal proximity sensor (Apple)

Figure 10. LEGO™ MINDSTORMS™ NXT robotics kit (LEGO)

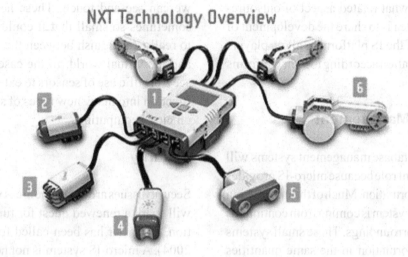

to a larger part of an ERP system and this enriches the operational data in ways we had not thought of just some decades ago. It is likely that the use of sensors in ERP systems will create a new sort of vendor lock-in, because it can be difficult to integrate or change ERP systems that are deeply connected to the company in various ways. This can further emphasize the need to evaluate carefully the chosen ERP package (Akkermans & van Helden, 2002), and even the set of critical success factors for ERP systems (Somers & Nelson, 2001).

Information Systems Development

Developing IS systems with sensors as integrated parts of the systems are different from creating a traditional PC-based system for instance. An interesting insight for micro-IS is to look toward an object oriented analysis and design method (OOA&D) (Mathiassen, Munk-Madsen, Nielsen, & Stage, 2001). Here the analysis is split into the problem area and the user area, and the book includes several examples of (micro) information systems. There is an example of a cruise control application, which is analyzed in terms of development and preparation for implementation. Micro-IS seeks to add a bridge from this method

via information systems development and right into the core of IS. It allows us to discuss more explicitly how to monitor the problem area using micro-IS technologies. Furthermore, micro-IS can enrich the user area in new ways by allowing the user to access, control and monitor information in new ways using sensors. These data provide new opportunities for developing distributed information systems covering vast numbers of actors, products and services and thus generating a new basis for business intelligence, coordination efficiencies and preventive measures to mention just a few.

Outsourcing

There is a tradition for outsourcing software development of systems. For now, we assume it is partly because it is fairly straightforward to exchange the digital information that constitutes the source files etc. of an IT project. It would appear that including the sensor systems in this equation results in something that is not yet sufficiently mature to lend itself to offshore outsourcing. So, it is a pertinent research question how the existing outsourcing theory can be used when micro-IS forms part of an IS system under development.

Many micro-IS platforms are open source, which is another somewhat related aspect of outsourcing, where the idea is to share the development of certain pieces of the IS platform to allow players access and adaptation according to their platforms and architectures.

Information Management

Database and database management systems will assume a different role because micro-IS provides a new kind of information. Much of the information from a micro-IS system is coming from continuous reading of the surroundings. These small systems do not store information in the same quantities as standard databases, but they rather *stream* information toward a central database leading to concepts such as real-time business intelligence. The micro-IS acts as the first intelligent filter to relay relevant data further down the network. Working with data streams is different since we cannot guarantee storage to all data in a database. Instead, the data stream is continuously monitored for valuable information or events. This is a different way of thinking about information and it introduces new challenges; the sensor-connected enterprise can react faster to changes in its surroundings and operating premises. It will have to foster a new kind of business intelligence and decision support systems. A recent surge in the direction of supporting a distributed IT infrastructure capable of processing and storing large data quantities is cloud computing. Companies such as Arista Networks offer such solutions handling gigabytes of data.

Human Computer Interaction

Numerous implications are in store for HCI as micro-IS enters IS, because we will someday become "one" with the systems. Where the human computer interaction (HCI) is mostly composed of a keyboard, mouse, and a computer monitor, micro-IS will provide new ways to interact with the system. We are used to evaluate things that we can see and touch. These new systems are sometimes so small that it could be impossible to really distinguish between the physical world and the virtual world. In the case of iPhone we see a prolific use of sensors to extend the phone's function into many new types of services relying on cloud computing.

Security

Security issues are one of the areas where micro-IS will spark a renewed quest for further investigation, as earlier has been called for (Baskerville, 2004). A micro-IS system is not necessarily connected to the main systems in the same way as we are used to. It can be so small that normal safety and security measures are simply not feasible. The embedded systems have significantly different properties than standard IT systems, and it is possible that the security issues have to be accounted for and balanced already in the end-to-end product design process, in order to address all possible threats from inception to end of the micro-IS product at a later stage.

Ethics and Corporate Social Responsibility

Recognizing the existence of micro-IS systems also brings focus to new hard questions. While engineers address the technical challenges, the IS perspective should not ignore ethical dilemmas. Embedded systems can monitor and control just about everything. The smaller and smarter these systems get, the more difficult questions will have to be addressed in due time. Most people will no doubt benefit from electronic systems controlling the emergency brakes of a car, but how should we feel about a similar system for controlling "how well" we drive in general and in regard to speeding in particularly? Or how would we feel if our employer asks for DNA samples to be analyzed with IBM's upcoming DNA transistor?

It is a delicate act of balance as also captured by John Elkington's triple bottom line: people, planet, and profit (Elkington, 1994). We indicate some possible ethical dilemmas and corporate social responsibility issues, later captured in our micro-IS model.

IS Education and IS Curriculum

It would be beneficial for students to acquire some managerial-level knowledge of embedded systems; i.e. what are the main properties and how do they with general management, business, and globalization practices?

Is it likely that changes in IS education evolve in parallel to research-driven micro-IS projects where the former is inspired by new methodologies and the latter is driven by micro- to nano-scale engineering? Will education keep the gap between research and practice more narrow? In order to deploy micro-IS in education and professional training, there must exist widely available open source platforms (R. U. Pedersen, 2007). A merge of engineering and IS disciplines is not straightforward as we have indicated. We suggest that a first step is to reckon the contributions from each camp and a second is to conceptualize a synthesis along new boundaries in design which we have practiced in education using an "intelligent toy."

Design Science

Micro-IS is especially interesting for design science research because there are many more degrees of freedom to be addressed than in traditional IS projects. We try to capture some of those degrees of freedom, or design parameters, in our model later. Even though this is not an 'opinion chapter' on design science, we will nevertheless note some connections to design science and soft systems methodology. For instance, the risk assessment of designing, developing, and selling embedded systems will require a new approach, perhaps such as the one found in the appendix of the Soft Design Science Methodology (Baskerville, Pries-Heje, & Venable, 2009). As described earlier, LEGO is known for creating toys like the MINDSTORMS that spark curiosity and innovation for its users. LEGO education uses a structured four phases learning process: connect, construct, contemplate, and continue. We believe that educational platforms like LEGO NXT can be important for design science projects (Pedersen 2008), and one convincing example is provided later in this chapter.

Figure 11. Micro-IS design model

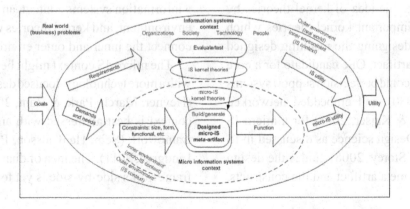

MICRO IS DESIGN MODEL

The micro-IS design model is a representation of how the search for an acceptable solution to a real world (business/society/natural sciences etc.) problem is conducted. Starting from the outside in, we begin by identifying a real-world (business) problem (see Figure 11). We have selected the design science topic and the society unit of analysis from Table 2.

At this point we want to create a small but completely working example of how energy management can be designed and used by non-technical end-users (such as those we would expect to find in "other corporate processes" -- where regulatory compliance is a requirement connecting to ongoing sensing of various emissions). We introduce two inner environment/ outer environment hierarchies (Simon, 1996). One is how the real world business problem (outer environment) regards the information system (inner environment) as a system to provide utility toward fulfillment of some goals. The other hierarchy is how an IS context (outer environment) regards the micro-IS context (inner environment) as a system to provide additional utility toward fulfillment of the aforementioned goals. We understand an information system context as a confluence of people, organizations, and technology (A. Lee, 1999). We add society to allow for a broader scope. The designed micro-IS meta-artifact is at the center of the design model.

We recognize the idea of kernel theories by showing three important kernel theories which are used when designing the resulting designed micro-IS meta-artifact. One candidate for a core IS kernel theory could be decision support systems (Sprague Jr, 1980), and embedded networked systems (Pottie & Kaiser, 2005) for a micro-IS kernel theory. Design science as discussed in IS (S. T. March & Storey, 2008) guides the design of the micro-IS meta artifact and the constructs, models, methods, and instantiations that sum up this meta-artifact.

We say that the real world setting includes some business(society/natural sciences etc) problems which form some goals for an information systems context project. These goals are translated to a set of demands and needs which are developed using the design science approach within the IS context "walls." Then the demands and needs are reformulated into constraints that relate to size, form, and function for the designed micro-IS meta-artifact. These constraints and the kernel theories form the search space for an acceptable solution to the part of the real world business problem that the micro-IS is intended to solve. An acceptable solution is reached by generating/building solution candidates and evaluating/testing them in the IS context. This approach will ensure that future micro-IS projects are understood from an IS rather than a technical perspective. This micro-IS meta-artifact provides some function which is to be aligned with the requirements of the IS context. This forms the combined utility of the information system.

The idea in the micro-IS design model is that a micro-IS meta-artifact does not stand alone; it's *raison d'être* stems from its inclusion in a larger IS context. A deep understanding of the inner environment (micro-IS) can be kept at a minimal basis yet the utility of including the micro-IS meta-artifact in the IS can be realized this way. It is the basic framing of the micro-IS design model: a real world setting, an outer environment in the form of a information systems context, an inner micro-IS environment, and kernel theories which span and connect the inner and outer environments.

The micro-IS context might be best addressed with a more technology-focused design framework (Hevner, March, Park, & Ram, 2004) and the IS context is best addressed with an action design framework (Sein, Henfridsson, Purao, Rossi, & Lindgren, 2011). The idea of dual design science frameworks side-by-side is yet to be explored.

Table 3. Micro-IS vocabulary

Vocabulary	Meaning
Object	An encapsulation of an artifact with properties to act on the object. Also called components, packages, configurations, classes, and modules.
Interface	A set of services forming a contract between the user and provider.
Transformation	Data that undergoes a change.
Sensor	Can monitor a physical phenomenon and convert it to a digital form.
Actuator	Can do something and act on a command triggering changes in the physical world.
Communication	Means for sending and receiving messages. Radio can be used as well.
Flow	There are two types of flow: Information flow and control flow. Both flows can be bi-directional.
Event	Something that occurs external to the system and is acted upon by the system.
Messages	An abstraction that means to send something in the form of information or commands.
Program	A set of commands to the embedded system.
Embedded system	A small computer system with chip that controls the behavior of the system, and a set of sensors and/or actuators. The chip is sometimes called a microcontroller or system on chip. This chip executes the program. It can also be called a device or controller.
Battery	A broad perspective on the energy that is needed to keep the embedded system running.
Micro Information System	Some collection of objects, interfaces, transformations, sensors, actuators, communications(s), events, messages, events, programs hosted on an embedded system and related to an IS.

Vocabulary: A Construct to Understand Micro-IS

The vocabulary is anchored in IS, but remains useful in communicating and co-creating solutions alongside other fields such as software engineering, computer science, and electrical engineering (Table 3):

Most of the vocabulary in Table 3 is self-explanatory, but the inclusion of flows merits more discussion. We identify two core flows related to micro-IS systems: information and control. Information flow usually originates from the micro-IS to, for example, an enterprise information system (EIS) (Walls, Widmeyer, & El Sawy, 1992). The flows can be bidirectional, and allow for explicit discussions of how raw data is captured, filtered, transformed, data mined, knowledge based, and presented to the end user. These transformations must be adaptable; that is why the information flow is bidirectional. A control flow can implicitly require an acknowledgement or a status message.

Generate/Evaluate Method

The premise of the method is that some problem exists, preferably an IS problem. The method we propose is an iterative process over the IS, SE, CS, and EE domains of the problem (Figure 12).

It is an important property of the micro-IS design model that the project is understood as an IS problem, and that is why we suggest a "return home" to IS after each foray into another field or discipline.

Micro-IS Instantiation

The micro-IS design model, vocabulary construct, and generate/evaluate method provides the core artifacts of a micro-IS framework. Only rarely can the core micro-IS design science framework be used without adaptation. Therefore we suggest a checklist for instantiating a new micro-IS meta-artifact for a selection of constructs, models, methods, and instantiations which match a given real-world (business) problem.

Figure 12. Micro-IS adapted cross-domain "generate/evaluate" (Hevner et al., 2004)

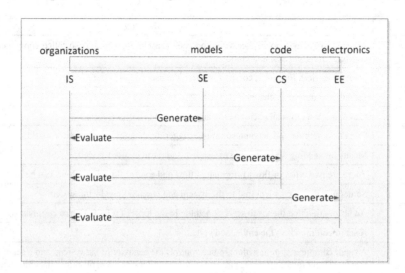

- Adapt the micro-IS design model to include the relevant environments, contexts, and kernel theories.
- Select a prototyping platform and design the new artifact: assemble, disassemble, construct, tear down, and work with the construction pieces while proceeding through the steps below.
- Refine the main IS problem and IS context and the information and control flows in the micro-IS system.
- What are the basic phenomena to be monitored? To be controlled?
- What set of sensors can monitor those phenomena?
- What set of actuators is needed to regulate the physical entity?
- Adapt the vocabulary to the problem.
- Upon completion of the micro-IS project, generalize the best micro-IS artifacts and update the core micro-IS framework accordingly.

To use the micro-IS framework, we suggest the constructs, models, and methods to be added, removed, or adapted. We suggest the use of a minimalistic approach: new artifacts should be added to the micro-IS framework only if they are essential to solve a given problem. The design theory nexus is needed here to adapt the core micro-IS framework to real business problems (Pries-Heje & Baskerville, 2008). It forms a method for adapting and extending the micro-IS framework.

With these implications in mind, we want to elaborate on the important role of the sensor itself in these systems by demonstration. That is the topic of the next sections.

Demonstrating the Micro-IS Framework

We demonstrate the synergy of combining the environmental informatics (Watson, Boudreau, & Chen, 2010) and micro-IS design science frameworks in a demand/response application. This then forms a representation of a design space model for green micro-IS (micro-IS-G) systems. This micro-IS-G framework can then be used as a point of reference for rigorous and relevant work. The source code is open source and can be provided in a zip file upon request. This addresses many of the small but important implementation questions that engineering audiences have.

Design of a Demand/Response Application

We want to create a prototype of a system which use the constructs, models, and methods we have provided. We identify the demand and supply in the environmental framework as central, and we instantiate a small demo system that makes use of that framework. (Figure 13)

The setup we use is a "household clothes dryer." That would be a sensitized object (Watson, Boudreau, & Chen, 2010) that we require to be turned off and on. How do we control peak demand in a network with such appliances? To meet this need, we use the OpenADR standard (Piette et al., 2009), which is a standard for automatic control of demand and response to promote common information exchange between the utility or Independent System Operator and electric customers using demand response price and reliability signals.

The household appliance in the form of Lego Mindstorms NXT is built to resemble a dryer, and we need a way to see this sensitized object

in a more generic manner. SensorML and TransducerML (Botts, Percivall, Reed, & Davidson, 2008) would be useful if we iterated the design over multiple generate/evaluate cycles; however, we note the interest in these standards after cycle 1. This information can be matched with the pricing events that are generated by the OpenADR client as provided by Akuacom.

The OpenADR events are configured in the OpenADR web interface (see Figure 13) for the account that was provided to us. We set up an event that notifies our system about price for electricity, and we then control our sensitized object accordingly. The events are configured to give the appliance warning when the event is imminent (NEAR) and then ACTIVE when the event is running in the timeslot that is defined in the OpenADR client program. The interface between the OpenADR event server and the sensitized object is XML, and the format for the DR signals is described in XML schemas.

The household gateway in the form of a laptop polls the OpenADR server for event information, and this information is then interpreted on the

Figure 13. Configuration of demand/response events

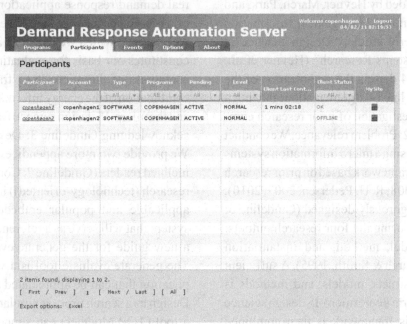

Figure 14. Research organization for a demand/response application

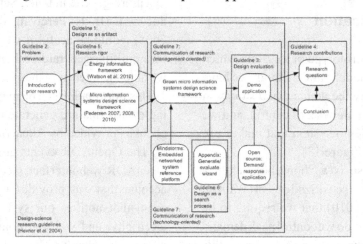

gateway program, which in turn queries the sensitized object under its control using SensorML coded messages. All communication takes place using the IP protocol. Inside the household, the UDP protocol is used and between the OpenADR server and the household gateway the HTTP protocol carries the XML formatted web service information (Figure 14).

The demonstration part of this chapter evaluates Watson et al.'s environmental framework (Watson et al., 2010) using the design science guidelines provided by Hevner, March, Park, and Ram in their seminal Management Information Systems Quarterly article, "Design Science in Information Systems Research" (Hevner et al., 2004). Figure 14 depicts the organization of the chapter and our line of argumentation; the introduction and investigation of prior research comprise Guideline 2: Problem relevance. We conduct this evaluation using a micro information systems design science framework based on prior research (R. Pedersen, 2008; R. U. Pedersen, 2007, 2010), which is then rigorously designed (Guideline 5: Research rigor) using the four research outputs: constructs, model, method, and instantiation (Salvatore T. March & Smith, 1995). A sufficient number of constructs, models, and methods is established to form a core micro-IS design science framework. This framework is then combined

with the energy informatics framework to form a new meta-artifact in the form of a green micro information systems (micro-IS-G) design science framework; this serves also as management-oriented communication, depicted in Guideline 7: Communication of research (management-oriented). The communication is accompanied by the instantiation of a demo application to exemplify the use of the micro-IS-G framework on a relevant problem within the environmental sustainability domain: a problem which shows a prototype of a real demand/response application. This application is based on an open source demand/response web service, which we use in an appendix and it constitutes our basis for evaluating the practical usefulness of the micro-IS-G framework – the combination of the energy informatics framework and the micro-IS design science framework – thus acknowledging Guideline 3: Design evaluation. We provide two more appendices for technically inclined readers (Guideline 7: Communication of research (technology-oriented)) in the form of an applicable and popular embedded networked system that will serve as a reference platform and a new guide for the generate/evaluate process. The generate/evaluate tool is a wizard-type application that can be appreciated as Guideline 6: Design as a search process similar to the idea that a tool (TOP Modeler) can support this process

(Markus, Majchrzak, & Gasser, 2002). Our arti-fact-driven approach in the creation of the micro-IS design framework, the combination with the energy informatics framework (Watson et al., 2010) to form the micro-IS-G green framework, the reference platform, the generate/evaluate tool, and the demo application are captured by Guideline 1: Design as an artifact. The instantiation is a demonstration of the usefulness of the energy informatics framework, and we use our acquired knowledge to answer the research questions in Watson et al.'s (Watson et al., 2010) paper. We summarize the research questions and offer our

conclusion that the micro-IS-G framework and the environmental informatics framework is a synergistic contribution to research and teaching within the nascent field of environmental infor-matics in the IS community (Guideline 4: Research contributions).

One of our design goals with the micro-IS design science framework is to use the best of embedded systems without getting lost in the technical details. We point to interfaces relevant to IS which will link naturally to other frameworks. In other words:

Figure 15. The OpenADR demo application

"[...] the purpose of abstraction is not to be vague, but to create a new semantic level in which one can be absolutely precise." Edsger W. Dijkstra, "The Humble Programmer" (1972).

This prototype was designed during the first round of generate/evaluation (Figure 15). It is programmed in Java using the open source Lego Mindstorms programming system LeJOS (Lew, Horton, & Sherriff, 2010).

The OpenADR demo application shows how the constructed prototype of a clothes dryer (a sensitized object) is controlled by the Lego Mindstorms. Lego Mindstorms is connected by USB to a laptop which uses the internet protocol to communicate with the residential gateway (a second laptop). This residential gateway is an OpenADR client using the provided Java software to compile a web service client; the client uses the REST protocol to poll the Open Demand Server (see Figure 13) in the United States. The events that we generated used a 10-minute waiting period before going into active state. The events contained price information, which we could use in making the prototype dependent on the right electricity price. Thus this application demonstrates how flow can be controlled (Watson et al., 2010) in a real prototype setting.

CONCLUSION

It is said that to understand our future, we must first understand our past. Since micro-IS is introduced as a potentially important part of our (IS) future, we might start to conclude by taking another look back in time. Before the advent of electricity, human networks and organizational ties were upheld with human-to-human contact and letters. The subsequent introduction of the telephone and similar technologies enabled us to maintain the same kind of networks but over greater distances. Presently, the Internet (including the mobile Internet) plays a growing role in human and organizational relationships. In the future, micro-IS, as we have presented it, will serve as a preliminary IS framework to analyze the physical connections to the real world in various ways: e.g. this will create a new source of information for human networks as indicated in Figure 16.

Whether or not micro-IS is perceived as promising or frightening, it should still be evident to everyone that we are increasingly surrounded by digital technology. Much of this technology can be useful in an IS setting, and the *micro-IS* concept holds potential of being one possible way to grow this area. Micro-IS can hopefully help to refine and redefine pieces of what we know already in

Figure 16. Micro-IS creates new information highways

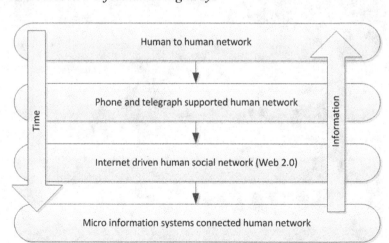

terms of IS. As future research platforms we are currently investigating the Go programming language from Google in relation to micro-IS.

Moreover, the prospects of micro-IS are to us so exciting, that we sincerely hope for an IS community to get a positive feeling of urgency and perhaps even obligation to put in the work required to shape this important area. It seems relevant to discuss ethical, environmental, and corporate guidelines *in parallel* with the technological development in the embedded systems communities. There is no particular reason why this area should be *pushed* forward by technology, rather than also being shaped by an IS application oriented *pull*.

We have contributed a preliminary model of micro-IS (see Figure 3), which addresses a number of the core IS topics (such as *IT and organizations*, *IS development*, *IT and individuals*, *IT and markets*, and *IT and groups*) (Sidorova et al., 2008). In our view, micro-IS is a fresh way to see something that has been somewhat hidden within IS, which can tie people, organizations, and technology together. Table 2 display many of these intersections where IS applications meet IS implications. It has not been our goal to mimic the great visions of pervasive and ubiquitous computing, but rather to take a step backwards and focus mainly on the fundamental aspects of micro-IS systems.

REFERENCES

Akkermans, H., & van Helden, K. (2002). Vicious and virtuous cycles in ERP implementation: A case study of interrelations between critical success factors. *European Journal of Information Systems*, *11*(1), 35–46. doi:10.1057/palgrave/ejis/3000418

Apple (n.d.). *Iphone*. Retrieved October 20th, 2011 from http://apple.com

Arch-Rock. (n.d.). *Image*. Retrieved October 20th 2011 from http://archrock.com

Baskerville, R. (2004, June 14-16). *Agile security for information warfare: A call for research*. Paper presented at the 13th European Conference on Information Systems, The European IS Profession in the Global Networking Environment, Turku, Finland.

Baskerville, R., Pries-Heje, J., & Venable, J. (2009). *Soft design science methodology*. Paper presented at the 4th International Conference on Design Science Research in Information Systems and Technology, Philadelphia, Pennsylvania.

Botts, M., Percivall, G., Reed, C., & Davidson, J. (2008). OGC® Sensor Web enablement: Overview and high level architecture. In Nittel, S., Labrinidis, A., & Stefanidis, A. (Eds.), *GeoSensor networks* (*Vol. 4540*, pp. 175–190). Berlin, Germany: Springer. doi:10.1007/978-3-540-79996-2_10

Culler, D. E., & Hong, W. (2004). Wireless sensor networks - Introduction. *Communications of the ACM*, *47*(6), 30–33. doi:10.1145/990680.990703

Denning, P. J. (2007). Computing is a natural science. *Communications of the ACM*, *50*(7), 13–18. doi:10.1145/1272516.1272529

Dijkstra, E. W. (1972). The humble programmer. *Communications of the ACM*, *15*(10), 859–866. doi:10.1145/355604.361591

Dwivedi, Y. K., & Kuljis, J. (2008). Profile of IS research published in the European Journal of Information Systems. *European Journal of Information Systems*, *17*(6), 678–693. doi:10.1057/ejis.2008.57

Elkington, J. (1994). Towards the sustainable corporation: Win-win-win business strategies for sustainable development. *California Management Review*, *36*(2), 90–100.

ELPRO. (n.d.). *Image*. Retrieved October 28th, 2011, from http://www.elpro.com

Fleisch, E., & Tellkamp, C. (2006). The business value of ubiquitous computing technologies. In Roussos, G. (Ed.), *Ubiquitous and pervasive commerce* (pp. 93–113). Springer. doi:10.1007/1-84628-321-3_6

Hevner, A., March, S., Park, J., & Ram, S. (2004). Design science in information systems research. *Management Information Systems Quarterly, 28*(1). IBM_Press_Room. (2009). *IBM research aims to build nanoscale DNA sequencer to help drive down cost of personalized genetic analysis*. Retrieved October 6th, 2009, from http://www-304.ibm.com/jct03001c/press/us/en/press-release/28558.wss, IBMSocialMedia, retrieved from IBM DNA Transistor at http://youtube.com

Lee, A. (1999). Inaugural editor's comments. *Management Information Systems Quarterly, 23*(1), v–xi.

Lee, E. E. (2006). *Cyber-physical systems - Are computing foundations adequate?* Paper presented at the Position Paper for NSF Workshop On Cyber-Physical Systems: Research Motivation, Techniques and Roadmap Austin.

LEGO. (n.d.). *Mindstorms*. Retrieved June 9th, 2010, from http://mindstorms.lego.com/

Lew, M. W., Horton, T. B., & Sherriff, M. S. (2010). *Using LEGO MINDSTORMS NXT and LEJOS in an advanced software engineering course*. Paper presented at the 2010 23rd IEEE Conference on Software Engineering Education and Training.

March, S. T., & Smith, G. F. (1995). Design and natural science research on information technology. *Decision Support Systems, 15*(4), 251–266. doi:10.1016/0167-9236(94)00041-2

March, S. T., & Storey, V. C. (2008). Design science in the information systems discipline: An introduction to the special issue on design science research. *Management Information Systems Quarterly, 32*(4), 725–730.

Markus, L., Majchrzak, A., & Gasser, L. (2002). A design theory for systems that support emergent knowledge processes. *Management Information Systems Quarterly, 26*(3), 179–212.

Mathiassen, L., Munk-Madsen, A., Nielsen, P. A., & Stage, J. (2001). *Object oriented analysis & design*. Aalborg, Denmark: Marko Publishers.

Pedersen, M. K. (2007). Case study 2: Distributed knowledge networks: Construction industry modernization. Innovating a digital model for the construction industry - a distributed knowledge management approach. In Wickramasinghe, N., & Lubitz, D. V. (Eds.), *Knowledge-based enterprise: Theories and fundamentals* (pp. 257–273). Hershey, PA: IGI Global.

Pedersen, M. K., & Larsen, M. H. (2005). Innocuous knowledge: Models of distributed knowledge networks. In Desouza, K. C. (Ed.), *New frontiers of knowledge management* (pp. 243–265). Palgrave Macmillan.

Pedersen, R. (2008). *Micro information systems: Toward an experimental platform*. Paper presented at the Ubiquitous Knowledge Discovery Workshop, European Conference on Machine Learning and Principles and Practice of Knowledge Discovery in Databases. Retrieved from September 14th, 2009, from http://www.ecmlpkdd2008.org/workshop-papers-ubiqkd

Pedersen, R. U. (2007). TinyOS education with LEGO MINDSTORMS NXT. In Gama, J., & Garber, M. M. (Eds.), *Learning from data streams* (pp. 231–241). Springer. doi:10.1007/3-540-73679-4_14

Pedersen, R. U. (2010). Micro information systems and ubiquitous knowledge discovery. In May, M., & Saitta, L. (Eds.), *Ubiquitous knowledge discovery (Vol. 6202*, pp. 216–234). Berlin, Germany: Springer. doi:10.1007/978-3-642-16392-0_13

Philips. (n.d.). *RFID image*. Retrieved October 20th, 2011 from http://www.nxp.com/

Piette, M. A., Ghatikar, G., Kiliccote, S., Koch, E., Hennage, D., Palensky, P., & McParland, C. (2009). *CEC OpenADR-Version 1.0 Report: Open automated demand response communications specification* (Version 1.0). California Energy Commission, PIER Program. CEC-500-2009-063 and LBNL-1779E.

Pottie, G., & Kaiser, W. (2005). *Principles of embedded networked systems design*. New York, NY: Cambridge University Press. doi:10.1017/CBO9780511541049

Pries-Heje, J., & Baskerville, R. (2008). The design theory nexus. *Management Information Systems Quarterly*, *32*(4), 731–755.

Sein, M. K., Henfridsson, O., Purao, S., Rossi, M., & Lindgren, R. (2011). Action design research. *Management Information Systems Quarterly*, *35*(1), 37–56.

Sidorova, A., Evangelopoulos, N., Valacich, J. S., & Ramakrishnan, T. (2008). Uncovering the intellectual core of the information systems discipline. *Management Information Systems Quarterly*, *32*(3), 467–482.

Simon, H. A. (1996). *The sciences of the artificial* (3rd ed.). Cambridge, MA: MIT Press.

Somers, T. M., & Nelson, K. (2001). *The impact of critical success factors across the stages of enterprise resource planning implementations*. Paper presented at the Hawaii International Conference on System Sciences, Maui, Hawaii.

Sprague, R. H. Jr. (1980). A framework for the development of decision support systems. *Management Information Systems Quarterly*, 1–26. doi:10.2307/248957

Walls, J. G., Widmeyer, G. R., & El Sawy, O. A. (1992). Building an information system design theory for vigilant EIS. *Information Systems Research*, *3*(1), 36–59. doi:10.1287/isre.3.1.36

Watson, R. T. (2001). Introducing MISQ review—A new department in MIS Quarterly. *Management Information Systems Quarterly*, *25*(1).

Watson, R. T., Boudreau, M.-C., & Chen, A. J. (2010). Information systems and environmentally sustainable development: Energy informatics and new directions for the IS community. *Management Information Systems Quarterly*, *34*(1), 23–38.

Wikipedia. (n.d.). *Mandelbrot set*. Retrieved November 10th, 2011, from http://en.wikipedia.org/wiki/Mandelbrot_set#Self-similarity

KEY TERMS and DEFINITIONS

Actuator: Can do something and act on a command.

Battery: A broad perspective on the energy that is needed to keep the embedded system running.

Communication: Means for sending and receiving messages. Radio can be used as well.

Embedded System: A small computer system and a related set of sensors and/or actuators.

Event: Something that occurs external to the system and is acted upon.

Flow: There are two types of flow: Information flow and control flow. Both flows can be bi-directional.

Interface: A set of services forming a contract between the user and provider.

Messages: An abstraction that means to send something in the form of information or commands.

Micro Information System: Objects, interfaces, transformations, sensors, actuators, communications(s), events, messages, events, programs hosted on an embedded system.

Object: An encapsulation of an artifact with properties to act on the object.

Program: A set of commands to the embedded system.

Sensor: Can monitor a physical phenomenon and convert it to a digital form.

Transformation: Data that undergoes a change.

Chapter 14
Mobile Communication in Hospitals:
What is the Problem?

Terje Solvoll
Norwegian Centre for Integrated Care and Telemedicine,
Tromsø Telemedicine Laboratory, University Hospital of North Norway
& Department of Computer Science, University of Tromsø, Norway

ABSTRACT

The work setting in hospitals is communication intensive and can lead to significant difficulties related to interruptions from co-workers. Physicians often need information fast, and any delay between the decision made and the action taken could cause medical errors. One suggested solution for this problem is to implement wireless phone systems. However, psychological theory and empirical evidence, both suggest that wireless phones have the potential of creating additional problems related to interruptions, compared to traditional paging systems. The fact that hospital workers prefer interruptive communication methods before non-interruptive methods, amplifies the risk of overloading people when phones are widely deployed. This challenge causes some hospital staff to resist the diffusion of wireless phones, and a key is how to handle the balance between increased availability, and increased interruptions. In this chapter, the authors present solutions based on context aware communication systems, aiming to reduce interruptions.

INTRODUCTION

We know from earlier studies within health care that physicians in hospitals are interrupted unnecessary by mobile devices in situations where such interruptions should be avoided (Scholl, Has-

vold, Henriksen, & Ellingsen, 2007; T. Solvoll & Scholl, 2008; Terje Solvoll, Scholl, & Hartvigsen, 2010, 2012). Unnecessary interruptions can cause concentration difficulties and disturb the activity performed (Hersh et al., 2002). Unwanted interruptions should be minimized in order to avoid

DOI: 10.4018/978-1-4666-2190-9.ch014

distraction that can lead to intolerable action or decisions, especially during surgery or patient examinations. This is a problem in today's hospital settings, and a solution to reduce such unnecessary interruptions from mobile devices is needed and wanted (T. Botsis, T. Solvoll, J. Scholl, P. Hasvold, & G. Hartvigsen, 2007; Scholl, et al., 2007; T. Solvoll & Scholl, 2008; Terje Solvoll, et al., 2012). A lot of research has been done within this area, some of this work will be presented in the next sections, but we cannot see that the situation has changed to the better. In this chapter we will present some earlier work on context sensitive systems for mobile communication in hospitals (internal communication systems, not including public networks (GSM/3G) enabling the use of Blackberries, Iphones, Ipads etc.) that aims to improve the communication situation and also reduce interruptions.

BACKGROUND

Physicians' working conditions rely on mobility. They move frequently between in-patient ward, out-patient ward, emergency ward, operating theatres, etc., and often do not stay more than a few minutes in the same location. High mobility requires mobile communication systems, which enables physicians to communicate with colleges at any time and place, to avoid any delay between the decision made and action taken. Such delays could result in medical errors (Hersh, et al., 2002), and mobile communication systems have been suggested as a solution to improve communication in hospitals (Coiera & Tombs, 1998). The challenge when deploying mobile communication systems is to handle the balance between the increased availability and possible interruptions (Scholl, et al., 2007; T. Solvoll & Scholl, 2008; Terje Solvoll, et al., 2010, 2012). Most hospitals still rely on a mobile communication infrastructure with dedicated devices for each

role, where pagers are the most dominant mobile communication device.

Pagers provide a cheap and reliable way for contacting staff. They are ubiquitous and several physicians carry numerous pagers simultaneously to cover the various work roles they have been assigned. Pagers suffer from a number of problems due to their simplicity. The most obvious limitation is that it requires the staff to locate a telephone (landline or wireless) in order to respond to a page. This might cause unnecessary delays and communication overhead, since the person placing the page is not always near the phone when the page is returned (Spurck, Mohr, Seroka, & Stoner, 1995). Pagers also create a large amount of unnecessary interruptions (Blum & Lieu, 1992; Katz & Schroeder, 1988), which is unpleasant and can cause medical errors (Hersh, et al., 2002).

The most intuitive solution to improve the communication situation in hospitals is to provide physicians with wireless phones. However, phones can be even more interruptive than pagers (Scholl, et al., 2007; T. Solvoll & Scholl, 2008; Terje Solvoll, et al., 2010, 2012). In (Scholl, et al., 2007) a physician states that; "with a pager you just have to glance down at your coat pocket to see who is paging, while with a phone, you have to pick it up from your pocket to see who is calling. Having done that, it is easier just answering and explaining that you are busy" (T. Solvoll & Scholl, 2008).

Preliminary studies points at a diversity of potential benefits from wireless phones in hospital settings, using both mobile text and voice services (Acuff, Fagan, Rindfleisch, Levitt, & Ford, 1997; Eisenstadt et al., 1998; Minnick, Pischke-Winn, & Sterk, 1994 ; Spurck, et al., 1995). These studies also reveal potential technological limitations that can explain some of the challenges of gaining acceptance. Text-chat is a less obtrusive medium than other forms of workplace communication (Bradner, Kellogg, & Erickson, 1999). It is therefore unlikely that mobile text-messaging creates the same amount of interruptions as mobile voice services. Improved asynchronous communication systems have in fact been recommended for improving hospital communication practices (Coiera & Tombs, 1998). In addition to mobile synchronous communication systems, mobile text-messaging systems are therefore an interesting medium to explore in hospitals settings.

However, the current generation of mobile-text messaging systems seems ill suited for hospital environments. Studies of mobile text-messaging usage in hospitals have, revealed difficulties related to small screen size (Eisenstadt, et al., 1998), and problems related to forcing doctors to carrying an additional device (Acuff, et al., 1997). It has to be taken into account that these studies are some years old. Today displays and keyboards are significantly improved, which might have changed the situation. A continual problem with mobile text messaging is that senders often need an acknowledgement that an asynchronous message has been read by the receiver (Coiera & Tombs, 1998). The acknowledgement challenge could be solved by a forced feedback when the message has been opened. Automatic suggestions for replies may ease the difficulties with text-messages. It has been reported that predefined messages can meet up to 90% of the mobile text-messaging needs for some hospital workers (Jakob E. Bardram & Hansen, 2004).

Mobile communication systems for hospitals, is an important research area since hospitals are noted to suffer from poor communication practices. The combination of wireless phones and fact that hospital workers prefer interruptive communication methods before non-interruptive methods (Blum & Lieu, 1992; Coiera & Tombs, 1998; Katz & Schroeder, 1988) and often exhibit "selfish" interruptive communication practices, may result in unnecessary interruptions for conversations that otherwise would' not occur (Parker & Coiera, 2000). This amplifies the risk of overloading limited resources with special knowledge, experience, and the power of taking medical decisions. The balance between getting immediate access to resources and causing interruptions in moments

where it is not appropriate, has similarities with the classical problems regarding collaboration and sharing of resources, such as of disparity in work and benefit, "prisoner's dilemma" and "the tragedy of the commons" (Grudin, 1994). A critical issue for voice services is the potential of make people "fatally available" (Spurck, et al., 1995), which cannot be overlooked since health care is a knowledge intensive activity where consulting colleagues or senior staff members is a necessity in many situations (Coiera, 2000).One way of attacking this problem is to provide the caller with context information from the receiver's situation. Context information could be any kind of information which helps to decide if the receiver is available or not, such as; location, activity, surrounding noise, role, etc. In a study by (Avrahami, Gergle, Hudson, & Kiesler, 2007) they revealed that if the caller is provided with context information about the receiver's situation, it reduces the mismatch between the caller's decision and the receiver's desires.

To address the conflict between physicians' needs for mobile communication and the interruptions from mobile devices in hospitals, we have been looking at context sensitive (also called context aware) systems for mobile communication first in general and then in hospital settings. A number of studies have focused on context-sensitive systems for hospitals; however, a lot of this work has focused on scopes not covered by this chapter, including issues related to mobile learning and privacy, accessing clinical data, or on multimedia communication at terminals with fixed locations (Mitchell, Spiteri, Bates, & Coulouris, 2000).

Context Sensitive Communication Systems

There have been many suggestions on how to reduce interruptions from mobile devices during the years. In this chapter we will focus on context sensitive/aware communication systems that aims to reduce interruptions, first in general, and then within hospital settings. But first of all we need to define context sensitive/aware systems. We will use the terms context aware and context sensitive as equal terms during this chapter.

Identifying Context Sensitive Systems

A system is a set of interacting or interdependent components forming an integrated whole. The behaviour of this whole has observable Inter-Process Communications. Further, to define what we mean by context, we had to look into some of the definitions defined during the years by the research community (Bisgaard, Heise, & Steffensen, 2004; Lieberman & Selker, 2000; Schilit, Adams, & Want, 1994), and came up with (Abowd et al., 1999) as the most suitable definition for this chapter:

Context is any information that can be used to characterize the situation of an entity. An entity is a person, place, or object that is considered relevant for the interaction between a user and an application, including the user and applications themselves.

This definition high lights the importance of which information that is relevant or not in a context sensitive system. A Context sensitive system could therefore be defined as a system allowing interactions between multiple entities using relevant information. Abowd, et al., (1999) states; "a system is context-aware if it uses context to provide relevant information and/or services to the user, where relevancy depends on the user's task". This definition shows that a context-aware system can change its behaviour and send some relevant information according to the context, which reflects our view. So, what is relevant information? What are the most common types of contextual information used by context aware applications? (Mizzaro, Nazzi, & Vassena, 2008) identified some common types of information:

- spatial
- temporal
- social situation
- resources that are nearby
- physiological measurements
- schedules and agendas
- activities
- identity

Only a small number of these crucial information types are applied in existing applications. Only the information that satisfies the requirements of the targeted application, technology available, and environmental constraints, is used. The trend has been to offer the user as much information as possible in order to provide more sophisticated and useful services, and at the same time making the users more available. A preliminary study on the Aware Media system by Jakob E. Bardram, Hansen, & Soegaard (2006), which is presented in this book, they suggest a classification that splits the above listed information along three main axes:

- **Social Awareness:** 'Where a person is', 'activity in which a person is engaged on', 'self-reported status'.
- **Spatial Awareness:** 'What kind of operation is taking place in a ward', 'level of activity', 'status of operation and people present in the room'.
- **Temporal Awareness:** 'Past activities', 'present and future activities' that is significant for a person.

This classification describes social aspects regarding knowledge about a person, spatial aspects regarding information about a specific place, and temporal aspects describing information about history and future plans of a subject.

The adoption of context-aware services based on these definitions is growing in a variety of domains, as mention in (Hristova, 2008):

- **Smart Homes:** Context aware applications provide useful services to the residents in order to increase their quality of life and help disabled or elderly people to be more independent, such as; supervising health care functions to monitor the person's biomedical functions: glucose levels, blood pressure, heartbeats or provide reminders about daily medication.

- **Airports:** Context-aware solutions are used to identify possible threats or emergency conditions providing automatic mechanisms aimed at delivering immediate security notification to the appropriate department such as maintenance, fire department or police. Services linked to passenger's behaviour have been developed as well. Most of them are able to send information to passengers' mobile devices about shopping zones, exits, gates, arrivals and departures delay according to their location.

- **Travel/Entertainment/Shopping:** Information provided, typically on mobile phone, is about nearby restaurants, theatres, festivals, events, shops and other data related to the area where the user is located.

- **Museum:** Context aware applications are often used to detect user's position within a building in order to guide visitors through a predefined path. Typically, these applications are developed on suitable portable devices able to sense the location and capable to provide video/audio information relating paintings, statues and other object within a museum.

- **Offices:** Context-aware systems are usually aimed at monitoring the status of the equipment and providing better allocation of human resources changing the shift schedules considering location and activity performed by workers.

Context Sensitive Communication Systems to Control Interruptions

One approach for generalizing context aware communication systems that aims to reduce interruptions, is to divide them into two categories (Ashraf Khalil & Connelly, 2006). The first category includes systems where the phone automatically changes configuration (Ashraf Khalil & Connelly, 2005; Nelson, Bly, & Sokoler, 2001; Schmidt, Takaluoma, & Mäntyjärvi, 2000; Siewiorek et al., 2003). This includes quiet calls where the receiver could negotiate with the caller through text or pre-recorded audio messages (Nelson, et al., 2001), which will not reduce personal interruptions due to the user is supposed to act upon the received call. SenSay (Siewiorek, et al., 2003) is an interesting context-aware mobile phone that adapts to dynamically changing environmental and physiological states. It combines information from several different sensors to catch the user's context, and adapt the ringer volume, the vibration and the feedback to the caller based on the phones context. It also makes call suggestion to users when they are idle. Contextual information is gathered by using 3-Axis accelerometers, Bluetooth, ambient microphones, and light sensors, mounted on different part of the user's body. A central hub mounted on the waist is the central component that receives and distributes data coming from the sensors to the decision logic module. The decision logic module analyzes the collected data and changes the state of the phone. The system provides four states: Uninterruptible, Idle, Active and Normal state. A number of settings on the phone are automatically changed within the different states. The uninterruptible state turns off the ringer and turn on the vibration only if the light level is below a certain threshold. This state is entered when the user is involved in a conversation (recognized by the environmental microphone) or is involved in a meeting recognized from the phones calendar. In this state, all incoming calls are blocked and with feedback messages sent to the caller. The caller does have an option to force the call in case of emergency. When high physical activity or high ambient noise level are detected by the accelerometer or microphones, the active state is entered. This means that the ringer is set to high and the vibration is turned on. When there activity level is low and the detected sounds of the surroundings are very low, the idle state is entered. In this state the phone reminds the user of pending calls. As the name indicates, the normal state will configure the ringer and vibration to default values. Figure 1 shows the overall architecture of the SenSay system, from sensor box to platform, to mobile phone. In another system presented in (Schmidt, et al., 2000), they use wireless application protocols (WAP) to automatically change the phones setting based on the recognized context, and in (Ashraf Khalil & Connelly, 2005) they use calendar information with the users scheduled activity stored, to automatically configure the phone.

The second category (Ashraf Khalil & Connelly, 2006) deals with systems that gives the caller information about the receivers context and thereby helps the caller to make decisions when it is appropriate to make the call (Milewski & Smith, 2000; Pedersen, 2001; Tang et al., 2001). In one study by (Avrahami, et al., 2007), they revealed that if they provided the caller with context information about the receiver's situation, it reduces the mismatch between the caller's decision and the receivers desires. In (Milewski & Smith, 2000) they provide information about the receiver's presence using the phone book and location, like the "buddy list" in instant messenger services. An interaction web-page that gives caller information about the receivers' situation and the available communication channels is used in (Pedersen, 2001), and in (Marmasse, Schmandt, & Spectre, 2004) they formed some kind of member-list combined with a prototype of a wristwatch that captures the user's context and share it to the members of the list, which use the information to check the availability before calling.

Context Sensitive Communication Systems for Hospitals

Context aware systems for hospitals are a promising application domain. Hospitals are dependent of a wide and reliable communication infrastructure for exchanging different kinds of data, such as patient reports, lab tests and working shifts, together with text, voice and alarm services. The management of this information is difficult and requires considering a wide variety of problems that should

Figure 1. SenSay; from sensor box, to platform, to mobile phone. This is a simplified version of the overall system architecture presented in(Siewiorek, et al., 2003).

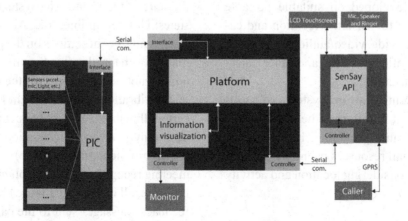

be avoided in order to properly meet the needs of hospital professionals. Context-aware applications for mobile communication seem to be a valid solution, which also can be used to move parts of the workers activities over to computers. While the society outside of hospitals have embraced mobile phones (GSM/3G), have health care only shown limited use of the technology. This is mainly due to a possible interference with medical equipment. However, some earlier studies showed that the benefits from this technology could outweigh the risk of interference (Kidd, Sharratt, & Coleman, 2004; Myerson & Mitchell, 2003). This has been challenged by Van Lieshout et al., (2007), which in 2007 classified incidents of electromagnetic interference (EMI) by mobile phones (GSM/3G) on critical care medical equipment.

Several other studies have been carried out within hospital settings, with improved communication and interruption reduction in mind (Acuff, et al., 1997; Coiera & Tombs, 1998; Eisenstadt, et al., 1998; Minnick, et al., 1994 ; Sammon, Karmin, Peebles, & Seligmann, 2006; Spurck, et al., 1995). In (Coiera & Tombs, 1998) they recommend a variety of approaches to improve communication, including support and asynchronous communication with acknowledgement. Different kind of text messaging systems for hospitals has also been revealed as positive (Acuff, et al., 1997; Eisenstadt, et al., 1998), but also showed concerns for character limits, small displays, and yet another device to carry. Of course, a lot have been improved within text messaging systems and mobile devices, regarding small displays and keyboards, since these studies were carried out, may obliterate these concerns. Other studies have shown positive results when providing nursing teams with wireless phones (Spurck, et al., 1995), wearable radio transmitters (Minnick, et al., 1994), and wireless hands-free headsets which interfaces the phone system (Sammon, et al., 2006). The feedback was; quicker updates to patient information, easier to locate nursing staffs,

and reduced noise levels, but also concerns about being too available.

Personal Digital Assistants (PDA) have been used by (Munoz, Rodriguez, Favela, Martinez-Garcia, & Gonzalez, 2003) in a contextual message exchange system. This solution, developed at IMSS General Hospital in Ensenada Mexico, uses handheld devices that allow users to specify when and where they want to send messages and/or data to other colleagues. Physicians' can, for example; specify who will be the recipient of a patient's lab test result, and thereby automatically send it when it is ready. Moreover, within this system it is enabled that physicians can send messages without knowing the names of the recipients. This is done by sending the lab tests to any physician in charge for the next shift, or to the first doctor who enters a specified room the next day. In another system by Holleran et al. (2003), they used PDAs for simple text services.

PDA's with built in mobile phones, web-browsers, electronic versions of commonly used UK medical reference text books, drug interactions compendium, anatomy atlases, International Classification of Diseases – 10 (ICD-10), guidelines, and medical calculators, has been used by (Aziz et al., 2005) to enrich communication between health care workers. The purpose of this study, carried out at the Academic Surgical Unit at St. Mary's Hospital (London), was to verify whether PDAs with built-in phones, could be an efficient solution to improve communication between hospital workers. This solution was also compared with pagers. During the assessment phase, Palm Tungsten PDAs were given to a surgical team. The information used to evaluate the communication efficiency gained with these devices, was the time clinicians needed to respond to a call. After 6 weeks of tests and questionnaires filled out by the involved participants, the results were encouraging. It showed a general benefit in replacing pagers with the new advanced PDA devices. In a study described in (Mendonca et al., 2004) they used PDA's with access to patent data and with virtual white boards, which allows health care workers assigned to the same patient know about each other's work progress.

In (Skov & Høegh, 2006) they evaluated a context-aware solution based on mobile phones capable to give nurses patient information. The provided information included the nurse's daily tasks, timing constraints and positions. Moreover, the mobile devices could also be used to insert collected data during the daily work, and to view previously stored patient's information in order to monitor changes. After the development, an assessment phase was conducted. The identified problems mainly concerned the complexity of the automatic update mechanism of the devices: Some subjects did not understand how to navigate between the different interfaces and they felt forced to undergo the information displayed on the phone. Others felt confused when the system suddenly changed the interface while they were reading the information displayed. Some of the nurses also expressed uncertainties about the validity of the data previously entered into the system, and they were not sure if the information was saved properly when using the device.

Intelligent Hospital, QoS Dream Platform, is an application proposed by (Mitchell, et al., 2000). It is based on wired touch-sensitive terminals ubiquitously scattered throughout the hospital. These terminals makes is possible for clinicians, after an authentication process, to request a video call with a colleague without knowing the location of the person they want to contact. The call is routed to the nearest terminal of the recipient, who can choose to accept the call, or refuse it. The user's location is tracked by an active badge system worn by the clinicians. The application is used for: Remote consultation between doctors (e.g. discussions regarding patients and their treatments), and consultation of patient's data enabled by an event notification infrastructure that allows pushing clinical data directly into the terminal's display. The Intelligent Hospital application was built to demonstrate a real application within the QoS Dream middleware platform. This platform supports context-aware, event driven applications, and solutions based on multimedia contents where user mobility is a predominant factor. It is based on four main conceptual components: Operating system with resource management and overall control functionality, a dynamic multimedia streaming component based on the DJINN platform used to re-route video streaming contents according to the movement of the participants, an event-based infrastructure based on the HERALD architecture, and a set of APIs for building applications using the technologies within the system.

Other systems like the AwareMedia and the AwarePhone systems to Bardram et al. (Jakob E. Bardram & Hansen, 2004; Jakob E. Bardram, et al., 2006), supports context aware communication. Figure 2 shows the AWARE system architecture divided into four layers: the Client layer, the Awareness layer, the Context layer, and the Monitor and Actuator layer (Jakob E. Bardram & Hansen, 2010). It was developed in centre for Pervasive Health care at the University of Aarhus in Denmark. These systems in combination, forms a complete communication system for clinicians in a surgical ward. The tracking system is tracking clinicians in selected areas, using Bluetooth tags/ devices worn by the clinicians. The AwareMedia shows information on a number of large interactive touch screen displays scattered throughout the hospital. The information includes; location from the tracking system along with the clinician's schedule, what kind of operation is currently performed at a specific ward, status of the operation, which physicians present in the room, actual stage of the operation through dynamic colored bars, and status of the work schedule (e.g. delays or cancellations) provided by displaying visual signs and text messages. Further, in a dedicated area of the display, the application shows the status on other physicians' activities, their location, status, and future schedules. The AwarePhone system is an application running on a mobile phone (GSM/3G), which allows clinicians to call or send a message

Figure 2. The AWARE system. This is a simplified version of the AWARE overall system architecture presented in (Jakob E. Bardram & Hansen, 2010).

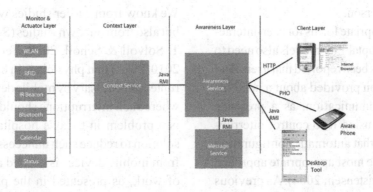

to a person in an operating theatre. Messages sent directly to the room, is shown to all people presented in that room through the AwareMedia Screen. The feedback from the use of these systems focusing on privacy issues as one of the big drawbacks deploying a system like this.

FUTURE RESEARCH DIRECTIONS

A number of studies have focused on context-sensitive systems for hospitals. Much of this work has focused on scopes not covered by this chapter, including issues related to mobile learning and privacy, accessing clinical data, or on multimedia communication at terminals with fixed locations (Mitchell, et al., 2000). The work done on context-sensitive mobile communication within hospital settings has identified some important elements of context, including location, role, delivery timing and artifact location, and user state (Munoz, et al., 2003). As presented in the previous section, this model has been applied to an instant messaging system based on PDAs enabling contact based on these contextual elements. This approach, however, requires workers to carry additional mobile devices in order to support voice and paging services, since it is not compatible with existing hospital communication infrastructure. Another issue, by our knowledge not covered in previous work on role-based contact, is how to

design interaction forms that allow users to easily switch work roles.

A variety of models for detecting interruptability have been created for stationary (Fogarty et al., 2005; Eric Horvitz & Apacible, 2003; E. Horvitz, Koch, Kadie, & Jacobs, 2002) and mobile settings (Bernstein, Vorburger, & Egger, 2005; Sawhney & Schmandt, 2000; Siewiorek, et al., 2003). In general, these models focused on office workers and social settings, and used information such as a user's calendar, interactions with computing devices, switches to determine if doors are open, accelerometers, microphones and motion sensors. Accuracy rates of approximately 80% to 90% have been reported for directly predicting interruptability and user state, such as "standing" or "walking", and social context, such as "lecture", "conversation" etc. None of these models, by our knowledge, has been explored in health care settings, and there are several factors which suggest that new health care relevant models need to be developed. First; studies on context aware communication for hospitals suggest information not included in these interruptability models, such as work role, are critical for detecting proper context in health care settings (Munoz, et al., 2003). Second; another issue is elements such as location and social relationships are inherently different within health care, and needs to be accounted for in health care appropriate models. For example, scenarios such as "visiting patients", "in surgery" etc. needs to be considered in combination with the work roles of the person initializing the contact and the contacted person.

In addition, appropriate forms for user-interaction with these interruptability models also need to be investigated. It has been reported that users tend to use the information provided about a person's availability for communication, as a presence indicator instead of using it to control interruptions. This suggests that automatic configuration of devices may be the most appropriate approach (Fogarty, Lai, & Christensen, 2004). As previous presented in this chapter, the "SenSay" context-aware mobile phone (Siewiorek, et al., 2003) uses a hybrid approach that automatically blocks calls, and also generates text messages notifying the caller that their call have been blocked. Then they are allowed to override the blocking by calling back within a predetermined number of minutes from the same phone number. This problem needs to be reinvestigated in health care settings, since there are some situations where certain calls should not be blocked (such as those for a specific role) whereas other calls may need to be restricted. Thus, the context of both the caller and person being called will need to be considered.

The use of semi-structured messages has shown to be particularly useful for work coordination (Malone, Grant, Lai, Rao, & Rosenblitt, 1987). Preliminary studies have estimated that up to 90% of mobile text-messages used by hospital workers could be met by the use of such messages (Jakob E. Bardram & Hansen, 2004). However, we have not been able to find any published work on the style and function of such messages, nor any studies that demonstrate if they would actually be adopted, or if they would have any effect during real work practice. The possibility to create automatic replies, and suggestions for replies, is also an advantage when using predefined messages, but the appropriate replies have not been studied in the context of mobile-text messaging. This could be particularly useful within health care settings, since such replies actually offers acknowledgement when a message has been read (Coiera & Tombs, 1998).

CONCLUSION

We know from earlier studies within health care, but also from our own studies (Scholl, et al., 2007; T. Solvoll & Scholl, 2008; Terje Solvoll, et al., 2010, 2012) that physicians in hospitals are interrupted unnecessary by mobile devices in situations where such interruptions should be avoided. This is a problem in today's hospital settings, and a solution to reduce such unnecessary interruptions from mobile devices is needed and wanted. A lot of work, as presented in the previous sections, has been done within the area during the years, but we cannot see that the situation has changed. We believe one of the problems applicable most of the earlier systems developed, requires both new devices and infrastructure, and/or is based on public networks like GSM/3G, which in both cases requires considerable investments. A system based on existing infrastructure and devices used in hospitals, would be much cheaper, and will probably require less training and maybe less resistance from health care workers when introduced. This is important since early studies shows that over half of medical informatics systems fail because of user and staff resistance (Anderson, 1993). We believe that; by knowing and understanding the physicians' work situation, the nature of unnecessary interruptions, and also by involving the participants in the design process, it is possible to build a system suited for their communication patterns and work situations, on top of an existing communication infrastructure, using devices already in use at hospitals. Our studies (Taxiarchis Botsis, Terje Solvoll, Jeremiah Scholl, Per Hasvold, & Gunnar Hartvigsen, 2007; Scholl, et al., 2007; T. Solvoll & Scholl, 2008; Terje Solvoll, et al., 2010) contributes to such knowledge, and is used as input in an ongoing work on designing and developing a context sensitive system for mobile communication in hospitals. Figure 3 presents the overall system architecture of the prototype developed. The system aims to reduce unnecessary interruptions from mobile devices in situations where interruptions should be avoided, like; when involved in a surgery (dressed in ster-

Figure 3. CallMeSmart overall system architecture

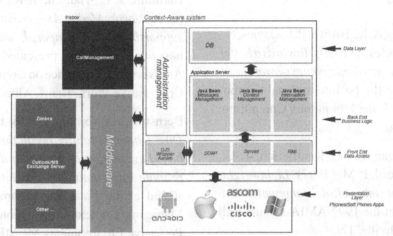

ile clothing), doing patient examination at the outpatient clinic, having serious conversations with patients/relatives in conversation rooms, etc.

The prototype focuses on context sensitive interfaces, middleware, and new interaction forms for mobile devices that support multi-modal communication in hospitals. These devices supports media such as voice services, text-messaging and paging services, in an efficient and non-interruptive manner, as well as enable support for individual and role-based contact on a single device. That is, the user only need to carry one device for both personal and role based communication, which enables other users to, for example, contact someone assigned as "on-call" duties at a specific department, even if they do not know who that person is. At the same time it aims to balance between availability and interruptions, while it enables acute calls and alarms be forced through. Currently, by our knowledge, similar devices are not generally available for internal communication systems in hospitals.

Our prototype senses the context automatically from different sensors, calendar information, work schedule, etc., to change the physicians'

availability and the phones profile, according to the collected context information.

At the same time, the caller is given feedback about the physicians' availability, and thereby it is possible for the caller to force through an emergency call, or forward the call to another physician at the same level, that is available. The system is based on the ideas from earlier studies on interruptions in combination with the ideas from (T. Botsis, et al., 2007; Terje Solvoll, Fasani, Ravuri, Tiemersma, & Hartvigsen, 2010; T. Solvoll & Scholl, 2008; Terje Solvoll et al., 2011; Talaei-Khoei, Solvoll, Ray, & Parameshwaran, 2011, 2012). A first version of the prototype is ready, and has been tested in lab-settings with physicians as test users. The tests were performed as scenarios observed from real situations. The feedback was mostly positive and has been used as input for improvement and further development of the prototype. This will be submitted as an article, titled CallMeSmart, to a journal during May 2012. The overall system architecture is presented in figure 3, and the system is ready for testing in clinical settings during May 2012, were the results is planned published in a journal, during 2013.

REFERENCES

Abowd, G. D., Dey, A. K., Brown, P. J., Davies, N., Smith, M., & Steggles, P. (1999). *Towards a better understanding of context and context-awareness.* Paper presented at the 1st International Symposium on Handheld and Ubiquitous Computing, Karlsruhe, Germany.

Acuff, R. D., Fagan, L. M., Rindfleisch, T. C., Levitt, B. J., & Ford, P. M. (1997). *Lightweight, mobile e-mail for intra-clinic communication.* Paper presented at the 1997 AMIA Annual Fall Symposium, Nashville, TN.

Anderson, J. G. (1993). *Evaluating health care information systems: Methods and applications.* Sage Publications, Inc.

Avrahami, D., Gergle, D., Hudson, S. E., & Kiesler, S. (2007). Improving the match between callers and receivers: A study on the effect of contextual information on cell phone interruptions. *Behaviour & Information Technology, 26*(3), 247–259. doi:10.1080/01449290500402338

Aziz, O., Panesar, S., Netuveli, G., Paraskeva, P., Sheikh, A., & Darzi, A. (2005). Handheld computers and the 21st century surgical team: A pilot study. *BMC Medical Informatics and Decision Making, 5*(1), 28. doi:10.1186/1472-6947-5-28

Bardram, J. E., & Hansen, T. R. (2004). *The AWARE architecture: Supporting context-mediated social awareness in mobile cooperation.* Paper presented at the 2004 ACM Conference on Computer Supported Cooperative Work, Chicago, Illinois, USA.

Bardram, J. E., & Hansen, T. R. (2010). Context-based workplace awareness. *Computer Supported Cooperative Work, 19*(2), 105–138. doi:10.1007/s10606-010-9110-2

Bardram, J. E., Hansen, T. R., & Soegaard, M. (2006). *AwareMedia: A shared interactive display supporting social, temporal, and spatial awareness in surgery.* Paper presented at the 2006 20th Anniversary Conference on Computer Supported Cooperative Work, Banff, Alberta, Canada.

Bernstein, A., Vorburger, P., & Egger, P. (2005). *Direct interruptablity prediction and scenario-based evaluation of wearable devices: Towards reliable interruptability predictions.* Paper presented at the First International Workshop on Managing Context Information in Mobile and Pervasive Environments MCMP-05.

Bisgaard, J. J., Heise, M., & Steffensen, C. (2004). *How is context and context-awareness defined and applied? A survey of context-awareness* (pp. 31–40). Department of Computer Science, Aalborg University.

Blum, N. J., & Lieu, T. A. (1992). Interrupted care. The effects of paging on pediatric resident activities. *American Journal of Diseases of Children, 146*(7), 806–808. doi:doi:10.1001/archpedi.146.7.806

Botsis, T., Solvoll, T., Scholl, J., Hasvold, P., & Hartvigsen, G. (2007). Context-aware systems for mobile communication in healthcare - A user oriented approach. *Proceedings of the 7th WSEAS International Conference on Applied Informatics and Communications*, (pp. 69-74).

Bradner, E., Kellogg, W. A., & Erickson, T. (1999). *The adoption and use of BABBLE: A field study of chat in the workplace.* Paper presented at the Sixth European Conference on Computer Supported Cooperative Work, Copenghagen, Denmark.

Coiera, E. (2000). When conversation is better than computation. *Journal of the American Medical Informatics Association, 7*(3), 277–286. doi:10.1136/jamia.2000.0070277

Coiera, E., & Tombs, V. (1998). Communication behaviours in a hospital setting: An observational study. *British Medical Journal, 316*(7132), 673–676. doi:10.1136/bmj.316.7132.673

Eisenstadt, S. A., Wagner, M. M., Hogan, W. R., Pankaskie, M. C., Tsui, F. C., & Wilbright, W. (1998). Mobile workers in healthcare and their information needs: Are 2-way pagers the answer? *Proceedings of the AMIA Symposium,* (pp. 135–139).

Fogarty, J., Hudson, S. E., Atkeson, C. G., Avrahami, D., Forlizzi, J., & Kiesler, S. (2005). Predicting human interruptibility with sensors. *ACM Transactions on Computer-Human Interaction, 12*(1), 119–146. doi:10.1145/1057237.1057243

Fogarty, J., Lai, J., & Christensen, J. (2004). Presence versus availability: The design and evaluation of a context-aware communication client. *International Journal of Human-Computer Studies, 61*(3), 299–317. doi:10.1016/j.ijhcs.2003.12.016

Grudin, J. (1994). Groupware and social dynamics: Eight challenges for developers. *Communications of the ACM, 37*(1), 92–105. doi:10.1145/175222.175230

Hersh, W., Helfand, M., Wallace, J., Kraemer, D., Patterson, P., & Shapiro, S. (2002). A systematic review of the efficacy of telemedicine for making diagnostic and management decisions. *Journal of Telemedicine and Telecare, 8*(4), 197–209. doi:10.1258/135763302320272167

Holleran, K., Pappas, J., Lou, H., Rubalcaba, P., Lee, R., Clay, S., et al. (2003). Mobile technology in a clinical setting. *AMIA Annual Symposium Proceedings,* 2003.

Horvitz, E., & Apacible, J. (2003). *Learning and reasoning about interruption.* Paper presented at the 5th International Conference on Multimodal Interfaces, Vancouver, British Columbia, Canada.

Horvitz, E., Koch, P., Kadie, C. M., & Jacobs, A. (2002). *Coordinate: Probabilistic forecasting of presence and availability.* Paper presented at the 18th Conference in Uncertainty in Artificial Intelligence (UAI'02).

Hristova, A. (2008). *Conceptualization and design of a context-aware platform for user centric applications. Master of Science in Communication Technology Master.* Trondheim: Norwegian University of Science and Technology.

Katz, M. H., & Schroeder, S. A. (1988). The sounds of the hospital. Paging patterns in three teaching hospitals. *The New England Journal of Medicine, 319*(24), 1585–1589. doi:10.1056/NEJM198812153192406

Khalil, A., & Connelly, K. (2005). Improving cell phone awareness by using calendar information. *Human-Computer Interaction - INTERACT 2005* (pp. 588-600).

Khalil, A., & Connelly, K. (2006). *Context-aware telephony: Privacy preferences and sharing patterns.* Paper presented at the CSCW'06, Banff, Alberta, Canada.

Kidd, A. G., Sharratt, C., & Coleman, J. (2004). Mobile communication regulations updated: How safely are doctors' telephones used? *Quality & Safety in Health Care, 13*(6), 478. doi:10.1136/qhc.13.6.478

Lieberman, H., & Selker, T. (2000). Out of context: Computer systems that adapt to, and learn from, context. *IBM Systems Journal, 39*(3, 4), 617-632. doi: 10.1147/sj.393.0617

Malone, T. W., Grant, K. R., Lai, K.-Y., Rao, R., & Rosenblitt, D. (1987). Semistructured messages are surprisingly useful for computer-supported coordination. *ACM Transactions on Information Systems, 5*(2), 115–131. doi:10.1145/27636.27637

Marmasse, N., Schmandt, C., & Spectre, D. (2004). WatchMe: Communication and awareness between members of a closely-knit group. *UbiComp 2004: Ubiquitous Computing* (pp. 214-231).

Mendonca, E., A., Chen, E., S., Stetson, P., D., McKnight, L. K., Lei, J., & Cimino, J. J. (2004). Approach to mobile information and communication for health care. *International Journal of Medical Informatics, 73*(7), 631–638. doi:10.1016/j.ijmedinf.2004.04.013

Milewski, A., & Smith, T. (2000). *Providing presence cues to telephone users.* Paper presented at the CSCW '00: 2000 ACM Conference on Computer Supported Cooperative Work.

Minnick, A., Pischke-Winn, K., & Sterk, M. B. (1994). Introducing a two-way wireless communication system. *Nursing Management, 25*(7), 42–47. doi:10.1097/00006247-199407000-00011

Mitchell, S., Spiteri, M. D., Bates, J., & Coulouris, G. (2000). *Context-aware multimedia computing in the intelligent hospital.* Paper presented at the 9th Workshop on ACM SIGOPS European Workshop: Beyond the PC: New Challenges for the Operating System, Kolding, Denmark.

Mizzaro, S., Nazzi, E., & Vassena, L. (2008). *Retrieval of context-aware applications on mobile devices: how to evaluate?* Paper presented at the Second International Symposium on Information Interaction in Context, London, United Kingdom.

Munoz, M. A., Rodriguez, M., Favela, J., Martinez-Garcia, A. I., & Gonzalez, V. M. (2003). Context-aware mobile communication in hospitals. *Computer, 36*(9), 38. doi:10.1109/MC.2003.1231193

Myerson, S. G., & Mitchell, A. R. J. (2003). Mobile phones in hospitals. *British Medical Journal, 326*(7387), 460–461. doi:10.1136/bmj.326.7387.460

Nelson, L., Bly, S., & Sokoler, T. (2001). *Quiet calls: Talking silently on mobile phones.* Paper presented at the CHI '01: SIGCHI Conference on Human Factors in Computing Systems.

Parker, J., & Coiera, E. (2000). Improving clinical communication: A view from psychology. *Journal of the American Medical Informatics Association, 7*(5), 453–461. doi:10.1136/jamia.2000.0070453

Pedersen, E. R. (2001). *Calls.calm: Enabling caller and callee to collaborate.* Paper presented at the CHI '01 Extended Abstracts on Human Factors in Computing Systems, Seattle, Washington.

Sammon, M. J., Karmin, L. S. B., Peebles, E., & Seligmann, D. D. (2006, 2006-09-29). *MACCS: Enabling communications for mobile workers within healthcare environments.* Paper presented at the MobileHCI'06.

Sawhney, N., & Schmandt, C. (2000). Nomadic radio: speech and audio interaction for contextual messaging in nomadic environments. *ACM Transactions on Computer-Human Interaction, 7*(3), 353–383. doi:10.1145/355324.355327

Schilit, B., Adams, N., & Want, R. (1994). *Context-aware computing applications.* Paper presented at the 1994 Workshop on Mobile Computing Systems and Applications.

Schmidt, A., Takaluoma, A., & Mäntyjärvi, J. (2000). Context-aware telephony over WAP. *Personal and Ubiquitous Computing, 4*(4), 225–229.

Scholl, J., Hasvold, P., Henriksen, E., & Ellingsen, G. (2007). *Managing communication availability and interruptions: A study of mobile communication in an oncology department* (pp. 234–250). Pervasive Computing. doi:10.1007/978-3-540-72037-9_14

Siewiorek, D., Smailagic, A., Furukawa, J., Krause, A., Moraveji, N., Reiger, K., et al. (2003). SenSay: A context-aware mobile phone. *Proceedings of the Seventh IEEE International Symposium on Wearable Computers, 2003.*

Skov, B., & Høegh, T. (2006). Supporting information access in a hospital ward by a context-aware mobile electronic patient record. *Personal and Ubiquitous Computing, 10*(4), 205–214. doi:10.1007/s00779-005-0049-0

Solvoll, T., Fasani, S., Ravuri, A. B., Tiemersma, A., & Hartvigsen, G. (2010, August 23-24, 2010). *Evaluation of an Ascom/trixbox system for context sensitive communication in hospitals.* Paper presented at the 8th Scandinavian Conference on Health Informatics, Copenhagen.

Solvoll, T., & Scholl, J. (2008). Strategies to reduce interruptions from mobile communication systems in surgical wards. *Journal of Telemedicine and Telecare, 14*(7), 389–392. doi:10.1258/jtt.2008.007015

Solvoll, T., Scholl, J., & Hartvigsen, G. (2010). Physicians interrupted by mobile devices – Relations between devices, roles and duties. *Studies in Health Technology and Informatics, 160,* 1365.

Solvoll, T., Scholl, J., & Hartvigsen, G. (2012). *Physicians interrupted by mobile devices in hospitals – Understanding the interaction between devices, roles and duties.* Unpublished work.

Solvoll, T., Tiemersma, A., Kerbage, E., Fasani, S., Ravuri, A. B., & Hartvigsen, G. (2011). Context-sensitive communication in hospitals: A user interface evaluation and redesign of Ascom wireless IP-DECT phones. *eTELEMED 2011, The Third International Conference on eHealth, Telemedicine, and Social Medicine,* Gosier, Guadeloupe, France (pp. 37–46).

Spurck, P. A., Mohr, M. L., Seroka, A. M., & Stoner, M. (1995). The impact of a wireless telecommunication system on time efficiency. *The Journal of Nursing Administration, 25*(6), 21–26. doi:10.1097/00005110-199506000-00007

Talaei-Khoei, A., Solvoll, T., Ray, P., & Parameshwaran, N. (2011). Policy-based awareness management (PAM): Case study of a wireless communication system at a hospital. *Journal of Systems and Software, 84*(10), 1791–1805. doi:10.1016/j.jss.2011.05.024

Talaei-Khoei, A., Solvoll, T., Ray, P., & Parameshwaran, N. (2012). Maintaining awareness using policies: Enabling agents to identify relevance of information. *Journal of Computer and System Sciences, 78*(1), 370–391. doi:10.1016/j.jcss.2011.05.013

Tang, J. C., Yankelovich, N., Begole, J., Kleek, M. V., Li, F., & Bhalodia, J. (2001). *ConNexus to awarenex: Extending awareness to mobile users.* Paper presented at the SIGCHI Conference on Human Factors in Computing Systems, Seattle, Washington, United States.

van Lieshout, E., van der Veer, S., Hensbroek, R., Korevaar, J., Vroom, M., & Schultz, M. (2007). Interference by new-generation mobile phones on critical care medical equipment. *Critical Care (London, England), 11*(5), R98. doi:10.1186/cc6115

Chapter 15

Thermo–Chemical Convection in Planetary Mantles:
Advection Methods and Magma Ocean Overturn Simulations

Ana-Catalina Plesa
German Aerospace Center (DLR), Germany & Westfälische Wilhelms-Universität Münster, Germany

Nicola Tosi
Technical University Berlin, Germany & German Aerospace Center (DLR), Germany

Christian Hüttig
Hampton University, USA

ABSTRACT

Thermo-chemical convection is the primary process that controls the large-scale dynamics of the mantle of the Earth and terrestrial planets. Its numerical simulation is one the principal tools for exploiting the constraints posed by geological and geochemical surface observations performed by planetary spacecrafts. In the present work, the authors discuss the modeling of active compositional fields in the framework of solid-state mantle convection using the cylindrical/spherical code Gaia. They compare an Eulerian method based on double-diffusive convection against a Lagrangian, particle-based method. Through a series of increasingly complex benchmark tests, the authors show the superiority of the particle method when it comes to model the advection of compositional interfaces with sharp density and viscosity contrasts. They finally apply this technique to simulate the Rayleigh-Taylor overturn of the Mars' and Mercury's primordial magma oceans.

INTRODUCTION

Our knowledge about planetary systems and bodies has significantly improved over the last 50 years thanks to the vast amount of information provided by Earth-based and space telescopes, orbiter and lander missions made possible by the efforts of national space agencies such as NASA, ESA, JAXA, etc. However, most data available have been derived from surface observations which offer an indirect and limited view of the deep interior and can thus provide only relatively poor constraints on the dynamics and thermal history of planetary bodies. Our main understanding

DOI: 10.4018/978-1-4666-2190-9.ch015

of the fluid dynamics of planetary mantles stems from laboratory experiments of convection and, in particular, from computer simulations. On the one hand, convection experiments are restricted to a small parameter range, not always relevant for planetary evolution. On the other hand, with the remarkable increase of computational power over the past years, numerical simulations have become the most powerful tool to model the temporal evolution of mantle flow with complex rheologies.

At the extreme conditions of planetary interiors, pressure- and temperature-activated deformation processes occurring at atomic level (e.g. Karato, 2008) allow rocks to flow like highly viscous fluids over geological time-scales ($\sim 10^6$ years and longer). The slow creep of the silicate materials that make up the mantle of terrestrial planets (i.e. Mercury, Venus, the Earth and Mars) is driven by a combination of thermal and compositional buoyancy. On the one hand, the primordial heat accumulated after accretion and core formation and the heat released by the decay of radiogenic isotopes are transported from the interior to the surface by thermal convection. This process involves the transfer of heat both via diffusion, which occurs mainly across thermal boundary layers, and advection due to fluid motion in the bulk of the mantle. On the other hand, density anomalies of non-thermal origin associated with chemical (i.e. compositional) heterogeneities provide an additional source of buoyancy that actively contributes to the transport of energy and mass.

Compositional heterogeneity in the mantle occurs at all spatial scales. It is an important factor in controlling the dynamics of regional- to medium-scale processes such as the flow in magma chambers (Verhoeven & Schmalzl, 2009), the rise of salt diapirs in sedimentary basins (Chemia et al., 2008), the dynamics of partial melt in the upper mantle (Fraeman & Korenaga, 2010), the subduction of lithospheric plates (Schmeling et al., 2008) or the dynamics of multi-component plumes (Samuel & Farnetani, 2003). It can also

contribute to the first order to shape the global-scale mantle circulation. Atop the core-mantle boundary (CMB) of the Earth, for example, seismic evidence indicates the existence of two broad antipodal regions characterized by higher than average density (Ishii & Tromp, 2004), which are interpreted as ascending thermo-chemical plumes (Tan & Gurnis, 2007) that represent a plausible source for hot-spots volcanism (Dechamps et al., 2011). Aside Earth, chemical heterogeneities are believed to play an essential role also in the evolution of other terrestrial bodies. Geochemical analysis of the so-called SNC meteorites suggests the existence of separate chemical reservoirs in the mantle of Mars, which have been preserved over the entire planetary evolution (Papike et al., 2009). The composition of some glasses on the Moon also suggests the migration of melt through a chemically heterogeneous mantle (Elkins-Tanton et al., 2011). On Mercury, the poor-iron oxide surface silicates and the high metallic iron fraction of the bulk planet hint at a complex thermo-chemical history of the mantle (Brown & Elkins-Tanton, 2009). Also, the fractional crystallization of a so-called magma ocean (see Section "Magma ocean cumulate overturn simulations"), which may take place early in the evolution of a terrestrial planet (e.g. Solomatov, 2007), produces a gravitationally unstable density stratification that can lead to a rapid overturn of the whole mantle and influence the onset and evolution of thermal convection (e.g. Elkins-Tanton et al., 2005; Brown & Elkins-Tanton, 2009).

In its simplest form, modeling of compositional heterogeneities requires the solution of the transport equation for a scalar, non-reactive field C:

$$\frac{\partial C}{\partial t} + \boldsymbol{v} \cdot \nabla C = 0 \qquad (1)$$

where t is the time and $\boldsymbol{v}$ a given velocity field. The accurate solution of Equation (1) is of primary importance especially if C is associated with buoyancy and/or rheological (i.e. viscosity) variations, as these enter the linear momentum conservation and affect to the first order the dynamics of the system (see Section "Model description"). Numerical methods for the solution of Equation (1) fall in two main categories. They are based either on a fixed computational grid (Eulerian methods) or on evolving grids or moving particles (Lagrangian methods).

Grid-based (GB) methods are a practical choice when it comes to model thermo-chemical convection since the same scheme can be adopted to discretize both Equation (1) and the energy conservation Equation (3) (see Section "Model description"). Low-order methods such as the classical up-wind scheme and its numerous extensions (e.g. LeVeque, 2004) are a viable choice but are prone to numerical diffusion and characterized by strict stability conditions that pose severe limits to the time-stepping. An alternative, which is also adopted in this work, is to add some amount of artificial diffusion to Equation (1) in order to make the field C smoother and employ correcting filters to suppress spurious oscillations (Lenardic & Kaula, 1993). More recent, high-order methods, such as essentially non-oscillatory (ENO) or weighted essentially non-oscillatory (WENO) schemes (e.g. Liu et al., 1994) can be extremely accurate but are also computationally demanding and difficult to implement on unstructured grids (Wolf & Azevedo, 2007).

As far as Lagrangian methods are concerned, the particle-in-cell (PIC) technique (see Section "Particle-in-cell advection") is probably the most widely used in geodynamics because of its accuracy and conceptual simplicity (e.g. van Keken et al., 1997; Tackley & King, 2003). Distinct advantages of this approach are the nearly negligible numerical diffusion and the possibility to resolve sub-grid structures. Nevertheless, in order to prevent the emergence of spurious noise, a relatively large number of particles per cell must be used, which results in markedly longer computational times with respect to simple Eulerian schemes, in particular for 3D simulations. Currently, beside Gaia, only a handful of numerical codes are capable to handle high-resolution simulations with particles in a 3D geometry. Notable examples in this sense are the recent models that employ the codes CitcomS (Tan et al., 2011) and StagYY (Nakagawa & Tackley, 2011; Dechamps et al., 2011) which helped to elucidate some key aspects of the role of chemical heterogeneities in shaping the dynamics of the Earth's lowermost mantle. Also, in the context of planetary mantle convection, CitcomS was recently employed to model self-consistently the formation of the Tharsis volcanic province and the so-called crustal dichotomy on Mars as a consequence of chemical differentiation due to partial melting (Šramek & Zhong, 2012). We refer the reader to the chapter by Noack and Tosi (this volume) for an up-to-date discussion on the state of the art of numerical modeling in geodynamics.

In this chapter, we model active compositional fields and compare the performance and accuracy of an Eulerian scheme based on double-diffusive convection against a PIC approach in solving a series of increasingly complex tests in a 2D cylindrical and 3D spherical geometry. We start introducing the set of equations governing thermo-chemical convection in planetary mantles and the numerical methods employed here to solve them. We then show different numerical tests: from the simple advection of a sharp interface in a rotational field to the entrainment of a dense layer by thermal convection. We finally apply the PIC approach to model the overturn of the primordial magma oceans of Mars and Mercury. The chapter is concluded by a summary of the results obtained and a discussion on possible future directions for the modeling of compositional fields in geodynamics.

MODEL DESCRIPTION

Governing Equations and Numerical Method

In first approximation, the mantle of terrestrial planets can be modeled as a highly viscous fluid heated from below because of the heat flowing out of the core, and from within, because of the decay of radiogenic isotopes. This task requires the solution of the full set of partial differential equations governing the motion and heat transfer in creeping (i.e. highly viscous) fluids (e.g. Landau & Lifshitz, 1987). To this end, we use the finite-volume code Gaia in 3D spherical (Hüttig & Stemmer, 2008a; Hüttig & Stemmer, 2008b) and 2D cylindrical geometry (Plesa, 2011) to perform numerical simulations of thermo-chemical mantle convection. In addition to the Equation (1) for the conservation of the composition, Gaia solves the conservation equations of mass, momentum and thermal energy (e.g. Schubert, 2001). Assuming an incompressible, Boussinesq fluid with Newtonian rheology and infinite Prandtl number, they respectively read:

$$\nabla \cdot \boldsymbol{v} = 0 \tag{2}$$

$$-\nabla p + \nabla \cdot (\eta(\nabla \boldsymbol{v} + (\nabla \boldsymbol{v})^T)) = (RaT - Ra_C C)\boldsymbol{e}_r \tag{3}$$

$$\frac{\partial T}{\partial t} + \boldsymbol{v} \cdot \nabla T = \nabla^2 T + \frac{Ra_Q}{Ra} \tag{4}$$

Symbols, parameters and scaling relations used in Equations (2)-(4) are explained in Table 1. The continuity Equation (2) describes the conservation of mass for an incompressible fluid. In the linear momentum Equation (3), viscous forces are instantaneously balanced by thermal and compositional buoyancy. In the thermal energy Equation (4), heat advection is balanced by heat diffusion and internal heating due to radioactive sources.

Gaia is based on a finite volume formulation with second-order accuracy in space and time. The space is discretized with a fixed grid based on a Voronoi tessellation of the 2D or 3D spherical shell (Hüttig & Stemmer, 2008b); both structured and unstructured grids can be used with Gaia. Following the well-known Courant-Friedrichs-Lewy (CFL) criterion, the time stepping *Δt*

is chosen in an adaptive way according to the maximum of velocity field v_{max}, the minimal mesh size Δx_{min} and the Courant number *Co*:

$$\Delta t = Co \frac{\Delta x_{min}}{v_{max}} \tag{5}$$

With a Courant number of 1, for a given velocity field, a fluid particle cannot travel beyond a neighboring grid cell in one time step. This value often represents a strict condition that must be met to satisfy stability criteria of several advection algorithms (e.g. LeVeque, 2004). In practice, to limit numerical diffusion and ensure a high accuracy, the Courant number is chosen smaller than unity no matter whether an Eulerian or Lagrangian advection method is used.

Gaia uses the SIMPLE algorithm (Patankar, 1980) to enforce the incompressibility constraint (2), a fully implicit three-levels time-scheme (Harder & Hansen, 2005) to solve the advection-diffusion Equation (4) and a modified-version of Equation (1) containing a diffusive term (see Equation (6) in the Section "Grid-based advection with filtering"). The systems of linear equations resulting from the discretization of Equations (1)-(4) are solved with the bi-conjugate gradient stabilized algorithm combined with a Jacobi preconditioner (e.g. Saad, 1996).

Gaia is written in C++, does not rely on external libraries and uses its own routines for mesh generation and matrix inversion. It is parallelized via domain decomposition using the message passing interface (MPI). A detailed description of the algorithms can be found in Hüttig and Stemmer (2008b).

Grid-Based Advection with Filtering

In the framework of thermal convection, a straightforward approach to solve for the advection of a compositional field is to use the same numerical method employed for the solution of Equation (4).

Table 1. Field variables, non-dimensional numbers and parameters with the corresponding scaling and units

Symbol	Description	Scaling /Unit
x	Position	D
v	Velocity	κ_0/D
η	Viscosity	η_0
p	Dynamic pressure	$\kappa_0\eta_0/D^2$
T	Temperature	ΔT
C	Composition	$\Delta\rho$
t	Time	D^2/κ_0
$Ra=\rho_0\alpha_0 g_0\Delta TD^3/\kappa_0\eta_0$	Thermal Rayleigh number	-
$Ra_Q=\rho^2_0\alpha_0 g_0 Q_0 D^5/\kappa_0\eta_0$	Internal heat sources Rayleigh number	-
$Ra_C=\Delta\rho_0 g_0 D^3/\kappa_0\eta_0$	Compositional Rayleigh number	-
$Le=\kappa_0/\lambda_0$	Lewis number	-
D	Mantle thickness	km
ΔT	Temperature drop across the mantle	K
$\Delta\rho$	Compositional density contrast	kg/m^3
ρ_0	Reference density	kg/m^3
η_0	Reference viscosity	Pa s
α_0	Reference thermal expansivity	1/K
g_0	Reference gravity acceleration	m/s^2
κ_0	Reference thermal diffusivity	m^2/s
λ_0	Chemical diffusivity	m^2/s
Q_0	Radiogenic heat production	W/kg

Instead of solving Equation (1) directly, one can add a diffusion term to avoid numerical instabilities and oscillations. The strength of the diffusive term is controlled by the Lewis number (Le):

$$\frac{\partial C}{\partial t} + v \cdot \nabla C = \frac{1}{Le}\nabla^2 C \qquad (6)$$

The choice of an optimal value for Le is somewhat problem-dependent and must be done carefully. On the one hand, a small Lewis number will induce excessive smoothing in regions where C varies sharply. On the other hand, too large values of Le will lead to strong differences between matrix elements, causing convergence problems. Another important issue are spurious undershoot and overshoot features, which are common when solving advection-diffusion equations with a very small diffusivity (i.e. a large Le). To suppress these unphysical oscillations, Lenardic and Kaula (1993) devised a filtering scheme which is also employed here (LK filter hereafter). First, the volume-averaged composition is computed. All under- and overshooting values are then corrected and a new volume-averaged composition is obtained. The difference between the two average compositions is then applied as a correction over the regions not affected by spurious oscillations in order to guarantee conservativeness of the scheme. Figure 1 illustrates the basic idea behind this filtering scheme.

One drawback of the filter, which however is irrelevant for our present purposes, is that it works only for conservative fields. As soon as a field changes over time, for example in the presence of sources or sinks, the method will produce erroneous results as it is no longer possible to identify the maximum and minimum spurious values.

Particle-in-Cell Advection

As discussed in the introductory section, the PIC method is a popular alternative to GB schemes. It has the distinct advantage of being essentially free of numerical diffusion and able to trace sub-grid structures. Moreover, particles can be the carriers of an arbitrary large number of different physical properties (density, viscosity, thermal conductivity, thermal expansivity, etc.). This greatly facilitates modeling of multi-material systems (e.g. Gerya & Yuen, 2007), thereby avoiding the need to solve a different advection equation for each material component, which is instead necessary if Eulerian schemes are employed.

Massless particles are first distributed within each domain cell. The initial conditions can be set directly on the particles by assigning to each of them a given value of C or, alternatively, C can

Figure 1. Filtering approach proposed by Lenardic and Kaula (1993). The composition field C is assumed to vary between 0 and 1. Grid points with C-values lower than 0 and greater than 1 are set to 0 and 1, respectively (red). C_{min} and C_{max} are the minimum and maximum spurious values observed. Grid points whose C-value is lower than $|C_{min}|$ or greater than $(2-C_{max})$ are also set to 0 and 1, respectively (blue). The C-value of all grid points that do not exhibit spurious oscillations (green) is then corrected according to the difference between the original average composition and that computed after the resetting of the spurious values.

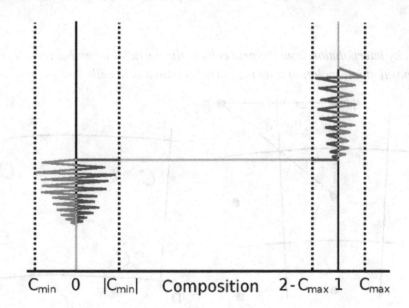

be first defined on the grid and then interpolated on the particles. After solving the momentum Equation (3), particles are advected by solving a trajectory equation:

$$\frac{dx_p}{dt} = v_p \qquad (7)$$

where x_p is the position vector of a particle with velocity v_p. After computing the new position x_p, a continuous C-field is reconstructed at grid level by employing an appropriate averaging scheme (e.g. Schmeling et al., 2008). To solve Equation (7), we use a Runge-Kutta integrator with first-order accuracy in time and fourth-order in space (Figure 2). In order to determine v_p, the velocity field, which is known only at grid level, must be interpolated at the location x_p. To this end, using barycentric coordinates, the particle is first located in its corresponding cell (Figure 2a). Its velocity is then calculated by averaging the velocities of the neighbouring cells with the corresponding barycentric weights:

$$v_p = \sum_{i=1}^{N_c} v_i d_i \qquad (8)$$

where N_c is the number of cell values used. The interpolation of the advected concentration from particles onto the grid points (Figure 2b) is simply obtained by locating all the N_p particles present in a given cell and interpolating their C-values at the cell center as follows:

$$C_i = \sum_{k=1}^{N_p} C_k d_k \qquad (9)$$

Note that in order to avoid the emergence of spurious statistical noise, about ten to a few tens of particles per grid cell are typically used. This can render the number of interpolations from particles to the grid and vice versa extremely large, which results in proportionally high computational costs. Also, at almost all supercomputing centers, the computational time allocated for a single run is usually limited. Therefore, in order to restart a simulation, snapshots must be written for each computational core every given number of time-steps. Storing particles values and positions in the snapshots does not result in a loss of accuracy upon restart since the exact state of the simulation can be restored. However, the size of the snapshots depends on the grid size and number of particles. Especially for high-resolution 3D simulations

Figure 2. a) Velocity interpolation from the grid cells to the particles using barycentric coordinates as weights. b) Composition interpolation from the particles onto a grid cell.

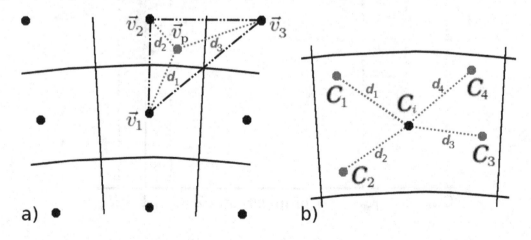

such as those described later (see section "Magma ocean cumulate overturn simulations"), the storage of all particles positions and physical properties can easily reach a few Gbyte. Typically, for a time-dependent simulation, around one to a few hundred time-steps need to be stored. Storing (and transferring) a few hundred Gbyte of data for a single simulation is clearly impractical. Therefore, at the cost of some loss of accuracy, an alternative is to avoid storing of the particles and to use Equation (7) to interpolate the composition from the grid back onto particles when a restart is done.

For 3D simulations employing particles, memory allocation also represents an important issue. In fact, upon initialization of the compositional field, particles are first loaded by a single computational core and then, if the simulation is run in parallel, redistributed among the remaining cores according to particles position. The maximum number of particles that can be used in a simulation is thus limited by the amount of memory that can be allocated for a single core. In a 3D run at medium to high resolution, it is not unusual to employ $\sim 10^7$-10^8 particles, which would demand ≥ 1-10 Gbyte of allocatable memory for a single core, a requirement which often cannot be met even at large computational facilities.

RESULTS

Benchmark Tests in 2D Cylindrical Geometry

In this section we present a series of benchmark tests performed using either the GB method with the filter correction or the PIC method. Two immiscible creeping fluids of different densities (i.e. compositions) and, in some cases, different viscosities, are used for the simulations. To compare the two advection methods, the following output quantities are used:

- Time-evolution of the root mean square (RMS) velocity
$$v_{rms} = \frac{1}{V} \int_V (v_x^2 + v_y^2 + v_z^2)^{1/2} dV,$$
- Radial or lateral profiles of the composition,
- Time-evolution of the entrainment e of one fluid above a certain depth d_e:
$e = \int_{V_{d_e}} C dV,$ where V_{de} is the domain volume above d_e.

The computational domain is a 2D cylindrical shell with a non-dimensional inner radius of 1.0 and an outer radius of 2.0 with free-slip velocity boundary conditions, unless explicitly stated. The mesh resolution varies among the tests. Since a projected grid with quadratic cells is used, the overall amount of grid points will be given as the number of radial shells N_s multiplied by the number of grid cells per shell N_{gs}, i.e. $N_s \times N_{gs}$.

Advection of a Sharp Interface

In this example, we compare the accuracy of the GB and PIC methods in advecting a sharp interface. We consider an isoviscous medium with a composition $C=0$ and advect a block with $C=1$ in a purely rotational velocity field (Figure 3). Figure 3a shows the initial setup of the composition. The momentum and energy equations are turned off and a constant angular velocity is set. As the block rotates, we analyze its deformation after completing several revolutions. In this test, high accuracy is obtained if the shape of the block is preserved during the rotations. For the GB method we choose $Le=10^{12}$ to minimize chemical diffusion. The LK filter is used to reduce overshoot and undershoot values in the composition. For the PIC solution we used 10 particles per cell. In both cases the Courant number is set to 0.1 and 64×584 grid points are used. Figure 3b shows lateral cross-section profiles of the block at the beginning and after one and two revolutions using both the GB and PIC methods.

The profiles in Figure 3b show that, for the PIC solution, the shape of the block is well preserved and exhibits minimal deformation. Other is the case when using the GB approach. Here, in spite of a Lewis number of 10^{12}, numerical diffusion cannot be suppressed and an increasing smoothing of the sides of the block is observed. As far as the computational time is concerned, the GB method is about two times faster than the PIC approach.

Sinking of a Viscous Cylinder

In the following test, we simulate the sinking of a dense cylinder in a less dense medium (Figure 4). The cylinder has $C=1$ and in the surrounding medium $C=0$. Differently from the previous test, only the energy equation is turned off, while the momentum and mass conservation are solved to compute the flow field. The compositional Rayleigh number Ra_C is set to 1. As the cylinder sinks through the less dense medium, it can deform or not depending on its viscosity contrast with respect to the surroundings. Figure 4a shows a case where the cylinder and the surrounding medium have the same viscosity whereas in Figure 4b the cylinder

is 100 times more viscous. The viscosity contrast is set using the composition values, i.e.

$$\eta = \exp(\log(\Delta\eta_C)C) \qquad (10)$$

where η is the viscosity and $\Delta\eta_c$ is the viscosity contrast (100 in this case). The tests were performed using both GB and PIC methods with 128 × 1188 computational grid points. For the GB method we used a Lewis number of 10^5, the LK filter and a Courant number of 10^{-2}. Compared to the previous test, the Lewis number is smaller in order to avoid strong oscillations in the compositional field. In fact, using a higher Le in conjunction with the fact that, as the composition, the velocity field is also highly localized in the domain, leads to a dramatic worsening of the conditioning of the C-field matrix. For the PIC calculation, we used 30 particles per cell (i.e $\sim 4.4 \times 10^6$ particles in the entire domain) and a Courant number of 0.3.

In the isoviscous case, a large deformation takes place. The cylinder does not preserve its initial shape and deforms into a drop-like structure. In Figure 4c we show the radial profiles of the composition for the isoviscous case at different time steps during the simulation. In the GB case, numerical diffusion can be clearly observed

Figure 3. Advection of a sharp interface: a) initial distribution of the composition, b) shape profiles at the initial time-step (solid line), after one revolution (dotted lines) and after two revolutions (dashed-dotted lines) obtained using the PIC method (black lines) and the GB approach (gray lines).

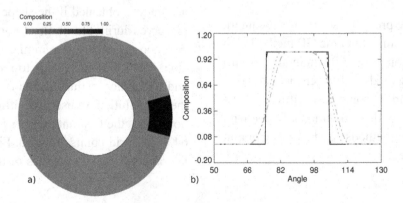

Figure 4. Sinking cylinder test: a) composition snapshot for the isoviscous case using the PIC method at time t=49.7; c) radial profiles for the composition through the middle of the sinking cylinder at time t=5.1 (solid lines), 49.7 (dotted lines), and 174.5 (dashed-dotted lines) for PIC approach (black lines) and GB approach (gray lines); e) RMS velocity over time for PIC method (black line) and GB method (gray line); b) composition snapshot for the non-isoviscous case using the PIC approach at time t=197; d) radial profiles for the composition at time t=71 (solid lines), 197 (dotted lines), and 276 (dashed-dotted lines) for PIC method (black lines) and GB method (gray lines); f) RMS velocity over time for PIC method (black lines) and GB method (gray lines).

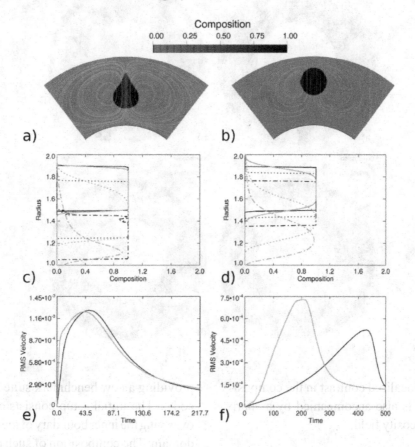

through the smoother transition in the compositional values compared to the PIC run. Figure 4e shows a relatively good agreement in the RMS velocity over time between the two methods.

By setting a viscosity contrast of two orders of magnitude or higher between the cylinder and the surrounding material, deformation does no longer occur and the cylinder sinks as if it were solid with a velocity that depends solely on the viscosity of the surrounding medium (Gerya, 2010). In this case however, problems arise when

using the GB method. Since the viscosity contrast is set using the composition values, when numerical diffusion takes place, the viscosity contrast between the cylinder and the surrounding medium cannot be maintained. Compared to the particle-based method, strong deformation takes place as Figure 4d clearly shows. As a consequence, also the cylinder's velocity increases, so that the two time-series of the RMS velocity differ considerably (Figure 4f). This test clearly exemplifies the inadequacy of the GB method in treating the

Figure 5. Rayleigh-Taylor instability benchmark: a) initial setup where the light layer (blue) is at the bottom of the domain, the heavy layer (red) at the top and a small perturbation is applied on the interface between the layers; b) composition field at time t=2000 using the GB approach with Le=10⁶; c) composition field at time t=2000 using the GB approach with Le=10¹²; d) composition field at time t=2000 using the PIC method.

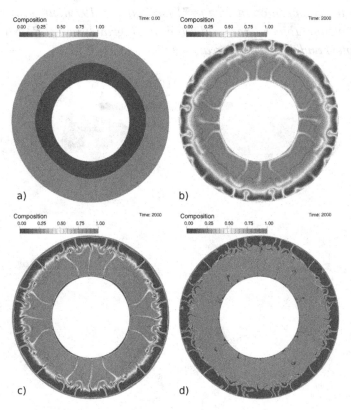

advection of a localized contrast in the composition when this is also accompanied by a sharp jump in the viscosity field.

Rayleigh-Taylor Instability

For the following benchmark test we consider two material layers with different densities (Figure 5). Similar tests have been shown in van Keken et al. (1997), Tackley and King (2003) and Gerya (2010), and are widely used to validate numerical codes that use active compositional fields. Differently from the results presented in the papers above, which were obtained only using a 2D Cartesian box geometry, here we carry out the simulations in a 2D cylindrical geometry, thereby providing a new benchmark suite for cylindrical codes. The initial setup consists of a light layer overlying the inner boundary of the computational domain. The composition of such a layer is set to 0 and its thickness is set to 0.4. The latter value is chosen in such a way that, assuming all light material to accumulate at the top boundary, the obtained thickness of the resulting layer is 0.2. A heavy layer with a composition of 1 occupies the upper part of the domain. We use no-slip boundary conditions for the velocity and do not solve the energy equation. A small perturbation is applied at the boundary between the two layers to trigger the gravitational instability. Figure 5a shows the initial setup for this test.

During the simulation, the light material rises towards the outer boundary because of Rayleigh-Taylor instability (e.g. Turner, 1980). However due to the no-slip boundary conditions, thin layers of light and heavy material stick at the bottom and top of the computational domain, respectively. This causes the formation of secondary diapirs which sink at a later time from the top towards the bottom (van Keken et al., 1997). For this benchmark, we compared several simulations using the GB method and different Lewis numbers against a case where the PIC approach was used. In all tests 128×1188 grid points are employed. As in the previous test, we used 30 particles per cell, resulting in a total of about 4.4×10^6 particles. Increasing the Lewis number shows the combined effects of numerical and chemical diffusion. In the first run a Lewis number of 10^6 was used (Figure 5b). Here the diffusion effects are clearly visible: although the flow pattern is similar to that obtained with the particle-method (Figure 5d),

small-scale structures cannot be captured. Secondary thin diapirs can be observed only when the Lewis number is increased to at least 10^8. Figure 5c shows the results of a simulation with $Le=10^{12}$. In Figure 6 we show the average radial profile of the composition in three cases displayed in Figure 5, i.e. GB with $Le=10^6$, $Le=10^{12}$ and PIC case. Using a Lewis number of 10^{12}, a good agreement with the radial profile from the PIC method is obtained. However, even in this case, sharp transitions in the profile are markedly smoothed. The radial profile from the case where $Le=10^6$ largely fails to approximate that obtained with the PIC method because of large diffusion. Yet the GB method is able to capture the time-evolution of the RMS velocity and entrainment quite precisely (Figures 6c and 6d).

Also note that the smoothing effects observed are due both to numerical and chemical diffusion. Nevertheless, a systematic series of tests (not displayed here) has shown minimal differences

Figure 6. Rayleigh-Taylor instability benchmark using the PIC method (black solid line), GB method with Le=10^6 (gray dotted line) and GB method with Le=10^{12} (gray dashed-dotted line): a) initial disturbance of the boundary between the two layers; b) average radial profiles of the composition at time t=2000 after the Rayleigh-Taylor overturn; c) time-series of the RMS velocity; d) time series of the entrainment of the light material above a height of 0.42 measured from the bottom of the domain.

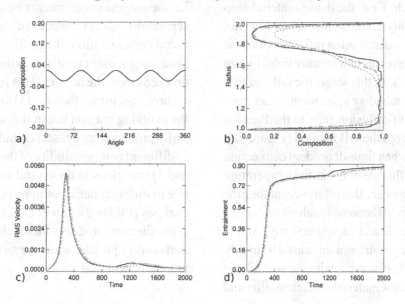

among the results when $10^8 \leq Le \leq 10^{18}$, indicating that the numerical diffusion induced by our GB method is hardly avoidable.

Entrainment by Thermo-Chemical Convection

This test deals with thermo-chemical convection in which the buoyancy due to chemical gradients works against the buoyancy due to thermal gradients. The grid resolution used for the test is 256×2394, which results in a total of ~6 × 10^5 computational points. Mechanical boundary conditions are free-slip for both boundaries. As initial condition, a compositional profile with a thin dense layer at the bottom of the domain is chosen. The thickness of this layer is 4% of the thickness of the computational domain. The initial non-dimensional temperature in the bulk of the domain is set to 0.2 with a small sinusoidal perturbation and two thermal boundary layers with a non-dimensional thickness of 0.2 are imposed. In the GB method, we use a Lewis number of 10^{12}, whereas in the PIC method we use 20 particles per cell resulting in a total of about 12×10^6 particles in the entire domain. In Figure 7, we show snapshots of the composition and temperature fields at two different time steps, obtained using both the GB and PIC approach. First, the dense material atop the inner boundary tends to pile up in four hot upwellings whose distribution reflects that of the initial perturbation of the temperature field (Figure 7a, 7c, 7e, and 7d). At this stage, the GB and PIC methods show qualitative agreement, apart from a small amount of diffusion seen in the thermo-chemical piles from the GB method (Figure 7a). At a later stage, when time-dependent convection sets in and the influence of the initial temperature perturbation disappears, the differences among the GB and PIC methods become much more evident (compare Figures 7b and 7d, respectively). While with the first a large entrainment caused by highly diffused plumes is observed, with the second, the entrainment of dense material is much smaller and caused exclusively by highly focused upwellings that exhibit negligible diffusion. Indeed, a more quantitative comparison of the time series of RMS velocity and entrainment (Figure 8) shows that, although the two methods behave similarly at the beginning of the simulation, their outcomes quickly diverge as the simulation advances in time.

Magma Ocean Cumulate Overturn Simulations

Early in the planetary evolution, the amount of heat released during accretion and core formation can be so large to cause melting of a significant part of, or perhaps even the whole mantle of a terrestrial planet, resulting in the formation of a liquid magma ocean. Subsequent planetary cooling causes the magma ocean to freeze. Freezing proceeds from the core-mantle boundary to the surface. In fact, since the slope of the adiabat is steeper than the solidus of the bulk magma ocean, the solidus is first intersected at depth (Solomatov, 2000; Elkins-Tanton et al., 2003). Freezing of the liquid magma ocean occurs either through equilibrium or fractional crystallization, which are equally plausible solidification mechanisms (Solomatov, 2000). In the equilibrium case, the magma ocean crystallizes without differentiating, i.e. the magma ocean freezes before crystal-melt separation can take place. In the case of fractional crystallization, the residual liquid evolves producing denser cumulates as the crystallization proceeds from the bottom. This is essentially due to three concurring factors. 1) Iron enrichment in the evolving magma ocean liquid (which necessarily produces the densest cumulates at the top), 2) different compressibility of the mineral phases and 3) variations in the crystal structure, all give rise to different densities in response to pressure changes (Elkins-Tanton et al., 2003). Fractional crystallization produces then a chemically stratified density profile, which turns out to be gravitationally unstable.

Figure 7. Thermo-chemical convection: a) composition and e) temperature at time t=0.012 and b) composition and f) temperature at time t=0.030 using the GB approach with a Lewis number of 10¹²; c) composition and g) temperature at time t=0.012 and d) composition and h) temperature at time t=0.030 using the PIC method with 20 particles per cell.

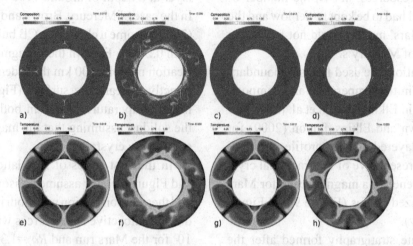

In the following set of calculations, we assume fractional crystallization and present PIC-based simulations of the cumulate overturn of the magma oceans of Mars and Mercury both in 2D cylindrical and 3D spherical geometry. The resolution used for the 2D, Mars-like simulations is 256 × 2394 grid points and 30 particles per cell, resulting in a total of ~6.1 × 10⁵ computational nodes and ~1.8 × 10⁷ particles. In 3D, we used 64 × 40962 grid points and 15 particles per cell,

resulting in ~2.7 × 10⁶ computational nodes and ~4 × 10⁷ particles. For the 2D, Mercury-like runs we used 96 × 2373 grid points and 30 particles per cell, i.e ~2 × 10⁵ computational nodes and 6 × 10⁶ particles, while, in 3D, we used 96 × 40962 grid points and 15 particles per cell, resulting in ~2 × 10⁶ grid points and ~3 × 10⁷ particles. The reason for the different grid resolutions are the different thicknesses of the mantles of Mars and Mercury. The thickness of Mars' mantle, in

Figure 8. Thermo-chemical convection: a) RMS velocity and b) entrainment (calculated above a depth of 0.3) as a function of time using the PIC method (black line) and the GB method with Le=10¹² (gray line).

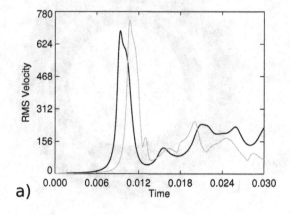
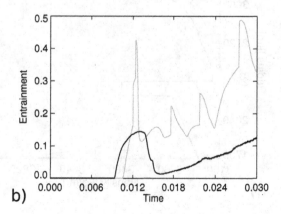

fact, is 1700 km, while that of Mercury's is only about 540 km. In 2D, it was possible to achieve similar resolutions. However, because of limited computational resources, in 3D, the number of particles per cell had to be kept rather low and the resolution of Mars' models could not be chosen as high as that of Mercury's.

In all simulations we used free-slip boundary conditions and initial temperature and composition profiles as in Elkins-Tanton et al. (2005) for Mars and Brown and Elkins-Tanton (2009) for Mercury. The layered density profile, prone to overturn, is representative of the fractional crystallization sequence of a magma ocean for Mars and Mercury-sized bodies (Figure 9 and Figure 10, respectively).

The cumulate stratigraphy formed after the fractional crystallization of a magma ocean depends not only on the depth of the magma ocean but is also influenced by the bulk mantle composition of the planetary body. In the case of Mars, the first minerals that crystallize are majorite and γ-olivine. Garnet, olivine and pyroxene follow in the crystallization sequence, with dense garnet crystals that settle between 12 and 14 GPa (Elkins-Tanton et al., 2005) and form a high density layer at a depth of around 1100 km (Figure 9a). In the case of Mercury, Brown and Elkins-Tanton (2009) assume a chondritic CB bulk composition with 0.2 wt% FeO. In their magma ocean solidification model a 100 km thick dense layer forms directly beneath the surface (Figure 10a). The initial temperature profile in both cases lies on the solidus, assuming that the magma ocean has completely crystallized.

In the first series of simulations (Figure 11 and Figure 12), we assume an isoviscous mantle and thermal convection with both internal heating due to radioactive heat-sources with $Ra_Q=6.83 \times 10^5$ for the Mars run and $Ra_Q=1.38 \times 10^5$ for the Mercury run, and bottom heating with $Ra=1.91 \times 10^4$ (i.e. $\eta_0=10^{23}$ Pa s) for the Mars run and $Ra=2.19 \times 10^4$ (i.e. $\eta_0=10^{21}$ Pa s) for the Mercury run. The unstable density stratification and the uniform viscosity cause a complete overturn of the whole mantle with the densest material

Figure 9. Magma ocean cumulate overturn for Mars-like parameters: a) density profile before (black line) and after (red line) overturn (i.e. at the end of the simulation) for the 2D simulation; b) density distribution after the fractional crystallization of the magma ocean (i.e. before the cumulate overturn) corresponding to the initial profile in panel a).

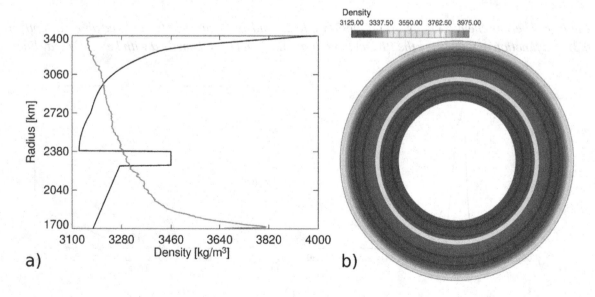

Figure 10. Magma ocean cumulate overturn for Mercury-like parameters: a) density profile before (black line) and after (red line) overturn (i.e. at the end of the simulation) for the 2D simulation; b) density distribution after the fractional crystallization of the magma ocean (i.e. before the cumulate overturn) corresponding to the initial profile in panel a).

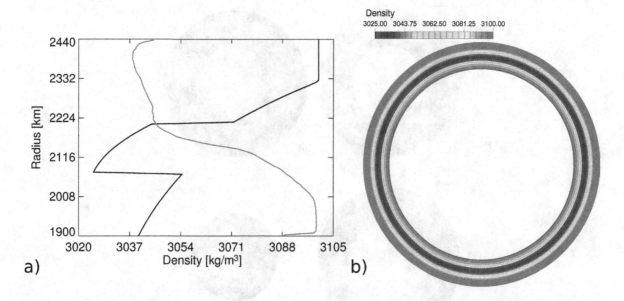

a)

b)

that accumulates at the bottom of the domain and the lightest that rises to the top. Reaching a stable density stratification after the overturn mainly depends on the value of the final density gradient and whether or not the strength of the thermal gradient is sufficient to allow thermal convection to continue. In the isoviscous case, where the complete mantle overturn takes place, we assume that thermal convection can continue after the overturn if the ratio of the thermal to compositional Rayleigh number is greater than 1. For the Mars-like parameters, using a thermal gradient of 0.676 K/km and a chemical gradient of 0.5 kg/m³km (Elkins-Tanton et al., 2005), an extremely large temperature difference ΔT higher than 13600 K is needed in order for thermal convection to continue after the overturn. Using Mercury-like parameters, with a thermal gradient of 1.279 K/km and a chemical gradient of 0.138 kg/m³km (Brown et al., 2009), the temperature difference needed in order for thermal convection to continue is ΔT=1239 K. Assuming a constant surface temperature set at the solidus, this value is hard to achieve since the ΔT across the mantle would be of only 691 K. However, if the surface temperature were quickly to decrease to values similar to present-day ones, the temperature difference across the mantle would be larger and thermal convection could restart.

In a second series of 2D cylindrical simulations, we investigate the effects of temperature-dependent viscosity on the overturn. In this case, because of the high viscosity contrast across the mantle (about 16 and 5 orders of magnitude in the Mars and Mercury runs, respectively) a stagnant layer forms in the coldest part of the mantle which prevents the uppermost dense layer to sink. In the case of Mars, a thin layer of dense material remains at the top while thermo-chemical convection develops beneath it (Figure 13). While the dense garnet layer, located in the initial setup at a depth of around 1100 km, sinks and accumulates at the CMB, the densest layer remains at the surface because of the stagnant lid formed by the

Figure 11. Magma ocean cumulate overturn for Mars-like parameters assuming an isoviscous medium: a) 2D density distribution during overturn; b) 3D density iso-surface during overturn; c) 2D density distribution after the overturn; d) 3D density iso-surface after the overturn.

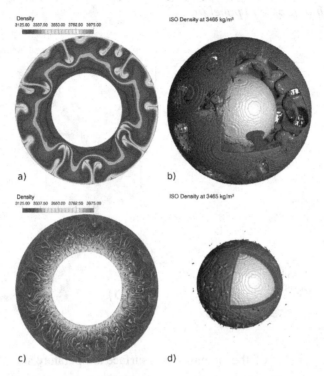

high viscosity contrast across the mantle. In Figure 13 we show three snapshots for the case with Mars-like parameters. The density distribution exhibits a stable configuration beneath the high density layer situated at the surface. Thermo-chemical plumes form because of both thermal and chemical buoyancy. The temperature dependence of the viscosity can be clearly observed in Figure 13c, where highly viscous regions correspond to the coldest temperatures.

In the case of Mercury, a similar behavior is observed. However, in this case, since the layer of dense material is thicker than the stagnant lid, parts of this layer are eroded and sink before settling at the CMB (Figure 14). Because of the smaller temperature contrast, the viscosity variations across the domain are about 11 orders of magnitude smaller than those of the Mars-run. Nevertheless, also in this case, the viscosity contrast is large enough to permit the formation of a

stagnant lid at the top which prevents the uppermost dense layer to sink.

In contrast to the isoviscous runs, when using a strong temperature dependence of the viscosity, the entire mantle overturn cannot take place and only the part of the mantle below the stagnant-lid can evolve into a stable chemical stratification. This can have important implications for the thermal history of both Mars and Mercury, since the surfaces of the two planets would present traces of incompatible elements enriched in the late solidified layers of the magma ocean.

CONCLUSION AND FUTURE DIRECTIONS

We have presented two different methods to simulate active compositional fields in thermo-chemical mantle convection simulations. The

Figure 12. Magma ocean cumulate overturn for Mercury-like parameters assuming an isoviscous medium: a) 2D density distribution during overturn; b) 3D density iso-surface during overturn; c) 2D density distribution after the overturn; d) 3D density iso-surface after the overturn.

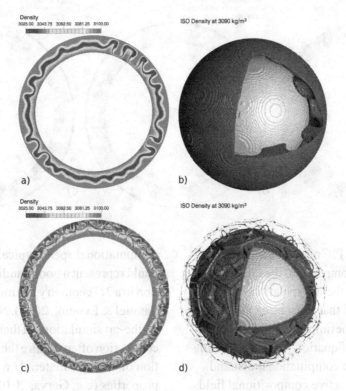

comparison tests show a high accuracy when using the diffusivity-free PIC method. Despite the use of both high Lewis numbers and of a dedicated filter to suppress spurious oscillations, the GB method, being prone to numerical diffusion, performs systematically worse than the PIC method, in particular if a viscosity contrast is associated with the compositional field to be advected. The

Figure 13. Magma ocean cumulate overturn for Mars-like parameters assuming a temperature-dependent viscosity: a) density, b) temperature and c) viscosity distributions after the overturn.

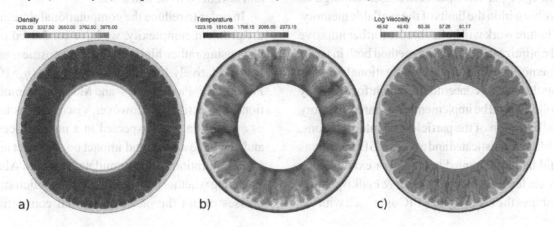

Figure 14. Magma ocean cumulate overturn for Mercury-like parameters assuming a temperature-dependent viscosity: a) density, b) temperature, and c) viscosity distributions after the overturn.

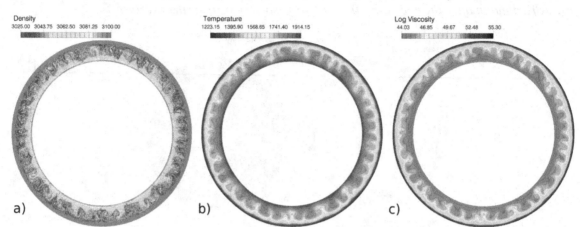

major drawback of the PIC method is the increased computational time compared to the GB method. This is mainly due to the interpolations from the particles onto the grid that must be carried out at each time step. Also, the time required for the solution of the trajectory Equation (6) is responsible for the increase of the computational demand.

The simulation of active compositional fields in a 3D geometry becomes essentially intractable with the GB method. A very high resolution, which in a 3D geometry can become prohibitively expensive, would be needed in this case in order to assure good accuracy of the advection. This kind of simulations can benefit of the PIC method where the grid resolution can be maintained relatively coarse compared with the GB method and the number of particles-per-cell chosen as large as possible within the limits of the available memory.

Future work will be devoted to further improve and optimize the PIC-based method both in terms of memory allocation and computational time. As far as the latter is concerned, a straightforward way to follow could be implementing a shared-memory parallelization of the particle-grid interpolations.

More sophisticated and accurate GB algorithms could be implemented in Gaia. For example, the particle level set method (Osher & Fedkiw, 2003) combines the accuracy of a PIC approach with the

computational speed typical of GB methods and could represent a good candidate to model advection in a 3D geometry in a more efficient way (e.g. Samuel & Evonuk, 2010). Nevertheless, as state-of-the-art simulations of thermo-chemical mantle convection often require the simultaneous advection of multiple materials with different physical properties (e.g. Gerya, 2010), we believe that, at present, a highly optimized PIC implementation still represents the most advantageous choice.

The magma ocean overturn simulations conducted in this study represent only a preliminary application of our PIC implementation. There are several important aspects related to the fluid dynamics of magma oceans that so far have received little attention from the geodynamics community and still need to be clarified.

In order to reduce the computational time and the problem complexity, we have conducted our tests using rather high reference viscosities, and hence relatively low Rayleigh numbers ($\eta_0 = 10^{23}$ Pa s and 10^{21} Pa s for Mars' and Mercury's simulations, respectively). However, viscosities as low as $\eta_0 = 10^{18}$ Pa s are expected in a magma ocean and can have a profound impact on the onset and overall duration of the cumulate overturn. Also, assessing whether compositional convection suppresses or not the onset of thermal convection when the overturn has completed is an issue of fundamental importance. All terrestrial planets, in fact, present signs of late volcanism, which is associated with thermal convection and can be hardly explained if this stops at a very early stage in the planetary evolution, e.g. after the magma ocean cumulate overturn. These kinds of questions will be the subject of future investigations that will be conducted with the aid of the numerical approach described in this study.

ACKNOWLEDGMENT

Ana-Catalina Plesa acknowledges support from the Helmholtz Association through the research alliance "Planetary Evolution and Life". Nicola Tosi acknowledges support from the Deutsche Forschungs Gemeinschaft (grant number TO 704/1-1). Part of the calculations presented was conducted thanks to resources of the Minnesota Supercomputing Institute which is gratefully acknowledged.

REFERENCES

Brown, S. M., & Elkins-Tanton, L. T. (2009). Compositions of Mercury's earliest crust from magma ocean models. *Earth and Planetary Science Letters*, *286*, 446–455. doi:10.1016/j.epsl.2009.07.010

Chemia, Z., Koyi, H., & Schmeling, H. (2008). Numerical modelling of rise and fall of a dense layer in salt diapirs. *Geophysical Journal International*, *172*(2), 798–816. doi:10.1111/j.1365-246X.2007.03661.x

Christensen, U. (1984). Convection with pressure- and temperature-dependent non-Newtonian rheology. *Geophysical Journal of the Royal Astronomical Society*, *77*, 343–384. doi:10.1111/j.1365-246X.1984.tb01939.x

Deschamps, F., Kaminski, E., & Tackley, P. J. (2011). A deep mantle origin for the primitive signature of ocean island basalt. *Nature Geoscience*, *4*, 879–882. doi:10.1038/ngeo1295

Elkins-Tanton, L. T., Burgess, S., & Yin, Q.-Z. (2011). The lunar magma ocean: Reconciling the solidification process with lunar petrology and geochronology. *Earth and Planetary Science Letters*, *304*, 326–336. doi:10.1016/j.epsl.2011.02.004

Elkins-Tanton, L. T., Parmentier, E. M., & Hess, P. C. (2003). Magma ocean fractional crystallization and cumulate overturn in terrestrial planets: Implications for Mars. *Meteoritics & Planetary Science*, *38*(13), 1753–1771. doi:10.1111/j.1945-5100.2003.tb00013.x

Elkins-Tanton, L. T., Zaranek, S. E., Parmentier, E. M., & Hess, P. C. (2005). Early magnetic field and magmatic activity on Mars form magma ocean cumulate overturn. *Earth and Planetary Science Letters*, *236*, 1–12. doi:10.1016/j.epsl.2005.04.044

Fraeman, A. A., & Korenaga, J. (2010). The influence of mantle melting on the evolution of Mars. *Icarus*, *210*, 43–57. doi:10.1016/j.icarus.2010.06.030

Gerya, T. V. (2010). *Introduction to numerical geodynamic modelling*. Cambridge University Press.

Gerya, T. V., & Yuen, D. A. (2003). Characteristics-based marker-in-cell method with conservative finite-differences schemes for modeling geological flows with strongly variable transport properties. *Physics of the Earth and Planetary Interiors*, *140*, 293–318. doi:10.1016/j.pepi.2003.09.006

Harder, H., & Hansen, U. (2005). A finite-volume solution method for thermal convection and dynamo problems in spherical shells. *Geophysical Journal International*, *161*, 522–532. doi:10.1111/j.1365-246X.2005.02560.x

Hüttig, C., & Stemmer, K. (2008a). The spiral grid: A new approach to discretize the sphere and its application to mantle convection. *Geochemistry Geophysics Geosystems*, *9*(2), Q02018. doi:10.1029/2007GC001581

Hüttig, C., & Stemmer, K. (2008b). Finite volume discretization for dynamic viscosities on Voronoi grids. *Physics of the Earth and Planetary Interiors*, *171*(1-4), 137–146. doi:10.1016/j.pepi.2008.07.007

Ishii, M., & Tromp, J. (2004). Constraining large-scale mantle heterogeneity using mantle and inner-core sensitive normal modes. *Physics of the Earth and Planetary Interiors*, *146*, 113–124. doi:10.1016/j.pepi.2003.06.012

Landau, L. D., & Lifshitz, E. M. (1987). *Fluid mechanics* (2nd ed.). Butterworth-Heinemann Course of Theoretical Physics.

Lenardic, A., & Kaula, W. M. (1993). Numerical treatment of geodynamic viscous flow problems involving the advection of material interfaces. *Journal of Geophysical Research*, *98*, 8243–8260. doi:10.1029/92JB02858

LeVeque, R. (2004). *Finite-volume methods for hyperbolic problems*. Cambridge University Press.

Liu, X.-D., Osher, S., & Chan, T. (1994). Weighted essentially non-oscillatory schemes. *Journal of Computational Physics*, *115*, 200–212. doi:10.1006/jcph.1994.1187

Nakagawa, T., & Tackley, P. J. (2011). Effects of low-viscosity post-perovskite on thermo-chemical mantle convection in a 3-D spherical shell. *Geophysical Research Letters*, *38*, L04309. doi:10.1029/2010GL046494

Noack, L., & Tosi, N. (2012). High-performance modelling in geodynamics. In C.-P. Rückemann, (Ed.), *Integrated information and computing systems for natural, spatial, and social sciences*. IGI Global

Osher, S., & Fedkiw, R. (2003). *Level set methods and dynamic implicit surfaces*. New York, NY: Springer. doi:10.1115/1.1760520

Papike, J. J., Karner, J. M., Shearer, C. K., & Burger, P. V. (2009). Silicate mineralogy of Martian meteorites. *Geochimica et Cosmochimica Acta*, *73*, 7443–7485. doi:10.1016/j.gca.2009.09.008

Patankar, S. V. (1980). *Numerical heat transfer and fluid flow. Hemisphere series on computational methods in mechanics and thermal science*. Taylor & Francis.

Plesa, A.-C. (2011). Mantle convection in a 2D spherical shell. In C.-P. Rückemann, W. Christmann, S. Saini, & M. Pankowska (Eds.), *Proceedings of the First International Conference on Advanced Communications and Computation (INFOCOMP 2011)*, October 23-29, 2011, Barcelona, Spain, (pp. 167–172). ISBN: 978-1-61208-161-8

Saad, Y. (1996). *Iterative methods for sparse linear systems*. Boston, MA: PWS Publishing.

Samuel, H., & Evonuk, M. (2010). Modeling advection in geophysical flows with particle level sets. *Geochemistry Geophysics Geosystems*, *11*(8), Q08020. doi:10.1029/2010GC003081

Samuel, H., & Farnetani, C. G. (2003). Thermo-chemical convection and helium concentrations in mantle plumes. *Earth and Planetary Science Letters*, *207*, 39–56. doi:10.1016/S0012-821X(02)01125-1

Schmeling, H., Babeyko, A. Y., Enns, A., Faccenna, C., Funiciello, F., & Gerya, T. (2008). A benchmark comparison of spontaneous subduction models – Towards a free surface. *Physics of the Earth and Planetary Interiors*, *171*, 198–223. doi:10.1016/j.pepi.2008.06.028

Schubert, G., Turcotte, D. L., & Olson, P. (2001). *Mantle convection in the Earth and planets*. Cambridge University Press. doi:10.1017/CBO9780511612879

Solomatov, V. (2000). Fluid dynamics of a terrestrial magma ocean . In Canup, R. M., & Righter, K. (Eds.), *Origin of the Earth and Moon*. Tucson, AZ: University of Arizona Press.

Solomatov, V. (2007). Magma oceans and primordial mantle differentiation. In D. J. Stevenson (Ed.), *Treatise on geophysics, volume 9 – Evolution of the Earth* (pp. 91-119). Amsterdam, The Netherlands: Elsevier.

Šramek, O., & Zhong, S. (2012). Martian crustal dichotomy and Tharsis formation by partial melting coupled to early plume migration. *Journal of Geophysical Research, 117*(E01005). doi:10.1029/2011JE003867

Tackley, P. J., & King, S. D. (2003). Testing the tracer ratio method for modeling active compositional fields in mantle convection simulations. *Geochemistry Geophysics Geosystems, 4*(4), 8302. doi:10.1029/2001GC000214

Tan, E., & Gurnis, M. (2007). Compressible thermochemical convection and application to lower mantle structures. *Journal of Geophysical Research, 112*(B06304). doi:10.1029/2006JB004505

Tan, E., Leng, W., Zhong, S., & Gurnis, M. (2011). On the location of plumes and lateral movement of thermochemical structures with high bulk modulus in the 3-D compressible mantle. *Geochemistry Geophysics Geosystems, 12*(7), Q07005. doi:10.1029/2011GC003665

Turner, J. S. (1980). *Buoyancy effects in fluids*. Cambridge University Press.

van Keken, P. E., King, S. D., Schmeling, H., Christensen, U. R., Neumeister, D., & Doin, M.-P. (1997). A comparison of methods for the modeling of thermochemical convection. *Journal of Geophysical Research, 102*, 22477–22495. doi:10.1029/97JB01353

Verhoeven, J., & Schmalzl, J. (2009). A numerical method for investigating crystal settling in convecting magma chambers. *Geochemistry Geophysics Geosystems, 10*, Q12007. doi:10.1029/2009GC002509

Wolf, W. R., & Azevedo, J. L. F. (2007). High-order ENO and WENO schemes for unstructured grids. *International Journal for Numerical Methods in Fluids, 55*(10), 917–943. doi:10.1002/fld.1469

Chapter 16
High-Performance Modelling in Geodynamics

Lena Noack
German Aerospace Center (DLR), Germany & Westfälische Wilhelms-Universität Münster, Germany

Nicola Tosi
Technical University Berlin, Germany & German Aerospace Center (DLR), Germany

ABSTRACT

Modelling of geodynamic processes like mantle or core convection has strongly improved over the last two decades thanks to the steady development of numerical codes that tend to incorporate a more and more realistic physics. High-performance parallel computations allow the simulation of complex problems, such as the self-consistent generation of tectonic plates or the formation of planetary magnetic fields. However, the need to perform broad explorations of the parameter space and the large computational demands imposed by the non-linear, multi-scale nature of convection, requires several simplifications, in the domain geometry as well as in the physical complexity of the problem. In this chapter, the authors give an overview of the state-of-the-art convection simulations in planetary mantles, the different models and geometries used, and various methods to simplify the computations.

INTRODUCTION

Planetary sciences embrace a wide variety of disciplines, among which astronomy, geology, geochemistry and geophysics are but a few of them, and involve the study of objects ranging in size from small meteorites and comets to giant gaseous planets, such as Jupiter and Saturn, or entire planetary systems. In this context, the study of terrestrial (i.e. rocky) bodies, such as Mercury, Mars, Venus, the Moon and the Earth, occupies a prominent role. On the one hand, the analysis of surface phenomena, like tectonic and atmospheric processes, can benefit of a large diversity of observations conducted both from Earth and from space. On the other hand, the deep interior of solid bodies can only be probed indirectly thanks to seismic observations, which however are available solely for the Earth and, to a lesser extent, for the Moon, or by investigating

DOI: 10.4018/978-1-4666-2190-9.ch016

the properties of minerals at extreme conditions of pressure and temperature.

In the first approximation, the Earth is composed of different material layers with distinct mechanical and chemical properties. The radial structure of the Earth has been known for some decades thanks to the study of earthquake-generated elastic waves that propagate through the interior of the planet (Dziewonski & Anderson, 1981). Seen from the centre to the surface, the Earth consists of a solid iron core, a fluid layer of iron mixed with lighter elements such as sulphur, and a rocky mantle composed of mostly solid, but also partially molten, silicate minerals. This is surrounded by thin, oceanic and continental plates of basaltic and felsic composition, respectively. The basic structure of the Earth is depicted in Figure 1 together with the assumed radial profile of the temperature in the mantle and the core.

A terrestrial planet is in general defined as a body differentiated into an iron core, a rocky mantle and a crust on top. Mercury, Mars, Venus, the Earth and the Moon, but also several moons of the Solar System and exo-planets orbiting other stars, are thought to possess the same basic internal structure.

Planets gain heat early during their formation process, where impacts and collisions lead to the accumulation of a vast amount of energy. Besides this form of primordial heat, thermal and compositional convection in the liquid core also deliver heat into the mantle. Moreover, radioactive elements, stored in the mantle during accretion, decay over time and supply the planet with additional thermal energy for billions of years. Because of thermal expansion and contraction, the material at the base of the mantle, heated by the core, is less dense than the material at the surface, which cools as it radiates heat to space. This results in gravitational instability, with hot and buoyant mantle rocks rising towards the surface, from which cooler and denser material descends back into the mantle. Even though the mantle is by all means solid, it behaves like a

Figure 1. A terrestrial planet is divided into an inner and outer iron core, a rocky mantle, and a crust (left). The mantle temperature (red line) increases sharply across two thermal boundary layers at the surface and at the core-mantle boundary (CMB), where heat is transported mostly by conduction. In the bulk of the mantle and in the core, instead, the temperature increase is essentially adiabatic. The Earth further has oceans and continents at the surface and a stable atmosphere (right).

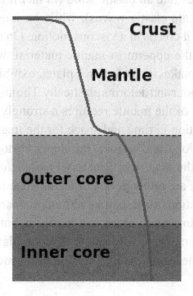

highly viscous fluid (the viscosity of rocks is typically larger than $10^{18}\,Pas$) on timescales of millions of years as a consequence of pressure- and temperature-activated deformation processes (e.g. Karato, 2008).

Sub-solidus thermal convection of the rocky mantle (i.e. at temperatures below the solidus, at which the mineral with the lowest melting temperature among those that form the mantle mixture starts to melt) is the principle mechanism that causes planets to cool with time, transporting heat from the mantle out to the surface. On Earth, it is the driving mechanism for plate tectonics, controls mountain building and sea-floor spreading and is responsible for the formation of partial melt in the upper mantle that ultimately determines the emergence of volcanism. Geodynamics deals with the thermo-mechanical modelling of all these processes resulting in a complexity that makes the use of numerical simulations an essential component to understand how the Earth evolved and to be able to transfer this knowledge to other terrestrial planets and moons. During the last two decades, planetary geodynamics has witnessed a dramatic improvement thanks to the development of high-performance codes. The use of super-computers has been shifting numerical models to a new level of sophistication, and some geophysical problems can now be investigated with unprecedented realism. Despite large uncertainties in the thermodynamic and transport properties of minerals at high pressures and temperatures of planetary interiors, modern mantle simulations can be performed (even in three dimensions) at a realistic convective vigour. Future development in high-performance modelling and numerical methods, as much as in high-pressure mineral physics, will help establishing more and more realistic simulations of the mantle.

In the convection of the liquid core or of the oceans and atmospheres, rotation and turbulence play a fundamental role. This makes global direct numerical simulations essentially intractable and requires, for instance, the use of complex parameterizations of the turbulent viscosity in atmosphere and ocean modelling (e.g. Marshall & Plumb, 2008) or of unrealistic modifications of certain material parameters in simulations of core dynamics (e.g. Christensen & Wicht, 2007). In mantle convection instead, which is the main topic treated in this chapter, viscous forces largely dominate over inertial and rotational forces because of the extremely high viscosity of rocks. As a consequence, the flow, albeit strongly time-dependent, is laminar, which greatly simplifies numerical models. Nevertheless, several other factors contribute to make mantle convection a highly complex process. The viscosity, in particular, is a non-linear function of temperature, pressure and strain-rate and can vary by several orders of magnitude across small distances (see Equation (1)). From the numerical point of view, this leads to extremely ill-posed problems characterized by stiff matrices, for which ad-hoc inversion strategies must be developed (e.g. Geenen et al., 2009). Furthermore, rock rheology imposes severe difficulties. The mantle is in fact a visco-elasto-plastic continuum in which different deformation mechanisms become of primary or secondary importance at different temporal and spatial scales. On short time scales, the mantle behaves like an elastic solid (in fact it is able to propagate elastic waves), while on longer time scales it creeps in a viscous motion. On the other hand, the uppermost mantle material, which on Earth makes up the tectonic plates, exhibits brittle behaviour and deforms plastically. The multi-scale nature of the mantle requires a strongly varying resolution in time and space for the treatment of both global and regional problems. On top of this, since the majority of material parameters in the mantle are rather poorly constrained, convection simulations must span a wide range of parameters. One simulation alone can hardly be interpreted in a conclusive way and tens of simulations are often necessary to draw meaningful conclusions.

The above-described complexities require the adoption of a number of simplifications, which we aim at examining in this chapter. We first review the basic equation system of mantle convection. After giving an overview of the traditional analytical approach used for parameterized models, we then discuss extensively state-of-the-art numerical solutions of geodynamical problems obtained with spectral, finite element and finite volume methods. Further, several possible geometrical reductions of the model domain are discussed and compared to each other. The subsequent section focuses on one example describing how to reduce the computational complexity of the problem by simplifying the viscosity law. The chapter concludes with some future developments that can be expected in the field of mantle convection.

MODELLING OF MANTLE CONVECTION

The basic core of mantle convection codes typically solves the conservation equations of thermal convection for a highly viscous Boussinesq fluid, in which compressibility, adiabatic effects and viscous dissipation on the temperature are neglected. The viscosity η is a non-linear function of the absolute temperature T, hydrostatic pressure P and strain-rate $\dot{\varepsilon}$. In its most general form, it is given by the Arrhenius law (e.g. Karato, 2008):

$$\eta\left(T, P, \dot{\varepsilon}\right) = \frac{1}{2A^{1/n}} \mu \dot{\varepsilon}^{(1-n)/n} \left(\frac{d}{b}\right)^{m/n} \exp\left(\frac{E^* + PV^*}{nRT}\right)$$

(1)

where A is a pre-factor, n the stress exponent, μ the shear modulus, d the grain size, b the length of the Burgers vector, m the grain-size exponent, E^* the activation energy and V^* the activation volume. R is the gas constant, while all other parameters above are material-dependent and are known from laboratory experiments (e.g. Karato & Wu, 1993; Hirth & Kohlstedt, 2003). In the basic equation system, only Newtonian fluids are considered and the viscosity is independent of stress and strain-rate, i.e. $n = 1$ in Equation (1). Further, basic models are also grain-size independent, so that $m = 0$. The expression for the viscosity of a Newtonian fluid is then readily obtained from Equation (1):

$$\eta\left(T, P\right) = B \exp\left(\frac{E^* + PV^*}{RT}\right)$$

(2)

where we set $B = \mu / 2A$.

Solid-state convection in a planetary mantle with variable viscosity and constant thermodynamic parameters is governed by the conservation equations of mass, linear momentum and thermal energy. In non-dimensional form, they respectively read (e.g. Schubert et al., 2001):

$$\nabla \cdot \mathbf{u}' = 0$$

(3)

$$-\nabla p' + \nabla \cdot \left[\eta'\left(\nabla \mathbf{u}' + (\nabla \mathbf{u}')^T\right)\right] + RaT'\mathbf{e}_r = 0$$

(4)

$$\frac{\partial T'}{\partial t'} + \mathbf{u}' \cdot \nabla T' = \nabla^2 T' + Q'$$

(5)

The convective velocity is denoted by $\mathbf{u}'$; p' is the dynamic pressure, T' the temperature, $\mathbf{e}_r$ the unit vector in the radial direction, t' the time, and Q' the internal heating rate. Equations (3)-(5) have been scaled using reference values for the super-adiabatic temperature difference across the mantle ΔT, surface temperature T_0, reference viscosity η_{ref}, mantle thickness D and thermal diffusivity κ_m (e.g. Christensen, 1984). The Rayleigh number Ra represents a measure of the vigour of convection in a fluid heated from below and is given by

$$Ra = \frac{\rho_m g \alpha_m \Delta T D^3}{\kappa_m \eta_{ref}} \qquad (6)$$

where ρ_m is the mantle density, g the gravity acceleration and α_m the coefficient of thermal expansion. The reference viscosity η_{ref} is determined from Equation (2) using predefined reference values for the temperature and hydrostatic pressure. Because of the high viscosity of the mantle, buoyancy forces due to thermal expansion are instantaneously balanced by the viscous resistance of the fluid. Therefore, in Equation (4), inertial forces are neglected.

Vigorous convection is an efficient mechanism to remove primordial heat due to accretion, heat from the core and heat due to the decay of radiogenic isotopes, from the interior of a planet out to its surface. In particular, in the terrestrial planets, uranium, thorium and potassium are the main contributors to the heat generated in the mantle by radioactive decay. The total non-dimensional internal heating rate Q' that appears in Equation (5) is given explicitly by

$$Q' = H \frac{D^2}{k_m \Delta T} \qquad (7)$$

where k_m is the mantle thermal conductivity and H the (dimensional) heat production rate per volume, defined as

$$H = \sum_{i=1}^{n} H_i \exp(-\lambda_i t) \qquad (8)$$

where H_i and λ_i are the heat production rate and decay constant of the i-th radioactive element, respectively (e.g. Breuer, 2009). When $Q' = 0$, the system of Equations (3)-(5) simply describes the Rayleigh-Bénard convection of a slow creeping fluid. The mantle is heated from below due to core cooling, triggering the upward motion of

hot and light material from the core-mantle boundary (CMB) towards the upper mantle and, similarly, the downward motion of heavier cool material towards the lower mantle.

Convection in Earth's mantle yet involves much more complicated processes. Density changes due to solid-solid phase transitions or the non-Newtonian, brittle nature of tectonic plates are only two of the ingredients that contribute to create a large variety of dynamical behaviours over a broad range of temporal and spatial scales. Wherever the mantle temperature exceeds the solidus partial melting occurs. This further affects convection and requires the solution – or the parameterization – of a two-phase flow problem for liquid molten material that flows through a solid, deformable matrix (e.g. Ricard, 2007). Depletion of mantle rocks by partial melting, alteration of the crust or the presence of chemically distinct minerals can be the source of compositional buoyancy that adds up to the buoyancy due to thermal expansion, requiring the accurate modelling and tracking of active compositional fields (Plesa et al., this volume). The rheology, which characterizes the way a continuum deforms in response to an applied stress, can greatly vary across the mantle. While in the coldest portions of the mantle (i.e. the crust and lithosphere) elasticity as well as plastic and ductile deformation play a prominent role (e.g. Ismail-Zadeh and Tackley, 2010), in the bulk of the mantle Newtonian diffusion (i.e. $n = 1$ in equ. (1)) or non-Newtonian dislocation creep (i.e. $n > 1$) are the dominant deformation mechanisms. Furthermore, even though most convection models treat the mantle as incompressible, the density can increase significantly with depth because of hydrostatic compression (in the Earth's mantle it almost doubles from the surface to the core-mantle boundary) and the change in volume due to pressure can exert an important influence on the convective behaviour and heat transport (e.g. King et al., 2010).

Taking into account all the above complexities would make the problem of mantle convection in terrestrial planets such as Earth, Mars and Venus essentially intractable. Therefore, a series of simplifications needs to be introduced. Models often concentrate on elucidating specific aspects of the problem such as the influence of phase transition on the convective behaviour (Peltier & Solheim, 1992) or the initiation of plate tectonics (Tackley, 2000b; Bercovici, 2003). The effects of two popular simplifications, namely the reduction in size and number of dimensions of the domain geometry (e.g. using 2D Cartesian or cylindrical models) and the approximation of the viscosity law (e.g. employing the so-called Frank-Kamenetskii approximation) are discussed later in this chapter.

Analytical Models

For simple convection problems, analytical solutions can be derived. These represent an important tool that provides a deep insight into the general behaviour of a dynamical system. One of the simplest problems that can be solved analytically is the boundary layer analysis of finite-amplitude convection in a plane layer of fluid heated from below. Assuming the fluid layer to be initially isothermal, conductive heat loss leads to the formation of thermal boundary layers (TBL) near the top and bottom boundaries. These grow thicker with time by conduction until they become gravitationally unstable and convection sets in. This model can be used to derive characteristic scaling relationships like the one between the Nusselt number (i.e. the ratio of the total to conductive heat flux) and the Rayleigh number or between the convective velocity and the Rayleigh number (e.g. Moresi & Solomatov, 1998). Here, we briefly review these two basic and widely used scaling laws, referring to standard convection monographs for their derivation and adaption to more general conditions (Schubert et al., 2001; Turcotte & Schubert, 2002).

Two different systems are typically investigated, depending on whether the fluid layer is heated from below (bottom-heated) or from within (internally heated) because of radioactive decay. On the one hand, in an internally heated system, no lower TBL forms and cold downwellings, which originate from the instability of the upper TBL, dominate the motion. In a bottom-heated system, on the other hand, a symmetry between bottom and top TBLs is established, and hot upwellings and cold downwellings become equally important. Nevertheless, in the high-Rayleigh number regime, such as that characterizing the Earth's mantle, convection soon leads to the formation of an isothermal mantle beneath the surface (neglecting the adiabatic temperature increase) that resembles the state obtained in internally heated cases (e.g. Sotin & Labrosse, 1999).

For deriving the basic scaling laws, the pressure-dependence of the viscosity (see Equation (2)) is usually neglected and the temperature is assumed to be constant everywhere, apart from the TBLs. At the top, either a stagnant lid, which characterizes one-plate planets like Mars, Mercury and other terrestrial bodies of the Solar System, or a mobile lid is assumed representing a planet like the Earth, which experiences plate tectonics. Considering a wholly mobile surface can lead to an overestimation of the cooling effect of plate tectonics, because of which only a relatively small portion of the cold crust is actually recycled into the mantle. Nevertheless this model fits better to the Earth than the one based on a stagnant lid (e.g. Schubert et al., 2001).

The Nusselt number is a measure of the non-dimensional heat flux that escapes the mantle and is an important global parameter that can be used to characterize the thermal evolution of a planet. On the base of boundary layer theory, the following relationship between Nusselt and Rayleigh numbers can be derived:

$$Nu = a\theta^c Ra^\beta \qquad (9)$$

In Equation (9), θ is defined as the natural logarithm of the viscosity contrast from the surface to the core-mantle boundary. Note that for isoviscous materials θ is set to one. If the viscosity contrast exceeds a certain limit (often defined to be 10^5), the high viscosity attained in the regions where the temperature is lowest leads to the formation of a stagnant lid that does not participate in the convection. Note that no matter whether a stagnant lid forms or not, the mantle itself is treated as an isoviscous fluid. The constants a, c and β vary with the boundary conditions and complexity of the problem. The exponent β is the most important parameter in Equation (9). For bottom-heated convection, the theory predicts $\beta = 1/3$. However, at high Rayleigh numbers, this value drops below this limit. A scaling relation can also be derived that connects the convective velocity with the Rayleigh number and depends on twice the exponent β that appears in Equation (9):

$$u = a\theta^c Ra^{2\beta} \qquad (10)$$

However, the two parameters a and c differ from those of Equation (9).

Parameterized Models

Parameterized models make use of the results described in the previous section to infer the thermal evolution of a planet without needing to explicitly solve the set of Equations (3)-(5). As prototype parameterized model, we can consider a simple configuration consisting of a single, internally-heated and isoviscous spherical layer that comprises the whole mantle. The evolution of the temperature T_m with time t of this layer can be obtained by solving a simple energy balance:

$$V_m \rho_m C_m \frac{\partial T_m}{\partial t} = V_m H - A_m q \qquad (11)$$

where V_m is the volume of the mantle, ρ_m the mantle density, C_m the heat capacity, H the heat production rate per unit volume (Equation (8)), A_m the area of the outer surface of the mantle and q the amount of heat that flows through it. The latter can be parameterized using appropriate scaling laws such as (9). In fact, the Nusselt number is defined as the ratio of the total heat flux to the conductive heat flux computed at the surface, i.e.

$$Nu = q \left(k_m \frac{T_m - T_s}{D} \right)^{-1} \qquad (12)$$

where T_s is the surface temperature, k_m the mantle thermal conductivity and D the mantle thickness. Thus, using Equation (9), we obtain:

$$q = \frac{k_m(T_m - T_s)}{D} Nu \sim \frac{k_m(T_m - T_s)}{D} Ra^\beta. \qquad (13)$$

Starting from the simple model above, fairly sophisticated one-dimensional models can be built that, for instance, take into account the thermal coupling between the mantle and metallic core (Stevenson et al., 1983), the possibility of mantle layering due to phase changes (Spohn & Schubert, 1982) or even the feedbacks induced by the outgassing and regassing of the mantle associated with the loss and recharge of volatiles in a coupled atmosphere-mantle context (Schubert et al., 1989; Phillips et al., 2001).

With respect to fully numerical models, parameterized models have the distinct advantage of requiring little computational resources. The model differential Equation (11) for the heat transfer needs to be solved in one dimension only and no actual convective motion must be simulated as in two or three dimensions. One-dimensional models of this kind also do not present significant numerical difficulties and permit to treat higher Rayleigh numbers than those that can be handled by solving the full set of conservation equations. The range of parameters that can be explored with parameterized models is therefore very large. However, although they represent a fundamental tool to get insight into the basic physics of mantle heat transport, they only permit to investigate global parameters. Even the most sophisticated scaling laws cannot accurately parameterize the heat transport associated with complex, multi-component flows with elaborate rheologies. Furthermore, they do not allow studying the dynamics of laterally varying structures such as plumes (McNamara & Zhong, 2004), subductions (Schellart et al., 2007), undulations of lid thickness or local lid failures (Noack et al., 2012). For these investigations, fully numerical convective models have to be used.

Spectral Codes

High accuracy and relative easiness of implementation make the spectral method (SM) an attractive alternative to finite element and finite volume methods (see next subsection) when the solution of the full set of partial differential Equations (3)-(5) is sought for. SMs are based upon the expansion of field variables and spatially varying parameters into truncated series of orthogonal eigenfunctions of differential operators defined on orthogonal curvilinear coordinate systems. Apart from regional crustal-scale problems, which often require either time-evolving boundaries and/ or a free surface (e.g. Schmeling et al., 2008), geodynamic problems are usually solved in simple, regular geometries, such as Cartesian boxes, cylindrical or spherical shells (see next section). For these domains, expansions in Fourier or spherical harmonics series represent a natural way to parameterize the horizontal spatial dependence of the field variables. In particular, for global models defined in a spherical shell, a

generic, square-integrable, scalar quantity f can be approximated as:

$$f(r,\vartheta,\varphi) = \sum_{\ell=0}^{\ell_{max}} \sum_{m=-\ell}^{\ell} f_{\ell m}(r) Y_{\ell m}(\vartheta,\varphi) \qquad (14)$$

where r, ϑ, φ are spherical coordinates (radius, latitude and longitude, respectively), $Y_{\ell m}(\vartheta,\varphi)$ are complex spherical harmonic functions of degree ℓ and order m, which are orthonormal on the unit sphere (e.g. Varshalovich et al., 1988), and $f_{\ell m}(r)$ are radially dependent spectral coefficients. The higher the value of ℓ_{max}, i.e. the number of terms retained in the series expansion, the higher is the lateral resolution that can be globally achieved. Vector and tensor quantities can be expressed in a similar fashion as Equation (14) by using instead a basis of vector or tensor spherical harmonics (e.g. Phinney & Burridge, 1973).

Prior to the widespread usage of medium to large parallel computing systems, SMs represented the most popular choice for global-scale geodynamics modelling. They have been - and still are - successfully employed in a variety of geophysical contexts such as mantle convection (e.g. Zhang & Yuen, 1996), magneto-hydrodynamics of the liquid core and geodynamo generation (Glatzmaier & Roberts, 1995), geomagnetic induction in the mantle (Velímský & Martinec, 2005) and post-glacial isostatic adjustment (Martinec, 2000). SMs are known to possess a generally better ratio of accuracy to computational costs when compared to finite techniques (e.g. Canuto et al., 2007). For convection problems defined in a spherical shell and under appropriate conditions, they also permit to reduce the set of partial differential Equations (3)-(5) to a system of weakly coupled first-order ordinary differential equations for each degree ℓ and order m, which can easily be integrated on a single-processor machine.

However, in order for the above simplification to hold, the viscosity must be either constant or, at most, radially (i.e. pressure-) dependent. In the presence of lateral viscosity variations due to temperature, in fact, the product between the viscosity and velocity gradient tensor (see Equation (4)) gives rise to a coupling of spectral modes. Separating the equations for each degree and order becomes no longer possible, with the consequence that a large and no longer sparse system matrix must be inverted. One way out of this problem consists in averaging the viscosity over the radial coordinate and treating the coupling terms in an iterative way (Zhang & Christensen, 1993). Nevertheless, iterations are unlikely to converge for lateral viscosity contrasts larger than a factor of about 10^3 (Čadek & Fleitout, 2003). Furthermore, partial sums of spherical harmonics are often prone to the Gibbs phenomenon (e.g. Canuto et al., 2007) close to strongly localized discontinuities of viscosity, which often occur, for example, when modelling the brittle nature of the lithosphere (Tackley, 2000b). An additional disadvantage of SMs regards the global nature of the basis functions employed, which makes local mesh refinement and simple parallelization via domain decomposition practically unfeasible. For these reasons, SMs are not as effective and promising as finite methods (see next subsection) for solving increasingly more realistic mantle convection problems.

Finite Element and Finite Volume Codes

Analogously to numerical codes based on the SM, codes based on the finite element (FE) or finite volume (FV) method solve explicitly the system of partial differential Equations (3)-(5).

The FE method owes its popularity to the ability to obtain accurate solutions of problems defined on complex geometries with strongly varying material properties. In order to apply the FE method, an integral (weak) formulation of the differential problem (3)-(5) must be first derived. This is accomplished by multiplying each equation by a suitable test function. The resulting product is then integrated by parts over the solution domain with the aid of Green's first identity (e.g. Hughes, 2000). The domain is partitioned into small, non-overlapping sub-domains (finite elements) over which the field variables are approximated by functions (generally polynomials) with local support. Solutions over each element then sum up to produce a global integral solution over the whole domain.

The FV method shares some common features with the FE method (e.g. Baranger et al., 1996). Even though it is not based on a weak formulation, it still requires an integration of the conservation equations over so-called control volumes (finite volumes). The application of the Gauss' theorem to the obtained volume integrals permits to reduce the order of the differential operators that must be then approximated at the walls of the control volumes using either grid-point values, in case of structured grids, or interpolated values, in case of irregular grids (e.g. Ferziger & Peric, 1999).

Both the FE and the FV method have been widely applied with equal success for modern, state-of-the-art geodynamic simulations. At present, none of them can be considered more apt than the other to treat convection problems at the global scale. Nevertheless, for regional scale problems of crustal dynamics, where complex geometries and a free-surface are routinely employed, the FE method is more popular and probably more effective (Kaus et al., 2008).

Both methods are used in global-scale convection codes. Baumgardner (1985) for example used the FE method to develop Terra. This was the first 3D code capable to treat time-dependent thermal convection in a spherical shell and is still in use (e.g. Schuberth et al., 2009). Today, the most robust and flexible FE code is arguably

CitComS (e.g. Zhong et al., 2008), which has been employed to solve a large variety of global geodynamical problems ranging from thermo-chemical convection in the Earth (e.g. Tan et al., 2011) to the modelling of convection in terrestrial planets such as Mercury (King, 2008) or Mars (Šrámek & Zhong, 2010). Furthermore, having been made freely available and extendable thanks to the Computational Infrastructure for Geodynamics (CIG, 2010), CitComS is also the spherical code most widely used by the geodynamic community.

The upcoming generation of FE mantle convection codes is probably best represented by Rhea (Burstedde et al., 2008), which possesses an outstanding parallel scalability, being capable to run efficiently on petascale supercomputers. Rhea also features an octree-based, parallel, adaptive mesh refinement (AMR) that enables it to tackle multi-scale problems in a global context. Stadler et al. (2010) used Rhea to perform simulations in which low viscosity plate boundaries could be resolved with a local element size as small as 1 km (Figure 2). An equivalent uniform resolution would have required about 10^{12} elements to cover the entire mantle. Thanks to the AMR,

the total size of the mesh could be reduced by more than three orders of magnitude. With a few hundred million elements, the problem became tractable with a large-scale supercomputer.

As far as FV codes are concerned, STAGYY by Tackley (2008) has proven to be highly flexible in treating a broad range of global geodynamical problems, amongst which the self-consistent generation of plate tectonics (van Heck & Tackley, 2008), the thermo-chemical evolution of the Earth (Nakagawa & Tackley, 2010) or the modelling of the crustal dichotomy of Mars (Keller & Tackley, 2009) are but a few examples. Developed by Choblet et al. (2007), Oedipus is another FV-based, 3D-spherical code that has found several interesting applications in the modelling of terrestrial bodies or icy moons in which convection is influenced by tidal effects such as tidal dissipation (e.g. Běhounková et al., 2010) or tidal despinning (e.g. Robuchon et al., 2010).

It is also important to point out that the application and development of advanced numerical tools need to be accompanied by adequate validation processes. Even though fluid dynamic experiments focusing on mantle convection problems form an

Figure 2. Viscosity field from a simulation performed with the FE code Rhea by Stadler et al. (2010). The resolution of a global Earth model can locally go down to 1 km. Such a high resolution cannot be achieved when using uniform grids. Regions where viscosity changes are smooth, such as in the lower mantle, are treated with a coarse discretization. Copyright by Science.

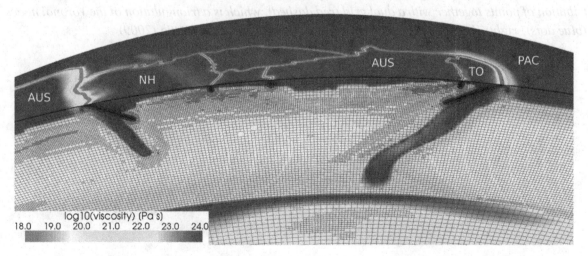

active research branch (e.g. Davaille & Limare, 2007; von Larcher et al., 2008), they are rarely compared against numerical solutions to assess the validity and accuracy of the latter. Instead, comparing solutions from different numerical codes is a more popular validation approach. However, only a handful of extremely simplified benchmark tests are currently available (Blankenbach et al., 1989; van Keken et al., 1997; Schmeling et al., 2008; King et al., 2010). Thorough comparisons of more sophisticated simulations in 2D as well as in 3D geometry have received so far no attention and would be highly desirable. In fact, while complex features such as non-linear rheologies, phase transitions or multiple materials with strongly varying mechanical and thermal properties are routinely included in modern mantle simulations, they have never been the subject of any systematic benchmark study.

Meshes, Parallelism, and Solvers

In the above described FV and FE codes, structured grids such as the Yin-Yang grid (Kageyama & Sato, 2004) used in STAGYY or the cubed sphere (Ronchi et al., 1996) used in Oedipus are the preferred choice. The FV code GAIA (Hüttig & Stemmer, 2008b) represents an interesting ex-

ception. GAIA is able to work both with projected icosahedral grids and fully unstructured grids like the so-called spiral grid introduced by Hüttig & Stemmer (2008a), which is based on a particular Voronoi decomposition (e.g. de Berg et al., 2008) that yields a nearly uniform resolution throughout the spherical domain (Figure 3).

On the one hand, apart from the above-mentioned code Rhea, no significant effort has been made so far, either in a FE or FV framework, to apply AMR to three-dimensional models. On the other hand, for simulations in two dimensions, Davies et al. (2007) implemented AMR in a finite element code, showing interesting applications to various geodynamic problems such as the modelling of mid-ocean ridges and subduction zones. Leng & Zhong (2011) compared the efficiency of an adaptive 2D finite element code to its uniform version and found a strong decrease in the required computational resources. The data handling is significantly more complicated when using adaptive grids compared to non-adaptive ones. Nevertheless, the reduction in computational time that can be gained is generally worth the effort, at least in two dimensions. In three dimensions, the trade-off between reduced computational time and additional time spent for

Figure 3. Discretization using Voronoi cells. Left: Voronoi grid (cell walls in blue) for an irregular distribution of points together with a dual grid (red dashed), which is a triangulation of the Voronoi nodes (blue dots); right: Voronoi cells for an irregular 3D spiral grid from Hüttig (2009)

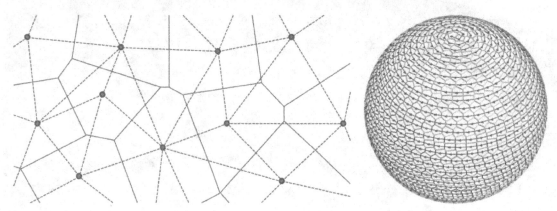

adaptive re-meshing must be considered with care and carried out in parallel (Burstedde et al., 2008).

To a certain extent, modern numerical simulations of mantle convection are still limited to the usage of unrealistic parameters (e.g. smaller Rayleigh numbers or viscosity approximations) or simplified domains (2D cylindrical or Cartesian). Despite these simplifications, present-day 3D models, but also high-resolution 2D models, almost always need to be run in parallel on supercomputers. Figure 4 shows an example of the parallel scalability (i.e. the speed-up of a code as a function of the number of processors) of the code GAIA using a 2D cylindrical geometry with different resolutions. Parallelization is attained via standard domain decomposition. The domain is divided into a number of subdomains equal to the number of processors in use. The boundaries of the subdomains overlap to allow for exchange of information. By increasing the mesh resolution, the ratio of boundary cells to total number of cells decreases, and the scaling improves if a larger amount of processors is used.

At present, even the most advanced 3D mantle convection simulations can be run on modern medium to large sized clusters, which are normally available at high performance computing (HPC) centres. To our knowledge, so far no effort has been made by the geodynamic community to port numerical codes originally designed for parallel HPC on large scale distributed grids, i.e. networks of computing systems at geographically distinct locations. Despite the disadvantages of increased latencies and the lack of high communication bandwidth, for those codes such as Rhea (Burstedde et al., 2008), with demonstrated excellent parallel scalability, the use of grid computing could represent an interesting

Figure 4. Speed-up factor of the code GAIA for six different 2D cylindrical grids from 16 shells (2112 grid points) up to 1024 shells (9863168 points). The growth of the speed-up factor with the number of processors has the same trend for less than 16 processors, after that the speed-up factor of the 16-shell grid starts to descend. For the largest investigated grid with 1024 shells, the parallelization is optimal for up to 500 processors and gets ineffective after that. Larger grids (e.g. 3D grids with 256 or more shells) can therefore efficiently be solved on several hundred up to some thousands of processors with the resolution itself being the limiter of the efficiency. The scaling tests have been done on the supercomputer of the North-German Supercomputing Alliance (HLRN).

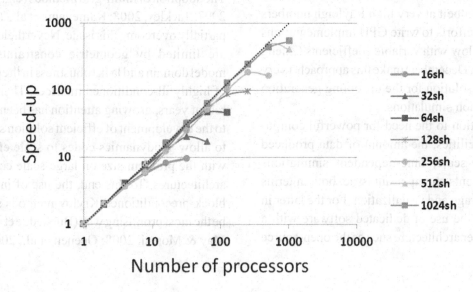

opportunity to explore new physics that may arise through the coupling of multi-scale processes requiring vastly different resolutions and an extremely large number of degrees of freedom. Nevertheless, large uncertainties in the initial conditions necessary to model planetary evolution as well as in the transport and thermal properties of key mantle materials demand broad explorations of the parameter space and hence a large number of simulation runs. This task can be best still best accomplished with parallel applications optimized to run on HPC clusters.

Besides high performance- and grid-computing, the introduction of the massively parallel architecture CUDA (e.g. Sanders & Kandrot, 2010) with its C and Fortran implementations has finally made possible the use of relatively cheap and easily accessible GPUs (Graphic Processing Units) for high performance scientific simulations. Sophisticated flows relevant for engineering applications have been successfully modelled on GPU (e.g. Elsen et al., 2008) showing dramatic performance improvement of one order of magnitude and more with respect to traditional CPU computations. As far as mantle dynamics is concerned, the first implementations of convection problems on GPU have started to appear (e.g. Sanchez et al., 2011). Even though these are mostly limited to flows with constant viscosity - albeit at very high Rayleigh numbers – ongoing efforts to write GPU implementations of Stokes flow with variable coefficients (Zheng et al., 2010, December) make this approach a very promising solution for the upcoming generation of convection simulations.

In addition to the need for powerful computational facilities, the amount of data produced with large-scale, time-dependent simulations also represents an important issue, both in terms of data storage and visualization. For the latter in particular, the use of dedicated software with a client-server architecture such as the open-source ParaView (Kitware, 2012) is becoming more and more popular. Carrying out in parallel the highly cpu-consuming steps of the data analysis on many-processors servers and using less powerful workstations for the final visualization is a very promising way to handle the largest 3D data sets.

Besides the issues related to resolution and gridding, the solution of the linear system arising from the discretization of the momentum Equation (4) presents significant challenges. The large viscosity variations occurring across the whole domain and, more importantly, across neighbouring cells, make the system matrix extremely ill-conditioned and demand the use of efficient direct or iterative solvers and preconditioners (e.g. Saad, 1996). Solving Equation (4) is indeed the main time-consuming step in a simulation of mantle convection. Also, methods that perform well for small- to medium-size problems (with up to $\sim 10^6$ degrees of freedom), such as Jacobi (Tackley, 2008), Gauss-Seidel (Zhong et al., 2008) or conjugate-gradient-based methods (Hüttig & Stemmer, 2008b), stop scaling linearly with the number of degrees of freedom when these exceed $\sim 10^7$ (Geenen et al., 2009), which is not unusual for high-resolution 3D problems. Note, however, that this does not affect the speed-up of the parallelization, but only the absolute computation times. The adoption of multi-grid methods (e.g. Choblet, 2007; Tackley, 2008; Kameyama et al., 2008) can partially overcome this issue. Nevertheless, these are limited by geometric constraints of the model domain and lack robustness in the presence of highly ill-conditioned matrices. Therefore, in recent years, growing attention has been devoted to the development of efficient solution strategies to allow geodynamics codes to scale efficiently with the problem size on large-scale computing architectures. To this end, the use of innovative block-preconditioned Krylov methods seems to be the most promising way (Burstedde et al., 2008; May & Moresi, 2008; Geenen et al., 2009).

VARIATION OF THE GEOMETRY

A straightforward approach to limit the computational complexity of the simulations is to decrease the total number of degrees of freedom of the problem by reducing either the number of dimensions or the size of the model domain. On the one hand, for a given resolution (i.e. mean distance between the centres of two neighbouring cells), a 3D spherical shell clearly needs a much larger number of grid points than a cylindrical shell or a 2D Cartesian box. At the resolutions typically employed to solve mantle convection problems, this difference amounts to at least a factor of a few hundreds. On the other hand, for certain problems, only a relatively small part of the mantle may be of interest, either because the process under study occurs at a regional scale or because the dynamics of a portion of the mantle can be considered as representative for the dynamics of the mantle as a whole. Recent high-performance modelling, conducted in 3D Cartesian or regional shell geometry, of subduction (Schellart et al., 2007), mid-ocean ridges and transform faults (Gerya, 2010a, 2010b) or planetary-scale mantle convection (e.g. Robuchon et al., 2010) hold good promises.

While simulations performed in Cartesian geometry (both in 2D and 3D) are perfectly suitable to model regional scale processes, they must be designed with particular care when it comes to model global scale mantle convection. In fact, in Cartesian models, the role of the bottom thermal boundary layer tends to be overestimated since, differently from spherical or cylindrical shell models, the upper and lower surfaces have the same size. Interesting efforts have been made to compensate the lack of sphericity of Cartesian simulations by introducing an appropriately scaled cooling term in the thermal energy budget (O'Farrell & Lowman, 2010). Nevertheless, curved geometries such as 2D axisymmetric (e.g. van Keken, 2001), 2D cylindrical (e.g. Hernlund & Tackley, 2008)

or 3D regional spherical shell domains represent a preferable choice.

In Figure 5 and Table 1 we compare the results of several simple 2D and 3D simulations of thermal convection of bottom-heated systems conducted in different geometries. The Rayleigh number is 10 at the surface. The viscosity is calculated according to the Frank-Kamenetskii approximation (see next section) assuming a contrast due to temperature of 10^5, which implies a local Rayleigh number of 10^6 at the bottom of the domain. In Cartesian geometry, we employed a 2D box model with different aspect ratios and boundary conditions (5a-5c) (e.g. Moresi et al., 2003; Tosi et al., 2010; King et al., 1990) and a 3D box with reflective boundaries (5d) (e.g. Stein et al., 2010; Tackley, 2000a; Gait & Lowman, 2007). In spherical geometry, we used a 3D spherical shell (5j) (e.g. Hüttig & Stemmer, 2008b; Tackley, 2008; Stadler et al., 2010; Stemmer et al., 2006; Choblet et al., 2007; Zhong et al., 2000) and different configurations of a 2D cylinder (5e-5i) (e.g. Ghias & Jarvis, 2007; Plesa, 2011; Li & Kiefer, 2007). Note, that simulations in a spherical axisymmetric shell (e.g. van Keken, 2001) are not considered, as this geometry is not implemented in the code GAIA, which was used for this study.

In general, upwellings in Cartesian geometry are rather flat, whereas the spherical geometry changes their shape to more mushroom-like structures. Furthermore, the number of plumes, which is representative of the characteristic wavelength of convection, varies strongly among the geometries used. The 2D box model with reflective boundary conditions shows one upwelling at the left boundary (5a) and two half-plumes if the aspect ratio of the box is doubled (5b). In a 3D box with the same boundary conditions, one plume rises in the centre of the box (5d) that closely resembles the one obtained in 2D using periodic sidewalls (5c). The situation is different for the spherical domains. In the more realistic 3D shell (5j), which should be considered as the reference case to be approximated, six axisymmetric upwell-

Figure 5. Thermal convection with temperature-dependent viscosity in different geometries along the lines of Blankenbach et al., (1989) but with a viscosity contrast of 10^5 and a surface Rayleigh number of 10. All calculations have been performed with the code GAIA (Hüttig & Stemmer, 2008b). See Table 1 for the description of the geometries.

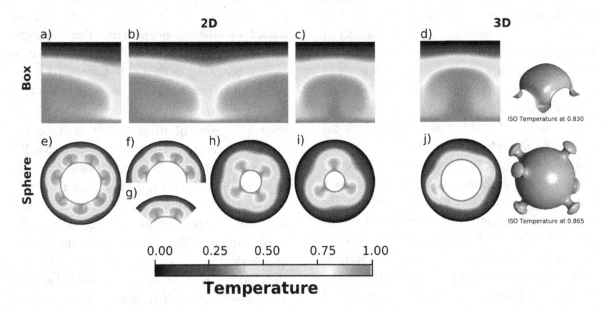

ings are observed. In 2D cylindrical geometry, instead, if the same ratio between inner and outer shell radius is assumed, several closely spaced plumes are formed, no matter whether a full (5e), a half (5f) or a quarter (5g) of the cylinder is considered.

The geometry and domain size further influence important parameters like the Nusselt number Nu, the average mantle temperature $|T_m|$ and the root mean square (rms) velocity v_{rms}. One reason for the observed differences is the mantle temperature itself. Higher temperatures, in fact, lead to lower viscosities and hence larger velocities that imply a more efficient convective heat transport (see Table 1). On the one hand, it should be noted that, when compared to each other, the standard 2D cylindrical models (cases e, f and g) do not exhibit significant differences, which is also what is observed when the 2D box models (cases a, b and c) are compared. On the other hand, both the standard 2D cylindrical cases e, f and g, and all the Cartesian cases a, b, c and d

differ significantly from the 3D spherical case. In particular, an analysis of the heat flux at the core-mantle boundary can explain the observed variations in the mantle temperatures. In a 3D spherical domain the heat flowing through an area of $4\pi r_c^2$ (the surface area of the core) heats up the mantle, whose volume is $4/3 \pi \left(r_p^3 - r_c^3\right)$, where r_c denotes the radius of the core and r_p the outer radius of the planet. In 2D, this translates to an area of $2\pi r_c$ compared to a volume of $\pi\left(r_p^2 - r_c^2\right)$. Therefore, the ratio between CMB area and mantle volume increases from 3D to 2D, leading to a warmer mantle in the 2D cylindrical case (Table 1). One possible way out of this problem is to reduce the radius of the core in the 2D simulations as discussed below (see Equation (3.1)). Note also that in Cartesian geometry, the difference between 2D and 3D is small, owing to the fact that the ratio between CMB area and mantle volume does not change.

Table 1. Global quantities for thermal convection simulations with temperature-dependent viscosity in different geometries along the lines of Blankenbach et al., (1989) but with a viscosity contrast of 10^5 and a surface Rayleigh number of 10. Letters in the 'Case' column correspond to those of Figure 5.

Case	Geometry	Nu	$|T_m|$	v_{rms}	A_c/A_m	A_c/V_m
a	2D box, 1:1, reflective BC	1.9555	0.6872	53.8057	1.0	2.0
b	2D box, 2:1, reflective BC	1.9555	0.6871	53.7893	1.0	2.0
c	2D box, 1:1, periodic BC	2.0135	0.6993	54.6189	1.0	2.0
d	3D box, 1:1:1, reflective BC	2.3627	0.6927	57.2126	1.0	2.0
e	2D cylinder	1.4394	0.5711	35.2505	0.5	1.333
f	2D 1/2 cylinder	1.4397	0.5725	34.8441	0.5	1.333
g	2D 1/4 cylinder	1.4400	0.5725	34.8691	0.5	1.333
h	2D cylinder, corrected volume	0.9948	0.4377	17.1118	0.273	0.857
i	2D cylinder, corrected radius	0.9136	0.4039	14.5119	0.25	0.8
j	3D sphere	0.7443	0.3374	16.1942	0.25	0.857

Let us consider a spherical shell with an inner to outer radius ratio of 0.5 (which is a good approximation for the Earth and most terrestrial planets) and assume, for simplicity, the non-dimensional values $r_p = 1$ and $r_c = 1/2$. For 2D and 3D boxes, the ratio of core surface area to mantle volume is 2, for the 2D cylindrical domain $4/3$, and for the full 3D sphere $6/7$. This trend can be directly observed in the averaged mantle temperature in Table 1. The smaller this value (i.e. the larger the volume where the heat from the core is distributed), the smaller is the mantle temperature. We have then carried out two additional 2D cylindrical simulations. In the first, shown in Figure 5h, the ratio of the core area A_c to mantle volume V_m is adjusted to the 3D case (corrected volume - CV):

$$\frac{A_{c,3D}}{V_{m,3D}} = \frac{A_{c,2D}}{V_{m,2D}} \quad \Leftrightarrow \quad \frac{3r_{c,3D}^2}{r_{p,3D}^3 - r_{c,3D}^3} = \frac{2r_{c,2D}}{r_{p,2D}^2 - r_{c,2D}^2} \quad (15)$$

The 2D cylindrical simulation with CV now better approaches the 3D spherical one. The rms-velocity in the mantle only differs by about 5% compared to 54% for the non-corrected version. The Nusselt number and mantle temperature

show more significant differences: 25% and 23%, respectively. However, these are again much smaller than those obtained when comparing the 2D and 3D sphere with equal radius ratio where the Nusselt number and average temperature differ by 48% and 41%.

The correction described above follows the one introduced by van Keken (2001) who similarly suggested to reduce r_c in such a way that the ratio between the core and surface area of a 3D spherical shell is maintained in 2D cylindrical geometry (corrected radius - CR):

$$\frac{A_{c,3D}}{A_{m,3D}} = \frac{A_{c,2D}}{A_{m,2D}} \quad \Leftrightarrow \quad \frac{r_{c,3D}^2}{r_{p,3D}^2} = \frac{r_{c,2D}}{r_{p,2D}} \quad (16)$$

This CR version has also been tested (Figure 5i). The results, listed in Table 1, even show a slight improvement for the Nusselt number (19%) and the average temperature (16%) with respect to those obtained with the CV version.

The simple investigations summarized in this section show the importance of the geometry and dimension of the domain employed. Given a set of parameters, simulations of thermal evolutions of terrestrial planets may show strong differences among different geometries. Scaling laws to be used in parameterized models are often derived from large ensembles of numerical simulations. In light of the simple results shown here, these should be conducted in a 3D spherical geometry. Alternatively, if the use of a 2D geometry cannot be avoided because of limited computational resources, a 2D cylindrical shell should be chosen after applying an appropriate radius correction.

The very first numerical models of mantle convection had to be based on reduced geometries. In the first studies (e.g. Parsons & McKenzie, 1978; Christensen, 1983) 2D box models were employed at coarse resolutions and only few parameter variations were possible since computational resources were strongly limited at that time (compared to later 2D parameter studies, e.g. by Moresi & Solomatov (1998) or Deschamps & Sotin (2000), who investigated about 100 model runs each). Also, the Rayleigh number could hardly exceed 10^6 and was thus much lower than those that can be currently handled. The first 3D spherical code was developed as early as in the 1985 (Baumgardner, 1985), even though it could not be used with realistic parameter sets due to limited resources. It is not unusual for present-day parameter studies (e.g. Hüttig & Breuer, 2011) to be based on up to ~100 3D spherical calculations with Raleigh numbers as large as 10^8. The steady improvement of calculations from past to present marks a clear trend, and it can be expected that in around one decade the use of both realistic parameters and high grid resolutions in 3D spherical geometry will represent a feasible task within the reach of the future generation of convection codes.

VARIATION OF THE VISCOSITY

The viscosity of a continuum is a measure of its resistance to deformation. Stresses induced by temperature and density gradients must overcome the viscous resistance of the material in order to deform, and hence to convect. The viscosity de-

pends strongly on the temperature, but it also increases with the hydrostatic pressure (Equation (2)). In the Earth's mantle, the viscosity increases with depth from the lithosphere to the CMB by a factor of 100 to 1000, as suggested by the inversion of various geodetic and geophysical observables (e.g. Mitrovica & Forte, 2004; Steinberger & Holme, 2008; van der Meer et al., 2010) and also by molecular dynamics simulations of diffusion in silicate minerals (e.g. Ito & Toriumi, 2010). It should be also noted that the adiabatic increase of the temperature with depth causes a reduction of the viscosity at the same time. Therefore, the actual increase of the viscosity solely due to pressure does not amount to a factor of 100 or 1000 only, but can be as large as a factor of 10^5 for Earth (assuming a CMB temperature of $3800K$ (Kawai & Tsuchiya, 2009) and an activation volume of $V^* = 2.5cm^3 / mol$ (Stamenkovic et al., 2011)).

An even larger effect on the viscosity is due to the fact that, at least on Earth, plastic yielding is the principal deformation mechanism of the uppermost layers of the mantle (i.e. the lithosphere and crust), where grains size strongly reduces in response to large applied stresses. Since the viscosity is a function of the grain size, it also decreases. In practice, sharp localizations of the deformation take place at weak zones of low viscosity, possibly leading to surface mobilization. Plates can thus slide into the mantle along such weak zones and subduction can take place (Bercovici, 2003).

The viscosity of the mantle is still far from being perfectly understood and Equation (1), which was introduced to describe it, may become inadequate in several circumstances. An interesting example is provided by the emerging field of exoplanetary research (e.g. Seager, 2011). During the past few years, a variety of planets have been discovered that orbit other stars and likely have an Earth-like composition but masses two to ten times larger than the mass of the Earth (hence super-Earths (Valencia et al., 2006)). Extrapolating our knowledge from Earth to simulate convection in the mantle of rocky super-Earths as for example CoRoT-7b (Hatzes et al., 2011) is therefore not straightforward, and studies of the possible viscosity variations with depth in massive exoplanets are highly controversial (Karato, 2011; Stamenkovic et al., 2011). Physical laws and laboratory experiments must be extrapolated to much higher pressures than the pressure attained at the Earth's CMB. Uncertainties in these extrapolations lead to different pressure-dependencies of the viscosity. Simulations of exoplanets therefore must span a large parameter space before robust conclusions can be drawn.

In the light of these issues, to simulate mantle convection, different simplifications in the viscosity law as well as assumptions about the underlying physical mechanisms need to be made. Small viscosities lead to large convective velocities, which typically require high grid resolution. Large and localized viscosity contrasts lead to stiff matrices and require sophisticated inversion algorithms. Typical simplifications adopted for convection simulations are

- To assume solely Newtonian behaviour (e.g. Stein et al., 2010; O'Neill et al., 2007; Rolf & Tackley, 2011; Stamenkovic et al., 2012),

- To neglect pressure-effects on the viscosity (e.g. O'Neill et al., 2007; van Heck & Tackley, 2008),

- To cut the viscosity above a predefined threshold value (e.g. Li & Kiefer, 2007; Michel & Forni, 2011),

- To reduce the viscosity contrast by assuming a higher surface temperature (e.g. Tackley, 2000b; Breuer et al., 1997),

- To reduce the viscosity contrast by assuming an arbitrary smaller activation energy (e.g. Roberts & Zhong, 2006; Nakagawa & Tackley, 2008),

- To approximate the viscosity law by a linearization of the exponential term in Equation (2) (Frank-Kamenetskii approximation (Frank-Kamenetskii, 1969]), so that the temperature dependence takes the form $\eta(T) \sim \exp(-aT)$ (e.g. Stein et al., 2010; Lenardic et al., 2008; Reese et al., 1999),

- To neglect lateral viscosity variations (e.g. Ziethe et al., 2009; Konrad & Spohn, 1997), or

- To use higher reference viscosities in order to reduce the convective vigour (e.g. van Heck & Tackley, 2008).

Note that those listed above are only simplifications of the viscosity formulation (1). A number of additional complexities such as compositional changes (e.g. McNamara & Zhong, 2004), anisotropy (Lev & Hager, 2008), hydration (Fraeman & Korenaga, 2010) or phase transitions (e.g. Tosi et al., 2010; Breuer et al., 1997) can further affect the distribution of viscosity, and thus the mantle dynamics, to the first order.

The simplifications above are routinely included in mantle convection codes. The interpretation of the outcome of the simulations, however, must be treated carefully. Using for example the Frank-Kamenetskii approximation of the viscosity helps to smooth the sharp gradients associated with the Arrhenius Equation (2) but may give rise to false convective regimes (Plesa & Breuer, 2010, May). For instance, as shown in Figure 6, a planet with a stagnant lid on top of the mantle, such as Mars, may suddenly migrate into an Earth-like plate tectonics regime if the Frank-Kamenetskii approximation instead of the Arrhenius law is employed.

Most realistic results for mantle convection models are expected when 3D spherical domain is used as well as a mixed Newtonian/non-Newtonian Arrhenius-like rheology without any approximation to reduce the viscosity contrast. However, since the present-day amount of computational resources is a strongly limiting factor to the complexity of problems to be investigated, a detailed comparison of the different viscosity laws with each other and especially with laboratory experiments is needed to understand, which simplifications tend to change the results. The simple investigation depicted in Figure 6 already showed that the use of the Frank-Kamenetskii approximation can lead to different numerical results. The same effect is expected when using higher reference viscosities (leading to rather sluggish convection), reduced activation energies or larger surface temperatures than the realistic values.

CONCLUSION AND FUTURE DIRECTIONS IN GEODYNAMICS

Many problems related to the numerical simulation of mantle convection have been solved in the past few years thanks to a growing community of geophysicists and computer scientists contributing to unravel the interior dynamics of the Earth and terrestrial planets. However, several open questions and challenges remain which will require strong efforts in the development of mantle convection codes in the near future.

Zhong et al. (2007) expect four major trends that will be followed by the forthcoming generation of high-performance mantle convection simulations:

Figure 6. Distribution of the non-dimensional temperature and viscosity fields of two 2D cylindrical simulations of mantle convection in a terrestrial planet using a temperature- and stress-dependent rheology. Note, that the viscosity scale is logarithmic. In the left panel, the Arrhenius law has been used. The right panel shows the same simulation but using the Frank-Kamenetskii approximation of the viscosity. Employing this approximation shifts the planet from a stagnant-lid regime to a plate-tectonics regime, with dramatic consequences for the surface and internal dynamics.

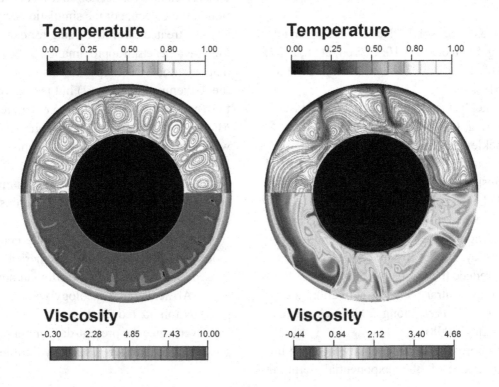

1. The study of the interplay between thermal and compositional convection will need further development both in terms of mesh resolution, which must be extremely high to accurately model mixing and stirring of buoyant chemical heterogeneities (e.g. Plesa et al., this volume), and in terms of the application of more sophisticated advection algorithms or the introduction of new and better ones.

2. The self-consistent generation of plate-tectonics will receive a growing attention. In particular, the strongly non-Newtonian behavior of the lithosphere that causes plastic deformation and shear localization can seriously affect the convergence properties of the solvers. Robust algorithms able to handle large and ill-conditioned systems will become more and more important.

3. Compressibility should be routinely incorporated in convection models. As far as the modeling of the Earth's mantle is concerned, this will allow for better comparisons against seismic and mineral physics models. Furthermore it will play a fundamental role in the newly born field of mantle convection in super-Earths.

4. The study of the multi-scale nature of mantle convection will play an increasingly important role and will clearly benefit of high resolutions and adaptive meshing.

Bercovici (2007) expects more research on the second point above, especially with regard to the initiation of plate tectonics and the difficulties to reproduce a realistic toroidal motion of tectonic plates.

He also lists the important issue of the coupling between planetary surfaces and atmospheres, which, so far, has received little attention from the community of numerical modellers.

It is often hypothesized that plate tectonics may play a role for the development of life (e.g. Parnell, 2004; Ward & Brownlee, 2000; Gilmour & Sephton, 2004). Also, the idea has been put forth that life itself might be the missing energy source (gained by photosynthesis) helping to produce the granite continents which make Earth so special (Rosing et al., 2006; Dyke et al., 2011). Only complex models coupling the interior to the atmosphere but also combining geochemistry, geophysics and biology in a new way can help to get a further insight into processes of this kind.

In addition, several constraints on parameters used for numerical studies are available from material physics (e.g. from mineralogy (Steinberger & Calderwood, 2006) or high-pressure physics (Grocholski et al., 2010)) but seldom used in convection studies. Incorporating experimental data as well as geophysical observations from Earth and other terrestrial bodies (e.g. constraints on crustal thickness (Grott & Breuer, 2008), geoid (Tosi et al., 2009), seismic tomography (King & Masters, 1992), surface mobilization (Lenardic et al., 2008), and atmospheric composition and density (Grott et al., 2011)) triggers a multi-disciplinary research path which is currently seldom followed but will be increasingly important in the future of mantle convection simulations. There is especially a need for a generally-applicable code which can not only be used to reveal specific observations but can be applied for all terrestrial planets fitting all available geophysical observations at once.

Since numerical codes are constantly extended to incorporate more and more sophisticated processes, the assessment of their accuracy and validity also represents a crucial issue. As only a handful of strongly simplified problems admit an analytical solution, codes are typically compared against each other. A few simple benchmarks have already been carried out for various geometries and focused on specific features like, for example, compressibility (King et al., 2010). A simple suite of benchmarks published by Blankenbach et al. (1989) still serves as a basic test for newly developed codes. Recently, Zhong et al., (2008) presented additional benchmark tests in a 3D spherical geometry, although only using one code

(CitComS). In the future, benchmarks in different geometries should be carried out to validate codes that account for complex rheologies and phase transitions, compressibility and chemical heterogeneities.

ACKNOWLEDGMENT

We thank the North-German Supercomputing Alliance (HLRN) for funding of the project "Scaling laws for mantle dynamics in exo-planets" under the leadership of Jürgen Oberst in the years 2010 and 2012. The research has also been funded by the Helmholtz Alliance "Planetary Evolution and Life". Nicola Tosi acknowledges support from the Deutsche Forschungs Gemeinschaft (grant number TO 704/1-1).

REFERENCES

Baranger, J., Matre, J. F., & Oudin, F. (1996). Connection between finite volume and mixed finite element methods. *Mathematical Modelling and Numerical Analysis, 30*(4), 445–465.

Baumgardner, J. R. (1985). Three dimensional treatment of convection flow in the Earth's mantle. *Journal of Statistical Physics, 39*(5/6), 501–511. doi:10.1007/BF01008348

Běhounková, M., Tobie, G., Choblet, G., & Čadek, O. (2010). Coupling mantle convection and tidal dissipation: Applications to Enceladus and Earth-like planets. *Journal of Geophysical Research, 115*, E09011. doi:10.1029/2009JE003564

Bercovici, D. (2003). The generation of plate tectonics from mantle convection. *Earth and Planetary Science Letters, 205*, 107–121. doi:10.1016/S0012-821X(02)01009-9

Bercovici, D. (2007). Mantle dynamics past, present and future: An introduction and overview. In D. Bercovici (Ed.), *Treatise on geophysics, volume 7 – Mantle dynamics* (pp. 1-30). Elsevier B.V.

Blankenbach, B., Busse, F., Christensen, U., Cserepes, L., Gunkel, D., & Hansen, U. (1989). A benchmark comparison for mantle convection codes. *Geophysical Journal International, 98*, 23–38. doi:10.1111/j.1365-246X.1989.tb05511.x

Breuer, D. (2009). Dynamics and thermal evolution. In Trümper, J. E. (Ed.), *Landolt-Börnstein astronomy and astrophysics 4b - Astronomy, astrophysics, and cosmology - Solar system* (pp. 254–280). Springer.

Breuer, D., Yuen, D. A., & Spohn, T. (1997). Phase transitions in the Martian mantle: Implications for partially layered convection. *Earth and Planetary Science Letters, 148*, 457–469. doi:10.1016/S0012-821X(97)00049-6

Burstedde, C., Ghattas, O., Gurnis, M., Stadler, G., Tan, E., Tu, T., et al. (2008). Scalable adaptive mantle convection simulation on petascale supercomputers. In *Proceedings of the 2008 ACM/IEEE Conference on Supercomputing* (pp. 1-15).

Čadek, O., & Fleitout, L. (2003). Effect of lateral viscosity variations in the top 300 km on the geoid and dynamic topography. *Geophysical Journal International, 152*, 566–580. doi:10.1046/j.1365-246X.2003.01859.x

Canuto, C., Hussaini, M. Y., Quarteroni, A., & Zang, T. A. (2007). *Spectral methods: Evolution to complex geometries and applications to fluid dynamics*. Springer.

Choblet, G., Čadek, O., Couturier, F., & Dumoulin, C. (2007). ŒDIPUS: A new tool to study the dynamics of planetary interiors. *Geophysical Journal International, 170*(1), 9–30. doi:10.1111/j.1365-246X.2007.03419.x

Christensen, U. R. (1983). Convection in a variable-viscosity fluid: Newtonian versus power-law rheology. *Earth and Planetary Science Letters, 64,* 153–162. doi:10.1016/0012-821X(83)90060-2

Christensen, U. R. (1984). Convection with pressure- and temperature-dependent non-Newtonian rheology. *Geophysical Journal of the Royal Astronomical Society, 77,* 343–384. doi:10.1111/j.1365-246X.1984.tb01939.x

Christensen, U. R., & Wicht, J. (2007). Numerical dynamo simulations. In P. Olsen (Ed), *Treatise on geophysics, Vol. 8 - Core dynamics* (245-282). Amsterdam, The Netherlands: Elsevier.

CIG. (2012). *Computational infrastructure for geodynamics for CitComS*. Retrieved January 12, 2012, from http://www.geodynamics.org/cig/software/citcoms

Davaille, A., & Limare, A. (2007). Laboratory studies of mantle convection. In D. Bercovici (Ed.), *Treatise on geophysics, Volume 7 – Mantle dynamics* (pp. 90-165). Elsevier B.V.

Davies, D. R., Davies, J. H., Hassan, O., Morgan, K., & Nithiarasu, P. (2007). Adaptive finite element methods in geodynamics - Convection dominated mid-ocean ridge and subduction zone simulations. *International Journal of Numerical Methods for Heat & Fluid Flow, 18*(7/8), 1015–1035. doi:10.1108/09615530810899079

de Berg, M., Cheong, O., van Kreveld, M., & Overmars, M. (2008). *Computational geometry: Algorithms and applications*. Germany: Springer.

Deschamps, F., & Sotin, C. (2000). Inversion of two-dimensional numerical convection experiments for a fluid with a strongly temperature-dependent viscosity. *Geophysical Journal International, 143,* 204–218. doi:10.1046/j.1365-246x.2000.00228.x

Dyke, J. G., Gans, F., & Kleidon, A. (2011). Towards understanding how surface life can affect interior geological processes: a non-equilibrium thermodynamics approach. *Earth System Dynamics, 2,* 139–160. doi:10.5194/esd-2-139-2011

Dziewonski, A. M., & Anderson, D. L. (1981). Preliminary reference Earth model. *Physics of the Earth and Planetary Interiors, 25,* 297–356. doi:10.1016/0031-9201(81)90046-7

Elsen, E., LeGresley, P., & Darve, E. (2008). Large calculation of the flow over a hypersonic vehicle using a GPU. *Journal of Computational Physics, 227,* 10148–10161. doi:10.1016/j.jcp.2008.08.023

Ferziger, J. H., & Peric, M. (1999). *Computational methods for fluid dynamics*. Germany: Springer. doi:10.1007/978-3-642-98037-4

Fraeman, A. A., & Korenaga, J. (2010). The influence of mantle melting on the evolution of Mars. *Icarus, 210,* 43–57. doi:10.1016/j.icarus.2010.06.030

Frank-Kamenetskii, D. (1969). *Diffusion and heat transfer in chemical kinetics*. Plenum Press.

Gait, A. D., & Lowman, J. P. (2007). Effect of lower mantle viscosity on the time-dependence of plate velocities in three-dimensional mantle convection models. *Geophysical Research Letters, 34,* L21304. doi:10.1029/2007GL031396

Geenen, T., ur Rehman, M., MacLachlan, S. P., Segal, G., Vuik, C., van den Berg, A. P., & Spakman, W. (2009). Scalable robust solvers for unstructured FE geodynamic modeling applications: Solving the Stokes equation for models with large localized viscosity contrasts. *Geochemistry Geophysics Geosystems, 10,* Q09002. doi:10.1029/2009GC002526

Gerya, T. (2010a). Dynamical instability produces transform faults at mid-ocean ridges. *Science, 329*(5995), 1047–1050. doi:10.1126/science.1191349

Gerya, T. (2010b). *Introduction to numerical geodynamic modelling*. Cambridge, UK: Cambridge University Press.

Ghias, S. R., & Jarvis, G. T. (2007). Mantle flow reversals in cylindrical Earth models. *Physics of the Earth and Planetary Interiors, 165*(3-4), 194–207. doi:10.1016/j.pepi.2007.09.004

Gilmour, I., & Sephton, M. A. (Eds.). (2004). *An introduction to astrobiology*. Cambridge, UK: Cambridge University Press.

Glatzmaier, G. A., & Roberts, P. H. (1995). A three-dimensional self-consistent computer simulation of a geomagnetic field reversal. *Nature, 377*, 203–209. doi:10.1038/377203a0

Grocholski, B., Shim, S.-H., & Prakapenka, V. B. (2010). Stability of the MgSiO3 analog NaMgF3 and its implication for mantle structure in super-Earths. *Geophysical Research Letters, 37*, L14204. doi:10.1029/2010GL043645

Grott, M., & Breuer, D. (2008). The evolution of the Martian elastic lithosphere and implications for crustal and mantle rheology. *Icarus, 193*, 503–515. doi:10.1016/j.icarus.2007.08.015

Grott, M., Morschhauser, A., Breuer, D., & Hauber, E. (2011). Volcanic outgassing of CO2 and H2O on Mars. *Earth and Planetary Science Letters, 308*(3-4), 391–400. doi:10.1016/j.epsl.2011.06.014

Hatzes, A. P. (2011). The mass of CoRoT-7b. *The Astrophysical Journal, 743*(1), 75–86. doi:10.1088/0004-637X/743/1/75

Hernlund, J. W., & Tackley, P. (2008). Modeling mantle convection in the spherical annulus. *Physics of the Earth and Planetary Interiors, 171*, 48–54. doi:10.1016/j.pepi.2008.07.037

Hirth, G., & Kohlstedt, D. L. (2003). Rheology of the upper mantle and the mantle wedge: A view from the experimentalists. In Eiler, J. (Ed.), *Inside the subduction factory* (pp. 83–105). doi:10.1029/138GM06

Hughes, T. J. R. (2000). *The finite element method: Linear static and dynamic finite element analysis*. Dover.

Hüttig, C. (2009). *Scaling laws for internally heated mantle convection*. Doctoral dissertation, University of Münster, Germany.

Hüttig, C., & Breuer, D. (2011). Regime classification and planform scaling for internally heated mantle convection. *Physics of the Earth and Planetary Interiors, 186*(3-4), 111–124. doi:10.1016/j.pepi.2011.03.011

Hüttig, C., & Stemmer, K. (2008a). The spiral grid: A new approach to discretize the sphere and its application to mantle convection. *Geochemistry Geophysics Geosystems, 9*(2), Q02018. doi:10.1029/2007GC001581

Hüttig, C., & Stemmer, K. (2008b). Finite volume discretization for dynamic viscosities on Voronoi grids. *Physics of the Earth and Planetary Interiors, 171*(1-4), 137–146. doi:10.1016/j.pepi.2008.07.007

Ismail-Zadeh, A., & Tackley, P. J. (2010). *Computational methods for geodynamics*. Cambridge, UK: Cambridge University Press. doi:10.1017/CBO9780511780820

Ito, I., & Toriumi, M. (2010). Silicon self-diffusion of MgSiO3 perovskite by molecular dynamics and its implication for lower mantle rheology. *Journal of Geophysical Research, 115*, B12205. doi:10.1029/2010JB000843

Kageyama, A., & Sato, T. (2004). The "Yin-Yang grid": An overset grid in spherical geometry. *Geochemistry Geophysics Geosystems, 5*, Q09005. doi:10.1029/2004GC000734

Kameyama, M., Kageyama, A., & Sato, T. (2008). Multigrid-based simulation code for mantle convection in spherical shell using Yin-Yang grid. *Physics of the Earth and Planetary Interiors, 171,* 19–32. doi:10.1016/j.pepi.2008.06.025

Karato, S.-I. (2008). *Deformation of Earth materials: An introduction to the rheology of solid earth.* Cambridge, UK: Cambridge University Press. doi:10.1017/CBO9780511804892

Karato, S.-I. (2011). Rheological structure of the mantle of a super-Earth: Some insights from mineral physics. *Icarus, 212*(1), 14–23. doi:10.1016/j.icarus.2010.12.005

Karato, S.-I., & Wu, P. (1993). Rheology of the upper mantle: A synthesis. *Science, 260,* 771–778. doi:10.1126/science.260.5109.771

Kaus, B. J. P., Steedman, C., & Becker, T. W. (2008). From passive continental margin to mountain belt: Insights from analytical and numerical models and application to Taiwan. *Physics of the Earth and Planetary Interiors, 171,* 235–251. doi:10.1016/j.pepi.2008.06.015

Kawai, K., & Tsuchiya, T. (2009). Temperature profile in the lowermost mantle from seismological and mineral physics joint modeling. *Proceedings of the National Academy of Sciences of the United States of America, 106*(52), 22119–22123. doi:10.1073/pnas.0905920106

Keller, T., & Tackley, P. J. (2009). Towards self-consistent modelling of the Martian dichotomy: The influence of low-degree convection on crustal thickness distribution. *Icarus, 202*(2), 429–443. doi:10.1016/j.icarus.2009.03.029

King, S. D. (2008). Pattern of lobate scarps on Mercury's surface reproduced by a model of mantle convection. *Nature Geoscience, 1,* 229–232. doi:10.1038/ngeo152

King, S. D., Lee, C., van Keken, P. E., Leng, W., Zhong, S., & Tan, E. (2010). A community benchmark for 2D Cartesian compressible convection in the Earth's mantle. *Geophysical Journal International, 180*(1), 73–87. doi:10.1111/j.1365-246X.2009.04413.x

King, S. D., & Masters, G. (1992). An inversion for radial viscosity structure using seismic tomography. *Geophysical Research Letters, 19*(15), 1551–1554. doi:10.1029/92GL01700

King, S. D., Raefsky, A., & Hager, B. H. (1990). Conman: Vectorizing a finite element code for incompressible two-dimensional convection in the Earth's mantle. *Physics of the Earth and Planetary Interiors, 59*(3), 195–207. doi:10.1016/0031-9201(90)90225-M

Kitware. (2012). *ParaView open-source code.* Retrieved January 31, 2012, from http://www.paraview.org

Konrad, W., & Spohn, T. (1997). Thermal history of the Moon: Implication for an early core dynamo and post-accretional magmatism. *Advances in Space Research, 19,* 1511–1521. doi:10.1016/S0273-1177(97)00364-5

Lenardic, A., Jellinek, A. M., & Moresi, L.-N. (2008). A climate induced transition in the tectonic style of a terrestrial planet. *Earth and Planetary Science Letters, 271,* 34–42. doi:10.1016/j.epsl.2008.03.031

Leng, W., & Zhong, S. (2011). Implementation and application of adaptive mesh refinement for thermochemical mantle convection studies. *Geochemistry Geophysics Geosystems, 12*(4), Q04006. doi:10.1029/2010GC003425

Lev, E., & Hager, B. (2008). Rayleigh-Taylor instabilities with anisotropic lithospheric viscosity. *Geophysical Journal International, 173*(3), 806–814. doi:10.1111/j.1365-246X.2008.03731.x

Li, Q., & Kiefer, W. S. (2007). Mantle convection and magma production on present-day Mars: Effects of temperature-dependent rheology. *Geophysical Research Letters, 34,* L16203. doi:10.1029/2007GL030544

Marshall, J., & Plumb, R. A. (2008). *Atmosphere, ocean, and climate dynamics – An introductory text.* China: Academic Press, Elsevier.

Martinec, Z. (2000). Spectral-finite element approach to three-dimensional viscoelastic relaxation in a spherical earth. *Geophysical Journal International, 142,* 117–141. doi:10.1046/j.1365-246x.2000.00138.x

May, D. A., & Moresi, L. (2008). Preconditioned iterative methods for Stokes flow problems arising in computational geodynamics. *Physics of the Earth and Planetary Interiors, 171*(1-4), 33–47. doi:10.1016/j.pepi.2008.07.036

McNamara, A. K., & Zhong, S. (2004). Thermo-chemical structures within a spherical mantle: Superplumes or piles? *Journal of Geophysical Research, 109,* B07402. doi:10.1029/2003JB002847

Michel, N., & Forni, O. (2011). Mars mantle convection: Influence of phase transitions with core cooling. *Planetary and Space Science, 59,* 741–748. doi:10.1016/j.pss.2011.02.013

Mitrovica, J. X., & Forte, A. M. (2004). A new inference of mantle viscosity based upon joint inversion of convection and glacial isostatic adjustment data. *Earth and Planetary Science Letters, 225,* 177–189. doi:10.1016/j.epsl.2004.06.005

Moresi, L., Dufour, F., & Mühlhaus, H. B. (2003). A Lagrangian integration point finite element method for large deformation modeling of viscoelastic geomaterials. *Journal of Computational Physics, 184,* 476–497. doi:10.1016/S0021-9991(02)00031-1

Moresi, L., & Solomatov, V. (1998). Mantle convection with a brittle lithosphere: Thoughts on the global tectonic styles of the Earth and Venus. *Geophysical Journal International, 133,* 669–682. doi:10.1046/j.1365-246X.1998.00521.x

Nakagawa, T., & Tackley, P. J. (2008). Lateral variations in CMB heat flux and deep mantle seismic velocity caused by a thermal–chemical-phase boundary layer in 3D spherical convection. *Earth and Planetary Science Letters, 271,* 348–358. doi:10.1016/j.epsl.2008.04.013

Nakagawa, T., & Tackley, P. J. (2010). Influence of initial CMB temperature and other parameters on the thermal evolution of Earth's core resulting from thermo-chemical spherical mantle convection. *Geochemistry Geophysics Geosystems, 11,* Q06001. doi:10.1029/2010GC003031

Noack, L., Breuer, D., & Spohn, T. (2012). Coupling the atmosphere with interior dynamics: Implications for the resurfacing of Venus. *Icarus, 217*(2), 484–498. doi:10.1016/j.icarus.2011.08.026

O'Farrell, K. A., & Lowman, J. P. (2010). Emulating the thermal structure of spherical shell convection in plane-layer geometry mantle convection models. *Physics of the Earth and Planetary Interiors, 182*(1-2), 73–84. doi:10.1016/j.pepi.2010.06.010

O'Neill, C., Jellinek, A. M., & Lenardic, A. (2007). Conditions for the onset of plate tectonics on terrestrial planets and moons. *Earth and Planetary Science Letters, 261,* 20–32. doi:10.1016/j.epsl.2007.05.038

Parnell, J. (2004). Plate tectonics, surface mineralogy, and the early evolution of life. *International Journal of Astrobiology, 3*(2), 131–137. doi:10.1017/S1473550404002101

Parsons, B., & McKenzie, D. (1978). Mantle convection and the thermal structure of the plates. *Journal of Geophysical Research, 83*(B9), 4485–4496. doi:10.1029/JB083iB09p04485

Peltier, W. R., & Solheim, L. P. (1992). Mantle phase transitions and layered chaotic convection. *Geophysical Research Letters, 19*(3), 321–324. doi:10.1029/91GL02951

Phillips, R. J., Bullock, M. A., & Hauck, S. A. II. (2001). Climate and interior coupled evolution on Venus. *Geophysical Research Letters, 28*(9), 1779–1782. doi:10.1029/2000GL011821

Phinney, R. A., & Burridge, R. (1973). Representation of the elastic - gravitational excitation of a spherical Earth model by generalized spherical harmonics. *Geophysical Journal International, 34*(4), 451–487. doi:10.1111/j.1365-246X.1973.tb02407.x

Plesa, A.-C. (2011). Mantle convection in a 2D spherical shell. *INFOCOMP 2011: First International Conference on Advanced Communications and Computation*, (pp. 167-172). ISBN 978-1-61208-161-8

Plesa, A.-C., & Breuer, D. (2010, May). *Mantle convection in a spherical shell: The problems of using Frank-Kamenetskii Approximation for the viscosity law*. Paper presented at the General Assembly of the European Geoscience Union, Vienna, Austria.

Plesa, A.-C., Tosi, N., & Hüttig, C. (2012). Thermo-chemical convection in planetary mantles: A comparison of advection methods in spherical domains. In Rückemann, C.-P. (Ed.), *Integrated information and computing systems for natural, spatial, and social sciences*. Hershey, PA: IGI Global.

Reese, C. C., Solomatov, V. S., & Moresi, L.-N. (1999). Non-newtonian stagnant lid convection and magmatic resurfacing on Venus. *Icarus, 139*, 67–80. doi:10.1006/icar.1999.6088

Ricard, Y. (2007). Physics and theory. In D. Bercovici (Ed.), *Treatise on geophysics, Volume 7 – Mantle dynamics* (pp. 31-87). Elsevier B.V.

Roberts, J. H., & Zhong, S. (2006). Degree-1 convection in the Martian mantle and the origin of the hemispheric dichotomy. *Journal of Geophysical Research, 111*, E06013. doi:10.1029/2005JE002668

Robuchon, G., Choblet, G., Tobie, G., Čadek, O., Sotin, C., & Grasset, O. (2010). Coupling of thermal evolution and despinning of early Iapetus. *Icarus, 207*, 959–971. doi:10.1016/j.icarus.2009.12.002

Rolf, T., & Tackley, P. J. (2011). Focussing of stress by continents in 3D spherical mantle convection with self-consistent plate tectonics. *Geophysical Research Letters, 38*, L18301. doi:10.1029/2011GL048677

Ronchi, C., Iacono, R., Paolucci, P. S., Hertzberger, B., & Serazzi, G. (1996). The "cubed sphere": A new method for the solution of partial differential equations in spherical geometry. *Journal of Computational Physics, 124*, 93–114. doi:10.1006/jcph.1996.0047

Rosing, M. T., Bird, D. K., Sleep, N. H., Glassley, W., & Albarede, F. (2006). The rise of continents—An essay on the geologic consequences of photosynthesis. *Palaeogeography, Palaeoclimatology, Palaeoecology, 232*, 99–113. doi:10.1016/j.palaeo.2006.01.007

Saad, Y. (1996). *Iterative methods for sparse linear systems*. Boston, MA: PWS Publishing.

Sanchez, D. A., Yuen, D. A., Sun, Y., & Wright, G. B. (2011). The role of floating point precision in two- and three-dimensional high Rayleigh-Bénard convection modeled on Fermi GPU. *Proceedings of the 14th IEEE International Conference on Computational Science and Engineering*, (pp. 606-610).

Sanders, J., & Kandrot, E. (2010). *CUDA by example: An introduction to general-purpose GPU programming*. Addison-Wesley.

Schellart, W. P., Freeman, J., Stegman, D. R., Moresi, L., & May, D. (2007). Evolution and diversity of subduction zones controlled by slab width. *Nature, 7133*(446), 308–311. doi:10.1038/nature05615

Schmeling, H., Babeyko, A. Y., Enns, A., Faccenna, C., Funiciello, F., & Gerya, T. (2008). A benchmark comparison of spontaneous subduction models – Towards a free surface. *Physics of the Earth and Planetary Interiors, 171*, 198–223. doi:10.1016/j.pepi.2008.06.028

Schubert, G., Turcotte, D. L., & Olson, P. (2001). *Mantle convection in the Earth and planets*. Cambridge, UK: Cambridge University Press. doi:10.1017/CBO9780511612879

Schubert, G., Turcotte, D. L., Solomon, S. C., & Sleep, N. H. (1989). *Coupled evolution of the atmospheres and interiors of planets and satellites: Origin and evolution of planetary and satellite atmospheres*. Tucson, AZ: University of Arizona Press.

Schuberth, B. S. A., Bunge, H.-P., Steinle-Neumann, G., Moder, C., & Oeser, J. (2009). Thermal versus elastic heterogeneity in high-resolution mantle circulation models with pyrolite composition: High plume excess temperatures in the lowermost mantle. *Geochemistry Geophysics Geosystems, 10*(1), Q01W01. doi:10.1029/2008GC002235

Seager, S. (2011). *Exoplanets*. Tucson, AZ: University of Arizona Press.

Sotin, C., & Labrosse, S. (1999). Three-dimensional thermal convection in an iso-viscous, infinite Prandtl number fluid heated from within and from below: Applications to the transfer of heat through planetary mantles. *Physics of the Earth and Planetary Interiors, 112*, 171–190. doi:10.1016/S0031-9201(99)00004-7

Spohn, T., & Schubert, G. (1982). Models of mantle convection and the removal of heat from the Earth's interior. *Journal of Geophysical Research, 87*, 4682–4696. doi:10.1029/JB087iB06p04682

Šrámek, O., & Zhong, S. J. (2010). Long-wavelength stagnant-lid convection with hemispheric variation in lithospheric thickness: Link between Martian crustal dichotomy and Tharsis? *Journal of Geophysical Research, 115*, E09010. doi:10.1029/2010JE003597

Stadler, G., Gurnis, M., Burstedde, C., Wilcox, L. C., Alisic, L., & Ghattas, O. (2010). The dynamics of plate tectonics and mantle flow: From local to global scales. *Science, 329*(5995), 1033–1038. doi:10.1126/science.1191223

Stamenkovic, V., Breuer, D., & Spohn, T. (2011). Thermal and transport properties of mantle rock at high pressure: Applications to super-Earths. *Icarus, 216*(2), 572–596. doi:10.1016/j.icarus.2011.09.030

Stamenkovic, V., Noack, L., Breuer, D., & Spohn, T. (2012). The influence of pressure-dependent viscosity on the thermal evolution of super-Earths. *The Astrophysical Journal, 748*(1), 41. doi:10.1088/0004-637X/748/1/41

Stein, C., Fahl, A., & Hansen, U. (2010). Resurfacing events on Venus: Implications on plume dynamics and surface topography. *Geophysical Research Letters, 37*, L01201. doi:10.1029/2009GL041073

Steinberger, B., & Calderwood, A. R. (2006). Models of large-scale viscous flow in the Earth's mantle with constraints from mineral physics and surface observations. *Geophysical Journal International, 167*, 1461–1481. doi:10.1111/j.1365-246X.2006.03131.x

Steinberger, B., & Holme, R. (2008). Mantle flow models with core-mantle boundary constraints and chemical heterogeneities in the lowermost mantle. *Journal of Geophysical Research, 113*, B05403. doi:10.1029/2007JB005080

Stemmer, K., Harder, H., & Hansen, U. (2006). A new method to simulate convection with strongly temperature- and pressure-dependent viscosity in a spherical shell: Applications to the Earth's mantle. *Physics of the Earth and Planetary Interiors, 157*, 223–249. doi:10.1016/j.pepi.2006.04.007

Stevenson, D. J., Spohn, T., & Schubert, G. (1983). Magnetism and thermal evolution of the terrestrial planets. *Icarus, 54*, 466–489. doi:10.1016/0019-1035(83)90241-5

Tackley, P. J. (2000a). Mantle convection and plate tectonics: Toward an integrated physical and chemical theory. *Science, 288*, 2002–2007. doi:10.1126/science.288.5473.2002

Tackley, P. J. (2000b). Self-consistent generation of tectonic plates in time-dependent, three-dimensional mantle convection simulations. *Geochemistry Geophysics Geosystems, 1*(8), 1021. doi:10.1029/2000GC000036

Tackley, P. J. (2008). Modelling compressible mantle convection with large viscosity contrasts in a three-dimensional spherical shell using the yin-yang grid. *Physics of the Earth and Planetary Interiors, 171*(1-4), 7–18. doi:10.1016/j.pepi.2008.08.005

Tan, E., Leng, W., Zhong, S., & Gurnis, M. (2011). On the location of plumes and lateral movement of thermochemical structures with high bulk modulus in the 3-D compressible mantle. *Geochemistry Geophysics Geosystems, 12*, Q07005. doi:10.1029/2011GC003665

Tosi, N., Čadek, O., Martinec, Z., Yuen, D. A., & Kaufmann, G. (2009). Is the long-wavelength geoid sensitive to the presence of postperovskite above the core-mantle boundary? *Geophysical Research Letters, 36*, L05303. doi:10.1029/2008GL036902

Tosi, N., Yuen, D. A., & Čadek, O. (2010). Dynamical consequences in the lower mantle with the post-perovskite phase change and strongly depth-dependent thermodynamic and transport properties. *Earth and Planetary Science Letters, 298*(1-2), 229–243. doi:10.1016/j.epsl.2010.08.001

Turcotte, D. L., & Schubert, G. (2002). *Geodynamics* (2nd ed.). New York, NY: Cambridge University Press.

Valencia, D., O'Connell, R. J., & Sasselov, D. (2006). Internal structure of massive terrestrial planets. *Icarus, 181*, 545–554. doi:10.1016/j.icarus.2005.11.021

van der Meer, D. G., Spakman, W., van Hinsbergen, D. J. J., Amaru, M. L., & Torsvik, T. H. (2010). Towards absolute plate motions constrained by lower-mantle slab remnants. *Nature Geoscience, 3*, 36–40. doi:10.1038/ngeo708

van Heck, H. J., & Tackley, P. J. (2008). Planforms of self-consistently generated plates in 3D spherical geometry. *Geophysical Research Letters, 35*, L19312. doi:10.1029/2008GL035190 van Keken, P. E. (2001). Cylindrical scaling for dynamical cooling models of the Earth. *Physics of the Earth and Planetary Interiors, 124*, 119–130. doi:10.1016/S0031-9201(01)00195-9

van Keken, P. E., King, S. D., Schmeling, H., Christensen, U. R., Neumeister, D., & Doin, M.-P. (1997). A comparison of methods for the modeling of thermochemical convection. *Journal of Geophysical Research, 102*, 22477–22495. doi:10.1029/97JB01353

Varshalovich, D. A., Moskalev, A. N., & Khersonskii, V. K. (1988). *Quantum theory of angular momentum*. World Scientific.

Velímský, J., & Martinec, Z. (2005). Time-domain, spherical harmonic-finite element approach to transient three-dimensional geomagnetic induction in a spherical heterogeneous Earth. *Geophysical Journal International, 161*(1), 81–101. doi:10.1111/j.1365-246X.2005.02546.x

von Larcher, T., Futterer, B., Egbers, C., Hollerbach, R., Chossat, P., & Beltrame, P. (2008). GeoFlow - European microgravity experiments on thermal convection in rotating spherical shells under influence of central force field. *Journal of the Japan Society of Microgravity Application, 25*(3), 121–126.

Ward, P. D., & Brownlee, D. (2000). *Rare Earth: Why complex life is uncommon in the universe.* New York, NY: Springer. doi:10.1063/1.1325239

Zhang, S., & Christensen, U. (1993). Some effects of lateral viscosity variations on geoid and surface velocities induced by density anomalies in the mantle. *Geophysical Journal International, 114*, 531–547. doi:10.1111/j.1365-246X.1993.tb06985.x

Zhang, S., & Yuen, D. A. (1996). Various influences on plumes and dynamics in time-dependent, compressible, mantle convection in 3-D spherical shell. *Physics of the Earth and Planetary Interiors, 94*, 241–267. doi:10.1016/0031-9201(95)03100-6

Zheng, L., Gerya, T., Yuen, D. A., Knepley, M. G., Zhang, H., & Shi, Y. (2010, December). *GPU implementation of Stokes equation with strongly variable coefficients*. Paper presented at the American Geophysical Union, Fall Meeting 2010, IN41A-1350.

Zhong, S., McNamara, A., Tan, E., Moresi, L., & Gurnis, M. (2008). A benchmark study on mantle convection in a 3-D spherical shell using CitComS. *Geochemistry Geophysics Geosystems, 9*(10), Q10017. doi:10.1029/2008GC002048

Zhong, S., Yuen, D. A., & Moresi, L. (2007). Computational methods. In D. Bercovici (Ed.), *Treatise on geophysics, Volume 7 – Mantle dynamics* (pp. 227-252). Elsevier B.V.

Zhong, S., Zuber, M. T., Moresi, L., & Gurnis, M. (2000). Role of temperature-dependent viscosity and surface plates in spherical shell models of mantle convection. *Journal of Geophysical Research, 105*, 11063–11082. doi:10.1029/2000JB900003

Ziethe, R., Seiferlin, K., & Hiesinger, H. (2009). Duration and extent of lunar volcanism: Comparison of 3D convection models to mare basalt ages. *Planetary and Space Science, 57*(7), 784–796. doi:10.1016/j.pss.2009.02.002

Section 4
Big Data Exploration, Visualisation, Education, and Social Media

Chapter 17
Space–Time Analytics for Spatial Dynamics

May Yuan
University of Oklahoma, USA

James Bothwell
University of Oklahoma, USA

ABSTRACT

The so-called Big Data Challenge poses not only issues with massive volumes of data, but issues with the continuing data streams from multiple sources that monitor environmental processes or record social activities. Many statistics tools and data mining methods have been developed to reveal embedded patterns in large data sets. While patterns are critical to data analysis, deep insights will remain buried unless we develop means to associate spatiotemporal patterns to the dynamics of spatial processes that essentially drive the formation of patterns in the data. This chapter reviews the literature with the conceptual foundation for space-time analytics dealing with spatial processes, discusses the types of dynamics that have and have not been addressed in the literature, and identifies needs for new thinking that can systematically advance space-time analytics to reveal dynamics of spatial processes. The discussion is facilitated by an example to highlight potential means of space-time analytics in response to the Big Data Challenge. The example shows the development of new space-time concepts and tools to analyze data from two common General Circulation Models for climate change predictions. Common approaches compare temperature changes at locations from the NCAR CCSM3 and from the CNRM CM3 or animate time series of temperature layers to visualize the climate prediction. Instead, new space-time analytics methods are shown here the ability to decipher the differences in spatial dynamics of the predicted temperature change in the model outputs and apply the concepts of change and movement to reveal warming, cooling, convergence, and divergence in temperature change across the globe.

NTRODUCTION

The example given in the abstract demonstrates the idea of new space-time analytics to dig down into massive amounts of spatiotemporal data to derive an understanding of spatial dynamics. While there is no unified definition, *analytics* is defined here as the science or method of examining something complex so as to determine its nature, structure, or essential features[1]. The Oxford English Dictionary quoted from R. Bisset Douglas (1800) "I teach

DOI: 10.4018/978-1-4666-2190-9.ch017

all the arts and sciences; Greek, Latin, Mathematics, Metaphysics, Analytics, Synthetics, and Arithmetic" which positions analytics in a progress of science's emphases (Table 1). While mathematics and metaphysics provide the basics of conceptual and symbolic abstraction, analytics is the first step towards data and computing. Analytics gains increasing popularity with the ever growing volumes of data from remote sensing satellites, environmental sensor networks, social surveys, surveillance systems and cyber media. Data deluge pushes the demand for analytical ability to take data, visualize it, understand it, process it, extract value from it, and communicate it.

Space-time analytics extends the definition of analytics to the use of space and time as frames of processing, extraction, visualization, understanding, and communication to simplify the complexity of spatial dynamics into elements and structures in space and time. Because every object or process exists in some space and time, data that provide measures of spatial objects or spatial processes must have location and time references. Hence, space-time naturally serves as a common framework for data integration. However, data are static; observations or samples are taken at specific location and instance. Space-time analytics aims not only to uncover patterns of properties captured by the data but also to reveal the underlying processes that drive the patterns. For example, analysis of temperature observations can reveal distributions of high and low temperatures. Insights about temperature change in a region are

acquired through the analyses of the movements of cold and warm fronts. Analyses of space-time tracks can lead to patterns of activities. Furthermore, analyses of the person's social and environmental resources provide the underlying constraints with which the person is operating, and subsequently the constraints lead to an understanding of the person's routine activity patterns.

Hence, the premise of the chapter posits the need of space-time analytics for understanding the underlying spatial dynamics. Ontological debates on spatiotemporal objects persist, but this chapter subscribes to the conceptual framework that consists of (1) change and movement as two fundamental spatiotemporal observables, and (2) activities, events, and processes are three spatiotemporal primitives that drive the observables (Yuan & Stewart, 2008). Change depicts the differentiation of properties or values over time, while movement involves changing locations over time. Humans observe change and movement to interpret the happening, transitions, or consequences of activities, events, and processes in space and time. In a nutshell, activities are actions taken by an agent, events denote what happens, and processes detail how it happens. The emphasis is to go beyond identification of space-time patterns of change and movement to the understanding of spatial dynamics about activities, events, and processes. The following sections include a conceptual framework for thinking about space-time analytics and highlights of space-time methods that represent key analytical emphases, arguments to support the premise for spatial dynamics with examples to illustrate alternative thoughts of space-time analytics, and suggestions for future research directions.

BACKGROUND

In geospatial domains, change and movement can only be observed in a space-time reference

Table 1. Sciences of methodology and logics

Science	Emphases
Mathematics	Space, number, quantity, and arrangement
Metaphysics	First principles of things or reality
Analytics	Element and structure
Synthetics	Whole, consequence, or particular instance
Arithmetic	Numbers and features

frame. Quantitative geographers and geospatial scientists have studied change and movement intensively. Brian Berry's geographic matrix considers change in three orthogonal dimensions of place, characteristics, and time (Berry, 1964). The geographic matrix is designed for regional analysis in which space-time observables are change-related measures; there is no movement in analysis. To incorporate movement, the geographic matrix is extended to six general approaches of analytics based on space, time, and theme (Table 2) Change is observed in three ways: (1) change to thematic or temporal characteristics over space, (2) change to thematic or spatial characteristics over time, and (3) changes to spatial or temporal characteristics over theme.

Changes to thematic or temporal characteristics over space are commonly depicted in thematic maps (e.g. soil map, population map, or hydrological map) or contours map (e.g. elevation maps or temperature isolines), which portray spatial distributions or spatial variations. Maps of temporal properties, such as flood maps showing areas of 500-year or 100-year flood zones or zones of traffic delays, characterize how the theme of interest changes time measurements over space. Measurements of time include starting time, ending time, duration, periodicity, and phases of transitions, for example. Time measurement is essential to risk forecasting which relies upon patterns elicited from time-series data to project future states or to determine natural variability

and departure from the norm. While temporal characteristics may vary, change over space is fundamentally static because spatial distributions or spatial variations are time-independent. Even the consideration of changes to time treats temporal characteristics as attributes of space, indifferent of themes as properties of space.

Changes to thematic properties over time when space is fixed represent histories at locations. Land use land cover change or temperature change are examples of change of thematic measurements over time in a specific area used to record thematic histories. While some relocation is possible, most in-situ observation networks remain stationary to assure the validity of long term records. For areal features, changes to thematic measurements inevitably lead to changes to spatial extent and therefore, shape, size, and spatial configuration of the space under study. Extensive changes to attributes and consequential changes to spatial properties lead to questions about changes to identities. Is a shopping mall still the same mall if 60% of the mall is converted to a charter school? Temporal GIS research to-date has investigated instantaneous or continuous changes to attributes, size, shape, topology, and identity (Hornsby & Egenhofer, 2002; Robertson, Nelson, Boots, & Wulder, 2007).

Changes to spatial and temporal characteristics over themes address the correlations or interactions among multiple phenomena and would be better to take a system perspective in space-time analytics.

Table 2. Extensions of Berry's geographic matrix to approaches to space-time analytics

Fix (hold constant)	Control (change over)	Measure (collect data)	Example
Time	Space	Theme	Spatial distributions of soils
Time	Theme	Space	Elevation contours
Space	Time	Theme	Observations at in-situ weather stations
Space	Theme	Time	Periodicity or return period of hurricanes or floods in a region
Theme	Space	Time	Predicting time of containment at wildfire fighting
Theme	Time	Space	Storm tracking, dispersion of pollution plume

Research on space-time analytics for autocorrelation or correlation has developed many advanced methods (Griffith, 2010; Griffith & Paelinck, 2009; Hardisty & Klippel, 2010), but few support analysis of the complexity of changes to system dynamics. An example of spatial and temporal change is the expansion and rate of expansion of urban and suburban areas into rural land. The urban expansion comes along with an increase in pavements which in turn lead to increasing surface runoff and triggering changes to spatiotemporal characteristics of flash floods. While many studies consider space and time as two orthogonal dimensions, interactions between spatial and temporal effects of changes to one theme can give rise to changes to another theme, and space-time is better defined based on the phenomenon of focus or the interactions. For example, emergency responses to a hurricane watch depend upon the progress and behavior of the hurricane in space and time. The changes across multiple themes and space-time manifestation of the themes involved in a system provide mechanistic explanations to system dynamics and lead to identification of *Kairos time*.

Time measurements are usually on chronological time (or *Chronos time*), which are based on movements of astronomical objects (e.g. the sun and moon), man-made objects (e.g. arms of clocks), or sand grains in an hour glass. Kairos time has largely been overlooked. Kairos time references to the time when the situation is ripe for a process to initiate or the moment is right for particular actions or an opportunity presents itself for fulfilling a particular quest. Kairos time emerges from the synergies among elements in a system, when all fit together creating a situation in which the collective outcome will be greater than the sum of individuals (Rife, 2010).

Movement is derived from changes in locations for an identified entity. Hence, space-time analytics needs to fix theme (i.e. the entity of interest) and track its spatial and temporal characteristics. While there are many possibilities of changes to spatial properties (e.g. shape, size, etc.), movement requires location change, which identification is

subject to spatial granularity of study. For point features, location change is determined by the delta between two points at different instances. For area or linear features, their centroids are commonly used to represent locations. The spatial extent or the shape of an area feature may change, but its centroid may remain the same and, therefore, there is no movement. In other situations, weighted centroids (e.g. by population, distance or other statistical measures) are more appropriate than geometric centroids alone.

Consideration of movement based on fixing theme, controlling space, and measuring time is uncommon in space-time analytics. An example will be decision making for emergency evacuation: when to start evacuating cities along a coast when a hurricane is moving onshore or in a region when a wildfire is raging towards a city (Cova & Goodchild, 2002). The rate and direction of movement is essential as well as how environmental factors may influence the movement.

Change and movement are driven by activities, events, and processes. *Activities are actions taken by actors*, usually with or for some purposes. Examples are go shopping, parade, or meet. *Events denote happening*: a severe weather event, a conference, a festival, or a traffic accident. *Processes emphasize the becoming: the development of something with transitions from one phase to another, such as*: the process of aging, the development of a hurricane, migration, desertification, and gentrification. While change and movement are what we can observe, space-time analytics lead to the understanding of activities, events, and processes that drive the change and movement. The following section outlines two examples to demonstrate the analytical needs and solutions.

SPACE-TIME ANALYTICS: FROM OBSERVABLES TO DRIVERS

Many studies have proposed methods or applications to discern patterns or clusters from space-time data (Ailliot, Thompson, & Thomson, 2009; G.

Andrienko et al., 2010; Chen et al., 2011; Griffith & Paelinck, 2009; Xie et al., 2011). These methods range from statistical to computational approaches, but few decipher the potential activities, events, and processes responsible for the patterns. The following example aims to show the need to consider spatial dynamics in space-time analytics. While the example is only an introduction, leaving out much computational details, the purpose here is to show what is possible when going beyond spatiotemporal patterns. Algorithmic details and analyses are discussed in Bothwell and Yuan (2011).

Temperature Change as an Example

Climate change models continue generating massive amounts of data for climate projections. Data animation or visual inspection quickly reaches its limits when searching for space-time patterns in the mountains of data. The limitation is particularly challenging for comparisons of model outputs. Basic measurements from climate change models are estimates of climate parameters at locations for a particular time, as monthly or annual means. Space-time analytics are applied by examining the change perspective of histories at location by: fixing location (individual model grid cells), controlling time (monthly or annually), and measuring theme (temperature, precipitation, etc.), or by the movement perspective based on how gradients among adjacent cells may lead to flows of climate properties. Histories at locations are common to temporal GIS applications since the early temporal GIS research (Langran, 1992; Yuan, 2009). Complimentary, we introduce an example of movement-based analytics with the concept of *flow*.

Flow and Movement for Space-Time Analytics of Temperature Change

The flow idea is based on the principle of kinematics that the direction and rate of change are primitives to characterize movement, and

further analysis of kinematic flows can lead to identification of space-time processes, such as divergence and convergence, which serve as the basis for interpretations of climate processes and comparison of climate model estimates. The case study is based on temperature data estimated for the International Panel for Climate Change (IPCC) A2 scenario, which assumes independent regional economic development with little technological development, from two popular Global General Circulation (GCM) models: the Center National Weather Research global ocean-atmosphere coupled system (CNRM-CM3) in France and the National Center for Atmospheric Research Community Climate System Model (NCAR-CCSM3) in the United States. Figure 1 shows an example of GCM temperature estimates.

Since the entities of interest must be identified prior to determine movement characteristics, isotherms are used as surrogate objects to capture the continuous and transitional nature of temperature fields (Figure 2). In a field-object view, cognition of objects is induced by spatial clusters or collections of high or low values that correspond to events or processes (Yuan, 2001). A closure of an isotherm demarks an area with temperature higher (hot spot) or lower (cold spot) than the temperature of the isotherm. Changes to the spatial distribution of isotherms and shifts of isotherms over time can provide summative assessment of climate trends. Certain isotherms carry physical meaning, such as $0°C$, and movement of the isotherm has ecological implications. While identification of corresponding isotherms to calculate movement is not trivial, the intent can be analogous to determining optical flow based on the patterns of motion from an objects, surfaces, or edges in a set of temporally ordered images (Horn & Schunk, 1981). The flow is assumed to follow the direction of the gradient from the origin point toward the corresponding object in the next time frame.

NCAR CCSM3 produces temperature estimates at $1.4°×1.4°$ resolution and the CNRM

CM3, at 2.8°x2.8° resolution. Kinematic analysis of movement is insensitive to differences in grid sizes because the emphasis is on the general pattern of flows rather than absolute properties at location (Bothwell & Yuan, 2010). The case study extracts two climatological means from 90 years (2000-2090) of monthly meteorological data using 30 year moving averages ending in 2030 and 2090. Based on the optical flow algorithm, we calculate longitudinal and latitudinal movements of isotherms (Figure 3).

Calculate Movement of Isotherms: Velocity, Local Gradient, and Displacement

The calculation is a multi-step process. Since temperature is continuous in space and time, movement of isotherms represents change in flows of air temperature. Kinematics concerns about movement, which can be measured as displacement or velocity. In the case of temperature, its spatial and temporal continuity leads to the ideas of flow and the rate of change of the flow as parameters to represent movement. Furthermore, velocity of a flow is the rate and direction of change in quantity at a given location. Along the reasoning, velocity of temperature flow is the rate and direction of change in degrees of temperature, which can be measured as changes in degrees of temperature in the longitudinal (x) and latitudinal (y) directions as well as the composite vector of both, which are named longitudinal displacement, latitudinal displacement, and vectors of displacement. Moreover, vectors of displacements can be used to determine convergence or divergence of temperature regions, objectively identified using *iso cluster* method. Figure 4 depicts the workflow of the multi-step process in the calculation. The following paragraphs highlight the concepts and methods presented in the workflow.

The conceptual framework and rationale for the conversion of static data to kinematic representation is rooted in the concept of flow. The total change of mass at a location is equal to the sum of local change and external input/output. Similarly, the total rate of change in flow at a given point ($\frac{\Delta F}{\Delta t}$) is equal to the sum of local

Figure 1. Mean temperature for the year range 2000-2030 from the CNRM CM3 GCM

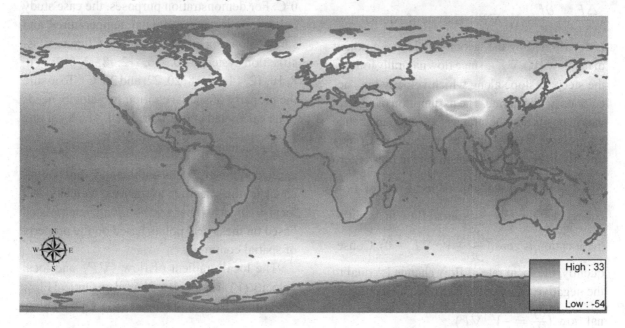

Figure 2. Use of isotherms as surrogate objects to measure movement. The direction and rate of movement is determined based on the optical flow algorithm by Horn and Schunk (1981).

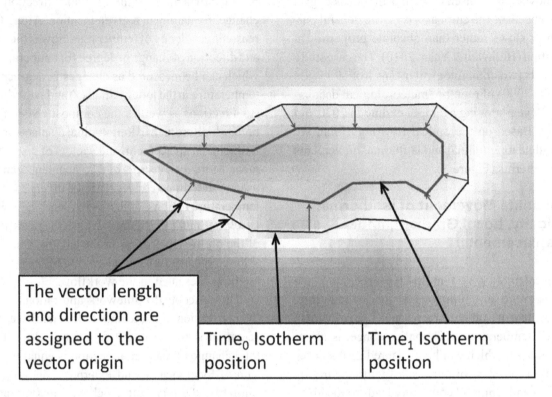

The vector length and direction are assigned to the vector origin

Time$_0$ Isotherm position

Time$_1$ Isotherm position

rate of change $(\frac{\partial f}{\partial t})$ and rate of change in external flows $(V \cdot \nabla F)$ in or out of the location $(\frac{\Delta F}{\Delta t} = \frac{\partial f}{\partial t} + V \cdot \nabla F)$. The rate of external flow is determined by the velocity and local gradient of the flow $(V \cdot \nabla F)$, since flow naturally follows the steepest slope along which velocity may accelerate or decelerate. The assumption of conservation posits that the air mass remains, and hence air pressure is constant at every location. Consequently, the net rate of total change in flow is zero $(\frac{\Delta F}{\Delta t} = 0)$, and the sum of local rate of flow change and the rate of external flow in or out of the location is zero $(\frac{\partial f}{\partial t} + V \cdot \nabla F = 0)$. Consequently, the local rate of flow change is equal to the negative value of the rate of change in external flow $(\frac{\partial f}{\partial t} = -V \cdot \nabla F)$.

The velocity at a location is determined by movement of isotherms. These isotherms should carry physical or ecological meanings, such as 0°C. For demonstration purposes, the case study below applies mean annual temperatures and subdivisions specified in Köppen Climate Classification system (-20, -16, -12, -8, -4, 0, 2, 4, 6, 8, 10, 12, 14, 16, 18, 20, 22, and 26 °C). To assure the property of spatial continuity, velocity needs to be calculated at every grid cell. The local rate of flow change equation $(\frac{\partial f}{\partial t} = -V \cdot \nabla F)$ is applied to the grid cells with temperature values equal to the specified isotherms. Velocity and local gradient at other grid points are interpolated based on these grid points based on the property of spatial continuity.

The local gradient of flow (∇F) and local velocity (V) are calculated based on Optical Flow Algorithm (Horn & Schunk, 1981). Optical Flow

Figure 3. Isotherm displacements in the longitudinal and latitudinal directions. Darker the colors represent higher displacement. Green shades represent north or west movement, and brown shades represent south or east movement.

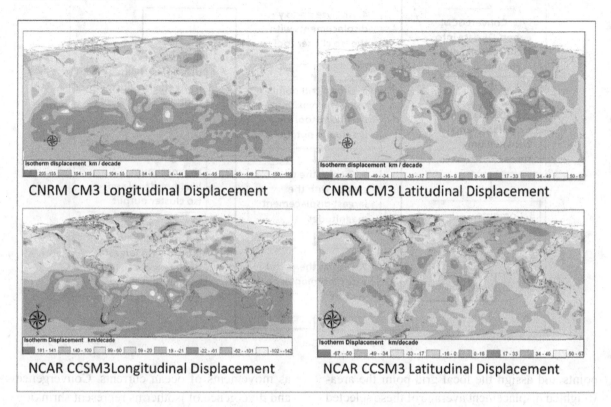

Algorithm is commonly used for digital image processing to generate velocity fields from sequential images with objects moved slightly from one image to another $(\frac{\partial I}{\partial t} + V \cdot \nabla I = 0)$

where I is the *image intensity*, of which *temperature* is used here instead. Following the algorithm, four 3×3 windows are applied to calculate the local gradient at each grid cell. Each 3×3 window is aligned with one edge of the cell to calculate the mean of temperature values within the window and then the vertical and horizontal differences to the mean. As such, velocity is represented by its components at u (west-east) and v (north or south) directions into rate at latitudinal direction (i.e. x displacement $/\partial t$) and rate at longitudinal direction (i.e. y displacement $/\partial t$) to reveal how temperature change towards the poles or along many coast lines that run north and south. The result consists of displacement tables for longitudinal and latitudinal displacements. Table 3 includes four grid cells as examples for latitudinal displacements calculated for CNRM data. The latitudes and longitudes are grid points from CNRM data, and the velocity is expressed as displacement vector along the latitudinal direction.

Spatial interpolation of velocity values to other grid cells not on the specified isotherms is based on the natural neighbor algorithm, which is a two-stage process for a given grid point (i.e. the focal grid point): (1) determine a neighborhood distance from the focal grid point and select all grid points that have known displacement values within the neighborhood distance; and (2) configure Thiessen polygons around the selected grid

Figure 4. Process to calculate movements and convert static data to kinematics representation

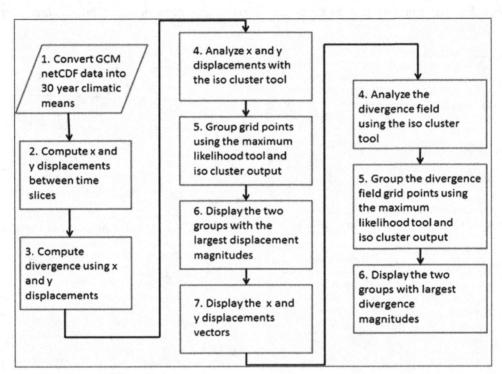

points and assign the focal grid point the area-weighted displacement average of these selected grid points based on associated Thiessen polygons. Natural Neighbor interpolation does not produce minima or maxima that are not present in the input samples (Gold, 1989).

The spatial interpolation generates three data sets for each climate change model (NCAR CCSM3 or CNRM CM3): longitudinal displacements, latitudinal displacements, and composite velocity with direction and magnitude that support identification of convergence, divergence, and rapid displacements. Longitudinal displacements summarize north or south movement of isotherms. In the northern hemisphere, south moving isotherms from the north pole suggest a cooling trend, and north moving isotherms from the equator suggest a warming trend. In the southern hemisphere, the implications reverse. Interpretations of east or west moving isotherms are likely subject to land-sea distributions as well

as movements of ocean currents. Convergence and divergence of isotherms represent shrinking or expanding hot or cold areas. Upwelling, for example, can be responsible for expanding cold area along the Peru coast, and ENSO may lead to warm expansion.

Divergence is calculated based on longitudinal velocity (v) and latitudinal velocity (u) using the centered difference formula. For location (i,j) divergence is:

$$Divergence_{(i,j)} = (\frac{u_{(i+1,j)} - u_{(i-1,j)}}{2\Delta x}) + (\frac{v_{(i,j+1)} - v_{(i,j-1)}}{2\Delta y})$$

'Δx' is the grid spacing in the latitudinal direction, and 'Δy' is the grid spacing in the longitudinal direction. Convergence occurs when the divergence value is less than zero. As mentioned previously, *iso cluster* analysis is to identify clusters of large displacements and the large areas of temperature convergence or divergence where displacements are low and movement inward or outward from a center. The *iso cluster* analysis makes an initial assignment of cluster classes using histogram peaks and then iteratively adjusts the assignments using variance and covariance based on an assumed normal distribution (de Smith *et al.* 2007). In each iteration, the *iso cluster* routine modifies the cluster assignment based on two criteria: (1) two clusters will be combined if their centers which are closer than a set tolerance level, and (2) clusters without a minimum number of members are dissolved with members assigned to surviving clusters. Clusters are further divided when they are overly large, have excessive standard deviation or when the average distance from cluster center is excessive. The *iso cluster* analysis results in clusters with low variance of divergence values within a cluster but high variance between clusters. Divergence and convergence zones are identified by extracting clusters with high positive and low negative values, respectively.

From Movement of Isotherms to Climate Process

Both models suggest that isotherms are moving towards the poles, but differences exist. NCAR CCSM3 projects that isotherms move faster in the Southern Ocean than CNRM CM3, which implies that NCAR CCSM3 expects the southern hemisphere has a broader distribution of warming than what CNRM CM3 estimates. In addition, CNRM suggests large patches of northward movements

(green spots) around the equatorial region with a stronger warming trend than what is suggested by NCAR CCSM3 model. Yet, CNRM shows an area of much darker and confined south-moving isotherms (in brown) in the mid-section of the U.S., Russia, Euroasia, and Siberia, suggesting the presence of local temperature minima, in contrast to a ligher but wider spread area of south-moving isotherms suggested by NCAR CCSM3. For latitudinal movement, CNRM CM3 expects an overall greater shift of isotherm eastward than what is suggested by NCAR CCSM3.

The two models estimate rather different patterns of divergence, convergence, and rapid movement of isotherms (Figure 5). Yet, around $67°$ N, both models suggest a wide band of rapid displacement northward in the North American Continent. The band in the CNRM model across the North American Continent with clusters in southern Greenland, a region in the western Indian Ocean and the southwest coast of Africa shows significantly large isotherm movement. The NCAR model extends the band to the northern portion of central Euroasia. These regions correspond well with the boundaries of the polar amplification (Holland & Bitz, 2003). Aside from the common patterns, CNRM model shows two interesting regions over Indonesia and at the center of the Niño 3 region. These locations for divergence hint that an ENSO process may be changing due to anthropomorphic climate change (IPCC 2001). The high change rate over the Arabian Sea is possibly due to an increase in monsoon strength leading to cooler than normal SSTs in the Arabian Sea and the influence of a strengthening Indian

Table 3. Examples of displacements calculated based on CNRM data

latitude	longitude	Latitudinal Displacement Vector
76.7065	-132.188	8.00296
73.9172	177.188	0.985113
73.9172	174.375	1.223
73.9172	171.563	0.99966

Ocean Dipole which affects zonal SST gradients along the Equator (Saji *et al.* 2006). The divergence region over the Arabian Sea indicates a possible warming region with rapid isotherm outflows in both the northern and southern directions. The rapid change in the south western coastal region of Africa may be the result of an increase in the western flow from the Sahara during summer brought about by global warming as suggested by Semazzi and Song (2001).

In comparison, NCAR model shows regions in the western Indian Ocean and the southwest coast of Africa with rapid isotherm movement southward. However, no support has been found for the band of rapid warming over the South Atlantic, Africa and the Indian Ocean east of Madagascar at ~15°S that corresponds to the region of rapid isotherm movement. Nevertheless, Carril *et al.* (1998) used an earlier version of the NCAR CCSM GCM and identified an area of more rapid warming in the south Atlantic just south of the ~15°S region. Divergence regions are scattered, and one area appears substantial: a tropical ocean region east of Brazil. The region east of Brazil is possibly a result of a shift in the Inter-Tropical Convergence Zone (ITCZ) due to changes in the Atlantic Ocean (Labraga 1997).

Solutions and Recommendations

Change and movement are space-time observables. Analysis of change or movement should aim at elicitation of activities, events, and processes that drive the change and movement in space and time. The climate change example is intended to demonstrate that the new perspective of movement in space-time analytics of temperature can enrich the findings with dynamic patterns of temperature change and potential climate processes that responsible for such change. Conventional approaches that focus on spatial distribution of temperature change (fixing time, controlling space, and measuring temperature) or temperature change at locations (fixing space, controlling time, and measuring temperature) are useful to provide the scalar view of temperature change. A switch to the focus on movement makes space and time an integral for the formation of flow patterns induced from isotherm movement. One key difference resides in the dependency of the theme of interest to space and time. Spatial distribution of temperature change or temperature change at locations considers temperature an attribute of space and time, in that temperature values are positioned to fill a space-time cube. From the movement's perspective, however, space and

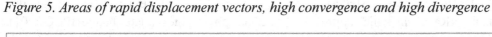

Figure 5. Areas of rapid displacement vectors, high convergence and high divergence

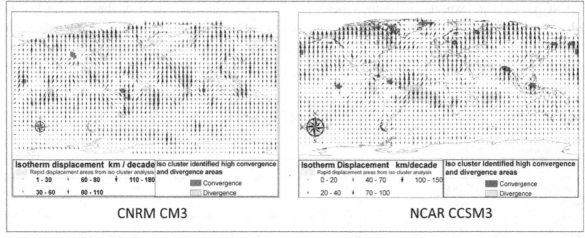

time become attributes of the entity of interest to specify the entity's locations over time. Hence, it is the entity that defines space and time of interest.

The switch in perspectives not only provides a new way of thinking about space and time but also offer new opportunities to identify patterns of dynamics. Because of activities, events, and processes operate at different scales, multiple levels of features may be extracted from a given data set with the finest level determined by the level of observations. The idea is consistent with Hierarchy Theory (Ahl & Allen, 1996), in which scale is the function that relates elements and behavior interconnections across levels. The scale of interest defines processes that are meaningful to analysis and hence determines what can be observed and measured in space and time. Hierarchy Theory recognizes two kinds of hierarchies: scalar hierarchy and specification hierarchy. A scalar hierarchy is built upon constraint relations among sub-systems (or parts) and super-systems (or wholes). To account for the scalar constraint relations, it requires explicitly represent at least three levels (i.e. the focal level, the higher level, and the lower level) simultaneously to model a scalar hierarchy system (Allen & Starr, 1982). The lower level situates possible dynamics at the focal level, while the higher level regulates the dynamics at the focal level. Behavior at the focal level is driven by "initiating conditions" arising from dynamics at the lower level, and is regulated by "boundary conditions" operating at the higher level (Salthe, 1991). On the other hand, a specification hierarchy is a nested system in which higher levels transitively integrate dynamics and phenomena at a lower level so that behavior at the higher level is determinable from knowledge of its component levels (Ahl & Allen, 1996).

Following the principle of Hierarchy Theory, space-time analytics can account for activities, events, and processes at different levels. The example of temperature change reveals regional characteristics of isotherm displacements and convergence/divergence. Global processes, like El Nino or Jet Streams, set the boundary conditions for the development of regional characteristics. Local processes, such as mesoscale convection or orographic lifting, may initiate the displacement or convergence/divergence processes. Space-time analytics with emphases on themes across multiple levels can bring new and rich insights into spatial dynamics.

FUTURE RESEARCH DIRECTIONS

Space-time analytics about movement has gained popularity in recent years, driven in part by the massive amount of space-time tracks from Global Positioning System (GPS)–enabled devices, like smart phones or in-car navigation systems. Space-time data from environmental modeling systems, surveys, and electronic transactions add to the ever-growing volumes. Both research and professional communities are afforded with innovative methods to visualize or analyze environmental changes and space-time trajectories (Ailliot, et al., 2009; G. Andrienko, et al., 2010; Gennady Andrienko et al., 2010; Demšar & Virrantaus, 2010; Shaw & Yu, 2009; Xia & Kraak, 2008; Xie, et al., 2011). Yet, a full system approach to address spatial dynamics is yet to be realized.

The chapter's premise posits that change and movement are space-time observables with which space-time analytics aims to uncover drivers of activities, events, and processes. A solid theoretical foundation and a thorough understanding of the system in consideration are critical to construct concepts of change and movement for the support of resolving space-time drivers. Research is needed to address the theoretical and methodological challenges of this system approach in space-time analytics and to go beyond chronological time to Kairos time that indicates opportunistic moments when situation is right for activities, events, and processes. Understanding the interactions of multiple themes in space and time demands a multidisciplinary collaboration and an integrated information and computational system.

CONCLUSION

The chapter explains the essence of space-time analytics. While many terms have not had unified definitions in academia, the chapter broadly defines space-time analytics and related key concepts. While the geographic matrix was proposed almost five decades ago, many contemporary GIS data models and space-time analysis methods are much aligned with the same concepts. More specifically, many data models and analysis methods take a space-centric perspective with time and theme treated as attributes of space. Expanding upon the geographic matrix, we stress the importance and novelty of change- and movement-based thinking. Six out of the eight analytical approaches in the geographic matrix correspond to change-based thinking, in which space and time form the analytical frame of references, and themes become the attributes of an imaginary space-time cube. Movement-based thinking requires the identification of entities in prior and associates the entities with spatial and temporal characteristics. When entities move in space and time, dynamics of their development and interaction naturally becomes the focus of space-time analytics.

An example using 90 years of monthly temperature projections is used to demonstrate the benefits of space-time analytics based on movement. Massive amounts of climate change model data require automatic means to discern patterns of interest, and we argue that the patterns need to be related to spatial dynamics. The concept of flow is used to capture spatiotemporal continuity of temporally ordered fields of temperature estimates, and movement of isotherms is used as space-time observables to characterize flow by displacement and rate of change. The approach identifies general trends of polar movement of isotherms as well as zones of rapid displacement, convergence, and divergence. The findings agree with processes identified in previous publications, and hence relate the movement patterns to spatial dynamics of processes responsible for the patterns.

Recent research in space-time analytics also exhibits a trend for movement-based analysis. Many studies propose new methods for visualizing space-time paths and for aggregating these paths into collective movement patterns. Most space-time path analyses are based on the conceptual framework of space-time cube, in which space-time paths connect spatial locations over time. When space-time analytics targets spatial dynamics, a system-based approach is required. Space-time paths are taken with inherent goals and hence are driven to achieve these goals, not in an empty space-time cube, but in a dynamic space-time complex. Hierarchy Theory can help us frame movement-based space-time analytics by addressing processes across multiple levels with constraints of boundary conditions and initial conditions for the processes at the focal level. The grand challenge of space-time analytics pushes our focus from static location-centric analysis of change to dynamic system-oriented analysis of movement. Much research is already heading in this direction, and useful outcomes are expected.

REFERENCES

Ahl, V., & Allen, T. F. H. (1996). *Hierarchy theory: A vision, vocabulary, and epistemology*. New York, NY: Columbia University Press.

Ailliot, P., Thompson, C., & Thomson, P. (2009). Space–time modelling of precipitation by using a hidden Markov model and censored Gaussian distributions. *Journal of the Royal Statistical Society. Series C, Applied Statistics*, 58(3), 405–426. doi:10.1111/j.1467-9876.2008.00654.x

Allen, T. F. H., & Starr, T. B. (1982). *Hierarchy: Perspectives for ecological complexity*. Chicago, IL: The University of Chicago Press.

Andrienko, G., Andrienko, N., Bremm, S., Schreck, T., von Landesberger, T., Bak, P., & Keim, D. (2010). Space-in-time and time-in-space self-organizing maps for exploring spatiotemporal patterns. *Computer Graphics Forum, 29*(3), 913–922. doi:10.1111/j.1467-8659.2009.01664.x

Andrienko, G., Andrienko, N., Demsar, U., Dransch, D., Dykes, J., & Fabrikant, S. I. (2010). Space, time and visual analytics. *International Journal of Geographical Information Science, 24*(10), 1577–1600. doi:10.1080/13658816.2010.508043

Berry, B. J. L. (1964). Approaches to regional analysis: A synthesis. *Annals of the Association of American Geographers. Association of American Geographers, 54*(1), 2–11. doi:10.1111/j.1467-8306.1964.tb00469.x

Bothwell, J., & Yuan, M. (2010). Apply concepts of fluid kinematics to represent continuous space-time fields in temporal GIS. *Annals of Geographic Information Science, 16*(1), 27–41.

Chen, J., Shaw, S.-L., Yu, H., Lu, F., Chai, Y., & Jia, Q. (2011). Exploratory data analysis of activity diary data: A space–time GIS approach. *Journal of Transport Geography, 19*(3), 394–404. doi:10.1016/j.jtrangeo.2010.11.002

Cova, T. J., & Goodchild, M. F. (2002). Extending geographical representation to include fields of spatial objects. *International Journal of Geographical Information Science, 16*(6), 509–532. doi:10.1080/13658810210137040

Demšar, U., & Virrantaus, K. (2010). Space-time density of trajectories: Exploring spatio-temporal patterns in movement data. *International Journal of Geographical Information Science, 24*(10), 1527–1542. doi:10.1080/13658816.2010.511223

Gold, C. M. (1989). Surface interpolation, spatial adjacency and G.I.S. In Raper, J. (Ed.), *Three dimensional applications in geographical information systems* (pp. 21–35). London, UK: Taylor and Francis.

Griffith, D. A. (2010). Modeling spatio-temporal relationships: Retrospect and prospect. *Journal of Geographical Systems, 12*(2), 111–123. doi:10.1007/s10109-010-0120-x

Griffith, D. A., & Paelinck, J. H. P. (2009). Specifying a joint space- and time-lag using a bivariate Poisson distribution. *Journal of Geographical Systems, 11*(1), 23–36. doi:10.1007/s10109-008-0075-3

Hardisty, F., & Klippel, A. (2010). Analysing spatio-temporal autocorrelation with LISTA-Viz. *International Journal of Geographical Information Science, 24*(10), 1515–1526. doi:10.1080/13658816.2010.511717

Holland, M. M., & Bitz, C. M. (2003). Polar amplification of climate change in the coupled model intercomparison project. *Climate Dynamics, 21*, 221–232. doi:10.1007/s00382-003-0332-6

Horn, B. K. P., & Schunk, B. G. (1981). Determining optical flow. *Artificial Intelligence, 17*, 185–203. doi:10.1016/0004-3702(81)90024-2

Hornsby, K., & Egenhofer, M. (2002). Modeling moving objects over multiple granularities. *Annals of Mathematics and Artificial Intelligence, 36*(1-2), 177–194. doi:10.1023/A:1015812206586

Langran, G. (1992). *Time in geographic information systems*. London, UK: Taylor & Francis.

Rife, M. C. (2010). Ethos, pathos, logos, kairos: Using a rhetorical heuristic to mediate digital-survey recruitment strategies. *IEEE Transactions on Professional Communication, 53*(3), 260–277. doi:10.1109/TPC.2010.2052856

Robertson, C., Nelson, T., Boots, B., & Wulder, M. (2007). STAMP: Spatial–temporal analysis of moving polygons. *Journal of Geographical Systems*, *9*(3), 207–227. doi:10.1007/s10109-007-0044-2

Salthe, S. N. (1991). Two forms of hierarchy theory in western discourses. *International Journal of General Systems*, *18*, 251–264. doi:10.1080/03081079108935149

Shaw, S.-L., & Yu, H. (2009). A GIS-based time-geographic approach of studying individual activities and interactions in a hybrid physical–virtual space. *Journal of Transport Geography*, *17*(2), 141–149. doi:10.1016/j.jtrangeo.2008.11.012

Xia, L., & Kraak, M.-J. (2008). The time wave. A new method of visual exploration of geo-data in time–space. *The Cartographic Journal*, *45*(3), 193–200. doi:10.1179/000870408X311387

Xie, Y., Koch, S., McGinley, J., Albers, S., Bieringer, P. E., Wolfson, M., & Chan, M. (2011). A space--time multiscale analysis system: A sequential variational analysis approach. *Monthly Weather Review*, *139*(4), 1224–1240. doi:10.1175/2010MWR3338.1

Yuan, M. (2001). Representing complex geographic phenomena with both object- and field-like properties. *Cartography and Geographic Information Science*, *28*(2), 83–96. doi:10.1559/152304001782173718

Yuan, M. (2009). Challenges and critical issues for temporal GIS research and technologies. In Karimi, H. A. (Ed.), *Handbook of research on geoinformatics* (pp. 144–153). doi:10.4018/978-1-59140-995-3.ch019

Yuan, M., & Stewart, K. (2008). *Computation and visualization for the understanding of dynamics in geographic domains: A research agenda*. Boca Raton, FL: CRC/Taylor and Francis.

KEY TERMS AND DEFINITIONS

Activity: Something which an actor (e.g. a person, animal, group, or chemical agent) chooses to do.

Change: Succession of one thing or property in place of another.

Event: Anything that happens or is contemplated as happening; an incident; an occurrence.

Movement: A change in place or position.

Process: The course of becoming, a succession of actions or events in order.

Space-Time Analytics: The use of space and time as frames of processing, extraction, visualization, understanding, and communication to simplify the complexity of spatial dynamics into elements and structures in space and time.

Spatial Dynamics: Change or movement in space due to activities, events, and processes.

ENDNOTES

[1] The definition is synthesized from entries of *analytics* and *analysis* in Oxford English Dictionary.

Chapter 18
An Ontology-Based Approach to Support Information Discovery in Spatial Data Infrastructures

Fabio Gomes de Andrade
Federal Institute of Education, Science, and Technology of Paraíba, Brazil

Cláudio de Souza Baptista
University of Campina Grande, Brazil

ABSTRACT

Currently, spatial data infrastructures (SDIs) are becoming the solution adopted by many organizations to facilitate discovery, access and integration of geographic information produced and provided by different agencies. However, the catalog services currently offered by these infrastructures provide keyword-based queries only. This may result on low recall and precision. Furthermore, these catalogs retrieve information based on the metadata records that describe either a service or a dataset. This feature brings limitations to more specific information discovery, such as those based on feature types and instances. This chapter proposes a solution that aims to overcome these limitations by using multiple ontologies to enhance the description of the information offered by SDIs. The proposed ontologies describe the semantics of several features of a service, enabling information discovery at level of services, feature types, and geographic data.

INTRODUCTION

In recent years, spatial data infrastructures (SDIs) (Williamson, Rajabifard, & Feeney, 2003) have been adopted by many government agencies as a solution to minimize problems of heterogeneity,

and to facilitate geographic data interoperability among different organizations. The popularity conquered by these infrastructures is evidenced by the large number of initiatives taken to develop SDIs worldwide. Spatial Data Infrastructures are being built, for example, in Australia ("Austra-

DOI: 10.4018/978-1-4666-2190-9.ch018

lian Spatial Data Infrastructure," 2011), Brazil ("Infraestrutura Nacional de Dados Espaciais," 2011), the United States of America ("National Spatial Data Infrastructure," 2011), Europe ("Infrastructure for Spatial Information in the European Community," 2011) and the world ("Global Spatial Data Infrastructure," 2011).

SDIs aim to enable the users to find easily the data and applications offered by their providers. To attain this goal, these infrastructures offer a catalog service, which can be used by both providers and clients. Providers of geographic data and applications may use this service to publish their resources. The clients of an infrastructure, in turn, may use this service to discover information of their interest. When a client submits a query to the catalog service, the service returns a collection of metadata records that match the query. With this information, clients may evaluate the retrieved resources and access them via their corresponding provider.

Current catalog services make information discovery easier, but also have some drawbacks. The main limitation is that their queries are usually keyword-based only, resulting in low precision and recall. This chapter proposes to improve information discovery in SDIs by using ontologies. Our main contribution concerns the modeling of a set of integrated ontologies that enable to describe formally the semantics of several features of the services offered by a given infrastructure. By using our approach it is possible to provide geographic information discovery at service, feature type and instance levels.

The remainder of the chapter is organized as follow. Section 2 discusses related works. Section 3 provides an overview of the main concepts and technologies addressed in the chapter. Section 4 describes geographic data integration in current SDIs. Section 5 presents the ontologies that aim to improve the information discovery process. Section 6 focuses on implementation issues. Finally, section 7 concludes the chapter and discusses further research directions.

RELATED WORK

Over the years, many works using ontologies were proposed to improve spatial data retrieval in spatial data infrastructures and geographic portals. The main difference between these works is the type of information that is discovered by each one.

Some works have been proposed concerning processing services discovery. Lemmens et al. (Lemmens et al., 2007) defined a framework for semantic interoperability of geo operations. Their work proposes ontologies to describe application domains and spatial features. Besides, an ontology for service classification is described and used to define a taxonomy of geographic services. Their work implements a matchmaker service enabled to discover services and service compositions automatically. By other hand, Lutz (Lutz, 2007) developed an approach that uses ontologies for the annotation and discovery of geo-services. In his work, the description of such services is done through semantic annotation of its input and output parameters, preconditions and effects. A semantic signature is generated to represent this information. During a query processing, a reasoner is used to discover services and service compositions using semantic relationships such as subsumption and plug-in. The main drawback of these works is that they do not address discovery of spatial feature types and data access services. Other important works regarding services discovery were proposed by Rezeg et al. (Rezeg, Laskri, & Servigne, 2010) and Yue et al. (Yue et al., 2011).

Other works, in turn, enable discovery of geographic data access services. Klien et al. (Klien, Lutz, & Kuhn, 2006) perform discovery of geo-services focusing on disaster management. In that approach, the functionality of spatial services is described by application ontologies. Services that implement these features are recorded in the system using metadata based on the Dublin Core metadata standard (Weibel & Koch, 2000). Another approach for discovery of geographic services is proposed by Stock et al. (Stock et al., 2010), where a feature type catalog is used to describe the operations that can be performed with various feature types. In the SWING project (Roman & Klien, 2007), the authors use an approach where spatial data provided by OGC WFS services are linked to concepts defined in an ontology through WSML. The project allows users to find spatial data by searching for concepts described in domain ontologies. The main drawback of these works is that they do not offer support to discovery at the level of feature types. Other works proposed to solve data access service discovery were proposed by Wiegand & Garcia (Wiegand & Garcia, 2007) and Lutz et al. (Lutz, Sprado, Klien, Schubert, & Christ, 2008).

As to feature types discovery, some solutions have been developed to it. Lutz & Klien (Lutz & Klien, 2006) propose a solution where each feature type and its respective properties can be associated to concepts defined in ontologies along mapping records. Another approach, based on similarity, was proposed by Zhang et al. (Zhang et al., 2010). In that work, the importance of a feature type being evaluated in a user's query is determined by the sum of the similarity degree of the following characteristics: the ontology concepts that they are related to, their properties, geometries (such as point, line and polygon), and bounding-boxes. Janowicz et al. (Janowicz, Wilkes, & Lutz, 2008) propose a similarity-based solution to discover feature types supplied by SDIs. Their work is based on a framework (Janowicz, 2006) that evaluates the similarity between the concepts of ontologies described in Description Logic (Baader, Calvanese, McGuinness, Nardi, & Patel-Schneider, 2003). In this work, the feature types offered by services are associated to the concepts defined in domain ontologies. During the searching process, the user selects the concepts that are most similar to the concept defined by the query. Andrade & Baptista (Andrade & Baptista, 2011) developed a search engine that uses ontologies and classic information retrieval techniques to improve feature types discovery. The drawback of these works is that they focus only in feature types discovery.

Lutz & Kolas (Lutz & Kolas, 2007) developed a work that implements information discovery at level of instances. Their work uses rules to associate feature types to concepts defined in domain ontologies. The rule-based approach generates a central knowledge base from data that are annotated with the concepts related to user submitted queries. Then, reasoning is performed to discover data that matched with the constraints defined in the query. The disadvantage of this approach is that only data available as Web Feature Service (WFS) can be discovered. In addition, this approach lacks support for seeking semantics of the functionality offered by the services.

Smits & Friis-Christensen (Smits & Friis-Christensen, 2007) use a thesaurus to improve information discovery in a European spatial data infrastructure. In that work, the descriptors of the resources registered in the infrastructure were associated with concepts defined by a thesaurus. In addition, users could do browsing through thesaurus concepts to retrieve resources that have descriptors associated with a particular concept. Another set of ontologies for geographic information discovery is proposed by Athanasis et al. (Athanasis, Kalabokidis, Vaitis, & Soulakellis, 2009). In that work, three kinds of ontologies were used. The first type was used to classify the format of geographic information. The second one was used to model application domains. Finally, the third one contained the elements of the ISO 19115 standard, which is a set of elements proposed by ISO to describe geographic information. Information retrieval is done through RQL ("The RDF Query Language," 2011) queries. The main drawback of these works is that they are too general, and there is no support to discovery of specific spatial data type and geographic services.

The analysis of the aforementioned related works shows that the use of semantics and ontologies to improve information discovery in SDIs is an open issue. Furthermore, most of the related works are focused on discovery of a specific resource type. Nonetheless, we believe that a complete solution for information discovery on SDIs should consider several resource types. In order to achieve this aim, it is necessary to describe the semantics of the various service features, such as their feature types and functional features.

BACKGROUND

This section describes the key concepts and technologies used to develop our solution. The highlighted topics are geographic information on the Web; Spatial Data Infrastructures as an integration tool; catalog services; and semantic Web and ontologies. It is important to mention that these following topics are addressed briefly, and references for further reading are provided.

Geographic Information on the Web

At the present, there is a plethora of geographic data stored in the web. These data can be produced and delivered by various levels of providers, such as: public agencies, private companies, nongovernmental organizations, academic institutions, and even by ordinary people. Similarly, information published by these providers can be accessed by various clients worldwide. Unfortunately, all this information is usually provided in a non-standardized manner, as data are highly heterogeneous. Such heterogeneity is due to the fact that information can be rendered in different formats, come under different data models, collected under different coordinate systems, represented in different scales and, documented in different ways, among other complications. All these heterogeneity problems reduce enormously the interoperability among all available information. Low interoperability, in turn, makes it difficult to reuse the available information to solve problems in different application domains. Besides, tasks such as integrating information

from different sources and data sharing among different applications will also end up being severely limited.

With the purpose of ameliorating the problems caused by geographic information heterogeneity, it was created, in 1994, the Open Geospatial Consortium (OGC) ("Open geospatial consortium," 2011). The OGC is a consortium of over 400 different organizations: public companies, private agencies and academic institutions, whose goals have been the development of standards that can be applied in the geospatial domain. All standards developed by this consortium are free, and have an open interface. This results in greater acceptance within the geospatial community; besides playing increasingly important role in the standardization of various processes. Other important standards for the geospatial domain are developed by the Technical Committee TC 211 of the International Organization for Standardization (ISO) ("International Organization for Standardization," 2011). However, unlike the standards proposed by the OGC, the ISO standards are private, and have no open interface. Examples of important standards developed by ISO for the geospatial domain include the ISO 19115 ("Geographic information-metadata," 2003) and the ISO 19139 ("Geographic information-metadata and XML schema implementation," 2007). ISO 19115 defines the set of metadata used for spatial data documentation. ISO 19139 defines the metadata used to document geographic services.

Since its creation, the OGC has developed a series of standards. From these standards, one can highlight a range of services aiming to standardize access to geographic information. Access services to geographic data are used for retrieving geographic information from a provider. The main objective of such services is to enable access to geographic information, offered in different formats, in a standardized manner. Currently, several types of access services to geographic data have been proposed by the OGC; however, each of these services is designed to data retrieval in some specific format. Some examples of these services include the Web Map Service (WMS) ("Web Map Service Interface," 2004), used for delivering layers of vector maps; the Web Map Service (WMS) ("Web Features Service implementation specification," 2008), used for providing geographic data mainly in the GML format; and the Web Coverage Service (WCS) ("Web Coverage Service implementation specification," 2008) used for retrieving data in the raster format.

Besides proposing standards on geographic information access services, the OGC also describes services that enable geographic data processing. Unlike data access services, responsible for geospatial information retrieval, these other services can process geographic data for the production of new information or new data sets. Geospatial processing services can be either generic, such as the services that convert data into different coordinates systems, or be targeted to one particular application domain, such as services that process satellite images to detect flooding areas. To implement such service category, the OGC proposes a standard service called Web Processing Service (WPS) ("Open GIS Web Processing Service," 2008).

According to WPS, each service operation is defined as a process with information such as: name, title, textual description, and sets of input and output parameters. Moreover, the WPS processes can be used to describe both simple services and service compositions, where one or more services are combined to provide a more complex service. In addition to WPS, processing services of geographic data can be provided in the form of web services (Alonso, Casati, Kuno, & Machiraju, 2004); a set of technologies used to implement service-oriented architectures (Erl, 2005).

Spatial Data Infrastructures as an Integration Tool

Ever since they were proposed, the services proposed by the OGC have gained wide acceptance and have become increasingly popular among geographic information providers. Although these services have facilitated access to information coming from different sources, they do not solve completely the problem of interoperability involving geographic information. This is because these services focus only on syntax, and do not consider the semantics of the information provided by these services. This limitation makes these services unable to detect and manage a number of heterogeneity problems that exists even with the adoption of the OGC services. For example, two map layers offered by different WMS services can be accessed in the same way; however, they may not be overlayed, because they use different coordinate systems; or because the data offered by the WFS services cannot be integrated directly, since these services use different measurement units for their attributes (for instance, a service describes a distance in meters; while another service presents it in miles). To overcome such limitations, many government agencies have developed spatial data infrastructures to enable the integration of geographic information provided by different agencies.

A spatial data infrastructure can be defined as the basis for the establishment of relevant political technologies, leading to institutional agreements aimed at facilitating the availability and access to geospatial data (Nebert, 2004). These infrastructures are being developed to facilitate the discovery, access and reuse of the geographic information created by different institutions. To achieve such goals, the SDIs have two central types of agents: the providers of geospatial information and services, who will use these infrastructures to present their resources, and the customers, who will use them to discover available information. Unlike the standards proposed by the OGC, the development of SDIs requires much more than simply the solution of technical problems. To improve interoperability between the information offered by providers, these infrastructures need as well to address several problems of some political and/or institutional order. The technical standards to be adopted by all sources of information, such as the specification of the information to be provided; units of measurement; coordinate system; and metadata standard. On the other hand, political and public order issues may include an institutional set of rules to govern these specifications: the agencies responsible for the information provided and the legislation concerning access restrictions to define what resources can be made available, what customers are to be granted access to information, and how this information can be used.

The increasing popularity of service-oriented architecture has contributed to build SDIs as a set of services that can be invoked over the network (Béjar, Latre, Nogueras-Iso, Muro-Medrano, & Zarazaga-Soria, 2009). In addition, OGC web services have been being increasingly used by these infrastructures to provide access to their data sets. Likewise, processing services for spatial data have been more and more used in spatial data processing. Another key facility for the implementation of SDIs is the catalog services, that is addressed in the following subsection.

Catalog Services

One of the main objectives of SDIs is to allow customers to find resources (either data or services) easily. To make this possible, these infrastructures provide a catalog service based on the OGC specification ("Open GIS Catalogue Services implementation," 2007). The catalog service may be used by both customers and providers of the infrastructure. The providers use the catalog service to advertise their resources. To benefit from this service, providers need to get all their resources registered in the catalog. During registration, they should provide metadata describing resource features, such as: the name, title, textual description, the geographical region covered, and URL. The metadata required for registration will depend on the type of service being registered, and must comply with the metadata standards adopted by the infrastructure.

The infrastructure clients, in turn, use the catalog services to find out information. For such, the client can set a series of constraints on some of the attributes defined for each metadata record. These constraints will be specified in some language filter, such as the Common Query Language (CQL) ("CQL: Contextual Query Language," 2011), which has a clause-based syntax similar to SQL, or the OGC Filter ("Filter encoding implementation specification," 2001), a XML-based language. While processing the user's request, the catalog service will compare the constraints defined against each record stored by the metadata service. The records that fulfill the search criteria are retrieved and returned to the client. Upon receiving the result, the client can use the metadata for each record retrieved in order to determine which from the retrieved resources best suit his/her needs. Afterwards, the client may use the information contained in the record to access the resource from its corresponding provider.

Current catalog services have some disadvantages that limit information discovery. The first of such disadvantages is that these services perform their search based only on keywords, and these affect the recall and precision of query results. Another serious limitation is that information retrieval is done based on metadata records alone, which impairs information discovery on the feature types offered by the service.

Semantic Web and Ontologies

The web has been growing steadily over the years. This has certainly propitiated an ever increasingly transmission of information worldwide. Besides the large number of sites, current web offers support to more complex contents. These include software applications (made available in the form of services), geographic data, and multimedia data, such as: images, video and audio. At present, the process of finding information on the web can only be done by means of keywords. Search engines, which use such methods, retrieve resources that have a certain set of keywords in their contents. Again the use of keywords for document retrieval can jeopardize both the recall and precision. Recall may reduce, because the relevant resources that retain in their contents terms representing synonyms, or terms that are related to those used in the query end up by not being retrieved. Precision can also drop since the resources, which are not relevant but do have the required term defined in their compositions, will be eventually retrieved.

In order to overcome these limitations, the semantic web (Berners-Lee, Hendler, & Lassila, 2001) was proposed. Using the semantic web, the resources offered are annotated with metadata describing their meanings, making them understandable for both man and machine. Furthermore, it is possible to describe the semantic relationships between the resources available on the network, and, at the same time, improve significantly the location of resources, enabling the automation of many services.

To implement the ideas proposed by the semantic web, it would be necessary to create instruments to formally describe the semantics of application domains related to resources that are available on the network. Such task has been resolved through the use of ontologies. Ontologies (Guarino, 1995) are used to conceptualize knowledge domains. The great advantage of using ontologies is that they permit the semantics of an application domain to be formally described through a language that can be understood both by humans and software applications. This allows the development of more powerful engines, and facilitates data sharing between applications.

In an ontology, an application domain is described by classes, properties, relationships and individuals. Classes represent entity types in the application domain. Properties represent the attributes that characterize entities. Relationships are structures that allow users to expound both the semantic relationship between entities. Finally, individuals are represented by the set of instances associated to the entities. Moreover, ontologies permit the definition of a set of axioms, enabling inference of new facts while processing a request.

Once created, ontologies can be used by search engines to improve the searching quality. When an information finding process is based on ontologies, two types of knowledge can be identified. The first type is called the *intentional* knowledge, and it represents the knowledge obtained through the analyses of the classes that make up the ontology. The second type is called *extensional* knowledge. This is obtained by analyzing the instances associated with the ontology. Over the years, several languages have been proposed for the development of ontologies. However, two languages have gained most prominence. They are the ones most used today for carrying out this kind of task: *Description Logic* and the Web Ontology Language (OWL) ("OWL Web Ontology Language Guide", 2004).

Ever since it was first proposed, the idea of a semantic web and the creation of ontologies have been largely in vogue for finding solutions for the discovery and integration of data problems. The application of these technologies may be verified in a number of application domains, such as: life sciences, tourism and digital libraries. Ontologies have also been widely used to solve research problems in geospatial domains. This application has been named geospatial semantic web (Egenhofer, 2002), (Kuhn, 2005).

INTEGRATING GEOGRAPHIC INFORMATION IN SDIS

As discussed in the previous section, for reasons of standardization, many SDIs offer access to their data and applications through the web services defined by the OGC standards. The use of these services allows one to discriminate geographic information at three levels of resources: services, feature types and instances. An overview of how these resources are organized in a SDI is shown in Figure 1.

An important feature of SDIs is that their catalog services may be accessed by different

Figure 1. Types of resources offered by SDIs

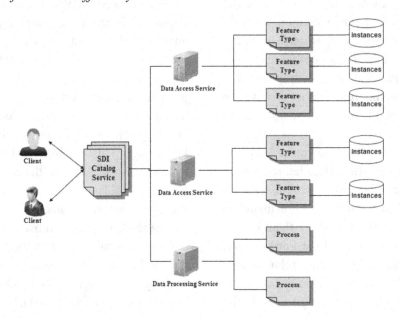

users with different perspectives. In order to satisfy these different classes of users these infrastructures should enable information discovery in several resource types. This necessity subdivides the problem of finding information in SDIs into smaller problems that can be organized hierarchically according to Figure 2. In this figure, each problem represents the discovery of one of the resource types offered by the infrastructure.

The first resource type corresponds to the services offered by the infrastructure. Services represent a software application that can be programmatically invoked by other software agents through the network. These services can be used to offer data or applications.

Data access services represent the services used to retrieve geographic data offered by a provider. Each service offers a set of geographic feature types. Some examples of requests for this type of services are *"Find WMS services that have data about rivers in the Paraíba state"* and *"Find WFS services that have data about airports available in the Amazon state"*. In current SDIs, to find this type of service, the user must enter with one or more keywords about the desired theme, and the

catalog service looks for services that contain these keywords in their description. As this search is based only on keywords, recall and precision are affected. Moreover, no means of discovering specific types of service (WMS, WFS e WCS) are offered, and the user should then be in charge of finding whether the services found offer data in the desired format.

Data processing services, in turn, handle geographic data to produce new information. These services are usually described by a set of input parameters, which must be informed such that the service can be executed, and a set of output parameters, which represents the data produced by the service execution. Examples of requests for this type of service could be *"Find services that calculate the geodetic distance between two locations"* or *"Find services capable of generating a map from a GML data set"*. Other research problem related to processing services retrieval is the discovery of service compositions (Alonso et al., 2004). Sometimes, there is not a single service that offers entire the functionality requested by the user. However, there are situations where two or more services can be combined to solve the user's

Figure 2. The SDI information discovery problem subdivision

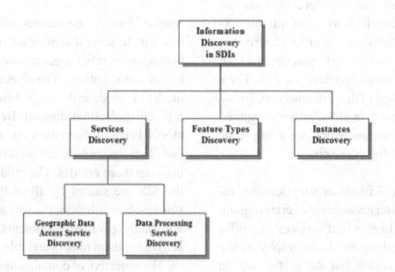

solicitation. Presently, data processing services are discovered by queries based on keywords.

A feature type represents a particular type of geo-referenced information provided by a geographic data access service. Each data access service offers a collection of feature types, usually related to the service application domain. For instance, a WMS offered by a hydrographic agency can provide feature types of water bodies, rivers and water reservoirs, while a WFS service, offered by a disaster management agency, can offer feature types, such as: fires, tsunamis, earthquakes and hurricanes. Geographic feature types are provided in different formats, according to the type of service by which they are offered. If the service is a WMS, then each feature type represents a vector map layer. However, if the service is a WFS, each feature type will be generally offered in the GML format.

Besides the lack of semantics, the retrieval of feature types in current SDIs has others drawbacks. Current catalog services fail in performing their queries using information contained in the metadata records. These records usually provide information about the service as a whole, and do not offer a detailed description of each feature type provided. Hence, services that offer feature types relevant to the user's query may not be retrieved if the keywords that describe the theme related to these feature types are not found in the service description. Besides, after a query is performed, the user evaluates each retrieved service; chooses the one that best fulfills his/her needs; finds where the chosen service is available; executes the *getCapabilities operation* to retrieve the data types offered; and analyzes each of the types to find which one is of interest. This task can be costly and tedious, since many services can be retrieved and each service can offer a large number of feature types.

The last resource type concerns to instances. The instances relates to geographic data provided by a feature type. In this case, each data object is a geo-referenced object. For example, a feature type that describes the hydrography of a given region contains a list of objects related to water bodies, for example, the river Amazon. Information relating to the data offered by a feature type is accessed via an operation provided by the service. However, the name of the operation varies with the type of service being used. For example, in WMS, the data is retrieved through an operation called *getMap*, while in WFS and WCS services information is retrieved, respectively, via the operations *getFeature* and *getCoverage*. In current SDIs, to obtain information at level of instances, the user must locate the service of interest; execute *getCapabilities* operation to identify the feature type that offer that information; and then execute the operation to retrieve the data. For a better understanding of the problems concerning information discovery in SDIs, we have assumed the following scenarios, which are going to be used in the remaining of the chapter:

Q₁: Mary is a Civil Engineer who develops research on water resources of a certain region. She would like to find services that offer layers describing the hydrography of the geographic region that she is studying. In this case, she looks for a data access service.

Q₂: Sam, in turn, needs a map that quickly shows the location of Indian tribes close to an area where a fire is occurring. In this case, instead of discovering services that offer this information, he would like to know which of the available feature types offer this kind of information.

Q₃: John is a civil defense agent. He has obtained a set of satellite images of a certain region and would like to discover a service that could process these images to detect flooding points. In this case, he looks for a data processing service.

THE PROPOSED SOLUTION

In this section we propose a solution to improve geographic information discovery in SDIs, using an ontology-based approach to enrich the description of the semantics of services offered by the infrastructure. This description is based on three types of ontologies: domain ontologies, geographic data ontologies and service ontologies. These ontologies are related to each other and are presented in Figure 3. Next subsections give more details about the goals and the structure of each one of these ontologies.

Domain Ontologies

Spatial data infrastructures offer data models referring to several application domains, such as hydrography, relief, weather, use of land, weather, health, among others. The objective of these data models is to describe the entities that compose a given application domain. Besides, each data model brings information about the properties that characterize each entity and the relationships between these entities. The models described by the SDI are shared by all of their information sources. Nevertheless, the way as these domains are usually specified (documents, UML diagrams, etc.) make them understandable only by humans.

The objective of domain ontologies is to offer a formal description of the semantics of these application domains. This description allows search engines to understand the semantics of these application fields. This enables the development of more accurate search engines. These ontologies are created from existing definitions in the data models described by the SDI. Each entity in the model is represented by a class; whereas their properties are modeled as attributes. The ontologies also describe the semantic relationships of generalization and composition between the entities. Figure 4 presents the extract of an ontology that describes the hydrographic field. This ontology was created from the document that describes how this application field is shown in the Brazilian Spatial Data Infrastructure. For reasons of simplicity, we have omitted the existing attributes for each entity. In this figure, the relationship "is-a" refers to generalizations. In turn, the relationship "part-of" represents a composition.

In the approach proposed in this chapter, domain ontologies are also used for the semantic annotation of feature types and processing services focused on a specific application domain. Besides, all the classes defined for these ontologies have a property called *hasSpatialFeatureType*, which enables the search engine to retrieve the feature type instances associated to each class in the ontology.

Figure 3. Ontologies used for information discovery

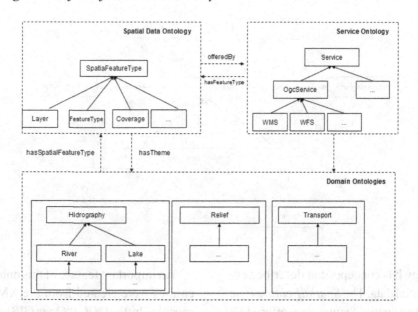

Spatial Data Ontology

Spatial data ontology is used to describe the spatial properties of the feature types offered by spatial services. Examples of such properties are the format (vector layer, GML feature, raster image), bounding-box, coordinate reference system, and so on. Differently from domain ontologies, this kind of ontology focuses only on spatial features that are common to all georeferenced information,

regardless the application domain which the data refer to. The goal of this ontology is to enable the inference of semantic relationships among geographic feature types. For example, it allows search tools to determine if a feature data type is offered in the format desired by the user, or if two or more map layers can be directly overlayed (in the case their coordinate reference systems comply among themselves). Figure 5 shows an excerpt of a spatial ontology.

Figure 4. Excerpt of an ontology for hydrography

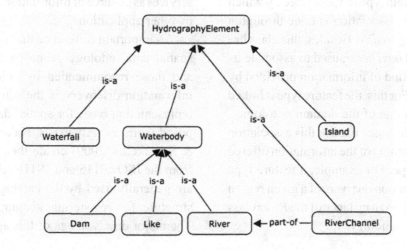

Figure 5. An excerpt of spatial ontology

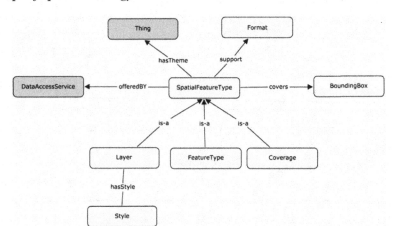

This ontology has concepts that describe several types of spatial data. The *SpatialFeatureType* entity represents a spatial feature type offered by an OGC data access service. It contains general properties common to all feature types, such as name, coordinate reference system, and bounding-box. This entity has also subclasses that represent specific types of spatial data. These subclasses are *Layer*, that is used to represent vector map layers offered by WMS; *FeatureType*, that is used to represent spatial features available by WFS; and *Coverage*, which represents raster images offered by WCS.

In the spatial ontology, each instance of *SpatialFeatureType* class is linked to one instance in the service ontology. The goal of this association is to connect each data type to the service by which it is offered. This association is done through a property called *offeredBy*. Besides, this class has a property called *hasTheme*, used to associate its instances to the kind of information provided by the feature type. For this, the feature type is linked to an instance in one of the domain ontologies. The class of the instance used in this association represents the meaning of the information offered by the feature type. For example, a feature type that offers information on rivers of a given region may be associated to an instance of the *River* class in a hydrography ontology.

An important feature of this ontology is that its entities were created from the XML schemas as specified by the OGC ("Open GIS schemas," 2011) for use in its services. This decision was taken to maintain the structure of the ontology aligned with the way information is structured within the services provided by the SDI. This alignment carries two important advantages to the approach in hand. The first advantage is that the information needed to instantiate the ontology classes (except for the theme) can be retrieved automatically from the service processing capabilities document. This facilitates the semantic annotation process, and increases the ontology usability. The second advantage is that this feature keeps the ontology compatible with other applications using OGC services as a source of information, enabling reuse by other applications.

An important difference that lies between the spatial data ontology proposed in this chapter and those recommended by other authors for information discovery is the scheme used as a representation basis for spatial data. Some proposed work, as (Athanasis, Kalabokidis, Vaitis, & Soulakellis, 2009) create their data ontology from the ISO 19115 and 19119 schemata, which are generally used by the catalog service infrastructure for registering geographic metadata. The major disadvantage of this approach is that the records stored in the catalogs usually contains information about the service as a whole, but, as described in the previous section, they provide little information on the feature types provided by the service. In turn, the use of OGC services in the way it is used in our approach as the basis for the spatial data ontology, allows us to retrieve all information efficiently, rendering information discovery far more accurate.

Service Ontology

The service ontology is used to describe the functional features of services registered in the infrastructure. Examples of these features include the meaning of their input and output parameters; the preconditions that must be obeyed for execution; and their resulting effects. This ontology was created by extending the OWL-S ontology (Martin et al., 2005), a general ontology to describe services independently from the application domain.

The main component of this ontology is the *Service* class that represents a service offered by the infrastructure. This class corresponds to *Service* class offered by OWL-S. In OWL-S, each service is described through three models: *ServiceProfile*, that describes the general features of the service; *ServiceModel*, that describes the functional features of the service; and *ServiceGrounding*, describing the service access information. During the creation of the service ontology, this class was extended through a class called *OgcService*. This new class is used for the specification of geographic services defined by the OGC.

The *OgcService* class has two subclasses: *DataAccessService* and *ProcessingService*. These classes represent, respectively, access and geographic data processing services. The class *DataAccessService* has a property called *hasFeatureType*, enabling the association of the instance of the service to the data types offered by the service itself. This property is the inverse of the *offeredBy* property, defined in the spatial data ontology. Since geographic data access services

are standardized and focused on the retrieval of specific information type, its definition is done through the constraints of the input/output parameters of its *ServiceModel*. For example, in the definition of the class that represents a WMS service, the ontology already constrains the range of its output parameter (*hasOutput*) to indicate that every instance of this service offer instances of *Layer* class. The same occurs to the WMS and WCS services, which are associated, respectively, to the *FeatureType* and *Coverage* concepts. In the case of WPS services, not constrained to specific feature types, the input and output parameters of the *ServiceModel* need to be defined by the service provider at the registration of the service. Geographic services offered by generic web services, without using any service defined by the OGC, are directly annotated as instances of the *Service* class.

In the service ontology, the properties *hasInput* and *hasOutput*, defined by the *ServiceModel* to describe the semantics of the input/output parameters, are used to connect the services to concepts defined in other ontologies. When processing services are generic, these parameters are associated to concepts defined in the spatial ontology. When the services are focused on a specific application domain, these parameters are associated to concepts defined by the domain ontology to which it is applied. Furthermore, a *hasFeatureType* property is defined for the *DataAccessService* class. Such property allows the connection of the service to each one of its feature types. An excerpt of service ontology is shown in Figure 6.

IMPLEMENTATION ISSUES

This section presents how the ontologies proposed can be used to enable information discovery. We address issues such as the semantic annotation process, information discovery and prototyping.

Figure 6. An excerpt of services ontology

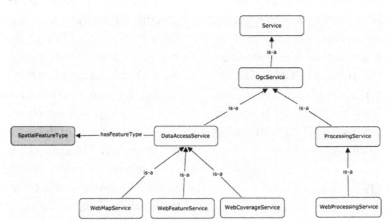

The Semantic Annotation Process

The ontologies described in the previous section are used to perform the semantic annotation of the resources offered by the SDI. The approach proposed in this chapter annotates three different types of resource: geographic data access service, feature types and spatial data processing services. All these annotations are done at the registration of the provider in the infrastructure catalog. To annotate a geographic data processing service, the provider just needs to associate the input and output parameters to the concepts that represent their meanings.

The semantic annotation of a geographic data access service is performed in several stages. In the first stage, an instance of the service which is being registered is created in the service ontology. After this instance is created, the operation *getCapabilities* of the service is executed to retrieve an XML document containing information about each feature type offered by the service. The retrieved document is processed for semantic annotation of each one of these feature types. This annotation is performed in two steps. In the first step, an instance is created in the spatial data ontology and filled with the information described in the document. The instanced class depends on the service type through which the data type is offered. For example, if the data type is offered by a WMS service, the *Layer* class is instanced, while instances of the classes *FeatureType* and *Coverage* are created at the annotation of types offered by WFS and WCS services, respectively. The instance set is also associated to its corresponding service. In the second step, the service provider needs to define the theme representing the information it offers. For that, it chooses, among the concepts defined in the domain ontologies used by the infrastructure, the one that best represents the type of information offered by the feature type. After that, a new instance of this concept is created and associated to the instance of the feature type. At the end of this annotation, the instances are stored in the database. Besides, a relational database with support to geographic data (PotgreSQL/Postgis) is used to store information about each spatial data type registered. This database is used for spatial filtering to improve performance.

The Information Discovery Process

The semantic annotation of spatial resources allows the development of search engines capable of understanding the information that describes them. The ontologies proposed in this chapter allow the discovery of services and feature types. The discovery of information is performed in two steps.

The first step consists in a spatial query, aiming to select the feature types the bounding-boxes of which intersect the geographic region defined in the user's query. The second step consists in the execution of a semantic query, applied only to instances retrieved in the first step. The execution of a spatial query, besides accelerating the resolution of this kind of query, enables to decrease the number of instances that will be analyzed during the process of semantic matchmaking. This reduces the cost of the reasoning operation and improves the overall performance of the solution.

The discovery of feature types, used to solve the query Q_1, is performed in the following manner. First, the client chooses the data format he is interest in (Layer, Feature Type or Coverage). After that, the client can define two types of constraint. The first constraint type refers to the feature type theme. It is performed through the selection of a concept defined in one of the domain ontologies offered by the infrastructure. The second type refers to spatial features and is defined through the application of constraints to the feature type attributes. Then, a SPARQL query ("SPARQL Query Language for RDF," 2008) is generated to represent these restrictions.

To perform the discovery of geographic data services, requested in query Q_2, the user selects the service type she wishes to retrieve (WMS, WFS or WCS). Then, she can add the feature types required for the service. For each feature type added, the user may define the same spatial and domain constraints used to retrieve the feature types. After defining all constraints, a SPARQL query is applied to the instances of the proposed ontologies.

To perform the discovery of geographic processing data services, requested in query Q_3, the user either selects the *ProcessingService* concept, in the case she is interested in more general service, or the WPS concept, in the case she is interested just in services offered as WPS processes. After that, the user selects the output type of interest. This is done through the selection of either a con-cept from the spatial data ontology, in the case of general services; or a concept defined in one of the domain ontologies, in the case of services focused on a specific application domain. The same way as in the other kinds of query, a SPARQL query is generated to retrieve the instances of services that offer the output parameters requested by the user.

PROTOTYPING

With the purpose of validating the approach proposed by this chapter, a prototype was implemented, using the Brazilian National SDI, called INDE. This prototype was implemented in Java. First, we created a set of domain ontologies. All of these ontologies were created from the data model documents specified by National Commission of Cartography, the agency responsible for developing standards for the Brazilian National SDI. Currently, we have ontologies for the following application domains: education, economy, hydrography, relief, transport, vegetation, energy and communication, geographic limits and public agencies. All the ontologies were created with the Protégé editor and OWL-DL language, which is the version of the OWL language that offers great expressiveness but keeps the computational decidability. We have opted for OWL because it is the ontology language recommended by W3C for the description of ontologies.

After being created, the ontologies were processed by the Jena framework and stored in a relational database implemented in the PostgreSQL DBMS. The ontologies were stored in a pre-parsed format, which enables to reduce the run-time parsing costs and, consequently, improving the performance of the semantic queries.

After creating the domain ontologies, a series of services offered by the INDE catalog service were collected. As the number of services registered in this service is still small, services offered by other public agencies in Brazil were also collected, at municipal, state and federal levels.

Each gathered service was stored in the database used by the prototype. After, the feature types offered by each service were manually annotated at the registering, according to concepts defined in the domain ontologies. The present database has 13 geographic data access services and 343 feature types. The first experiments performed involving discovery of geographic data services and feature types are fulfilling our expectations, since the information is being retrieved in a short and acceptable time interval, and precision and recall were enhanced.

CONCLUSION

Spatial data infrastructures play an increasingly important role in the dissemination and reuse of geographic information coming from different sources. These infrastructures provide access to geographic information via the standard services provided by the OGC. This allows us to split the crucial problem of geographic information discovering into various minor problems. The catalog services currently offered by these infrastructures aim at easing resource discovering, but they do not solve this predicament completely. These limitations are due to the lack of formal means to represent the semantics of the features offered by servers, and the lack of efficient mechanisms for the information discovery at different levels of service, feature types and instances.

In order to overcome the limitation of current catalog services, we propose in this chapter an ontology-based approach to enrich the semantic description of services offered by SDIs. The approach proposed here creates a semantic database that offers the necessary support for the discovery of information in data access service and feature type levels. The semantic infrastructure built by the approach proposed by the chapter is composed of three types of ontologies: domain ontologies, spatial data ontology and services ontology. Besides, all of these ontologies are integrated among themselves, enabling to improve the search process by the analysis of the semantic relationships between the instances in each one of these ontologies.

Further research directions include the implementation of information discovery at instance level. This kind of discovery is applied just to data offered by WFS services. Although the domain ontologies proposed in this chapter already allow the discovery of this kind of information, this kind of discovery requires efficient means to translate data in GML format to OWL instances. Another important improvement in our proposal is the use of existing information in the description of these resources to automatize (or semi-automatize) the annotation task. This will reduce the users' effort to perform the annotation and will increase the usability of the solution.

REFERENCES

Alonso, G., Casati, F., Kuno, H., & Machiraju, V. (2004). *Web services: Concepts, architectures and applications*. Berlin, Germany: Springer Verlag.

Andrade, F. G., & Baptista, C. S. (2011). Using semantic similarity to improve information discovery in spatial data infrastructures. *Journal of Information and Data Management*, *2*(2), 181–194.

ANZLIC Spatial Information Council. (2011). *Australian spatial data infrastructure*. Retrieved October 16, 2011, from http://www.anzlic.org.au/ASDI_quick.html

Athanasis, N., Kalabokidis, K., Vaitis, M., & Soulakellis, N. (2009). Towards a semantics-based approach in the development of geographic portals. *Computers & Geosciences*, *35*(2), 301–308. doi:10.1016/j.cageo.2008.01.014

Baader, F., Calvanese, D., McGuinness, D. L., Nardi, D., & Patel-Schneider, F. (2003). *The description logic handbook: Theory, implementation, applications*. Cambridge, UK: Cambridge University Press.

Béjar, R., Latre, M. A., Nogueras-Iso, J., Muro-Medrano, P. R., & Zarazaga-Soria, F. J. (2009). An architectural style for spatial data infrastructures. *International Journal of Geographical Information Science, 23*(3), 271–294. doi:10.1080/13658810801905282

Berners-Lee, T., Hendler, J., & Lassila, O. (2001). The Semantic Web. *Scientific American*. Retrieved October 16, 2011, from http://www.scientificamerican.com/article.cfm?id=the-semantic-web

Egenhofer, M. (2002). Towards the geospatial Semantic Web. In A. Voisard & S. Chen (Eds.), *ACM International Symposium on Advances in Geographic Information Systems,* Vol. 1 (pp. 1-4). McLaen, VA: ACM Press.

Erl, T. (2005). *Service-oriented architecture: concepts, technology and design*. Upper Saddle River, NJ: Prentice Hall.

Federal Geographic Data Committee. (2011). *National spatial data infrastructure*. Retrieved October 16, 2011, from http://www.fgdc.gov/nsdi/nsdi.html

Forth Institute of Computer Science. (2011). *The RDF query language*. Retrieved October 16, 2011, from http://139.91.183.30:9090/RDF/RQL/

Global Spatial Data Infrastructure Association. (2011). *Global spatial data infrastructure*. Retrieved October 16, 2011, from http://www.gsdi.org/

Guarino, N. (1995). Formal ontology, conceptual analysis and knowledge representation. *International Journal of Human-Computer Studies, 43*(5), 625–640. doi:10.1006/ijhc.1995.1066

Infraestrutura Nacional de Dados Espaciais. (2011). *Infraestrutura nacional de dados espaciais*. Retrieved October 16, 2011, from: http://www.inde.gov.br/

International Organization for Standardization. (2003). *Geographic information – Metadata*. Technical Committee 211. Retrieved October 16, 2011, from http://www.iso.org/iso/catalogue_detail.htm?csnumber=26020

International Organization for Standardization. (2007). *Geographic information: Metadata and XML schema implementation*. Technical Committee 211. Retrieved October 16, 2011, from http://www.iso.org/iso/catalogue_detail.htm?csnumber=32557

International Organization for Standardization. (2011). *International Organization for Standardization*. Retrieved October 16, 2011, from http://www.iso.org/

Janowicz, K. (2006). Sim-DL towards a semantic similarity measurement theory for the description logic ALCNR in geographic information retrieval. In Meersman, R., Tari, Z., & Herrero, P. (Eds.), *On the Move to Meaningful Internet Systems: OTM 2006 (Vol. 4278,* pp. 1681–1692). Lecture Notes in Computer Science Berlin, Germany: Springer. doi:10.1007/11915072_74

Janowicz, K., Wilkes, M., & Lutz, M. (2008) Similarity-based information retrieval and its role within spatial data infrastructures. In T. J. Cova, J. J. Miller, K. Beard, A. U. Frank, M. F. Goodchild (Eds.), *Fifth International Conference on Geographic Information Science, Lecture Notes in Computer Science 5266* (pp. 151-167). Berlin, Germany: Springer.

Joint Centre Research. (2010). *Infrastructure for spatial information in the European community*. Retrieved October 16, 2011, from http://inspire.jrc.ec.europa.eu/

Klien, E., Lutz, M., & Kuhn, W. (2006). Ontology-based discovery of geographic information services - An application in disaster management. *Computers, Environment and Urban Systems*, *30*(1), 102–123. doi:10.1016/j.compenvurbsys.2005.04.002

Kuhn, W. (2005). Geospatial semantics: why, of what, and how? In Spaccapietra, S., & Zimányi, E. (Eds.), *Journal of Data Semantics* (pp. 1–24). Berlin, Germany: Springer. doi:10.1007/11496168_1

Lemmens, R., de By, R. A., Gould, M., Wytzisk, A., Grannell, C., & van Oosterom, P. (2007). Enhancing geo-service chaining through deep service descriptions. *Transactions in GIS*, *11*(6), 849–871. doi:10.1111/j.1467-9671.2007.01079.x

Library of Congress. (2011). *CQL: Contextual query language*. Retrieved October 16, 2011, from http://www.loc.gov/standards/sru/specs/cql.html

Lutz, M. (2007). Ontology-based descriptions for semantic discovery and composition of geoprocessing services. *GeoInformatica*, *11*(1), 1–36. doi:10.1007/s10707-006-7635-9

Lutz, M., & Kolas, D. (2007). Rule-based in spatial data infrastructure. *Transactions in GIS*, *11*(1), 317–336. doi:10.1111/j.1467-9671.2007.01048.x

Lutz, M., Sprado, J., Klien, E., Schubert, C., & Christ, I. (2008). Overcoming semantic heterogeneity in spatial data infrastructures. *Computers & Geosciences*, *35*(4), 739–752. doi:10.1016/j.cageo.2007.09.017

Martin, D., Paolucci, M., McIlraith, S., Burstein, M., McDermott, D., & McGuinness, D. (2005). Bringing semantics to Web services: The OWL-S approach. In Cardoso, J., & Sheth, A. (Eds.), *Semantic Web services and Web process composition* (pp. 26–42). Berlin, Germany: Springer. doi:10.1007/978-3-540-30581-1_4

Nebert, D. (Ed.). (2004). *Developing spatial data infrastructures: The SDI cookbook*. Global Spatial Data Infrastructure.

Open Geospatial Consortium. (2001). *Filter encoding implementation specification*. Retrieved October 16, 2011, from http://www.opengeospatialorg./standards/filter

Open Geospatial Consortium. (2004). *Web map service interface*. Retrieved October 16, 2011, from http://www.opengeospatialorg./standards/wms

Open Geospatial Consortium. (2007). *Open GIS catalogue services specification*. Retrieved October 16, 2011, from http://www.opengeospatialorg./standards/csw

Open Geospatial Consortium. (2008). *Open GIS web processing service*. Retrieved October 16, 2011, from http://www.opengeospatialorg./standards/wps

Open Geospatial Consortium. (2008). *Web coverage service implementation standard*. Retrieved October 16, 2011, from http://www.opengeospatialorg/standards/wcs

Open Geospatial Consortium. (2008). *Web feature service implementation specification*. Retrieved October 16, 2011, from http://www.opengeospatialorg./standards/wfs

Open Geospatial Consortium. (2011). *Open geospatial consortium*. Retrieved October 16, 2011, from http://www.opengeospatialorg

Open Geospatial Consortium. (2011). *Open GIS schemas*. Retrieved October 16, 2011, from http://schemas.opengis.net

Rezeg, K., Laskri, M. T., & Servigne, S. (2010). Geospatial web services semantic discovery approach using quality. *Journal of Convergence Information Technology*, *5*(2), 28–35. doi:10.4156/jcit.vol5.issue2.3

Roman, D., & Klien, E. (2007). SWING – A semantic framework for geospatial Web services. In Scharl, A., & Tochtermann, K. (Eds.), *The Geospatial Web: How GeoBrowsers, social software and the Web 2.0 are shaping the network society* (pp. 229–234). London, UK: Springer.

Smits, P., & Friis-Christensen, A. (2007). Resource discovery in a European spatial data infrastructure. *IEEE Transactions on Knowledge and Data Engineering, 19*(1), 85–95. doi:10.1109/TKDE.2007.250587

Stock, K. M., Atkinson, R., Higgins, C., Small, M., Woolf, A., & Millard, K. (2010). A semantic registry using a feature type catalogue instead of ontologies to support spatial data infrastructures. *International Journal of Geographical Information Science, 24*(2), 231–252. doi:10.1080/13658810802570291

Weibel, S. L., & Koch, T. (2000). *The Dublin core metadata initiative: Mission, current activities, and future directions*. Retrieved October 16, 2011, from http://www.dlib.org/dlib/december00/weibel/12weibel.html

Wiegand, N., & Garcia, C. (2007). A task-based ontology approach to automate geospatial data retrieval. *Transactions in GIS, 11*(3), 355–376. doi:10.1111/j.1467-9671.2007.01050.x

Williamson, I., Rajabifard, A., & Feeney, M. F. (2003). *Developing spatial data infrastructures: From concept to reality*. London, UK: Taylor & Francis. doi:10.1201/9780203485774

World Wide Web Consortium. (2004). *OWL web ontology language guide*. Retrieved October 16, 2011, from http://www.w3.org/TR/owl-guide/

World Wide Web Consortium. (2008). *SPARQL query language for RDF*. Retrieved October 16, 2011, from http://www.w3.org/TR/rdf-sparql-query/

Yue, P., Gong, J., Di, L., Lianlian, H., & Wei, Y. (2011). Integrating semantic web technologies and geospatial catalog services for geospatial information discovery and processing in cyber-infrastructure. *GeoInformatica, 15*(2), 273–303. doi:10.1007/s10707-009-0096-1

Zhang, C., Zhao, T., Li, W., & Osleeb, J. P. (2010). Towards logic-based geospatial feature discovery and integration using web feature service and geospatial Semantic Web. *International Journal of Geographical Information Science, 24*(6), 903–923. doi:10.1080/13658810903240687

KEY TERMS AND DEFINITIONS

Catalog: Service that allows data discovery on SDIs.

Data Integration: Represents the problem of combining data provided by different local sources.

Distributed Databases: Database whose data are spread over several data sources.

Ontology: Formal conceptualization of application domain.

Semantic Web: Extension of the current web, which aims to describe the semantic of the resources published in the web.

Spatial Data Infrastructure: Framework that aims facilitating discovery and integration of spatial data provided by different organizations.

Spatial Data: Data that owns a geospatial reference.

Chapter 19

Integration of a Visualization Solution with a 3-D Simulation Model for Tissue Growth

Belgacem Ben Youssef
King Saud University, Saudi Arabia & Simon Fraser University, Canada

ABSTRACT

Visualizing time-varying phenomena is paramount to ensure correct interpretation and analysis, provoke insights, and communicate those insights to others. In particular, visualization allows us the freedom to explore the spatial and temporal domains of such phenomena. The task of visualizing tissue growth is challenging due to the amount of data that needs to be visualized and the large simulation parameter space. Further, many problems and their solution strategies tend to be extremely heterogeneous: in their models, codes, and applications. Such solutions must be designed to manage this heterogeneity in an integrated way, so that the user is presented with a predictable and consistent computing environment. In this book chapter, the author presents an application of visualization to a three-dimensional simulation model for tissue growth. The chapter reports on the different components of the model where cellular automata is used to model populations of cells that execute persistent random walks on the computational grid, collide, and proliferate until they reach confluence. It discusses the main issues regarding the parallelization of the model and its implementation on a parallel machine. The author then elaborates on the integration of visualization with the said simulation model. This includes presenting the system architecture of the developed visualization solution and the employed rendering techniques. Finally, the chapter demonstrates some of the preliminary performance results and discusses the encountered challenges in this undertaking.

DOI: 10.4018/978-1-4666-2190-9.ch019

INTRODUCTION

Tissue growth is a complex process affected by many factors including cell activities like adhesion or migration, scaffold properties, and external stimuli that modulate cellular functions. For these reasons the development of bioartificial tissue substitutes involves *extensive* and *time-consuming* experimentation. The complexity of biological behavior is the result of dynamic interactions occurring not only among the various components of a cell, but also among the populations of cells that form human tissues. As such, systems-based approaches must be used to study biocomplexity at the cell population and tissue levels. These approaches must consider cells as system components that migrate, proliferate and interact to generate the complex behavior observed in living systems (Marée & Hogeweg, 2001; Lysaght & Hazlehurst, 2004).

Computational models can provide powerful frameworks for studying biocomplexity at the cell population and tissue level (Levin et al., 1997; Law, 2007). The simulation of biological systems, however, differs in significant ways from traditional computer-science problems. Models of biological systems must be based on a thorough understanding of the fundamental mechanisms governing the behavior of the cellular components of such systems. In addition, such models must accurately describe the dynamic interactions among the multitude of cells forming most biological systems of practical interest. Therefore, employing systems-based approaches could lead to models with high complexity whose solution poses significant computational challenges (Lauffenburger & Linderman, 1993; Lee et al., 1995; Soll & Wessels, 1998). The availability of computational models with *predictive* abilities could greatly speed up progress in this area. Such models will assist us in predicting the dynamic response of cell populations to external stimuli,

and in assessing the effect of various system parameters on the overall tissue growth rates.

The fundamental advances in 3-D modeling, simulation, and data capture technologies as well as the tremendous increases in computing power have allowed users to take advantage of the many innovations in algorithmic techniques to generate ever more complex models and datasets. As such, visualization has become an important tool, not only in computational science and engineering but also in many other areas, in using and dealing with these massive amounts of data (Johnson & Weinstein, 2006). However, the modeling and simulation process, which represents one of the many sources of this data, is still seen as quite separate from the visualization process. Integrating the two into one computational environment would allow the user to think in terms of the overall task of problem solving in order to analyze the obtained results, gain further insight, and support important decision making. Having a readily available visualization component would allow the user to enhance his understanding in real time (Telea, 2008). In addition, the ability to interactively change the parameters of the simulation model allows for a form of computational steering that is becoming ever more in demand lately (Wright et al., 2010).

We have developed a three-dimensional computational model for tissue growth using cellular automata. This is a stochastic model that accounts for mammalian cell migration, division, and collision. In this chapter, we begin by presenting some background material on the building of three-dimensional bioartificial tissues. We review the computational model and present its corresponding algorithm next. We then discuss some aspects related to its parallelization and present our work up to this point regarding the integration of visualization with the said simulation model for 3-D tissue growth. We conclude this chapter by providing our summary and future directions for research.

BUILDING 3-D BIOARTIFICIAL TISSUES

The growth of three-dimensional tissues with proper structure and function is the main goal of tissue engineering. Tissue engineers draw on the knowledge gained in the fields of biology, biochemistry, engineering and the medical sciences to develop bioartificial implants or to induce tissue remodeling in order to replace, repair or enhance the function of a particular tissue or organ (Palsson & Bhatia, 2004). The three-dimensional structure of natural tissues is supported by the *extracellular matrix* (ECM). This matrix often has the form of a three-dimensional network of cross-linked protein strands. In addition to determining the mechanical properties of a tissue, the ECM plays many important roles in tissue development. Biochemical and biophysical signals from the ECM modulate fundamental cellular activities, including adhesion, migration, proliferation, as well as differentiation and programmed cell death (Langer & Vacanti, 1993).

Since bioartificial constructs must reproduce the architecture of the tissues they replace, they are always built on three-dimensional scaffolds made from suitable biomaterials. Very often, the scaffolds used for tissue engineering applications are made from synthetic materials like polymers with or without surface modification to improve their biocompatibility (Vacanti & Vacanti, 1997). Biomaterials must play multiple roles in tissue-engineered constructs. Besides serving as the structural component, they provide:

- The proper three-dimensional architecture of the construct;
- A three-dimensional matrix for *guided cell migration* and *proliferation*; and
- Growth factors to induce and maintain differentiated cell function.

The dynamic process for generating cellularized tissue substitutes can be summarized as follows (see Figure 1).

1. A small tissue sample is harvested from the patient or donor.
2. Cells are isolated, cultured and seeded into a three-dimensional scaffold with the proper structure and surface properties. The scaffold may contain growth factors to induce and maintain the proper differentiated cellular function.

Figure 1. Tissue engineering strategy for the generation of cellularized tissue substitutes

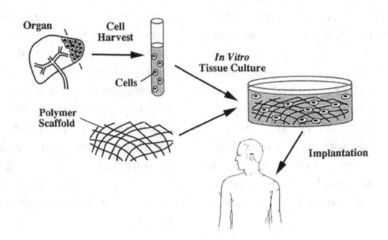

3. The cells migrate in all directions and proliferate to populate the scaffold. Cell migration speeds and proliferation rates are controlled by the surface properties and the morphology of the scaffold. Bioactive agents may also be used to regulate cell migration and proliferation.

4. The bioartificial tissue substitute is implanted in the patient.

THE SIMULATION MODEL

Tissue regeneration is a highly dynamic process. When cells are seeded in a 3-D scaffold, they migrate in all directions, interact with each other and proliferate until they completely fill the space available to them. This assumes that enough nutrients are always available to sustain cell growth everywhere in the interior of the scaffold. To model this dynamic process, we consider cellular automata (Tchuente, 1987; Toffoli & Margolus, 1988; Wolfram, 1994) consisting of three-dimensional grids with N total cubic computational sites. Each site is a *finite automaton* that can exist at one of a finite number of states at each time interval. That is, a site may be either:

- Empty and available for a cell to move in, or

- Occupied by a cell, which is at a given point in its mitotic cycle and moves in a certain direction. No other cell can move or divide into an already occupied site.

Proliferating cells execute *persistent random walks* in space. This process consists of the following stages:

1. Each cell in the population moves in one direction for a certain period of time (*persistence*). At the end of this interval, the cell stops and turns to continue its migration in another direction. The persistence is a ran-

dom variable whose density function can be determined experimentally.

2. When two cells *collide*, they stop for a short period of time before resuming their migration to move away from each other.

3. At the end of its cycle, a cell stops to divide into two daughter cells. The cell cycle or *division time* is another random variable whose density function can be experimentally measured.

4. This process is repeated until the cell population has completely □lled the scaffold or until the cells cannot migrate and divide any further (Ben Youssef, 2004).

To simulate these dynamics, the state $x_i(t)$ of each cellular automaton takes values from a set of integer numbers that code all the required information about cell migration speed, the direction of movement, and the time remaining until the next direction change and the next cell division. Our model also considers that cell division time is a random variable whose probability density function can be obtained experimentally using the procedure described by Lee and coworkers (Lee et al., 1994). Hence, every automaton has its state evolving at discrete time steps Δt through interactions with neighboring automata. Let us consider the j-th automaton that contains a cell at time t^r. Its state $x_j(t^r)$ is specified by the following numbers:

1. Migration index m_j: If $m_j = 1, 2, ..., 6$, then the cell is migrating in one of the six directions (east, north, west, south, up and down). If $m_j = 0$, the cell is stationary.

2. Division counter $k_{d,j}$: The time that must elapse before the cell divides is equal to $t_d = k_{d,j}\Delta t$. For each iteration, this counter is decremented by one and the cell divides when $k_{d,j} = 0$.

3. Persistence counter $k_{p,j}$: The time that must elapse before the cell changes its direction

of movement is equal to $t_p = k_{p,j} \Delta t$. For each iteration, this counter is decremented by one and the cell turns when $k_{p,j} = 0$.

For every automaton i ($1 \leq i \leq N^3$), the application of these rules defines a local transition function specifying the state $x_i(r+1)$ of the automaton at t^{r+1} as a function of the states of its neighbors at t^r:

$$x_i(r+1) = f_i\left[\left(x_i(r), x_{i+1}(r), x_{i+2}(r), ..., x_{i+6}(r)\right)\right]$$
(1)

where $i=1,2,...,N$ and $x_{i+1}(r), x_{i+2}(r), ..., x_{i+6}(r)$ are the states of the six neighbors of automaton i. The application of the local transition functions to all the automata in a cellular space transforms a configuration $X(r) = [x_1(r), x_2(r), ..., x_N(r)]$ of the cellular automaton to another one $X(r+1)$ according to Equation (1). Thus, a global transition function F acting on the entire array can be defined as:

$$X(r+1) = F(X(r)) \quad r = 0, 1, 2, ...$$
(2)

Starting from an initial configuration $X(0)$, the cellular automaton follows a trajectory of configurations $X(1), X(2), ..., X(r), ...$ defined by the global transition function F. At each time level, the states of all the cells of an automaton are updated in parallel.

SEQUENTIAL ALGORITHM

Initial Condition

1. Select the sites that will be occupied by cells at time t^0. The assignment of seed cells to the grid sites may be done either randomly (using, for example, a uniform distribution like the one shown in Figure 2 below) or according to rules that emulate special cases

of tissue regeneration like wound healing (Majno & Joris, 2004).

2. Assign a state $x_j(t^0)$ to each occupied site j by randomly selecting the migration index m_j, by choosing the proper value of the persistence counter $k_{p,j}$, and by setting the cell division counter $k_{d,j}$ according to the experimentally determined distribution of cell division times. The integer counters $k_{p,j}$ and $k_{d,j}$ will be decremented at every iteration and the cell will change its direction of movement or divide when $k_{p,j} = 0$ or $k_{d,j} = 0$ respectively.

Iterative Operations

At each time step $t^r = t^{r-1} + \Delta t, \quad r = 1,2,...$

1. Randomly select a site (an automaton).
2. If this site contains a cell that is ready to divide, execute the *division routine* and go to step 5.
3. If this site contains a cell that is ready to change its direction of movement, execute the *direction change routine* and go to step 5.
4. Otherwise, try to move the cell to a neighboring site in the direction indicated by the migration index of its current state:
   a. If this site is free, *mark* it as the site that will contain the cell at the next time step and decrement the persistence and cell phase counters by one.
   b. If this site is occupied, we have a cell-cell collision. The cell will remain at the present site (thus, entering the *stationary state*) and execute the *direction change* routine after a pre-specified number of iterations.
5. Select another site and repeat steps 2–4 until all sites have been examined.
6. Update the states of all sites so that the locations of all cells are set for the next time step.

Division Routine

1. Scan the neighborhood of the current site to determine if there are any free adjacent sites. If all adjacent sites are occupied, the cell will not divide. The cell division counter gets a new value.

2. If there are free sites in the neighborhood, select one of these sites to place the second daughter cell. The other daughter cell will occupy the current location. The selection algorithm may assign either the same probability to each of the free neighbors of a cell or "bias" the division process by assigning higher probabilities to some neighbors.

3. Mark the selected site that will contain one of the daughter cells in the next time step. Once a site has been marked, no other cell can move in it during this iteration. Set the state of this site $x_j(t')$ by defining the migration index as well as the persistence and cell division counters.

4. Return.

Direction Change Routine

1. Scan the neighborhood of the current site to determine if there are any free adjacent sites. If all adjacent sites are occupied, the cell remains at the present site. The cell is also assigned a new persistence counter.

2. If there are free sites in the neighborhood, select one of these sites by using a random algorithm based on the experimentally determined transition probabilities.

3. Mark the selected site that will contain the cell in the next time step (once a site has been marked in this fashion, no other cell can move in it at this iteration). Set the persistence counter to its appropriate initial value and decrement the cell phase counter by one.

4. Return.

PARALLELIZATION AND OPTIMIZATION

The parallel algorithm we developed to simulate the dynamics of tissue growth was implemented on a distributed-memory cluster machine using the Message Passing Interface (MPI). Our discussion will focus on the main issues we faced during the different steps comprising the parallelization task. We begin by looking at the architecture of the application at hand. Our application falls in the category of *loosely synchronous* applications (Fox et al., 1994). Such applications exhibit certain characteristics where the amount of computation could vary from one partition and time step to another because it depends on the amount of useful data (Pancake, 1996). A single processor experiences different workloads from the early time steps to the later ones. The need to exchange data among processors necessitates that each processor be able to determine when the other nodes are ready for this exchange so that data not yet used is not overwritten. Between these exchange points, the different nodes proceed at their own rates. Since the workload now varies both temporally and spatially, much effort must be spent to evenly distribute it among the nodes. In order to minimize overhead, we used a *static* and cell distribution-dependent *load-balancing* strategy whereby each node stays responsible for a fixed part of the cellular space where data may change. This is known as the *Eulerian method* (van Hanxleden & Scott, 1991). Static methods are uncomplicated, but can have difficulty handling subsequent load imbalances. The major advantage of using static load balancing is that the entire overhead of the load-balancing process is incurred at compile time, resulting in less overall overhead and more efficiency.

We were interested in solutions which are easily scalable, that is, the solutions should be efficient for a wide range of number of processors, with the goal of minimizing the overall execution time of the program, while minimizing the communication delays. Our choice of static strategies was based on the fact that the behavior (division and migration) of cells is random. We observed that the computational load fluctuations between neighboring sub-domains tend to average out, thus maintaining a load-balanced computation. Moreover, the choice of a cell distribution-dependent balancing technique fulfilled the objective of not only conserving the required load balancing but also maintaining the efficiency of the parallel computation.

Below, we list the main steps of the parallelization task including a description of the issues we faced in devising and implementing our parallel algorithm:

Domain Decomposition

According to the most common seeding mode, cells are uniformly and randomly distributed in the cellular array as shown in Figure 2. This type of distribution is amenable to a slab decomposition achieved by dividing the cellular array in slabs along the z dimension. The area of the boundary between any two sub-domains is equal to $N_x \times N_y$ sites. Except for the sub-domains at both ends of the decomposition, all remaining sub-domains have two neighbors. Therefore, the maximum amount of data communication from a sub-domain to its neighbors is $2 \times N_x \times N_y$ data elements at each time step. In this decomposition method, the boundary between any two sub-domains remains the same as we increase the number of processors P, provided that the size of the cellular array is not changed.

Mapping and Tuning

To achieve the slab decomposition, the sub-domains were logically mapped onto a one-dimensional processor grid. In our application, this topology reflects the logical communication pattern of the processes. In this regard, MPI

provides a class of collective communication operations called *reduction operations* (Quinn, 2004). We used global reduction operations for the calculation of the needed simulation parameters and to minimize the communication to computation ratio. We also note that the decomposition of the cellular space in the parallel algorithm of our application influences the order of events. If our parallel algorithm does not preserve the exact order of events of the serial algorithm, then it will only be an approximation. The mode and frequency of communication between the neighboring processors can affect the ordering of events and therefore the accuracy and efficiency of the parallel algorithm.

Dealing with Correctness

Our objective is to solve the same problem with the parallel code as with the serial code (Page & Nance, 1994). *Correctness* for the scope of our application is related to the kind of problem our code solves, not to the exact results we get from the machine. This means that two algorithms A1 and A2 may give different cell population distributions after a certain number of steps, but both distributions could be correct solutions to the problem if they were achieved according to the rules of our automaton. Our algorithm defines the transition from one array configuration $X(r)$ to the next $X(r + 1)$ by a set of allowed movements and divisions (birth of cells) within a defined neighborhood. A possible input I is an array configuration $X(0) = \left[x_1\left(0\right), x_2\left(0\right), ..., x_N\left(0\right)\right]$ giving the initial cell population distribution and assigning to each occupied site an appropriate state. The corresponding set of possible outputs O_I after r iterations consists of all array configurations computed according to the previously defined rules of mammalian cell proliferation and migration. Since the same rules were used to compute all configurations belonging to O_I, they are correct solutions to our problem.

Figure 2. An example of a uniform cell distribution of 80 cells in a 20 x 20 x 20 cellular array with a 1% cell seeding density

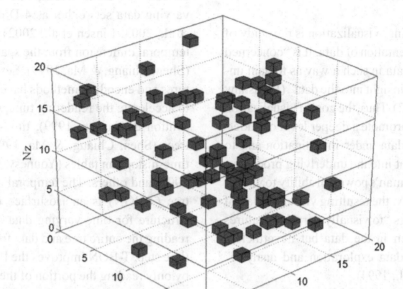

Parallelization of the Random Number Generator

The serial algorithm uses often a pseudo-random number generator (PRNG) to select a site of the domain and to reset the state of a site occupied by a living cell. A parallel implementation of the PRNG on one node would be very inefficient and would constitute a bottleneck. Instead, we parallelized the random number generator in a way that keeps our computation deterministic, even if the order of the generation of the parallel subsequences by the different nodes is not fixed. The key for this is the parallelization strategy and, consequently, the seeds used. We employed the leaping strategy (Fox et al., 1988) which interleaves the parallel subsequences of random numbers, reducing them to a single sequence that is almost equivalent to the sequential one. Given a seed for a serial simulation run, deterministic and unique parallel seeds were then obtained for the parallel simulation runs.

Splitting Cell Movement and Division

Performing cell movement and division in one step will lead to correctness problems. The solution is to use a "splitting" technique that consists of two steps: the first computes the next position of a cell or its daughter cell, while the second step is the one that actually moves/divides the cell and updates the state. The sequential implementation inherently uses this splitting technique so that there is no possibility of conflicts (Hoshino et al., 1989). To *preserve* the semantics of the serial algorithm, the parallel algorithm must communicate with the neighboring processors between the first and second step. If we do not communicate with neighboring processors between these two steps, we lose correctness since this leads to having more than one cell occupy a given site, which is a violation of one of the rules of our cellular automaton.

VISUALIZATION OF TIME-VARYING DATA

Generally speaking, visualization is the study of the visual representation of data. It is "concerned with exploring data in such a way as to gain understanding and insight into the data" (Earnshaw & Wiseman, 1992). Thus, the goal of visualization is in essence to promote a deeper level of understanding of the data under investigation and to foster new insight into the underlying processes, relying on the human's powerful ability to visualize. Consequently, the resulting visual display of data enables users "to visually perceive features which are hidden in the data but nevertheless are needed for data exploration and analysis" (Rosenblum et al., 1994).

Research on the visualization of time-varying data has generally focused on three major components related to encoding and compression, feature extraction, and rendering. There are two types of time-varying volume data compression methods: value-based encoding and physically-based feature extraction methods. Value-based encoding methods transform, and potentially compress, data by exploiting coherence. The value-based encoding and compression methods could reduce the size of the datasets and therefore make storage more manageable (Lum, Ma, & Clyne, 2001; Shen, Chiang, & Ma, 1999). Exploiting coherence is the key to value-based encoding methods. Data features, such as vortices or shocks, can also be represented in a more compact fashion (Post et al., 2003; Silver & Wang, 1997). The data can be represented as a set of features instead of just a collection of voxels, which provides a higher level view of the data. Woodring et al. (2003) proposed an approach which computes projections from a 4-D to a 3-D hyperplane by considering time-varying volumetric data as a four-dimensional data field. The 3-D hyperplane projections are then visualized by volume rendering.

Depending on the discrepancy between time steps, the visualization of time-varying data can also be classified as homogeneous or inhomogeneous. In other words, one can treat time-varying data sets either as 4-D data (Woodring et al., 2003; Linsen et al., 2002) or separate the temporal dimension from the spatial dimensions (Shen, Chiang, & Ma, 1999). Several data structures and encoding methods have been proposed to accelerate the rendering time, such as T-BON (Sutton & Hansen, 1999), time-space partition trees (Shen, Chiang, & Ma, 1999), differential time-histogram tables (Younesy, Möller, & Carr, 2005) and others. The temporal branch-on-need tree (T-BON) is an isosurface extraction data structure for time-varying data sets. Instead of reading the entire tree and data from disk at each time step, T-BON improves the I/O performance by only reading the portion of the data necessary to construct the isosurface of the current time step. The geometry-based tree structure can also help to explore spatial coherence and therefore increase the performance.

The time-space partition (TSP) tree is a time-supplemented octree, which treats spatial and temporal dimensions equally. This is a data structure proposed to accelerate the volume rendering of time-varying data sets. The user is able to control the trade-off between image quality and rendering speed by providing different error tolerances (Shen, Chiang, & Ma, 1999; Ellsworth, Chiang, & Shen, 2000). The differential time-histogram table (DTHT) is another data structure which encodes the temporal coherence and histogram distribution of time-varying data sets. DTHT is used to reduce the data loaded from disk between adjacent time steps by a given error tolerance. Further, spatial distribution is also used to accelerate rendering (Younesy, Möller, & Carr, 2005).

Ma et al. (2005) give a survey of different time-varying data visualization techniques. This survey focuses on how time-varying volume data can be efficiently rendered to achieve interactive frame rates by employing data encoding, hardware acceleration, and parallel pipelined rendering. The motivation for most of this research is rooted in massive data volumes, which are common in many engineering and scientific problems and are typically produced by simulations of complex physical phenomena. The ability to understand such phenomena is important to solve many of those problems. Most time-varying data sets are directly rendered as an animation sequence which shows how the underlying structures change over time. Tzeng and Ma (2005) present a new time-varying data visualization system by employing a machine learning approach. Machine learning algorithms are used to *learn* to extract and track features in time-varying flow field data sets. A transfer function for the entire time series is given by applying transfer functions from a few key time steps. Tory et al. (2001) discuss several methods to visualize specifically time-varying medical data. They explore visualization methods, which include isosurfaces, direct volume rendering and vector visualization using glyphs, to produce an animation of consecutive time steps that illustrate how the intensity and gradient changes along the time. They argue that these visualization techniques could provide new insight into the information contained in the time-varying medical image data and therefore help improve diagnosis or treatment.

RELATED WORK ON VISUALIZATION OF TISSUE GROWTH

Previous research on visualization that relates to our work primarily focuses on the modeling and visualization of plant life and plant ecosystems (Deussen et al., 1998; Měch & Prusinkiewicz, 1996; Prusinkiewicz, Hammel, & Mjolsness, 1993). This work resulted in the development of a modeling framework for the simulation and visualization of a wide range of interactions at the level of plant architecture. The framework extended the formalism of *Lindenmayer* systems (L-systems) with the needed constructs to model bi-directional information exchanges between plants and their environment.

Other works deal with the modeling of porous materials such as ECMs and related heterogeneous structures using stochastic geometry and functions. This new technique for solid modeling can be employed in the design of such structures to represent 3-D objects with complex internal shape and material properties (Schroeder et al., 2003). Yet another contribution deals with the possibility of a versatile soft tissue model. The aim of this work done by Wang and Devarajan (2004) is the modeling of human organs for use in surgery simulation software where realistic graphics and haptics must be delivered in real time. This is crucial to users to help them with depth perception and hand-eye coordination by obtaining accurate visual and force feedback.

The recent work in genome research has brought forward many proposed visualization solutions and algorithmic techniques to extract the required information, such as gene expression data, from large databases. The primary application areas include the classification of samples and evaluation of gene clusters for DNA microarray datasets using supervised and unsupervised clustering methods as well as multidimensional support vector machines (Komura et al., 2004; Zhang et al., 2003).

Volume rendering is a flexible technique for visualizing scalar fields with widespread applicability in medical imaging and scientific visualization. Researchers have investigated volume rendering for some time now and have developed a wide range of algorithms that include ray tracing, surface rendering, and other compositing techniques that map the data onto the image plane (Levoy, 1990; Totsuka & Levoy, 1993; Lacroute & Levoy, 1994; Engel, Kraus, & Ertl, 2001; Westover, 1990). Most of these algorithms operate on static volumes while our simulations of tissue growth produce 3-D time-varying datasets containing massive amounts of data. Instead of just one dataset of 512^3 or 1024^3, there could now be hundreds and possibly more of such datasets. Nonetheless, these algorithms can be adapted to our particular simulation by making use of some of the data encoding and compression methods, reviewed in the previous section, to enable interactive visualization of the simulation data (Ma & Camp, 2000).

ENCOUNTERED CHALLENGES

The simulation of realizable tissue objects requires very large amounts of memory. The extent of the memory intensiveness of our application can be further illustrated by the fact that simulating a $1cm^3$ of tissue requires a volume of 1000^3 since a mammalian cell is assumed to have a size of $10\mu m$. Visualization is necessary to enhance our understanding of the underlying phenomena of the model and to analyze the massive amount of data more effectively.

On a medium resolution volume of 512^3 which has 134,217,728 voxels and assuming a one byte scalar value per voxel, 134 MB of memory is required to store and manipulate these volumetric data. The visualization algorithm must be able to render as fast as 30 frames per second to produce a smooth animation of the simulation. Since for every frame the data has to be processed in the processor, this means that every $1/30^{th}$ of a second the volume must be transferred and displayed to the user on the screen. This in turn necessitates a bus bandwidth of around 4 GB/s. Hence, most of the available bandwidth on a system's bus is consumed by the rendering processes, leaving very little capacity to the simulation tasks.

To the best of our knowledge, there is little previous work done in visualizing tissue growth data. Our intent is to provide a tool that users can experiment with and explore the effect of varying system input parameters on the simulation of tissue growth. In addition, we expect that enhancing the usability of the tool will become more prominent as the simulation engine takes on added complexity when extending the model to include the simulation of multi-cellular tissue growth with each cell type having its own division and migratory characteristics.

IMPLEMENTED VISUALIZATION SOLUTION

The integrated application is divided into three major components: a simulation module, a transfer-function module, and a visualization engine. Each voxel output by the simulation module provides multiple state variables for each cell. The state of a cell contains information regarding its direction of motion, its persistence counter, and its cell phase counter as mentioned previously. Therefore, we need to apply the requisite transfer function to extract the appropriate data and map it to a scalar/vector quantity to be utilized by the visualization engine. Such data will be also more meaningful to the user. Currently, we have implemented the following transfer functions: a scalar-to-scalar transfer function used to display occupied or empty sites, a scalar-to-distance-field transfer function to be utilized by the isosurface extractor, and a scalar-to-color transfer function to display the age of a cell. Each one of these is used as needed by the volume renderer.

The visualization component contains an implementation of two different volume renderers: a point renderer and an isosurface extractor. The point renderer shows each voxel as a discrete point or cube element in space. The point renderer also shows the age of the cells in the visualization domain and maps it to colors. This rendering shows the approximate distribution of the cells during the simulations, giving some insight into how the cells move and divide over time. The block diagram of this component is shown in Figure 3 and an instance of this type of rendering is displayed in Figure 4. Further, the scalar-to-color transfer function uses the cell phase counter present in the cell's state information to display the age of a cell: from a young cell (blue) to a cell that is ready to divide (red). As noted above, the cell phase counter is the remaining time before a cell must give birth to two daughter cells. A higher value for this counter means that the cell must wait longer before it can divide. The colour varies linearly with the value of the cell phase counter to provide

Figure 3. The point-renderer component of the visualization tool

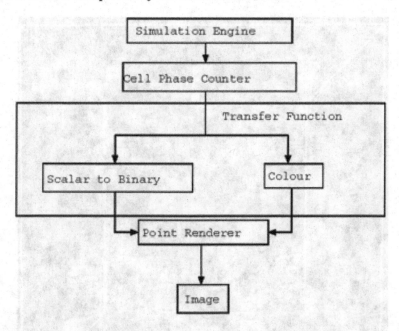

a smooth mapping between values. In addition, the marching cube algorithm (Lorensen & Cline, 1987) was used to display the clustering of cells (colonies of cells). This stage of tissue growth can be easily observed when the outer surface of a cluster is rendered instead of the individual cells. Isosurfaces at the boundary interface between the "outer" and "inner" cells were successfully obtained. The results from our renderer show a good clustering effect (see Figure 5).

EVALUATION OF VISUALIZATION RESULTS

Research in the dynamics of large cell populations (Zygourakis, Bizios, & Markenscoff, 1991) has revealed the following observations related to the stages of contact-inhibited cell proliferation during tissue growth:

1. **Phase 1: Exponential Growth of Cells:** At low seeding densities, cells grow at normal rates until they form colonies.

2. **Phase 2: Formation and Growth of Isolated Colonies:** Small isolated colonies form and grow without (or with only a few) colony-colony merging events. Cell proliferation rates fall below the levels observed in Phase 1, since only the cells on the perimeter of the colonies can divide.

3. **Phase 3: Merging of Growing Colonies:** As isolated colonies grow, they merge with adjacent enlarging colonies. These colony-colony mergings result in further decreases of proliferation rates as more cells become completely surrounded and stop dividing.

Figure 6 clearly shows that the visualization of simulation data reproduces the aforementioned empirical observations from the growth of migrating tissue cells. This verification using visualization further enhances the validity of the simulation model. These three phases of tissue growth are respectively illustrated in the left, center, and right images of the same figure.

Figure 4. An example of point rendering applied to the simulation data showing cells as cubical elements

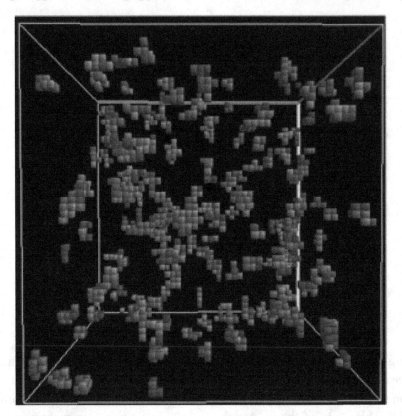

PERFORMANCE EVALUATION

The time complexity of our implementation of the sequential algorithm is of the order of $O(N^3)$. In addition, our implementation of the parallel algorithm based on the slab decomposition has a time complexity of the order of $O(N^3/P)$, using P processors. Speedup, denoted by S, is one of the most commonly accepted performance measurements of an application running on a parallel computer system. The sequential execution time is obtained by running the serial algorithm on a single node of the cluster. We were limited by the available memory capacity per node on the cluster. For instance, the largest cellular array size for the sequential runs was 330×330×330. The following performance results were obtained for a uniform distribution with an initial seeding den-

sity of 0.5% and cell migration speeds of 10 μm/hr.

For each cellular array size, we vary the number of processors P from 2 to 25 and for each selected number of processors in this range, we vary the size of the cellular array such that $N \in \{150, 200, 250, 300, 330\}$, where $N = N_x = N_y = N_z$. The execution time for different cellular array sizes and numbers of processors are shown in Table 1. These data are plotted and presented in Figure 7 to show a comparison of the values of the speedup for various cellular array sizes and numbers of processors.

The performance results show that for a given number of processors and as the cellular array size increases, the speedup values increase as well. This is due to the fact that as the size of the cellular array increases, the ratio of the computation time over the communication time on each

Figure 5. Isosurface rendering of cell data clearly depicting the cell clustering effect during tissue growth

node increases. In addition, these results show that for a fixed cellular array size and as the number of processors increases (up to 25), the speedup value increases. The increase in speedup values is due to the fact that increasing the num-

ber of processors yields, for most cases, smaller execution times. It is interesting to note that for the cellular array of 150×150×150, the speedup reaches its maximum value of approximately 3.94 when P is in the range from 10 to 20 processors

Figure 6. The visualization of the three phases of tissue growth (Left, Center, and Right images, respectively) is obtained using a uniform cell-seeding distribution

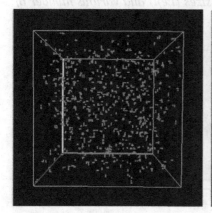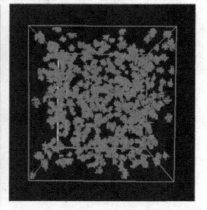

Table 1. Execution times in seconds for various cellular array sizes and different number of processors

Cellular Array Size	Number of Processors						
	1	2	4	8	10	20	25
150x150x150	2124	1441.6	861.0	570.5	538.9	539.2	571.1
200x200x200	5413	3568.6	1942.2	1181.0	1047.2	838.8	816.8
250x250x250	11382	7389.2	3911.5	2292.2	1925.3	1361.5	1255.0
300x300x300	21211	13199.7	6884.0	3838.3	3291.8	2029.9	1833.5
330x330x330	29156	17873.0	9255.1	5072.3	4266.5	2615.0	2298.9

and then starts to decrease for larger values of P due to the impact of *Amdahl's law* (Grama et al., 2003). In this instance, and according to our performance data, we observe that the communication time dominates the parallel execution time and accounts for most of it (approximately 83%). As a result, the parallel execution time at $P = 25$ starts to increase and is noticeably greater than the parallel execution time at $P = 20$ as illustrated in Table 1. For $N = 150$, we could hypothesize that the parallel algorithm has a performance sweet spot defined by $P \in [10,20]$ (Kuck, 1996).

SUMMARY AND FUTURE RESEARCH DIRECTIONS

We have presented the integration of a visualization solution with our three-dimensional simulation model for tissue growth, which was preceded by a description of the main issues dealt with during its parallelization. The ability to visualize time-varying 3-D data is crucial in ensuring the correct interpretation, analysis, and understanding of the underlying phenomena of the model. Our objective is to provide a mechanism to integrate modeling, simulation, data analysis, and visualization of tissue growth. Using a uniform cell-seeding distribution, we were able to visually corroborate the presence of the experimentally observed stages in the proliferation of mammalian tissue cells. These preliminary results enhance the validity of the simulation model.

Since natural tissues are multi-cellular, our future work includes extending both the computational model and its integrated visualization solution to support multiple types of cells. As we delve into the visualization of multi-cellular tissues, a new set of challenges is presented to the visualization process. The use of direct volume

Figure 7. Comparison of speedup curves for various cellular array sizes (Left) and various number of processors (Right)

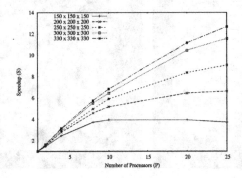
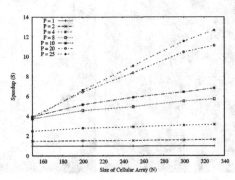

rendering algorithms becomes necessary in order to be able to show the internal structures as well as the global features of the newly grown tissue. Moreover, there are currently over 20 tunable parameters for the simulation model using one cell type. Therefore, the use of high-level parameter abstraction to reduce the size of the parameter space would enhance the usability of the visualization tool when this extension to the model is carried out. Other supporting features for the design space exploration that can be added include undo, redo, and fast tissue preview capabilities.

ACKNOWLEDGMENT

This research was originally funded by the Natural Sciences and Engineering Research Council (NSERC) of Canada via a Discovery Grant, under project number 31-611407, at Simon Fraser University. Ongoing research work is gratefully supported by the Research Center in the College of Computer & Information Sciences at King Saud University, Riyadh, Saudi Arabia.

REFERENCES

Ben Youssef, B. (2004, September). Simulation of cell population dynamics using 3D cellular automata. *Lecture Notes in Computer Science, 3305*, (pp. 561–570). Springer-Verlag GmbH.

Burgess, B. T., Myles, J. L., & Dickinson, R. B. (2000). Quantitative analysis of adhesion-mediated cell migration in three-dimensional gels of RGD-grafted collagen. *Annals of Biomedical Engineering, 28*(1), 110–118. doi:10.1114/1.259

Deussen, O., Hanrahan, P., Lintermann, B., Měch, R., Pharr, M., & Prusinkiewicz, P. (1998). Realistic modeling and rendering of plant ecosystems. In *SIGGRAPH '98: Proceedings of the 25th Annual Conference on Computer Graphics and Interactive Techniques*, (pp. 275–286). New York, NY: ACM Press.

Earnshaw, R. A., & Wiseman, N. (1992). *An introductory guide to scientific visualization*. Springer-Verlag. doi:10.1007/978-3-642-58101-4

Ellsworth, D., Chiang, L.-J., & Shen, H.-W. (2000). Accelerating time-varying hardware volume rendering using TSP trees and color-based error metrics. In *VolVis '00: Proceedings of the 2000 IEEE Symposium on Volume Visualization*, (pp. 119–128). New York, NY: ACM Press.

Engel, K., Kraus, M., & Ertl, T. (2001). High-quality pre-integrated volume rendering using hardware-accelerated pixel shading. In *HWWS '01: Proceedings of the ACM SIGGRAPH/EUROGRAPHICS Workshop on Graphics Hardware*, (pp. 9–16). New York, NY: ACM Press.

Fox, G. C., Johnson, M. A., Lyzenga, G. A., Otto, S. W., Salmon, J. K., & Walker, D. W. (1988). Solving problems on concurrent processors: *Vol. I. General techniques and regular problems*. Englewood Cliffs, NJ: Prentice Hall.

Fox, G. C., Williams, R. D., & Messina, P. C. (1994). *Parallel computing works!* Morgan Kaufmann Publishers, Inc.

Grama, A., Gupta, A., Karypis, G., & Kumar, V. (2003). *Introduction to parallel computing* (2nd ed.). New York, NY: Addison-Wesley.

Hoshino, T., Hiromoto, R., Sekiguchi, S., & Majima, S. (1989). Mapping schemes of the particle-in-cell method implemented on the PAX computer. *Parallel Computing, 9*(1), 53–75. doi:10.1016/0167-8191(88)90018-X

Johnson, C. R., & Weinstein, D. M. (2006). Biomedical computing and visualization. In *Proceedings of the 29th Australasian Computer Science Conference (ACSC 2006),* (Vol. 48, pp. 3-10). Hobart, Australia.

Komura, D., Nakamura, H., Tsutsumi, S., Aburatani, H., & Ihara, S. (2004). Multidimensional support vector machines for visualization of gene expression data. In *SAC '04: Proceedings of the 2004 ACM Symposium on Applied Computing,* (pp. 175–179). New York, NY: ACM Press.

Kuck, D. J. (1996). *High performance computing: Challenges for future systems.* New York, NY: Oxford University Press, Inc.

Lacroute, P., & Levoy, M. (1994). Fast volume rendering using a shear-warp factorization of the viewing transformation. In *SIGGRAPH '94: Proceedings of the 21st Annual Conference on Computer Graphics and Interactive Techniques,* (pp. 451–458). New York, NY: ACM Press.

Langer, R., & Vacanti, J. (1993). Tissue engineering. *Science, 260*(5110), 920–926. doi:10.1126/science.8493529

Lauffenburger, D. A., & Linderman, J. J. (1993). *Receptors: Models for binding trafficking and signaling.* New York, NY: Oxford University Press.

Law, A. M. (2007). *Simulation modeling & analysis* (4th ed.). Boston, MA: McGraw-Hill, Inc.

Lee, Y., Markenscoff, P., McIntire, L. V., & Zygourakis, K. (1995). Characterization of endothelial cell locomotion using a Markov chain model. *Biochemistry and Cell Biology, 73,* 461–472. doi:10.1139/o95-052

Lee, Y., McIntire, L. V., & Zygourakis, K. (1994). Analysis of endothelial cell locomotion: Differential effects of motility and contact inhibition. *Biotechnology and Bioengineering, 43*(7), 622–634. doi:10.1002/bit.260430712

Levin, S. A., Grenfell, B., Hastings, A., & Perelson, A. S. (1997). Mathematical and computational challenges in population biology and ecosystems science. *Science, 275*(5298), 334–343. doi:10.1126/science.275.5298.334

Levoy, M. (1990). Efficient ray tracing of volume data. *ACM Transactions on Graphics, 9*(3), 245–261. doi:10.1145/78964.78965

Linsen, L., Pascucci, V., Duchaineau, M. A., Hamann, B., Joy, K. I., & Coquillart, S. … Hu, S.-M. (2002). Hierarchical representation of time-varying volume data with 4th-root-of-2 subdivision and quadrilinear B-spline wavelets. In *Proceedings of the Tenth Pacific Conference on Computer Graphics and Applications – Pacific Graphics,* (p. 346).

Lorensen, W. E., & Cline, H. E. (1987). Marching cubes: A high resolution 3-D surface construction algorithm. In *SIGGRAPH '87: Proceedings of the 14th Annual Conference on Computer Graphics and Interactive Techniques,* (pp. 163–169). ACM Press.

Lum, E., Ma, K.-L., & Clyne, J. (2001). Texture hardware assisted rendering of time-varying volume data. *Proceedings of IEEE Visualization, 2001,* 263–270.

Lysaght, M. J., & Hazlehurst, A. L. (2004). Tissue engineering: The end of the beginning. *Tissue Engineering, 10*(1-2), 309–320. doi:10.1089/107632704322791943

Ma, K.-L., & Camp, D. M. (2000). High performance visualization of time-varying volume data over a wide-area network status. In *Supercomputing '00: Proceedings of the 2000 ACM/IEEE Conference on Supercomputing (CDROM),* Washington, DC: IEEE Computer Society.

Ma, K.-L., & Lum, E. B. (2005). Techniques for visualizing time-varying volume data. In Hansen, C. D., & Johnson, C. R. (Eds.), *The visualization handbook* (pp. 511–531). Boston, MA: Elsevier. doi:10.1016/B978-012387582-2/50028-9

Majno, G., & Joris, I. (2004). *Cells, tissues and disease: Principles of general pathology.* Oxford, UK: Oxford University Press.

Marée, A. F., & Hogeweg, P. (2001). How amoeboids self-organize into a fruiting body: Multicellular coordination in Dictyostelium discoideum. *Proceedings of the National Academy of Sciences of the United States of America, 98*(7), 3879–3883. doi:10.1073/pnas.061535198

Měch, R., & Prusinkiewicz, P. (1996). Visual models of plants interacting with their environment. In *SIGGRAPH '96: Proceedings of the 23rd Annual Conference on Computer Graphics and Interactive Techniques,* (pp. 397–410). New York, NY: ACM Press.

Page, E. H., & Nance, R. E. (1994). Parallel discrete event simulation: A modeling methodological perspective. In *Proceedings of the 1994 Workshop on Parallel and Distributed Simulation,* (pp. 88-93).

Palsson, B. O., & Bhatia, S. N. (2004). *Tissue engineering.* Upper Saddle River, NJ: Pearson Prentice Hall.

Pancake, C. M. (1996). Is parallelism for you? *IEEE Computational Science & Engineering, 3*(2), 18–37. doi:10.1109/99.503307

Post, F. H., Vrolijk, B., Hauser, H., Laramee, R. S., & Doleisch, H. (2003). The state of the art in flow visualization: Feature extraction and tracking. *Computer Graphics Forum, 22*(4), 775–792. doi:10.1111/j.1467-8659.2003.00723.x

Prusinkiewicz, P., Hammel, M. S., & Mjolsness, E. (1993). Animation of plant development. In *SIGGRAPH '93: Proceedings of the 20th Annual Conference on Computer Graphics and Interactive Techniques,* (pp. 351–360). New York, NY: ACM Press.

Quinn, M. J. (2004). *Parallel programming in C with MPI and OpenMp.* Dubuque, IA: McGraw-Hill.

Rosenblum, L., Earnshaw, R. A., Encarnacao, J., Hagen, H., Kaufman, A., & Klimenko, S. V. … Thalmann, D. (1994). *Scientific visualization: Advances and challenges.* London, UK: Academic Press.

Schroeder, S., Regli, W. C., Shokoufandeh, A., & Sun, W. (2003). Representation of porous artifacts for bio-medical applications. In *SM '03: Proceedings of the Eighth ACM Symposium on Solid Modeling and Applications,* (pp. 254–257). New York, NY: ACM Press.

Shen, H.-W., Chiang, L.-J., & Ma, K.-L. (1999). A fast volume rendering algorithm for time-varying fields using a time-space partitioning (TSP) tree. *Proceedings of IEEE Visualization, 99,* 371–378.

Silver, D., & Wang, X. (1997). Tracking and visualizing turbulent 3-D features. *IEEE Transactions on Visualization and Computer Graphics, 3*(2), 129–141. doi:10.1109/2945.597796

Soll, D., & Wessels, D. (1998). *Motion analysis of living cells: Techniques in modern biomedical microscopy.* New York, NY: Wiley-Liss.

Sutton, P., & Hansen, C. D. (1999). Isosurface extraction in time-varying fields using a temporal branch-on-need tree (T-BON). In *Proceedings of the IEEE Conference on Visualization '99,* (pp. 147–153). IEEE Computer Society Press.

Tchuente, M. (1987). Computation on automata networks. In Fogelman-Soulie, F., Robert, Y., & Tchuente, M. (Eds.), *Automata networks in computer science: Theory and applications*. Princeton, NJ: Princeton University Press.

Telea, A. C. (2008). *Data visualization: Principles and practice*. Wellesley, MA: A. K. Peters, Ltd.

Toffoli, T., & Margolus, N. (1988). *Cellular automata machines: A new environment for modeling*. Cambridge, MA: The MIT Press.

Totsuka, T., & Levoy, M. (1993). Frequency domain volume rendering. In *SIGGRAPH '93: Proceedings of the 20th Annual Conference on Computer Graphics and Interactive Techniques*, (pp. 271–278). New York, NY: ACM Press.

Troy, M., Röber, N., Möller, T., Celler, A., & Stella Atkins, M. (2001). 4D space-time techniques: A medical imaging case study. In *Proceedings of IEEE Visualization 2001 Conference*, (pp. 473–476).

Tzeng, F.-Y., & Ma, K.-L. (2005). Intelligent feature extraction and tracking for visualizing large-scale 4D flow simulations. In *Proceedings of the ACM/IEEE SC 2005 Supercomputing Conference*, (p. 6).

Vacanti, J. P., & Vacanti, C. A. (1997). The challenge of tissue engineering. In Lanza, R. P., Langer, R. L., & Chick, W. L. (Eds.), *Principles of tissue engineering*. San Diego, CA: Academic Press.

van Hanxleden, R., & Scott, L. R. (1991, November). Load balancing on message passing architectures. *Journal of Parallel and Distributed Computing*, *13*(3), 312–324. doi:10.1016/0743-7315(91)90078-N

Wang, X., & Devarajan, V. (2004). A honeycomb model for soft tissue deformation. In *VRCAI '04: Proceedings of the 2004 ACM SIGGRAPH International Conference on Virtual Reality Continuum and its Applications in Industry*, (pp. 257–260). New York, NY: ACM Press.

Westover, L. (1990). Footprint evaluation for volume rendering. In *SIGGRAPH '90: Proceedings of the 17th Annual Conference on Computer Graphics and Interactive Techniques*, (pp. 367–376). New York, NY: ACM Press.

Wolfram, S. (1994). *Cellular automata and complexity: Collected papers*. Addison-Wesley.

Woodring, J., Wang, C., & Shen, H.-W. (2003). High-dimensional direct rendering of time-varying volumes. *Proceedings of IEEE Visualization*, *2003*, 417–424.

Wright, H., Crompton, R. H., Kharche, S., & Wenisch, P. (2010). Steering and visualization: Enabling technologies for computational science. *Future Generation Computer Systems*, *26*(3), 506–513. doi:10.1016/j.future.2008.06.015

Younesy, H., Möller, T., & Carr, H. (2005). Visualization of time-varying volumetric data using differential time-histogram table. In *Proceedings of the Fourth International Workshop on Volume Graphics 2005*, (pp. 21–29).

Zhang, L., Tang, C., Song, Y., Zhang, A., & Ramanathan, M. (2003). Vizcluster and its application on classifying gene expression data. *Distributed and Parallel Databases*, *13*(1), 73–97. doi:10.1023/A:1021517806825

Zygourakis, K., Bizios, R., & Markenscoff, P. (1991, August). Proliferation of anchorage-dependent contact-inhibited cells: I. Development of theoretical models based on cellular automata. *Biotechnology and Bioengineering, 38*(5), 459–470. doi:10.1002/bit.260380504

KEY TERMS AND DEFINITIONS

Correctness: For the scope of this project, correctness is related to the kind of problem our simulation model solves, not to the exact results obtained. Hence, an algorithm is correct for a given problem, if for a given input, the output of this algorithm is valid.

Model: To model is to abstract from reality a description of a dynamic system. Modeling is the process of establishing interrelationships between important entities of a system, where models are represented in terms of goals, performance criteria, and constraints. Modeling has an iterative character that is the result of many feedback loops emanating from the different stages of the modeling process.

Parallelism: It refers to the simultaneous execution of several operations or instructions at a given time instant. A parallel computer allows us to specify that several tasks may be overlapped (pipelining) or performed simultaneously (multiprocessing). The overriding objective of using parallelism is to reduce the overall time required to carry out and complete given computations.

Rendering: In the context of visualization, this term means the realization of an abstract object as an image on a display device.

Simulation: Computer simulation is the discipline of designing a model of an actual or theoretical system, executing the model on a computer, and analyzing the execution output. Simulation embodies the principle of learning by doing as well as role playing.

Speedup: In parallel computing, speedup is the performance gain that can be obtained by executing a task or program on multiple processors as opposed to a single processor. It is equal to the ratio of the sequential execution time to the parallel execution time.

Tissue: From a cellular organizational level, tissues fall between cells and organisms. Thus, a tissue is a collection of cells that are from the same origin, but can be non-identical. This ensemble of cells carries out a specific (and identical) function. At a higher level, the grouping of multiple tissues forms an organ.

Visualization: In general terms, visualization is the study of the visual representation of data with the goal of promoting a deeper level of understanding of the data under investigation and to foster new insight into the underlying processes while relying on the human's powerful ability to visualize.

Voxel: A voxel is a volume element, which represents a value in three-dimensional space. Contrast this with the term pixel, which defines a picture element and represents 2-D image data in a bitmap.

Chapter 20

Information System Prosumption Development and Application in e-Learning

Malgorzata Pankowska
University of Economics in Katowice, Poland

ABSTRACT

In order to reduce risks and increase the speed of new information technology (IT) product or service development as well as to satisfy customers' demand, end users' involvement has become one of the most important issues. The chapter aims at the presentation of the user role in information system development and the activities of prosumers in e-learning. The first part of the chapter covers literature review referring to studies on end users' involvement in the information system (IS) development process. In the second part of the chapter the opportunities of prosumption development on the Internet are discussed. Particularly, the author focuses on e-learning purposes development and IT-supported communication among e-learners. The third part of the chapter covers a proposal of the architecture model as well as a discussion on methods of information system design for the prosumption development.

INTRODUCTION: CUSTOMER INVOLVEMENT IN PRODUCTION PROCESS

As consumerism rises, traditional development models are unable to quickly and accurately satisfy the needs of customer. Therefore, it is necessary that customers play a critical role in the manufacturing, research and marketing process. Companies invite them to the value exchange processes and treat them as partners in product development processes.

For companies in the service sector, customers' perception might seriously affect the quality of service delivery. Customer involvement can take different forms, i.e.:

DOI: 10.4018/978-1-4666-2190-9.ch020

- Customer participation in the new service development process directly (Martin & Horne, 1995);
- Co-development of technology providers and users on exploration of the use of the technology in a specific industry (Anderson & Crocca, 1993);
- Partnership i.e. a formal relationship between the customers and the company (Campbell & Cooper, 1999);
- Prosumption i.e. the dual roles played by the customer as a provider as well as a consumer (Matthing *et al*., 2004).

Generally, customer involvement help companies better understand customer needs, provide differentiated services, reduce the development time, facilitate user education, and improve innovation diffusion. According to Schiel the good customers for the co-development of products and services are:

- Willing to participate, without a prejudice, in discussions, handle critical feedback, and constructively assert the advantages of their position;
- Open minded to learn or to teach the product designers as well as to change their minds or to challenge the rest of the work team with their ideas;
- Willing to work on backlog tasks, because they can be easily guided in writing use cases and gathering evidence concerning their demands (Schiel, 2010).

The chapter is to support the creation of a theory of activation of IS users for co-development of information systems values in e-learning area. Therefore, social interactions, perceived IS development methods, their accessibility, transparency and risks are discussed. The second part covers analysis of e-learners activities and their communication problems. The last part aims towards proposal of information system architecture model.

Users involved in an information system development process are different, so they can be included in three classes:

- Lead users;
- Normal users;
- Community users (Tidd & Bessant, 2009).

Lead users are defined as members having two characteristics. First, they anticipate obtaining relatively high benefits from developed solution according to their needs. Second, they are at the leading edge of important trends in a marketplace under study. Normal users are less involved in the development process. Although normal user involvement might help provide innovative ideas, the limited understanding of new technologies could threaten the executability of the ideas, therefore there is a need to carefully select normal users for further co-development of products. Community users, unlike normal users, usually seem to have expertise in a specific field. They are interested in information technology and are willing to spend more time online on innovations. Organizations are now exploring ways to ensure a platform (i.e. Website) through which users can generate and contribute content, resulting in a cooperative experience between users and organizations. Thus, the research questions guiding the chapter concern the user role in information system development and the activities of prosumers in e-learning.

BACKGROUND: INFORMATION SYSTEMS USER ACTIVATION APPROACHES

Historically, there are several kinds of adaptive methods of information system development that build a model of users' knowledge and their involvement in that process. Active participation of a person in a community is a powerful indicator of the person's interests, preferences, beliefs and social and demographic context. Community members are a part of users' model and can contribute to tasks like personalized services, assistance and recommendations. Involvement of the end users in IT projects covering IS development is presented in Table 1.

Passive users and users-evaluators are oriented towards the observation and acceptance of other people efforts. But partnership and participatory design has focused on the design of end user applications or the co-realization of a more holistic composition of new and existing technologies and practices. Infrastructural design issues like software languages, programming languages, communication, security and resource models do not seem to be in need of partnership and participatory design. Participatory design tools were adapted from human-computer interaction methods. The tools were to:

- Involve designers and users in the design process,
- Capture as much of the rich context of use as possible,
- Require no prior knowledge on user-centred design methods and be pragmatic in approach,

- Provide applicability and specificity to a given design problem (Bonner, 2009).

Innovation methods that involve customers and enable companies to deduce their needs are therefore widely discussed. Prahalad and Ramaswamy developed a co-creation model based on dialogue, access, risk reduction and transparency of information between customers and software company (Prahalad & Ramaswamy, 2000). Von Zedtwitz and Gassman consider problems of management of customer-oriented research and links between research scientists and development team (Von Zedtwitz & Gassman, 2002). Von Hippel developed the lead user method and he argues that some customers are more appropriate to co-develop new products and services than others (Von Hippel, 1986; Urban & Von Hippel, 1988). Therefore, the IT suppliers and end users have created opportunities to be integrated and to exchange their knowledge and competencies needed for joint information system development.

Collaborative engineering is an emerging approach to designing collaborative work practices for high-value recurring tasks (Kolfschoten, 2010). To implement a collaborative work practice,

Table 1. Participation of users in Information Technology projects

	Information System (IS) vendor domination				User domination	
	USER					
	Passive	**Evaluator**	**Partner**	**Co-creator**	**Producer**	**Prosumer**
Goal specification Project concepts			X	X	X	X
Business logic analysis Business process modelling			X	X	X	X
Requirements Engineering			X	X	X	X
IS Design				X	X	X
IS Implementation					X	X
IS Testing		X	X	X	X	X
IS Deployment		X	X	X	X	X
IS Exploitation	X	X	X	X	Internet Users	X

groups need to be trained or require facilitation support. A key requirement is the users' willingness to change. In the information system life cycle, the designers analyse the system and basing on design patterns derived from their expertise, they propose changes, that are evaluated by the user community and then implemented. However, in collaborative engineering the end users are still dominated by the producer. They are still considered less experienced, even though they do not always behave in the same way. They are characterised by the following criteria:

- Involvement in the information system development process: strongly involved or just watching and not very useful;
- Environment: personal (home) users, work (corporate, organizational, enterprise) users;
- Frequency of use: occasional, frequent, extensive;
- Software used: word editors, email, graphics, accounting;
- Educational level: basic, intermediate, advanced;
- Relationship: internal users (co-workers), external users (clients) (Lukosch, 2010; Beisse, 2010).

Differentiation of expertise and experience of users creates the need to support users in the information system development processes. Although helpdesk systems and computer user support provide services to workers or clients to help them use computers more productively in their job or at home, the strategy that a specific organization selects to ensure user support often depends on the organization size, type, functions, location, financial conditions, skill levels, and goals for computer support services. A challenge that continually confronts user support staff is the need to develop an IT platform to enable software applications creation by end users and for them. Knowledge, skill and abilities are necessary to perform the job. However, the use of support Websites to communicate with end users has lately increased dramatically and open systems environments enable information systems prosumption development. Consequently, developing and implementing a customer collaboration capability is not merely a matter of implementing the framework, it is oriented towards the development of motivations for end users to enable them active participation in the value creation process. End users acting as individuals need tools for application development by them and for them. The cooperation with end users as corporate workers should be clearly established. Interaction with the customers could involve an element of commerce. Firms recognize an opportunity to engage customers in information system design. So, the companies develop forums, chat rooms, or they try to leverage existing social media sites like Facebook or Twitter. Companies believe they can engage customers in social media sites, like Facebook and it will be useful for the further product development (Bhalla, 2011). For example, social networking and social media provide great opportunity for locating and satisfying niche audience for a wide variety of movies. Film makers, using the new digital social networking technologies are taking production and distribution in their own hands by building their own audiences. By linking with already existing Websites, blogs and virtual communities film makers can find interested people regardless of their location (Einav, 2010).

User innovation begins when one or more users recognize a set of new opportunities. While it is clear that many users innovate, the evidence on the role of user-innovators in the commercialization of their innovations is mixed. IT companies depreciate the users' competencies as partners. As prosumers, user-innovators should develop new information systems designs for their own personal usage or (in case of user firms) for internal corporate benefit. They do not anticipate selling goods, however they can consider subcontracting the production or testing (Baldwin *et al.*, 2006). Prosumers stimulated by their own needs are willing to pay the design cost, apply the viral marketing and invest a small capital in manufacturing. Prosumption implies that buyers produce products for their own consumption. The emergent orientation towards consumers as active value-creators reflects a new trend in marketing and production practice (Xie *et al.*, 2008).

MAIN FOCUS OF THE CHAPTER: OPEN BUSINESS MODEL

Openness and Open Systems

Organizations are beginning to develop interactive business models, termed an open business model, where the absorption of external resources for value creation is permitted. In the open business model, the organizations can receive (for free or purchase) intellectual capital from competitors, merge with or acquire other organizations, cooperate with partners within research projects at universities, and engage users of IT products and services. The open business model occurs when individual users and user communities as prosumers produce and consume value from and for each other through content contributions that create mutual benefits. Social media -and open source tools create for end users the opportunities to be producers of their own content and Web 2.0 applications. In open business model the boundary acts as the interaction point between users and the organization and facilitates the development of user experience. The users are seeking personalized expertise and practices that are derived from relationships rather than products or services. The essential elements of the user culture in open source based projects appear to be sharing of the activity tools by the socio-technical system and further development of activity tools by the users, while activity tools cover technology and guidelines for users (Kokkonen, 2009). In his essay titled The Cathedral and the Bazaar, Eric

Raymond uses the image of a bazaar to contrast the collaborative development model of open source software with traditional software development (Raymond, 2000). The bazaar is a place where the community of users itself exchanges goods and services. However, there is a problem that open source software provides few direct benefits for normal users, because of their lack of the requisite technical skills to do their own information system development. But instead open source tools are best suited for technically proficient users with strong motivations for customization. Evidence suggests that the major reason open source projects fail is a lack of normal user contribution to the system development (West, 2002). On the other side, open source technology platforms such as the TCP/IP protocol suite and utilities created as part of Unix, as well as Linux, Apache and MySQL, and open source programming languages i.e. Perl, Python, PHP are built and maintained by collaborative communities of advanced users. A clear definition for open source explains that software code is available for redistribution without restriction and without charge and the license must allow derivatives to be redistributed under the same terms as the original works (Dargan, 2005). Nowadays, a group of terms describe the trend of the openness of innovation activities: open source, open standard, open research, user-driven innovation. In contrast to open source, open innovation typically implies the payment of license fees as well as other financial arrangement.

Open business models have been implemented in industries ranging from high-tech corporations (e.g. Dell, Google, IBM), online social networks (e.g. MySpace, LinkedIn), corporations (e.g. Procter & Gamble), pharmaceutical companies (e.g. Eli Lily/ Innocentive), automobile manufacturers (e.g. Chevrolet and Ford Motors) to traditional news media (e.g. CNN and the New York Times). So, the new business models occur when both consumers and producers generate and consume values from each other through knowledge contribution that create mutual benefits.

The shift in value propositions has been caused by three key enablers that have emerged - i.e., networked individualism, growth of social media, user generated online content, and potential context collapse with the digital media development (Di Gangi & Wasko, 2009).

Open source software, open standards, open information (e.g. public information) encourage Internet users to the innovativeness. User innovation is highly democratised, because users of products and services are increasingly able to innovate on their own, owing to their access to easy-to-use tools and components. Users innovate for themselves because they want something that is not available on the market, because professional services are too expensive, or just because of the pleasure of learning. Empirical studies show that 10-50% of users engage in developing and modifying products and services (Leadbeater, 2007). The open innovation is more attractive for autonomous activity, because of the necessity to share the codified information and co-ordination of activities among different parties is easier for innovations that can be pursued independently. Anyway, the key problem in managing innovation in networks (open innovation) consists of providing coordination of activities that are reciprocally independent. Another important issue of openness is the users' willingness to cooperate and development of stimulants for collaboration. The information available on the Internet and the Web, as well as the tools by which this information is accessible, have led to the establishment of a number of distinct Internet communities and belonging to these communities (via Facebook, Twitter) is a social requirement.

The individual users influence the way new services are created and incorporated into their daily practices. IT service innovations are to a large extent user-driven and directed towards providing a specific user experience. They are interactive processes, in which multiple actors, including customers play a significant roles. Service innovation requires co-creation i.e., users providing feedback with regard to existing information systems. They suggest alternative solutions or even they are able to propose their own services or contents. So, the intensified interaction with customers will improve the effectiveness of IT service innovations.

User innovation means innovation of the use and of the implementation, innovation in IT products and services, innovation in configuration of technologies and finally the innovation of technologies themselves. As it was noticed by Piercy the new, easier to end users technologies and the new channels of communication are making it much easier for user innovation to occur and have an impact (Piercy, 2009). Virtual business environment allows companies to interact with their customers in various phases of product development. Contemporarily, the majority of people consume what they produced. It is a production for own usage of producer. For many years it was a marginal activity, covering mostly agriculture activities. Toffler named them prosumers (a combination of producer and consumer) (Klen, 2009). Originally in economy the producers were consumers and their surplus production was sold by them on the market. However, because of work dividing, task sharing and specialisation the producers have provided goods and services to the market and they develop series and mass production. Although, the ability to produce large quantities of products has improved in the tome and with the studies, later, a low proficiency of mass production encouraged producers to a customised products development. Therefore, the prosumption can be considered as a next step in market products' development. Consumers start behave as prosumers and this movement creates an environment based on innovators and value creation models where collaboration and co-designing predominate. The interaction between these people generates valuable information for the productive sector and with the support of the currently available technologies. Contemporary user of Internet can act as:

- Information provider, working also on information retrieval and filtering through browsers,
- Medical practitioner, able of self-diagnosing and self-therapy,
- Marketer, looking for information on product and diffusing the product information through viral marketing,
- Researcher, involved in observations, delivering information for further research and filling questionnaires,
- Teacher in self-learning processes and knowledge recipient in online courses,
- Application designer, tester and implementer,
- Publisher and author of newsletters, journals, music and films.

e-Learning Goals and Processes

New modes of innovation require an openness which is an ability to access and integrate other's ideas in their own research. Globalization and the use of the Internet have enhanced these effects. Other sources of innovation can mean other firms, nonprofit organizations, universities, but also users, consumers, amateurs and volunteers influencing the demand. e-Learners as innovators look for the development of new design of teaching materials for their own personal usage. They do not anticipate a sale of the educational services or course manuals, although they can teach other users online. Creating personal learning environment and collecting learning artifacts in own personal repositories are the essential characteristics of e-learners as innovators. Although, they need an e-moderator support, they are not passive recipients of a course content or listeners of teacher's monologue. Nowadays, the Internet design space is described as an abstract territory where the course design is realized by professionals and volunteers. e-Learners are motivated to explore an Internet space because they believe that their new learning object designs enhance their learning. There is no

one to pay e-learners for searching and designing on the Internet. Every new learning object is an innovative option and e-learners as innovators have the right but not the obligation to solve some problems in a new way. They can create for themselves a certain portfolio of Internet learning objects and the portfolio structure depends upon them. The use of learning object portfolio by one person does not preclude another from using it too, although with respecting the property rights e.g. patents and copyrights. Further usage of learning objects is a guarantee of further knowledge development, therefore preventing e-learners from using the other designs is not a sufficient barrier of plagiarism. It should be noticed, that property rights are a feature of specific institutional regimes, not an intrinsic characteristic of learning objects (Baldwin *et al.*, 2006). An important feature of e-learning innovativeness on the Internet is a necessity, because the necessity is the mother of invention, therefore many e-learners will create their own learning object portfolio to solve the problem their encountered.

Web 2.0 Opportunities

Nowadays, business organizations are exploring ways to provide a platform (Website) through which users generate and contribute content, resulting in a co-created experience between users and online schools. However, organizations interested in leveraging user-generated websites are facing a new challenge, getting users to actively engage through content contribution, retrieval and exploration.

Websites such as Twitter, Facebook, MetaCafe, Wikipedia, Flickr among others have all been introduced within the last decade and rapidly grew in user membership. Business organizations are beginning to invest time and effort in developing a social media presence, to capitalize on a growing user population that is interested in creating, retrieving and exploring the websites. Organizations recognized the potential benefits such as marketing insights, cost savings, brand awareness and idea generation.

Users benefit from a positive user experience that fulfills personal needs and interests, although there is a risk, that if an organization fails to emphasize a positive user experience, negative consequences can occur i.e., negative publicity and loss of user engagement.

In recent years, the rise of portable or time-shifted media (such as podcasts, the iTunes Music Store and the video equivalents), blogs and social networks have created changes in traditional relationships to everything from media, to education, to consumer and political behavior (Polaine & Bennett, 2010). A wiki is the most important, online collaborative writing tool with which anyone can add content and anyone can edit content that has already been published. Web 2.0 provides capabilities and fostering social norms that allow large groups of temporally and geographically dispersed people to self-organize and to co-create value in a decentralized manner (Briggs, 2009). Under the Web 2.0, new media for delivery, participation and sharing information, shopping digital goods, searching tools and WebTV are included. The data suggest that the changes in traditional media are driven by the new media companies and that traditional media adopt and promote these changes (Bjorn-Andersen *et al.*, 2008).

The term Enterprise 2.0 introduced by McAfee is used to describe the nature of an enterprise where social and technological changes support management of information (McAfee, 2006). Social networking capabilities there help organizations in capturing unstructured tacit knowledge. The main challenge is on how to differentiate meaningful and re-usable knowledge from the contents like blogs, online communities and wikis. Engineering 2.0 implies that the innovation ecosystem includes open networks of peers. Engineering 2.0 technologies offer the potential to leverage on spontaneous and decentralized forms of collaboration (Larsson *et al.*, 2010).

Project Management 2.0 or Social Project Management is a next step in an evolution of project management practices and software built on Web 2.0 technologies. Such software applications comprise blogs, wikis and other collaborative and social software and share abilities to upload data and media. In the literature, Project Management 2.0 is often associated with agile project management methods (Romero & Molina, 2009).

CUSTOMER ORIENTED ARCHITECTURE DEVELOPMENT

e-Learning 2.0

Web technologies revolutionize the way people access information, broadcast it and interact. They enable teleworking, networking and socializing. Informal learning has received a special attention as an important part of one's learning experience. In the Web learning community, establishing contacts and learning relationships with individuals interested in the same area and development of shared understanding and even practice are available. While the success of Web learning still requires a careful selection of appropriate communication and collaboration tools, the underlying learning and teaching methodology is shifting from passive content reading towards active content creation. e-Learners have opportunities to collect, select and share drawings, animations, pictures, digital videos, texts and sounds among users. According to Spaniol et al. Learning as a Service (LaaS) aims at the flexible orchestration of social software within a web-based learning framework according to the professionals' needs (Spaniol *et al.*, 2008).

The Web learning has revealed the social learning processes, which are very community specific. Some non-technical communities of professionals are usually not able to express their needs in the very beginning of technology enhanced learning application usage. Thus, the communities have to gain experiences on their own learning processes while using the systems. A personal learning environment enables the usage of social software for informal learning which is learner-driven, problem-based and motivated by e-learners' interests. Personal learning environments are associated with flexible learning methods. Teachers used to play a role of e-moderator or e-advisor, or even their role is not clearly specified. For example, Edmodo (www.edmodo.com) is a communication platform for teachers and students. It provides a way for teachers and students to share knowledge, links and files.

Social learning online is the practice of working in groups. It takes place in response to problems and it is driven by the interests of the e-learner. It is sequenced and controlled by e-learner in terms of time. It is built on unique and personal knowledge bases and realized in communities of practice. A community of practice supports the apprenticeship by interacting regularly and sharing experiences (Healy, 2009).

e-Learning Communication

Today, students are believed to become autonomous, independent and self-directed learners who take responsibility for their own personal and professional development thus changing the teacher's role from expert to moderator, coach and facilitator.

Figure 1 presents communication in e-learning environment. A student group is a special group, in which people work interdependently to accomplish a goal. Students in a group are interconnected to share knowledge. Formal and informal rules and roles specified for the group control the interaction among group members.

Usually the e-learning content providers are interested in minimizing the time for course creating, therefore many course e-moderators provide only a stimulating element structure. The e-learners should be persuaded that they are bright and creative and they do not be very fearful of change. Usually students are afraid of something new or difficult to read, catch and cope. They fear failing in the exam process. So, the e-learners should be informed about the general rules and principles in a certain domain. They should be given examples on how to solve problems, presentations of methodologies, methods. The course content is changed frequently and by the e-learner, who is the owner of the course content. For other e-learners dissemination of the e-learning content is necessary for further education. So, conclusions and considerations included in the works of the earlier e-learners should be suggested as needed to read by the next student group. Therefore, the e-learning courses are constantly developed and verified by students processes.

However, not all the courses are appropriate for participative e-learning. Good candidates for e-learning are:

- Projects that need extensive simulations, like industrial control systems, flight simulators
- Content that needs a lot of collaborative expertise to develop like specialized graphics, simulations or programming,
- Generic topics demanding creative thinking like management training, financial training or time management,
- Specific topics demanding careful analysis like images in medicine for diagnosis and therapy.

e-Learning in groups is effective when it allows for identification of learning competencies. The e-learners have an opportunity to commonly practice their skills, but they are working as self-organizing and self-controlled group. They focus on the future and the learning is transformed from the training session to the work environment.

In e-learning in groups the creativity development is particularly important. The teachers' and moderators' role is to encourage e-learners to creative thinking. In e-learning environment, the

Figure 1. Communication in e-learning community

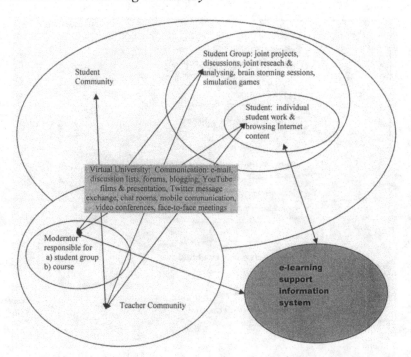

online communication is realized among e-learners, e-teachers and e-moderators. The e-teachers are responsible for the content provision and for the course realization. The e-moderators support e-students in their learning processes. e-Learning 2.0 is an opportunity to provide learning methods and material by e-learner. Figure 2 presents the simplest use case to reveal roles of that actors in e-learning system.

Traditional e-learning platforms usually accept only active role of e-teacher for the content providing. e-Learning 2.0 rejects this approach and includes an option of changing the roles among e-teacher and e-learner.

The e-learning task motivation includes personal intrinsic motivation, the social environment impact and the attitude towards the task and the communication online. Creativity is a problem for both individuals and groups, so different inventive techniques are demanded. Brainstorming, - the best known technique for encouraging group creativity has been criticized as being ineffective. However

it depends on the problems to be solved. Tasks range from cooperative activities, where members work together (e.g. generating creative ideas) to difference analysis, where members compete or negotiate.

Effective e-learning group has a shared understanding of the group's goals, norms and resources, including understanding of their roles, knowledge, and skills of each team members. The shared understanding is essential for coordination among group members, especially for tactical operations. Therefore, the action learning seems to be the most appropriate for e-learning when students are directly dealing with real life issues. The basic idea of action learning is to develop a group that can analyze and solve an important, real problem in joint activities online.

Levi argues that action learning combines training with developing innovative solutions to existing organizational problems. In the process of joint problem solving students learn how to create and operate as effective problem solving

Figure 2. e-Learning use case

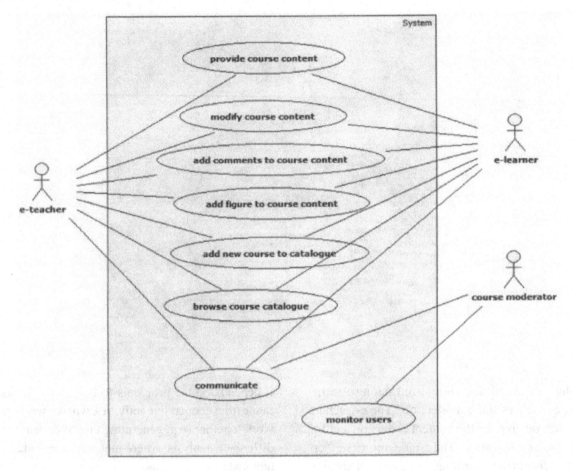

teams (Levi, 2007). So, problem is a challenge, learning is developed around the problem or a task that need solving as important. Students learn best from taking action and reflecting in the results. The problem should be valuable and oriented towards improving quality, reducing turnover, recognizing the situation, analysis of an incident, designing an organizational process. The action learning approach should encourage to experimentation, offer a certain support, promote feedback and provoke to questioning.

Classical learning theory conceptualized the interactive relationships between teachers and learners i.e., between producers and consumers. It is argued that education is a service-oriented activity, producing active interaction. Luckily,

Internet and Web development ensure that the recipients of educational services are conceptualized as active co-producers and they are not passive receptors. The learning environment should be designed in a way that makes it possible for learners to express their demands and preferences as part of the constructive process.

Architecture Model

Generally, models are a purposeful abstraction of reality. There is no single correct way to create models and many different methodologies have been proposed. They share a common goal of defining the rules and requirements of the context of use and communicating the understanding in one or more modeling artifacts.

A model is an abstract and unambiguous conception of something in the real world that focuses on specific aspects or elements and abstracts from other elements, based on the purpose for which the model is created (Lankhorst, 2005). In this context, models are presented using formalized graphical or textual means. In the context of information system development, models can be utilized for various kinds of information processing, visualization, analysis, testing and simulation. Modeling is the act of purposely abstracting a model from the detailed descriptions of reality. The iterative modeling approach seems to be very helpful to handle the complexity of enterprise modeling by allowing the use of different levels of abstraction. Through abstraction levels you can capture the key concepts and key relations in an enterprise model, before its further application for diagnosis and prediction. Nowadays, the enterprise architecture or corporate architecture is proposed as a methodology to develop IT implementation model. The term 'enterprise' can be interpreted as an overall concept to identify a company, business organization or governmental institution. Therefore, a virtual education institution can also be analyzed as an enterprise. According to Robbins, an enterprise is considered as a 'consciously coordinated social entity, with a relatively identifiable boundary, that functions on a relatively continuous basis to achieve a common goal' (Hoogervorst, 2009). So the enterprise is understood as a social entity, where people are responsible for realizing the pre-specified goals. Communication is evidently vital for them to coordinate their collaborative activities. The basic communication patterns form an essential aspect of the enterprise engineering theory and modeling methodology. Goal orientation is the second important characteristic. Interaction among people within an enterprise, their activities' coordination, their cooperation and competition are in consequence to determine the level of enterprise goal achievement. The interaction patterns can be spontaneous, however, from the point of view of goal achievement it is better to have them planned and designed.

Enterprise architecture is defined as a coherent and consistent set of principles and standards that guide system design (Lankhorst, 2005). For an enterprise, IT architecture provides normative design guidance for the enterprise information systems. Architectural framework as a conceptual structure related to a certain system type consists of areas of concern and a necessary and sufficient set of design domains. Enterprise architecture is also defined as a strategic information asset base, which defines the business mission, the information and technology necessary to perform the mission, the transitional processes for implementing new technologies in response to the changing mission needs (Updating, 2003). According to McGovern *et al.*, enterprise architecture identifies the main components of an organization and how components in the organization's nervous system function together to achieve defined business objectives (McGovern *et al.*, 2003). These components include personnel, business processes, technology, financial information and other resources. Business architecture involves a specification of the business mission, strategy, business components, organizational structure, business process models and business functions. Information architecture (also named data architecture) defines who requires what information to achieve their mission and how the information is accessible. The application architecture covers the application of a portfolio that is necessary for the business mission and the information needs of the organization. Information technology architecture reveals which IT services are necessary for the application portfolio, as well as the hardware and network products. Enterprise architecture processes can range from something that is very formal and prescriptively defined to something that is very simple yet still effective.

According to Op't Land *et al.*, enterprise architecture focuses on shaping and governing the design of the future enterprise using principles to stipulate future direction and models to underpin and visualize future states. The authors specified three important perspectives on the role of enterprise architecture (Op't Land *et al.*, 2009). A regulation-oriented perspective is to emphasize the notion governing the design of an enterprise. Taking this perspective, an enterprise architect should focus on principles, leading to rules, guidelines and standards, heading in the direction of the success of enterprise design chosen by the enterprise itself. The design-oriented perspective emphasizes the comprehensive and cohesive specification of an enterprise in all its aspects on a high level design. The pattern-oriented perspective focuses on the use of design patterns, which form a bridge between the regulative and the design perspectives.

The enterprise architecture is a process as well as a product. As a product, the architecture serves to guide managers in designing business processes and it supports system developers in building applications in a way that is in line with business objectives and policies. The effects of the architecture as a process reach further that the mere creation of the architecture product – the awareness of stakeholders with respect to business objectives and information flows will be raised.

The enterprise architecture development is supported by a structured collection of methods and techniques. Methods usually specify the various phases of architecture's life cycle, what deliverables should be produced at each stage, and how they are verified or tested. In literature, the following methods for the enterprise architecture development are considered:

- The Rational Unified Process (RUP) as an iterative process for software realization with adding functionality to the architecture at each increment.
- The Enterprise Unified Process (Ambler, 2005).
- The UN/CEFACT Modeling Methodology (UMM) as an incremental business pro-

cess and information model construction methodology.
- The TOGAF (The Open Group Architecture Framework) (Hugoson et al., 2008; Lankhorst, 2005).
- The Zachman framework as a logical structure for classifying and organizing the descriptive representations of an enterprise (Noran, 2003).

The Zachman enterprise architecture framework is considered as one of the best known of all frameworks. Although it was developed in 1987 it has had substantial influence on modern understanding of enterprise architecture (Hanschke, 2010). The Zachman framework, as it was underlined by Noran (Noran, 2003) assumes a different approach towards the architecture model development, presenting the life cycle phases as perspective of the various stakeholders involved in the enterprise architecture engineering.

The Zachman enterprise architecture framework presents various views and aspects of the enterprise architecture in a matrix structure. It differentiates between the levels "Scope", "Enterprise Model" "System Model", "Technology Model" and "Detailed Representations". The model covers six aspects of the enterprise architecture: "Data", "Function", "Network", "People", "Time" and "Motivation". Taken together, the matrix cells create a complete picture of the enterprise (Figure 2). The DATA view describes the entities established in each perspective of the social institutions. Examples cover business objects, system data, relational tables. The FUNCTION view presents the functions within each perspective. Examples include business processes, software application and computer hardware function, or language control loop. The NETWORK view reveals locations and interconnections within the social institution. This view comprises major business geographic locations, logistics network sections and allocation of system nodes and repositories. The PEOPLE view describes the people relationships within the enterprise. The design of the social institution should reveal the allocation of work units and the structure of power and authority as well as the structure of responsibility. In the institutional structure presentation the hierarchy presentation shows delegation of authority, and the horizontal, flat structure is to represents the assignment of responsibility. The TIME view is to represent time and event relationships that establish performance criteria and enterprise resources exploitation in long time. This is useful for designing schedules, the processing architecture and control architecture as well as timing devices. The last MOTIVATION view is to reveal the motivations of the social institution. This view covers description of the enterprise goals and objectives, business plan, knowledge architecture and knowledge design (Minoli, 2008).

The SCOPE in the Zachman framework intents to provide an executive summary for a planner who wants to estimate the size, cost and functionality of the proposed information system. The ENTERPRISE MODEL is to show all the business entities and processes and their interaction from the point of view of business people. The SYSTEM MODEL is for system analyst and designer who must determine the data elements and software functions that represent the business model. However, the user, supported by tools and techniques can be involved in the activities of this stage. The TECHNOLOGY MODEL covers consideration on the constraints of tools, technology and materials. The DETAILED REPRESENTATIONS of components is to represent individual, independent modules that can be allocated to system implementers. The FUNCTIONING ENTERPRISE describes the operating system from two points of view i.e., the aspect of user-moderator and the aspect of user-exploiter. User-moderator is to make sure that information system is working correctly and for the realization of established goals. User-exploiter is permitted to exploit the information system fully. This differentiation of users is used

to support better control of information processing, storage and transmission.

The presented in Table 2 modification of the Zachman enterprise architecture framework allows for a good introduction for the venture of the architecture development by professionals and the information system users. Initial specification of roles and responsibilities allows to cope with the highly complex subject matter of enterprise architectures. However, the model covers considerations on a very abstract level, therefore for each cell the specification of methods, techniques, guidelines and tools seems to be necessary to ensure the rolling out a customised architecture.

User Centred Design

Customer participation in information system development is the degree to which the end user is involved in taking actions to respond to information processing needs. In very customized service contexts, customers may need to be more physically present or at least they provide some input into the design process. Ability in future co-creation refers to customers' knowledge and skills that enable them to perform effectively. The factors underlying customer involvement cover customer ability and role clarity in future co-operation. First, the software company people should understand the user roles as consultants and advisers and they should learn how to act in the information technology service encounter.

According to the product experience theory, as the customers increase their level of participation in information systems development, the software firm has an opportunity to shape their perceptions about IT service delivery and influence their total service experiences through value co-creation (Dong *et al.*, 2008).

User centred system design (UCSD) approach emphasizes that the information system is to serve the user, not a specific technology. It is a process focusing on usability throughout the entire development process and further throughout the

Table 2. The Zachman framework modification to emphasize the role of user

	DATA What?	FUNCTION How?	NETWORK Where?	PEOPLE Who?	TIME When?	MOTIVATION Why?
SCOPE (CONTEXTUAL) Planner	Information requirements model	Business processes' list	Territorial structure of institutional units	List of key business units	Critical events and business lifecycle list	Strategies and goals list
ENTERPRISE MODEL (CONCEPTUAL) Owner	Semantic model, list of concepts	Data Flow Diagram, Business Process Model,	Business Logistics System, Logistic network	Work flow model	Master Schedule	Business Plan
SYSTEM MODEL (LOGICAL) Designer	Logical Data Model	Application Architecture	Distributed System Architecture	Human Interface Architecture	Data warehouse and data base uploading schedule	Business rules model
User - Designer	Business Object Model	Use case model, task model, business object model	Distributed system component list	User interface prototypes	Processing structure	Business Rules list. Corporate knowledge concepts
TECHNOLOGY MODEL (PHYSICAL) Builder	Physical data model	System design	Technology architecture	Presentation architecture	Control structure	Rule Design
User-builder	Data specification	Application prototype interaction models	Network infrastructure model	Interaction standards, access regulation system	Time of key transaction realization in OLTP system	Good practices and business standards
DETAILED REPRESENTATION (OUT-OF-CONTEXT) Subcontractor	Data definition	Program	Network architecture	Security Architecture	Timing definition	Rule definition
User- subcontractor	Data validation	4GL application	Infrastructure requirements	Security requirements	Timing validation	Rule validation
FUNCTIONING ENTERPRISE User -moderator	Data	Function	Network	Organization	Schedule	Institutional Strategy
User - exploiter	Data base exploitation	Application access for exploitation	Internet and Other network communication	Co-operation with other users	Plan of exploitation of system	Business unit strategy compliance with institutional strategy

Source of the Zachman Framework: (Minoli, 2008; Hanschke, 2010).

system life cycle. Usability means ease-of-use or user-friendliness. According to ISO 9241-11:1998 usability is the extent to which a product can be used by specified users to achieve specified goals with effectiveness, efficiency and satisfaction in a specified context of use. Usability should be considered from the very beginning of the development when a ground plan of the system is decided. The human-computer interaction community has developed a variety of approaches and methods for involving users. User centred design, participatory design, ethnography and contextual design are considered as the main approaches (Kujala, 2005). Usability is perceived by many as a concept associated with the design of the user interface and has received little attention from software architects. To ensure cost-efficiency of the usability of software system, the integration of usability should be included in the initial discussion of quality requirements. Usability is expressed by different other features i.e., learnability, efficiency of computing, reliability of information system, satisfaction as a measure of positive attitude toward the use of the system. The usability properties can guide the requirements gathering and cover principles e.g. providing feedback to the user, providing explicit user control or providing guidance. Usability patterns for information systems development suggest some abstract mechanism that could be used to improve usability i.e., wizard, undo, alert.

The key principles of UCSD are as follows: user focus, active user involvement, evolutionary system development, simple design representations, prototyping, evaluation of use in a context, holistic design, process customization (Gulliksen et al., 2005). Active user involvement means that representative users should be directly involved, both in the development project and in related activities, such as, organizational development and designing new work practices. User design representations and terminology are understood by all users and stakeholders, so they can fully appreciate the consequences of the design on their future use situation. Abstract notions, such as use case, UML diagrams or requirements specifications are not sufficient to give the users a concrete understanding of the future use situation. Therefore, prototypes must be used to visualize and evaluate ideas and design solutions in cooperation with the end users in a real context. The principles for UCSD can be used for explanation model analysis and communicating, business process development, assessment and customization, as well as for knowledge transfer and procurement support. User centred design is

currently defined in the ISO 13407:1999 standard and typically entails involving users in the design and evaluation of the system. In UCSD, tasks are often modelled using scenarios, most commonly expressed in the form of plausible story narratives. A special form of use case, the task case or essential use case was invented to serve the needs of user interface and interaction design by distilling interaction to its simplest, abstract essence. Users who interact with a system are referred to as actors, and UCSD models roles instead of users. It is an approach focused on the end users of a product. The philosophy is that the product should suit the user, rather than making the user suit the product (Courage & Baxter, 2005). The approach offers some advantages for users i.e., maximization of the ease of use, avoiding unnecessary repetition of information, elimination of useless information and inconsistencies. Practitioners are able to focus early on users' tasks, understand users' cognitive, behavioural and attitudinal characteristics revealed in a particular environment. The opportunities to apply the UCSD for learning online were discussed in the literature (Daniel et al., 2009).

Agility and Agile Methods

Involving end user in the development process requires that users and developers can communicate using a common language. This language has to allow them to identify and specify requirements as well as solutions. A lack of end user participation when designing software often leads to invalid requirements. The IS complexity can only be managed by fostering interaction between end-users and developers during the whole IS life cycle. The interaction can be supported by the agile methods' application for IT project management and IS design.

Agility means an effective and efficient execution of business processes. Agile methods are oriented towards achievement of user satisfying effects in short time. The success of agile methods is based on the 12 core principles i.e. responsive planning, business-value-driven work, hands-on business outputs, direct stakeholder engagement, immovable deadlines, management by self-motivation, just-in-time communication, immediate status tracking, waste management, constantly measurable quality, continuous improvement and inevitability of change (Cooke, 2010). The change is an essential part of any business. Responsive planning to accommodate inevitable internal and external changes is central for agile methods of information system development. They are based around the iterative delivery of business value in short periods of time (i.e. two to four weeks) with planning based on the feedback received from key stakeholders at each iteration. In each iteration, stakeholders are requested to provide a business value, so that the organization can benefit frequently and quickly from investment in people. Agile methods rely on the mutual trust and dependency between users and delivery team members for prioritization of the business requirements and regular production of outcomes that meet user requirements. Agile software development methods focus on values identified in the Agile Alliance's Manifesto:

- Individuals and interactions over processes and tools.
- Working software over comprehensive documentation.
- Customer collaboration over contract negotiation.
- Responding to change over following a plan (Cockburn, 2004; Bonner, 2010; Baskerville *et al.*, 2005).

The most important property of any IT project, large or small, is that of delivering running, tested code to real users frequently, every few months. The advantages of this approach are numerous. The sponsors of IT project get critical feedback on the rate of progress of the working team. Users get an opportunity to discover whether their original request was for what they actually need and to get their discoveries fed back into development. Developers can recognize the weaknesses of proposed solutions. The designers and programmers can debug their solutions and get a morale boost through accomplishments. Frequent delivery of the system prototypes allows to reduce the risk of missing a real problem with integration or deployment. Otherwise, they would encounter the problems, when it is very late, that is, at the moment of deploying the system.

Agile software development methods, with values and principles expressed in the Agile Manifesto, have a focus on people and teams, frequent delivery of high quality release, intensive customer collaboration and responding to change, with minimal planning. Although, the agile methods are oriented towards involvement of end users in production process, there is lack of emphasizing the dominant role of end user in information systems development process and in the best case end user plays a role of a project partner.

The agile software development includes, as examples, the following methods: Dynamic Systems Development Method (DSDM), Scrum, Extreme Programming (XP), Crystal, Feature Driven Development (FDD), Adaptive Software Development.

Dynamic Systems Development Method (DSDM) is an iterative and interactive approach to agile software delivering, that has its roots in Rapid Application Development (RAD) resulting in a strong emphasis on building prototypes and confirming the feasibility of the solution prior to undertaking full development activities. The DSDM practice includes active user involvement throughout the process, iterative and incremental development, frequent delivery of tangible outputs and empowering the delivery team. Testing and quality control in the software development process are also emphasized. The agile organizations consider a customer to be a person to whom the outcomes are delivered, although in the traditional business environment, customer is a user of products and services. The agile organization exposes the user experience as important for designing the right system to support them. Activities of the system development team cover user research and analysis, high-level design of the system as experienced and expressed by the users, specification of system functionalities and behaviour, high-level interaction design and screen layout and testing proposed designs with users. So, in user centred agile methods, user or end user is the person who interacts directly with the produced system to generate a desired result (Beyer, 2010).

Both Scrum and DSDM have the same core objective - the delivery of high business-value outcomes in controlled, iterative timeframes. Scrum provides a high-level framework for achieving the objectives, and relies on communication between the participants to ensure that work undertaken meets the business needs (Pries & Quigley, 2011). The DSDM method assumes a more structured framework to achieve the information system design objectives, requires the proposed work to be documented and confirmed prior to the continuation in the further stage.

In Extreme Programming (XP) method customer is empowered to decide what is or is not useful in the software product. They determine the priority of features and set the order of implementation. Here, the customer is a role played by one person or a team, including the product owner and project manager, and business analysts. In XP approach customer is responsible for delivering the user story cards describing everything that seems to be needed in the next release of the software product. The best practices for integrating user expertise and experience with agile methods still cover techniques of passive behaviour of end users i.e. interviews, questions, user story cards. The designers assume that users are not good at articulating what they want, therefore there is a strong necessity to elicit the requirements from them. In situation, where users want to be helpful and are available, they attempt to use the system

to do their own work, they discover and report problems.

Like XP, Scrum is both an iterative and incremental process. As an iterative process it enables the progress through successive refinement and frequent contact with users. The project team iteratively refines the system areas until the final product is satisfactory. Each iteration in software development life cycle is to improve the product through the addition of greater details.

In agile methods i.e., Scrum, XP, it is not important for the product owner to identify all of the requirements at the beginning of the software development process. However, there is often a benefit of gathering together as many themes as possible. Constantine and Lockwood proposed agile usage-centred design as a solution applied in requirement management (Constantine & Lockwood, 2002). Agile usage-centred design is driven by essential use cases or task cases rather than user stories. Agile usage centred design focuses on user role modelling, prioritizes stories, organizes stories into groups, creates and refines prototypes.

The Crystal Clear method gives people an opportunity to share their discoveries. Osmotic communication gives stakeholders the greatest chance to elicit important information from each other. Easy access to expert users gives them the opportunity to quickly discover relevant information. Frequent delivery creates feedback to the system's requirements and the development process. The Crystal Clear team covers people working together very close, so they can communicate informally in a more casual style. The role model is created jointly by a designer-programmer, a business expert, and an expert user. Although responsibility can move between these roles, the expert user is the most important person in this process (Cohn, 2004). In Crystal Clear method the role model is applied to prioritize work, write appropriate use cases, make specific decisions about user-interface and interaction design as well as to test the software system.

Feature Driven Development (FDD) is known as a client-centric, architecture-centric, and pragmatic software process. The client in FDD method is used to represent project stakeholders or customers (i.e., recipient of project effects). In FDD method six primary roles are identified i.e. project manager, chief architect, development manager, chief programmer, class owner and domain expert. A person can take one or more roles in the projects. User or end users are not included in role specification (Palmer & Felsing, 2002).

Adaptive Software Development (ASD) is oriented towards the economy of increasing returns, high speed and high change in the Internet economy. ASD method was developed by Highsmith, who uses the Complex Adaptive Systems (CAS) theory and transfers the CAS model to software development, therefore for him the development organization consists of the environment, its members as agents, and the product as the result of competition and cooperation (Riehle, 2001). The ASD method covers three different roles i.e. developers, managers and customers. The last provide input to steer process. Users are not considered. In ASD, people use technology as they see proper and human relationships are assumed to be a key enabler of emergent results.

CONCLUSION

Information technology project stakeholders as well as software designers strongly emphasize the important role of end user in information system development process. Mostly, users are involved in software requirements specification, interface designing, and testing. Traditional as well as agile methods allow them to be a partner, expert i.e. advisor in the development process, but the main role is played by the IT team. However, nowadays, user participatory design approach and user centred system design create new opportunities to strongly involve user in application development. A great opportunity for end user activation is Web 2.0 environment development. Therefore, nowadays end users can be responsible for providing contents and simple applications to the Internet. These possibilities allow for creation of new e-learning environments where e-learner takes the role of e-teacher. So, they can prosume i.e., create and utilize teaching materials. Opportunities to act independently on the Internet are very persuasive and encourage users to be involved in open system development. Their activation is limited to niche software and simple applications development, because of the lack of expertise and experience. The enterprise architecture approaches allow for identification of roles of information systems stakeholders and support specification of business and IT relationships.

REFERENCES

Ambler, S. W. (2005). *An overview of the enterprise unified process* (EUP). Retrieved October 13, 2011, from http://www.enterpriseunifiedprocess.com/

Anderson, W. L., & Crocca, W. T. (1993). Engineering practice and co-development of product prototypes. *Communications of the ACM, 36*(6), 49–56. doi:10.1145/153571.256015

Appelo, J. (2011). *Management 3.0 leading agile developers developing agile leaders.* Upper Saddle River, NJ: Addison-Wesley.

Baldwin, C., Hienerth, C., & Von Hippel, E. (2006). How user innovations become commercial products: A theoretical investigation and case study. *Research Policy, 35*(9), 1291–1313. doi:10.1016/j.respol.2006.04.012

Beisse, F. (2010). *A guide to computer user support for help desk and support specialist.* Boston, MA: Course Technology, Cengage Learning.

Beyer, H. (2010). *User-centred agile methods.* London, UK: Morgan & Claypol.

Bhalla, G. (2011). *Collaboration and co-creation, new platforms for marketing and innovation.* London, UK: Springer-Verlag.

Bjorn-Andersen, N., Rasmussen, L. B., & Rasmusssen, S. (2008). Web 2.0 adoption by Danish newspapers - Urgent need for new business models? *Proceedings of I-KNOW'08 and I-MEDIA'08,* Graz, Austria, September 3-5, 2008. Retrieved September 15, 2011, from http://i-know.tugraz.at/wp-content/uploads/2008/11

Bonner, J. V. H. (2009). Lessons learned in providing product designers with user-participatory interaction design tools. In Voss, A., Hartswood, M., Procter, R., Rouncefield, M., Slack, R. S., & Buscher, M. (Eds.), *Use-designer relations, interdisciplinary perspective* (pp. 87–110). London, UK: Springer-Verlag.

Briggs, C. (2009). Web 2.0 business models ad decentralized value creation systems. In Lytras, M. D., Damiani, E., & Ordonez de Pablos, P. (Eds.), *Web 2.0: The business model* (pp. 133–147). Berlin, Germany: Springer-Verlag.

Campbell, A. J., & Cooper, R. G. (1999). Do customer partnerships improve new product success rates? *Industrial Marketing Management, 28*(5), 507–519. doi:10.1016/S0019-8501(99)00058-9

Cockburn, A. (2004). *Crystal clear a human-powered methodology for small teams.* Upper Saddle River, NJ: Pearson Education.

Cohn, M. (2004). *User stories applied: For agile software development.* New York, NY: Addison Wesley.

Constantine, L. L., & Lockwood, L. A. D. (2002). Usage-centred engineering for Web applications. *IEEE Software, 19*(2), 42–50. doi:10.1109/52.991331

Cooke, J. L. (2010). *Agile productivity unleashed, proven approaches for achieving real productivity gains in any organization.* Ely, UK: IT Governance Publishing.

Courage, C., & Baxter, K. (2005). *Understanding your users: A practical guide to user requirements, method, tools and techniques.* Amsterdam, The Netherlands: Elsevier.

Daniel, B. K., O'Brien, D., & Sarkar, A. (2009). User-centred design principles for online learning communities: A sociotechnical approach for the design of a distributed community of practice. In Lytras, M. D., & Ordonez de Pablos, P. (Eds.), *Social Web evolution: Integrating semantic applications with Web 2.0 technologies* (pp. 267–279). Hershey, PA: Information Science Reference. doi:10.4018/978-1-60566-272-5.ch019

Dargan, P. A. (2005). *Open systems and standards for software product development.* Boston, MA: Artech House Computing Library.

Di Gangi, P. M., & Wasko, M. (2009). The co-creation of value: Exploring user engagement in user-generated content websites. *Proceedings of JAIS Theory Development Workshop, Sprouts-Working Papers on Information Systems, 9*(50). Retrieved January 15, 2011, from http://sprouts.aisnet.org/9-50

Dong, B., Evans, K. R., & Zou, S. (2008). The effects of customer participation in co-created service recovery. *Journal of the Academy of Marketing Science, 36,* 123–137. doi:10.1007/s11747-007-0059-8

Einav, G. (2010). *Transitioned media: A turning point into the digital realm.* Berlin, Germany: Springer-Verlag.

Gulliksen, J., Goransson, B., Boivie, I., Persson, J., Blomkvist, S., & Cajander, A. (2005). Key principles for user-centred systems design. In Seffah, A., Gulliksen, J., & Desmarais, M. C. (Eds.), *Human-centred software engineering - Integrating usability in the software development lifecycle* (pp. 17–37). Berlin, Germany: Springer-Verlag. doi:10.1007/1-4020-4113-6_2

Hanschke, I. (2010). *Strategic IT management: A toolkit for enterprise architecture management.* Berlin, Germany: Springer-Verlag.

Healy, A. (2009). Communities of practice as a support function for social learning in distance learning programs. In Lytras, M. D., Ordonez de Pablos, P., Damiani, E., Avison, D., Naeve, A., & Horner, D. G. (Eds.), *Best practices for the knowledge society knowledge, learning, development and technology for all* (pp. 49–56). Berlin, Germany: Springer-Verlag. doi:10.1007/978-3-642-04757-2_6

Hoogervorst, J. P. (2009). *Enterprise governance and enterprise engineering.* Berlin, Germany: Springer-Verlag. doi:10.1007/978-3-540-92671-9

Hugoson, M. A., Magoulas, T., & Pess, K. (2008). Interoperability strategies for business agility, advances. In Dietz, J. L. G., Albami, A., & Barjis, J. (Eds.), *Enterprise Engineering I* (pp. 108–122). Berlin, Germany: Springer-Verlag. doi:10.1007/978-3-540-68644-6_8

ISO 13407. (1999). *Human-centred design processes for interactive systems.* Retrieved February 12, 2012, from http://www.iso.org/iso/catalogue_detail.htm?csnumber=21197

ISO 9241-11. (1998). *Ergonomic requirements for office work with visual display terminals (VDTs) - Part 11: Guidance on usability.* Retrieved February 12, 2012, from http://www.iso.org/iso/cataloque_detail.htm?csnumber=16883

Klen, E. R. (2009). Co-creation and co-innovation in collaborative networked environment. In Camarinha-Matos, L. M., Paraskakis, I., & Afsarmanesh, H. (Eds.), *Leveraging knowledge for innovation in collaborative networks* (pp. 33–42). Berlin, Germany: Springer-Verlag. doi:10.1007/978-3-642-04568-4_4

Kokkonen, J. (2009). User culture, user-system relation and trust: The case of Finnish Wikipedia. In Niiranen, S., Yli-Hietanen, J., & Lugmayr, A. (Eds.), *Open information management, applications of interconnectivity and collaboration* (pp. 326–343). Hershey, PA: Information Science Reference. doi:10.4018/978-1-60566-246-6.ch015

Kolfschoten, G. L., Briggs, R. O., & de Vreede, G. J. (2010). A technology for pattern-based process design and its application to collaboration engineering. In Rummler, S., & Bor, N. G. K. (Eds.), *Collaborative technologies and applications for interactive information design: Emerging trends in user experiences* (pp. 1–19). Hershey, PA: Information Science Reference. doi:10.4018/978-1-60566-727-0.ch001

Kujala, S. (2005). Linking user needs and use case-driven requirements engineering. In Seffah, A., Gulliksen, J., & Desmarais, M. C. (Eds.), *Human-centred software engineering - Integrating usability in the software development life cycle* (pp. 113–127). Berlin, Germany: Springer-Verlag. doi:10.1007/1-4020-4113-6_7

Lankhorst, M. (2005). *Enterprise architecture at work, modelling, communication and analysis.* Berlin, Germany: Springer-Verlag.

Larsson, A., Ericson, A., Larsson, T., Isaksson, O., & Bertoni, M. (2010). Engineering 2.0: Exploring lightweight technologies for the virtual enterprise. In Randall, D., & Salembier, P. (Eds.), *From CSCW to Web 2.0 European Developments in Collaborative Design* (pp. 173–192). Berlin, Germany: Springer-Verlag. doi:10.1007/978-1-84882-965-7_9

Leadbeater, C. (2007). *Open platform to develop and share innovative new business ideas*. Retrieved December 20, 2010, from http://www.openbusiness.cc/2007/03/14/two-faces-of-open-innovation/

Levi, D. (2007). *Group dynamics for teams*. London, UK: Sage Publications, Inc.

Lukosch, S. (2010). Pattern-based tool design for shared knowledge construction. In Rummler, S., & Bor, N. G. K. (Eds.), *Collaborative technologies and applications for interactive information design: Emerging trends in user experiences* (pp. 19–39). Hershey, PA: Information Science Reference. doi:10.4018/978-1-60566-727-0.ch002

Martin, C. R., & Horne, D. A. (1995). Level of success inputs for service innovations in the same firm. *International Journal of Service Industry Management, 6*(4), 40–56. doi:10.1108/09564239510096894

Matthing, J., Sandem, B., & Edvardsson, B. (2004). New service development: learning from and with customers. *International Journal of Service Industry Management, 15*(5), 479–498. doi:10.1108/09564230410564948

McAfee, A. P. (2006). Enterprise 2.0: The dawn of emergent collaboration. [Spring.]. *MIT Sloan Management Review, 47*(3), 21–28.

McGowern, J., Ambler, S. W., Stevens, M. E., Linn, J., Sharan, V., & Jo, E. K. (2003). *Practical guide to enterprise architecture*. Upper Saddle River, NJ: Prentice Hall PTR.

Minoli, D. (2008). *Enterprise architecture A to Z. Frameworks, business process modeling, SOA, and infrastructure technology*. London, UK: CRC Press, Taylor & Francis Group. doi:10.1201/9781420013702

Noran, O. (2003). Mapping of individual architecture frameworks (GRAI, PERA, C4ISR, CIMOSA, ZACHMAN, ARIS) onto GERAM. In Bernus, P., Nemes, L., & Schmidt, G. (Eds.), *Handbook on enterprise architecture* (pp. 65–212). Berlin, Germany: Springer-Verlag.

Op't Land, M., Proper, E., Waage, M., Cloo, J., & Steghuis, C. (2009). *Enterprise architecture, creating value by informed governance*. Heidelberg, Germany: Springer-Verlag.

Palmer, S. R., & Felsing, J. M. (2002). *A practical guide to feature-driven development*. Upper Saddle River, NJ: Prentice Hall Inc.

Piercy, N. F. (2009). *Marketing-led strategic change: Transforming the process of going to market*. Amsterdam, The Netherlands: Elsevier.

Polaine, A., & Bennett, R. (2010). Creative waves: Exploring emerging online cultures, social networking and creative collaboration through e-learning to offer visual campaigns for local Kenyan Health Needs. In Rummler, S., & Bor, N. G. K. (Eds.), *Collaborative technologies and applications for interactive information design: Emerging trends in user experiences* (pp. 39–51). Hershey, PA: Information Science Reference.

Prahalad, C. K., & Ramaswamy, V. (2000). Co-opting customer competence. *Harvard Business Review, 78*, 79–87.

Pries, K. H., & Quigley, J. M. (2011). *Scrum project management*. London, UK: CRC Press Taylor & Fraxis Group.

Raymond, E. S. (2000). *The cathedral and the bazaar*. Retrieved January 21, 2011, from http://www.catb.org/~esr/writings/homesteading/

Romero, D., & Molina, A. (2009). Value co-creation and co-innovation: Linking networked organizations and customer communities. In Mamarinha-Matos, L. M., Paraskakis, I., & Afsarmanesh, H. (Eds.), *Leveraging knowledge for innovation in collaborative networks* (pp. 401–415). Berlin, Germany: Springer-Verlag. doi:10.1007/978-3-642-04568-4_42

Schiel, J. (2010). *Enterprise-scale agile software development.* London, UK: CRC Press, Taylor & Francis Group.

Seffah, A., Gulliksen, J., & Desmarais, M. C. (2005). An introduction to human-centred software engineering, integrating usability in the development process. In Seffah, A., Gulliksen, J., & Desmarais, M. C. (Eds.), *Human-centred software engineering - Integrating usability in the software development lifecycle* (pp. 3–12). Berlin, Germany: Springer-Verlag. doi:10.1007/1-4020-4113-6_1

Spaniol, M., Klamma, R., & Cao, Y. (2008). Learning as a service: A Web-based learning framework for communities of professionals on the Web 2.0. In *Advances in Web based learning - ICWL 2007* (*Vol. 4823*, pp. 160–173). Lecture Notes in Computer Science Berlin, Germany: Springer-Verlag. doi:10.1007/978-3-540-78139-4_15

Tidd, J., & Bessant, J. (2009). *Managing innovations, integrating technological, market and organizational change.* Chichester, UK: John Wiley and Sons.

Urban, G. L., & Von Hippel, E. (1988). Lead user analyses for the development of new industrial products. *Management Science, 5*(34), 569–582. doi:10.1287/mnsc.34.5.569

Von Hippel, E. (1986). Lead users: A source of novel product concepts. *Management Science, 32*(7), 791–805. doi:10.1287/mnsc.32.7.791

Von Zedtwitz, M., & Gassman, O. (2002). Market versus technology drive in R&D internationalization: Four different patterns of managing research and development. *Research Policy, 31,* 569–588. doi:10.1016/S0048-7333(01)00125-1

West, J. (2002). *How open is open enough? Melding proprietary and open source platform strategies.* December. Retrieved January 15, 2011, from http://www.joelwest.org/Pa-pers/West2003a-WP.pdf

Xie, B., Bagozzi, R. P., & Troye, S. V. (2008). Trying to prosume: Toward a theory of consumers as co-creators of value. *Journal of the Academy of Marketing Science, 36,* 109–122. doi:10.1007/s11747-007-0060-2

KEY TERMS AND DEFINITIONS

Agility: Ability to achieve goals in short time and in a smart way.

e-Learning: Learning online in Internet, learning on computer and with interactive media and Information Technology.

Enterprise Architecture: An integrated collection of models and documents that include presentations of business activities, information, applications and technologies in a certain social organization. An enterprise architecture is developed to describe the interconnections among IT and business issues. It enables that business decisions on IT can be analysed and a strong evidence for taking investement decisions is ensured.

Information System Development: Information system engineering, a process realized by a system analyst and designer to develop an information system. The process consists of the following stages: analysis, design, implementation, testing and evaluation.

Prosumption: In economics production for the own use, niche activity. In business science impact of very active consumer on production process and results.

User Centred Design: Information system development strategy, characterized as a multi-stage process that requires designers to test the information system in the real world with actual users as well as to analyze and foresee the usage of information system.

Web 2.0: Web applications that enable participatory information sharing, interoperability, user website design, collaboration on the World Wide Web, content providing, reading and browsing.

Chapter 21
The Impact of Social Media in Web–Based Information Management and Digital Media

Monika Steinberg
University of Applied Sciences and Arts Hannover, Germany

ABSTRACT

The availability of Social Media has changed the way we handle requested resources in interactive media contexts and how we operate with each other on the Web. New challenges in the area of information management, Digital Media processing, and knowledge engineering have arisen such as, how to query or effectively embed Social Media into information and knowledge management concerns effectively. In addition, interactivity and the focus on interaction between users and resources in Social Media contexts create new ways of enriching and annotating content collectively following the wisdom of crowds and helpful intelligent automatic analysis. In this chapter the impact of Social Media concepts and distributed resources in web-based information management, knowledge engineering, and Digital Media applications is introduced. The relation between traditional web application design, distributed resource utilization, changes, and challenges in current interactive Digital Media systems will be regarded.

INTRODUCTION

During the last decade, the quantity and quality of information has changed drastically. We now talk about Information Society instead of Industrial Society. Today, the Web offers the biggest and

fastest growing information space, which is accessible to almost everyone on demand, anytime and anywhere (24/7 paradigm). Figure 1 shows world Internet penetration rates by geographic region in 2009 (Internet World Stats, 2010). According to statistics, today more than 50% of Europeans use

DOI: 10.4018/978-1-4666-2190-9.ch021

Figure 1. World Internet penetration rates by geographic regions in 2009 (Internet World Stats, 2010)

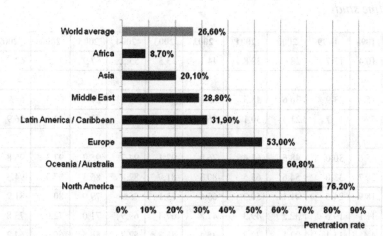

the Internet. In comparison, only North America and Australia showed a higher penetration rate than Europe in 2009. In Europe, Germany ranks third after Great Britain and France regarding current Internet penetration. Germans aged 60 and older accounted for 30% of total internet penetration in 2009. The development of online usage in Germany from 1997 until 2009 is shown in percent in Table 1 (ARD/ZDF-Online study). The number of internet users increased enormously in the past and will very likely continue to do so in the future. Especially remarkable is the online usage of younger people between the ages of 14 and 29, which will probably reach 100% very soon in Germany.

Motivation and Scope of Problem

The Web is omnipresent and used as a source of information and knowledge worldwide. This practice is growing continuously and is here to stay. Web 2.0 (also called Social Media) and online communities are being used more and more by the Digital Native generation.

Some of the questions arising as a result of Social Media are:

- How can the Web as a rapidly growing and distributed knowledge base remain sustainable in higher-layered web applications?
- How can more motivation, incentive, fun and participation be brought into web-based applications and communities?
- How can the wide range of available content be transformed into enhanced knowledge representations and distributed knowledge bases on demand?
- Which concepts and techniques are most suitable to address these challenges in current web applications?

Of course, we can read a Wikipedia article sentence by sentence, or we can click through Flickr image collections, but are there methods of user interaction that are better suited to transfer the knowledge and information contained in resources?

If we found a web resource that seems to be suitable because the content matches our topic of interest, the next question we would probably ask ourselves would be about the quality and source of the content, e.g. who wrote it, how current the information is, and whether it is correct. Some of

Table 1. Development in percent of online usage in Germany between 1997 and 2009 (occasional usage) (ARD/ZDF-online study)

	1997	1998	1999	2000	2001	2002	2003	2004	2005	2006	2007	2008	2009
Total	6.5	10.4	17.7	28.6	38.8	44.1	53.5	55.3	57.9	59.5	62.7	65.8	67.1
Gender													
Male	10.0	15.7	23.9	36.6	48.3	53.0	62.6	64.2	67.5	67.3	68.9	72.4	74.5
Female	3.3	5.6	11.7	21.3	30.1	36.0	45.2	47.3	49.1	52.4	56.9	59.6	60.1
Age													
14–19 years	6.3	15.6	30.0	48.5	67.4	76.9	92.1	94.7	95.7	97.3	95.8	97.2	97.5
20–29 years	13.0	20.7	33.0	54.6	65.5	80.3	81.9	82.8	85.3	87.3	94.3	94.8	95.2
30–39 years	12.4	18.9	24.5	41.1	50.3	65.6	73.1	75.9	79.9	80.6	81.9	87.9	89.4
40–49 years	7.7	11.1	19.6	32.2	49.3	47.8	67.4	69.9	71.0	72.0	73.8	77.3	80.2
50–59 years	3.0	4.4	15.1	22.1	32.2	35.4	48.8	52.7	56.5	60.0	64.2	65.7	67.4
60+	0.2	0.8	1.9	4.4	8.1	7.8	13.3	14.5	18.4	20.3	25.1	26.4	27.1
Employment													
In education	15.1	24.7	37.9	58.5	79.4	81.1	91.6	94.5	97.4	98.6	97.6	96.7	98.0
Employed	9.1	13.8	23.1	38.4	48.4	59.3	69.6	73.4	77.1	74.0	78.6	81.8	82.3
Pensioner/ unemployed	0.5	1.7	4.2	6.8	14.5	14.8	21.3	22.9	26.3	28.3	32.0	33.6	34.7

these questions might be able to be answered by automated mechanisms, e.g. metadata analysis.

What is the motivation for users to interact continuously with resources in communities and other applications on the Web? Maybe we can enable a user's interoperations for some higher purpose, in addition to fulfilling his request. Can we embed a user's output directly into the knowledge cycle of requested resources? User activity with a global purpose would be helpful to transfer information and to enrich content with valuable metadata in the background. Maybe users would interact more if their activities were rewarded in some global way.

Obviously, many different tasks are required to utilize arbitrarily available distributed resources for higher level, extensible and standardized applications with rich interoperation for knowledge transfer. Dissertation research work (Steinberg, 2011) showed that there are several knowledge bases, services and software components avail-

able that are required for subtasks. Therefore, the challenge is to merge, model and expand existing services and distributed web resources to perform these tasks.

Further Background

The indexed Web contains at least 20.57 billion web pages. The Web can be thought of as a source of unlimited content that continues to grow on a daily basis in an enormous manner. The increasing interconnectivity between persons, daily life, buildings or cities with technical devices (hyper connectivity), and the amount of information created by related daily interaction, grows continuously. Powerful information and communication technologies have drastically changed our society. The Internet has emerged as an everyday tool and serves as a universal network for knowledge acquisition, information exchange and working together. The line between real and virtual life is becoming increasingly blurry. Mobile devices and the growing convergence of electronic media is opening up new possibilities with the Internet of Things, and often seem to be pervasively integrated into our daily routine.

To bring global interconnectivity and the related flood of information under control over the long term, intelligent, smart systems and services have been, and are continuing to be developed. These intelligent services have proactive knowledge available to communicate and interact with their environment. Intelligent services can make daily life, spare time, learning and working easier for users of these services. Even access to resources or knowledge transfer can be simplified. Personalization of one's own information space becomes possible and new ways of managing information and knowledge can be developed with the help of intelligent services. Users can be assisted in the area of knowledge acquisition; the preparation and presentation of information and knowledge can be improved and conveyed, thereby creating more incentive and motivation.

The quality and relevance of web content can be enhanced by web-based, intelligent services and applications. However, there is still a strong need for further investigation and research, especially regarding new user interaction concepts and services in knowledge engineering and transfer that make use of distributed resources as a dynamic knowledge base. The Web of Content is on its way to becoming the Web of Applications with on-demand infrastructure and on-demand software (Software as a Service or SaaS). Service-oriented offers are also appearing in the area of knowledge and learning management, but the Web as a globally and locally connected knowledge base, consisting of intertwined, distributed resources, has not been adequately involved so far. The content required for knowledge and learning is still created manually from scratch – often without careful attention and integration of existing and powerful web-based knowledge.

In the last few years, the principle of hybrid intelligence came about with the advent of Social Media and Web 2.0 (Berners-Lee, 2009). Hybrid interaction structures in the form of social networks combined with collective intelligence and calculable machine intelligence emerged to allow collaborative filtering and extraction of semantic meaning from our environment stemming from the overload of information. The principle of hybrid Intelligence allows computers and humans to do what they are best at, which means that an effective mixture of implicit and social knowledge can be realized. Especially in the context of Web 2.0, we can find several examples of collectively created content (collective intelligence), such as wiki communities, video portals, photo collections and weblogs. Table 2 shows occasional usage of Web 2.0 offers in Germany represented in percent. With 94%, usage of Wikipedia (Wikipedia, 2010) and

Table 2. Usage of Web 2.0 offers in percent by gender and age in Germany in 2009 (occasional usage; ARD/ZDF-Online study)

	Total	Women	Men	14–19	20–29	30–39	40–49	50–59	60+
Wikipedia	65	64	67	94	77	70	62	50	39
Video portals	52	45	58	93	79	55	45	27	12
Private networks	34	36	32	81	67	29	14	12	7
Photo communities	25	25	26	42	41	20	19	19	14
Job networks	9	8	11	6	16	13	8	7	1
Weblogs	8	6	10	12	16	10	5	4	1
Bookmark collections	4	4	4	9	6	4	2	2	2

video portals is highest among German teenagers between the ages of 14 and 19.

Table 3 shows the development of frequent and occasional Web 2.0 usage in Germany between 2007 and 2009 (ARD/ZDF-Online study):

Noticeable here is the overall increasing usage for all Web 2.0 offers. It can be assumed that this trend will continue. Occasional usage of the wiki community, Wikipedia (Wikipedia, 2011), is rather high with 65% in 2009. A good half of German users sometimes view video portals like YouTube (YouTube, 2011) and even every fourth user browses web-based photo collections like Flickr (Flickr, 2011) or Panoramio (Panoramio, 2011) now and then. Average usage of Web 2.0 offers also increased in almost every area. It is obvious that omnipresent New Media plays, and will continue to play a very important role in the current and future web. Furthermore, the Web influences nearly every aspect of society, such as culture, education, collaboration, communication, business, lifestyle, social habits and privacy.

The Web as a digital, computerized, interactive information and communication tool is the most powerful and pervasive example of today's New Media. In contrast, television, traditional movies and books are not part of the definition of New Media anymore.

This chapter provides insight into current social and interactive web application issues that serve as a basis for the design and implementation of nowadays highly interactive web-based systems in information management and Digital Media. Further on the main phenomena and problems while integrating Social Media aspects, distributed resources and technologies into web-based interactive systems will be discussed.

Main Issues and Superior Hypotheses

During dissertation research (Steinberg, 2011) regarding the mentioned areas, the following hypotheses emerged:

- There are many (free) resources available on the Web that should be utilized as a distributed knowledge base for further purposes, especially in the area of information and knowledge transfer.
- Without suitable and motivating user interaction and incentive, available web resources are useless or even boring for the user.
- Web-based games can be designed as interactive knowledge systems. They are suit-

*Table 3. Development of occasional and frequent usage of Web 2.0 offers in percent in Germany from 2007 to 2009 (*users with own profile). (ARD/ZDF-online study)*

	Seldom to Occasional Usage			Frequent Usage (at least once a week)		
	2007	**2008**	**2009**	**2007**	**2008**	**2009**
Wikipedia	47	60	65	20	25	28
Video portals	34	51	52	14	21	26
Private networks	15	25	34	6	18*	24*
Photo communities	15	23	25	2	4	5
Job networks	10	6	9	4	2*	5*
Weblogs	11	6	8	3	2	3
Bookmark collections	3	3	4	O	1	2
Virtual gaming worlds	3	5	-	2	2	-

able for improving knowledge engineering tasks, and for increasing attendance and motivation.

- The quality of interaction and information is important for the current and future web.
- Every user interaction or activity with a resource means implicit enrichment of the resource.

The main aspects of these hypotheses will be outlined in the following. For more details regarding the concept and its prototypically implementation please refer to the dissertation *"Utilizing Distributed Web Resources for Enhanced Knowledge Representation"* (Steinberg, 2011). The dissertation finally combines all aspects shortly mentioned in this chapter into an overall concept to utilize distributed web resources for enhanced knowledge representation and higher-layered applications (by the implementation of the qKAI mashup framework).

THE IMPACT OF SOCIAL MEDIA IN INTERACTIVE SYSTEMS

This section provides insight into current social and interactive web application issues that serve as a basis for the design and implementation of contemporary highly interactive web-based systems in information and knowledge management or Digital Media.

The Web as Distributed Knowledge Base

The challenge while integrating distributed web resources as a linked knowledge base in web-based interactive system is to accomplish, improve and simplify access, representation and user motivation regarding interaction with autonomous, distributed web resources (instead of creating new resources from scratch). To utilize distributed resources like Wikipedia articles or multimedia from Flickr, semantic annotation (Linked Data (Bizer, 2008) can be used to interlink and enrich the provenance sources by the output of user interaction and automated analysis. Game mechanics are interpreted here as a subset of user interaction design (Human Computer Interaction) with enhanced user interaction quality. Enhanced knowledge representation here means e.g. to offer web-based gaming scenarios as an interactive knowledge system that relies on distributed web resources.

The World Wide Web is a hypermedia system consisting of interactive, non-linear media with distributed, intertwined resources. Current web content is much more than just hypertext created only by experts (like it was at the very beginning of the Web in 1991 (Wikipedia, World Wide Web, 2009). Next to pure text elements, today's Web consists of a great deal of collectively created multimedia content like pictures, videos, animations, sounds or maps that offer a wide range of opportunities, which can be used for many purposes. We can find related and helpful content on the Web for practically anything, whether it be a nice hotel to spend our next holiday, the meaning of a French word, the architectural history of Berlin, or the best price for a book, the Web is a vast information space that meets our information needs. In Web 2.0 (Wikipedia, Web 2.0, 2009) we do not just find the information itself, we even find other people's opinions and experiences with it, e.g. rating and ranking mechanisms, comments and reviews. These activities and contributions play a central role in how the Web is used. Figure 2 shows a tag cloud of currently involved areas in developing web applications.

This section provides insight into current web concepts as a basis for the design and implementation of nowadays web-based interactive systems in information management and Digital Media.

Figure 2. Web 3.0 tag cloud (created with Wordle (Wordle, 2009))

Web 3.0 and Social Media

Current web trends can be summarized under the term Web 3.0 or Social Semantic Web (Social Semantic Web, 2011), in which user-centered interaction is being intertwined with standardized data formats. First best practice applications, which are combining user interactivity with semantic data standards in a web context, are Freebase (Freebase, 2011), DBpedia (DBpedia, 2012), and DBpedia mobile respectively (Becker & Bizer, 2008).

The term Social Media is used as a synonym for Web 2.0. Currently, the line between the Semantic Web and Web 2.0 is becoming much more fluid, allowing us to create new synergies in a Web 3.0 or Social Semantic Web environment. The combination of social user involvement, employing desktop-like interfaces with rich user experience (Rich Internet Applications or RIA) and the Semantic Web with technologically oriented operability for data representation and processing, is a promising conceptual basis to solve two current problems:

- On the one hand, there is still a lack of lightweight user participation in Semantic Web contexts because hurdles need to be overcome and fancy interoperation ability is missing.
- On the other hand, there are claims for less trivial and more unitary content in Web 2.0 and Social Media contexts.

DBpedia and Freebase have started to address these issues by offering collaborative content collection, creation, and refinement, or semantic interlinking to increase freely available and distributed resources that can be interpreted successfully by humans and machines. Both integrate content from the online encyclopedia, Wikipedia – currently the most famous community using wiki technology:

"Wikipedia is a free, web-based, collaborative, multilingual encyclopedia project supported by the non-profit Wikimedia Foundation. Its 16 million articles (over 3.4 million in English) have been written collaboratively by volunteers around the world, and almost all of its articles can be edited by anyone with access to the site." (Wikipedia, 2010)

Figure 3 shows an example of a Wikipedia article and a Freebase site.

What all of the available solutions still have in common is a missing knowledge-oriented focus

Figure 3. Example of a Wikipedia article about Hannover and a Freebase site about architecture in 2010

with emphasis on enhanced user interaction, incentive and motivation for interoperation and feedback. The conjunction between virtual resources and real world resources currently happens, for example, by the principle of geocoding. Assigning latitude and longitude as geographical positions in real life allows interlinking virtual resources with real places, objects and persons. With the help of Global Positioning System (GPS) devices, localization and positioning of real resources becomes possible and traceable. Also virtual worlds and 3D environments reflect the real world as a digital simulation of real world tasks and situations.

Online Communities and Social Networks

The traditional understanding of a community was once mainly the local area or neighborhood, since villages or cities needed to communicate with each other and get information. Today, when we speak of virtual communities or online communities (network communities), the local vicinity is not that important anymore. Via the Internet, people can engage with each other in communities across geographical and cultural boundaries in different ways.

In the area of intelligent media systems, communities can be used in a supportive, advisory or informational knowledge capacity, which can in turn be integrated into a variety of thematic relationships and everyday life for counseling and help.

In particular, mobile communities can be used as a ubiquitous reference and as active collections of knowledge. Communities have a wide range of synchronous and asynchronous forms of communication (email, forums, chat, news boards, wikis, blogs, reviews, comments, content collections and grouping, short messages), which can be used effectively for interaction and collaboration in a community.

There are many communities with a leisure-oriented focus, but the number of communities that follow sober economic interests, specialist, or interest-oriented objectives is rising steadily.

In the existing literature, various categorizations of communities can be found, such as commercial, theme-oriented or method-oriented communities, depending on the nature of the community, its purpose and type of audience. Parent is often divided into the following three types of communities (Rotz, 2010):

- **Communities of Interest (CoI):** communities that are formed from a common interest like hobbies or sports;
- **Communities of Practice (CoP):** communities that are formed from a common problem like diseases or legal issues;
- **Communities of Association (CoA):** communities that are formed from similarities, such as inhabitants of a particular city, a former school, or fans of a certain pop star.

Current research projects are concerned with the combination of collective user intelligence and lexical or semantic data collections to arrive at the use of controlled vocabulary for tagging (DBpedia, 2009) (Faviki, 2009).

According to the study 'European Communication Monitor 07,' by 2010 'Social Media' will be a mission-critical communications tool, more important than sponsorship, events or corporate publications. Online communities have become a successful business model; this is proved by the horrendous sums, which were offered for communities like Flickr or YouTube. (Rotz, 2010)

Online communities as a source of collective information and knowledge, such as Wikipedia, as an amusing exchange of messages such as Twitter (Twitter, 2010), or as communication and exchange tools such as forums or chats, have become indispensable. They are committed to the social web culture. The different types of communities and Social Media have huge potential as a counseling, assistance and exchange platform or as a source of support in everyday life.

Online networks are represented on the current web by Social Networks, such as Twitter to post short messages, Facebook to connect with friends (Facebook, 2011), Last.fm to listen to music (Last.fm, 2011) Foursquare to locate things and friends (Foursquare, 2010), LinkedIn for business contacts (Linkedin, 2011) or Dailymile to share sports training information (Dailymile, 2011).

Regardless of which term is used - Web 2.0, Social Software, Social Media, Social Networks - a high degree of associated social interactivity is typical for all of them. Interaction takes place as communication between users, but users are also actively involved in content creation, feedback and enrichment.

Common to all Social Media is that users exchange information and resources on these platforms. The social network is used to create content, i.e. User Generated Content (UGC).

Social networks are slang for a form of network communities, which house technical web applications or portals. (Wikipedia, Social Network, 2010)

Web 2.0 and the increasing use of Social Media are changing the way people deal with information on the web. An increasing number of users are not only information consumers (consumer), but produce and publish their own content simultaneously (prosumer = consumer + producer). User generated content (UGC) with community feedback is widely used in the Social Web. Interactive information and knowledge offers are comfortably available via Internet at any time and place (24/7). Web-based user interaction, like wikis in Wikipedia, forums, weblogs or games, lets distributed knowledge grow as an open information space. Statistical and empirical evaluations are also possible; in addition to interaction and communication components, Web 2.0 capabilities include evaluation mechanisms, tools for providing exchange and feedback, groups and support in documentation and education.

Folksonomies

A particular phenomenon within communities, which came about in 2003 with Del.icio.us (Del.icio.us, 2010), the social bookmarking application in Web 2.0, was the concept of folksonomy (folk + taxonomy), which are features that allow lay people to collectively classify and index content freely and collectively (social tagging). The totality of the tags of all users is known as folksonomy.

Here, users interact mostly in open communities and there are no set rules for indexing. Each newly assigned keyword, such as a photo or blog entry increases findability when searching for tagged contents. However, the disadvantages of folksonomies are clear; ambiguity, subjectivity, and small deviations in the associated tags (e.g. singular vs. plural or different languages) can diminish the relevance (precision) of results, since a specific controlled vocabulary is not required. Many resources in folksonomies are not found because there is a lack of relevant tags. Famous examples of folksonomies are Deli.cio.us und Flickr (see Figure 4).

Open Content

There are many resources available on the Web, but should resources be used over and over again without any restrictions? A huge knowledge base that is available for reuse without complicated copyright restrictions is called Open Content. Open Content is here defined according to the description of Open Knowledge in *"Defining the Open in Open Data, Open Content and Open Information"* by the Open Knowledge Foundation (Open Knowledge Foundation, 2009):

"A piece of knowledge is open if you are free to use, reuse, and redistribute it."

Here we add processing differentiation between Open Content as raw input information and Open Knowledge, which represents qualified information that has been checked or enriched. The Semantic Web of Data and User Generated Content (wikis, communities or weblogs) grow in a structured, unstructured and semi-structured manner. DBpedia offers an extensive knowledge base in Resource Description Framework (RDF) format (W3C, 2008) (generated from Wikipedia content), allows semantic browsing and detailed thematic inquiries with SPARQL (W3C, 2010) queries for refinishing and further assignment.

The aim of the Semantic Web is to provide unique descriptions of entities, their relations and properties on the Internet according to a standardized formula. This is an example of a resource or *"thing"* if we are talking about the renewed *"Internet of Things."* Access to resources is always carried out using representations. One resource can have several representations, such as extensible Hypertext Markup Language (xHTML),

Figure 4. Delicio.us tags and Flickr images about the architecture in Hannover

Resource Description Framework (RDF) (Fensel, 2005), Extensible Markup Language (XML) or JavaScript Object Notation (JSON) (JSON, 2010).

Open shared databases like Freebase offer a free Application Programming Interface (API) to reuse its content with its own Metaweb Query Language (MQL). Relational databases can be easily converted into Web of Data by embedding existing components like a D2R server (Bizer & Cyganiak, 2009). Additionally, many unstructured sources like HTML sites or PDF files do not apply to machine interpretable web concepts yet. Serializing this data to standardized formats with open access is the first step towards enhanced machine and user interpretability. Aperture (Aduna & Deutsches Forschungszentrum für Künstliche Intelligenz GmbH (DFKI), 2009) and Virtuoso Spongers (Openlink, 2012) for example, enable comprehensive solutions for these tasks. In case more text engineering is needed, there are comprehensive solutions for standard Natural Language Processing (NLP) tasks (e.g. OpenNLP (OpenNLP, 2012) to perform sentence detection, NER (Named Entity Recognition), POS (Part-Of-Speech) tagging or even semantic chunking.

Linked Open Data (LOD) and Semantic Web

With the Linked Open Data (LOD) community around DBpedia (DBpedia, 2012), a huge knowledge base in standardized and machine interpretable format is available, which represents a semantic representation of the Wikipedia online encyclopedia. Another advantage of LOD is that resources are extendable and reusable without copyright restrictions under the GNU license, in terms of Open Content and Open Knowledge (see Figure 5).

The Semantic Web, increasingly described as Linked Data or the Web of Data, is supposed to bring a new aspect to the Internet. What used to be known as internet pages for use by human beings only, will now be applied to automatic processes. In order to achieve this, the former will be classified as continuous text existent data and its properties will be transformed into defined forms, the aggregation of which will be connected through labeled links.

The Resource Description Framework (RDF, 2012) structure developed for this purpose fol-

Figure 5. DBpedia linked open data cloud (DBpedia, 2012)

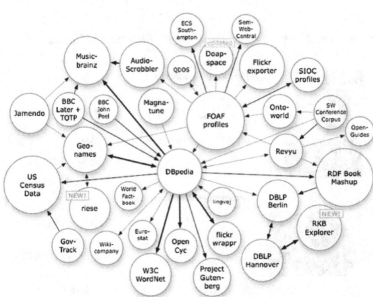

lows a natural speaking sentence structure. It consists of the following information carrier: The subject, resource or node is presented as a URI (Unified Resource Identifier), just like a predicate and object. All of them might contain properties following their description. The properties themselves are typed and if we imagine RDF as a tree, they would represent the leaves. Their type is normally described, for example, as a number, like 42, which is of the type integer, which is functionally dependent on its predicate. The relation of the information carriers is modeled implicitly and always directed and qualified through the predicate. Instead of speaking about subject, predicate and object (the object might be a subject as well), it is more efficient to name them properties that are assigned to resources. Resources are connected to relations in three ways relations: As source, target and identifier.

The Web behind the Scenes: A Technical View

The following passages explain the techniques, which are seen as some of the most important current web technologies and concepts. The Web is regarded as a distributed, partially free, available and rich knowledge base delivering Open Content (as an example).

SPARQL

With SPARQL (SPARQL Protocol and RDF Query Language as recursive acronym) (W3C, 2008) a search and query language for RDF repositories was designed. SPARQL has been a W3C specification since the beginning of 2008. SPARQL's syntax is similar to SQL, which allows columns to be defined to answer requests. Filtering expressions are possible in SPARQL that are placed in the WHERE clause in SQL for example. Up to now, there has not been an efficient functionality to implement full text search. Aside from ASK, there are no aggregate functions available in the

SPARQL specification at this time. ASK allows only a true/false statement about whether a request delivers a result or not. Abandoning the special case of identity, regular expressions should be used for full text search. Such expressions do not fit a large amount of data properly because there are still no database indices available to speed them up to text. That is why every expression for any RDF property has to be evaluated and all of the properties have to be fully loaded also. To get more aggregate functionality in addition to ASK, many providers use additional, proprietary extensions. These extensions, which are not yet standardized, use the strength of the traditional, relational query language SQL and a combination of SPARQL and SQL. Temporary query results are often stored in a relational database, and SQL is utilized for effective, internal data processing.

The Central Principle of Resources

A web resource is a virtual entity that is available for consumption by users to benefit from it. Web resources contain different types of content and formats like text or multimedia (image, sound or video). In the web context, every resource is identified by a name in the form of a Uniform Resource Identifier/Locater (URI or URL). This identification enables interaction and interlinking of distributed resources over the Web. One resource can offer different representations to suit the needs of different consumers like a machine or a human being.

The amount of valuable resources is enormous. There are several platforms and communities offering resources in every domain and format for nearly any purpose. Especially in Web 2.0 and Semantic Web, the amount of freely available and collectively created resources has increased. Overall, the Web offers many (free) available resources that should be utilized as a distributed knowledge base for interactive information exchange, learning purposes and knowledge transfer. The challenge is to facilitate, improve and simplify access, representation and user interaction regarding autonomous, distributed web resources.

A new generation of intelligent tools and services for interactive information and knowledge transfer, collaboration and learning has to be developed, which relies on semantically interlinked and distributed resources.

There are still no comprehensive application scenarios or enhanced user interaction concepts available in information and knowledge transfer that are based upon existing web content. Extensive web-based resources are available (most are open to the public), but are not yet embedded as interactive knowledge bases in higher-layered applications in information and knowledge transfer with sustainability and mutual benefits for all areas.

The challenge lies in the utilization of existing web resources through collaboration, standardization, modeling, and enhanced representation instead of new content creation to allow innovative user interaction scenarios in an incentive way with the web-based knowledge base available.

Linked Data Principle: Informational and Non-informational Resources

Here we find an interesting context, in which resources and how they are handled on the Web is discussed. In the following excerpt, H. Halpin and V. Presutti describe the classification of information and non-information resources in relation to Uniform Resource Identifiers (URIs):

The primary goal of the Semantic Web is to use URIs as a universal space to name anything, expanding from using URIs for web pages to URIs for real objects and imaginary concepts,' as phrased by Berners-Lee. This distinction has often been tied to the distinction between information resources, like web pages and multimedia, and non-information resources, which are everything from real people to abstract concepts like 'the integers.' Furthermore, the W3C has recom-

mended not to use the same URI for information resources and non-information resources, and several communities like the Linked Data initiative are deploying this principle. The definition put forward by the W3C, that information resources are things whose essential nature is information is a distinction at best. (Halpin & Presutti, 2009)

RESTful Web Services

Representational State Transfer (REST) (Fielding, 2000) is an architectural style in software design that is not tied to any particular technology, although it is used as a guide for designing system architectures that follow constraints.

Web services are *"software systems designed to support interoperable machine-to-machine interaction over a network."* (Wikipedia, Web services, 2009) They are identified by an URI (Uniform Resource Identifier) and can be accessed via HTTP (Hyper Text Transfer Protocol) by using XML-based communications protocols like SOAP (Simple Object Access Protocol) or XML-RPC (Extensible Markup Language Remote Procedure Call). Web services greatly support the collaboration of applications running on different platforms because they abstract from specific programming languages and operating systems; and by doing so, constitute a type of distributed system.

Beside SOAP and XML-RPC, the REST architectural style of web services has caught the media's attention over the past decade. In his dissertation *"Architectural Styles and the Design of Network based Software Architectures,"* Roy Thomas Fielding describes a style of software architecture comprised of distributed hypermedia systems, which he calls Representational State Transfer, REST for short. Fielding has designed this architectural style by starting with a *"Null style"* (Fielding, 2000) that does not impose any constraints on those elements that are part of a system having the respective architecture and he then applies constraints that *"differentiate the design space*" incrementally. Any service that complies with these types of constraints can, in a strict sense, be referred to as RESTful.

The central principle of resources, users and interaction between them is interpreted by the semantic annotation of resources following Linked Data principles and Representational State Transfer (REST) constraints.

RESTful web services can be interpreted as an adapted, utilized representation of a resource or a resource collection, respectively. Web services can aggregate distributed web resources (e.g. querying, modeling, representing or annotating them) and interacting with the users.

THE CONVERGENCE OF USER INTERACTION AND GAME DESIGN ON THE WEB

Gaming can be interpreted as the supreme discipline of interaction, because a player will play only if important aspects of the quality of the interaction like functionality, design, usability, incentive and fun, are fulfilled.

Review of the literature (Huizinga, 1971) (Prensky, 2001)(Kim, 2009)(Ahn, Blum, Ginosar, Kedia & Liu, 2006) and research work showed that gaming principles are suitable for several different tasks:

- To enrich content
- To transfer knowledge
- To increase users' ongoing participation and motivation in web-based applications

Therefore, new concepts combining knowledge engineering, distributed web resources and gaming mechanics can be derived to take the most feasible advantage of it in every single field (Steinberg, 2011). Up to now, the combination of quality focused and social, game-oriented user interaction relying on distributed web resources has not been covered very well. In regards to knowledge transfer based on distributed web resources, the research also showed a strong need for concepts, implementations and further use case studies.

Distributed web resources can be turned into gaming content for example, to simplify information access, transfer knowledge and annotate content with the interaction output.

Game design principles are finding their way into other fields like advertising, marketing, learning software or social web applications with increasing frequency (Kim, 2010). The reason behind this trend is simple; people love to play games. Games manage to keep users motivated for a longer time than other activities, because they do not perceive playing as something they have to do; it is something they like to do. This, of course, only applies if the game follows properly incorporated game design principles. Obviously, fun is a great motivator (Nov, 2007); therefore, it is natural that users would be attracted to areas other than game design if they think it will be fun.

By applying simple game principles to other types of activities, like reward points to a "*boring*" vocabulary trainer, the vocabulary trainer becomes a vocabulary learning game. Students or other users of such (and other) learning games stay motivated and learn quickly because they do not perceive it as learning, but playing. Companies use Advergames to promote their products on the Internet. Whereas banner ads are something that most users feel uncomfortable with, Advergames have the ability to pique user's interest and this is a basic requirement for customer acquisition. For (social) web applications like Flickr or YouTube, motivated users are essential because they create the (open) content that is presented to users and without such content these web applications would be "*unviable*." It is therefore no surprise that web applications tend to use game design principles to keep their users motivated.

For this purpose, a global interaction rewarding model (GIAR) (Ullmann, 2010) has been designed which classifies typical activities within web applications and rewards those activities with points and special awards. The meta-rewarding system rewards users for any kind of interaction/ activity within any kind of web application. It is implemented via RESTful web services, which executes two tasks: activity logging and rewarding, and generating activity stats, which are known from game design (user rankings, level progression, etc.) (Steinberg, 2011).

Interweaving Gaming Principles with Web Applications

Since the first days of the World Wide Web, web design process has been developing continuously. The first available websites presented the user with static content; today, users are able to create new content interactively. Web design has evolved into web application design, where the internet browser acts as the operating system and websites act as the applications with which the user interacts. As websites become more and more interactive, principles and methodologies known from inter-action design (id) must be considered during the design process of a web application. One basic principle is that there is not "*the*" solution to a known interface design problem; there are always more solutions. Therefore, designing interfaces is always an iterative process of building prototypes and testing them with users to validate or dismiss a solution (Wikipedia, Interaction design, 2010).

In the past few years, a new trend can be ob-served in popular web applications like Twitter (Twitter, 2010) or Flickr, in which game design principles are used to motivate and encourage users to keep active within their applications. The great benefit of games is that people enjoy playing them (for hours or even days) because it is fun; it is something they like to do since "*playing is something one chooses to do.*" (Prensky, 2001)

More and more web applications make use of simple game mechanics like collecting points or providing leaderboards to "*put the fun in functional*" (Kim, 2009) and by doing so, users are kept motivated since they perceive the application as a game and have fun using it.

Interaction Design and Gaming Mechanics

Designers of modern, interactive and engag-ing websites must incorporate tenets from the previously mentioned disciplines, such as web design, interaction design and game design into their websites. Incorporating even simple game mechanics like rewarding points, leaderboards or level systems causes significant overhead during the design process of web applications. One has to choose which interactions to reward, and develop algorithms and models for leaderboards or level systems and compute activity statistics for users.

In Games People Play, E. Berne defined games as a series of interactions (Berne, 2010):

A game is an ongoing series of complementary ulterior transactions progressing to a well-de-fined, predictable outcome. Descriptively, it is a recurring set of transactions... with a concealed motivation... or gimmick.

To re-state Berne's definition, one can think of a game as a series of interactions (words, body language, facial expressions, etc.) between two or more people that follow a predictable pattern. The interactions ultimately progress to an outcome in which one individual obtains a 'payoff' or 'goal'. In most cases, the participants of the games are unaware that they are 'playing.'

Data management efforts increase as the need to manage the content that users create interactively also increases. Creation of interactive content is still the main purpose of web applications, as well as providing the data needed for applied game mechanics. In some cases, the work involved in applying game principles does not pay off, e.g. for short-term online surveys where the main purpose is to aggregate data. Especially for these kinds of applications, the quantity of data is important and this can only be accomplished by motivated participants.

The quality of data is crucial for applications, which utilize information based on Open Data for interactive knowledge transfer. Assessing certain criteria regarding the quality of information can hardly be managed automatically because these criteria are subjective. Therefore, it is up to motivated users to contribute information about such criteria.

Utilizing game mechanics without the need to integrate them into an application can be achieved by using an independent global interaction rewarding service that deals with the whole "*game*" management. One only needs to choose which interactions to reward and integrate corresponding service calls into the application to be developed. The service manages interaction logging and rewarding, the evaluation of activity stats like leaderboards, level rankings and other kinds of information that have the ability to encourage people. The rewarding service acts completely independently of a specific web application and can therefore aggregate activities within the different applications that a person is actively using. This can be used to derive some kind of a global WWW-activity ranking that reflects how active users are on the internet and could motivate them to become more active in the various web applications in which they have accounts (Steinberg, 2011).

The Competition for Attention and Feedback

One main problem regarding user interaction in web-based applications and systems is how to motivate users to engage in ongoing interoperation and to build compelling and addictive scenarios with incentive and rewarding. Without the adequate ability to user interaction, available resources remain useless for the end user. Particularly in the area of Social Media and Online Communities, we can talk of competing for the user's attention, ongoing participation and feedback.

In all managing disciplines regarding information, learning or knowledge management, gaming principles are becoming more and more important

in motivating users to participate continuously and to get users to deal with learning material in a more incentive way.

On the one hand, there are solutions that deploy gaming for content enrichment ("*Games with a purpose*" (Ahn, 2006)) there are also solutions that deploy gaming for learning and there are some gaming mechanics adapted in the interaction concepts of Web 2.0 applications. A combination of these approaches remains to be seen. In the thesis "*Utilizing Distributed Web Resources for Enhanced Knowledge Representation*" (Steinberg, 2011) for example, they are combined and adapted to web-based, knowledge-oriented scenarios related to distributed web resources to gain the advantages inherent in each approach.

In addition to the simple fun factor, game-oriented user interaction is suitable for several tasks in web applications, knowledge engineering and learning:

- To transfer knowledge and to learn (especially fact-related knowledge);
- To bring ongoing incentive and motivation to participate in web applications;
- To deduce new information about a resource and its interacting user (enhance content).

There are still only a few connections between these different areas. Combining them could have advantages and create symbiosis in all areas (Steinberg, 2011).

Gaming mechanics have just started to be interwoven with web applications in Web 2.0. Online communities like Flickr, Foursquare, Dailymile or Amazon embed interaction design components from game design to increase motivation, incentive and participation. In other words, we can talk about "*Functional Fun,*" while combining gaming mechanics with useful tasks like learning or enhancing content.

Games are introduced as interactive knowledge systems here. This means a knowledge-oriented derivation of the concept "*Games as systems of information*" by Salen and Zimmermann (Salen & Zimmermann, 2003). Gaming mechanics are well suited as an aid in the many steps involved in knowledge engineering, e.g. annotation, evaluation, acquisition or representation.

Every kind of user interaction with a resource brings new information with it (inference and feedback) about the quality of the resource or the interoperating users themselves. Therefore, every activity in relation to a resource can be stored and traced in connection with the interacting user and the interaction task to allow further processing and analysis (Steinberg, 2011).

Game-based interaction can be seen as a highly sophisticated form of user interaction. High design and high functionality are necessary to motivate users to continue playing a game. Current user interaction design in the area of social web applications shows a convergence between traditional web interaction and adapted game mechanics (e.g. Flickr, Amazon).

For example, leaderboard functionality is established to increase user participation and motivation. Collecting, points, feedback, exchange and customization are some of the primary principles in gaming that can be useful for interaction design in web applications. Basic gaming mechanics in web applications can serve as a tool to keep up the user's motivation to continuing participation and feedback.

In social web applications the first aim is to get the user's attention and then enable the user to interact with content and other users. The next important aim is to get resonance or feedback by the user and about the user. Without any response, the users' attention would remain useless in a community. From this it follows that an important question in social web application design is, how to persuade users to give active and immediate feedback. Here, we find another common aspect between web applications and game design: feedback is a crucial part.

Game mechanics and Gamification (Wikipedia, Gamification, 2010) are increasingly finding their way into social web applications – sometimes quite obviously, such as by using a point or badge system. Collecting, feedback, exchange and customization are some of the most feasible game mechanics that can be adapted to web application activity. Incentive in relation to ongoing activity is very important and can be reached by badges and further in-game awards in the first step. Regarding the long term, getting virtual badges only might get boring, so other types of awarding concepts are necessary.

THE ISSUE OF QUALITY

As we have seen in the last sections, the quantity of web resources is not a problem. The Web offers autonomous and frequently useful resources in a growing manner. User Generated Content (UGC) like wikis, weblogs or webfeeds often do not have one responsible authorship or declared experts who check the created content for accuracy, availability, objectivity or reliability. The user is not able to control the quality of the content he receives easily. If we want to utilize the distributed information flood as a linked knowledge base for higher-layered applications (e.g. for knowledge transfer and learning), information quality (iq) is a very important and complex aspect to analyze, personalize and annotate resources.

The problem of contents quality arises if someone can declare himself an expert in a specific area, however, the state of the art, regarding the Wikipedia community, for example, shows that the mechanisms of social and collective control are working very well. A comparison of Encyclopedia Britannica (Britannica, 2010) and Wikipedia showed that they are both similar in quality (Heise, 2008).

Nevertheless, in general, low information quality (iq) is one of the main discriminators of data sources on the Web (Naumann, 2002). Assessing information quality with measurable parameters can offer an extended personalized, smart view on a broad, global knowledge base.

If we want to embed web content into information and knowledge transfer, the issue of data quality is unavoidable. Information quality is an important concern if we want to build knowledge out of information to use it for educational purposes. Currently, web users are clamoring for content that is more sophisticated, and less triviality (Kruse, Warnke, Dittler & Gebel, 2007). Utilizing autonomous web resources by qualitative assessment is becoming more and more important.

To let users interact with Social Media and Open Content out of distributed web resources, enhanced inquiry, selection, storage and buffering are important prerequisites. Nevertheless, statements about the resources' iq enhance its fitness for use. The more we know about a resource, the better we can reuse it. The implementation of a hybrid data layer for acquiring, storing and representing Open Content out of distributed resources is essential to determine, enhance and assure quality of content (Steinberg, 2011).

FUTURE RESEARCH DIRECTIONS

The work presented in this chapter opens up several directions for future research in the related areas of information management and knowledge engineering utilizing distributed resources like Social Media as a global knowledge base while applying gaming mechanics and information quality criteria in RESTful web applications.

Prototypical implementations of knowledge engineering services enabling semantic resource annotation, enhanced knowledge representation and global interaction rewarding have been prototypically developed in e.g. the qKAI mashup framework (Steinberg, 2011).

The main features of the qKAI mashup framework are:

- Support for hybrid data handling of distributed web resources as a global knowledge base, while combining a traditional relational data model with semantic resource annotation.
- Support for the global integration of gaming principles as enhanced user interaction concepts into web applications.
- Support for enhancing information quality of distributed web resources by user interaction and automatically deployed algorithms.

The derived taxonomy called Global Interaction Rewarding (GIAR) system uses principles and mechanics known from game design. A social interaction rewarding community, Squirl, has been implemented as an example use case of the positive conversion of gaming principles and user interaction in web-based applications (Ullmann, 2009)

Basic game mechanics and reward types have been successfully applied in order to reward user interactions or to give feedback on their effect on a user's progress. The thesis (Steinberg, 2011) presents a concept that integrates an application independent model for globally rewarding user interaction tasks. The Social Interaction Taxonomy can be integrated into web applications through RESTful web services.

The taxonomy serves as a foundation for activity monitoring, interaction rewarding or analysis. It is also useful for increasing incentive and motivation to ongoing participation in social web applications are further use cases in global interaction rewarding. Basic game mechanics and reward types are presented and have been applied in order to reward user interactions or to give feedback on their effect on a user's progression. Interaction rewarding acting independently from specific web applications and especially from the interactions they offer is implemented by the Global Interaction rewarding model (GIAR).

An exemplary foundation has been laid upon which to build web-based social network applications and further mashup scenarios with a focus on Open Content out of distributed resources, information quality concerns and incentive to ongoing user attendance and interoperation.

The assessment of information quality can be extended by e.g. analyzing more metadata about resources automatically by implementing state of the art algorithms and technologies. The evaluation in (Steinberg, 2011) for example showed promising results for further work while at the same time integrating game mechanics and aspects of information quality into knowledge engineering based on distributed resources of Social Media and Linked Open Data.

CONCLUSION AND OUTLOOK

The Web is omnipresent as an information and knowledge base, which is continuously increasing. The challenges involved in simplifying access to distributed web resources, to enhance their representation and interconnectivity and to create motivating user interoperation with regard to these resources are growing in importance.

This chapter presented a short insight into current technologies to utilize distributed web resources for enhanced knowledge representation in e.g. social web applications and knowledge engineering. Web-based game mechanics can be deployed as interactive knowledge systems that rely on Open Content.

New challenges in the area of knowledge engineering have arisen like how to query or embed Social Media into knowledge management concerns effectively. In addition, interactivity and the focus on interaction between users and resources in Social Media contexts create new ways of enriching and annotating content collectively following the wisdom of crowds and helpful intelligent automatic analysis.

The convergence of game mechanics, interaction design and web applications is currently a hot topic, but one that still presents some challenges for web developers and interaction designers. With Social Media the competition for the user's attention, attendance and feedback plays a very important role and can be regarded as the motivating force of social communities and online marketing strategies.

The question of the content's quality is more important than ever because of the vast information flood generated by various users and often non-experts in the social web. Information quality criteria like relevance or popularity can be used as a tool to better reuse qualified Open Content in interactive systems (Steinberg, 2011).

Web 2.0 mechanisms can be helpful for new concepts in fulfilling the knowledge life cycle and its single tasks. Users can be involved in the standard tasks of knowledge engineering in a collaborative and collective way (hybrid intelligence). User interaction tasks can be mapped to these knowledge engineering tasks. Some of the ways that a user's interaction can help is to create, edit, annotate, evaluate or qualify knowledge and information resources. The web is on its way to becoming a global, distributed and all-embracing knowledge base for nearly every purpose and domain.

REFERENCES

W3C. (2008). *Resource description framework* (RDF). Retrieved May 25, 2010, from http://www.w3.org/RDF/

W3C. (2010). *SPARQL protocol and RDF query language*. Retrieved May 25, 2010, from http://www.w3.org/TR/rdf-sparql-query/

Aduna & Deutsches Forschungszentrum für Künstliche Intelligenz GmbH (DFKI). (2009). *Aperture.* Retrieved May 27, 2009 from http://aperture.sourceforge.net/ ARD/ZDF-Online study 1997—2009 (2009). Retrieved May 15, 2009 from http://www.ard-zdf-onlinestudie.de/?id=onlinenutzung.

Becker, C., & Bizer, C. (2008). *DBpedia mobile: A location enabled linked data browser.* 17th International World Wide Web Conference, WWW2008, China.

Berne, E. (2009). *Games people play.* Retrieved May 25, 2009, from http://www.ericberne.com/Games_People_Play.htm

Berners-Lee, T., & W3C. (2009). *Web 2.0 and Semantic Web.* Retrieved April 10, 2009, from http://www.w3.org/2006/Talks/1108-swui-tbl/#(1)

Bizer, C. (2009). *DBpedia: A project aiming to extract structured information from the information created as part of the Wikipedia project.* Retrieved May 20, 2009, from http://dbpedia.org/About

Bizer, C., & Cyganiak, R. (2010). D2R server: Publishing relational databases on the Semantic Web. Retrieved May 27, 2009, from http://www4.wiwiss.fu-berlin.de/bizer/d2r-server/

Bizer, C., Heath, T., & Berners-Lee, T. (2008). *Linked data: Principles and state of the art.* 17th International World Wide Web Conference, WWW2008, China.

Britannica: Online Encyclopedia. (2010). Retrieved from May 20, 2010, http://www.britannica.com/

Dailymile: Track your workouts, a social networking website. (2010). Retrieved October 27, 2010, from http://www.dailymile.com/

DBpedia: The DBpedia Knowledge Base. (2012). Retrieved January 1, 2012, from http://dbpedia.org/

Del.icio.us: A social bookmarking service. (2010). Retrieved November 22, 2010, from http://delicio.us

Facebook: A social network service and website. (2011). Retrieved August 22, 2010, from http://www.facebook.com.

Faviki: Tags that make sense. (2009). Retrieved May 25, 2009, from http://www.faviki.com/pages/welcome/

Fensel, J. H. D., Lieberman, H., & Wahlster, W. (2005). *Spinning the Semantic Web: Bringing the World Wide Web to its full potential.* The MIT Press.

Fielding, R. (2000). *Architectural styles and the design of network-based software architectures.* Dissertation, UC Irvine.

Flickr: Share your photos — Watch the world. (2011). Retrieved May 16, 2010, from http://www.flickr.com/

Foursquare: A location-based social networking website. (2010). Retrieved May 20, 2010, from http://www.foursquare.com

Freebase: A large collaborative knowledge base. (2011). Retrieved May 5, 2009, from http://www.freebase.com

Gamification. (2011). Wikipedia. Retrieved February 2, 2011, from http://en.wikipedia.org/wiki/Gamification.

Halpin, H., & Presutti, V. (2009). *An ontology of resources for linked data.* LDOW 2009. Madrid, Spain. ACM. 978-1-60558-487-4/09/04

Huizinga, J. (1971). *Homo ludens: A study of the play-element in culture.* Beacon Press.

Interaction design. (2010). Wikipedia. Retrieved October 5, 2010, from http://en.wikipedia.org/wiki/Interaction_design#Interaction_design_domains

Internet World Stats. (2010). Retrieved April 10, 2009, from http://www.internetworldstats.com

JSON (JavaScript Object Notation). (2010). Retrieved October 5, 2010, from http://www.json.org/

Kim, A. J. (2010). *Putting the fun in functional - Applying game mechanics to social media.* Retrieved October 10, 2010, from http://www.slideshare.net/amyjokim/fun-in-functional-2009-presentation

Kleinz, T. (2009). Nature: Wikipedia nahe an Encyclopaedia Britannica. *Heise Online News.* Retrieved July 20, 2009, from http://www.heise.de/newsticker/meldung/Nature-Wikipedia-nahe-an-Encyclopaedia-Britannica-158194.html

Kruse, P., Warnke, T., Dittler, A., & Gebel, T. (2010). *Wertewelt Medien.* Retrieved April 10, 2008, from http://www.nextpractice.de/fileadmin/studien/medienstudie2007/Medienstudie_Nov2007.pdf

Last.fm: A music website. (2011). Retrieved August 22, 2010 from http://www.last.fm/

LinkedIn: A business-oriented social networking site. (2011). Retrieved May 20, 2011, from http://www.likedin.com

Naumann, F. (2002). Lecture Notes in Computer Science: *Vol. 2261. Quality-driven query answering for integrated information systems.* Springer. doi:10.1007/3-540-45921-9

Nov, O. (2007). What motivates Wikipedians. *Communications of the ACM, 50*(11), 60–64. doi:10.1145/1297797.1297798

Open Knowledge Foundation. (2009). *The open knowledge definition.* Retrieved May 25, 2009, from http://opendefinition.org/

Openlink Virtuoso. (2010). Retrieved May 27, 2009, from http://virtuoso.openlinksw.com/

OpenNLP. (2009). Retrieved May 27, 2009, from http://opennlp.sourceforge.net/

Panoramio: A photo sharing community. (2011). Retrieved January 20, 2012, from http://www.panoramio.com

Prensky, M. (2001). *Digital game-based learning.* New York, NY: McGraw-Hill.

Rotz, B. v. (2010). *Erfolgreiche Online Communities I.* Retrieved August 15, 2010, from http://www.contentmanager.de/magazin/artikel_1766_online_communities.html

Salen, K., & Zimmerman, E. (2003). *Rules of play: Game design fundamentals.* MIT Press.

Social Semantic Web. (2011). Wikipedia. Retrieved November 20, 2011, from http://en.wikipedia.org/wiki/Social_Semantic_Web

Soziales Netzwerk. (2010). Wikipedia. Retrieved October 11, 2010, from http://de.wikipedia.org/wiki/Soziales_Netzwerk_(Internet)

Steinberg, M. (2011). *Utilizing distributed web resources for enhanced knowledge representation.* Unpublished doctoral dissertation, Leibniz Universität Hannover, Germany.

Twitter: A microblogging service. (2012). Retrieved January 15, 2012, from http://www.twitter.com

Ullmann, N. (2010). *Design and implementation of a global rewarding model based on user interaction tasks.* Master thesis, Leibniz Universität Hannover, Germany

von Ahn, L. (2006). Games with a purpose. *Computer, 39*(6), 92–96. doi:10.1109/MC.2006.196

von Ahn, L., Ginosar, S., Kedia, M., Liu, R., & Blum, M. (2006). *Improving accessibility of the Web with a computer game.* International Conference for Human-Computer Interaction, CHI 2006, Canada.

Web, W. W. (2009). Wikipedia. Retrieved May 27, 2009 from http://en.wikipedia.org/wiki/World_Wide_Web

Web 2.0. (2011). Wikipedia. Retrieved May 20, 2011 from http://en.wikipedia.org/wiki/Web_2.0.

Web services. (2009). Wikipedia. Retrieved May 27, 2010, from http://en.wikipedia.org/wiki/Web_service

Wikipedia (about itself). (2010). Wikipedia. Retrieved May 8, 2010, from http://en.wikipedia.org/wiki/Wikipedia

Wordle: A toy for generating word clouds. (2009). Retrieved May 18, 2009 from http://www.wordle.net

YouTube: A video sharing community. (2011). Retrieved May 27, 2011 from http://www.youtube.com

Compilation of References

Abowd, G. D., Dey, A. K., Brown, P. J., Davies, N., Smith, M., & Steggles, P. (1999). *Towards a better understanding of context and context-awareness.* Paper presented at the 1st International Symposium on Handheld and Ubiquitous Computing, Karlsruhe, Germany.

Abras, C., Maloney-Krichmar, D., & Preece, J. (2004). User-centered design. In Bainbridge, W. S. (Ed.), *Berkshire encyclopedia of human-computer interaction.* Great Barrington, MA: Berkshire Publishing Group.

Accenture. (2006). *Executives report that mergers and acquisitions fail to create adequate value.* Accenture.

Acuff, R. D., Fagan, L. M., Rindfleisch, T. C., Levitt, B. J., & Ford, P. M. (1997). *Lightweight, mobile e-mail for intra-clinic communication.* Paper presented at the 1997 AMIA Annual Fall Symposium, Nashville, TN.

Adams, M., ter Hofstede, H. M. A., Edmond, D., & van der Aalst, W. M. P. (2006). *Implementing dynamic flexibility in workflows using worklets.* Technical Report BPM-06-06. BPM Center.

Adaptive Computing. (2011). *Moab adaptive computing suite data sheet.* Retrieved March 1, 2012, from http://www.adaptivecomputing.com/docs/1450

Aduna & Deutsches Forschungszentrum für Künstliche Intelligenz GmbH (DFKI). (2009). *Aperture.* Retrieved May 27, 2009 from http://aperture.sourceforge.net/ARD/ZDF-Online study 1997—2009 (2009). Retrieved May 15, 2009 from http://www.ard-zdf-onlinestudie.de/?id=onlinenutzung.

Agarwal, A., Miller, J., Eastep, J., Wentziaff, D., & Kasture, H. (2010). *Self-aware computing.* Retrieved July 11, 2011, from http://www.defensetechbriefs.com/component/content/article/8259

Ahl, V., & Allen, T. F. H. (1996). *Hierarchy theory: A vision, vocabulary, and epistemology.* New York, NY: Columbia University Press.

Ailliot, P., Thompson, C., & Thomson, P. (2009). Space–time modelling of precipitation by using a hidden Markov model and censored Gaussian distributions. *Journal of the Royal Statistical Society. Series C, Applied Statistics, 58*(3), 405–426. doi:10.1111/j.1467-9876.2008.00654.x

Akkermans, H., & van Helden, K. (2002). Vicious and virtuous cycles in ERP implementation: A case study of interrelations between critical success factors. *European Journal of Information Systems, 11*(1), 35–46. doi:10.1057/palgrave/ejis/3000418

Akram, A., Meredith, D., & Allan, R. (2006). Evaluation of BPEL to scientific workflows. *Sixth IEEE International Symposium on Cluster Computing and the Grid (CCGRID'06),* (pp. 269-274). IEEE. doi:10.1109/CCGRID.2006.44

Albers, S. (2010). Energy-efficient algorithms. *Communications of the ACM, 53.*

Allen, T. F. H., & Starr, T. B. (1982). *Hierarchy: Perspectives for ecological complexity.* Chicago, IL: The University of Chicago Press.

Alonso, G., Casati, F., Kuno, H., & Machiraju, V. (2004). *Web services: Concepts, architectures and applications.* Berlin, Germany: Springer Verlag.

Ambler, S. W. (2005). *An overview of the enterprise unified process* (EUP). Retrieved October 13, 2011, from http://www.enterpriseunifiedprocess.com/

AMD. (2005). *AMD secure virtual machine architecture reference manual,* Rev. 3.01.

Amir, E., Anderson, M. L., & Chaudhri, C. K. (2004). *Report on DARPA Workshop on Self-Aware Computer Systems.* Retrieved August 18, 2011, from http://citeseerx. ist.psu.edu (document 10.1.1.120.6684.pdf)

An Electronic Health Record for every South African. (2011). Retrieved December 28, 2011, from http://ehr. co.za/main.php

Andersen, R., Ruland, C., Slaughter, L., Andersen, T., & Jacobsen, W. (2005). Clustering techniques for organizing cancer-related concepts into meaningful groups for patients. *AMIA Annual Symposium Proceedings*, (p. 882).

Andersen, K. V. (2006). E-government: Five key challenges for management. *The Electronic. Journal of E-Government, 4*(1), 1–8.

Anderson, J. G. (1993). *Evaluating health care information systems: Methods and applications.* Sage Publications, Inc.

Anderson, W. L., & Crocca, W. T. (1993). Engineering practice and co-development of product prototypes. *Communications of the ACM, 36*(6), 49–56. doi:10.1145/153571.256015

Andrade, F. G., & Baptista, C. S. (2011). Using semantic similarity to improve information discovery in spatial data infrastructures. *Journal of Information and Data Management, 2*(2), 181–194.

Andrienko, G., Andrienko, N., Bremm, S., Schreck, T., von Landesberger, T., Bak, P., & Keim, D. (2010). Space-in-time and time-in-space self-organizing maps for exploring spatiotemporal patterns. *Computer Graphics Forum, 29*(3), 913–922. doi:10.1111/j.1467-8659.2009.01664.x

Andrienko, G., Andrienko, N., Demsar, U., Dransch, D., Dykes, J., & Fabrikant, S. I. (2010). Space, time and visual analytics. *International Journal of Geographical Information Science, 24*(10), 1577–1600. doi:10.1080/1 3658816.2010.508043

Ane, B. K., & Roller, D. (2011). An architecture of adaptive product data communication system for collaborative design. *Proceedings of the 4th International Conference on Advances in Computer-Human Interactions (ACHI'11)*, (pp. 182-187).

Ane, B. K. (2010). *Automation of design for reverse engineering in a collaborative design environment: Development of STEP neutral format translator for product data exchange. Research Report.* Stuttgart, Germany: IRIS, Universität Stuttgart.

Angelopoulos, S., Kitsios, F., & Papadopoulos, T. (2010). New service development in e-government: Identifying critical success factors. *Transforming Government: People. Process and Policy, 1*(1), 95–118.

Antonakopoulou, A., Lioudakis, G. V., Gogoulos, F., Kaklamani, D. I., & Venieris, I. S. (2012). Leveraging access control for privacy protection: A survey. In Yee, G. (Ed.), *Privacy protection measures and technologies in business organizations: Aspects and standards* (pp. 65–94). Hershey, PA: IGI Global.

ANZLIC Spatial Information Council. (2011). *Australian spatial data infrastructure.* Retrieved October 16, 2011, from http://www.anzlic.org.au/ASDI_quick.html

Appari, A., Anthony, D. L., & Johnson, E. M. (2009). *HIPAA compliance: An examination of institutional and market forces.* Paper presented at the 8th Workshop on Economics of Information Security, London.

Appelo, J. (2011). *Management 3.0 leading agile developers developing agile leaders.* Upper Saddle River, NJ: Addison-Wesley.

Apple (n.d.). *Iphone.* Retrieved October 20th, 2011 from http://apple.com

Apple iCloud. (n.d.). Retrieved March 2, 2012, from http:// www.apple.com/icloud/

Arch-Rock. (n.d.). *Image.* Retrieved October 20th 2011 from http://archrock.com

Armbrust, M., Fox, A., Griffith, R., Joseph, A. D., Katz, R. H., & Konwinski, A. ... Zaharia, M. (2009). *Above the clouds: A Berkeley view of cloud computing.* University of California, (UCB/EECS-2009-28), 07-013. EECS Department, University of California, Berkeley. Retrieved March 2, 2012, from http://www.eecs.berkeley.edu/Pubs/ TechRpts/2009/EECS-2009-28.html

Arnone, D., Lazzaro, M., & Rossi, A. (2010). *GAMES deliverable 5.1 [GAMES D5.1], Specification of the ESMI interface*. Retrieved March 1, 2012, from http://www.green-datacenters.eu

Asanovic, K., Bodik, R., Catanzaro, B. C., Gebis, J. J., Husbands, P., et al. (2006). *The landscape of parallel computing research: A view from Berkeley*. Retrieved March 1, 2012, from http://www.eecs.berkeley.edu/Pubs/TechRpts/2006/EECS-2006-183.pdf

Ashby, W. R. (1956). *An introduction to cybernetics*. London, UK: Chapman & Hall Ltd.

ASIP Santé project. (2011). Retrieved January 09, 2012, from http://esante.gouv.fr/en

As-Saber, S., Srivastava, A., & Hossain, K. (2006). Information technology law and e-government: A developing country perspective. *Journal of Administration & Governance, 1*(1), 84–101.

Astrova, I., Koschel, A., & Kruessmann, T. (2010). Comparison of enterprise service buses based on their support of high availability. *Proceedings of the 2010 ACM Symposium on Applied Computing - SAC '10*, (p. 2495). New York, NY: ACM Press. doi:10.1145/1774088.1774605

Athanasis, N., Kalabokidis, K., Vaitis, M., & Soulakellis, N. (2009). Towards a semantics-based approach in the development of geographic portals. *Computers & Geosciences, 35*(2), 301–308. doi:10.1016/j.cageo.2008.01.014

Avrahami, D., Gergle, D., Hudson, S. E., & Kiesler, S. (2007). Improving the match between callers and receivers: A study on the effect of contextual information on cell phone interruptions. *Behaviour & Information Technology, 26*(3), 247–259. doi:10.1080/01449290500402338

Aziz, O., Panesar, S., Netuveli, G., Paraskeva, P., Sheikh, A., & Darzi, A. (2005). Handheld computers and the 21st century surgical team: A pilot study. *BMC Medical Informatics and Decision Making, 5*(1), 28. doi:10.1186/1472-6947-5-28

Baader, F., Calvanese, D., McGuinness, D. L., Nardi, D., & Patel-Schneider, F. (2003). *The description logic handbook: Theory, implementation, applications*. Cambridge, UK: Cambridge University Press.

Baldwin, C., Hienerth, C., & Von Hippel, E. (2006). How user innovations become commercial products: A theoretical investigation and case study. *Research Policy, 35*(9), 1291–1313. doi:10.1016/j.respol.2006.04.012

Baranger, J., Matre, J. F., & Oudin, F. (1996). Connection between finite volume and mixed finite element methods. *Mathematical Modelling and Numerical Analysis, 30*(4), 445–465.

Bardram, J. E., & Hansen, T. R. (2004). *The AWARE architecture: Supporting context-mediated social awareness in mobile cooperation*. Paper presented at the 2004 ACM Conference on Computer Supported Cooperative Work, Chicago, Illinois, USA.

Bardram, J. E., Hansen, T. R., & Soegaard, M. (2006). *AwareMedia: A shared interactive display supporting social, temporal, and spatial awareness in surgery*. Paper presented at the 2006 20th Anniversary Conference on Computer Supported Cooperative Work, Banff, Alberta, Canada.

Bardram, J. E., & Hansen, T. R. (2010). Context-based workplace awareness. *Computer Supported Cooperative Work, 19*(2), 105–138. doi:10.1007/s10606-010-9110-2

Barkema, H., & Schijven, M. (2008). How do firms learn to make acquisitions? A review of past research and an agenda for the future. *Journal of Management, 34*(3), 594. doi:10.1177/0149206308316968

Barlow-Zambodla, A. (2009). Mobile technology for learner support in open schooling. *SAIDE Newsletter, 15*(1). Retrieved October 20, 2011, from http://www.saide.org.za/resources/newsletters/Vol_15_no.1_2009/Content/Mobile%20Technology%20for%20Learner%20Support.htm

Basile, C., Lioy, A., Perez, G. M., Clemente, F. J. G., & Skarmeta, A. F. G. (2007). POSITIF: A policy-based security management system. In *POLICY 2007: Proceedings of the 8th IEEE International Workshop on Policies for Distributed Systems and Networks*. Washington, DC: IEEE Computer Society.

Baskerville, R. (2004, June 14-16). *Agile security for information warfare: A call for research.* Paper presented at the 13th European Conference on Information Systems, The European IS Profession in the Global Networking Environment, Turku, Finland.

Baskerville, R., Pries-Heje, J., & Venable, J. (2009). *Soft design science methodology.* Paper presented at the 4th International Conference on Design Science Research in Information Systems and Technology, Philadelphia, Pennsylvania.

Bass, T., Freyre, A., Gruber, D., & Watt, G. (1998). E-mail bombs and countermeasures: Cyber attacks on availability and brand integrity. *IEEE Network,* (March/April): 10–17. doi:10.1109/65.681925

Baumgardner, J. R. (1985). Three dimensional treatment of convection flow in the Earth's mantle. *Journal of Statistical Physics, 39*(5/6), 501–511. doi:10.1007/BF01008348

Baun, C., Kunze, M., Nimis, J., & Tai, S. (2011). *Cloud computing: Web-based dynamic IT services.* Heidelberg, Germany: Springer-Verlag.

Becker, C., & Bizer, C. (2008). *DBpedia mobile: A location enabled linked data browser.* 17th International World Wide Web Conference, WWW2008, China.

Beisse, F. (2010). *A guide to computer user support for help desk and support specialist.* Boston, MA: Course Technology, Cengage Learning.

Béjar, R., Latre, M. A., Nogueras-Iso, J., Muro-Medrano, P. R., & Zarazaga-Soria, F. J. (2009). An architectural style for spatial data infrastructures. *International Journal of Geographical Information Science, 23*(3), 271–294. doi:10.1080/13658810801905282

Belobaba, P., Odoni, A., & Barnhart, C. (2009). *The global airline industry.* Chichester, UK: John Wiley & Sons, Ltd. doi:10.1002/9780470744734

Ben Youssef, B. (2004, September). Simulation of cell population dynamics using 3D cellular automata. *Lecture Notes in Computer Science, 3305,* (pp. 561–570). Springer-Verlag GmbH.

Běohounková, M., Tobie, G., Choblet, G., & Čadek, O. (2010). Coupling mantle convection and tidal dissipation: Applications to Enceladus and Earth-like planets. *Journal of Geophysical Research, 115,* E09011. doi:10.1029/2009JE003564

Bercovici, D. (2007). Mantle dynamics past, present and future: An introduction and overview. In D. Bercovici (Ed.), *Treatise on geophysics, volume 7 – Mantle dynamics* (pp. 1-30). Elsevier B.V.

Bercovici, D. (2003). The generation of plate tectonics from mantle convection. *Earth and Planetary Science Letters, 205,* 107–121. doi:10.1016/S0012-821X(02)01009-9

Berenson, H., Bernstein, P., Gray, J., Melton, J., O'Neil, E., & O'Neil, P. (1995). A critique of ANSI SQL isolation levels. *Proceedings of the ACM SIGMOD Conference,* (pp. 1-10).

Berger, E. (2010). The iPad: Gadget or medical godsend? *Annals of Emergency Medicine, 56*(1), 21A–22A. doi:10.1016/j.annemergmed.2010.05.010

Bernd, B., Heiko, G., & Michael, W. (2007). Aktives Semantiches Konstruktions- und Zuverlässigkeitsnetz. In Bertsche, B., & Bullinger, H.-J. (Eds.), *Entwicklung und Erprobung Innovativer Produkte-Rapid Prototyping: Grundlagen, Rahmenbedingungen und Realisierung* (pp. 130–158). Berlin, Germany: Springer-Verlag.

Berne, E. (2009). *Games people play.* Retrieved May 25, 2009, from http://www.ericberne.com/Games_People_Play.htm

Berners-Lee, T., & W3C. (2009). *Web 2.0 and Semantic Web.* Retrieved April 10, 2009, from http://www.w3.org/2006/Talks/1108-swui-tbl/#(1)

Berners-Lee, T., Hendler, J., & Lassila, O. (2001). The Semantic Web. *Scientific American*. Retrieved October 16, 2011, from http://www.scientificamerican.com/article.cfm?id=the-semantic-web

Bernstein, A., Vorburger, P., & Egger, P. (2005). *Direct interruptablity prediction and scenario-based evaluation of wearable devices: Towards reliable interruptability predictions*. Paper presented at the First International Workshop on Managing Context Information in Mobile and Pervasive Environments MCMP-05.

Berry, B. J. L. (1964). Approaches to regional analysis: A synthesis. *Annals of the Association of American Geographers. Association of American Geographers, 54*(1), 2–11. doi:10.1111/j.1467-8306.1964.tb00469.x

Bertino, E., Catania, B., Damiani, M. L., & Perlasca, P. (2005). GEO-RBAC: A spatially aware RBAC. In *Proceedings of the 11th ACM Symposium on Access Control Models and Technologies (SACMAT '06)* (pp. 29-37). New York, NY: ACM.

Bertino, E., Martino, L., Paci, F., & Squicciarini, A. (2010). *Security for Web services and service-oriented architectures*. Berlin, Germany: Springer-Verlag. doi:10.1007/978-3-540-87742-4

Bethencourt, J., Sahai, A., & Waters, B. (2007). Ciphertext-policy attribute-based encryption. In *S&P 2007: Proceedings of the 2007 IEEE Symposium on Security and Privacy* (pp. 321-334). Washington, DC: IEEE Computer Society.

Beyer, H. (2010). *User-centred agile methods*. London, UK: Morgan & Claypol.

Bhalla, G. (2011). *Collaboration and co-creation, new platforms for marketing and innovation*. London, UK: Springer-Verlag.

Bhatti, R., Ghafoor, A., Bertino, E., & Joshi, J. B. D. (2005). X-GTRBAC: An XML-based policy specification framework and architecture for enterprise-wide access control. *Journal of ACM Transactions of Information and System Security, 8*(2), 187–227. doi:10.1145/1065545.1065547

Bisgaard, J. J., Heise, M., & Steffensen, C. (2004). *How is context and context-awareness defined and applied? A survey of context-awareness* (pp. 31–40). Department of Computer Science, Aalborg University.

Bizer, C. (2009). *DBpedia: A project aiming to extract structured information from the information created as part of the Wikipedia project*. Retrieved May 20, 2009, from http://dbpedia.org/About

Bizer, C., & Cyganiak, R. (2010). D2R server: Publishing relational databases on the Semantic Web. Retrieved May 27, 2009, from http://www4.wiwiss.fu-berlin.de/bizer/d2r-server/

Bizer, C., Heath, T., & Berners-Lee, T. (2008). *Linked data: Principles and state of the art*. 17th International World Wide Web Conference, WWW2008, China.

Bjorn-Andersen, N., Rasmussen, L. B., & Rasmusssen, S. (2008). Web 2.0 adoption by Danish newspapers - Urgent need for new business models? *Proceedings of I-KNOW '08 and I-MEDIA '08*, Graz, Austria, September 3-5, 2008. Retrieved September 15, 2011, from http://i-know.tugraz.at/wp-content/uploads/2008/11

Blankenbach, B., Busse, F., Christensen, U., Cserepes, L., Gunkel, D., & Hansen, U. (1989). A benchmark comparison for mantle convection codes. *Geophysical Journal International, 98*, 23–38. doi:10.1111/j.1365-246X.1989.tb05511.x

Blum, N. J., & Lieu, T. A. (1992). Interrupted care. The effects of paging on pediatric resident activities. *American Journal of Diseases of Children, 146*(7), 806–808. doi:doi:10.1001/archpedi.146.7.806

BOINC. (2012). *Berkeley Open Infrastructure for Network Computing*. Retrieved March 25, 2012, from http://boinc.berkeley.edu

Boneh, D., & Franklin, M. K. (2003). Identity-based encryption from the Weil pairing. *SIAM Journal on Computing, 32*(3), 586–615. doi:10.1137/S0097539701398521

Bonham, G., Seifert, J., & Thorson, S. (2001). *The transformational potential of e-government: At the role of political leadership*. Paper read at the 4th Pan European International Relations Conference, University of Kent.

Bonner, J. V. H. (2009). Lessons learned in providing product designers with user-participatory interaction design tools. In Voss, A., Hartswood, M., Procter, R., Rouncefield, M., Slack, R. S., & Buscher, M. (Eds.), *Use-designer relations, interdisciplinary perspective* (pp. 87–110). London, UK: Springer-Verlag.

Boomer, D., Broussard, K., & Meseke, M. (2011). *HPSS 8 metadata services evolution to meet the demands of extreme scale computing* [PDF document]. Retrieved June 26, 2011, from http://www.pdsi-scidac.org/events/PDSW10/resources/posters/HPSS8.pdf

Borghoff, U. M., & Schlichter, J. H. (2000). *Computer-supported cooperative work: Introduction to distributed applications*. Heidelberg, Germany: Springer-Verlag.

Bothwell, J., & Yuan, M. (2010). Apply concepts of fluid kinematics to represent continuous space-time fields in temporal GIS. *Annals of Geographic Information Science, 16*(1), 27–41.

Botsis, T., Solvoll, T., Scholl, J., Hasvold, P., & Hartvigsen, G. (2007). Context-aware systems for mobile communication in healthcare - A user oriented approach. *Proceedings of the 7th WSEAS International Conference on Applied Informatics and Communications,* (pp. 69-74).

Botts, M., Percivall, G., Reed, C., & Davidson, J. (2008). OGC® Sensor Web enablement: Overview and high level architecture. In Nittel, S., Labrinidis, A., & Stefanidis, A. (Eds.), *GeoSensor networks (Vol. 4540,* pp. 175–190). Berlin, Germany: Springer. doi:10.1007/978-3-540-79996-2_10

Boulon, J. Konwinski, Qi, R., A., Rabkin, A., Yang, E., & Yang, M. (2008). Chukwa – A large-scale monitoring system. In *Proceedings of the First Workshop on Cloud Computing and its Applications (CCA 2008)*. Retrieved February 29, 2012, from http://www.cca08.org/papers/Paper-13-Ariel-Rabkin.pdf

Bourn, J. (2002). *Better public services through e-government*. London, UK: The National Audit Office.

Bowen, J. A. (2011). *Legal issues in cloud computing* (pp. 593–613). Cloud Computing Principles and Paradigms. doi:10.1002/9780470940105.ch24

Box, D. (1998). *Essential COM*. Upper Saddle River, NJ: Addison-Wesley.

BPEL Designer Project. (2012). Retrieved February 10, 2012, from http://www.eclipse.org/bpel/

Bradner, E., Kellogg, W. A., & Erickson, T. (1999). *The adoption and use of BABBLE: A field study of chat in the workplace*. Paper presented at the Sixth European Conference on Computer Supported Cooperative Work, Copenghagen, Denmark.

Brandenburger, A., & Nalebuff, B. (1996). *Co-opetition*. New York, NY: Doubleday.

Brechlerova, D., & Candik, M. (2008). *New trends in security of electronic health documentation*. Paper presented at the ICCST 2008, 42nd Annual IEEE International Carnahan Conference on Security Technology, 2008.

Breibart, Y., Garcia-Molina, H., & Silberschatz, A. (1992). Overview of multidatabase transaction management. *The VLDB Journal, 2*, 181–239. doi:10.1007/BF01231700

Breuer, D. (2009). Dynamics and thermal evolution. In Trümper, J. E. (Ed.), *Landolt-Börnstein astronomy and astrophysics 4b - Astronomy, astrophysics, and cosmology - Solar system* (pp. 254–280). Springer.

Breuer, D., Yuen, D. A., & Spohn, T. (1997). Phase transitions in the Martian mantle: Implications for partially layered convection. *Earth and Planetary Science Letters, 148*, 457–469. doi:10.1016/S0012-821X(97)00049-6

Briggs, C. (2009). Web 2.0 business models ad decentralized value creation systems. In Lytras, M. D., Damiani, E., & Ordonez de Pablos, P. (Eds.), *Web 2.0: The business model* (pp. 133–147). Berlin, Germany: Springer-Verlag.

Britannica: Online Encyclopedia. (2010). Retrieved from May 20, 2010, http://www.britannica.com/

Brown, S. M., & Elkins-Tanton, L. T. (2009). Compositions of Mercury's earliest crust from magma ocean models. *Earth and Planetary Science Letters, 286*, 446–455. doi:10.1016/j.epsl.2009.07.010

Bullen, M., & Janes, D. P. (2007). Preface. In Bullen, M., & Jane, D. P. (Eds.), *Making the transition to e-learning: Strategies and issues* (pp. vii–xvi). Hershey, PA: Information Science Publishing.

Bundesministerium für Bildung und Forschung (BMBF). (2009). *Ergebnisse der ersten HPC- Fördermaßnahme, HPCSoftware für skalierbare Parallelrechner* [PDF document]. Retrieved June 23, 2011, from http://www.pt-it.pt-dlr.de/_media/HPC_Infoblatt.pdf

Bundesministerium für Umwelt, Naturschutz und Reaktorsicherheit (BMU). (2009). *Energieeffiziente Rechenzentren, Best-Practice-Beispiele aus Europa, USA und Asien.*

Burgess, B. T., Myles, J. L., & Dickinson, R. B. (2000). Quantitative analysis of adhesion-mediated cell migration in three-dimensional gels of RGD-grafted collagen. *Annals of Biomedical Engineering, 28*(1), 110–118. doi:10.1114/1.259

Burstedde, C., Ghattas, O., Gurnis, M., Stadler, G., Tan, E., Tu, T., et al. (2008). Scalable adaptive mantle convection simulation on petascale supercomputers. In *Proceedings of the 2008 ACM/IEEE Conference on Supercomputing* (pp. 1-15).

C2C-CC Manifesto. (2007). *Report of the CAR 2 CAR Communication Consortium.* Retrieved June 12, 2011, from http://www.car-to-car.org

Čadek, O., & Fleitout, L. (2003). Effect of lateral viscosity variations in the top 300 km on the geoid and dynamic topography. *Geophysical Journal International, 152,* 566–580. doi:10.1046/j.1365-246X.2003.01859.x

Cain and Abel. (2012). *Password recovery tool.* Retrieved February 15, 2012, from http://www.oxid.it

Caldwell, N. H. M., & Rodgers, P. A. (1998). WebCADET: Facilitating distributed design support. *Proceedings of the IEEE Colloquium on Web-Based Knowledge Servers,* (pp. 9/1–9/4).

Campbell, A. J., & Cooper, R. G. (1999). Do customer partnerships improve new product success rates? *Industrial Marketing Management, 28*(5), 507–519. doi:10.1016/S0019-8501(99)00058-9

Campbell, M. I., Cagan, J., & Kotovsky, K. (1999). A-design: An agent-based approach to conceptual design in a dynamic environment. *Research in Engineering Design, 11,* 172–192. doi:10.1007/s001630050013

Canuto, C., Hussaini, M. Y., Quarteroni, A., & Zang, T. A. (2007). *Spectral methods: Evolution to complex geometries and applications to fluid dynamics.* Springer.

Chadwick, A., & May, C. (2003). Interaction between states & citizens of the age of the internet: E-government in the United States, Britain. *Governance: An International Journal of Policy, Administration and Institutions, 16*(2), 271–300. doi:10.1111/1468-0491.00216

Chakrabarti, A. (2007). *Grid computing security* (1st ed.). Berlin, Germany: Springer.

Challenor, R., & Deegan, S. (2009). What service users want: a new clinic results service. Can we satisfy both patients' needs and wants? *International Journal of STD & AIDS, 20*(10), 701–703. doi:10.1258/ijsa.2009.009077

Chappel, D. A. (2004). In Hendrickson, M. (Ed.), *Enterprise service bus: Theory in practice* (1st ed., p. 352). O'Reilly Media.

Charness, N., & Bosman, E. A. (1990). Human factors and design for older adults. In Birren, J. E., & Schaie, K. W. (Eds.), *Handbook of the psychology of aging* (3rd ed., pp. 446–463). San Diego, CA: Academic Press.

Chemia, Z., Koyi, H., & Schmeling, H. (2008). Numerical modelling of rise and fall of a dense layer in salt diapirs. *Geophysical Journal International, 172*(2), 798–816. doi:10.1111/j.1365-246X.2007.03661.x

Chen, J., Shaw, S.-L., Yu, H., Lu, F., Chai, Y., & Jia, Q. (2011). Exploratory data analysis of activity diary data: A space–time GIS approach. *Journal of Transport Geography, 19*(3), 394–404. doi:10.1016/j.jtrangeo.2010.11.002

Chen, T. M. (2010). Stuxnet, the real start of cyber warfare? *IEEE Network, 24*(6), 2–3. doi:10.1109/MNET.2010.5634434

Chen, Y. C., & Knepper, R. (2005). Digital government development strategies. Lessons for policy makers from a comparative perspective. In Huang, W., Siau, K., & Kwok, K. W. (Eds.), *Electronic government strategies and implementation* (pp. 394–420). Hershey, PA: Idea Group Publishing.

Chevaleyre, Y., Endriss, U., Estivie, S., & Maudet, N. (2005). Welfare engineering in practice: On the variety of multi-agent resource allocation problems. In M.-P. Gleizes, A. Omicini, & F. Zambonelli (Eds.), *Engineering Societies in the Agents World V,* (LNAI 3451, pp. 335–347). Berlin, Germany: Springer-Verlag.

Chiou, C.-K., Tseng, J. C. R., Hwang, G.-J., & Heller, S. (2010). An adaptive navigation support system for conducting context-aware ubiquitous learning in museums. *Computers & Education, 55*(2), 834–845. doi:10.1016/j.compedu.2010.03.015

Choblet, G., Čadek, O., Couturier, F., & Dumoulin, C. (2007). ŒDIPUS: A new tool to study the dynamics of planetary interiors. *Geophysical Journal International, 170*(1), 9–30. doi:10.1111/j.1365-246X.2007.03419.x

Choudrie, J., & Lee, H. (2004). Broadband development in South Korea: Institutional and cultural factor. *European Journal of Information Systems, 13*(2), 103–114. doi:10.1057/palgrave.ejis.3000494

Chowbe, V. S. (2011). The concept of cyber-crime: Nature and scope. *Global Journal of Enterprise Information System, 3*(1), 72–84.

Christensen, U. R., & Wicht, J. (2007). Numerical dynamo simulations. In P. Olsen (Ed), *Treatise on geophysics, Vol. 8 - Core dynamics* (245-282). Amsterdam, The Netherlands: Elsevier.

Christensen, K., & Moloney, N. (2005). *Complexity and criticality*. London, UK: Imperial College Press.

Christensen, U. (1984). Convection with pressure- and temperature-dependent non-Newtonian rheology. *Geophysical Journal of the Royal Astronomical Society, 77,* 343–384. doi:10.1111/j.1365-246X.1984.tb01939.x

Christensen, U. R. (1983). Convection in a variable-viscosity fluid: Newtonian versus power-law rheology. *Earth and Planetary Science Letters, 64,* 153–162. doi:10.1016/0012-821X(83)90060-2

Christensen, U. R. (1984). Convection with pressure- and temperature-dependent non-Newtonian rheology. *Geophysical Journal of the Royal Astronomical Society, 77,* 343–384. doi:10.1111/j.1365-246X.1984.tb01939.x

Christmann. (2009). *Description for resource efficient computing system* (RECS). Retrieved March 1, 2012, from http://shared.christmann.info/download/project-recs.pdf

Christmann. (2012). *Christmann website*. Retrieved March 1, 2012, from at http://christmann.info/

Chua, H. H. (2011, 15 May). Social media: The new voice of GE. *The Straits Times*.

Chung, M. K. (2007). *Singapore e-government experience*. Paper presented at Asia e- Government Forum 2007, 20 September 2007, Seoul, Korea.

CIG. (2012). *Computational infrastructure for geodynamics for CitComS*. Retrieved January 12, 2012, from http://www.geodynamics.org/cig/software/citcoms

Clarke, N. L., & Furnell, S. M. (2005). Authentication of users on mobile telephones - A survey of attitudes and practices. *Computers & Security, 24*(7), 519–527. doi:10.1016/j.cose.2005.08.003

Clarke, N. L., Furnell, S. M., Rodwell, P. M., & Reynolds, P. L. (2002). Acceptance of subscriber authentication methods for mobile telephony devices. *Computers & Security, 21*(3), 220–228. doi:10.1016/S0167-4048(02)00304-8

Cliver, R. (2011). Tremors in the Web of trade: Complexity, connectivity and criticality in the mid-eighth century Eurasian world. *The Middle Ground Journal, 2,* 1–39.

COBIT. (n.d.). *IT governance framework – Information assurance control*. ISACA. Retrieved March 2, 2012, from http://www.isaca.org/Knowledge-Center/COBIT/Pages/Overview.aspx

Cockburn, A. (2004). *Crystal clear a human-powered methodology for small teams*. Upper Saddle River, NJ: Pearson Education.

Cohn, M. (2004). *User stories applied: For agile software development*. New York, NY: Addison Wesley.

Coiera, E. (2000). When conversation is better than computation. *Journal of the American Medical Informatics Association, 7*(3), 277–286. doi:10.1136/jamia.2000.0070277

Coiera, E., & Tombs, V. (1998). Communication behaviours in a hospital setting: An observational study. *British Medical Journal, 316*(7132), 673–676. doi:10.1136/bmj.316.7132.673

Commission of the European Communities (CEC). (2009). *Commission recommendation of 9.10.2009 on mobilising information and communications technologies to facilitate the transition to an energy-efficient, low-carbon economy.*

Committee on Financial Services U.S. House of Representatives. (2006). *Sarbanes-Oxley at four: protecting investors and strengthening markets*. Washington, DC: Author.

Conci, M., Pianesi, F., & Zancanaro, M. (2009). *Useful, social and enjoyable: Mobile phone adoption by older people*. Paper presented at the 12th IFIP TC 13 International Conference on Human-Computer Interaction: Part I.

Condor. (2008). *High throughput computing*. Retrieved January 2, 2011, from http://www.cs.wisc.edu/condor/

Constantine, L. L., & Lockwood, L. A. D. (2002). Usage-centred engineering for Web applications. *IEEE Software, 19*(2), 42–50. doi:10.1109/52.991331

Contini, S., & Yin, Y. L. (2006). Forgery and partial key-recovery attacks on HMAC and NMAC using hash collisions. *Proceedings of the Twelfth International Conference on the Theory and Application of Cryptology and Information Security (AsiaCrypt), Lecture Notes in Computer Science, 4284*, December 3-7, 2006, Shanghai, China, (pp. 37-53). ISBN 3-540-49475-8

Cooke, J. L. (2010). *Agile productivity unleashed, proven approaches for achieving real productivity gains in any organization*. Ely, UK: IT Governance Publishing.

Coratella, A., Hirsch, R., & Rodriguez, E. (2002). A framework for analyzing mobile transaction models. In K. Siau (Ed.), *Advanced topics in database research*, Vol. 2, ed. Hershey, PA: IGI Global.

Council for Excellence in Governance. (2001). *E-government, the next American revolution*. Washington, DC: Council for Excellence in Governance.

Courage, C., & Baxter, K. (2005). *Understanding your users: A practical guide to user requirements, method, tools and techniques*. Amsterdam, The Netherlands: Elsevier.

Coursey, D., & Norris, D. (2008). Models of e-government: Are they correct? An empirical assessment. *PAR, 68*, 523–536.

Couture, A. W. (2009). *Invest in storage professional services, not more hardware*. Gartner RAS Core Research Note G00165133. Retrieved October 18, 2011, from http://www.gartner.com/DisplayDocument?doc_cd=165133&ref=g_rss

Cova, T. J., & Goodchild, M. F. (2002). Extending geographical representation to include fields of spatial objects. *International Journal of Geographical Information Science, 16*(6), 509–532. doi:10.1080/13658810210137040

Cox, R. W., Rinnen, P., Zaffos, S., & Chang, J. (2010, November 15). *Magic quadrant for midrange and high-end modular disk arrays*. Gartner RAS Core Research Note G00207396. Retrieved October 18, 2010, from http://www.gartner.com/technology/media-products/reprints/hitachi/vol3/article2/article2.html?WT.ac=us_hp_sp1r21&_p=v

Culler, D. E., & Hong, W. (2004). Wireless sensor networks - Introduction. *Communications of the ACM, 47*(6), 30–33. doi:10.1145/990680.990703

Cundy, H. M., & Rollet, A. P. (1961). *Mathematical models* (2nd ed.). Oxford, UK: Oxford University Press.

Cuppens-Boulahia, N., Cuppens, F., Autrel, F., & Debar, H. (2009). An ontology-based approach to react to network attacks. *International Journal of Information and Computer Security, 3*(3/4), 280–305. doi:10.1504/IJICS.2009.031041

Cuppens, F., & Cuppens-Boulahia, N. (2008). Modelling contextual security policies. *International Journal of Information Security, 7*(4), 285–305. doi:10.1007/s10207-007-0051-9

Currle-Linde, N., Adamidis, P., Resch, M., Bos, F., & Pleiss, J. (2006). GriCoL: A language for scientific grids. *2006 Second IEEE International Conference on e-Science and Grid Computing (e-Science '06)* (pp. 62-62). Amsterdam, Netherlands: IEEE. doi:10.1109/E-SCIENCE.2006.261146

Cutkosky, M. R., Engelmore, R. S., Fikes, R. E., Genesereth, M. R., Gruber, T. R., & Mark, W. S. (1993). PACT: An experiment in integrating concurrent engineering systems. *IEEE Computer, 26*, 28–37. doi:10.1109/2.179153

Dailymile: Track your workouts, a social networking website. (2010). Retrieved October 27, 2010, from http://www.dailymile.com/

Daniel, B. K., O'Brien, D., & Sarkar, A. (2009). User-centred design principles for online learning communities: A sociotechnical approach for the design of a distributed community of practice. In Lytras, M. D., & Ordonez de Pablos, P. (Eds.), *Social Web evolution: Integrating semantic applications with Web 2.0 technologies* (pp. 267–279). Hershey, PA: Information Science Reference. doi:10.4018/978-1-60566-272-5.ch019

Darcy, M. (2010, February 11). *IBM announces new scale-out storage system to access billions of files.* IBM Press Release. Retrieved October 16, 2010, from http://www-03.ibm.com/press/us/en/pressrelease/29786.wss#release

Dargan, P. A. (2005). *Open systems and standards for software product development.* Boston, MA: Artech House Computing Library.

Davaille, A., & Limare, A. (2007). Laboratory studies of mantle convection. In D. Bercovici (Ed.), *Treatise on geophysics, Volume 7 – Mantle dynamics* (pp. 90-165). Elsevier B.V.

Davies, D. R., Davies, J. H., Hassan, O., Morgan, K., & Nithiarasu, P. (2007). Adaptive finite element methods in geodynamics - Convection dominated mid-ocean ridge and subduction zone simulations. *International Journal of Numerical Methods for Heat & Fluid Flow, 18*(7/8), 1015–1035. doi:10.1108/09615530810899079

Davies, P. B. (2007). Models for e-government. *Transforming Government: People. Process and Policy, 1*(1), 7–28.

Dawes, S. S., & Pardo, T. (2002). Building collaborative digital government systems. In McIver, W. J., & Elmagarmid, A. K. (Eds.), *Advances in digital government technology, human factors and policy.* Norwell, MA: Kluwer Academic Publishers. doi:10.1007/0-306-47374-7_16

DBpedia: The DBpedia Knowledge Base. (2012). Retrieved January 1, 2012, from http://dbpedia.org/

de Berg, M., Cheong, O., van Kreveld, M., & Overmars, M. (2008). *Computational geometry: Algorithms and applications.* Germany: Springer.

Deelman, E., & Chervenak, A. (2008). Data management challenges of data-intensive scientific workflows. *2008 Eighth IEEE International Symposium on Cluster Computing and the Grid (CCGRID)*, (pp. 687-692). IEEE. doi:10.1109/CCGRID.2008.24

Deelman, E., Gannon, D., Shields, M., & Taylor, I. (2009). Workflows and e-science: An overview of workflow system features and capabilities. *Future Generation Computer Systems, 25*(5), 528-540. Elsevier B.V. doi:10.1016/j.future.2008.06.012

Deelman, E., Blythe, J., Gil, Y., Kesselman, C., Mehta, G., & Patil, S. (2004). Lecture Notes in Computer Science: *Vol. 3165. Pegasus: Mapping scientific workflows onto the grid* (pp. 131–140). doi:10.1007/978-3-540-28642-4_2

Degenring, A. (2005). Enterprise service bus. *JavaSPEKTRUM, 4*, 16-18. Retrieved February 10, 2012, from http://www.sigs-datacom.de/fachzeitschriften/javaspektrum/archiv/artikelansicht.html?tx_mwjournals_pi1[pointer]=0&tx_mwjournals_pi1[mode]=1&tx_mwjournals_pi1[showUid]=1612

Del.icio.us: A social bookmarking service. (2010). Retrieved November 22, 2010, from http://delicio.us

Deliverable, G. A. M. E. S. 7.4. (2011). *First GAMES trial results.* To appear on http://www.green-datacenters.eu

Demšar, U., & Virrantaus, K. (2010). Space-time density of trajectories: Exploring spatio-temporal patterns in movement data. *International Journal of Geographical Information Science, 24*(10), 1527–1542. doi:10.1080/13658816.2010.511223

Denning, D. E. R. (1982). *Cryptography and data security.* Addison-Wesley Publication.

Denning, P. J. (2007). Computing is a natural science. *Communications of the ACM, 50*(7), 13–18. doi:10.1145/1272516.1272529

Deschamps, F., Kaminski, E., & Tackley, P. J. (2011). A deep mantle origin for the primitive signature of ocean island basalt. *Nature Geoscience, 4*, 879–882. doi:10.1038/ngeo1295

Deschamps, F., & Sotin, C. (2000). Inversion of two-dimensional numerical convection experiments for a fluid with a strongly temperature-dependent viscosity. *Geophysical Journal International, 143*, 204–218. doi:10.1046/j.1365-246x.2000.00228.x

Deussen, O., Hanrahan, P., Lintermann, B., Měch, R., Pharr, M., & Prusinkiewicz, P. (1998). Realistic modeling and rendering of plant ecosystems. In *SIGGRAPH '98: Proceedings of the 25th Annual Conference on Computer Graphics and Interactive Techniques*, (pp. 275–286). New York, NY: ACM Press.

Deutsches Klimarechenzentrum (DKRZ). (2011). Data archive. Retrieved June 18, 2011, from http://www.dkrz.de/Klimarechner-en/datenarchiv

D-Grid. (2008). *The German Grid initiative.* Retrieved October 21, 2008, from http://www.d-grid.de

Di Gangi, P. M., & Wasko, M. (2009). The co-creation of value: Exploring user engagement in user-generated content websites. *Proceedings of JAIS Theory Development Workshop, Sprouts- Working Papers on Information Systems, 9*(50). Retrieved January 15, 2011, from http://sprouts.aisnet.org/9-50

Dijkstra, E. W. (1972). The humble programmer. *Communications of the ACM, 15*(10), 859–866. doi:10.1145/355604.361591

Dimitrakos, T., Golby, D., & Kearney, P. (2004). *Towards a trust and contract management framework for dynamic virtual organisations.* eAdoption and the Knowledge Econ- omy: eChallenges 2004. Retrieved February 10, 2012, from http://epubs.cclrc.ac.uk/bitstream/701/E2004-305-TRUSTCOM-OVERVIEW-FINAL[1].pdf

Dobbertin, H., Bosselaers, A., & Preneel, B. (1996). Ripemd-160: A strengthened version of RIPEMD. *Proceedings of the Third International Workshop on Fast Software Encryption, Lecture Notes in Computer Science, 1039,* (pp. 71-82). February 21-23, 1996, Cambridge, United Kingdom. ISBN: 3-540-60865-6

Dolan, B. (2010). *Number of smartphone health apps up 78 percent.* Retrieved August 3, 2011, from http://mobihealthnews.com/9396/number-of-smartphone-health-apps-up-78-percent/

Dong, B., Evans, K. R., & Zou, S. (2008). The effects of customer participation in co-created service recovery. *Journal of the Academy of Marketing Science, 36,* 123–137. doi:10.1007/s11747-007-0059-8

Dropbox. (n.d.). Retrieved March 2, 2012, from https://www.dropbox.com/

Dutta, S., & Mia, I. (2011). *Global information technology.* Geneva, Switzerland: World Economic Forum.

Dwivedi, Y. K., & Kuljis, J. (2008). Profile of IS research published in the European Journal of Information Systems. *European Journal of Information Systems, 17*(6), 678–693. doi:10.1057/ejis.2008.57

Dyke, J. G., Gans, F., & Kleidon, A. (2011). Towards understanding how surface life can affect interior geological processes: a non-equilibrium thermodynamics approach. *Earth System Dynamics, 2,* 139–160. doi:10.5194/esd-2-139-2011

Dziewonski, A. M., & Anderson, D. L. (1981). Preliminary reference Earth model. *Physics of the Earth and Planetary Interiors, 25,* 297–356. doi:10.1016/0031-9201(81)90046-7

Earnshaw, R. A., & Wiseman, N. (1992). *An introductory guide to scientific visualization.* Springer-Verlag. doi:10.1007/978-3-642-58101-4

Ebrahim, Z., & Irani, Z. (2005). E-government adoption: Architecture and barriers. *Business Management Process, 11*(5), 589–611. doi:10.1108/14637150510619902

Economic Intelligence Unit. (2009). *E-readiness ranking 2009. The usage imperative.* London, UK: Economic Intelligence Unit.

Edmiston, K. D. (2003). State and local e-government: Prospects and challenges. *American Review of Public Administration, 33,* 20–45. doi:10.1177/0275074002250255

Edwards, G. (1996). Geocognostics - A new paradigm for spatial information? *Proceedings of the AAAI Spring Symposium 1996.*

Egenhofer, M. (2002). Towards the geospatial Semantic Web. In A. Voisard & S. Chen (Eds.), *ACM International Symposium on Advances in Geographic Information Systems,* Vol. 1 (pp. 1-4). McLaen, VA: ACM Press.

Einav, G. (2010). *Transitioned media: A turning point into the digital realm.* Berlin, Germany: Springer-Verlag.

Eisenstadt, S. A., Wagner, M. M., Hogan, W. R., Pankaskie, M. C., Tsui, F. C., & Wilbright, W. (1998). Mobile workers in healthcare and their information needs: Are 2-way pagers the answer? *Proceedings of the AMIA Symposium,* (pp. 135–139).

Ekker, N., Coughlin, T., & Handy, J. (2009). *Solid stat storage 101: An introduction to solid state storage,* (p. 7). Storage Networking Industry Association (SNIA). Retrieved October 18, 2011, from https://members.snia.org/apps/group_public/download.php/35796/SSSI%20Wht%20Paper%20Final.pdf

Elkington, J. (1994). Towards the sustainable corporation: Win-win-win business strategies for sustainable development. *California Management Review, 36*(2), 90–100.

Elkins-Tanton, L. T., Burgess, S., & Yin, Q.-Z. (2011). The lunar magma ocean: Reconciling the solidification process with lunar petrology and geochronology. *Earth and Planetary Science Letters, 304*, 326–336. doi:10.1016/j. epsl.2011.02.004

Elkins-Tanton, L. T., Parmentier, E. M., & Hess, P. C. (2003). Magma ocean fractional crystallization and cumulate overturn in terrestrial planets: Implications for Mars. *Meteoritics & Planetary Science, 38*(13), 1753–1771. doi:10.1111/j.1945-5100.2003.tb00013.x

Elkins-Tanton, L. T., Zaranek, S. E., Parmentier, E. M., & Hess, P. C. (2005). Early magnetic field and magmatic activity on Mars form magma ocean cumulate overturn. *Earth and Planetary Science Letters, 236*, 1–12. doi:10.1016/j.epsl.2005.04.044

Ellaway, R. (2011). eMedical teacher. *Medical Teacher, 33*, 258–260. doi:10.3109/0142159X.2011.561696

Ellsworth, D., Chiang, L.-J., & Shen, H.-W. (2000). Accelerating time-varying hardware volume rendering using TSP trees and color-based error metrics. In *VolVis '00: Proceedings of the 2000 IEEE Symposium on Volume Visualization,* (pp. 119–128). New York, NY: ACM Press.

Elmasri, R., & Navather, S. B. (1989). *Fundamentals of database systems*. New York, NY: Benjamin Cummings Publishing Company Inc.

Elmroth, E., Galán, F., Henriksson, D., & Perales, D. (2009). Accounting and billing for federated cloud infrastructures. In J. E. Guerrero (Ed.), *Proceedings of the Eighth International Conference on Grid and Cooperative Computing* (GCC 2009), (pp. 268-275). IEEE Computer Society Press.

ELPRO. (n.d.). *Image*. Retrieved October 28th, 2011, from http://www.elpro.com

Elsen, E., LeGresley, P., & Darve, E. (2008). Large calculation of the)ow over a hypersonic vehicle using a GPU. *Journal of Computational Physics, 227*, 10148–10161. doi:10.1016/j.jcp.2008.08.023

Elwood, D., Diamond, M. C., Heckman, J., Bonder, J. H., Beltran, J. E., Moroz, A., & Yip, J. (2011). Mobile health: Exploring attitudes among physical medicine and rehabilitation physicians toward this emerging element of health delivery. *The American Academy of Physical Medicine and Rehabilitation, 3*, 678–680.

Engel, K., Kraus, M., & Ertl, T. (2001). High-quality pre-integrated volume rendering using hardware-accelerated pixel shading. In *HWWS '01: Proceedings of the ACM SIGGRAPH/EUROGRAPHICS Workshop on Graphics Hardware,* (pp. 9–16). New York, NY: ACM Press.

Erickson, T. (2010). *IDC prognostiziert 35 Zettabyte für das Jahr 2020*. SearchStorage.com. Retrieved October 18, 2011, from http://www.searchstorage.de/themenbereiche/management/daten/articles/262827/

Erl, T. (2005). *Service-oriented architecture: concepts, technology and design*. Upper Saddle River, NJ: Prentice Hall.

ETK - BMW Group. (2010). *Electronic parts catalogue. Database version: ETK 2.32*. Munich, Germany: BMW Group.

EUROCONTROL. (2010). *Call sign similarity project update*. Retrieved May 5, 2011, from www.eurocontrol.int

Europe's Information Society. (2011). *Radio Frequency IDentification and the Internet of Things*. Retrieved July 20, 2011, from http://ec.europa.eu/information_society/policy/rfid/index_en.htm

European Commission. (2010). *EU code of conduct for data centres*. Retrieved March 1, 2012, from http://re.jrc.ec.europa.eu/energyefficiency/html/standby_initiative_data_centers.htm

Evans, D., & Yen, D. C. (2006). E-government: Evolving relationship of citizens and government, domestic, and international development. *Government Information Quarterly, 23*(2), 207–235. doi:10.1016/j.giq.2005.11.004

Exascale Project. (2012). Retrieved March 25, 2012, from http://www.exascale.org.

Exascale Report. (2011). Retrieved November 27, 2011, from http://theexascalereport.com

Facebook: A social network service and website. (2011). Retrieved August 22, 2010, from http://www.facebook.com.

Faviki: Tags that make sense. (2009). Retrieved May 25, 2009, from http://www.faviki.com/pages/welcome/

Federal Geographic Data Committee. (2011). *National spatial data infrastructure.* Retrieved October 16, 2011, from http://www.fgdc.gov/nsdi/nsdi.html

Felten, E. W. (2003). Understanding trusted computing. *IEEE Security & Privacy, 1*(3), 60–66. doi:10.1109/MSECP.2003.1203224

Fensel, J. H. D., Lieberman, H., & Wahlster, W. (2005). *Spinning the Semantic Web: Bringing the World Wide Web to its full potential.* The MIT Press.

Ferraiolo, D. F., Sandhu, R., Gavrila, S., Kuhn, R. D., & Chandramouli, R. (2001). Proposed NIST standard for role-based access control. *ACM Transactions on Information and System Security, 4*(3), 224–274. doi:10.1145/501978.501980

Ferrini, R., & Bertino, E. (2009). Supporting RBAC with XACML+OWL. In *SACMAT 2009: Proceedings of the 14ᵗʰ ACM Symposium on Access Control Models and Technologies* (pp. 145-154). New York, NY: ACM.

Ferziger, J. H., & Peric, M. (1999). *Computational methods for fluid dynamics.* Germany: Springer. doi:10.1007/978-3-642-98037-4

Fielding, R. (2000). *Architectural styles and the design of network-based software architectures.* Dissertation, UC Irvine.

File System. (n.d.). In *Wikipedia.* Retrieved January 22, 2012, from http://en.wikipedia.org/wiki/File_system

Finin, T., Joshi, A., Kagal, L., Niu, J., Sandhu, R., Winsborough, W., & Thuraisingham, B. (2008). ROWLBAC: Representing role based access control in OWL. In *Proceedings of the 13ᵗʰ ACM Symposium on Access Control Models and Technologies* (pp. 73-82). New York, NY: ACM.

Fleisch, E., & Tellkamp, C. (2006). The business value of ubiquitous computing technologies. In Roussos, G. (Ed.), *Ubiquitous and pervasive commerce* (pp. 93–113). Springer. doi:10.1007/1-84628-321-3_6

Flickr: Share your photos — Watch the world. (2011). Retrieved May 16, 2010, from http://www.flickr.com/

Fogarty, J., Hudson, S. E., Atkeson, C. G., Avrahami, D., Forlizzi, J., & Kiesler, S. (2005). Predicting human interruptibility with sensors. *ACM Transactions on Computer-Human Interaction, 12*(1), 119–146. doi:10.1145/1057237.1057243

Fogarty, J., Lai, J., & Christensen, J. (2004). Presence versus availability: The design and evaluation of a context-aware communication client. *International Journal of Human-Computer Studies, 61*(3), 299–317. doi:10.1016/j.ijhcs.2003.12.016

Fornyings-, administrasjons- og kirkedepartementet. (2008). *Rammeverk for autentisering og uavviselighet i elektronisk kommunikasjon med og i offentlig sektor.* Retrieved July 25, 2011, from http://www.regjeringen.no/nb/dep/fad/dok/lover-og-regler/retningslinjer/2008/rammeverk-for-autentisering-og-uavviseli.html?id=505958

Forth Institute of Computer Science. (2011). *The RDF query language.* Retrieved October 16, 2011, from http://139.91.183.30:9090/RDF/RQL/

Fouque, P. A., Leurent, G., & Nguyen, P. Q. (2007). Full key recovery attacks on HMAC/NMAC-MD4 and NMAC-MD5. *Proceedings of the Twenty Seventh International Cryptology Conference, Lecture Notes in Computer Science, 4622,* August 19-23, 2007, Santa Barbara, California, United States of America, (pp. 13-30). ISBN: 978-3-540-74142-8

Foursquare: A location-based social networking website. (2010). Retrieved May 20, 2010, from http://www.foursquare.com

Fox, G. C., Johnson, M. A., Lyzenga, G. A., Otto, S. W., Salmon, J. K., & Walker, D. W. (1988). Solving problems on concurrent processors: *Vol. I. General techniques and regular problems.* Englewood Cliffs, NJ: Prentice Hall.

Fox, G. C., Williams, R. D., & Messina, P. C. (1994). *Parallel computing works!* Morgan Kaufmann Publishers, Inc.

Fraeman, A. A., & Korenaga, J. (2010). The influence of mantle melting on the evolution of Mars. *Icarus, 210,* 43–57. doi:10.1016/j.icarus.2010.06.030

Francis, M. (2010). *High performance storage user forum (HUF)*. UK Met Office, September 28, 2010, Hamburg, Germany.

Frank, L. (2003). Data cleaning for datawarehouses built on top of distributed databases with approximated ACID properties. *Proceedings of the International Conference on Computer Science and its Applications,* National University US Education Service, (pp. 160-164).

Frank, L. (2008). Smooth and flexible ERP migration between both homogeneous and heterogeneous ERP systems/ERP modules. *Proceedings of the 2nd Workshop on 3rd Generation Enterprise Resource Planning Systems,* Copenhagen business School.

Frank, L. (2011). Architecture for integrating heterogeneous distributed databases using supplier integrated e-commerce systems as an example. *Proceedings of the International Conference on Computer and Management (CAMAN 2011),* May, Wuhan, China.

Frank, L., & Munck, S. (2008). An overview of architectures for integrating distributed electronic health records. *Proceeding of the 7th International Conference on Applications and Principles of Information Science (APIS2008),* (pp. 297-300).

Frank-Kamenetskii, D. (1969). *Diffusion and heat transfer in chemical kinetics.* Plenum Press.

Frank, L. (2004). Architecture for integration of distributed ERP systems and e-commerce systems. [IMDS]. *Industrial Management & Data Systems, 104*(5), 418–429. doi:10.1108/02635570410537507

Frank, L. (2010). *Design of distributed integrated heterogeneous or mobile databases* (pp. 1–157). Germany: LAP LAMBERT Academic Publishing AG & Co. KG.

Frank, L. (2011). Architecture for ERP system integration with heterogeneous e-government modules. In Chhabra, S., & Kumar, M. (Eds.), *Strategic enterprise resource planning models for e-government: Applications & methodologies.* Hershey, PA: IGI Global. doi:10.4018/978-1-60960-863-7.ch007

Frank, L. (2011). *Countermeasures against consistency anomalies in distributed integrated databases with relaxed ACID properties. Proceeding of Innovations in Information Technology (Innovations 2011).* Abu Dhabi: UAE.

Frank, L., & Zahle, T. (1998). Semantic ACID properties in multidatabases using remote procedure calls and update propagations. *Software, Practice & Experience, 28,* 77–98. doi:10.1002/(SICI)1097-024X(199801)28:1<77::AID-SPE148>3.0.CO;2-R

Freebase: A large collaborative knowledge base. (2011). Retrieved May 5, 2009, from http://www.freebase.com

Freitas, R., Slember, J., Sawdon, W., & Chiu, L. (2011). *GPFS scans 10 billion files in 43 minutes.* IBM Advanced Storage Laboratory, IBM Almaden Research Center, San Jose, CA [PDF document]. Retrieved October 18, 2011, from http://www.almaden.ibm.com/storagesystems/resources/GPFS-Violin-white-paper.pdf

Fruchter, R., Reiner, K. A., Toye, G., & Leifer, L. J. (1996). Collaborative mechatronic system design. *Concurrent Engineering. Research and Applications, 4,* 401–412.

Gait, A. D., & Lowman, J. P. (2007). Effect of lower mantle viscosity on the time-dependence of plate velocities in three-dimensional mantle convection models. *Geophysical Research Letters, 34,* L21304. doi:10.1029/2007GL031396

Gallagher, R. H. (1975). *Element analysis: Fundamentals.* Prentice Hall.

Gamification. (2011). Wikipedia. Retrieved February 2, 2011, from http://en.wikipedia.org/wiki/Gamification.

Garcia-Molina, H., & Salem, K. (1987). Sagas. *ACM SIGMOD Conference,* (pp. 249-259).

Garcia-Molina, H., & Polyzois, C. (1990). *Issues in disaster recovery. IEEE Compcon* (pp. 573–577). New York, NY: IEEE.

Garrison, D. R., Anderson, T., & Archer, W. (2000). Critical inquiry in a text-based environment: Computer conferencing in higher education. *The Internet and Higher Education, 2*(2-3), 87–105. doi:10.1016/S1096-7516(00)00016-6

Geenen, T., ur Rehman, M., MacLachlan, S. P., Segal, G., Vuik, C., van den Berg, A. P., & Spakman, W. (2009). Scalable robust solvers for unstructured FE geodynamic modeling applications: Solving the Stokes equation for models with large localized viscosity contrasts. *Geochemistry Geophysics Geosystems, 10,* Q09002. doi:10.1029/2009GC002526

Gellman, R. (2009), Privacy in the Clouds: Risks to Privacy and Confidentiality from cloud Computing, Febuary 23, 2009. Retrieved March 2, 2012, from http://www.world-privacyforum.org/pdf/WPF_cloud_Priavacy_Report.pdf.

Gercke, M. (2007). *Internet-related identity theft*. Strasbourg, France: Economic Crime Division, Directorate of Human Rights and Legal Affairs, Council of Europe.

Gerecke, K. (2010). *IBM systems storage-Kompendium*. Mainz, Germany: IBM Deutschland GmbH.

Gerry, J. A., Hulen, H., Schaefer, P., & Coyne, B. (2009). *High performance storage system overview* [PDF document]. Retrieved from http://www.hpss-collaboration.org/documents/HPSSIntroduction2009.pdf

Gerya, T. (2010). Dynamical instability produces transform faults at mid-ocean ridges. *Science, 329*(5995), 1047–1050. doi:10.1126/science.1191349

Gerya, T. (2010). *Introduction to numerical geodynamic modelling*. Cambridge, UK: Cambridge University Press.

Gerya, T. V., & Yuen, D. A. (2003). Characteristics-based marker-in-cell method with conservative finite-differences schemes for modeling geological flows with strongly variable transport properties. *Physics of the Earth and Planetary Interiors, 140*, 293–318. doi:10.1016/j.pepi.2003.09.006

GEXI. (2012). *Geo exploration and information*. Retrieved January 29, 2012, from http://www.user.uni-hannover.de/cpr/x/rprojs/de/#gexi

Ghias, S. R., & Jarvis, G. T. (2007). Mantle flow reversals in cylindrical Earth models. *Physics of the Earth and Planetary Interiors, 165*(3-4), 194–207. doi:10.1016/j.pepi.2007.09.004

Giacomazzi, F., Panella, C., Pernici, B., & Sansoni, M. (1997). Information systems integration in mergers and acquisitions: A normative model. *Information & Management, 32*, 289–302. doi:10.1016/S0378-7206(97)00031-1

Gilmour, I., & Sephton, M. A. (Eds.). (2004). *An introduction to astrobiology*. Cambridge, UK: Cambridge University Press.

Glatzmaier, G. A., & Roberts, P. H. (1995). A three-dimensional self-consistent computer simulation of a geomagnetic field reversal. *Nature, 377*, 203–209. doi:10.1038/377203a0

Global Footprint Network. (2011). *Footprint basics – Overview*. Retrieved October 12, 2011, from http://www.footprintnetwork.org/en/index.php/GFn/page/footprint_basics_overview/

Global Spatial Data Infrastructure Association. (2011). *Global spatial data infrastructure*. Retrieved October 16, 2011, from http://www.gsdi.org/

Göhner, M., & Rückemann, C.-P. (2006). *Accounting-Ansätze im Bereich des Grid-Computing*. D-Grid Integration project, D-Grid document, 24 pp. Retrieved December 28, 2007, from http://www.d-grid.de/fileadmin/dgi_document/FG2/koordination_mab/mab_accounting_ansaetze.pdf

Göhner, M., & Rückemann, C.-P. (2006). *Konzeption eines Grid-Accounting-Systems*. D-Grid Integration project, D-Grid document, 45 pp. Retrieved December 28, 2007 from http://www.d-grid.de/fileadmin/dgi_document/FG2/koordination_mab/mab_accounting_system.pdf

Gold-Bernstein, B., & Ruh, W. A. (2005). *Enterprise integration: The essential guide to integration solutions*. Addison-Wesley.

Gold, C. M. (1989). Surface interpolation, spatial adjacency and G.I.S. In Raper, J. (Ed.), *Three dimensional applications in geographical information systems* (pp. 21–35). London, UK: Taylor and Francis.

Gollol Raju, N. S., Anthony, J. P., Jamadagni, R. S., Istepanian, R., Suri, J., & Laxminarayan, S. (2004). *Status of mobile computing in health care: An evidence study*. Paper presented at the 26th Annual International Conference of the IEEE Engineering in Medicine and Biology Society (IEMBS '04).

Goodchild, M. F. (1989). Modelling error in objects and fields. In Goodchild, M. F., & Gopal, S. (Eds.), *The accuracy of spatial databases*. London, UK: Taylor & Francis.

Google App Engine. (n.d.). Retrieved March 2, 2012, from http://appengine.google.com.

Google News. (2009). *Favorite passwords: '1234' and 'password'*. Retrieved December 20, 2009, from http://www.google.com/hostednews/afp/article/ALeqM-5jeUc6Bblnd0M19WVQWvjS6D2puvw

Görlach, K., Sonntag, M., Karastoyanova, D., Leymann, F., & Reiter, M. (2011). Conventional simulation workflow technology for scientific conventional workflow technology for scientific simulation. In X. Yang, L. Wang, & J. Lizhe (Ed.), *Guide to e-science* (pp. 0-31).

Gosain, S., Malhotra, A., & El Sawy, O. A. (2004). Coordinating for flexibility in e-business supply chains. [Armonk, NY: M. E. Sharpe, Inc.]. *Journal of Management Information Systems*, 21(3), 7–45.

Goyal, V., Pandey, O., Sahai, A., & Waters, B. (2006). Attribute-based encryption for fine-grained access control of encrypted data. In *CCS 2006: Proceedings of the 13th ACM Conference on Computer and Communications Security* (pp. 89–98). New York: ACM.

Graf, S., & Hommel, W. (2010). Organisationsübergreifendes Management von Föderations-Sicherheitsmetadaten auf Basis einer Service-Bus-Architektur. *Informationsmanagement in Hochschulen* (4th ed., pp. 233-246). Retrieved February 10, 2012, from http://dx.doi.org/10.1007/978-3-642-04720-6_20

Grama, A., Gupta, A., Karypis, G., & Kumar, V. (2003). *Introduction to parallel computing* (2nd ed.). New York, NY: Addison-Wesley.

Gray, J., & Reuter, A. (1993). *Transaction processing*. Morgan Kaufman, 1993.

Greif, I. (1988). *Computer-supported cooperative work: A book of readings*. San Mateo, CA: Morgan Kaufmann Publishers.

Griffith, D. A. (2010). Modeling spatio-temporal relationships: Retrospect and prospect. *Journal of Geographical Systems*, 12(2), 111–123. doi:10.1007/s10109-010-0120-x

Griffith, D. A., & Paelinck, J. H. P. (2009). Specifying a joint space- and time-lag using a bivariate Poisson distribution. *Journal of Geographical Systems*, 11(1), 23–36. doi:10.1007/s10109-008-0075-3

Grocholski, B., Shim, S.-H., & Prakapenka, V. B. (2010). Stability of the MgSiO3 analog NaMgF3 and its implication for mantle structure in super-Earths. *Geophysical Research Letters*, 37, L14204. doi:10.1029/2010GL043645

Grott, M., & Breuer, D. (2008). The evolution of the Martian elastic lithosphere and implications for crustal and mantle rheology. *Icarus*, 193, 503–515. doi:10.1016/j.icarus.2007.08.015

Grott, M., Morschhauser, A., Breuer, D., & Hauber, E. (2011). Volcanic outgassing of CO_2 and H_2O on Mars. *Earth and Planetary Science Letters*, 308(3-4), 391–400. doi:10.1016/j.epsl.2011.06.014

Grudin, J. (1994). Groupware and social dynamics: Eight challenges for developers. *Communications of the ACM*, 37(1), 92–105. doi:10.1145/175222.175230

gSOAP. (2012). Retrieved February 10, 2012, from http://www.cs.fsu.edu/~engelen/soap.html

Guarino, N. (1995). Formal ontology, conceptual analysis and knowledge representation. *International Journal of Human-Computer Studies*, 43(5), 625–640. doi:10.1006/ijhc.1995.1066

Gulliksen, J., Goransson, B., Boivie, I., Persson, J., Blomkvist, S., & Cajander, A. (2005). Key principles for user-centred systems design. In Seffah, A., Gulliksen, J., & Desmarais, M. C. (Eds.), *Human-centred software engineering - Integrating usability in the software development lifecycle* (pp. 17–37). Berlin, Germany: Springer-Verlag. doi:10.1007/1-4020-4113-6_2

Günther, W., & ten Hompel, M. (2010). *Internet der Dinge in der Intralogistik*. Berlin, Germany: Springer-Verlag. doi:10.1007/978-3-642-04896-8

Hafner, M., & Breu, R. (2009). *Security engineering for service-oriented architectures*. Berlin, Germany: Springer-Verlag.

Hagalisletto, A., & Riiber, A. (2007) *Using the mobile phone in two-factor authentication. UbiComp 2007 Workshop Proceedings.*

Hague, M. J., & Taleb-Bendiab, A. (1998). Tool for management of concurrent conceptual engineering design. *Concurrent Engineering. Research and Applications*, 6, 111–129.

Ha, H. (2011). Security and privacy in e-consumer protection in Victoria, Australia. In Wakeman, I. (Eds.), *IFIPTM 2011, IFIP AICT 358* (pp. 240–252). Berlin, Germany: Springer-Verlag. doi:10.1007/978-3-642-22200-9_19

Ha, H., & Coghill, K. (2006). E-government in Singapore: A SWOT and PEST analysis. [APSSR]. *Asia-Pacific Social Science Review, 6*(2), 103–130.

Haleblian, J., Devers, C., Mcnamara, G., Carpenter, M., & Davison, R. (2009). Taking stock of what we know about mergers and acquisitions: A review and research agenda. *Journal of Management, 35*(3), 469. doi:10.1177/0149206308330554

Halpin, H., & Presutti, V. (2009). *An ontology of resources for linked data.* LDOW 2009. Madrid, Spain. ACM. 978-1-60558-487-4/09/04

Hanschke, I. (2010). *Strategic IT management: A toolkit for enterprise architecture management.* Berlin, Germany: Springer-Verlag.

Harder, H., & Hansen, U. (2005). A finite-volume solution method for thermal convection and dynamo problems in spherical shells. *Geophysical Journal International, 161*, 522–532. doi:10.1111/j.1365-246X.2005.02560.x

Hardisty, F., & Klippel, A. (2010). Analysing spatio-temporal autocorrelation with LISTA-Viz. [Article]. *International Journal of Geographical Information Science, 24*(10), 1515–1526. doi:10.1080/13658816.2010.511717

Harmer, C., & Bandulet, C. (2011). *The file system evolution,* (p. 3). [PDF document]. Retrieved January 22, 2012, from http://www.snia.org/sites/default/education/tutorials/2011/fall/FileSystemsManagement/CraigHarmer_File_Systems_Evolution_v1-3.pdf

Harrell, H., & Higgins, L. (2002). IS integration: Your most critical m&a challenge? *Journal of Corporate Accounting & Finance, 13*(2), 23–31. doi:10.1002/jcaf.1220

Hatzes, A. P. (2011). The mass of CoRoT-7b. *The Astrophysical Journal, 743*(1), 75–86. doi:10.1088/0004-637X/743/1/75

Healy, A. (2009). Communities of practice as a support function for social learning in distance learning programs. In Lytras, M. D., Ordonez de Pablos, P., Damiani, E., Avison, D., Naeve, A., & Horner, D. G. (Eds.), *Best practices for the knowledge society knowledge, learning, development and technology for all* (pp. 49–56). Berlin, Germany: Springer-Verlag. doi:10.1007/978-3-642-04757-2_6

Heart, T., & Kalderon, E. (2011). Older adults: Are they ready to adopt health-related ICT? *International Journal of Medical Informatics, 8*, 8.

Heeks, R. (2001). *Understanding e-governance for development*, Working Papers Series, No. 12/2001. Manchester, UK: Institute for Development, Policy and Management Information Systems, Technology and Government, University of Manchester.

Heeks, R. (2005). E-government as a career of context. *Journal of Public Policy, 25*, 51–74. doi:10.1017/S0143814X05000206

Hellman, M. E. (1980). A cryptanalytic time-memory trade-off. *IEEE Transactions on Information Theory, IT-26*(4), 401-406. ISSN: 0018-9448

Helse- og omsorgsdepartementet. (2008). *Samspill 2.0 Nasjonal strategi for elektronisk samhandling i helse- og omsorgssektoren 2008 – 2013*. Retrieved August 3, 2011, from http://www.helsedirektoratet.no/samspill/publikasjoner/samspill_2_0__nasjonal_strategi_for_elektronisk_samhandling_i_helse__og_omsorgssektoren_2008___2013_744694

Henningsson, S., Svensson, C., & Wallén, L. (2007). *Mastering the integration chaos following frequent m&as: Is integration with SOA technology*. In 40th Hawaii International Conference on System Science Waikoloa, Hawaii, US.

Hermana, B., & Sulfianti, W. (2011). Evaluating e-government implementation by local government: Digital divide in Internet-based public services in Indonesia. *International Journal of Business and Social Sciences, 2*(30), 156–163.

Hernlund, J. W., & Tackley, P. (2008). Modeling mantle convection in the spherical annulus. *Physics of the Earth and Planetary Interiors, 171,* 48–54. doi:10.1016/j.pepi.2008.07.037

Hersh, W., Helfand, M., Wallace, J., Kraemer, D., Patterson, P., & Shapiro, S. (2002). A systematic review of the efficacy of telemedicine for making diagnostic and management decisions. *Journal of Telemedicine and Telecare, 8*(4), 197–209. doi:10.1258/135763302320272167

Hevner, A., March, S., Park, J., & Ram, S. (2004). Design science in information systems research. *Management Information Systems Quarterly, 28*(1). IBM_Press_Room. (2009). *IBM research aims to build nanoscale DNA sequencer to help drive down cost of personalized genetic analysis.* Retrieved October 6th, 2009, from http://www-304.ibm.com/jct03001c/press/us/en/pressrelease/28558.wss, IBMSocialMedia, retrieved from IBM DNA Transistor at http://youtube.com

Hiegl, M. (April 23, 2010). *Sun/Oracle bereitet das Ende von Lustre vor* [Blog]. Retrieved January 22, 2012, from https://www-304.ibm.com/connections/blogs/Martin_Hiegl/tags/gpfs?lang=en_us

Hiegl, M. (May 5, 2009). *IBM general parallel file system.* Blog. Retrieved January 22, 2012, from https://www-304.ibm.com/connections/blogs/Martin_Hiegl/tags/gpfs?lang=en_us

Hirth, G., & Kohlstedt, D. L. (2003). Rheology of the upper mantle and the mantle wedge: A view from the experimentalists. In Eiler, J. (Ed.), *Inside the subduction factory* (pp. 83–105). doi:10.1029/138GM06

HLRN. (2012). *The North-German Supercomputing Alliance.* Retrieved January 29, 2012, from http://www.hlrn.de

Hochberger, C., Waldschmidt, K., & Ungerer, T. (2008). *Grand challenge 6: HW -, SW-Architekturen und Werkzeuge für Multi-Core- und Many-Core-Prozessoren* (p. 41). Grand Challenges der Technischen Informatik.

Hoffmann, C. M., & Joan-Arinyo, R. (2005). *A brief on constraint solving.* West Lafayette, IN: Purdue University.

Hohpe, G., & Woolf, B. (2004). *Enterprise integration patterns.* Addison-Wesley.

Holland, M. M., & Bitz, C. M. (2003). Polar amplification of climate change in the coupled model intercomparison project. *Climate Dynamics, 21,* 221–232. doi:10.1007/s00382-003-0332-6

Holleran, K., Pappas, J., Lou, H., Rubalcaba, P., Lee, R., Clay, S., et al. (2003). Mobile technology in a clinical setting. *AMIA Annual Symposium Proceedings, 2003.*

Hoogervorst, J. P. (2009). *Enterprise governance and enterprise engineering.* Berlin, Germany: Springer-Verlag. doi:10.1007/978-3-540-92671-9

Horn, B. K. P., & Schunk, B. G. (1981). Determining optical flow. *Artificial Intelligence, 17,* 185–203. doi:10.1016/0004-3702(81)90024-2

Hornsby, K., & Egenhofer, M. (2002). Modeling moving objects over multiple granularities. *Annals of Mathematics and Artificial Intelligence, 36*(1-2), 177–194. doi:10.1023/A:1015812206586

Horvitz, E., & Apacible, J. (2003). *Learning and reasoning about interruption.* Paper presented at the 5th International Conference on Multimodal Interfaces, Vancouver, British Columbia, Canada.

Horvitz, E., Koch, P., Kadie, C. M., & Jacobs, A. (2002). *Coordinate: Probabilistic forecasting of presence and availability.* Paper presented at the 18th Conference in Uncertainty in Artificial Intelligence (UAI'02).

Hoshino, T., Hiromoto, R., Sekiguchi, S., & Majima, S. (1989). Mapping schemes of the particle-in-cell method implemented on the PAX computer. *Parallel Computing, 9*(1), 53–75. doi:10.1016/0167-8191(88)90018-X

Hotham, P. (2011). *SESAR & NextGen working together for aviation interoperability.* Presentation to the Royal Aeronautical Society Annual Conference, London, April 14th 2011; Retrieved October 5, 2011, http://www.sesarju.eu/news-press/news/sesar-ju-royal-aeronautical-society-annual-conference-815

HPSS Collaboration. org, (2010). *What is high performance storage system?* Retrieved June 18, 2011, from http://www.hpsscollaboration.org/index.shtml

Hristova, A. (2008). *Conceptualization and design of a context-aware platform for user centric applications.* Master of Science in Communication Technology Master. Trondheim: Norwegian University of Science and Technology.

http://science.energy.gov/~/media/ascr/ascac/pdf/reports/Exascale_subcommittee_report.pdf.

Huang, K., Li, X., Cao, S., Yang, B., & Pan, W. (2001). Co-DARFAD: The collaborative mechanical product design system. *Proceedings of the 6th International Conference on Computer Supported Cooperative Work In Design,* (pp. 163-168).

Huang, G. Q., Lee, S. W., & Mak, K. L. (1999). Web-based product and process data modelling in concurrent 'Design for X'. *Robotics and Computer-integrated Manufacturing, 15,* 53–63. doi:10.1016/S0736-5845(98)00028-3

Huang, G. Q., & Mak, K. L. (1999). Web-based morphological charts for concept design in collaborative product development. *Journal of Intelligent Manufacturing, 10,* 267–278. doi:10.1023/A:1008999908120

Huang, G. Q., & Mak, K. L. (1999). Design For manufacture and assembly on the internet. *Computers in Industry, 38,* 17–30. doi:10.1016/S0166-3615(98)00105-5

Hughes, T. J. R. (2000). *The finite element method: Linear static and dynamic finite element analysis.* Dover.

Hugoson, M. A., Magoulas, T., & Pess, K. (2008). Interoperability strategies for business agility, advances. In Dietz, J. L. G., Albami, A., & Barjis, J. (Eds.), *Enterprise Engineering I* (pp. 108–122). Berlin, Germany: Springer-Verlag. doi:10.1007/978-3-540-68644-6_8

Huizinga, J. (1971). *Homo ludens: A study of the play-element in culture.* Beacon Press.

Hulen, H. (n.d.). *Basics of the high performance storage system* [PDF document]. Retrieved June 18, 2011, from http://www.isi.edu/~annc/classes/grid/papers/HPSS-Basics.pdf

Hulen, H., & Jaquette, G. (2011). *Operational concepts and methods for using RAIT in high availability tape archives* [PDF document]. Retrieved June 8, 2011, from http://www.storageconference.org/2011/Papers/MSST.Hulen.pdf

Hummel, K. E., & Brooks, S. L. (1986). Symbolic representation of manufacturing features for an automated process planning system. In Lu, S., & Komanduri, R. (Eds.), *Knowledge-based expert systems for manufacturing* (pp. 233–243). ASME.

Hüttig, C. (2009). *Scaling laws for internally heated mantle convection.* Doctoral dissertation, University of Münster, Germany.

Hüttig, C., & Breuer, D. (2011). Regime classification and planform scaling for internally heated mantle convection. *Physics of the Earth and Planetary Interiors, 186*(3-4), 111–124. doi:10.1016/j.pepi.2011.03.011

Hüttig, C., & Stemmer, K. (2008). The spiral grid: A new approach to discretize the sphere and its application to mantle convection. *Geochemistry Geophysics Geosystems, 9*(2), Q02018. doi:10.1029/2007GC001581

Hüttig, C., & Stemmer, K. (2008). Finite volume discretization for dynamic viscosities on Voronoi grids. *Physics of the Earth and Planetary Interiors, 171*(1-4), 137–146. doi:10.1016/j.pepi.2008.07.007

Hwang, G. J., & Chang, H. F. (2011). A formative assessment-based mobile learning approach to improving the learning attitudes and achievements of students. *Computers & Education, 56*(1), 1023–1031. doi:10.1016/j.compedu.2010.12.002

Hwang, G. J., & Tsai, C. C. (2011). Research trends in mobile and ubiquitous learning: A review of publications in selected journals from 2001 to 2010. *British Journal of Educational Technology, 42*(4), 65–70. doi:10.1111/j.1467-8535.2011.01183.x

IBM Dictionary of Computing. (2008). *IBM terminology.* Retrieved January 20, 2011, from http://www-01.ibm.com/ software/globalization/terminology/d.html

IBM System Storage DS8000 series. (2011). Retrieved October 16, 2011, from http://www-03.ibm.com/systems/storage/disk/ds8000/overview.html

IBM Systems and Technology. (2010). *Optimize storage capacity with IBM Real-time compression* [PDF document]. Retrieved June 18, 2011, from ftp://public.dhe.ibm.com/common/ssi/ecm/en/tsb03020usen/TS-B03020USEN.PDF

IDC. (2011). *IDC predictions 2011: Welcome to the new mainstream.* Retrieved October 20, 2011 from http://www.idc.com/research/viewdocsynopsis.jsp?containerId=225878

Inden, U., & Franken, F. (2011). *Final report: CES-SAR – Configuration and evaluation of service systems with RFID.* Gefördert durch das Bundesministerium für Wirtschaft und Technologie (BMWi) Project Number: MT06005) – Cologne Business Working Paper – Publication Series of the Faculty of Economics and Business Administration, Cologne University of Applied Sciences, (in publication) ISSN-Print 2192-7944, ISSN-Internet 2192-7944

Inden, U., Tieck, S., & Rückemann, C.-P. (2011). Rotation-oriented collaborative air traffic management. In C.-P. Rückemann, W. Christmann, S. Saini, & M. Pankowska, (Eds.), *Proceedings of The First International Conference on Advanced Communications and Computation (INFOCOMP 2011)*, October 23-29, 2011, Barcelona, Spain, (pp. 25-30). ISBN: 978-1-61208-161-8

Infocomm Development Authority of Singapore. (2002). Equipping public officers for an e-government through ICT education. *eGovernment, 6*(2002), 1-2.

Infocomm Development Authority of Singapore. (2006). *Singapore: A world class e-government.* Singapore: Infocomm Development Authority of Singapore.

Infocomm Development Authority of Singapore. (2010). *Realising the iN2015 Vision. Singapore: An intelligent nation, a global city, powered by Infocomm.* Singapore: Infocomm Development Authority of Singapore.

Infocomm Development Authority of Singapore. (2011). *Annual survey on infocomm usage in householders for 2010.* Singapore: Infocomm Development Authority of Singapore.

Infocomm Development Authority of Singapore. (2011). *Singapore egov: Connecting people – Enriching lives.* Singapore: Infocomm Development Authority of Singapore.

Infocomm Development Authority of Singapore. (n.d.). *Singapore's e-Government journey.* Singapore. *Infocomm Development Authority of Singapore.*

Infraestrutura Nacional de Dados Espaciais. (2011). *Infraestrutura nacional de dados espaciais.* Retrieved October 16, 2011, from: http://www.inde.gov.br/

Inspector Colombo. (1962-2011). Retrieved October 12, 2011 from http://www.famous-detectives.com/inspector-columbo.htm

Interaction design. (2010). Wikipedia. Retrieved October 5, 2010, from http://en.wikipedia.org/wiki/Interaction_design#Interaction_design_domains

International Organization for Standardization / International Electrotechnical Commission – ISO/IEC (2009). *Information technology – Trusted platform module – Part 1: Overview.* International Standard, Reference number ISO/IEC 11889-1:2009(E).

International Organization for Standardization. (2003). *Geographic information – Metadata.* Technical Committee 211. Retrieved October 16, 2011, from http://www.iso.org/iso/catalogue_detail.htm?csnumber=26020

International Organization for Standardization. (2007). *Geographic information: Metadata and XML schema implementation.* Technical Committee 211. Retrieved October 16, 2011, from http://www.iso.org/iso/catalogue_detail.htm?csnumber=32557

International Organization for Standardization. (2011). *International Organization for Standardization.* Retrieved October 16, 2011, from http://www.iso.org/

International Standard Organization (ISO). (1992). *Industrial automation system and integration – Product data representation and exchange. Technical Report.* Geneva, Switzerland: ISO Central Secretariat.

International Telecommunication Union. (2010). *The international public telecommunication numbering plan.* Retrieved July 19, 2011, from http://www.itu.int/rec/T-REC-E.164/en

Internet World Stats. (2010). Retrieved April 10, 2009, from http://www.internetworldstats.com

Irani, S., Sandeep, S., & Gupta, R. (2003). Strategies for dynamic power management in systems with multiple power-saving states. *ACM Transactions on Embedded Computing Systems, 2*(3), 325–346. doi:10.1145/860176.860180

Ishi, H., Paradiso, J., & Picard, R. (2010). *TTT vision statement.* MIT Media Lab. Retrieved February 29, 2012, from http://ttt.media.mit.edu/vision/vision.html

Ishii, M., & Tromp, J. (2004). Constraining large-scale mantle heterogeneity using mantle and inner-core sensitive normal modes. *Physics of the Earth and Planetary Interiors, 146,* 113–124. doi:10.1016/j.pepi.2003.06.012

Ismail-Zadeh, A., & Tackley, P. J. (2010). *Computational methods for geodynamics.* Cambridge, UK: Cambridge University Press. doi:10.1017/CBO9780511780820

ISO 13407. (1999). *Human-centred design processes for interactive systems.* Retrieved February 12, 2012, from http://www.iso.org/iso/catalogue_detail.htm?csnumber=21197

ISO 9241-11. (1998). *Ergonomic requirements for office work with visual display terminals (VDTs) - Part 11: Guidance on usability.* Retrieved February 12, 2012, from http://www.iso.org/iso/cataloque_detail.htm?csnumber=16883

Ito, I., & Toriumi, M. (2010). Silicon self-diffusion of MgSiO3 perovskite by molecular dynamics and its implication for lower mantle rheology. *Journal of Geophysical Research, 115,* B12205. doi:10.1029/2010JB000843

Jacobson, V., Smetters, D. K., Thornton, J. D., Plass, M. F., Briggs, N. H., & Braynard, R. L. (2009). Networking named content. In *CoNEXT 2009: Proceedings of the 5th International Conference on Emerging Networking Experiments and Technologies* (pp. 1-12). New York, NY: ACM.

Jagannathan, V., Almasi, G., & Suvaiala, A. (1996). Collaborative infrastructures using the WWW and CORBA-based environments. *Proceedings of the IEEE Workshops on Enabling Technologies Infrastructure for Collaborative Enterprises* (*WET ICE'96*), (pp. 292-297).

Jagannathan, V., Dodhiawala, R., & Baum, L. S. (1989). *Blackboard architectures and applications.* San Diego, CA: Academic Press.

Jähnert, J., Mandic, P., Cuevas, A., Wesner, S., Moreno, J. I., & Villagra, V. (2010). A prototype and demonstrator of Akogrimo's architecture: An approach of merging grids, SOA, and the mobile Internet. *Computer Communications, 33*(11), 1304–1317. doi:10.1016/j.comcom.2010.03.003

Janowicz, K., Wilkes, M., & Lutz, M. (2008) Similarity-based information retrieval and its role within spatial data infrastructures. In T. J. Cova, J. J. Miller, K. Beard, A. U. Frank, M. F. Goodchild (Eds.), *Fifth International Conference on Geographic Information Science, Lecture Notes in Computer Science 5266* (pp. 151-167). Berlin, Germany: Springer.

Janowicz, K. (2006). Sim-DL towards a semantic similarity measurement theory for the description logic ALCNR in geographic information retrieval. In Meersman, R., Tari, Z., & Herrero, P. (Eds.), *On the Move to Meaningful Internet Systems: OTM 2006* (*Vol. 4278,* pp. 1681–1692). Lecture Notes in Computer ScienceBerlin, Germany: Springer. doi:10.1007/11915072_74

Jansen, W., & Grance, T. (2011). *Guidelines on security and privacy in public cloud computing.* Director, 144, 800–144, NIST. Retrieved March 2, 2012, from http://www.securityvibes.com/servlet/JiveServlet/downloadBody/1322-102-1-1327/Draft-SP-800-144_cloud-computing.pdf

Jawahitha, S. (2004). Consumer protection in e-commerce: Analyzing the statutes in Malaysia. *Journal of American Academy of Business, 4*(1/2), 55.

Jeneson, A., Andersen, T., & Ruland, C. M. (2007). *Comparing messages in an online communication forum for cancer patients with patients' messages to a clinical nurse specialist.* Paper presented at the Medinfo 2007 Congress, Brisbane.

Jensen, M., Schwenk, J., Gruschka, N., & Iacono, L. L. (2009). On technical security issues in cloud computing. *2009 IEEE International Conference on Cloud Computing,* (pp. 109-116). IEEE. Retrieved March 2, 2012, from http://ieeexplore.ieee.org/lpdocs/epic03/wrapper.htm?arnumber=5284165

Jiang, T., Kipp, A., et al. (2010). *Layered green performance indicators definition.* GAMES Deliverable 2.1 [DAMES D2.1]. Retrieved March 1, 2012, from http://www.green-datacenters.eu

John the Ripper. (2012). *Password cracker.* Retrieved February 15, 2012, from http://www.openwall.com

Johnson, C. R., & Weinstein, D. M. (2006). Biomedical computing and visualization. In *Proceedings of the 29th Australasian Computer Science Conference (ACSC 2006)*, (Vol. 48, pp. 3-10). Hobart, Australia.

Joint Centre Research. (2010). *Infrastructure for spatial information in the European community*. Retrieved October 16, 2011, from http://inspire.jrc.ec.europa.eu/

Jones, L. A., Anton, A. I., & Earp, J. B. (2007). *Towards understanding user perceptions of authentication technologies*. Paper presented at the 2007 ACM Workshop on Privacy in Electronic Society.

Joshi, J. B. D., Shafiq, B., Ghafoor, A., & Bertino, E. (2003). Dependencies and separation of duty constraints in GTRBAC. In *Proceedings of the Eighth ACM Symposium on Access Control Models and Technologies (SACMAT '03)* (pp. 51-64). New York, NY: ACM.

JSON (JavaScript Object Notation). (2010). Retrieved October 5, 2010, from http://www.json.org/

Kageyama, A., & Sato, T. (2004). The "Yin-Yang grid": An overset grid in spherical geometry. *Geochemistry Geophysics Geosystems, 5*, Q09005. doi:10.1029/2004GC000734

Kailas, A., Chia-Chin, C., & Watanabe, F. (2010). From mobile phones to personal wellness dashboards. *Pulse, IEEE, 1*(1), 57–63. doi:10.1109/MPUL.2010.937244

Kameyama, M., Kageyama, A., & Sato, T. (2008). Multigrid-based simulation code for mantle convection in spherical shell using Yin-Yang grid. *Physics of the Earth and Planetary Interiors, 171*, 19–32. doi:10.1016/j.pepi.2008.06.025

Kannoju, P. K., Sridhar, K. V., & Prasad, K. S. R. (2010). *A new paradigm of electronic health record for efficient implementation of healthcare delivery*. Paper presented at the 2010 IEEE EMBS Conference on Biomedical Engineering and Sciences (IECBES).

Karato, S.-I. (2008). *Deformation of Earth materials: An introduction to the rheology of solid earth*. Cambridge, UK: Cambridge University Press. doi:10.1017/CBO9780511804892

Karato, S.-I. (2011). Rheological structure of the mantle of a super-Earth: Some insights from mineral physics. *Icarus, 212*(1), 14–23. doi:10.1016/j.icarus.2010.12.005

Karato, S.-I., & Wu, P. (1993). Rheology of the upper mantle: A synthesis. *Science, 260*, 771–778. doi:10.1126/science.260.5109.771

Karlin, A. R., Manasse, M. S., McGeoch, L. A., & Owicki, S. S. (1994). Competitive randomized algorithms for nonuniform problems. *Algorithmica, 11*, 542–571. doi:10.1007/BF01189993

Katz, M. H., & Schroeder, S. A. (1988). The sounds of the hospital. Paging patterns in three teaching hospitals. *The New England Journal of Medicine, 319*(24), 1585–1589. doi:10.1056/NEJM198812153192406

Kauffman, S. (1995). *At home in the universe: The search for the laws of self-organization and complexity*. Oxford, UK: Oxford University Press.

Kaus, B. J. P., Steedman, C., & Becker, T. W. (2008). From passive continental margin to mountain belt: Insights from analytical and numerical models and application to Taiwan. *Physics of the Earth and Planetary Interiors, 171*, 235–251. doi:10.1016/j.pepi.2008.06.015

Kawai, K., & Tsuchiya, T. (2009). Temperature profile in the lowermost mantle from seismological and mineral physics joint modeling. *Proceedings of the National Academy of Sciences of the United States of America, 106*(52), 22119–22123. doi:10.1073/pnas.0905920106

Keegan, D. (2002). *The future of learning: From eLearning to mLearning*. Retrieved October 20, 2011 from http://learning.ericsson.net/mlearning2/project_one/book.html

Keller, T., & Tackley, P. J. (2009). Towards self-consistent modelling of the Martian dichotomy: The influence of low-degree convection on crustal thickness distribution. *Icarus, 202*(2), 429–443. doi:10.1016/j.icarus.2009.03.029

Kemptner, H.-P. (2007). *Storage Architekturen – Datenmanagement im Mittelpunkt*, V3, (Unpublished). IBM Deutschland GmbH, Mainz.

Kephard, J. O., & Chess, D. M. (2003). The vision of autonomic computing. *IEEE Computer, 36*(1), 41–50. doi:10.1109/MC.2003.1160055

Kettle, D. F. (2002). *The transformation of governance: Public administration for twenty-first century America*. John Hopkins University Press.

Khalaf, R. (2007). *Note on syntactic details of split BPEL-D Business Processes Institut für Architektur von Anwendungssystemen, Elektrotechnik Und Informationstechnik* (p. 13). Stuttgart. Retrieved February 10, 2012, from http://elib.uni-stuttgart.de/opus/volltexte/2007/3230/index.html

Khalil, A., & Connelly, K. (2005). Improving cell phone awareness by using calendar information. *Human-Computer Interaction - INTERACT 2005* (pp. 588-600).

Khalil, A., & Connelly, K. (2006). *Context-aware telephony: Privacy preferences and sharing patterns.* Paper presented at the CSCW'06, Banff, Alberta, Canada.

Khurana, H., Hadley, M., Lu, N., & Frincke, D. A. (2010). Smart-Grid security issues. *IEEE Security & Privacy*, *8*(1), 81–85. doi:10.1109/MSP.2010.49

Kidd, A. G., Sharratt, C., & Coleman, J. (2004). Mobile communication regulations updated: How safely are doctors' telephones used? *Quality & Safety in Health Care*, *13*(6), 478. doi:10.1136/qhc.13.6.478

Kim, A. J. (2010). *Putting the fun in functional - Applying game mechanics to social media.* Retrieved October 10, 2010, from http://www.slideshare.net/amyjokim/fun-in-functional-2009-presentation

Kim, Y., Kelly, T., & Raja, S. (2010). *Building broadband: Strategies and policy for the developing world.* Washington, DC: Global Information and Communication Technologies (GICT) Department, World Bank.

King, S. D. (2008). Pattern of lobate scarps on Mercury's surface reproduced by a model of mantle convection. *Nature Geoscience*, *1*, 229–232. doi:10.1038/ngeo152

King, S. D., Lee, C., van Keken, P. E., Leng, W., Zhong, S., & Tan, E. (2010). A community benchmark for 2D Cartesian compressible convection in the Earth's mantle. *Geophysical Journal International*, *180*(1), 73–87. doi:10.1111/j.1365-246X.2009.04413.x

King, S. D., & Masters, G. (1992). An inversion for radial viscosity structure using seismic tomography. *Geophysical Research Letters*, *19*(15), 1551–1554. doi:10.1029/92GL01700

King, S. D., Raefsky, A., & Hager, B. H. (1990). Conman: Vectorizing a finite element code for incompressible two-dimensional convection in the Earth's mantle. *Physics of the Earth and Planetary Interiors*, *59*(3), 195–207. doi:10.1016/0031-9201(90)90225-M

King, W. R., & He, J. (2006). A meta-analysis of the technology acceptance model. *Information & Management*, *43*(6), 740–755. doi:10.1016/j.im.2006.05.003

Kipp, A., & Schubert, L. (2011). eBusiness interoperability and collaboration. In E. Kajan (Ed.), *Electronic business interoperability: Concepts, opportunities, and challenges* (pp. 153-184). Hershey, PA: IGI Global. doi:10.4018/978-1-60960-485-1

Kipp, A., Schubert, L., & Geuer-Pollmann, C. (2009). Dynamic service encapsulation. *Proceedings of the First International Conference on Cloud Computing* (pp. 217-230). Munich. doi:10.1007/978-3-642-12636-9_15

Kipp, A., Schubert, L., Liu, J., et al. (2011). Energy consumption optimisation in HPC service centres. *Proceedings of the Second International Conference on Parallel, Distributed, Grid and Cloud Computing for Engineering*, Ajaccio, Corsica, France, (pp. 1-16). Retrieved March 1, 2012, from http://www.ctresources.info/ccp/paper.html?id=6281

Kipp, A., Jiang, T., Liu, J., Fugini, M., Anghel, I., & Cioara, T. (2012 in press). Energy-aware provisioning of HPC services with virtualised web services. In Khan, S. U., & Kolodziej, J. (Eds.), *Evolutionary based solutions for green computing.* Berlin, Germany: Springer Verlag.

Kitware. (2012). *ParaView open-source code.* Retrieved January 31, 2012, from http://www.paraview.org

Kleiboer, A., Gowing, K., Holm Hansen, C., Hibberd, C., Hodges, L., & Walker, J. (2010). Monitoring symptoms at home: What methods would cancer patients be comfortable using? *Quality of Life Research*, *19*(7), 965–968. doi:10.1007/s11136-010-9662-0

Kleinz, T. (2009). Nature: Wikipedia nahe an Encyclopaedia Britannica. *Heise Online News*. Retrieved July 20, 2009, from http://www.heise.de/newsticker/meldung/Nature-Wikipedia-nahe-an-Encyclopaedia-Britannica-158194.html

Klen, E. R. (2009). Co-creation and co-innovation in collaborative networked environment. In Camarinha-Matos, L. M., Paraskakis, I., & Afsarmanesh, H. (Eds.), *Leveraging knowledge for innovation in collaborative networks* (pp. 33–42). Berlin, Germany: Springer-Verlag. doi:10.1007/978-3-642-04568-4_4

Klien, E., Lutz, M., & Kuhn, W. (2006). Ontology-based discovery of geographic information services - An application in disaster management. *Computers, Environment and Urban Systems*, *30*(1), 102–123. doi:10.1016/j.compenvurbsys.2005.04.002

Knaf, H. (2011). *EMERGENT*. Retrieved September 22, 2011, from http://www.itwm.fraunhofer.de/en/departments/system-analysis-prognosis-and-control/decision-support-in-the-medical-sciences-and-in-technology/emergent.html

Koestler, A. (1967). *The ghost in the machine*. New York, NY: Macmillan.

Koh, C. E., Ryan, S., & Prybutok, V. R. (2005). Creating value through managing knowledge in an e-government to constituency (G2C) environment. *Journal of Computer Information Systems*, *45*, 32–41.

Kokkonen, J. (2009). User culture, user-system relation and trust: The case of Finnish Wikipedia. In Niiranen, S., Yli-Hietanen, J., & Lugmayr, A. (Eds.), *Open information management, applications of interconnectivity and collaboration* (pp. 326–343). Hershey, PA: Information Science Reference. doi:10.4018/978-1-60566-246-6.ch015

Kolfschoten, G. L., Briggs, R. O., & de Vreede, G. J. (2010). A technology for pattern-based process design and its application to collaboration engineering. In Rummler, S., & Bor, N. G. K. (Eds.), *Collaborative technologies and applications for interactive information design: Emerging trends in user experiences* (pp. 1–19). Hershey, PA: Information Science Reference. doi:10.4018/978-1-60566-727-0.ch001

Komura, D., Nakamura, H., Tsutsumi, S., Aburatani, H., & Ihara, S. (2004). Multidimensional support vector machines for visualization of gene expression data. In *SAC '04: Proceedings of the 2004 ACM Symposium on Applied Computing*, (pp. 175–179). New York, NY: ACM Press.

Konrad, W., & Spohn, T. (1997). Thermal history of the Moon: Implication for an early core dynamo and post-accretional magmatism. *Advances in Space Research*, *19*, 1511–1521. doi:10.1016/S0273-1177(97)00364-5

Koomey, J. (2008). Worldwide electricity used in data centers. *Environmental Research Letters*, *3*(034008).

Koomey, J., Berard, S., Sanchez, M., & Wong, H. (2010). Stanford University implications of historical trends in the electrical efficiency of computing. *Annals of the History of Computing*, *33*(3), 46–54. doi:10.1109/MAHC.2010.28

Koponen, T., Chawla, M., Chun, B., Ermolinskiy, A., Kim, K. H., Shenker, S., & Stoica, I. (2007). A data-oriented (and beyond) network architecture. *ACM SIGCOMM Computer Communication Review*, *37*(4), 181–192. doi:10.1145/1282427.1282402

Kor, K. B. (2011, 22 September). Singapore to set up national cyber security centre. *The Straits Times*.

Koszlaka, T. A., & Ntloedibe-Kuswani, G. S. (2010). Literature on the safe and disruptive potential of mobile technologies. *Distance Education*, *31*(2), 139–157. doi:10.1080/01587919.2010.498082

Koukovini, M. N., Papagiannakopoulou, E. I., Lioudakis, G. V., Kaklamani, D. I., & Venieris, I. S. (2011). A workflow checking approach for inherent privacy awareness in network monitoring. In *DPM 2006: Proceedings of the 6th Workshop on Data Privacy Management* (LNCS 7122, under publication). Berlin, Germany: Springer-Verlag.

Kraemer, F. (2011). *Advanced clustered and parallel storage system technologies in action* [PDF document]. Retrieved October 16, 2011, from http://www.linuxtag.org/2011/fileadmin/www.linuxtag.org/slides/Frank%20Kraemer%20-%20Advanced%20Clustered%20and%20Parallel%20Storage%20System%20Technologies%20in%20Action.pdf

Kranzlmüller, D. (2011). *SuperMUC – PetaScale HPC at the Leibniz Supercomputing Centre* (LRZ). Retrieved March 1, 2012, from http://www.nm.ifi.lmu.de/~kranzlm/vortraege/2011-10-17%20Linz%20-%20SuperMUC%20-%20PetaScale%20HPC%20at%20the%20Leibniz%20Supercomputing%20Centre.pdf

Kruse, P., Warnke, T., Dittler, A., & Gebel, T. (2010). *Wertewelt Medien*. Retrieved April 10, 2008, from http://www.nextpractice.de/fileadmin/studien/medienstudie2007/Medienstudie_Nov2007.pdf

Kuck, D. J. (1996). *High performance computing: Challenges for future systems*. New York, NY: Oxford University Press, Inc.

Kuhn, W. (2005). Geospatial semantics: why, of what, and how? In Spaccapietra, S., & Zimányi, E. (Eds.), *Journal of Data Semantics* (pp. 1–24). Berlin, Germany: Springer. doi:10.1007/11496168_1

Kujala, S. (2005). Linking user needs and use case-driven requirements engineering. In Seffah, A., Gulliksen, J., & Desmarais, M. C. (Eds.), *Human-centred software engineering - Integrating usability in the software development life cycle* (pp. 113–127). Berlin, Germany: Springer-Verlag. doi:10.1007/1-4020-4113-6_7

Kurbel, K., Jankowska, A. M., & Dabkowski, A. (2005). Architecture for multi-channel enterprise resource planning system. In J. Krogstie, K. Kautz, & D. Allen (Eds.), *Mobile information systems II*, 191, (pp. 245-259). New York, NY: Springer-Verlag. Retrieved from http://www.springerlink.com/content/6717916mw6081610/

Kurniawan, S. (2008). Older people and mobile phones: A multi-method investigation. *International Journal of Human-Computer Studies*, 66(12), 889–901. doi:10.1016/j.ijhcs.2008.03.002

Lacroute, P., & Levoy, M. (1994). Fast volume rendering using a shear-warp factorization of the viewing transformation. In *SIGGRAPH '94: Proceedings of the 21st Annual Conference on Computer Graphics and Interactive Techniques*, (pp. 451–458). New York, NY: ACM Press.

Landau, L. D., & Lifshitz, E. M. (1987). *Fluid mechanics* (2nd ed.). Butterworth-Heinemann Course of Theoretical Physics.

Langer, R., & Vacanti, J. (1993). Tissue engineering. *Science*, 260(5110), 920–926. doi:10.1126/science.8493529

Langran, G. (1992). *Time in geographic information systems*. London, UK: Taylor & Francis.

Lankhorst, M. (2005). *Enterprise architecture at work, modelling, communication and analysis*. Berlin, Germany: Springer-Verlag.

Larsson, A., Ericson, A., Larsson, T., Isaksson, O., & Bertoni, M. (2010). Engineering 2.0: Exploring lightweight technologies for the virtual enterprise. In Randall, D., & Salembier, P. (Eds.), *From CSCW to Web 2.0 European Developments in Collaborative Design* (pp. 173–192). Berlin, Germany: Springer-Verlag. doi:10.1007/978-1-84882-965-7_9

Last.fm: A music website. (2011). Retrieved August 22, 2010 from http://www.last.fm/

Latre, M. A., Lopez-Pellicer, F. J., Nogueras-Iso, J., B'ejar, R., & Muro-Medrano, P. R. (2010). Facilitating e-government services through SDIs: An application for water abstractions authorizations. In Andersen, K. N., Francesconi, E., Grönlund, A., & van Engers, T. M. (Eds.), *Electronic government and the information systems perspective* (pp. 108–119). Berlin, Germany: Springer Verlag. doi:10.1007/978-3-642-15172-9_11

Lauffenburger, D. A., & Linderman, J. J. (1993). *Receptors: Models for binding trafficking and signaling*. New York, NY: Oxford University Press.

Law, A. M. (2007). *Simulation modeling & analysis* (4th ed.). Boston, MA: McGraw-Hill, Inc.

LCPSoft. (2012). *LCPSoft programs*. Retrieved February 15, 2012, from http://www.lcpsoft.com

Leadbeater, C. (2007). *Open platform to develop and share innovative new business ideas*. Retrieved December 20, 2010, from http://www.openbusiness.cc/2007/03/14/two-faces-of-open-innovation/

Lee, E. E. (2006). *Cyber-physical systems - Are computing foundations adequate?* Paper presented at the Position Paper for NSF Workshop On Cyber-Physical Systems: Research Motivation, Techniques and Roadmap Austin.

Lee, A. (1999). Inaugural editor's comments. *Management Information Systems Quarterly, 23*(1), v–xi.

Lee, A. (2010). Retrospect and prospect: Information systems research in the last and next 25 years. *Journal of Information Technology, 25*, 336–348. doi:10.1057/jit.2010.24

Lee, Y., Markenscoff, P., McIntire, L. V., & Zygourakis, K. (1995). Characterization of endothelial cell locomotion using a Markov chain model. *Biochemistry and Cell Biology, 73*, 461–472. doi:10.1139/o95-052

Lee, Y., McIntire, L. V., & Zygourakis, K. (1994). Analysis of endothelial cell locomotion: Differential effects of motility and contact inhibition. *Biotechnology and Bioengineering, 43*(7), 622–634. doi:10.1002/bit.260430712

LEGO. (n.d.). *Mindstorms*. Retrieved June 9th, 2010, from http://mindstorms.lego.com/

Lemmens, R., de By, R. A., Gould, M., Wytzisk, A., Grannell, C., & van Oosterom, P. (2007). Enhancing geo-service chaining through deep service descriptions. *Transactions in GIS, 11*(6), 849–871. doi:10.1111/j.1467-9671.2007.01079.x

Lenardic, A., Jellinek, A. M., & Moresi, L.-N. (2008). A climate induced transition in the tectonic style of a terrestrial planet. *Earth and Planetary Science Letters, 271*, 34–42. doi:10.1016/j.epsl.2008.03.031

Lenardic, A., & Kaula, W. M. (1993). Numerical treatment of geodynamic viscous flow problems involving the advection of material interfaces. *Journal of Geophysical Research, 98*, 8243–8260. doi:10.1029/92JB02858

Leng, W., & Zhong, S. (2011). Implementation and application of adaptive mesh refinement for thermochemical mantle convection studies. *Geochemistry Geophysics Geosystems, 12*(4), Q04006. doi:10.1029/2010GC003425

Lev, E., & Hager, B. (2008). Rayleigh-Taylor instabilities with anisotropic lithospheric viscosity. *Geophysical Journal International, 173*(3), 806–814. doi:10.1111/j.1365-246X.2008.03731.x

LeVeque, R. (2004). *Finite-volume methods for hyperbolic problems*. Cambridge University Press.

Levi, D. (2007). *Group dynamics for teams*. London, UK: Sage Publications, Inc.

Levin, S. A., Grenfell, B., Hastings, A., & Perelson, A. S. (1997). Mathematical and computational challenges in population biology and ecosystems science. *Science, 275*(5298), 334–343. doi:10.1126/science.275.5298.334

Levoy, M. (1990). Efficient ray tracing of volume data. *ACM Transactions on Graphics, 9*(3), 245–261. doi:10.1145/78964.78965

Lew, M. W., Horton, T. B., & Sherriff, M. S. (2010). *Using LEGO MINDSTORMS NXT and LEJOS in an advanced software engineering course*. Paper presented at the 2010 23rd IEEE Conference on Software Engineering Education and Training.

Library of Congress. (2011). *CQL: Contextual query language*. Retrieved October 16, 2011, from http://www.loc.gov/standards/sru/specs/cql.html

Lieberman, H., & Selker, T. (2000). Out of context: Computer systems that adapt to, and learn from, context. *IBM Systems Journal, 39*(3, 4), 617 - 632. doi: 10.1147/sj.393.0617

Li, G., Muthusamy, V., & Jacobsen, H.-A. (2010). A distributed service-oriented architecture for business process execution. *ACM Transactions on the Web, 4*(1), 1–33. doi:10.1145/1658373.1658375

Lim, L., & Koh, A. (2008). *The acceleration of SOA adoption in Singapore: Challenges and issues*. Paper read at the 19th Australian Conference on Information Systems, 3-5 Dec 2008, Christchurch, New Zealand.

Lin, J., Fox, M. S., & Bilgic, T. (1996). *A requirement ontology for engineering design*. Unpublished technical report, University of Toronto, Canada.

LinkedIn: A business-oriented social networking site. (2011). Retrieved May 20, 2011, from http://www.likedin.com

Lin, S. P., & Yang, H. Y. (2009). Exploring key factors in the choice of e-health using an asthma care mobile service model. *Telemedicine Journal of Electronic Health, 15*(9), 884–890. doi:10.1089/tmj.2009.0047

Linsen, L., Pascucci, V., Duchaineau, M. A., Hamann, B., Joy, K. I., & Coquillart, S. ... Hu, S.-M. (2002). Hierarchical representation of time-varying volume data with 4th-root-of-2 subdivision and quadrilinear B-spline wavelets. In *Proceedings of the Tenth Pacific Conference on Computer Graphics and Applications – Pacific Graphics*, (p. 346).

Linthicum, D. (2004). *Next generation application integration*. Addison-Wesley.

Liou, K. T. (2011). *The role of governance and evolution of the concept of governance over the last 100 years*. Paper presented at the 3rd International Conference in Public Policy and Management, 23 Oct 2011, School of Public Policy and Management, Tsinghua University, Beijing, China.

Lioudakis, G. V., Gogoulos, F., Antonakopoulou, A., Kaklamani, D. I., & Venieris, I. S. (2009). Privacy protection in passive network monitoring: an access control approach. In *Proceedings of the IEEE 23rd International Conference on Advanced Information Networking and Applications (AINA-09)* (pp. 109-116). Washington, DC: IEEE Computer Society Press.

Lioudakis, G. V., Koutsoloukas, E. A., Dellas, N., Kapitsaki, G. M., Kaklamani, D. I., & Venieris, I. S. (2008). A semantic framework for privacy-aware access control. In M. Ganzha, M. Paprzycki, & T. Pełech-Pilichowski (Eds.), *Proceedings of the 3rd International Workshop on Secure Information Systems (SIS'08) – International Multiconference on Computer Science and Information Technology* (pp. 813-820). Los Alamitos, CA: IEEE Computer Society Press.

Lioudakis, G. V., Tropea, G., Kaklamani, D. I., Venieris, I. S., & Blefari-Melazzi, N. (2010). Combining monitoring and privacy-protection perspectives in a semantic model for IP traffic measurements. In E. Gelenbe, R. Lent, G. Sakellari, A. Sacan, H. Toroslu, & A. Yazici (Eds.), *Computer and Information Sciences: Proceedings of the 25th International Symposium on Computer and Information Sciences* (LNEE 62, pp. 187–190). Amsterdam, Netherlands: Springer-Verlag.

Li, Q., & Kiefer, W. S. (2007). Mantle convection and magma production on present-day Mars: Effects of temperature-dependent rheology. *Geophysical Research Letters*, *34*, L16203. doi:10.1029/2007GL030544

List of File System. (n.d.). In *Wikipedia*. Retrieved January 22, 2012, from http://en.wikipedia.org/wiki/List_of_file_systems#Distributed_parallel_fault-tolerant_file_systems

Liu, J., Kipp, A., Arnone, D., vor dem Berge, M., et al. (2010). *Validation scenarios*. GAMES Deliverable 7.2 [GAMES D7.2]. Retrieved March 1, 2012, from http://www.green-datacenters.eu

Liua, C. L., Lua, Z. Z., Xub, Y. L., & Yuec, Z. F. (2005). Reliability analysis for low cycle fatigue life of the aeronautical engine turbine disc structure under random environment. *Materials Science and Engineering A*, 218–225. doi:10.1016/j.msea.2004.12.014

Liu, X.-D., Osher, S., & Chan, T. (1994). Weighted essentially non-oscillatory schemes. *Journal of Computational Physics*, *115*, 200–212. doi:10.1006/jcph.1994.1187

Liu, Y., Li, H., & Carlsson, C. (2010). Factors driving the adoption of m-learning: An empirical study. *Computers & Education*, *55*, 1211–1219. doi:10.1016/j.compedu.2010.05.018

Li, W. D., Ong, S. K., & Nee, A. Y. C. (2006). *Integrated and collaborative product development environment: Technologies and implementation*. Singapore: World Scientific.

Logic Supply Inc. (2011). *Transcend commercial 2.5" SATA SSD, 64 GB*. Retrieved July 3, 2011, from http://www.logicsupply.com/products/64gssd25s_m

Lorensen, W. E., & Cline, H. E. (1987). Marching cubes: A high resolution 3-D surface construction algorithm. In *SIGGRAPH'87: Proceedings of the 14th Annual Conference on Computer Graphics and Interactive Techniques*, (pp. 163–169). ACM Press.

Lorenz, A., & Oppermann, R. (2009). Mobile health monitoring for the elderly: Designing for diversity. *Pervasive and Mobile Computing*, *5*(5), 478–495. doi:10.1016/j.pmcj.2008.09.010

Lovelace, M., Boucher, V., Nayak, S., Neal, C., Razmuk, L., Sing, J., & Tarella, J. (2010, November 17). *IBM scale out network attached storage: Architecture, planning, and implementation basics*, (p. 9). IBM Redbook SG24-7875-00 [PDF document]. Retrieved October 16, 2011, from http://www.redbooks.ibm.com/redpieces/pdfs/sg247875.pdf

Luck, M., McBurney, P., Shehory, O., & Willmott, S. (2005). *Agent technology: Computing as interaction (a roadmap for agent based computing)*. Southampton, UK: University of Southampton (on behalf of AgentLink III).

Ludäscher, B., Altintas, I., Berkley, C., Higgins, D., Jaeger, E., Jones, M., & Lee, E. a, et al. (2006). Scientific workflow management and the Kepler system. *Concurrency and Computation, 18*(10), 1039–1065. doi:10.1002/cpe.994

Ludäscher, B., Weske, M., McPhillips, T., & Bowers, S. (2009). Lecture Notes in Computer Science: *Vol. 5701. Scientific workflows: Business as usual?* (pp. 31–47).

Luethy, R. (2010, December 17). *Price trends of HDDs Vs. SSDs*. Retrieved October 16, 2011, from http://rogerluethy.wordpress.com/2010/12/07/price-trends-of-hdds-vs-ssds/

Luethy, R. (2011, January 18). *Gartner magic quadrant midrange and high-end modular disk arrays*. Retrieved October 16, 2011, from http://rogerluethy.wordpress.com/2011/01/18/gartner-magic-quadrant-midrange-and-high-end-modular-disk-arrays/

Luhmann, N. (1968). *Vertrauen - ein Mechanismus der Reduktion sozialer Komplexität* (4th ed.). Stuttgart, Germany: Lucius & Lucius.

Lukosch, S. (2010). Pattern-based tool design for shared knowledge construction. In Rummler, S., & Bor, N. G. K. (Eds.), *Collaborative technologies and applications for interactive information design: Emerging trends in user experiences* (pp. 19–39). Hershey, PA: Information Science Reference. doi:10.4018/978-1-60566-727-0.ch002

Lum, E., Ma, K.-L., & Clyne, J. (2001). Texture hardware assisted rendering of time-varying volume data. *Proceedings of IEEE Visualization, 2001*, 263–270.

Lunker, M. (2005). *Cyber laws: A global perspective*. New York, NY: United Nations Public Administration Network.

Luo, N., Koh, W. P., Ng, W. Y., Yau, J. W., Lim, L. K., & Sim, S. S. (2009). Acceptance of information and communication technologies for healthcare delivery: A SingHealth Polyclinics study. *Annals of the Academy of Medicine, Singapore, 38*(6), 529–528.

Lutz, M. (2007). Ontology-based descriptions for semantic discovery and composition of geoprocessing services. *GeoInformatica, 11*(1), 1–36. doi:10.1007/s10707-006-7635-9

Lutz, M., & Kolas, D. (2007). Rule-based in spatial data infrastructure. *Transactions in GIS, 11*(1), 317–336. doi:10.1111/j.1467-9671.2007.01048.x

Lutz, M., Sprado, J., Klien, E., Schubert, C., & Christ, I. (2008). Overcoming semantic heterogeneity in spatial data infrastructures. *Computers & Geosciences, 35*(4), 739–752. doi:10.1016/j.cageo.2007.09.017

Lu, Y.-C., Xiao, Y., Sears, A., & Jacko, J. (2004). A review and framework of handheld computer adoption in healthcare. *International Journal of Medical Informatics, 74*, 409–422. doi:10.1016/j.ijmedinf.2005.03.001

LX Project. (2012). Retrieved January 29, 2012, from http://www.user.uni-hannover.de/cpr/x/rprojs/de/index.html

Lysaght, M. J., & Hazlehurst, A. L. (2004). Tissue engineering: The end of the beginning. *Tissue Engineering, 10*(1-2), 309–320. doi:10.1089/107632704322791943

Ma, K.-L., & Camp, D. M. (2000). High performance visualization of time-varying volume data over a wide-area network status. In *Supercomputing '00: Proceedings of the 2000 ACM/IEEE Conference on Supercomputing (CDROM)*, Washington, DC: IEEE Computer Society.

MacDonald, J. A. (2008). *Cellular authentication - Key agreement for service providers*. Paper presented at the Second International Conference on Pervasive Computing Technologies for Healthcare, 2008 (PervasiveHealth 2008).

Maehle, E., & Waldschmidt, K. (2008). *Grand challenge 3: Vertrauenswürdigkeit und Zuverlässigkeit* (p. 30). Grand Challenges der Technischen Informatik.

Mahendra, J. (1998). *What is archive? Definition from "Whatis.com"*. Retrieved June 17, 2011, from http://searchstorage.techtarget.com/definition/archive

Mahmood, Z., & Hill, R. (2011). *Cloud computing for enterprise architectures.* London, UK: Springer-Verlag.

Majno, G., & Joris, I. (2004). *Cells, tissues and disease: Principles of general pathology.* Oxford, UK: Oxford University Press.

Ma, K.-L., & Lum, E. B. (2005). Techniques for visualizing time-varying volume data. In Hansen, C. D., & Johnson, C. R. (Eds.), *The visualization handbook* (pp. 511–531). Boston, MA: Elsevier. doi:10.1016/B978-012387582-2/50028-9

Malone, T. W., Grant, K. R., Lai, K.-Y., Rao, R., & Rosenblitt, D. (1987). Semistructured messages are surprisingly useful for computer-supported coordination. *ACM Transactions on Information Systems, 5*(2), 115–131. doi:10.1145/27636.27637

March, S. T., & Smith, G. F. (1995). Design and natural science research on information technology. *Decision Support Systems, 15*(4), 251–266. doi:10.1016/0167-9236(94)00041-2

March, S. T., & Storey, V. C. (2008). Design science in the information systems discipline: An introduction to the special issue on design science research. *Management Information Systems Quarterly, 32*(4), 725–730.

Marée, A. F., & Hogeweg, P. (2001). How amoeboids self-organize into a fruiting body: Multicellular coordination in Dictyostelium discoideum. *Proceedings of the National Academy of Sciences of the United States of America, 98*(7), 3879–3883. doi:10.1073/pnas.061535198

Markus, L., Majchrzak, A., & Gasser, L. (2002). A design theory for systems that support emergent knowledge processes. *Management Information Systems Quarterly, 26*(3), 179–212.

Marmasse, N., Schmandt, C., & Spectre, D. (2004). WatchMe: Communication and awareness between members of a closely-knit group. *UbiComp 2004: Ubiquitous Computing* (pp. 214-231).

Marquie, J. C., Jourdan-Boddaert, L., & Huet, N. (2002). Do older adults underestimate their actual computer knowledge? *Behaviour & Information Technology, 21*(4), 273–280. doi:10.1080/0144929021000020998

Marshall, J., & Plumb, R. A. (2008). *Atmosphere, ocean, and climate dynamics – An introductory text.* China: Academic Press, Elsevier.

Martin, C. R., & Horne, D. A. (1995). Level of success inputs for service innovations in the same firm. *International Journal of Service Industry Management, 6*(4), 40–56. doi:10.1108/09564239510096894

Martin, D., Paolucci, M., McIlraith, S., Burstein, M., McDermott, D., & McGuinness, D. (2005). Bringing semantics to Web services: The OWL-S approach. In Cardoso, J., & Sheth, A. (Eds.), *Semantic Web services and Web process composition* (pp. 26–42). Berlin, Germany: Springer. doi:10.1007/978-3-540-30581-1_4

Martinec, Z. (2000). Spectral-finite element approach to three-dimensional viscoelastic relaxation in a spherical earth. *Geophysical Journal International, 142*, 117–141. doi:10.1046/j.1365-246x.2000.00138.x

Martins, J. (2011, March 1). *The hot new storage technology for 2011 is... tape?* Data Mobility Group [PDF document]. Retrieved October 17, 2011, from http://public.dhe.ibm.com/common/ssi/ecm/en/tsl03052usen/TSL03052USEN.PDF

Mashman, W. (2011). Editor's page. The iPad in Cardiology: Tool or toy? *JACC: Cardiovascular Interventions, 4*(2), 258–259. doi:10.1016/j.jcin.2011.01.001

Mathe, J. L., Duncavage, S., Werner, J., Malin, B. A., Ledeczi, A., & Sztipanovits, J. (2007). Towards the security and privacy analysis of patient portals. *SIGBED Review, 4*(2), 5–9. doi:10.1145/1295464.1295467

Mathiassen, L., Munk-Madsen, A., Nielsen, P. A., & Stage, J. (2001). *Object oriented analysis & design.* Aalborg, Denmark: Marko Publishers.

Matsuoka, Y., Schaumont, P., Tiri, K., & Verbauwhede, I. (2004). *Java cryptography on KVM and its performance and security optimization using HW/SW co-design techniques.* Paper presented at the 2004 International Conference on Compilers, Architecture, and Synthesis for Embedded Systems.

Matthing, J., Sandem, B., & Edvardsson, B. (2004). New service development: learning from and with customers. *International Journal of Service Industry Management, 15*(5), 479–498. doi:10.1108/09564230410564948

Maturana, H., & Varela, F. (1992). *The tree of knowledge: Biological roots of human understanding (original: El árbol del conocimiento. Bases biológicas del entendimiento humano)*. Boston, MA: Shambhala Publications, Inc.

May, D. A., & Moresi, L. (2008). Preconditioned iterative methods for Stokes flow problems arising in computational geodynamics. *Physics of the Earth and Planetary Interiors, 171*(1-4), 33–47. doi:10.1016/j.pepi.2008.07.036

Mayhew, D. J. (1999). *The usability engineering lifecycle*. Paper presented at the CHI '99 Extended Abstracts on Human Factors in Computing Systems.

McAfee, A. P. (2006). Enterprise 2.0: The dawn of emergent collaboration. [Spring.]. *MIT Sloan Management Review, 47*(3), 21–28.

McCarthy, D. R., & Dayal, U. (1989). The architecture of an active database management system. *Proceedings of ACM SIGMOD International Conference on Management of Data*, (pp. 215-224).

McGowern, J., Ambler, S. W., Stevens, M. E., Linn, J., Sharan, V., & Jo, E. K. (2003). *Practical guide to enterprise architecture*. Upper Saddle River, NJ: Prentice Hall PTR.

McNamara, A. K., & Zhong, S. (2004). Thermochemical structures within a spherical mantle: Superplumes or piles? *Journal of Geophysical Research, 109*, B07402. doi:10.1029/2003JB002847

Měch, R., & Prusinkiewicz, P. (1996). Visual models of plants interacting with their environment. In *SIGGRAPH '96: Proceedings of the 23rd Annual Conference on Computer Graphics and Interactive Techniques*, (pp. 397–410). New York, NY: ACM Press.

Mehandjiev, N., & Grefen, P. (Eds.). (2010). *Dynamic business process formation for instant virtual enterprises*. London, UK: Springer-Verlag.

Mehrotra, S., Rastogi, R., Korth, H., & Silberschatz, A. (1992). A transaction model for multi-database systems. *Proceedings of the International Conference on Distributed Computing Systems*, (pp. 56-63).

Mehta, M., & Hirschheim, R. (2007). Strategic alignment in mergers & acquisitions: Theorizing is integration decision making. *Journal of the Association for Information Systems, 8*(3), 143–174.

Mell, P., & Grance, T. (2011). *The NIST definition of cloud computing* (Draft), January, 2001. Retrieved March 2, 2012, from http://www.worldprivacyforum.org/pdf/WPF_cloud_Priavacy_Report.pdf

Mendonca, E., A., Chen, E., S., Stetson, P., D., McKnight, L. K., Lei, J., & Cimino, J. J. (2004). Approach to mobile information and communication for health care. *International Journal of Medical Informatics, 73*(7), 631–638. doi:10.1016/j.ijmedinf.2004.04.013

Michel, N., & Forni, O. (2011). Mars mantle convection: Influence of phase transitions with core cooling. *Planetary and Space Science, 59*, 741–748. doi:10.1016/j.pss.2011.02.013

Microsoft Case Studies. (2011). *Egyptian Ambulance Organization: Ambulance agency improves emergency service delivery with electronic fleet management*. Retrieved August 03, 2011, from http://www.microsoft.com/casestudies/Case_Study_Detail.aspx?CaseStudyID=4000010726

Microsoft Case Studies. (2011). *First choice home health and hospice of Utah, home health provider saves $500,000 annually, doubles cash flow, with mobile solution*. Retrieved July 19, 2011, from http://www.microsoft.com/casestudies/Case_Study_Detail.aspx?CaseStudyID=4000010753

Milewski, A., & Smith, T. (2000). *Providing presence cues to telephone users*. Paper presented at the CSCW '00: 2000 ACM Conference on Computer Supported Cooperative Work.

Ming, C., Jinfei, L., Qinghua, K., & Yuan, Y. (2010). Study on collaborative product design based on modularity and multi-agent. *Proceedings of the 2010 14th International Conference on Computer Supported Cooperative Work in Design*, (pp. 274-279).

Ministry of Education. Singapore. (2010). *Greater support for cyber wellness projects*. Singapore: Ministry of Education, Singapore.

Ministry of Internal Affairs and Communications. (n.d.). *Japan's e-government initiatives*. Japan: Ministry of Internal Affairs and Communications.

Minnick, A., Pischke-Winn, K., & Sterk, M. B. (1994). Introducing a two-way wireless communication system. *Nursing Management*, *25*(7), 42–47. doi:10.1097/00006247-199407000-00011

Minoli, D. (2008). *Enterprise architecture A to Z. Frameworks, business process modeling, SOA, and infrastructure technology*. London, UK: CRC Press, Taylor & Francis Group. doi:10.1201/9781420013702

Mirkovic, J., Bryhni, H., & Ruland, C. (2009). *Review of projects using mobile devices and mobile applications in healthcare*. Paper presented at the Scandinavian conference on Health Informatics, Arendal, Norway.

Mirkovic, J., Bryhni, H., & Ruland, C. (2011). *Designing user friendly mobile application to assist cancer patients in illness management*. Paper presented at the eTELEMED 2011, The Third International Conference on eHealth, Telemedicine, and Social Medicine, Gosier, Guadeloupe, France.

Mirkovic, J., Bryhni, H., & Ruland, C. M. (2011). *Secure solution for mobile access to patient's health care record*. Paper presented at the 2011 IEEE 13th International Conference on e-Health Networking, Applications and Services, Columbia, Missouri, USA.

Mitchell, S., Spiteri, M. D., Bates, J., & Coulouris, G. (2000). *Context-aware multimedia computing in the intelligent hospital*. Paper presented at the 9th Workshop on ACM SIGOPS European Workshop: Beyond the PC: New Challenges for the Operating System, Kolding, Denmark.

Mitrovica, J. X., & Forte, A. M. (2004). A new inference of mantle viscosity based upon joint inversion of convection and glacial isostatic adjustment data. *Earth and Planetary Science Letters*, *225*, 177–189. doi:10.1016/j.epsl.2004.06.005

Mizzaro, S., Nazzi, E., & Vassena, L. (2008). *Retrieval of context-aware applications on mobile devices: how to evaluate?* Paper presented at the Second International Symposium on Information Interaction in Context, London, United Kingdom.

Mobile Learning Group. Athabasca University. (n.d.). *Mobile learning and pervasive computing*. Retrieved October 1, 2011, from http://adlib.athabascau.ca/

Modafferi, S., Mussi, E., Maurino, A., & Pernici, B. (2004). A framework for provisioning of complex e-services. *Proceedings IEEE International Conference on Services Computing, SCC 2004* (pp. 81-90). IEEE. doi:10.1109/SCC.2004.1357993

Montello, D. R. (1993). Scale and multiple psychologies of space. In A. Frank & L. Campari (Eds.), *Spatial information theory: A theoretical basis for GIS. Lecture Notes in Computer Science, No. 716*, COSIT'93, (pp. 312-321). Springer.

Moon, M. J. (2002). The evolution of e-government among municipalities: Rhetoric or reality. *Public Administration Review*, *62*(4), 424–433. doi:10.1111/0033-3352.00196

Moon, M. J., & Norris, D. F. (2005). Does managerial orientation matter? The adoption of reinventing government and e-government at the municipal level. *Information Systems Journal*, *15*, 43–60. doi:10.1111/j.1365-2575.2005.00185.x

Moore, G. E. (1965). Cramming more components onto integrated circuits. *Electronics Magazine, 4.* openQRM. (2012). *OpenQRM website*. Retrieved March 1, 2012, from http://www.openqrm.com/

Moresi, L., Dufour, F., & Mühlhaus, H. B. (2003). A Lagrangian integration point finite element method for large deformation modeling of viscoelastic geomaterials. *Journal of Computational Physics*, *184*, 476–497. doi:10.1016/S0021-9991(02)00031-1

Moresi, L., & Solomatov, V. (1998). Mantle convection with a brittle lithosphere: Thoughts on the global tectonic styles of the Earth and Venus. *Geophysical Journal International*, *133*, 669–682. doi:10.1046/j.1365-246X.1998.00521.x

Moser, O., Rosenberg, F., & Dustdar, S. (2008). Non-intrusive monitoring and service adaptation for WS-BPEL. *Proceeding of the 17th International Conference on World Wide Web - WWW'08*, (p. 815). New York, NY: ACM Press. doi:10.1145/1367497.1367607

Mottram, B. (2008). *Pergamum – "New age" storage clustering takes aim at disk based archival storage, a brief*. [PDF Document]. Retrieved January 22, 2012, from http://www.veridictusassociates.com/images/Pergamum_Brief.pdf

Müller-Schloer, C., Schmeck, H., Bringschulte, U., Feldbusch, F., Trumler, W., & Ungerer, T. (2008). *Grand Cahallenge 4: 'Organic computing' Techniken*. Grand Challenges der Technischen Informatik.

Müller-Stewens, G., & Fleisch, E. (2008). High-resolution-management: Konsequenzen des "Internet der Dinge" auf die Unternehmensführung. *Führung und Organisation, 77*(5), 272–281.

Munoz, M. A., Rodriguez, M., Favela, J., Martinez-Garcia, A. I., & Gonzalez, V. M. (2003). Context-aware mobile communication in hospitals. *Computer, 36*(9), 38. doi:10.1109/MC.2003.1231193

Myerson, S. G., & Mitchell, A. R. J. (2003). Mobile phones in hospitals. *British Medical Journal, 326*(7387), 460–461. doi:10.1136/bmj.326.7387.460

Naismith, L., Lonsdale, P., Vavoula, G., & Sharples, M. (2006). *Literature review in mobile technologies and learning (Futurelab Series Report 11)*. Bristol, UK: Futurelab.

Nakagawa, T., & Tackley, P. J. (2008). Lateral variations in CMB heat flux and deep mantle seismic velocity caused by a thermal–chemical-phase boundary layer in 3D spherical convection. *Earth and Planetary Science Letters, 271*, 348–358. doi:10.1016/j.epsl.2008.04.013

Nakagawa, T., & Tackley, P. J. (2010). Influence of initial CMB temperature and other parameters on the thermal evolution of Earth's core resulting from thermo-chemical spherical mantle convection. *Geochemistry Geophysics Geosystems, 11*, Q06001. doi:10.1029/2010GC003031

Nakagawa, T., & Tackley, P. J. (2011). Effects of low-viscosity post-perovskite on thermo-chemical mantle convection in a 3-D spherical shell. *Geophysical Research Letters, 38*, L04309. doi:10.1029/2010GL046494

Narayanan, A., & Shmatikov, V. (2005). Fast dictionary attacks on passwords using time-space tradeoff. *Proceedings of the Twelfth ACM Conference on Computer and Communications Security*, November 7-11, 2005, Alexandria, Virginia, United States of America, (pp. 364-372). ISBN: 1-59593-226-7

NASCIO. (2007). *Attention state CIOS: It security awareness and training may avert your next crisis!* Lexington, KY: NASCIO.

National Energy Research Scientific Computing (NERSC) Facility. Extreme Scale Workshop. (2009). *HPSS in the extreme scale era* [PDF document]. Retrieved June 18, 2011, from http://www.nersc.gov/assets/HPC-Requirements-for-science/HPSSExtremeScaleFINALpublic.pdf

National Fire Protection Organisation. (1996). *Abschließender Bericht über den Brandhergang - Brand im Terminal des Flughafens*, Düsseldorf, Deutschland 11. Retrieved October 17, 2011, from www.nfta.org

National Institute of Standards and Technology. (2012). *The NIST definition of cloud computing*. Retrieved February 3, 2011, from http://csrc.nist.gov/publications/nistpubs/800-145/SP800-145.pdf

National Institute of Standards and Technology. NIST. (2002). Secure hash standard. *Federal Information Processing Standards Publication, 180*(2), 1-75. Retrieved February 21, 2012, from http://csrc.nist.gov/publications/fips/fips180-2/fips180-2.pdf

Naumann, F. (2002). Lecture Notes in Computer Science: *Vol. 2261. Quality-driven query answering for integrated information systems*. Springer. doi:10.1007/3-540-45921-9

Ndou, V. (2004). E-government for developing countries: Opportunities and challenges. *Electronic Journal of Information Systems in Developing Countries, 18*, 1–24.

Nebert, D. (Ed.). (2004). *Developing spatial data infrastructures: The SDI cookbook*. Global Spatial Data Infrastructure.

Nelson, L., Bly, S., & Sokoler, T. (2001). *Quiet calls: Talking silently on mobile phones*. Paper presented at the CHI '01: SIGCHI Conference on Human Factors in Computing Systems.

Newman, H. (2009). *LBL HPSS Workshop for DOE/SC, CTO/Instrumental Inc.*, July 2009.

Nielsen, J. (1995). *Usability engineering*. San Francisco, CA: Morgan Kaufmann Publishers Inc.

Nkosi, M. T., & Mekuria, F. (2010). *Cloud computing for enhanced mobile health applications*. Paper presented at the IEEE Second International Conference on Cloud Computing Technology and Science (CloudCom 2010).

Noack, L., Breuer, D., & Spohn, T. (2012). Coupling the atmosphere with interior dynamics: Implications for the resurfacing of Venus. *Icarus, 217*(2), 484–498. doi:10.1016/j.icarus.2011.08.026

Noack, L., & Tosi, N. (2012). High-performance modelling in geodynamics. In Rückemann, C.-P. (Ed.), *Integrated information and computing systems for natural, spatial, and social sciences.*

Noorollahi Ravari, A., Amini, M., & Jalili, R. (2008). A semantic aware access control model with real time constraints on history of accesses. In M. Ganzha, M. Paprzycki, & T. Pełech-Pilichowski (Eds.), *Proceedings of the International Multiconference on Computer Science and Information Technology* (pp. 827-836). Los Alamitos, CA: IEEE Computer Society Press.

Noorollahi Ravari, A., Jafarian, J., Amini, M., & Jalili, R. (2010). GTHBAC: A generalized temporal history based access control model. *Journal of Telecommunication Systems, 45*(2), 111–125. doi:10.1007/s11235-009-9239-9

Noran, O. (2003). Mapping of individual architecture frameworks (GRAI, PERA, C4ISR, CIMOSA, ZACHMAN, ARIS) onto GERAM. In Bernus, P., Nemes, L., & Schmidt, G. (Eds.), *Handbook on enterprise architecture* (pp. 65–212). Berlin, Germany: Springer-Verlag.

Nordbotten, N. A. (2009). XML and Web services security standards. *IEEE Communications Surveys & Tutorials, 11*(3), 4–21. doi:10.1109/SURV.2009.090302

Norman, D. (2002). *The design of everyday things.* Basic Books.

Norris, F., Fletcher, P. D., & Holden, S. H. (2001). *Is your local government plugged in? Highlights of the 2000 electronic government survey.* Baltimore, MD: University of Maryland.

Nov, O. (2007). What motivates Wikipedians. *Communications of the ACM, 50*(11), 60–64. doi:10.1145/1297797.1297798

O'Farrell, K. A., & Lowman, J. P. (2010). Emulating the thermal structure of spherical shell convection in plane-layer geometry mantle convection models. *Physics of the Earth and Planetary Interiors, 182*(1-2), 73–84. doi:10.1016/j.pepi.2010.06.010

O'Neill, C., Jellinek, A. M., & Lenardic, A. (2007). Conditions for the onset of plate tectonics on terrestrial planets and moons. *Earth and Planetary Science Letters, 261*, 20–32. doi:10.1016/j.epsl.2007.05.038

Object Management Group. (2008). *Common object request broker architecture (CORBA) Specification: Version 3.1.* Needham, MA: OMG.

OECD. (2003). *The e-government imperative.* Paris, France: OECD.

Oechslin, P. (2003). Making a faster cryptanalytic time-memory trade-off. *Proceedings of the Twenty Third International Cryptology Conference (CRYPTO), Lecture Notes in Computer Science, 279*, August 17-21, 2003, Santa Barbara, California, United States of America, (pp. 617-630). ISBN: 978-3-540-40674-7

Oinn, T., Greenwood, M., Addis, M., Alpdemir, M. N., Ferris, J., & Glover, K. (2006). Taverna: Lessons in creating a workflow environment for the life sciences. *Concurrency and Computation, 18*(10), 1067–1100. doi:10.1002/cpe.993

Ojo, A., Janowski, T., Estevez, E., & Khan, I. K. (2007). *Human capacity development for e-government.* UNU-IIST Report No. 362. Tokyo, Japan: United Nations University, International Institute for Software Technology.

Ong, C. E. (2005). Jurisdiction in B2C e-commerce redress in the European community. *Journal of Electronic Commerce in Organizations, 3*(4), 75–87. doi:10.4018/jeco.2005100105

Op't Land, M., Proper, E., Waage, M., Cloo, J., & Steghuis, C. (2009). *Enterprise architecture, creating value by informed governance.* Heidelberg, Germany: Springer-Verlag.

Open Geospatial Consortium. (2001). *Filter encoding implementation specification.* Retrieved October 16, 2011, from http://www.opengeospatialorg./standards/filter

Open Geospatial Consortium. (2004). *Web map service interface.* Retrieved October 16, 2011, from http://www.opengeospatialorg./standards/wms

Open Geospatial Consortium. (2007). *Open GIS catalogue services specification.* Retrieved October 16, 2011, from http://www.opengeospatialorg./standards/csw

Open Geospatial Consortium. (2008). *Open GIS web processing service*. Retrieved October 16, 2011, from http://www.opengeospatialorg./standards/wps

Open Geospatial Consortium. (2008). *Web coverage service implementation standard*. Retrieved October 16, 2011, from http://www.opengeospatialorg/standards/wcs

Open Geospatial Consortium. (2008). *Web feature service implementation specification*. Retrieved October 16, 2011, from http://www.opengeospatialorg./standards/wfs

Open Geospatial Consortium. (2011). *Open geospatial consortium*. Retrieved October 16, 2011, from http://www.opengeospatialorg

Open Geospatial Consortium. (2011). *Open GIS schemas*. Retrieved October 16, 2011, from http://schemas.opengis.net

Open Knowledge Foundation. (2009). *The open knowledge definition*. Retrieved May 25, 2009, from http://opendefinition.org/

Openlink Virtuoso. (2010). Retrieved May 27, 2009, from http://virtuoso.openlinksw.com/

OpenNebula. (2010). *About the OpenNebula technology*. Retrieved March 3, 2012, from http://www.opennebula.org/about:technology

OpenNLP. (2009). Retrieved May 27, 2009, from http://opennlp.sourceforge.net/

Ophcrack. (2012). *Ophcrack rainbow tables*. Retrieved February 15, 2012, from http://ophcrack.sourceforge.net/tables.php

Oracle. (2009). *Java card 3.0.1 platform specification*. Retrieved October 20, 2011, from http://www.oracle.com/technetwork/java/javacard/specs-jsp-136430.html

Or, C. K., & Karsh, B. T. (2009). A systematic review of patient acceptance of consumer health information technology. *Journal of the American Medical Informatics Association, 16*(4), 550–560. doi:10.1197/jamia.M2888

Osher, S., & Fedkiw, R. (2003). *Level set methods and dynamic implicit surfaces*. New York, NY: Springer. doi:10.1115/1.1760520

Page, E. H., & Nance, R. E. (1994). Parallel discrete event simulation: A modeling methodological perspective. In *Proceedings of the 1994 Workshop on Parallel and Distributed Simulation*, (pp. 88-93).

Palmer, S. R., & Felsing, J. M. (2002). *A practical guide to feature-driven development*. Upper Saddle River, NJ: Prentice Hall Inc.

Palsson, B. O., & Bhatia, S. N. (2004). *Tissue engineering*. Upper Saddle River, NJ: Pearson Prentice Hall.

Pancake, C. M. (1996). Is parallelism for you? *IEEE Computational Science & Engineering, 3*(2), 18–37. doi:10.1109/99.503307

Panoramio: A photo sharing community. (2011). Retrieved January 20, 2012, from http://www.panoramio.com

Panteli, N., Pitsillides, B., Pitsillides, A., & Samaras, G. (2010). An e-healthcare mobile application: A stakeholders' analysis experience of reading. In Khoumbati, K., Dwivedi, Y. K., Srivastava, A., & Lal, B. (Eds.), *Handbook of research on advances in health informatics and electronic healthcare applications: Global adoption and impact of information communication technologies* (pp. 433–445).

Papazoglou, M. P., & van den Heuvel, W.-J. (2007). Service oriented architectures: Approaches, technologies and research issues. *The VLDB Journal, 16*(3), 389–425. doi:10.1007/s00778-007-0044-3

Papike, J. J., Karner, J. M., Shearer, C. K., & Burger, P. V. (2009). Silicate mineralogy of Martian meteorites. *Geochimica et Cosmochimica Acta, 73*, 7443–7485. doi:10.1016/j.gca.2009.09.008

Parker, J., & Coiera, E. (2000). Improving clinical communication: A view from psychology. *Journal of the American Medical Informatics Association, 7*(5), 453–461. doi:10.1136/jamia.2000.0070453

Parnell, J. (2004). Plate tectonics, surface mineralogy, and the early evolution of life. *International Journal of Astrobiology, 3*(2), 131–137. doi:10.1017/S1473550404002101

Parsons, B., & McKenzie, D. (1978). Mantle convection and the thermal structure of the plates. *Journal of Geophysical Research, 83*(B9), 4485–4496. doi:10.1029/JB083iB09p04485

Pascual, P. (2003). *E-government.* Philippines and Malaysia: e-ASEAN Task Force and UNDP-APDIP.

Patankar, S. V. (1980). *Numerical heat transfer and fluid flow. Hemisphere series on computational methods in mechanics and thermal science.* Taylor & Francis.

Patterson, M. (2001). *E-commerce law.* Paper read at the Free Trade Agreement - Opportunities and Challenges Conference, 21st June, 2001, at Hyatt Hotel, Canberra.

Patterson, M. K., & Fenwick, D. (2008). *The state of data center cooling.* Retrieved March 1, 2012, from ftp://download.intel.com/technology/EEP/data-center-efficiency/state-of-date-center-cooling.pdf

Patterson, M. K. (2008). The effect of data center temperature on energy efficiency. *Thermal and Thermomechanical Phenomena in Electronic Systems, ITHERM, 2008.* doi:10.1109/ITHERM.2008.4544393

Patterson, M. K. (2009). *Data center energy: Going forward.* The Green Grid Technical Forum.

Pedersen, E. R. (2001). *Calls.calm: Enabling caller and callee to collaborate.* Paper presented at the CHI '01 Extended Abstracts on Human Factors in Computing Systems, Seattle, Washington.

Pedersen, R. (2008). *Micro information systems: Toward an experimental platform.* Paper presented at the Ubiquitous Knowledge Discovery Workshop, European Conference on Machine Learning and Principles and Practice of Knowledge Discovery in Databases. Retrieved from September 14th, 2009, from http://www.ecmlpkdd2008.org/workshop-papers-ubiqkd

Pedersen, M. K. (2007). Case study 2: Distributed knowledge networks: Construction industry modernization. Innovating a digital model for the construction industry - a distributed knowledge management approach. In Wickramasinghe, N., & Lubitz, D. V. (Eds.), *Knowledge-based enterprise: Theories and fundamentals* (pp. 257–273). Hershey, PA: IGI Global.

Pedersen, M. K., & Larsen, M. H. (2005). Innocuous knowledge: Models of distributed knowledge networks. In Desouza, K. C. (Ed.), *New frontiers of knowledge management* (pp. 243–265). Palgrave Macmillan.

Pedersen, R. U. (2007). TinyOS education with LEGO MINDSTORMS NXT. In Gama, J., & Garber, M. M. (Eds.), *Learning from data streams* (pp. 231–241). Springer. doi:10.1007/3-540-73679-4_14

Pedersen, R. U. (2010). Micro information systems and ubiquitous knowledge discovery. In May, M., & Saitta, L. (Eds.), *Ubiquitous knowledge discovery* (*Vol. 6202*, pp. 216–234). Berlin, Germany: Springer. doi:10.1007/978-3-642-16392-0_13

Peltier, W. R., & Solheim, L. P. (1992). Mantle phase transitions and layered chaotic convection. *Geophysical Research Letters, 19*(3), 321–324. doi:10.1029/91GL02951

Perkins, M. (2007). *High-end storage array specifications.* SearchStorage.com, Retrieved October 16, 2011, from http://searchstorage.techtarget.com/tutorial/High-end-storage-array-specifications

Philips. (n.d.). *RFID image.* Retrieved October 20th, 2011 from http://www.nxp.com/

Phillips, R. J., Bullock, M. A., & Hauck, S. A. II. (2001). Climate and interior coupled evolution on Venus. *Geophysical Research Letters, 28*(9), 1779–1782. doi:10.1029/2000GL011821

Phinney, R. A., & Burridge, R. (1973). Representation of the elastic - gravitational excitation of a spherical Earth model by generalized spherical harmonics. *Geophysical Journal International, 34*(4), 451–487. doi:10.1111/j.1365-246X.1973.tb02407.x

Piercy, N. F. (2009). *Marketing-led strategic change: Transforming the process of going to market.* Amsterdam, The Netherlands: Elsevier.

Piette, M. A., Ghatikar, G., Kiliccote, S., Koch, E., Hennage, D., Palensky, P., & McParland, C. (2009). *CEC OpenADR-Version 1.0 Report: Open automated demand response communications specification* (Version 1.0). California Energy Commission, PIER Program. CEC-500-2009-063 and LBNL-1779E.

Pinnock, H., Slack, R., Pagliari, C., Price, D., & Sheikh, A. (2006). Professional and patient attitudes to using mobile phone technology to monitor asthma: questionnaire survey. *Primary Care Respiratory Journal, 15*(4), 237–245. doi:10.1016/j.pcrj.2006.03.001

Pitsillides, A., Samaras, G., Pitsillides, B., Georgiades, D., Andreou, P., & Christodoulou, E. (2006). Ditis: Virtual collaborative teams for home healthcare. *Journal of Mobile Multimedia*, 23-26.

Plaza, I., Martin, L., Martin, S., & Medrano, C. (2011). Mobile applications in an aging society: Status and trends. *Journal of Systems and Software*, *84*(11), 1977–1988. doi:10.1016/j.jss.2011.05.035

Plesa, A.-C. (2011). Mantle convection in a 2D spherical shell. *INFOCOMP 2011: First International Conference on Advanced Communications and Computation*, (pp. 167-172). ISBN 978-1-61208-161-8

Plesa, A.-C., & Breuer, D. (2010, May). *Mantle convection in a spherical shell: The problems of using Frank-Kamenetskii Approximation for the viscosity law*. Paper presented at the General Assembly of the European Geoscience Union, Vienna, Austria.

Plesa, A.-C., Tosi, N., & Hüttig, C. (2012). Thermochemical convection in planetary mantles: A comparison of advection methods in spherical domains. In Rückemann, C.-P. (Ed.), *Integrated information and computing systems for natural, spatial, and social sciences*. Hershey, PA: IGI Global.

Podgurski, A. (2010). *Evidence-based validation and improvement of electronic health record systems*. Paper presented at the FSE/SDP Workshop on Future of Software Engineering Research.

Polaine, A., & Bennett, R. (2010). Creative waves: Exploring emerging online cultures, social networking and creative collaboration through e-learning to offer visual campaigns for local Kenyan Health Needs. In Rummler, S., & Bor, N. G. K. (Eds.), *Collaborative technologies and applications for interactive information design: Emerging trends in user experiences* (pp. 39–51). Hershey, PA: Information Science Reference.

Polyzois, C., & Garcia-Molina, H. (1994). Evaluation of remote backup algorithms for transaction-processing systems. *ACM TODS*, *19*(3), 423–449. doi:10.1145/185827.185836

Post, F. H., Vrolijk, B., Hauser, H., Laramee, R. S., & Doleisch, H. (2003). The state of the art in flow visualization: Feature extraction and tracking. *Computer Graphics Forum*, *22*(4), 775–792. doi:10.1111/j.1467-8659.2003.00723.x

Pottie, G., & Kaiser, W. (2005). *Principles of embedded networked systems design*. New York, NY: Cambridge University Press. doi:10.1017/CBO9780511541049

Poullet, Y. (2006). The directive 95/46/EC: Ten years after. *Computer Law & Security Report*, *22*(3), 206–217. doi:10.1016/j.clsr.2006.03.004

Poynton, T. A. (2005). Computer literacy across the lifespan: A review with implications for educators. *Computers in Human Behavior*, *21*(6), 861–872. doi:10.1016/j.chb.2004.03.004

Prahalad, C. K., & Ramaswamy, V. (2000). Co-opting customer competence. *Harvard Business Review*, *78*, 79–87.

Prananto, A., & McKemmish, S. (2007). *Critical success factors for the establishment of e-government*. RISO Working Paper. Melbourne, Victoria: Faculty of Information and Communication Technologies, Swinburne University of Technology.

Preda, S., Cuppens, F., Cuppens-Boulahia, N., Garcia-Alfaro, J., & Toutain, L. (2011). Dynamic deployment of context-aware access control policies for constrained security devices. *Journal of Systems and Software*, *84*(7), 1144–1159. doi:10.1016/j.jss.2011.02.005

Preece, J., Rogers, Y., & Sharp, H. (2002). *Interaction design* (1st ed.). New York, NY: John Wiley & Sons, Inc.

Prensky, M. (2001). *Digital game-based learning*. New York, NY: McGraw-Hill.

Pries-Heje, J., & Baskerville, R. (2008). The design theory nexus. *Management Information Systems Quarterly*, *32*(4), 731–755.

Pries, K. H., & Quigley, J. M. (2011). *Scrum project management*. London, UK: CRC Press Taylor & Fraxis Group.

Prusinkiewicz, P., Hammel, M. S., & Mjolsness, E. (1993). Animation of plant development. In *SIGGRAPH '93: Proceedings of the 20th Annual Conference on Computer Graphics and Interactive Techniques*, (pp. 351–360). New York, NY: ACM Press.

Public Company Accounting Oversight Board. (n.d.). Retrieved March 2, 2012, from http://pcaobus.org

Purnell, N. (2011). *Singapore moving on data protection law; Early '12 passage, effective date delay seen.* Bethesda, MD: Bureau of National Affairs, Inc.

Quinn, C. N. (2011). *Designing mLearning: Tapping into the mobile revolution for organizational performance.* San Francisco, CA: Pfeiffer.

Quinn, M. J. (2004). *Parallel programming in C with MPI and OpenMp.* Dubuque, IA: McGraw-Hill.

Rab, A. (Ed.). (2009). *Information society policies. Annual world report 2009.* Paris, France: UNESCO.

Rabbitt, P. (1993). Does it all go together when it goes? The Nineteenth Bartlett Memorial Lecture. *The Quarterly Journal of Experimental Psychology. A, Human Experimental Psychology, 46*(3), 385–434. doi:10.1080/14640749308401055

Raddum, H., Nestås, L. H., & Hole, K. J. (2010). *Security analysis of mobile phones used as OTP generators.* Paper presented at the Workshop in Information Security Theory and Practice.

RainbowCrack. (2012). *RainbowCrack project.* Retrieved February 15, 2012, from http://project-rainbowcrack.com

Rashid, N., & Rahman, S. (2010). An investigation into critical determinants of e-government implementation in the context of a developing nation. In Andersen, K. N., Francesconi, E., Grönlund, A., & van Engers, T. M. (Eds.), *Electronic government and the information systems perspective* (pp. 9–21). Berlin, Germany: Springer Verlag. doi:10.1007/978-3-642-15172-9_2

Rasmussen, N. (2011). *Eco-mode: Benefits and risks of energy-saving modes of UPS operation.* Retrieved March 1, 2012, from http://www.apc.com/whitepaper?wp=157

Raymond, E. S. (2000). *The cathedral and the bazaar.* Retrieved January 21, 2011, from http://www.catb.org/~esr/writings/homesteading/

Reese, C. C., Solomatov, V. S., & Moresi, L.-N. (1999). Non-newtonian stagnant lid convection and magmatic resurfacing on Venus. *Icarus, 139,* 67–80. doi:10.1006/icar.1999.6088

Reynolds, R., Walker, K., & Speight, C. (2010). Web-based museum trails on PDAs for university-level design and evaluation. *Computers & Education, 55*(3), 994–1003. doi:10.1016/j.compedu.2010.04.010

Rezeg, K., Laskri, M. T., & Servigne, S. (2010). Geospatial web services semantic discovery approach using quality. *Journal of Convergence Information Technology, 5*(2), 28–35. doi:10.4156/jcit.vol5.issue2.3

Ribstein, L. E., & Butler, H. N. (2006). The Sarbanes-Oxley debacle: What we've learned; how to fix it. U Illinois Law & Economics Research Paper No. LE06-017. Retrieved March 2, 2012, from http://ssrn.com/abstract=911277

Ricard, Y. (2007). Physics and theory. In D. Bercovici (Ed.), *Treatise on geophysics, Volume 7 – Mantle dynamics* (pp. 31-87). Elsevier B.V.

Richards, M., & Dequenne, F. (2010). *HPSS at ECMWF: High performance storage system user forum* (HUF), September 28, 2010, Hamburg, Germany.

Rieger, F. (2009). *Security nightmares 2009.* Retrieved February 29, 2012, from http://www.golem.de/print.php?a=64350.

Rieger, F. (2012). *Security nightmares 2012.* Retrieved February 29, 2012, from http://www.golem.de/print.php?a=88727.

Rife, M. C. (2010). Ethos, pathos, logos, kairos: Using a rhetorical heuristic to mediate digital-survey recruitment strategies. *IEEE Transactions on Professional Communication, 53*(3), 260–277. doi:10.1109/TPC.2010.2052856

Rivest, R. (1992). *The MD5 message-digest algorithm.* IETF RFC 1321, Retrieved February 21, 2012, from http://www.ietf.org/rfc/rfc1321.txt

Robbins, S., & Stylianou, A. (1999). Post-merger systems integration: The impact on is capabilities. *Information & Management*, *36*, 205–212. doi:10.1016/S0378-7206(99)00018-X

Roberts, J. H., & Zhong, S. (2006). Degree-1 convection in the Martian mantle and the origin of the hemispheric dichotomy. *Journal of Geophysical Research*, *111*, E06013. doi:10.1029/2005JE002668

Robertson, C., Nelson, T., Boots, B., & Wulder, M. (2007). STAMP: Spatial–temporal analysis of moving polygons. *Journal of Geographical Systems*, *9*(3), 207–227. doi:10.1007/s10109-007-0044-2

Robuchon, G., Choblet, G., Tobie, G., Čadek, O., Sotin, C., & Grasset, O. (2010). Coupling of thermal evolution and despinning of early Iapetus. *Icarus*, *207*, 959–971. doi:10.1016/j.icarus.2009.12.002

Rodríguez-Haro, F., Freitag, F., & Navarro, L. (2009). Enhancing virtual environments with QoS aware resource management. *Annales des Télécommunications*, *64*, 289–303. doi:10.1007/s12243-009-0106-1

Rogers, E. (1995). *Diffusion of innovations* (4th ed.). New York, NY: The Free Press.

Rolf, T., & Tackley, P. J. (2011). Focussing of stress by continents in 3D spherical mantle convection with self-consistent plate tectonics. *Geophysical Research Letters*, *38*, L18301. doi:10.1029/2011GL048677

Roller, D., & Eck, O. (1997). Constraint propagation using an active semantic network. *Proceedings of 1st International Workshop on Geometric Constraint Solving & Applications.*

Roller, D., Bihler, M., & Eck, O. (1997). SN: Active, distributed knowledge base for rapid prototyping. *Proceedings of 30th ISATA - Volume "Rapid Prototyping in the Automotive Industries"*, (pp. 253-262).

Roller, D., & Eck, O. (1998). Constraint propagation using an active semantic network. In Brüderlin, B., & Roller, D. (Eds.), *Geometric constraints solving and applications*. Berlin, Germany: Springer-Verlag. doi:10.1007/978-3-642-58898-3_3

Roller, D., Eck, O., Bihler, M., & Stolpmann, M. (1995). *An active semantic network for supporting rapid prototyping. ISATA Proceedings on Mechatronics - Efficient Computer Support for Engineering* (pp. 41–48). Manufactoring, Testing & Reliability.

Rollins, J. M. (2012). *Speed of a piston.* Retrieved March 15, 2012 from http://www.camotruck.net/ rollins/piston.html

Roman, D., & Klien, E. (2007). SWING – A semantic framework for geospatial Web services. In Scharl, A., & Tochtermann, K. (Eds.), *The Geospatial Web: How Geo-Browsers, social software and the Web 2.0 are shaping the network society* (pp. 229–234). London, UK: Springer.

Romero, D., & Molina, A. (2009). Value co-creation and co-innovation: Linking networked organizations and customer communities. In Mamarinha-Matos, L. M., Paraskakis, I., & Afsarmanesh, H. (Eds.), *Leveraging knowledge for innovation in collaborative networks* (pp. 401–415). Berlin, Germany: Springer-Verlag. doi:10.1007/978-3-642-04568-4_42

Ronchi, C., Iacono, R., Paolucci, P. S., Hertzberger, B., & Serazzi, G. (1996). The "cubed sphere": A new method for the solution of partial differential equations in spherical geometry. *Journal of Computational Physics*, *124*, 93–114. doi:10.1006/jcph.1996.0047

Rosenblum, L., Earnshaw, R. A., Encarnacao, J., Hagen, H., Kaufman, A., & Klimenko, S. V. … Thalmann, D. (1994). *Scientific visualization: Advances and challenges.* London, UK: Academic Press.

Rosing, M. T., Bird, D. K., Sleep, N. H., Glassley, W., & Albarede, F. (2006). The rise of continents—An essay on the geologic consequences of photosynthesis. *Palaeogeography, Palaeoclimatology, Palaeoecology*, *232*, 99–113. doi:10.1016/j.palaeo.2006.01.007

Rotchanakitumnuai, S. (2008). Measuring e-government service value with the E-GOVSQUAL-RISK model. *Business Process Management Journal*, *14*(5), 724–737. doi:10.1108/14637150810903075

Rotz, B. v. (2010). *Erfolgreiche Online Communities I.* Retrieved August 15, 2010, from http://www.contentmanager.de/magazin/artikel_1766_online_communities.html

Rückemann, C.-P. (2010). Future geo-exploration information and computing systems created by academia-industry collaboration. In *Proceedings of the 9th International Scientific-Practical Conference 2010 (HTFR 2010)*, April 22-23, 2010, (pp. 254-258). Saint Petersburg, Russia: Saint Petersburg University Press.

Rückemann, C.-P. (2010). Integrating high end computing and information systems using a collaboration framework respecting implementation, legal issues, and security. *International Journal on Advances in Security, 3*(3&4), 91-103. Retrieved November 06, 2011, from http://www.iariajournals.org/security/sec_v3_n34_2010_paged.pdf

Rückemann, C.-P. (2010). Legal issues regarding distributed and high performance computing in geosciences and exploration. In *Proceedings of the Fourth International Conference on Digital Society (ICDS 2010)*, (pp. 339-344). Retrieved April 30, 2011, from http://www.computer.org/portal/web/csdl/doi/10.1109/ICDS.2010.56

Rückemann, C.-P. (2011). Envelope interfaces for geoscientific processing with high performance computing and information systems. In C.-P. Rückemann & O. Wolfson (Eds.), *Proceedings International Conference on Advanced Geographic Information Systems, Applications, and Services (GEOProcessing 2011), February 23-28, 2011*, Gosier, Guadeloupe, France, (pp. 23-28). Retrieved April 30, 2011, from http://www.thinkmind.org/download.php?articleid=geoprocessing_2011_2_10_30030

Rückemann, C.-P. (2011). *Securing privacy for future information and computing systems.* Panel on Privacy Invasion and Protection in Digital Society at Digital World 2011, February 26, 2011, Gosier, Guadeloupe, France, ICDS-GEO-CYBERLAWS Panel, The International Conference on Digital Society (ICDS 2010), February 23-28, 2011, Gosier, Guadeloupe, France / Digital World 2011. Retrieved November 20, 2011, from http://www.iaria.org/conferences2011/ProgramGEOProcessing11.html

Rückemann, C.-P. (2011). Implementation of integrated systems and resources for information and computing. In C.-P. Rückemann, W. Christmann, S. Saini, & M. Pankowska (Eds.), *Proceedings International Conference on Advanced Communications and Computation (INFOCOMP 2011)*, October 23-29, 2011, Barcelona, Spain, (pp. 1-7). ISBN: 978-1-61208-161-8

Rückemann, C.-P., & Gersbeck-Schierholz, B. F. S. (2011). Object security and verification for integrated information and computing systems. In L. Berntzen, A. Villafiorita, & M. Perry (Eds.), *Proceedings of the Fifth International Conference on Digital Society (ICDS 2011), Proceedings of the International Conference on Technical and Legal Aspects of the e-Society (CYBERLAWS 2011)*, February 23-28, 2011, Gosier, Guadeloupe, France, (pp. 1-6). Retrieved November 20, 2011, from http://www.thinkmind.org/download.php?articleid=cyberlaws_2011_1_10_70008

Rückemann, C.-P., Göhner, M., & Baur, T. (2007). *Towards integrated grid accounting/billing for D-Grid.* Grid Working Paper.

Rückemann, C.-P. (2011). Queueing aspects of integrated information and computing systems in geosciences and natural sciences. In Chen, D. (Ed.), *Advances in data, methods, models and their applications in geoscience* (pp. 1–26). doi:10.5772/29337

Ruland, C. M., Borosund, E., & Varsi, C. (2009). User requirements for a practice-integrated nurse-administered online communication service for cancer patients. *Studies in Health Technology and Informatics, 146*, 221–225.

Ruland, C. M., Jeneson, A., Andersen, T., Andersen, R., Slaughter, L., & Bente Schjodt, O. (2007). Designing tailored Internet support to assist cancer patients in illness management. *AMIA... Annual Symposium Proceedings / AMIA Symposium. AMIA Symposium, 11*, 635–639.

Russell, S., & Norvig, P. (2010). *Artificial intelligence: A modern approach* (3rd ed.). Upper Saddle River, NJ: Prentice Hall/Pearson Education.

Rzevski, G. (2011). A practical methodology for managing complexity. *Emergence: Complexity & Organization, 13*(1-2), 38–56.

Saad, Y. (1996). *Iterative methods for sparse linear systems*. Boston, MA: PWS Publishing.

Sahai, A., & Waters, B. (2005). Fuzzy identity-based encryption. In R. Cramer (Ed.), *Advances in Cryptology: Proceedings of EUROCRYPT 2005, 24th Annual International Conference on the Theory and Applications of Cryptographic Techniques* (LNCS 3494, pp. 457–473). Berlin, Germany: Springer-Verlag.

Salen, K., & Zimmerman, E. (2003). *Rules of play: Game design fundamentals*. MIT Press.

Salesforce.com. (n.d.). *Manage sales*. Retrieved March 2, 2012, from http://www.salesforce.com

Salomie, I., Cioara, T., Anghel, I., et al. (2010). *Run-time energy-aware adaptivity model*. GAMES Deliverable 4.1 [GAMES D4.1]. To appear on http://www.green-datacenters.eu

Salthe, S. N. (1991). Two forms of hierarchy theory in western discourses. *International Journal of General Systems, 18*, 251–264. doi:10.1080/03081079108935149

Samarati, P., & de Capitani di Vimercati, S. (2001). Access control: Policies, models and mechanisms. In G. Goos, J. Hartmanis, & J. van Leeuwen (Eds.), *Foundations of Security Analysis and Design* (LNCS 2171, pp. 137–196). Berlin, Germany: Springer-Verlag.

Sammon, M. J., Karmin, L. S. B., Peebles, E., & Seligmann, D. D. (2006, 2006-09-29). *MACCS: Enabling communications for mobile workers within healthcare environments*. Paper presented at the MobileHCI'06.

Samuel, H., & Evonuk, M. (2010). Modeling advection in geophysical flows with particle level sets. *Geochemistry Geophysics Geosystems, 11*(8), Q08020. doi:10.1029/2010GC003081

Samuel, H., & Farnetani, C. G. (2003). Thermochemical convection and helium concentrations in mantle plumes. *Earth and Planetary Science Letters, 207*, 39–56. doi:10.1016/S0012-821X(02)01125-1

Sanchez, D. A., Yuen, D. A., Sun, Y., & Wright, G. B. (2011). The role of floating point precision in two- and three-dimensional high Rayleigh-Bénard convection modeled on Fermi GPU. *Proceedings of the 14th IEEE International Conference on Computational Science and Engineering*, (pp. 606-610).

Sanders, J., & Kandrot, E. (2010). *CUDA by example: An introduction to general-purpose GPU programming*. Addison-Wesley.

Sandholm, T. (1993). An implementation of the contract net protocol based on marginal cost calculation. In R. Fikes, & W. G. Lehnert (Eds.), *Proceedings of the 11th National Conference on Artificial Intelligence* (pp. 256-262) Menlo Park, CA: AAAI Press.

Sang, S., Lee, J.-D., & Lee, J. (2009). E-government adoption in ASEAN: The case of Cambodia. *Internet Research, 19*(5), 517–534. doi:10.1108/10662240910998869

Sarrazin, H., & West, A. (2011). Understanding the strategic value of it in m&a. *McKinsey Quarterly*.

Sasaki, Y., Wang, L., Ohta, K., & Kunihiro, N. (2008). Security of MD5 challenge and response: Extension of APOP password recovery attack. *Proceedings of RSA Conference, The Cryptographers' Track, Lecture Notes in Computer Science, 4964, Topics in Cryptology*, April 8-11, 2008, San Francisco, United States of America, (pp. 1-18). Retrieved February 21, 2012, from http://www.springerlink.com/content/y368t967v5168586/

Sasaki, Y., Yamamoto, G., & Aoki, K. (2008). Practical password recovery on an MD5 challenge and response. *Cryptology ePrint Archive*, Report 2007/101, (pp. 101-111), Retrieved February 21, 2012, from http://eprint.iacr.org/2007/101.pdf

Sawhney, N., & Schmandt, C. (2000). Nomadic radio: speech and audio interaction for contextual messaging in nomadic environments. *ACM Transactions on Computer-Human Interaction, 7*(3), 353–383. doi:10.1145/355324.355327

Schellart, W. P., Freeman, J., Stegman, D. R., Moresi, L., & May, D. (2007). Evolution and diversity of subduction zones controlled by slab width. *Nature, 7133*(446), 308–311. doi:10.1038/nature05615

Scherer, C. (2011, January 14). Aircraft must be smart swimmers to make next-gen ATM work. *Flight International.*

Schiel, J. (2010). *Enterprise-scale agile software development.* London, UK: CRC Press, Taylor & Francis Group.

Schilit, B., Adams, N., & Want, R. (1994). *Context-aware computing applications.* Paper presented at the 1994 Workshop on Mobile Computing Systems and Applications.

Schmeling, H., Babeyko, A. Y., Enns, A., Faccenna, C., Funiciello, F., & Gerya, T. (2008). A benchmark comparison of spontaneous subduction models – Towards a free surface. *Physics of the Earth and Planetary Interiors, 171*, 198–223. doi:10.1016/j.pepi.2008.06.028

Schmeling, H., Babeyko, A. Y., Enns, A., Faccenna, C., Funiciello, F., & Gerya, T. (2008). A benchmark comparison of spontaneous subduction models – Towards a free surface. *Physics of the Earth and Planetary Interiors, 171*, 198–223. doi:10.1016/j.pepi.2008.06.028

Schmidt, A., Takaluoma, A., & Mäntyjärvi, J. (2000). Context-aware telephony over WAP. *Personal and Ubiquitous Computing, 4*(4), 225–229.

Schmidt, M.-T., Hutchison, B., Lambros, P., & Phippen, R. (2005). The enterprise service bus: Making service-oriented architecture real. *IBM Systems Journal, 44*(4), 781–797. doi:10.1147/sj.444.0781

Schnoor, I. (October 23, 2011). Real-time processing and archiving strategies. In *Proceedings International Conference on Advanced Communications and Computation* (INFOCOMP 2011), October 23-29, 2011, Barcelona, Spain, (pp. 155-160). ISBN: 978-1-61208-161-8

Scholl, J., Hasvold, P., Henriksen, E., & Ellingsen, G. (2007). *Managing communication availability and interruptions: A study of mobile communication in an oncology department* (pp. 234–250). Pervasive Computing. doi:10.1007/978-3-540-72037-9_14

Schroeder, S., Regli, W. C., Shokoufandeh, A., & Sun, W. (2003). Representation of porous artifacts for bio-medical applications. In *SM '03: Proceedings of the Eighth ACM Symposium on Solid Modeling and Applications*, (pp. 254–257). New York, NY: ACM Press.

Schubert, G., Turcotte, D. L., & Olson, P. (2001). *Mantle convection in the Earth and planets.* Cambridge, UK: Cambridge University Press. doi:10.1017/CBO9780511612879

Schubert, G., Turcotte, D. L., Solomon, S. C., & Sleep, N. H. (1989). *Coupled evolution of the atmospheres and interiors of planets and satellites: Origin and evolution of planetary and satellite atmospheres.* Tucson, AZ: University of Arizona Press.

Schuberth, B. S. A., Bunge, H.-P., Steinle-Neumann, G., Moder, C., & Oeser, J. (2009). Thermal versus elastic heterogeneity in high-resolution mantle circulation models with pyrolite composition: High plume excess temperatures in the lowermost mantle. *Geochemistry Geophysics Geosystems, 10*(1), Q01W01. doi:10.1029/2008GC002235

Seager, S. (2011). *Exoplanets.* Tucson, AZ: University of Arizona Press.

Seffah, A., Gulliksen, J., & Desmarais, M. C. (2005). An introduction to human-centred software engineering, integrating usability in the development process. In Seffah, A., Gulliksen, J., & Desmarais, M. C. (Eds.), *Human-centred software engineering - Integrating usability in the software development lifecycle* (pp. 3–12). Berlin, Germany: Springer-Verlag. doi:10.1007/1-4020-4113-6_1

Sein, M. K., Henfridsson, O., Purao, S., Rossi, M., & Lindgren, R. (2011). Action design research. *Management Information Systems Quarterly, 35*(1), 37–56.

Shah, J. J., & Mantyla, M. (1995). *Parametric and feature-based CAD/CAM: Concepts, techniques, and applications.* Toronto, Canada: John Wiley & Sons, Inc.

Shamji, A., & Law, M. (2011). The role of technology in medical education: Lessons from the University of Toronto. *UMTJ, 88*(3), 150–153.

Shanmugam, M., Thiruvengadam, S., Khurat, A., & Maglogiannis, I. (2006). *Enabling secure mobile access for electronic health care applications.* Paper presented at the Pervasive Health Conference and Workshops, 2006.

Sharma, S., & Gupta, J. (2002). Transforming to e-government: A framework. *2nd European Conference on E-Government, Public Sector Times* (pp. 383-390), 1-2 October 2002, St. Catherine's College Oxford, United Kingdom.

Shaw, S.-L., & Yu, H. (2009). A GIS-based time-geographic approach of studying individual activities and interactions in a hybrid physical–virtual space. *Journal of Transport Geography, 17*(2), 141–149. doi:10.1016/j. jtrangeo.2008.11.012

Shen, W., & Barthes, J. P. (1995). DIDE: A multi-agent environment for engineering design. *Proceedings of the 1st International Conference on Multi-Agent Systems (ICMAS'95)*, (pp. 344-351).

Shen, H.-W., Chiang, L.-J., & Ma, K.-L. (1999). A fast volume rendering algorithm for time-varying fields using a time-space partitioning (TSP) tree. *Proceedings of IEEE Visualization, 99,* 371–378.

Shen, W., Hao, Q., & Li, W. (2008). Computer supported collaborative design: Retrospective and perspective. *Computers in Industry, 59,* 855–862. doi:10.1016/j. compind.2008.07.001

Shieh, Y. Y., & Tsai, F. Y. Arash, Wang, M. D., & Lin, C. M. C. (2007). *Mobile healthcare: Opportunities and challenges.* Paper presented at the International Conference on the Management of Mobile Business, Toronto, Canada.

Shields, M., & Taylor, I. (2006). Programming scientific and distributed workflow with Triana Services. *Concurrency and Computation: Practice & Experience - Workflow in Grid Systems, 18*(10), 1-10. doi:10.1002/cpe.v18:10

Shmoo. (2012). *The Shmoo Group rainbow tables.* Retrieved February 15, 2012, from http://rainbowtables. shmoo.com

Shneiderman, B. (1986). *Designing the user interface: Strategies for effective human-computer interaction.* Boston, MA: Addison-Wesley Longman Publishing Co., Inc.doi:10.1145/25065.950626

Shue, V. (2011). *Philosophies and styles of public leadership in China.* Paper presented at the 3rd International Conference in Public Policy and Management, 23 Oct 2011, School of Public Policy and Management, Tsinghua University, Beijing, China.

Sidorova, A., Evangelopoulos, N., Valacich, J. S., & Ramakrishnan, T. (2008). Uncovering the intellectual core of the information systems discipline. *Management Information Systems Quarterly, 32*(3), 467–482.

Siek, K. A., Khan, D. U., Ross, S. E., Haverhals, L. M., Meyers, J., & Cali, S. R. (2011). Designing a personal health application for older adults to manage medications: A comprehensive case study. *Journal of Medical Systems, 12,* 12.

Siewiorek, D., Smailagic, A., Furukawa, J., Krause, A., Moraveji, N., Reiger, K., et al. (2003). SenSay: A context-aware mobile phone. *Proceedings of the Seventh IEEE International Symposium on Wearable Computers, 2003.*

Silver, D., & Wang, X. (1997). Tracking and visualizing turbulent 3-D features. *IEEE Transactions on Visualization and Computer Graphics, 3*(2), 129–141. doi:10.1109/2945.597796

Simon, H. (1991). Bounded rationality and organizational learning. *Organization Science, 2*(1), 125–134. doi:10.1287/orsc.2.1.125

Simon, H. A. (1996). *The sciences of the artificial* (3rd ed.). Cambridge, MA: MIT Press.

Singh, S. H. (2003). *Government in the digital era and human factors in e-governance.* Paper read the Regional Workshop on e-Government, 1-3 December 2003, Sana'a.

Sipior, J., & Ward, B. (2005). Bridging the digital divide for e-government inclusion: A United States case study. *The Electronic.Journal of E-Government, 3*(3), 137–146.

Skobelev, P. (2011). Bio-inspired multi-agent technology for industrial applications. In F. Alkhateeb, E. Al Maghayreh, & I. Abu Doush (Eds.), *Multi-Agent Systems - Modeling, Control, Programming, Simulations and Applications.* Rijeka, Croatia: InTech. Retrieved February 29, 2012, from http://www.intechopen.com/articles/show/title/bio-inspired-multi-agent-technology-for-industrial-applications

Skov, B., & Høegh, T. (2006). Supporting information access in a hospital ward by a context-aware mobile electronic patient record. *Personal and Ubiquitous Computing, 10*(4), 205–214. doi:10.1007/s00779-005-0049-0

Smith, S., & Jamieson, R. (2006). Determining key factors in e-government information system security. *Information Systems Management,* (Spring): 23–32. doi:10.1201/107 8.10580530/45925.23.2.20060301/92671.4

Smits, P., & Friis-Christensen, A. (2007). Resource discovery in a European spatial data infrastructure. *IEEE Transactions on Knowledge and Data Engineering, 19*(1), 85–95. doi:10.1109/TKDE.2007.250587

Smyth, S. M. (2009). Searches of computers and computer data at the United States border: The need for a new framework following United States V. Arnold. *Journal of Law, Technology and Policy, 2009*(1), 69-105. Retrieved February 21, 2012, from http://papers.ssrn.com/sol3/papers.cfm?abstract_id=1345927

Snell, A. (April 8, 2011). *LSI und Whamcloud bieten gemeinsam Lustre Support Service für HPC Storagesysteme.* Press Release LSI Corp. Retrieved January 23, 2012, from http://www.lsi.com/emea/newsroom/Pages/ge_20110408pr.aspx

Social Semantic Web. (2011). Wikipedia. Retrieved November 20, 2011, from http://en.wikipedia.org/wiki/Social_Semantic_Web

Solid-state drive. (n.d.). *Wikipedia, the free encyclopedia.* Retrieved October 16, 2011 from http://en.wikipedia.org/wiki/Solid-state_drive.

Soll, D., & Wessels, D. (1998). *Motion analysis of living cells: Techniques in modern biomedical microscopy.* New York, NY: Wiley-Liss.

Solomatov, V. (2007). Magma oceans and primordial mantle differentiation. In D. J. Stevenson (Ed.), *Treatise on geophysics, volume 9 – Evolution of the Earth* (pp. 91-119). Amsterdam, The Netherlands: Elsevier.

Solomatov, V. (2000). Fluid dynamics of a terrestrial magma ocean. In Canup, R. M., & Righter, K. (Eds.), *Origin of the Earth and Moon.* Tucson, AZ: University of Arizona Press.

Solvoll, T., Fasani, S., Ravuri, A. B., Tiemersma, A., & Hartvigsen, G. (2010, August 23-24, 2010). *Evaluation of an Ascom/trixbox system for context sensitive communication in hospitals.* Paper presented at the 8th Scandinavian Conference on Health Informatics, Copenhagen.

Solvoll, T., Scholl, J., & Hartvigsen, G. (2012). *Physicians interrupted by mobile devices in hospitals – Understanding the interaction between devices, roles and duties.* Unpublished work.

Solvoll, T., Tiemersma, A., Kerbage, E., Fasani, S., Ravuri, A. B., & Hartvigsen, G. (2011). Context-sensitive communication in hospitals: A user interface evaluation and redesign of Ascom wireless IP-DECT phones. *eTELEMED 2011, The Third International Conference on eHealth, Telemedicine, and Social Medicine,* Gosier, Guadeloupe, France (pp. 37–46).

Solvoll, T., & Scholl, J. (2008). Strategies to reduce interruptions from mobile communication systems in surgical wards. *Journal of Telemedicine and Telecare, 14*(7), 389–392. doi:10.1258/jtt.2008.007015

Solvoll, T., Scholl, J., & Hartvigsen, G. (2010). Physicians interrupted by mobile devices – Relations between devices, roles and duties. *Studies in Health Technology and Informatics, 160,* 1365.

Somers, T. M., & Nelson, K. (2001). *The impact of critical success factors across the stages of enterprise resource planning implementations.* Paper presented at the Hawaii International Conference on System Sciences, Maui, Hawaii.

Sonntag, M., & Karastoyanova, D. (2010). *Next generation interactive scientific experimenting based on the workflow technology.* 21st IASTED International Conference Modelling and Simulation (MS 2010). ACTA Press.

Sonntag, M., Currle-Linde, N., Görlach, K., & Karastoyanova, D. (2010). Towards simulation workflows with BPEL: Deriving missing features from GRICOL. *21st IASTED International Conference on Modelling and Simulation MS 2010.* ACTA Press.

Sonntag, M., Karastoyanova, D., & Deelman, E. (2010). Lecture Notes in Computer Science: Vol. 6470. *BPEL4Pegasus : Workflows combining business and BPEL4Pegasus : Combining business* (pp. 728–729). doi:10.1007/978-3-642-17358-5_75

Sotin, C., & Labrosse, S. (1999). Three-dimensional thermal convection in an iso-viscous, infinite Prandtl number fluid heated from within and from below: Applications to the transfer of heat through planetary mantles. *Physics of the Earth and Planetary Interiors*, *112*, 171–190. doi:10.1016/S0031-9201(99)00004-7

Soziales Netzwerk. (2010). Wikipedia. Retrieved October 11, 2010, from http://de.wikipedia.org/wiki/Soziales_Netzwerk_(Internet)

Spaniol, M., Klamma, R., & Cao, Y. (2008). Learning as a service: A Web-based learning framework for communities of professionals on the Web 2.0. In *Advances in Web based learning - ICWL 2007* (*Vol. 4823*, pp. 160–173). Lecture Notes in Computer ScienceBerlin, Germany: Springer-Verlag. doi:10.1007/978-3-540-78139-4_15

SPEC. (2008). *SPECpower_ssj2008 description*. Retrieved March 1, 2012, from http://www.spec.org/power_ssj2008/index.html

SPEC. (2008-2010). *All published SPECpower_ssj2008results*. Retrieved March 1, 2012, from http://www.spec.org/power-ssj2008/results/power-ssj2008.html

Special Committee for e-Government, Republic of Korea (2003). *Korea's e-government completion of e-government framework*. Korea: Special Committee for e-Government, Republic of Korea.

Spil, T. A. M., & Katsma, C. P. (2007). *Balancing supply and demand of an electronic health record in the Netherlands; Not too open systems for not too open users*. Paper presented at the 40th Annual Hawaii International Conference on System Sciences, 2007 (HICSS 2007).

Spohn, T., & Schubert, G. (1982). Models of mantle convection and the removal of heat from the Earth's interior. *Journal of Geophysical Research*, *87*, 4682–4696. doi:10.1029/JB087iB06p04682

Sprague, R. H. Jr. (1980). A framework for the development of decision support systems. *Management Information Systems Quarterly*, 1–26. doi:10.2307/248957

Sprow, E. (1992). Chrysler's concurrent engineering challenge. *Manufacturing Engineering*, *108*, 35–42.

Spurck, P. A., Mohr, M. L., Seroka, A. M., & Stoner, M. (1995). The impact of a wireless telecommunication system on time efficiency. *The Journal of Nursing Administration*, *25*(6), 21–26. doi:10.1097/00005110-199506000-00007

Šramek, O., & Zhong, S. (2012). Martian crustal dichotomy and Tharsis formation by partial melting coupled to early plume migration. *Journal of Geophysical Research*, *117*(E01005). doi:10.1029/2011JE003867

Šramek, O., & Zhong, S. J. (2010). Long-wavelength stagnant-lid convection with hemispheric variation in lithospheric thickness: Link between Martian crustal dichotomy and Tharsis? *Journal of Geophysical Research*, *115*, E09010. doi:10.1029/2010JE003597

Stadler, G., Gurnis, M., Burstedde, C., Wilcox, L. C., Alisic, L., & Ghattas, O. (2010). The dynamics of plate tectonics and mantle flow: From local to global scales. *Science*, *329*(5995), 1033–1038. doi:10.1126/science.1191223

Stake, R. E. (2005). Qualitative case studies. In Denzin, N. K., & Lincoln, Y. S. (Eds.), *The Sage handbook of qualitative research* (3rd ed., pp. 443–466). Thousand Oaks, CA: Sage.

Stamenkovic, V., Breuer, D., & Spohn, T. (2011). Thermal and transport properties of mantle rock at high pressure: Applications to super-Earths. *Icarus*, *216*(2), 572–596. doi:10.1016/j.icarus.2011.09.030

Stamenkovic, V., Noack, L., Breuer, D., & Spohn, T. (2012). The influence of pressure-dependent viscosity on the thermal evolution of super-Earths. *The Astrophysical Journal*, *748*(1), 41. doi:10.1088/0004-637X/748/1/41

Standing, S., & Standing, C. (2008). Mobile technology and healthcare: The adoption issues and systemic problems. *International Journal of Electronic Healthcare*, *4*(3-4), 221–235. doi:10.1504/IJEH.2008.022661

Steinberg, M. (2011). *Utilizing distributed web resources for enhanced knowledge representation*. Unpublished doctoral dissertation, Leibniz Universität Hannover, Germany.

Steinberger, B., & Calderwood, A. R. (2006). Models of large-scale viscous flow in the Earth's mantle with constraints from mineral physics and surface observations. *Geophysical Journal International, 167*, 1461–1481. doi:10.1111/j.1365-246X.2006.03131.x

Steinberger, B., & Holme, R. (2008). Mantle flow models with core-mantle boundary constraints and chemical heterogeneities in the lowermost mantle. *Journal of Geophysical Research, 113*, B05403. doi:10.1029/2007JB005080

Stein, C., Fahl, A., & Hansen, U. (2010). Resurfacing events on Venus: Implications on plume dynamics and surface topography. *Geophysical Research Letters, 37*, L01201. doi:10.1029/2009GL041073

Stemmer, K., Harder, H., & Hansen, U. (2006). A new method to simulate convection with strongly temperature- and pressure-dependent viscosity in a spherical shell: Applications to the Earth's mantle. *Physics of the Earth and Planetary Interiors, 157*, 223–249. doi:10.1016/j.pepi.2006.04.007

Stevenson, D. J., Spohn, T., & Schubert, G. (1983). Magnetism and thermal evolution of the terrestrial planets. *Icarus, 54*, 466–489. doi:10.1016/0019-1035(83)90241-5

Stockinger, H. (1999). Data replication in distributed database systems. *CMS Note*. Retrieved from http://cdsweb.cern.ch/record/687136

Stock, K. M., Atkinson, R., Higgins, C., Small, M., Woolf, A., & Millard, K. (2010). A semantic registry using a feature type catalogue instead of ontologies to support spatial data infrastructures. *International Journal of Geographical Information Science, 24*(2), 231–252. doi:10.1080/13658810802570291

Storage magazine/SearchStorage.com (2011, March). *NetApp tops enterprise arrays field again*. Retrieved October 16, 2010, from http://searchstorage.techtarget.com/magazineContent/NetApp-tops-enterprise-arrays-field-again.

Storer, M. W., Greenan, K. M., Miller, E. L., & Voruganti, K. (2008, February). *Pergamum: Replacing tape with energy efficient, reliable, disk-based archival storage.* [PDF Document]. Retrieved January 22, 2012, from http://www.ssrc.ucsc.edu/Papers/storer-fast08.pdf

Sudarsanam, P. (2003). *Creating value from mergers and acquisitions: The challenges: An integrated and international perspective.* Prentice Hall.

Sulaiman, R., Sharma, D., Wanli, M., & Tran, D. (2008). *A security architecture for e-health services.* Paper presented at the 10th International Conference on Advanced Communication Technology (ICACT 2008).

Sulaiman, R., Xu, H., & Sharma, D. (2009). *E-health services with secure mobile agent.* Paper presented at the Seventh Annual Communication Networks and Services Research Conference (CNSR '09).

Sutton, P., & Hansen, C. D. (1999). Isosurface extraction in time-varying fields using a temporal branch-on-need tree (T-BON). In *Proceedings of the IEEE Conference on Visualization '99*, (pp. 147–153). IEEE Computer Society Press.

Tackley, P. J. (2000). Mantle convection and plate tectonics: Toward an integrated physical and chemical theory. *Science, 288*, 2002–2007. doi:10.1126/science.288.5473.2002

Tackley, P. J. (2000). Self-consistent generation of tectonic plates in time-dependent, three-dimensional mantle convection simulations. *Geochemistry Geophysics Geosystems, 1*(8), 1021. doi:10.1029/2000GC000036

Tackley, P. J. (2008). Modelling compressible mantle convection with large viscosity contrasts in a three-dimensional spherical shell using the yin-yang grid. *Physics of the Earth and Planetary Interiors, 171*(1-4), 7–18. doi:10.1016/j.pepi.2008.08.005

Tackley, P. J., & King, S. D. (2003). Testing the tracer ratio method for modeling active compositional fields in mantle convection simulations. *Geochemistry Geophysics Geosystems, 4*(4), 8302. doi:10.1029/2001GC000214

Taifur, S. (2006). *SICT's steps towards good governance through ICTs: E-governance strategies. Bangladesh.* Bangladesh: Ministry of Planning.

Talaei-Khoei, A., Solvoll, T., Ray, P., & Parameshwaran, N. (2011). Policy-based awareness management (PAM): Case study of a wireless communication system at a hospital. *Journal of Systems and Software, 84*(10), 1791–1805. doi:10.1016/j.jss.2011.05.024

Talaei-Khoei, A., Solvoll, T., Ray, P., & Parameshwaran, N. (2012). Maintaining awareness using policies: Enabling agents to identify relevance of information. *Journal of Computer and System Sciences, 78*(1), 370–391. doi:10.1016/j.jcss.2011.05.013

Tan, E., & Gurnis, M. (2007). Compressible thermo-chemical convection and application to lower mantle structures. *Journal of Geophysical Research, 112*(B06304). doi:10.1029/2006JB004505

Tan, E., Leng, W., Zhong, S., & Gurnis, M. (2011). On the location of plumes and lateral movement of thermochemical structures with high bulk modulus in the 3-D compressible mantle. *Geochemistry Geophysics Geosystems, 12*, Q07005. doi:10.1029/2011GC003665

Tang, J. C., Yankelovich, N., Begole, J., Kleek, M. V., Li, F., & Bhalodia, J. (2001). *ConNexus to awarenex: Extending awareness to mobile users.* Paper presented at the SIGCHI Conference on Human Factors in Computing Systems, Seattle, Washington, United States.

Tanriverdi, H., & Uysal, V. (2011). Cross-business information technology integration and acquirer value creation in corporate mergers and acquisitions. *Information Systems Research, 22*(4). doi:10.1287/isre.1090.0250

Tape, I. B. M. (2011). *Why IBM?* Retrieved October 16, 2011, from http://www-03.ibm.com/systems/storage/tape/why/index.html

Tassabehji, R., & Elliman, T. (2006). *Generating citizen trust in e-government using a trust verification agent: A research note.* Paper read at the European and Mediterranean Conference on Information Systems (EMCIS) 2006, July 6-7 2006, Costa Blanca, Alicante, Spain.

Taylor, I. J., Deelman, E., Gannon, D. B., Gannon, D., Shields, M., & Taylor, I. (2007). *Workflows for e-science - Scientific workflows for grids.* Springer Business. Retrieved February 10, 2012, from http://books.google.de/books?hl=de&lr=&id=-ZEtM2YKwEYC&oi=fnd&pg=PR7&dq=Workflows++for++e-+Science&ots=HMdPzLt37Q&sig=l65IfOlX9Km2GOOn3kKpFMAiruw#v=onepage&q&f=false

Taylor, H. (2006). *The joy of SOX: Why Sarbanes-Oxley and service-oriented architecture may be the best thing that ever happened to you.* Wiley Pub.

Tchuente, M. (1987). Computation on automata networks. In Fogelman-Soulie, F., Robert, Y., & Tchuente, M. (Eds.), *Automata networks in computer science: Theory and applications.* Princeton, NJ: Princeton University Press.

Technologies, C. A. (2010). *Turnkey cloud computing.* Retrieved September 14, 2011, from http://www.3tera.com/AppLogic

Techrepublic.com. (2011). *Pergamum: Replacing tape with energy efficient, reliable, disk-based archival storage.* Retrieved June 17, 2011, from http://www.techrepublic.com/whitepapers/pergamum-replacing-tape-with-energy-efficient-reliable-disk-based-archival-storage/1294097.

Telea, A. C. (2008). *Data visualization: Principles and practice.* Wellesley, MA: A. K. Peters, Ltd.

ten Hompel, M. (2008). *Logistics by design – Ein Ansatz für zukunftsfähige Intralogistik: Serviceorientierte Architektur als Grundlage* (Vol. 5, pp. 236–240). Hebezeuge-Fördermittel / HF Forschung.

The 3rd Generation Partnership Project. (2011). *The mobile broadband standards.* Retrieved September 23, 2011, from http://www.3gpp.org/

The Climate Group on behalf of the Global eSustainability Initiative GeSI [Climate Group]. (2008). *SMART 2020: Enabling the low carbon economy in the information age.*

Thiel, S., Dalakakis, S., & Roller, D. (2005). A learning agent for knowledge extraction from an active semantic network. *World Academy of Science, Engineering and Technology, 7.*

Thing, V. L. L., & Ying, H. M. (2009). A novel time-memory trade-off method for password recovery. *International Journal of Digital Forensics and Incident Response, 6,* S114-S120. Retrieved February 21, 2012, from www.dfrws.org/2009/proceedings/p114-thing.pdf

Thorp, J. (2010). Europe's E-health initiatives. *Journal of American Health Information Management Association, 81*(9), 56–58.

Tidd, J., & Bessant, J. (2009). *Managing innovations, integrating technological, market and organizational change.* Chichester, UK: John Wiley and Sons.

Todorov, D. (2007). *Mechanics of user identification and authentication: Fundamentals of identity management.* Auerbach Publications. doi:10.1201/9781420052206

Toffoli, T., & Margolus, N. (1988). *Cellular automata machines: A new environment for modeling.* Cambridge, MA: The MIT Press.

Tolbert, C. J., & Mossberger, K. (2006). The effects of e-government on trust and confidence in government. *Public Administration Review, 66*(3), 354–369. doi:10.1111/j.1540-6210.2006.00594.x

Tonti, G., Bradshaw, J. M., Jeffers, R., Montanari, R., Suri, N., & Uszok, A. (2003). Semantic Web languages for policy representation and reasoning: A comparison of KAoS, Rei, and Ponder. In D. Fensel, K. Sycara, & J. Mylopoulos (Eds.), *The Semantic Web: Proceedings of the Second International Semantic Web Conference (ISWC 2003)* (LNCS 2870, pp. 419-437). Berlin, Germany: Springer-Verlag.

Tosi, N., Čadek, O., Martinec, Z., Yuen, D. A., & Kaufmann, G. (2009). Is the long-wavelength geoid sensitive to the presence of postperovskite above the core-mantle boundary? *Geophysical Research Letters, 36*, L05303. doi:10.1029/2008GL036902

Tosi, N., Yuen, D. A., & Čadek, O. (2010). Dynamical consequences in the lower mantle with the post-perovskite phase change and strongly depth-dependent thermodynamic and transport properties. *Earth and Planetary Science Letters, 298*(1-2), 229–243. doi:10.1016/j.epsl.2010.08.001

Totsuka, T., & Levoy, M. (1993). Frequency domain volume rendering. In *SIGGRAPH '93: Proceedings of the 20th Annual Conference on Computer Graphics and Interactive Techniques,* (pp. 271–278). New York, NY: ACM Press.

Toye, G., Cutkosky, M., Leifer, L., Tenenbaum, J., & Glicksman, J. (1993). SHARE: A methodology and environment for collaborative product development. *Proceedings of the IEEE 2nd Workshop on Enabling Technologies: Infrastructure for Collaborative Enterprises,* (pp. 33-47).

Transaction_processing_system. (n.d.). *Wikipedia, the free encyclopaedia.* Retrieved June 17, 2011 from http://en.wikipedia.org/wiki/Transaction_processing_system

Transport & Travel @ eCitizen. (2010). *NSMen.* Singapore: Singapore Government.

Traunmuller, R. (2010). Web 2.0 creates a new government. In In K. N. Andersen, E. Francesconi, A. Grönlund, & T. M. van Engers (Eds.), *Electronic government and the information systems perspective,* (pp. 77-83). Berlin, Germany: Springer Verlag.

Tropea, G., Lioudakis, G. V., Blefari-Melazzi, N., Kaklamani, D. I., & Venieris, I. S. (2011). Introducing privacy-awareness in network monitoring ontologies. In Salgarelli, L., Bianchi, G., & Blefari-Melazzi, N. (Eds.), *Trustworthy Internet* (pp. 317–331). Milan, Italy: Springer-Verlag. doi:10.1007/978-88-470-1818-1_24

Troy, M., Röber, N., Möller, T., Celler, A., & Stella Atkins, M. (2001). 4D space-time techniques: A medical imaging case study. In *Proceedings of IEEE Visualization 2001 Conference,* (pp. 473–476).

Turcotte, D. L., & Schubert, G. (2002). *Geodynamics* (2nd ed.). New York, NY: Cambridge University Press.

Turner, J. S. (1980). *Buoyancy effects in fluids.* Cambridge University Press.

Tversky, B. (1993). Cognitive maps, cognitive collages, and spatial mental models. *Lecture Notes in Computer Science,* (716): 14–24. doi:10.1007/3-540-57207-4_2

Twitter: A microblogging service. (2012). Retrieved January 15, 2012, from http://www.twitter.com

Tzeng, F.-Y., & Ma, K.-L. (2005). Intelligent feature extraction and tracking for visualizing large-scale 4D flow simulations. In *Proceedings of the ACM/IEEE SC 2005 Supercomputing Conference,* (p. 6).

U. S. Department of Health and Human Services. (2003). *Summary of the HIPAA privacy rule.* Retrieved January 06, 2012, from http://www.hhs.gov/ocr/privacy/hipaa/understanding/summary/index.html

U. S. Department of Health and Human Services. (2003). *Summary of the HIPAA security rule*. Retrieved January 06, 2012, from http://www.hhs.gov/ocr/privacy/hipaa/understanding/srsummary.html

U.S. Department of Energy (DOE). (2009). *HPSS in the extreme scale era* [PDF document]. Retrieved October 19, 2011, from http://www.nersc.gov/assets/HPC-Requirements-for-Science/HPSSExtremeScaleFINALpublic.pdf

U.S. Department of Energy (DOE). (2010). *The opportunities and challenges of exascale computing* [PDF document]. Retrieved October 19, 2011, from

UDCC. (2011). Universal decimal classification. Universal Decimal Classification Consortium (UDCC). Retrieved November 27, 2011, from http://www.udcc.org

Ullmann, N. (2010). *Design and implementation of a global rewarding model based on user interaction tasks*. Master thesis, Leibniz Universität Hannover, Germany

United Nations Division for Public Economics and Public Administration, American Society for Public Administration. (2002). *Benchmarking e-government: A global perspective. Assessing the progress of the UN member states*. New York, NY: United Nations–DPEPA and ASPA.

United Nations Public Administration Network. (n.d.). *United Nations e-government survey 2010 special awards*. New York, NY. *United Nations Public Administration Network*.

United States Congress House Committee on Small Business. (2007). *Full committee hearing on Sarbanes-Oxley section 404: Will the SEC's and PCAOB's new standards lower compliance costs for small companies?* Committee on Small Business, United States House of Representatives. Washington, DC: Author.

United States Congress Senate Committee on Banking, Housing, and Urban Affairs. (2009). *The state of the securities markets [electronic resource]: Hearing before the Committee on Banking, Housing, and Urban Affairs, United States Senate, One Hundred Tenth Congress, first session on examining current issues and matters raised in previous securities hearings*. Washington, DC: Author.

United States Congress. (1999). *Financial Services Modernization Act* (Gramm-Leach-Bliley). Pub. L. No. 106-102,11 Stat. 1338, codified at 15 U.S.C. 6801-09.

United States Congress. (1999). *Gramm-Leach-Bliley safeguards rule-Subtitle A- Disclosure of nonpublic personal information*. Codified 15 U.S.C. 6801-09.

United States Congress. (2003). *The Fair and Accurate Credit transactions Act of 2003* (FACT). Pub. L. No. 108-159,117 Stat. 1952.

University Corporation for Atmospheric Research (UCAR). (2011). *CISL HPSS*. Retrieved June 18, 2011, from http://www2.cisl.ucar.edu/book/export/html/964

University of Cambridge, & China Mobile. (2011). *Mobile communication for medical care - Final report. Case study A: mHealth in Guangdong Province*. Retrieved August 3, 2011, from http://www.csap.cam.ac.uk/media/uploads/files/1/mobile-communications-for-medical-care.pdf

Urban, G. L., & Von Hippel, E. (1988). Lead user analyses for the development of new industrial products. *Management Science*, *5*(34), 569–582. doi:10.1287/mnsc.34.5.569

Vacanti, J. P., & Vacanti, C. A. (1997). The challenge of tissue engineering. In Lanza, R. P., Langer, R. L., & Chick, W. L. (Eds.), *Principles of tissue engineering*. San Diego, CA: Academic Press.

Valencia, D., O'Connell, R. J., & Sasselov, D. (2006). Internal structure of massive terrestrial planets. *Icarus*, *181*, 545–554. doi:10.1016/j.icarus.2005.11.021

van Brussel, H., Wyns, J., Valckenaers, P., Bongaerts, L., & Peeters, P. (1998). Reference architecture for holonic manufacturing systems: PROSA. *Computers in Industry*, *37*(3), 255–274. doi:10.1016/S0166-3615(98)00102-X

van der Meer, D. G., Spakman, W., van Hinsbergen, D. J. J., Amaru, M. L., & Torsvik, T. H. (2010). Towards absolute plate motions constrained by lower-mantle slab remnants. *Nature Geoscience*, *3*, 36–40. doi:10.1038/ngeo708

van Hanxleden, R., & Scott, L. R. (1991, November). Load balancing on message passing architectures. *Journal of Parallel and Distributed Computing*, *13*(3), 312–324. doi:10.1016/0743-7315(91)90078-N van Heck, H. J., & Tackley, P. J. (2008). Planforms of self-consistently generated plates in 3D spherical geometry. *Geophysical Research Letters*, *35*, L19312. doi:10.1029/2008GL035190

van Keken, P. E. (2001). Cylindrical scaling for dynamical cooling models of the Earth. *Physics of the Earth and Planetary Interiors*, *124*, 119–130. doi:10.1016/S0031-9201(01)00195-9

van Keken, P. E., King, S. D., Schmeling, H., Christensen, U. R., Neumeister, D., & Doin, M.-P. (1997). A comparison of methods for the modeling of thermochemical convection. *Journal of Geophysical Research*, *102*, 22477–22495. doi:10.1029/97JB01353

van Keken, P. E., King, S. D., Schmeling, H., Christensen, U. R., Neumeister, D., & Doin, M.-P. (1997). A comparison of methods for the modeling of thermochemical convection. *Journal of Geophysical Research*, *102*, 22477–22495. doi:10.1029/97JB01353

van Lieshout, E., van der Veer, S., Hensbroek, R., Korevaar, J., Vroom, M., & Schultz, M. (2007). Interference by new-generation mobile phones on critical care medical equipment. *Critical Care (London, England)*, *11*(5), R98. doi:10.1186/cc6115

Varshalovich, D. A., Moskalev, A. N., & Khersonskii, V. K. (1988). *Quantum theory of angular momentum*. World Scientific.

Vasich, T. (2012). *The age of electronic medicine*. Retrieved January 27, 2012 from http://www.uci.edu/features/2010/08/feature_ipad_100813.php

Vector Fabrics, B. V. (2011). *Using vfAnalyst to parallelize your program*. Whitepaper. Retrieved October 3, 2011, from http://www.vectorfabrics.com/

Velímský, J., & Martinec, Z. (2005). Time-domain, spherical harmonic-finite element approach to transient three-dimensional geomagnetic induction in a spherical heterogeneous Earth. *Geophysical Journal International*, *161*(1), 81–101. doi:10.1111/j.1365-246X.2005.02546.x

Venkatesh, V., Morris, M., Davis, G., & Davis, F. (2003). User acceptance of information technology: Toward a unified view. *Management Information Systems Quarterly*, *27*(3), 425–478.

Verhaeghen, P., & Salthouse, T. A. (1997). Meta-analyses of age-cognition relations in adulthood: Estimates of linear and nonlinear age effects and structural models. *Psychological Bulletin*, *122*(3), 231–249. doi:10.1037/0033-2909.122.3.231

Verhoeven, J., & Schmalzl, J. (2009). A numerical method for investigating crystal settling in convecting magma chambers. *Geochemistry Geophysics Geosystems*, *10*, Q12007. doi:10.1029/2009GC002509

Verroust, A., Schonek, F., & Roller, D. (1992). A rule oriented method for parametrized computer aided design. *Computer Aided Design*, *24*, 531–540. doi:10.1016/0010-4485(92)90040-H

Vintar, M., Kunstelj, M., Decman, M., & Bercic, M. (2003). Development of e-government in Slovenia. *Information Polity*, *8*, 133–149.

VMware. (2010). *VMware distributed power management: Concepts and usage*. Retrieved March 1, 2012, from http://www.vmware.com/files/pdf/Distributed-Power-Management-vSphere.pdf

von Ahn, L., Ginosar, S., Kedia, M., Liu, R., & Blum, M. (2006). *Improving accessibility of the Web with a computer game*. International Conference for Human-Computer Interaction, CHI 2006, Canada.

von Ahn, L. (2006). Games with a purpose. *Computer*, *39*(6), 92–96. doi:10.1109/MC.2006.196

Von Hippel, E. (1986). Lead users: A source of novel product concepts. *Management Science*, *32*(7), 791–805. doi:10.1287/mnsc.32.7.791

von Larcher, T., Futterer, B., Egbers, C., Hollerbach, R., Chossat, P., & Beltrame, P. (2008). GeoFlow - European microgravity experiments on thermal convection in rotating spherical shells under influence of central force field. *Journal of the Japan Society of Microgravity Application*, *25*(3), 121–126.

Von Zedtwitz, M., & Gassman, O. (2002). Market versus technology drive in R&D internationalization: Four different patterns of managing research and development. *Research Policy*, *31*, 569–588. doi:10.1016/S0048-7333(01)00125-1

Vygotsky, L. S. (1978). *Mind in society*. Cambridge, MA: Harvard University Press.

W3C. (2008). *Resource description framework* (RDF). Retrieved May 25, 2010, from http://www.w3.org/RDF/

W3C. (2010). *SPARQL protocol and RDF query language*. Retrieved May 25, 2010, from http://www.w3.org/TR/rdf-sparql-query/

Wallis, A., Haag, Z., & Foley, R. (1998). A multi-agent framework for distributed collaborative design. *Proceedings of the IEEE Workshops on Enabling Technologies Infrastructure for Collaborative Enterprises (WET ICE'98)*, (pp. 282-287).

Walls, J. G., Widmeyer, G. R., & El Sawy, O. A. (1992). Building an information system design theory for vigilant EIS. *Information Systems Research, 3*(1), 36–59. doi:10.1287/isre.3.1.36

Wang, L., Shen, W., Xie, H., Neelamkavil, J., & Pardasani, A. (2000). Collaborative conceptual design: A state-of-the-art survey. *Proceedings of the 6th International Conference on Computer Supported Cooperative Work in Design*, (pp. 204-209).

Wang, X., & Devarajan, V. (2004). A honeycomb model for soft tissue deformation. In *VRCAI '04: Proceedings of the 2004 ACM SIGGRAPH International Conference on Virtual Reality Continuum and its Applications in Industry*, (pp. 257–260). New York, NY: ACM Press.

Wang, L. (2009). *Virtual environments for grid computing*. Karlsruhe, Germany: Universitaetsverlag Karlsruhe.

Ward, P. D., & Brownlee, D. (2000). *Rare Earth: Why complex life is uncommon in the universe*. New York, NY: Springer. doi:10.1063/1.1325239

Watson, D. (2006). *Yes, Virginia, there is an HPSS in your future*. [PDF Document]. Retrieved January 24, 2012, from http://www.hpss-collaboration.org/documents/WatsonSalishan2007.pdf.

Watson, R. T. (2001). Introducing MISQ review—A new department in MIS Quarterly. *Management Information Systems Quarterly, 25*(1).

Watson, R. T., Boudreau, M.-C., & Chen, A. J. (2010). Information systems and environmentally sustainable development: Energy informatics and new directions for the IS community. *Management Information Systems Quarterly, 34*(1), 23–38.

Web 2.0. (2011). Wikipedia. Retrieved May 20, 2011 from http://en.wikipedia.org/wiki/Web_2.0.

Web services. (2009). Wikipedia. Retrieved May 27, 2010, from http://en.wikipedia.org/wiki/Web_service

Web, W. W. (2009). Wikipedia. Retrieved May 27, 2009 from http://en.wikipedia.org/wiki/World_Wide_Web

Weibel, S. L., & Koch, T. (2000). *The Dublin core metadata initiative: Mission, current activities, and future directions*. Retrieved October 16, 2011, from http://www.dlib.org/dlib/december00/weibel/12weibel.html

Weikum, G., & Schek, H. (1992). Concepts and applications of multilevel transactions and open nested transactions. In Elmagarmid, A. (Ed.), *Database transaction models for advanced applications* (pp. 515–553). Morgan Kaufmann.

Wein, B. B. (2003). IHE (Integrating the Healthcare Enterprise): A new approach for the improvement of digital communication in healthcare. *Rofo, 175*(2), 183–186. doi:10.1055/s-2003-37238

Weiss, G. (1999). *Multiagent systems: A modern approach to distributed artificial intelligence*. Massachusetts, USA: MIT Press.

Welytok, J. G. (2006). *Sarbanes-Oxley for dummies*. Wiley Pub.

Wescott, D. (2004). E-government and the transformation of service delivery and citizen attitudes. *Public Administration Review, 64*(1), 15–27. doi:10.1111/j.1540-6210.2004.00343.x

Wesner, S. (2005). Towards an architecture for the mobile grid (Architektur für ein Mobiles Grid). *it - Information Technology, 47*(6), 336-342. doi:10.1524/itit.2005.47.6.336

West, J. (2002). *How open is open enough? Melding proprietary and open source platform strategies.* December. Retrieved January 15, 2011, from http://www.joelwest.org/Pa-pers/West2003a-WP.pdf

Westover, L. (1990). Footprint evaluation for volume rendering. In *SIGGRAPH '90: Proceedings of the 17th Annual Conference on Computer Graphics and Interactive Techniques,* (pp. 367–376). New York, NY: ACM Press.

White, J. (1996). *Mobile agent white papers.* Retrieved March 25, 2011, from http://www.klynch.com/documents/agents/

Wiegand, N., & Garcia, C. (2007). A task-based ontology approach to automate geospatial data retrieval. *Transactions in GIS, 11*(3), 355–376. doi:10.1111/j.1467-9671.2007.01050.x

Wieland, M., Gorlach, K., Schumm, D., & Leymann, F. (2009). Towards reference passing in web service and workflow-based applications. *2009 IEEE International Enterprise Distributed Object Computing Conference,* (pp. 109-118). IEEE. doi:10.1109/EDOC.2009.17

Wijnhoven, F., Spil, T., Stegwee, R., & Fa, A. (2006). Post-merger it integration strategies: An IT alignment perspective. *The Journal of Strategic Information Systems, 15*(1), 5–28. doi:10.1016/j.jsis.2005.07.002

Wikipedia (about itself). (2010). Wikipedia. Retrieved May 8, 2010, from http://en.wikipedia.org/wiki/Wikipedia

Wikipedia. (n.d.). *Mandelbrot set.* Retrieved November 10th, 2011, from http://en.wikipedia.org/wiki/Mandelbrot_set#Self-similarity

Williamson, I., Rajabifard, A., & Feeney, M. F. (2003). *Developing spatial data infrastructures: From concept to reality.* London, UK: Taylor & Francis. doi:10.1201/9780203485774

Windows Azure. (n.d.). *Website.* Retrieved March 2, 2012, from http://www.windowsazure.com/

wiseGEEK.com. (2011). *What is data transfer rate?* Retrieved June 23, 2011, from http://www.wisegeek.com/what-is-datatransfer-rate.htm

Wohlstadter, E., & Tai, S. (2009). *Web services, reference entry. Encyclopedia of Database Systems (EDBS).* Heidelberg, Germany: Springer.

Wolfram, S. (1994). *Cellular automata and complexity: Collected papers.* Addison-Wesley.

Wolf, W. R., & Azevedo, J. L. F. (2007). High-order ENO and WENO schemes for unstructured grids. *International Journal for Numerical Methods in Fluids, 55*(10), 917–943. doi:10.1002/fld.1469

Wong, P., & Cha, V. (2009). *The evolution of government infocomm plans: Singapore's e-government journey (1980 – 2007).* Singapore: Institute of Systems Science, National University of Singapore.

Woodring, J., Wang, C., & Shen, H.-W. (2003). High-dimensional direct rendering of time-varying volumes. *Proceedings of IEEE Visualization, 2003,* 417–424.

Wordle: A toy for generating word clouds. (2009). Retrieved May 18, 2009 from http://www.wordle.net

World Wide Web Consortium. (2002). *Web services architecture requirements.* W3C Working Draft 29 April 2002. Retrieved February 10, 2011, from http://www.w3.org/TR/2002/WD-wsa-reqs-20020429

World Wide Web Consortium. (2004). *OWL web ontology language guide.* Retrieved October 16, 2011, from http://www.w3.org/TR/owl-guide/

World Wide Web Consortium. (2004). *Web Ontology Language (OWL).* Retrieved October 20, 2011, from http://www.w3.org/2004/OWL/

World Wide Web Consortium. (2008). *SPARQL query language for RDF.* Retrieved October 16, 2011, from http://www.w3.org/TR/rdf-sparql-query/

Wright, H., Crompton, R. H., Kharche, S., & Wenisch, P. (2010). Steering and visualization: Enabling technologies for computational science. *Future Generation Computer Systems, 26*(3), 506–513. doi:10.1016/j.future.2008.06.015

Wu, I.-L., Li, J.-Y., & Fu, C.-Y. (2011). The adoption of mobile healthcare by hospital's professional: An integrative perspective. *Decision Support Systems, 51,* 587–596. doi:10.1016/j.dss.2011.03.003

Wu, J. H., Wang, S. C., & Lin, L. M. (2007). Mobile computing acceptance factors in the healthcare industry: A structural equation model. *International Journal of Medical Informatics*, 76(1), 66–77. doi:10.1016/j.ijmedinf.2006.06.006

Xia, L., & Kraak, M.-J. (2008). The time wave. A new method of visual exploration of geo-data in time–space. *The Cartographic Journal*, 45(3), 193–200. doi:10.1179/000870408X311387

Xie, H. (2001). Tracking of design changes for collaborative product development. *Proceedings of the 6th International Conference on Computer Supported Cooperative Work in Design*, (pp. 175-180).

Xie, B., Bagozzi, R. P., & Troye, S. V. (2008). Trying to prosume: Toward a theory of consumers as co-creators of value. *Journal of the Academy of Marketing Science*, 36, 109–122. doi:10.1007/s11747-007-0060-2

Xie, Y., Koch, S., McGinley, J., Albers, S., Bieringer, P. E., Wolfson, M., & Chan, M. (2011). A space--time multiscale analysis system: A sequential variational analysis approach. *Monthly Weather Review*, 139(4), 1224–1240. doi:10.1175/2010MWR3338.1

Xuan, W., Xue, S., & Ma, T. (2009). Architecture of collaborative design based on grid. *Proceedings of the Third International Conference on Genetic and Evolutionary Computing*, (pp. 244-247).

Yamada, H. (2010, July). Current status of e-government in Japan and its future direction - Electronic application services. *The Quarterly Review*, 36, 19–33.

Yildiz, M. (2007). E-government research: Reviewing the literature, limitations, and ways forward. *Government Information Quarterly*, 24, 646–665. doi:10.1016/j.giq.2007.01.002

Ying, H. M., & Thing, V. L. L. (2011). A novel rainbow table sorting method. *Proceedings of The Second International Conference on Technical and Legal Aspects of the e-Society* (CYBERLAWS), February 23-28, 2011, Gosier, Guadeloupe, France, (pp. 35-40). ISBN: 978-1-61208-122-9

Yin, L., Shaw, S.-L., Wang, D., Carr, E. A., Berry, M. W., Gross, L. J., & Comiskey, E. J. (2011). A framework of integrating GIS and parallel computing for spatial control problems - A case study of wildfire control. *International Journal of Geographical Information Science*, 26(4). do i:doi:10.1080/13658816.2011.609487

Younesy, H., Möller, T., & Carr, H. (2005). Visualization of time-varying volumetric data using differential time-histogram table. In *Proceedings of the Fourth International Workshop on Volume Graphics 2005*, (pp. 21–29).

YouTube: A video sharing community. (2011). Retrieved May 27, 2011 from http://www.youtube.com

Yu, W. D., Gummadikayala, R., & Mudumbi, S. (2008). *A web-based wireless mobile system design of security and privacy framework for u-Healthcare*. Paper presented at the 10th International Conference on e-health Networking, Applications and Services (HealthCom 2008).

Yuan, M. (2001). Representing complex geographic phenomena with both object- and field-like properties. *Cartography and Geographic Information Science*, 28(2), 83–96. doi:10.1559/152304001782173718

Yuan, M. (2009). Challenges and critical issues for temporal GIS research and technologies. In Karimi, H. A. (Ed.), *Handbook of research on geoinformatics* (pp. 144–153). doi:10.4018/978-1-59140-995-3.ch019

Yuan, M., & Stewart, K. (2008). *Computation and visualization for the understanding of dynamics in geographic domains: A research agenda*. Boca Raton, FL: CRC/Taylor and Francis.

Yue, P., Gong, J., Di, L., Lianlian, H., & Wei, Y. (2011). Integrating semantic web technologies and geospatial catalog services for geospatial information discovery and processing in cyberinfrastructure. *GeoInformatica*, 15(2), 273–303. doi:10.1007/s10707-009-0096-1

Zdrahal, Z., & Domingue, J. (1997). The world wide design lab: An environment for distributed collaborative design. *Proceedings of the 1997 International Conference on Engineering Design*, (pp. 19-21).

Zhang, A., Nodine, M., Bhargava, B., & Bukhres, O. (1994). Ensuring relaxed atomicity for flexible transactions in multidatabase systems. *Proceedings of ACM SIGMOD Conference,* (pp. 67-78).

Zhang, C., Zhao, T., Li, W., & Osleeb, J. P. (2010). Towards logic-based geospatial feature discovery and integration using web feature service and geospatial Semantic Web. *International Journal of Geographical Information Science, 24*(6), 903–923. doi:10.1080/13658810903240687

Zhang, L., Tang, C., Song, Y., Zhang, A., & Ramanathan, M. (2003). Vizcluster and its application on classifying gene expression data. *Distributed and Parallel Databases, 13*(1), 73–97. doi:10.1023/A:1021517806825

Zhang, S., & Christensen, U. (1993). Some effects of lateral viscosity variations on geoid and surface velocities induced by density anomalies in the mantle. *Geophysical Journal International, 114,* 531–547. doi:10.1111/j.1365-246X.1993.tb06985.x

Zhang, S., & Yuen, D. A. (1996). Various influences on plumes and dynamics in time-dependent, compressible, mantle convection in 3-D spherical shell. *Physics of the Earth and Planetary Interiors, 94,* 241–267. doi:10.1016/0031-9201(95)03100-6

Zheng, L., Gerya, T., Yuen, D. A., Knepley, M. G., Zhang, H., & Shi, Y. (2010, December). *GPU implementation of Stokes equation with strongly variable coefficients.* Paper presented at the American Geophysical Union, Fall Meeting 2010, IN41A-1350.

Zhong, S., Yuen, D. A., & Moresi, L. (2007). Computational methods. In D. Bercovici (Ed.), *Treatise on geophysics, Volume 7 – Mantle dynamics* (pp. 227-252). Elsevier B.V.

Zhong, S., McNamara, A., Tan, E., Moresi, L., & Gurnis, M. (2008). A benchmark study on mantle convection in a 3-D spherical shell using CitComS. *Geochemistry Geophysics Geosystems, 9*(10), Q10017. doi:10.1029/2008GC002048

Zhong, S., Zuber, M. T., Moresi, L., & Gurnis, M. (2000). Role of temperature-dependent viscosity and surface plates in spherical shell models of mantle convection. *Journal of Geophysical Research, 105,* 11063–11082. doi:10.1029/2000JB900003

Zhu, H. (2005). *Building reusable components with service-oriented architectures.* In 2005 IEEE International Conference on Information Reuse and Integration (IEEE IRI-2005), Las Vegas, Nevada, USA.

Ziethe, R., Seiferlin, K., & Hiesinger, H. (2009). Duration and extent of lunar volcanism: Comparison of 3D convection models to mare basalt ages. *Planetary and Space Science, 57*(7), 784–796. doi:10.1016/j.pss.2009.02.002

Zivadinovic, D. (2007). *IPv6: Das Mega-Netz.* Retrieved August 15, 2011, from http://www.heise.de/netze/artikel/IPv6-Das-Mega-Netz-221708.html

ZIVHPC. (2009). Retrieved October 23, 2011, from https://www.uni-muenster.de/ZIV/Technik/ZIVHPC/index.html

ZIVSMP. (2009). Retrieved October 23, 2011, from https://www.uni-muenster.de/ZIV/Technik/ZIVHPC/ZIVSMP.html

Zygourakis, K., Bizios, R., & Markenscoff, P. (1991, August). Proliferation of anchorage-dependent contact-inhibited cells: I. Development of theoretical models based on cellular automata. *Biotechnology and Bioengineering, 38*(5), 459–470. doi:10.1002/bit.260380504

About the Contributors

Claus-Peter Rückemann, Dr. rer. nat., is a lecturer and researcher at the Leibniz Universität Hannover and the Westfälische Wilhelms-Universität Münster (WWU), Germany. He holds an University-Diplom degree in geophysics and a Doctorate degree for natural sciences in geoinformatics, informatics, and geosciences from the Faculty of Mathematical and Natural Sciences, WWU. Dr. Rückemann teaches Information Science, Security, and Computing at the University of Hannover, in the European Legal Informatics Study Programme. He studied geophysics, theoretical and applied physics, mathematics, computer science, and archaeology. For the last two decades he is in professional practice in natural and information sciences, advanced scientific and High Performance Computing (HPC), in research, management, and supervising positions. He is the head of research of the LX Foundation, director of the GEXI Consortium, serves in international scientific advisory boards, research grants committees, and panels and as an auditor. He is the general chair of the International Conference on Advanced Communications and Computation (INFOCOMP), advisory chair of the GEOProcessing and CYBERLAWS conferences and advisory board and board member of international scientific journals and editor of scientific proceedings and books. He is also on duty for HLRN, managing the largest supercomputer resources in Northern Germany. He has been distinguished with the Grade IARIA Fellow of the International Academy, Research, and Industry Association for his scientific research on the state of the art improvement in HPC, Information Systems, Distributed Computing, and international collaboration.

* * *

Ajith Abraham is the Director of Machine Intelligence Research Laboratory (MIR Labs), which has members from more than 80 countries. Currently, he is also Research Professor at Faculty of Electrical Engineering and Computer Science, VSB-TU Ostrava, Czech Republic. He has a worldwide academic experience with formal appointments in Australia, China, Czech Republic, France, Hungary, Korea, Norway, Spain and USA. His research and development experience includes more than 20 years in the industry and academia. He works in a multidisciplinary environment involving machine intelligence, network security, various aspects of networks, e-commerce, Web intelligence, Web services, computational grids, data mining, and their applications to various real-world problems. He has published more than 750 publications. Presently, he is the Chair of IEEE Systems Man and Cybernetics Society Technical Committee on Soft Computing and also a Distinguished Speaker of the IEEE Computer Society. At the same time, he also serves as the editorial board of over 50 International journals and has also guest edited 40 special issues on various topics.

Fabio Gomes de Andrade is an Adjunct Professor at the Computer Science Department of Federal Institute of Education, Science and Technology of Paraiba, Brazil, where he has been since 2002. He received his Master degree in Computer Science from University of Campina Grande in 2006. Actually, Mr. Andrade is a PhD student at the Computer Science Department of University of Campina Grande, under supervision of Dr. Cláudio de Souza Baptista, and his thesis focuses on the use of semantics to enhance geographic data discovery on spatial data infrastructures. Besides, his research interests include spatial data integration, Semantic Web, distributed databases, and information retrieval.

Bernadetta Kwintiana Ane is a Senior Researcher at the Institute of Computer-aided Product Development Systems, Universität Stuttgart, Germany. She has been 17 years working experiences in industry and academy. She published more than 60 scientific papers in referred international journals and conferences, as well as book chapters, white papers, scientific oratio, and owner of international patent. Presently, as a Humboldtian as well as an IEEE member she serves internationally as a research fellow at several research centers in Europe, US, Japan, and India. Meantime, she also contributes as an associate editor for the *Journal of Intelligent Automation and Soft Computing*, and *Journal of Information Assurance and Security* in USA, as well as research grant assessor for the Czech Science Foundation and reviewers for IEEE and several well-known referred international journals.

Douglas Archibald, Dr., is the Educational Researcher Scientist at the C.T. Lamont Centre for Research in Primary Care, Elisabeth Bruyère Research Institute and the Department of Family Medicine, University of Ottawa. Dr. Archibald has a PhD in Education (University of Ottawa) and a Master's of Arts in Education (Ontario Institute for Studies in Education). His program of research incorporates various facets of medical education which include interprofessional education, research methodology, and eLearning. Some recent projects have included the assessment of an online training program involving simulation to improve medical residents' knowledge and skills to manage patients with inflammatory arthritis; and the development and validation of assessment instruments for interprofessional education. Doug has recent publications in the fields of eLearning and health care education.

Cláudio de Souza Baptista is an Associate Professor at the Computer Science Department of University of Campina Grande, Brazil, where he has been since 1994. He is also the Coordinator of the Information Systems Laboratory at the same university. He received his PhD degree in Computer Science from University of Kent at Canterbury, United Kingdom, in 2000. From 1991-1993 he worked as a Software Engineer at the Vale Company in Brazil. His research interests include database, distributed databases, digital libraries, geographical information systems, information retrieval, data warehouses, and multimedia databases. He has authored more than 40 papers in international conferences, book chapters and journals.

Belgacem Ben Youssef received his PhD from the Cullen College of Engineering at the University of Houston (Houston, Texas, USA). He is currently an Associate Professor of Computer Engineering in the College of Computer & Information Sciences at King Saud University in Riyadh, Saudi Arabia. Prior to that, he was an Assistant Professor in both the TechOne Program and the School of Interactive Arts & Technology at Simon Fraser University (Vancouver, British Columbia, Canada). His research interests include parallel computing, computational tissue engineering, visualization, digital signal processing, and spatial thinking in learning and design. Dr. Ben Youssef has also two years of industrial experience in software development and technical project management in the telecommunications and business sectors. He is a member of both the IEEE Computer Society and the ACM.

James Bothwell, Ph.D., is a research affiliate of the Geoinformatics Department and of the Center for Spatial Analysis at the University of Oklahoma, and a teaching professor of Computer Science at the Oklahoma City Community City College. James received his PhD in GIScience from the University of Oklahoma in 2011 under the guidance of May Yuan. James' research combines GIScience with Artificial Intelligence, from his MS, to advance representation and analysis of geographic kinematics. Climate change, both observed and modeled, is the current domain of his geographic kinematics research. James' research project was funded by the National Science Foundation (NSF# 0416208 Collaborative Research: Integration of Geographic Complexity and Dynamics in Geographic Information Systems) and by Dr. David Karoly, ARC Federation Fellow in the School of Earth Sciences at the University of Melbourne.

Haakon Bryhni holds a PhD in high speed communication and multiprocessor server systems from the University of Oslo and a MSc in Telematics from Norwegian Institute of Technology. His professional experience includes research in packet radio protocols at the Norwegian Defence Research Establishment, and high speed internet protocols at Apple Research Labs. Bryhni was co-founder of Advanced Communication Technology in 1998 where he was a pioneer in mobile Internet technology. Bryhni co-founded Nunatak in 2001 and commenced full time engagement from 2006 and holds several board positions in the portfolio. In addition, Bryhni is Assistant Professor at the University of Oslo, Department of Informatics and has a research interest in mobile communication systems, wireless communication, and security. Bryhni received the Telenor nordic research prize for his research within mobile technologies august 2005, holds several patents and is an active researcher in combination with seed capital investments.

Lars Frank, Associate Professor, Dr. Merc., works in the Department of IT Management Copenhagen Business School, Frederiksberg, Denmark. After studying computer science, Professor Frank worked for 15 years as a database consultant primarily in the banking sector, where problems of integration of banking systems were an important part of his work. This interest he had the opportunity to extend with his employment at CBS (CBS) in 1993, where he has specifically researched the problems of integration of large IT systems so they work as a single consistent system to its users. Theoretically, it is an easy task to get a single integrated IT system, since you can just develop or purchase such a system. In practice, however, in reality it is a difficult task, since the conversion of large comprehensive IT systems is very risky if it is done from one day to the next. Therefore, Lars Frank focused his research on the integration of different IT systems, taking it enables to convert over a longer period of time and opportunity to integrate new systems with existing systems. Since this is a very complex area of research, Lars Frank is working with companies interested in developing more integration-friendly software.

Wolfgang Christmann is founder and CEO of Christmann Informationstechnik & Medien GmbH & Co. KG. He studied Engineering at the University Hanover, Germany and took his way into the IT over first steps in CNC programming. With an energy-efficient RFID server project (running as an appliance with 10 Watts) he startet focussing on the vision of a resource efficient IT infrastructure. The RECS® | Box is the visible outcome of this. He is engaged in international conferences and research projects.

Huong Ha, Dr., PhD (Monash University), MPP (National University of Singapore), ILA Cert. (United Nations University/International Leadership Academy), BA, is currently affiliated with the University of Newcastle. She has been Director of Research & Development, and was the Dean of TMC Business School, TMC Academy. She is also the Chief Editor of *TMC Academic Journal*, a peer-reviewed journal with an ISNN and registered with the National Library Board of Singapore. It is listed on Ulrichsweb. com, the Directory of Open Access Journals and the Australian ERA 2010 list. Her research interests include corporate governance, sustainability, and e-consumer protection. Her research activities have resulted in research and international travel grants, awards, refereed journal articles, book chapters and encyclopaedia articles and several conference papers. She has been a reviewer of many academic journals and conferences. She is a member of the Chinese American Scholars Association Board (Canada/ USA), the Scientific Committee of the 1st International Conference for Graduate Research in Tourism, Hospitality and Leisure (Albania), and others.

Rebecca Hogue is pursuing a PhD in Education at the University of Ottawa. Her professional background is in instructional design and software quality assurance. She holds a Master of Arts Degree in Distributed Learning (Distance Education), and a Bachelor of Science Degree in Computer Science. Her passion is for teaching learning professionals how to integrate technology into their teaching practice. Her research involves creating faculty development resources for integrating mobile technology into university teaching.

Christian Hüttig obtained a Master degree in Computer Science from HTWM Mittweida in 2004. He completed his PhD studies at University of Münster. He is currently employed as a post-doctoral fellow at the Hampton University, Virginia USA. His principal research interests are high performance computing and numerical simulations of mantle convection in terrestrial planets and icy satellites.

Udo H. Inden is a self-employed Consultant and Lecturer since 1996 at the Faculty for Business Administration and Economics of Cologne University of Applied Sciences. His fields of expertise are the management of complex service systems, managerial skills, augmented intelligence and learning in organizations, lead-user programs and methodological support of investor relations in ventures of up to 400 Million €. He initiated, consulted, or managed more than 150 projects in applied sciences with a particular focus on the use of ontology-based multi-agent systems supporting organizational effectiveness. His background includes about twenty years in different fields of aviation industry as well as large scale venture management on the development of innovative transportation technology. Before, he served for about 15 years in senior positions as instructor and in the management of non-profit organizations.

Alexander Kipp is the Deputy Head of the Intelligent Service Infrastructure (ISIS) research department at the High Performance Computing Centre (HLRS) of the University of Stuttgart. He holds a Diploma in Computer Science. Since 2006 he is employed at the High Performance Computing Centre (HLRS) of the University of Stuttgart, working at Cloud-/VO-/Web Service-related research projects on both national and international level. He is the deputy head of the "Intelligent Service Infrastructures" department at HLRS, which focuses on realising next generation cross domain service infrastructures. In this context, he is responsible for the Green-IT activities of HLRS. His research interest lies in the area of adaptive and energy aware service infrastructures, in particular in the area of service virtualization and the corresponding technologies.

Solomon Lasluisa is a Ph.D. student at Rutgers University. He received his undergraduate degree from Rutgers School of Engineering majoring in Electrical & Computer Engineering. His research interests are in legal issues in cloud computing, big data analysis, and parallel and distributed computing. He has been work in Rutgers' Center for Autonomic Computing since 2010. He has been working on projects which look to provision and schedule resources by tracking data clusters in monitoring data using distributed clustering algorithms. This work is now being expanded to explore its uses in scientific computing in order to provide real time data analysis in scientific simulations.

Georgios V. Lioudakis, Dr., is a Senior Research Associate of the Intelligent Communications and Broadband Networks Laboratory (ICBNet) of the National Technical University of Athens (NTUA), Greece. He received his Dr.-Ing. degree in Electrical and Computer Engineering from the NTUA in 2008. As a research fellow of the NTUA since 2000, he has participated in several European and national research projects. His research interests include security and privacy protection, software engineering, middleware and distributed technologies, mobile networks and services; he has several publications related to these fields. Since 2009, Dr. Lioudakis is also an Adjunct Lecturer at the Department of Telecommunications Science and Technology, University of Peloponnese, Greece.

Colla MacDonald, Dr., is a Full Professor in the Faculty of Education, cross appointed with the Faculty of Medicine, and a Senior Researcher at the Bruyère Research Institute. Her research concentrates on curriculum design, evaluation and eLearning. She has published over 80 refereed articles, book chapters and conference proceedings. Colla has been principal investigator of SSHRC, Ministry of Health and Long-Term Care, Inukshuk Wireless, Canadian Foundation for Innovation, Office of Learning Technologies and CIHR funded research projects. Currently, seven PhD students work with her to conduct research on various aspects of emerging technologies. She published the *Demand-Driven Learning Model* and *W(e)Learn* framework which have been as quality standards to design, delivery and assess programs. Colla has won the International WebCt Exemplary Course Award (twice) the Business/ Professional 2010 International e-Learning Award, and the Faculty of Education's top researcher award. She is on an advisory committee with the World Health Organization.

Jay Mercer, Dr., is the Medical Chief, Department of Family Medicine and Medical Director of the Bruyere Family Medicine Centre. He has worked as a clinician in urban and rural practices with varying degrees of automation. He has worked as Medical Director of cma.ca, the Canadian Medical Association's Internet Portal. In this role he was also the project leader for the CMA's Physician Website initiative and patient portal initiatives, as well as several other activities which integrate technology into patient care. Prior to becoming a doctor, Jay was trained in strategic analysis and worked in the areas of data security, information systems and data management in both military and civilian environments. Jay has spoken and written frequently about data security, confidentiality, and practice automation for physician groups across Canada.

Jelena Mirkovic is a Ph.D. student and Research Assistant at the Center for Shared Decision Making and Collaborative Care Research, Oslo University Hospital, Oslo, Norway since April 2008. She received her M.S. and B.Sc. in Electrical and Computer Engineering from the Faculty of Technical Sciences, University of Novi Sad, Serbia. Her research interests are mobile applications and systems, security, usability and user-friendliness, and application and terminal mobility. She has published papers in several areas including development and integration of mobile services in healthcare information systems; security issues in emerging healthcare services; user-friendliness and usability of mobile healthcare applications; development of seamless healthcare applications.

Lena Noack is a PhD student at the Institute of Planetology of the Westfälische Wilhelms-Universität Münster and currently works at the German Aerospace Center (DLR) in the Institute of Planetary Research. She graduated in Numerical Mathematics at the Humboldt University of Berlin in 2008. Her research is concerned with the mechanism of renewing the surface of a terrestrial body and its implications for the habitability of a planet. The work focuses on the existence of plate tectonics and in particular on the probability of plate tectonics on super-Earths, as well as on a reasonable explanation for the young resurfacing on Venus.

Malgorzata Pankowska is an Assistant Professor of the Department of Informatics at the Karol Adamiecki University of Economics in Katowice, Poland. She received the qualification in Econometrics and Statistics from the Karol Adamiecki University of Economics in Katowice in 1981, the Ph.D. degree in 1988 and the Doctor Habilitatus degree in 2009, both from the Karol Adamiecki University of Economics in Katowice. She participated in EU Leonardo da Vinci Programme projects as well as gave lectures within the Socrates Program Teaching Staff Exchange in Braganca, Portugal, Trier, Germany, Brussels, Belgium, and in Vilnius, Lithuania. She is a member of ISACA and the Secretary in the Board of the Polish Scientific Society of Business Informatics. Her research interests include virtual organization development, ICT project management, IT outsourcing, information governance, and business information systems design and implementation.

Manish Parashar is Professor of Electrical and Computer Engineering at Rutgers University. He is also founding Director of the Center for Autonomic Computing and The Applied Software Systems Laboratory (TASSL), and Associate Director of the Rutgers Center for Information Assurance (RUCIA). Manish received a BE degree from Bombay University, India and MS and Ph.D. degrees from Syracuse University. His research interests are in the broad area of parallel and distributed computing and include computational and data-enabled science and engineering, autonomic computing, and power/energy management. A key focus of his research is on addressing the complexity or large-scale systems and applications through programming abstractions and systems. Manish has published over 350 technical papers, serves on the editorial boards and organizing committees of a large number of journals and international conferences and workshops, and has deployed several software systems that are widely used. He has also received numerous awards and is Fellow of IEEE/IEEE Computer Society and Senior Member of ACM.

Mogens Kühn Pedersen, Professor, works in the Department of Operations Management, Copenhagen Business School, Frederiksberg, Denmark. Research areas include ICT innovation, open source software, standards and standardization, IT governance and strategic development, digital government and business services, economics of information, digital technology and -organization, distributed knowledge systems, and networks.

Rasmus Ulslev Pedersen, Associate Professor, works in the Department of IT Management, Embedded Software Laboratory, Copenhagen Business School, Frederiksberg, Denmark. Research areas include business intelligence, data mining, and wireless sensor networks. Recent project focus is on providing open source experimental platforms for stream data mining. The first open source toolkit for LEGO MINDSTORMS NXT was provided by this author, and it is now used for experimentation with sensor information in relation to creating business value in associated IS processes.

Ana-Catalina Plesa earned a Master's degree in Computer Science from the University of Passau in 2008. She is now a PhD student at the Institute of Planetology of the Westfälische Wilhelms-Universität Münster and currently works at the German Aerospace Center (DLR) in the Institute of Planetary Research. She works on the numerical modeling of mantle convection in terrestrial planets with focus on the partial melting processes and their implications for the habitability.

Ivan Rodero is currently a Research Associate at the Center for Autonomic Computing at Rutgers, the State University of New Jersey. From September 2009 to July 2011 he also was a Visiting Assistant Professor of the Department of Electrical and Computer Engineering. He received an integrated BS/MS degree in Computer Science and Engineering in 2004 and a PhD degree in February 2009 from Technical University of Catalonia (UPC). Before joining Rutgers, Ivan Rodero was researcher at Barcelona Supercomputing Center and part-time Adjunct Professor of the Computer Architecture Department of UPC. He has published several papers in international conferences, journals and workshops. He also has served in organizational and program committees of international conferences and workshops, and has served as a referee for journals. His research interests are in the broad area of parallel and distributed computing and include high performance computing, autonomic computing, grid/cloud computing, and green computing. He is member of IEEE.

Dieter Roller holds the position of Director of the Institute of Computer-aided Product Development at the Universität Stuttgart, Germany. He is full Professor and Chair of Computer Science Fundamentals. Additionally, he has been awarded the distinction as Honorary Professor of the University of Kaiserslautern and also serves as Liaison Professor of the German Computer Science Society "Gesellschaft für Informatik e.V." for the Universität Stuttgart. As former R&D manager with world-wide responsibility for CAD-technology within an international computer company, he gathered a comprehensive industrial experience. He is the inventor of several patents and is well-known through numerous technical talks in countries all over the world, 70 published books, and over 160 contributions to journals and proceedings books. Currently, he serves as reviewer for the Commission of the European Communities in Brussels as well as for the Baden-Württemberg Ministry of Science and Research for project grants. He is also reviewer for well-known scientific journals and member of several national and international programme committees.

Ralf Schneider is a Ph.D. student in the field of *Computer supported analysis and diagnostics for medical problems* at the High Performance Computing Center Stuttgart since May 2007. In 2006 he worked in a student research project in the field of static and dynamics under the topic *Modeling of the inhomogeneous orthotropic material behavior of the cortical femur structure based on clinical CT- respectively density data* at the Institut für Statik- und Dynamik der Luft- und Raumfahrtkonstruktionen. In February 2007 he obtained his diploma in Aerospace Engineering at the University of Stuttgart.

Isabel Schwerdtfeger holds a Master's Degree in Economics with a Minor in International Management from the University of Hamburg, Germany. She is a Senior Solution Sales Professional for Data Center Services at IBM and is responsible for selling IBM solutions directly to customers. Formerly, she has executed the role as Client Representative for the Telecommunications and Media Industry, where she was responsible for managing the total customer relationship of one strategic or several clients. In 1999 she started her sales career as a Professional Sales Representative for E-Commerce Solutions at IBM. Since 2008 she has specialised in the field of Storage and Data Solutions, especially for High Performance Computing and innovative solutions for clients in the Public Sector. She is responsible for closing the sale and managing customer satisfaction with respect to the engagement. Her key reference projects are Deutsches Klimarechenzentrum, Deutscher Wetterdienst, and various financial institutions in Germany.

Lutz Schubert is Head of the Intelligent Service Infrastructure (ISIS) research department at the High Performance Computing Centre (HLRS) of the University of Stuttgart. He holds a Diploma in Computer Science and Philosophy. He is actively working on distributed systems related research in renowned national and international research teams. As such he has participated in shaping the Grid concepts, later Web services, and now Cloud Computing. His specific research focus thereby rests on efficient distributed execution frameworks and operating systems. Lutz Schubert has given many keynotes and invited talks in the areas of high performance computing and cloud computing, and has contributed to several reports, panels and roadmaps. He furthermore acts as independent expert for the European Commission and acts as designated rapporteur for the EC Cloud Computing expert working group and the EC's white paper "The Future of Cloud Computing, the Future of European Cloud Computing" (2010).

Terje Solvoll is at his end of his PhD studies and works as a Researcher at the Norwegian Centre for Integrated Care and Telemedicine (NST), Tromsø Telemedicine Laboratory (TTL), and is affiliated to the Department of Computer Science at the University of Tromsø, Norway. He has been working as a Researcher/Project Manager at NST/TTL since 2006, and started his PhD work in 2007. Before this he worked at Telenor R&D as a Researcher within communication systems, and later in the industry with satellite communication systems. He has a Master's degree in Computer Science and his research interests concentrates on telemedicine, ehealth and computer science. He has published his work within journals like: *Journal of Telemedicine and Telecare, Acta Pædiatrica, BMCResearchNotes, Journal of Systems and Software, Journal of Computer Systems and Sciences*, and conferences including: WSEAS07, TTeC08, SHI 2010, MedInfo 2010, eTELEMED 2011, and 2012.

Monika Steinberg is Deputy Professor in Information Management for Audiovisual and Multimedia Content at the University of Applied Sciences and Arts in Hannover (Faculty of Media, Design and Information). She received a PhD (Dr.-Ing.) from the Leibniz Universität Hannover for interdisciplinary research work in architectural informatics and computer science in 2011. Her research focuses on digital (social) media, web application development, distributed data, and interactive systems.

Vrizlynn L. L. Thing received her Ph.D. degree in Computing from Imperial College London, United Kingdom, for her work on the adaptive detection and mitigation of Distributed Denial-of-Service attacks, and her M.Eng. and B.Eng. (Hons) degrees in Electrical and Electronics Engineering from Nanyang Technological University, Singapore. She currently leads the Digital Forensics Group at the Institute for Infocomm Research, A*STAR (Agency for Science, Technology and Research), Singapore. She is also an Adjunct Assistant Professor at the School of Computing, National University of Singapore. She teaches "Systems security and forensics" and "Topics in information security" to undergraduate and postgraduate students at the university. Her research interests include digital (multimedia, network and mobile) forensics, and systems and network security.

Nicola Tosi earned a Master degree in Physics from the University of Milan (Italy). After completing his PhD studies at the Geo-Forschungs-Zentrum Potsdam (Germany), he spent two years as Marie Curie postdoctoral fellow at the Charles University in Prague (Czech Republic). He is now research scientist jointly at the Technical University and German Aerospace Center in Berlin (Germany). His primary research interest is the numerical modeling of mantle convection in the Earth and terrestrial planets.

Micha vor dem Berge studied Technical Information Technology at the University of Applied Sciences Wolfenbüttel, Germany, and graduated with a Master's degree. He works at Christmann Informationstechnik + Medien in the Research & Development department, being responsible for research on energy-efficiency in data centres and intelligent monitoring and management, as well as for development of servers.

Hwei-Ming Ying received the B.Sc. degree in Mathematics from the Imperial College London, U.K., in 2006 and the M.Sc. degree in Mathematics from University of Michigan, USA, in 2011. He joined the Institute for Infocomm Research, A*STAR (Agency for Science, Technology and Research), Singapore, in 2006. He was in the Cryptography Group before joining the Digital Forensics Group in 2008. After completing his M.Sc. degree, he returned to the Digital Forensics Group at the Institute for Infocomm Research in 2011. His research interests include applied mathematics, discrete mathematics, probability theory, combinatorics, as well as various areas of mathematical sciences.

May Yuan, PhD, is Edith Kinney Gaylord Presidential Professor and Brandt Professor of Atmospheric and Geographic Sciences, the Director of Geoinformatics Program, and the Director of Center for Spatial Analysis at the University of Oklahoma. May's research interest is in temporal GIS, geographic representation, spatiotemporal information modeling, and applications of geographic information and spatial thinking to dynamic systems. Her research projects center on representation models, algorithms for spatiotemporal analysis, and modeling of spatial dynamics in human-environment systems. She explores multiple perspectives of dynamics, examines the influences of space syntax on human activities, analyzes spatiotemporal patterns and behavioral structures of dynamic systems, and draws insights into the system development and evolution to derive an integrated understanding, interpretation, and prediction of activities, events, and processes.

Index